INTEGRATIVE ACTIVITY OF THE BRAIN

INTEGRATIVE ACTIVITY OF THE BRAIN

An Interdisciplinary Approach

By

JERZY KONORSKI, M.D.

Professor of Neurophysiology, Nencki Institute
of Experimental Biology, Warsaw, Poland

CHICAGO AND LONDON
THE UNIVERSITY OF CHICAGO PRESS

International Standard Book Number: 0–226–45054–6
Library of Congress Catalog Card Number: 67–16776

THE UNIVERSITY OF CHICAGO PRESS, CHICAGO 60637
The University of Chicago Press, Ltd., London

CONTENTS

Chapter III

Categories of Perceptions in Particular Analyzers   111

Chapter IV

General Physiology of Associations   166

PREFACE TO THE SECOND IMPRESSION

When rereading my book after it was published, I discovered a number of shortcomings which need to be corrected: some expressions seemed not quite adequate, some statements not clear, and a few substantive errors were overlooked. Also a few errors in the Index were found. I owe my sincere apologies to the reader for these lapses.

I take the opportunity of the second printing of the book to rectify the most important errors, without changing the essential text. Among other things the diagram in Figure II–16 has been redrawn, since its previous version was not quite clear, and Figure VII–12 illustrating the kymographic record of an experiment has been replaced by Table VII–1 giving the corresponding protocols.

Two and a half years have elapsed from the time when this book was submitted for publication. This period is too short to make any serious evaluation of the ideas included in it; therefore I resisted the temptation to comment on new experimental data confirming or questioning my concepts, leaving this task to a more remote future.

J. K.

December 1969

ACKNOWLEDGMENTS

Both the undertaking of writing this book and the possibility of its completion are due to the help, sympathy, and encouragement of a number of my friends and colleagues. Here I may express my thanks and acknowledgment only to some of them whose assistance was of particular importance to me.

The ideas advanced in this book are based to a large extent on the experimental work performed by my associates in the Neurophysiological Department of the Nencki Institute of Experimental Biology. Since their names and papers are quoted in the text I do not need to enumerate them now, but it is a great pleasure for me to convey them my sincere gratitude. I also owe very much to the close scientific cooperation of the Department of Neurosurgery of the Polish Academy of Sciences (head L. Stępień). Our common work on the physiological mechanisms of aphasias and agnosias enabled me to acquire a first-hand knowledge on this most important source of information in brain research. My recent cooperation with R. Gawroński in the field of bionics helped me considerably to crystallize my ideas on the physiological mechanisms of perceptions.

Many of my colleagues in the United States helped me in various ways by their constructive and friendly criticism and comments. I am particularly indebted to Neal E. Miller, who gave me most valuable advice in many problems and helped me to avoid some errors in my argumentation. He organized for me a series of lectures in the Department of Psychology of Yale University in which I had the opportunity to discuss the problems of classical and instrumental conditioning, which was of great help for the clearer formulation of my concepts. I owe very much to H. Enger Rosvold, who was most helpful in clarifying the exposition of my ideas and in removing a number of inconsistencies and redundancies in the text. I am very grateful to John Seward, Mortimer Mishkin, and Philipp Liss for reading parts of

the manuscript and making valuable comments. It goes without saying that all these scientists do not necessarily share all my ideas and
conclusions.

The generosity of the Foundation Fund in Psychiatry has made it
possible for me to spend several months in the United States, which
was indispensable at certain stages of my work. An office in the Na-
tional Medical Library was most kindly made available to me so that
I was able to make profit of their immense resources.

INTRODUCTION

If we compare the history of the physiology of the brain with that of the spinal cord, we may observe that each of these disciplines developed in a quite different way.

The physiology of the spinal cord was founded chiefly by Sherrington in his early research work presented in his classical treatise *The Integrative Action of the Nervous System.*[1] Sherrington's experimental methods in his original study were purely "behavioristic": he applied stimuli acting upon the receptive surface of the skin and recorded somatic responses of the decerebrate animal. Accepting as the basis of his considerations the idea of neuronal organization of the vertebrate nervous system advanced by Ramón y Cajal, Sherrington drew conclusions from his experimental results about those central processes which controlled spinal reflexes. Although the intimate nature of these processes was not known, no one doubted that they were real physiological events and not arbitrary "constructs" invented for the systematization of the empirical material. When, with the introduction of refined electrophysiological methods, it became possible to record directly the processes occurring in the nerve cells of the spinal cord, the general principles of the functioning of this organ were already firmly established and the new discoveries fit perfectly in Sherrington's general scheme.

Quite different was the development of the physiology of the brain. The first major attempt to establish the foundation of the integrative activity of this organ was made by Pavlov in his research presented in his famous work *Conditioned Reflexes: An Investigation of the Physiological Activity of the Cerebral Cortex.*[2] His experimental approach was exactly the same as that of Sherrington, the only difference being that, since the cerebral cortex was thought to be the organ controlling not the innate but the acquired activity of the organism, the *conditioned* reflexes were taken as fundamental phenomena representing this activity.

The fate of Pavlov's theory of cortical processes was different from that of Sherrington's theory of spinal functions. This was mainly due to the fact that Pavlov's theory, developed in the period when the concept of the neuronal organization of the nervous system was not generally acknowledged, contained basic hypotheses incompatible with this concept. In consequence, whereas the huge body of facts collected by Pavlov's co-workers had a tremendous impact upon the development of the behavioral sciences, his physiological theory of cortical processes was abandoned, because it could not serve as a foundation for further investigation of brain functions. Thus, when electrophysiological methods, facilitating the direct study of the activity of the brain, were introduced, there was no general conceptual framework within which the collected data could be coherently organized.

As the result of this somewhat anomalous development, we are now confronted with two distinct scientific disciplines concerned with the functions of the brain. One discipline is concerned with electrical signs of brain activity in the anesthetized animal with little attempt to throw light on the actual functioning of that organ in normal condition. On the other hand, in the research work of physiologically minded psychologists occasional attempts are made to interpret the results of behavioral experiments by reference to physiological processes. This tendency is now gaining in importance *pari passu* with the increasing application of neurophysiological techniques in waking animals.

In my previous monograph *Conditioned Reflexes and Neuron Organization*[3] I made an attempt to show that the extensive experimental material gathered by Pavlov's school *can* be reorganized and explained on the basis of Sherrington's principles of the central nervous activity, and thus be incorporated into the framework of present-day neurophysiology. Moreover, conditioned reflexes, when already established, function according to principles surprisingly similar to those governing spinal reflexes. Although some hypotheses proposed in my earlier work were disproved by further experimentation, our analysis *has* shown that by applying the input-output methodology the integrative action of the brain in normal animals can be investigated in the same way as that of the spinal cord in decerebrate animals.

The present work is not concerned with merely offering the reader a revised version of my previous discussion based on new behavioral data and enriched by the tremendous progress in neurophysiology made in recent years. The principal change in respect to my previous approach to the subject is that I now go beyond the relatively narrow and rigid range of phenomena dealt with in the experimental work on conditioned reflexes and utilize also other sources of information whenever they are likely to throw light on the mechanisms of brain processes.

What are these additional sources?

First, if we take into account the normal behavior of higher animals, particularly of human beings in everyday life, we may easily observe a tremendous discrepancy between this behavior and the primitive stereotyped performances manifested in conditioned reflex experiments. This means that our everyday behavior may provide an immense amount of data highly informative about our own cerebral processes. This bulk of data is even further increased if we include the behavior of brain-damaged human subjects, particularly those whose lesions are anatomically verified.

Whereas the utilization of behavioral acts, motor and autonomic, observed in human beings as a source of information on their brain function certainly does not raise any opposition, there is another source, much more debatable—namely, introspection.

I do not wish to enter here into a discussion of the role of introspection in modern human psychology or to discuss the tendency, prevailing in some psychological circles, to base this science on purely objective, and not subjective, information. My point is whether we should utilize the introspective data as a source of information on the cerebral processes in addition to, or even on a level equal with, the data obtained from overt behavioral performances.

None of us doubts that our mental experiences, which we know from our own introspection, do depend on our cerebral activity—that if this activity is blocked or abolished, the mental processes disappear. Moreover, we believe that different mental experiences depend on different cerebral processes—that is, that exactly the same process cannot give rise to two different psychic phenomena. But if this is true, then why not infer the occurrence of particular nervous processes from our mental experiences in exactly the same way as we infer them from behavioral acts? To give a simple example, if from the fact that a subject salivates in response to the conditioned stimulus heralding the presentation of food we infer that the corresponding nervous structures have entered into the functional connection (whatever the intimate mechanism of this connection is), so I can as well infer the existence of this connection in my own brain from the fact that hearing from another room the sounds of a dinner being served I clearly visualize it in my imagination. As a matter of fact, the proposed approach does not differ essentially from that used with striking scientific success in psychophysics, where the large amount of important physiological data was obtained on the basis of subjective experience of experimental subjects. Of course the introspective observations utilized for our analysis should be no less reliable and their reproducibility no less rigorous than the reliability and reproducibility of objective observations. Furthermore, we should clearly realize that the occurrence of a certain subjective experience, similar to the occurrence of a certain objectively observed behavioral act, is not the explanation itself but, on the contrary, a phenomenon which *requires* explanation in terms of physiological processes. In other words, we maintain that true physiology of the brain should be capable of explaining mental experiences of the subject in the same way as it explains his observable responses.

The utilization of the subjective phenomena as the source of information about the cerebral processes becomes even more important in our time when we are able to correlate more and more these phenomena with the electrical signs of brain function. For instance, if we can establish a close correlation between the threshold of the fusion of cortical potentials to flicker and the threshold of the subjective experience of fusion, then we can infer that the latter phenomenon is probably the effect of the former. In this way the ultimate goal of brain physiology, consisting in conclusions about the mental experiences of a subject from the electrical activity of his brain, ceases to be mere fantasy and begins to be a real possibility. But this would never be achieved if we did not return to observing subjective experiences of human beings.

From this we can make a further step which is even more "dangerous" (I mean, for the scientific reputation of the author)—that of concluding both from the electrical signs of brain function and from particular behavioral manifestations about the psychic experiences of *animals*.

Fortunately we deal in this book only with higher mammals, and therefore we are not obliged to give an answer to the question as to whether the protozoa, for instance, are endowed with psychic processes. Our aim is much more modest. We claim that if in man the psychic experience of perception of a given stimulus-object is manifested by a definite behavioral act and/or a definite evoked potential in the brain, and if in a given animal (monkey or cat) that stimulus-object produces exactly the same set of responses, we are justified in assuming that the animal experiences perception of the object in much the same way. Similarly, if the animal returns to a food-tray from which he was pulled away by force, just as we return to an unfinished meal from which we were called by a telephone message, we can assume that the animal has an image of the unfinished portion just as we do. To deny such an assumption would mean to draw a sharp border between the brain function in man and in the higher verte-brates, which would be inadmissible from the biological point of view.

Since in a part of our analysis of brain processes we shall consider it fruitful to resort to mental experiences of animals, we shall provide corresponding terms with strictly operational definitions in order not to shock those readers who object to this extrapolation.

To sum up, the task posed in this work is to present the general architecture of the brain activity of higher animals on the basis of *all* available evidence which can be utilized for this purpose. According to whether the stress is placed on the information provided by the experimental work on animals or on information derived from the observation of subjective experiences and behavior of human beings, the book is composed of two parts. The part based largely on experi-mental data from the field of animal behavior is concerned with the organization of basic (innate) activities of the organism (Chapter I), and with acquired activities superimposed upon them in the form of classical and instrumental conditioned reflexes (Chapters VI–XI). The other part, founded mostly on psychological and neuropathological data collected on human beings, deals with physiological mechanisms of perceptions (Chapters II and III) and associations (Chapters IV and V). The discussion on recent memory (Chapter XII) and recapitula-tion (Chapter XIII) have a mixed character.

These two parts, although conceptually closely related, *can* be con-sidered by the reader separately—he may concentrate on one and neglect the other.

The present work does not intend to embrace all the literature rele-vant to its subject in order to draw from it some conciliatory conclu-sions which would fit in with all findings in the best possible way. Many excellent surveys fulfill this purpose. Since our purpose is to present a coherent concept of the integrative activity of the brain, the evidence we use must have a selective character and disregard those findings which seem to us debatable or not pertinent to our con-siderations. Experimental data obtained in our own laboratory natu-rally play a major role in our discussion, because they have largely shaped our ideas.

A few comments are needed about our attitude to the anatomical controversies concerning the localization of various functionally de-fined "centers" or regions. Here we follow the prudent thesis of von Holst[4] that at the present stage of the development of brain physi-ology the questions "how" and "why" are more important than that of "where." In order to be consistent, when dealing with the prob-lems of functional organization of particular systems, we shall make use of block models devoid of too precise anatomical specifications.

If anyone should say that in this work we are dealing with the "conceptual" nervous system, we shall readily accept this definition without considering it a reproof. In fact, as long as our concepts on the functioning of the nervous system do not contain essential errors, this way of dealing with it seems to be more profitable for our purpose than dealing with all the intricacies of actual anatomical relations.

For the sake of brevity, we are also not concerned here with the critical evaluation of those concepts which are incompatible with ours or with comparing our views with those which are similar. It should be emphasized that the theory of integrative processes of the brain proposed in this work does not pretend to be entirely original. It is composed of statements of which some are generally accepted; others have been similarly advanced by other authors; and still others have probably not been advanced before.

In dealing with the theoretical analysis of one field of science, two opposite attitudes are possible, both equally important for its development. One attitude is that the author tries to *explain* as many facts as possible in the given domain, at the risk that some of his explanations are insufficiently founded or provisory. In the other attitude the author tries to be the devil's advocate discovering all the weaknesses and inconsistencies of the accepted views.

The present study clearly represents the first attitude with all the hazards and difficulties it implies. It is thought that at the present stage of the development of our discipline this very approach is badly needed because of the lack of any general framework which would organize and systematize the rapidly growing experimental findings. Therefore, the theories satisfactorily accounting for the facts found and predicting new data are equally important when they are confirmed as when they are disproved by further research. Perhaps in the latter case they are even more helpful because they stir our curiosity drive indispensable for any scientific research.

References to Introduction

1. C. S. Sherrington. 1906. *The Integrative Action of the Nervous System*. 1st ed. New York: Charles Scribner's Sons.
2. I. P. Pavlov. 1927. *Conditioned Reflexes: An Investigation of the Physiological Activity of the Cerebral Cortex*. Translated and edited by G. V. Anrep. London: Oxford University Press.
3. J. Konorski. 1948. *Conditioned Reflexes and Neuron Organization*. Cambridge: Cambridge University Press.
4. E. von Holst. 1954. Relations between the central nervous system and the peripheral organs. *Br. J. Anim. Behav.*, 2: 89–94.

CHAPTER 1

BASIC ACTIVITIES OF ORGANISMS

1. Introductory remarks

It is generally accepted that the central nervous system of higher animals is endowed with two principal properties which are referred to as reactivity and plasticity. Reactivity of the system is its capacity to be activated by stimulation of receptive organs; plasticity is the capacity to change its reactive properties as the result of successive activations.[1]

The principle of reactivity is based on definite fundamental features of neural tissue—excitability, conductivity, and transmissibility—whose biochemical and biophysical mechanisms have recently been thoroughly explored. The intimate mechanism of plasticity is so far poorly understood: although a number of hypotheses have been proposed to account for plastic phenomena in the nervous system, none of them has yet been verified by any clear experimental evidence.

Since the intimate mechanism of plasticity is not known, we have no answer to the question of whether this property is inherent to nervous tissue in general, being manifested on all levels of the neural axis, or whether it is specific only to its highest levels—that is, the cerebral cortex and the basal ganglia. Whatever the final solution to this problem, there is no doubt that, according to the overwhelming mass of experimental evidence, plastic phenomena are most common and conspicuous in normal animals, much more limited in decorticated animals, and still uncertain and debatable in decapitated preparations. Because of this, Pavlov[2] held the view that the property we call plasticity is inherent only in the higher parts of the nervous system and that the cerebral cortex should be considered *the* organ controlling plastic processes.

Although this radical point of view seems now to be abandoned, there is no doubt that plastic phenomena play a dominant role in the integrative activity of the cerebral cortex. These phenomena will be the main subject of the present study.

Before embarking on this topic, we should, however, first consider those activities of the organisms which are not due to plasticity but are the product of ontogenic development of the individual determined by its phylogeny.

In speaking of innate activities of the organisms, we should have clearly in mind that their occurrence in the pure form is nearly nonexistent in the normal behavior of animals and man, because soon after birth the individual begins to modulate his innate responses by the feedback provided by their immediate consequences. In fact, relatively few primitive responses, mostly depending on the lower parts of the nervous axis—such as myotatic reflexes, swallowing, sneezing, and coughing—are rigid and preserve the same pattern both in various species and in various periods of life.

The same mixed nature characterizes all activities that are acquired during life through individual experience. Since all learned activities are developed on the basis of the phylogenetically predetermined structures whose modulation, but not whose existence, is conditioned by experience, they should always be considered a combination of innate and acquired components. As an obvious example, the language which we learned is a matter of individual experience, but the capacity to learn *any* language is innate and particular only to human species.

Despite this relativity of our division of the activities of the nervous system according to their origins, we shall, at least for the sake of clarity of further exposition, consider first the mechanisms controlling basic innate activities of the organisms and only then turn to the analysis of the mechanisms that underlie their learned behavior.

2. Categories of basic activities of the nervous system

Living organisms are machines of a particular type whose activity is directed in principle toward their preservation and perpetuation. To achieve this task, organisms have developed through phylogeny a number of particular mechanisms, each designed to fulfill particular roles in securing their well-being. Following Pavlov, these mechanisms will be referred to as unconditioned reflexes (UR).*

* To avoid misunderstanding, it should be made clear that we shall here designate as a reflex every process originating in receptive organs or higher levels of the afferent

Unconditioned reflexes may be classified into particular categories according to different criteria. First, they may be divided according to *stimuli* eliciting them; second, according to their *biological role;* third, according to their *sequence* in the given activity of the organism.

The first classification (according to stimuli) will not be discussed in detail here. Although it is undoubtedly important to procure the complete inventory of all unconditioned reflexes proper to particular species, this task is beyond the scope of the present study.

Much more important is the division of reflexes on the basis of their biological role. Here we may classify all reflexes into those which are absolutely indispensable to the preservation of the organisms (or species) whatever the conditions in which they exist, and those which are thrown into action only in states of emergency, when the organism is confronted with, or endangered by, a harmful agent. The first category of reflexes will be called *preservative* reflexes; the second, *protective reflexes.***

Preservative reflexes include the following groups: (1) reflexes concerned with assimilation of necessary materials (inspiratory and ingestive reflexes); (2) reflexes concerned with excretion of waste or unused materials (expiration, urination, defecation); (3) reflexes concerned with recuperation (sleep); (4) reflexes concerned with preservation of species (copulation, bearing progeny, and nurture of progeny).

Protective reflexes include: (1) reflexes concerned with the withdrawal of the whole body or any part from the operation of a noxious or endangering stimulus (retractive or retreat reflexes); (2) reflexes concerned with the rejection of harmful agents from the surface

---

part of the nervous system, mediated by nervous centers and terminating on some level of the efferent part of that system. We shall use this term for denoting those functions which are poly-effector, involving even the action of the whole organism, as well as those functions which are mono-effector or in which we deliberately select only a particular effect; we shall use this term, not only for "phasic" actions, in which both stimulus and response last for a relatively short time and are temporally locked, but also for "tonic" actions (often called "states"), in which the response is durable and may outlast the operation of a stimulus. Depending on the context we call particular reflexes either by the types of the stimuli eliciting them (for example, food reflex, pinprick reflex), or by the types of the functions produced by them (for example, alimentary reflex, defensive reflex), or finally by the types of their particular effects (for example, salivary reflex, flexion reflex). The aggregate of neurons mediating a given reflex, whatever its distribution in the nervous system, will be referred to as the "center" of this reflex.

** In the present work we shall not use the well-known Hess division of the basic activities of the organisms into trophotropic and ergotropic (cf. W. R. Hess, *The Functional Organization of the Diencephalon,* 1954), because its main criterion is their parasympathetic and sympathetic characteristics. As will be seen below, protective activities are not necessarily sympaticomimetic and preservative activities are not necessarily parasympaticomimetic.

of, or inside, the body (rejective reflexes); (3) reflexes concerned with annihilating or disarming harmful agents (offensive reflexes).

Some of the preservative reflexes are directed *toward* the objects to be utilized (food, the opposite sex); they will be referred to as *appetitive* reflexes; the stimuli which elicit them will be called *attractive* stimuli. Most of the protective reflexes are directed *away* from a noxious or dangerous stimulus; these will be called *defensive* reflexes; the stimuli concerned, *aversive* stimuli.

Division into preservative and protective reflexes should not be considered absolute, since organisms are usually confronted in their life with a continuum of conditions from which they choose those which are optimal for their well-being. In consequence, both these categories of reflexes serve the purpose of shifting the subject from a less favorable to a more favorable condition. For instance, low temperature acts as a harmful stimulus; hence it elicits a protective reflex. On

TABLE I-1

CLASSIFICATION OF BASIC ACTIVITIES
OF ORGANISMS

preservative preparatory	preservative consummatory
protective preparatory	protective consummatory

the other hand, aiming at the optimal temperature may be considered a preservative reflex. Similarly, grooming may be considered protection from parasites or the maintenance of a clean body. In spite of these reservations, the above division will prove useful, since most of the reflexes we shall discuss in this work may be conveniently classified within its framework.

The third way of dividing the basic activities of organisms is that concerning their sequential occurrence. If we take into account preservative activities, we shall see that unconditioned reflexes leading to certain profitable effects are usually preceded by preliminary actions directed to *providing* the appropriate stimuli eliciting these reflexes. Thus food intake is preceded by looking for food, going to sleep is preceded by looking for a secure place, and coitus is preceded by finding a partner of the opposite sex. The situation is somewhat different in protective unconditioned reflexes, because here preliminary actions are directed toward the *avoidance* of a noxious stimulus or at least toward making it less harmful. Accordingly, we shall divide the basic activities of the organisms, both preservative and protective, into *consummatory* reflexes—those elicited by the specific stimuli requiring an appropriate adaptive response—and *preparatory* reflexes—those tending to provide the attractive stimuli or to forestall the aversive stimuli.

According to this dual division, we can discern four categories of basic activities of the organisms: preservative-preparatory, preservative-consummatory, protective-preparatory and protective-consummatory (Table I-1). Below we shall discuss successively each of these categories.

3. Consummatory alimentary unconditioned reflex

As a model of basic preservative activities, we shall utilize the alimentary UR because this reflex plays a substantial role in experiments on the acquired behavior of animals (to be discussed in Chapters VI–XI).

By the consummatory food UR, we shall denote the course of events which start at the moment when the edible substance makes contact with the mouth, particularly when it is put into the oral cavity, and which end in swallowing. In other words, we shall exclude from the consummatory ingestive reflex the preceding phase when the perception of food (by vision or smell) leads to definite motor activities that cause its being placed in the mouth. We shall see later that this phase constitutes the last stage of the preparatory feeding activity and is based on mechanisms different from those involved in the consummatory reflex itself.

The ingestive UR produced by solid food is composed of two stages. In the first stage, the food evokes masticatory movements accompanied by salivation until the bolus—the slimy pellet that is a mixture of chewed food, mucus, and liquid—is formed. The bolus is then moved to the back part of the mouth, and the second stage of the reflex follows—swallowing. When the food is liquid, its presence in the mouth immediately causes deglutition.

According to the experimental work of Sherrington,[3] who studied the masticatory reflex in decerebrate cats, this reflex occurs in the following way.

In the decerebrate preparation the mouth is tonically closed, as it is in normal animals in the waking state. Tactile stimuli, consisting of touch or pressure of some parts of the oral cavity, cause the mouth to open by contraction of the jaw-opening muscles and reciprocal relaxation of the jaw-closing muscles. The optimal reflexogenic zone for the jaw-opening reflex is the gum bordering the teeth of either the upper or the lower jaw and the front part of the hard palate. The cessation of stimulation of these regions immediately produces a strong rebound: the jaw-opening muscles are relaxed, and the jaw-closing muscles are contracted, causing the mouth to close vigorously. Since with the mouth closed the solid unchewed food again presses onto the gums and the walls of the oral cavity, the next act of opening the mouth follows, again succeeded by its closing. In this way the masticatory rhythmic movements are repeated until the morsel of food is completely chewed.

Although this mechanism provides the basis for the masticatory reflex, it is obviously still too crude and rigid to be fully effective. The higher levels of the nervous axis (particularly the sensori-motor mouth area of the cerebral cortex) contribute greatly to making this primitive mechanism more flexible and adjusting it to the particular size, shape, and consistency of the morsel of food throughout mastication. In this respect the observation of dogs in which the sensori-motor mouth area (situated in the coronal gyrus) has been bilaterally removed is most instructive. These dogs are greatly handicapped in chewing, and the food often falls out of their mouths. The movements of the jaws, although even more vigorous than in normal dogs, lack skill and precision. Therefore the act of mastication lasts for a much longer time and remains less effective than normally, because the animal is deprived of the proper feedback concerning the location of the morsel of food in the mouth and its consistency, and also of the skillful manipulation of food by coordinate delicate movements of the tongue and the jaws.

We have clear evidence that the main stimuli controlling mastication are somatic stimuli—touch, pressure, and possibly proprioception. Taste plays no role in the act of mastication, except that of determining whether the substance should be masticated or rejected. When the gustatory sensation is reduced or abolished after the removal of the taste area, the animals properly chew the material put into their mouths, although it may be inedible, such as cotton or paper. The common habit of masticating chewing gum is another illustrative example which shows that taste is not indispensable to the chewing reflex: since chewing gum cannot form a bolus because it is water-repellent, the reflex continues indefinitely when the substance is in the mouth and stimulates the appropriate reflexogenic zones.

Another reflex produced by the presence of food in the mouth is salivation, which was studied in great detail by Pavlov[4] at the turn of the century. Although the taste of food plays no role in the masticatory reflex, it does play perhaps the most dominant role in the salivary reflex. In fact, salivation is elicited by both solid and liquid substances if they act on chemoreceptors of the mouth. If the substance put into the mouth is tasteless (such as water), no salivation occurs.

The lower center controlling the salivary reflex is in the medulla.[5] Messages from taste receptors in the mouth run mainly through the lingual nerve and reach the nucleus of the solitary fasciculus; hence they are carried to the nuclei innervating the salivary glands.

The higher center of the salivary reflex is within the somato-sensory mouth area of the cerebral cortex. The ascendant pathways run from the *nucleus solitarius* via the medial postero-ventral nucleus of the thalamus and reach the cortical taste area. Stimulation of that area elicits salivation; its ablation produces a dramatic impairment in taste discrimination and a strong decrease in salivary reflexes.[6]

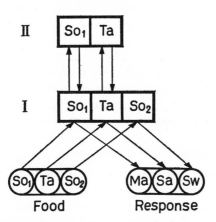

FIG. I-1. BLOCK MODEL OF THE FOOD CONSUMMATORY UR

I, lower level of integration; II, higher level of integration. Squares, nervous centers, circles, peripheral stimuli and responses. So_1, tactile and postural stimuli within the mouth, and their centers; Ta, taste stimuli and their centers; So_2, tactile stimuli of the back part of the mouth, and their centers; Ma, mastication; Sa, salivation; Sw, swallowing.

Note that the center of swallowing is thought to be localized on the lower level only.

When, owing to the conjoint act of mastication and salivation, the bolus is formed, the next stage of the ingestive reflex occurs, namely, deglutition, which was studied in great detail by Miller and Sherrington[7] in decerebrate cats.

The reflexogenic zone for deglutition is situated in the posterior part of the tongue, the soft palate, and the pharynx. It is interesting to note that in the decerebrate preparation the swallowing reflex is promptly elicited by water or water solutions within a large range of temperature but not by oil. A solution of alcohol seems to be the most effective stimulus for deglutition, eliciting repeated swallowing movements. On the other hand, a bolus, even placed in the optimal reflexogenic zone for swallowing, either fails completely to elicit this reflex or elicits it irregularly and with long latency. Evidently either the swallowing response to a bolus requires the presence of some higher centers, or the reflex must be facilitated by the preceding chewing reflex. In normal conditions the swallowing reflex is produced by fluids and by slimy objects but not by dry ones. This explains why we do not swallow chewing gum and have great difficulties in swallowing dry pills, even if they are much smaller than the usual boluses. In order to swallow a pill, we must take into the mouth a sufficient amount of water to prevent the dry object from touching our oral receptors. Dry, rough, or sharp-edged objects reaching the reflexogenic swallowing zone elicit the antagonistic reflex—vomiting. The lowest center integrating the swallowing act is in the medulla.

This short survey of the central mechanism of the ingestive reflexes is summarized in the block model in Figure I-1. In this model each block is a "black box" representing afferent neurons receiving messages from the periphery, internuncial neurons, and efferent neurons transmitting the patterned message to the executive centers.

4. Consummatory protective unconditioned reflexes

As stated above, the protective URs may be divided into: (1) retreat or retractive reflexes, (2) rejection reflexes, and (3) offensive reflexes. The first and the second categories, in contradistinction to the third, will be denoted as defensive reflexes, according to the original meaning of this term used by Pavlov and Bechterev.

(1) Among many forms of retractive reflexes, the best known in experimental practice is the flexor reflex. Its biological role is obvious, since terrestrial animals are permanently exposed to the danger of operation of noxious stimuli on the ground and therefore had to develop the appropriate mechanism for coping with such accidents. The fact that the mechanism controlling this reflex is in the spinal cord shows how fundamental and primitive this defensive mechanism is. However, as is true of nearly all the basic activities of the organism, the flexor reflex, being relatively simple in the spinal preparation, grows in complication and precision when higher nervous structures, including the cerebral cortex, are involved.

Retractive reflexes are elicited not only by the operation of pain-producing stimuli but also by those of other modalities. For instance, an unpleasant odor or the touch of objects eliciting disgust (slimy or muddy objects) consistently evoke withdrawal of the head or the limb, not only in humans but in other organisms as well.

(2) The protective consummatory reflexes of the second category

reject aversive stimuli from the surface or inside the body. Included in this category are the following types of reflexes:

(a) Vomiting reflex, produced either by irritation of the back part of the mouth and pharynx with dry or sharp objects or by ingestion of aversive substances (or their odor).

(b) Sneezing and coughing reflexes, produced by irritation of the nasal mucosa or respiratory tract.

(c) Rejecting reflexes, produced by introduction into the mouth of such aversive substances as dry sand or solutions of chinine or acids. This type of reflex, which rarely occurs in natural life, was used by Pavlov in his studies on conditioning. The effect of the reflex consists of mouthing movements and copious salivation.

(d) Shaking reflex of the entire body or limbs. Here we may include shaking the head in response to an air-puff into the ear and rhythmic extensor thrusts in response to a band tightly attached to the hindleg.

(e) Scratch reflex, which was investigated in great detail by Sherrington[8] at the turn of the century as the model of spinal reflexes. Although the scratch reflex can be easily elicited even in the low spinal preparation, it is rudimentary in this condition and consists simply of rhythmic movements of the hindleg executed in the air without touching the body. Only in the normal animal does this reflex achieve the necessary precision and skill to reach, by means of appropriate bodily posture, without losing the balance of the body, the exact spot on the skin which is irritated.

The scratch reflex is never elicited by a true painful agent (which evokes retractive or offensive reflexes) but rather by a light tactile stimulus preferably moving from one place to another. Its biological role is to fight against skin parasites. As such it might be included in the next category of protective activities—the offensive reflexes.

(3) The offensive or aggressive reflexes are directed toward the destruction of the source of a harmful stimulus. In natural life harmful stimuli are often provided by other animals of a different, or even of the same, species. The biologically adequate response may sometimes be not escaping but fighting. As a result, the same noxious stimuli may elicit either defensive reflexes or aggressive reflexes, depending on the conditions in which they operate.

A striking example of this dual role of a noxious stimulus was provided in experiments on rats.[9] If rats or mice are subjected to painful stimuli provided by an electrified floor, they usually display a regular retraction reflex consisting of jumping or climbing the walls. If, however, two animals are placed together in the same small compartment, their response to the electrified floor changes radically; instead of dis-

playing the retractive reflex, they begin to fight. This reflex stops immediately when the stimulation is discontinued.

No less instructive are observations on rats, cats, and dogs on the
effects of squeezing the distal part of the tail or the limb. As a rule the
animals do not display any attempt to escape but rather strong aggression, even if the painful stimulus is provided by an inanimate object.
Similarly, a dog usually exhibits a strong aggression toward the apparatus producing the air-puff into the ear and attempts to bite the experimenter if his hand is near the ear. Aggressive reflexes are also displayed by a decorticated dog if its back is touched.

To conclude this cursory survey of the consummatory reflexes,
both preservative and protective, we should like to draw attention to
an important characteristic of the stimuli by which they are elicited.
These stimuli always have a refined and discriminative character and
differ from those stimuli which are utilized by neurophysiologists for
studying receptive mechanisms of the anesthetized animals. As mentioned above, slimy and fluid objects (but not oil) touching the soft
palate produce deglutition, whereas dry objects produce the vomiting
reflex; pain administered to the feet produces in rats a different effect
from the same pain plus the vicinity of another subject; the scratch
reflex, even on the spinal level, is evoked by an extremely refined stimulus whose full characteristic in terms of receptors is still not known.
In other words, these simple and seemingly primitive reflexes require
for their elicitation very fine and elaborate stimulus-patterns which
must fit them as exactly as a key fits a lock, to use Sherrington's ingenious comparison. The realization of this point is of prime importance, because no physiological theory of higher nervous activity can be
considered adequate if it does not provide its satisfactory explanation.

5. Consummatory unconditioned reflexes to biologically neutral
stimuli (targeting reflexes)

So far we have been concerned with a rather limited group of stimuli
which have a definite biological role and as such elicit particular unconditioned responses. In this group belong: nociceptive stimuli of
various character administered to particular parts of the body; specific
somatic stimuli administered to the mucosa of the mouth; various
categories of taste stimuli; aversive odors; vestibular stimuli producing
postural responses; somatic stimuli applied to sexual organs; increased
pressure in the urinary bladder or in the rectum. Yet, an incomparably larger number of stimuli impinging upon receptive organs are
not directly connected with any definite biological significance. Nevertheless, these originally "neutral" or "indifferent" stimuli produce a

number of highly elaborated reflexes directed to their optimal inspection for the purpose of their association with biologically significant stimuli. In this section we shall discuss those specific responses produced by the neutral stimuli which can be classified as consummatory responses.

If a new indifferent stimulus is presented to the animal, the only biologically reasonable response to it is that providing information as to what may be the use of this stimulus, or what danger it carries. For this purpose the animal has to adjust the corresponding receptive organs in such a way as to perceive this stimulus most effectively. In psychological terms we say that the subject "pays attention" to the presented stimulus. Since the corresponding physiological term "orienting reflex" is used in various senses, usually referring to *all* elements comprised in the reaction to novelty, we would propose a new term *targeting reflex*, which will specifically denote *the adjustment of a given analyzer to the better perception of a stimulus*. The whole array of unspecific somatic and autonomic responses usually elicited by a new stimulus—such as startle, increase of heart rate, change in skin resistance—will be called, following Pavlov, *orientation reflex* (to be discussed in a later section).

What are the effects of targeting reflexes elicited by stimuli of particular modalities?

Visual stimuli provided by presentation of particular visual patterns produce a number of responses by which the given pattern is focused upon the foveae of both eyes. This is achieved by turning the eyes and head toward the object (fixation reflex), converging the eyeballs, and adjusting the lenses and pupils to the best reception of the pattern (accommodation). When the stimulus-pattern changes its place, the eyes and head follow it, to hold it in the field of precise vision.

There is good anatomical and physiological evidence to show that the visual targeting reflex is mediated by the superior colliculi and adjacent structures as the lower level, and the visual area of the cerebral cortex as the higher level of its controlling mechanism. Superior colliculi receive fibers from (and probably send fibers to) the visual cortex, particularly from the parastriate area (area 18), through the internal corticotectal tract, and send fibers to the oculomotor nuclei. Unilateral lesions in the superior colliculi lead to a complete or relative neglect of contralateral visual stimuli, whereas bilateral collicular lesions produce an enduring deficit in fixation and following reflexes.[10] Bilateral occipital lesions produce a similar deficit.[11] Stimulation of the striate and parastriate area produces conjugate eye deviations in various planes.

The mechanism of the auditory targeting reflex is similar to that of the visual targeting reflex. The reflex consists of pricking up the ears, turning the head toward the source of the sound, and contracting the middle ear muscles in proportion to the intensity of the stimulus.

It may be assumed that the control of the auditory targeting reflex is again accomplished on two levels; in the inferior colliculi, and in the auditory area of the cortex. In fact, the inferior colliculi are bidirectionally linked through the medial geniculate body (and perhaps also directly) with the auditory cortex and send descending fibers by way of the tectospinal tract. The physiological evidence of the cortical control of the auditory targeting reflex is provided by the results of ablations of the auditory projective area. It has been shown that bilateral ablation of this area produces a striking impairment of the localization of the source of sound,[12] and nearly total abolition of the tensor tympani reflex to the auditory stimuli.[13]

The olfactory targeting reflex is accomplished by repeated sniffing movements observed in those animals in which smell plays an important role as the source of information about the external world. The central control of this reflex is not known.

Finally, the physiological mechanism of tactile targeting reflexes is also poorly understood. Subjectively, we can easily concentrate our attention on a definite tactile stimulus when we palpate an object in dark, but it is not clearly known what mechanism is then in operation. The role of the somato-sensory cortex in the occurrence of the tactile targeting reflex is documented by the so-called extinction phenomenon: if in a patient with a somato-sensory cortical lesion two symmetrical points on the skin are simultaneously touched, he does not perceive the tactile stimulus on the side contralateral to the lesion.

We may conclude that according to the available evidence the projective areas of the cerebral cortex seem to play an important role in appropriate targeting reflexes. The significance of this fact will be further discussed in connection with the physiology of perceptions.

An important property of targeting reflexes is that they are not stimulus-bound. Beginning with the presentation of a given stimulus, the targeting reflex decreases with its duration and eventually disappears. Psychologically, the subject is no longer interested in the stimulus and stops paying attention to it. This process, called habituation, will be discussed in detail in Chapter II, Section 10.

6. Preparatory alimentary unconditioned reflex (hunger)

Having analyzed the representative consummatory URs to attractive, aversive, and "neutral" stimuli, we turn now to the discussion of preparatory URs. Again we shall begin by considering a preparatory

preservative reflex, and we shall choose for our analysis the preparatory activity connected with food intake.

It is generally accepted that the preparatory activity leading to the
consummatory alimentary reflex is controlled by *hunger*. From the
physiological point of view, hunger may be considered a *definite pattern of central nervous processes manifested by particular effects directed to procuring food and discontinued after food has been ingested ad libitum*. The latter state, opposite to hunger, is referred to
as *satiation*.

According to our definition, hunger is not identical either with
starvation—that is, simple deprivation of food for a length of time—or
with physiological need of food manifested by the physical symptoms
of starvation. Rather, it is a control mechanism of a particular reflex action which we shall call the *hunger reflex*. Accordingly, our immediate
task will be the specification of those stimuli which elicit hunger and
those responses which are produced by it. Then we shall turn to the
analysis of the central mechanism mediating the hunger reflex. In this
chapter we shall speak only of unconditioned hunger reflexes.

The question of what *stimuli* elicit the hunger UR is not simple,
chiefly because, as we shall see in our further discussion, hunger can
be produced by a number of factors acting either separately or, most
often, in various combinations. In consequence, it is not possible totally to discard any single factor suspected as eliciting hunger on the
basis of mere evidence indicating that this factor alone was not effective in producing it. Thus, any monistic theory of the origin of
hunger does not seem to be very likely.

First, the appearance of hunger depends to a great extent on both
the length of time elapsed from the last meal and the amount of food
eaten at that meal. Accordingly, hunger may be ascribed either to the
information transmitted to the brain from interoceptors in the digestive tract or to the changes in the composition of the blood affecting
the neurons of the appropriate centers, or to both these factors.

In the lengthy discussion on the origin of hunger, Cannon[14] has
shown that hunger is not correlated with emptiness of the stomach.
On the other hand, his own concept—that hunger is due to afferent
messages concerning *contractions* of the empty stomach—must be
abandoned on the basis of evidence indicating that neither vagotomy,
which totally abolishes these contractions,[15] nor total resection of the
stomach affects the hunger reflex. The close correlation of hunger
contractions with the sensation of hunger demonstrated by Cannon
must be attributed to the fact that the contractions are the *effect* of
the hunger reflex rather than its *source*. Since, however, these contractions appear when the stomach is empty and stop when it is filled,

and since extension of the gastric wall is a factor producing satiation, we can conclude that the emptiness of the stomach *can* be treated as one of the agents contributing to the occurrence of hunger.

The role of blood composition as a hunger-producing factor is much better documented. The "glucostatic theory" of hunger has been proposed, according to which hunger depends on the contents of glucose in blood or, more precisely, on the capacity of its utilization measured by the difference between the level of sugar in the arterial and venous blood.[16]

The question may, however, be raised as to whether the gluco-receptors in the central nervous system are the only chemoreceptors that determine whether the subject is or is not hungry, or whether other nutritive substances contained in the blood and passing the cerebro-spinal barrier also play a role in its determination.

We have much evidence to show that in both animals and man there is no single hunger directed to obtaining any food but, rather, selective hungers directed to definite kinds of food and neglecting other kinds. Although this selectivity may depend on other factors which will be discussed later, there is no doubt that specific hungers are also produced by humoral factors—that is, by relative deprivation or need of particular nutritive substances, such as proteins or their components, salts, and the like.[17] The fact that a person, after having been on a strict diet for a long time because of an illness, or because of unfavorable life conditions, or being in a state of particular nutritive needs (for example, in pregnancy), "craves" a certain kind of food to the exclusion of others may be explained only by assuming that specific lacks produce specific hungers. Another fact substantiating this view is that the injection of insulin produces not an increase of hunger in general but selective hunger for sweets. Thus the afferent side of the hunger system represents a highly differentiated chemoreceptive field in which "receptors" of various kinds, although probably anatomically intermingled, react to particular molecules.

Considering the humoral factors as important hunger-producing stimuli, we should, however, clearly realize that they are not the only determinants of the hunger reflex. Leaving those factors which produce hunger by way of conditioning for later discussion (Chapter VI), we shall deal here only with those stimuli which may be considered as having an unconditional character. The most prominent of these stimuli is provided by *offering a small portion of food to a subject which is not fully satiated.*

The experiment illustrating this fact runs as follows. A dog is well habituated to the experimental chamber, where he remains for a long time but never gets food. His behavior does not display any hunger;

on the contrary, he is impassive and calm. If we now offer the animal a small portion of tasty food, his whole attitude is changed; immediately after the consummatory food response is terminated, he displays a strong hunger reflex lasting for several minutes.

The same thing is observed in human beings. It is our common experience that if we sit down to a routine meal without being at all hungry because the previous meal was too recent or was too abundant, one piece of tasty food is enough to evoke hunger. The proverb "l'appétit vient en mangeant" illustrates this phenomenon. Thus, a briefly operating taste stimulus eliciting the consummatory reaction immediately produces the hunger UR if the subject is not oversatiated.

Further analysis of this phenomenon may reveal that the appetizing effect of a small portion of food is highly selective, arousing hunger directed specifically to that food which has been just tasted. This fact may be easily tested by self-observation, and is clearly shown by the so-called peanut phenomenon—in which one nut will arouse a selective appetite for eating another. Experimentally this fact has been proved in the following way.[18] A dog was trained to perform two different movements: one for procuring bread, and the other for procuring water from the same bowl. When the animal was thirsty but food-satiated, he performed only the water movements; when he was hungry but water-satiated, he performed only the food movements. When, however, he was both hungry and thirsty, he performed both movements alternately, but each appeared repeatedly in rather long series. In other words, when he started working for food, he continued to do so for some time; only then, after a moment of hesitation, did he switch to working for water, or vice versa. Priming the animal by food or water unmistakably led to the performance of the food movement or the water movement respectively. The same switching occurred if after the food movement water was offered instead of food, or vice versa. Exactly the same relations were observed in Wyrwicka's experiments on rabbits which were fed by two kinds of food, each provided by a different instrumental act.*

Hunger evoked by priming plays a most important role in the normal life of animals and man, and bears directly upon the problem of the so-called palatability of food.

When we discussed the role of taste in consummatory reflexes, the problem of its attractiveness did not enter the picture. In discussing

---

* Apparent contradiction to this thesis is seen in the human type of feeding in which complex dishes are served in our usual menu. These dishes are of course carefully combined and may be compared with fugues or accords in the acoustic analyzer. The principle of selectivity of the appetites produced by "priming" may be, however, manifested in man by a series of separate dishes served at our dinners: we would hardly accept a feast in which single gulps of each dish were offered in alternating sequence.

hunger, however, this aspect of taste is of prime importance. Generally speaking, the more hungry we are for a given food, the greater is the satisfaction when this food is put into the mouth, and a more intense hunger for that food is aroused when a portion of it is consumed. Analogously, when a dog is given bread in the experimental chamber, and then a portion of meat is substituted for the bread, the animal immediately becomes animated and his hunger is greatly increased.

Finally, we can ask ourselves whether there are other external unconditioned stimuli beyond taste stimuli which also contribute to the elicitation of hunger reflexes. Although the direct evidence to that issue is still lacking it is probable that the *smell* of food seems to belong to that category of stimuli, at least in some species of animals. In the protocols of old experiments by Cytovich[18a] it was indicated that when the young dogs which had been fed so far only on milk were for the first time confronted with meat, its odor (in contradistinction to its sight) was by no means neutral, but exhibited a strong attractive effect and the tendency to take the piece of meat into the mouth. Similarly it was proved by Coustan that in newborn animals the smell of nipples plays a most important role in feeding behavior.[18b]

It is quite possible that in particular species of animals some other exteroceptive stimuli (e.g., visual) may play a role in innate hunger reflexes, as they do in protective preparatory activity (see next section).

For the sake of terminological convenience we shall denote by *appetite* hunger determined by taste of food, its smell or other exteroceptive stimuli, both unconditioned and conditioned. Hunger produced by purely humoral factors affecting directly intraneural chemoreceptors will be called *humoral hunger*. It should be emphasized that both categories of hunger-producing factors usually operate jointly with the relative preponderance of one of them.

We turn now to the description of the *effects* produced by hunger.

The most conspicuous effect of hunger is a general *motor restlessness*. This effect is observed in all laboratory animals, such as mice, rats, cats, dogs, and monkeys. It is also easily noticed in zoo animals just before feeding time. In normal human adults it is usually inhibited by social factors, but it is clearly manifest in infants, who "announce" hunger by their excitement. Both in human infants and in many species of animals, vocalization belongs to the most usual symptoms of hunger.

If we closely observe the restlessness of animals during hunger we may notice that it does not have a character of hyperkinesis (chaotic muscle contractions) but rather of hyperactivity, consisting of a series of behavioral acts specific for a given animal and following one another in a changing order. Since, as will be discussed in later chapters, we have some reasons to believe that there is a common system in the brain in which the "programing" of the behavioral acts occurs, we can assume that the effect of hunger is to facilitate or mobilize that system. Accordingly, we shall refer to this state of restlessness as the *arousal of the motor behavioral system.*

In proportion to the motor hyperactivity produced by hunger we also observe in this state the increased *efficiency* of the motor system in general and of the masticatory muscles in particular. Hungry animals living in free conditions are amazingly capable of strong physical efforts when they are hungry; the same is true of humans in particular situations. A good experimental example of this fact was provided by experiments by Hananashvili,[19] who trained dogs to jump over a high barrier in order to get food. He noticed that the ability to overcome this barrier was closely related to the degree of hunger. When hunger was moderate and they were primed by bread, the dogs tried in vain to jump over; but when hunger was primed by meat, they immediately succeeded in doing so.

Although in most animals used in behavioristic experiments, as well as in human beings, the preparatory alimentary behavior controlled by hunger is further shaped according to individual experience, in some instances we observe also the inherited, rigid forms of this behavior. Hunting activity (stalking, attacking, and so on) observed in predators is a typical example of such behavior.

In this connection the question arises as to whether the act of seizing food by mouth in response to its sight or smell should be considered an unconditioned hunger response or a conditioned response acquired by a natural training in early life.

It is difficult to answer this question without performing special experiments. In those birds which peck at all small objects immediately after hatching, the response is certainly innate, and only its discriminatory character is due to experience. According to numerous observations made by Slonim and his associates[20] on mammals, it may be supposed that the response is mixed, and that in various species either the innate or the acquired element takes the upper hand.

Another manifestation of the hunger UR is the arousal of particular *afferent* systems—that is, increased attention to stimuli of various modalities. There is no doubt that in the state of hunger the excitability of the gustatory analyzer is strongly increased, and the same is true of the olfactory analyzer; a subject, who in a state of satiation does not pay any attention to weak odors, does so when he is in a state of hunger. Further, we have good reason to believe that the hunger reflex elicits strong arousal in the visual analyzer and/or in the auditory analyzer in those animals in which visual or auditory perceptions play a dominant role in the search for food.

Whereas these two effects of hunger—arousal of the motor behavioral system, and arousal of the afferent systems—are well known from general observation of animals and men as well as from the role they play in conditioning, we have, unfortunately, only meager knowledge of the particular effects of hunger upon the autonomic system. The only well-established fact concerns the so-called hunger contractions of the stomach (hunger pangs) observed both in humans with gastric fistula and in animals. These slow contractions involve the whole stomach, and increase in frequency and duration with the increase of hunger. They have nothing to do with peristaltic movements of the stomach produced when it is filled with food. Other alimentary autonomic responses, such as salivation or gastric secretion, are elements of the food consummatory reflex and are certainly not produced by hunger itself (cf. Chapter IX).

The question may be asked as to what kind of *general* autonomic activation is produced by hunger. Does hunger give rise to the preponderance of the sympathetic system, of the parasympathetic system, or is it autonomically neutral?*

Unfortunately, we cannot give an answer to this important question because of a lack of direct experimental evidence. The fact that hunger is connected with an increase of the general motor activity and augmented muscular efficiency seems to suggest that it produces an increase of the sympathetic tonus. If this supposition is confirmed by further experimental data, preservative activities would not be obligatorily "trophotropic" in Hess's sense.

Having discussed in brief the afferent and efferent sides of the hunger UR, let us turn now to the consideration of its central mechanism. Not long ago such a consideration could have been based merely on conjectures, because we had to infer the mechanism of this reflex only from the properties of its input and output. The situation has, however, changed radically in recent years. It has now become possible, by

---

* It should be emphasized that when we speak of the sympathetic or parasympathetic character of a certain activity, we utilize these terms with great reservation, indicating only a relative preponderance of this or that outflow. As a matter of fact, in nearly all physiological states the autonomic responses follow some definite complex patterns which cannot be characterized as purely sympathetic or parasympathetic, because they are usually mixed. The situation here is similar to that encountered in the somatic system, in which hardly any natural movement can be considered as consisting of pure contraction of flexors with relaxation of extensors, or vice versa.

means of electrical stimulation of the areas involved in controlling hunger in waking animals, and appropriate lesions, to localize the relevant areas of the brain and to learn directly their functional properties.

In this book we do not intend to go into details of all these data, or to evaluate various discrepancies and differences of opinions which still exist among the investigators. We would like only to outline those conclusions which can at this time be safely drawn and which allow us to understand the functional mechanism of the alimentary preparatory system.

There is a large body of evidence that the preparatory alimentary activity is controlled by two reciprocally related subsystems, which may be called the hunger subsystem and the satiation subsystem.

The lower level of both subsystems is represented in the hypothalamus. The hypothalamic hunger center is in the lateral nucleus, whereas the hypothalamic satiation center is in the ventromedial nucleus. Stimulation of the lateral hypothalamus produces a typical picture of hunger which does not differ from that observed in natural conditions. It is best seen in animals which were previously satiated, because then it contrasts sharply with the opposite state.

The goat is a good subject for such observation.[21] A satiated goat is quiet and apathetic, with a tendency to lie down in a drowsy state. When the lateral hypothalamus is stimulated, the animal becomes alert and, with increasing stimulation, more and more restless. It displays a searching type of behavior, looks around, attempts to climb the walls of the partition, grasps the clothes of persons in the vicinity. When food is offered, the animal eats it voraciously and during the act of eating remains calm, becoming restless again when the food is removed. The cessation of stimulation causes an immediate termination of the act of eating or restlessness, and the animal returns to the previous apathetic state.

On the contrary, stimulation of the hypothalamic satiation center causes an immediate cessation of the act of eating, and the goat becomes quiet and apathetic. Often he turns away from the food and lies down. The cessation of stimulation causes an immediate return to the food and more intensive ingestion, apparently due to rebound.[22]

Experiments concerned with hypothalamic lesions were performed chiefly on rats and gave the opposite results. Lesions affecting the lateral hypothalamus produce at first total aphagia, which thereafter sooner or later changes into anorexia.[23] In that period the animals take only the most palatable food but refuse to ingest the ordinary laboratory food which they readily consumed before the surgery. The period of recovery depends largely on the extent of the lesion. The consummatory food reflex is preserved: when food is placed into the mouth, the animal is able to swallow it.

Lesions sustained in the ventromedial hypothalamus give rise to hyperphagia: the animals eat much more than before the surgery, and, if allowed to eat *ad libitum*, gain considerable weight. Then the food intake returns to slightly above normal, and the weight of the animal becomes constant. Interestingly, the obese animals, like the hypophagic ones, become very finicky. If food is mixed with non-nutritive material, they stop eating completely, whereas normal animals increase their food intake. They also stop eating when a small amount of quinine, not disturbing the consummatory response of normal animals, is added to the food. On the contrary, if the diet is flavored with dextrose, the food intake is considerably increased in the ventromedial animals whereas it is slightly decreased in normal rats.[24]

The higher levels of the hunger and satiation subsystems are represented in the limbic brain. Although the localization of appropriate centers is still poorly understood, their existence is documented by both ablation and stimulation experiments. There is some evidence to show that lesions in the baso-lateral part of the amygdaloid complex produce hyperphagia.[25] Stimulation of the same structures gives rise to a dramatic inhibition of food intake, which lasts for a considerable period of time and may even remain permanent for the food that was consumed during stimulation.[26] Aphagia turning into anorexia is produced by lesions in more medial parts of the amygdala.[27]

What is the organization of this whole preparatory alimentary system? Of course, we are still far from the answer, but can offer tentative suggestions.

The first question is where the intracentral chemoreceptors regulating hunger reflexes to particular nutritive substances are situated. The most reasonable assumption seems to be that the molecules of these substances act directly upon corresponding chemoreceptors of the hypothalamic satiation center. It may be further assumed that neurons of the satiation center send inhibitory impulses to corresponding neurons of the hunger center which produce hunger for particular alimentary substances. Thus the aggregate of neurons in the satiation center excited by the appropriate molecules inhibits the corresponding neurons of the hunger center. On the contrary, the lack of these molecules in the surrounding fluid releases the given part of the hunger center from their inhibitory influence (Figure I-2).

The interrelations described seem now to be substantiated by the direct electrophysiological evidence.[28] They do not, however, imply that the hypothalamic hunger center, or for that matter the whole hunger subsystem, depends fully on the humoral factors acting upon the satiation center. First, there is some evidence that nutritive substances, in particular glucose, may also act directly on the hunger center and cause its inhibition.[29] Second, as indicated before, we can effectively stimulate artificially the hypothalamic hunger center in a fully satiated animal and produce a normal act of eating. This indicates that this center *can* be activated *in spite* of the inhibitory influence exerted upon it from the satiation center. Third, the relative independence of the hunger subsystem from the satiation subsystem is documented by the fact that even if the hunger subsystem *is* released from the inhibitory

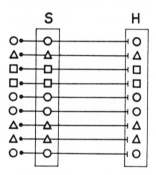

Fig. I-2. Schematic Representation of the Influence of Satiation Center upon Hunger Center

S, satiation center; H, hunger center. Circles, triangles, and squares denote various molecules of nutritive substances. They are assumed to stimulate the appropriate chemoreceptors in the satiation center. The units of this center send inhibitory impulses to the corresponding units of the hunger center. Possible direct inhibitory influence of the molecules upon the hunger center is not indicated.

influence of the latter, it is not *ipso facto* activated. There are other powerful agents, both unconditioned and conditioned, which influence the hunger subsystem independently of the humoral factors. As stated before, the chief unconditioned factor activating the hunger subsystem is represented by the consumption of a small portion of food in a not oversatiated subject. Another factor that contributes to activating the hunger center is provided by the smell of food. On the other hand, the extension of the gastric wall caused by food in the stomach inhibits the hunger center. Inhibition of this center is also produced by increased body temperature and by antagonistic reflexes (cf. Section 12, below). The mode of operation of these factors is still not clear.

Thus we see that the level of hunger at each particular moment is the result of the combination of all these positive and negative influences.

The chief functional significance of the higher level of the preparatory alimentary system is associative—by its mediation the alimentary conditioned reflexes are formed (cf. Chapter VI). We assume that each center of this higher level is connected bidirectionally with the corresponding center of the lower level. The ascending connections transmit the messages informing the higher centers of the hunger-satiation interrelations produced in the lower centers; the descending connections transmit orders which correct and modulate the activity of these centers according to the particular information concerning the environmental situation of the organism in the given moment and its previous experiences. A block model of the hunger-satiation system, showing its chief functional properties, is represented in Figure I-3.

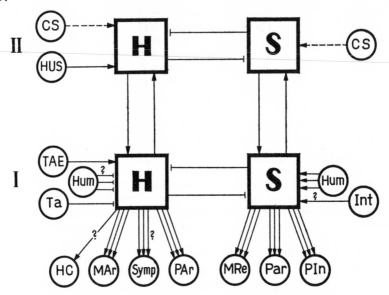

FIG. I-3. BLOCK MODEL OF THE HUNGER-SATIATION SYSTEM (SIMPLIFIED)

I, lower level of the system; II, higher level of the system. H, hunger centers; S, satiation centers. →, excitatory connections; —|, inhibitory connections;-→, conditioned connections. Ta, effect of taste (see Section 10); TAE, taste aftereffect; Int, interoceptive stimuli; Hum, humoral stimuli; CS, conditioned stimulus; HUS, hunger US (e.g., smell of food); HC, hunger contractions; MAr, motor arousal; Symp, sympathetic outflow; PAr, perceptual arousal; MRe, motor relaxation; Par, parasympathetic outflow; PIn, perceptual indifference.

Since it was reported that hunger contractions are present after lateral hypothalamic lesions (J. Mayer and S. Sudsaneh, Mechanism of hypothalamic control of gastric contractions in rat, *Amer. J. Physiol.*, 197 [1959]: 274–85), they may depend also on a lower (vagal) reflex-arc probably thrown into action by irritation of the stomach by the balloon.

On the basis of these considerations we can easily explain a number of experimental findings concerning the food intake in normal and brain-lesioned animals. Here we shall deal only with those phenomena which have an unconditioned character (or nearly so), leaving those findings which involve conditioning to later chapters.

The food intake in normal animals living in a uniform situation (such as rats in their cages) is regulated both by hunger provided by the deficit of nutritive substances in blood and by appetite provided by the palatability of the food consumed. In normal conditions the first factor is sufficient for eliciting the hunger reflex, and therefore the animal takes a sufficient quantity of food, even if its gustatory value is reduced by the addition of non-nutritive substances. After a lesion in the hypothalamic hunger center, the animal is initially aphagic but gradually recovers, probably because the center is only partly destroyed. However, since the hunger mechanism is impaired, the elicitation of the hunger reflex requires a more intense stimulation, which is provided by increasing the palatability of the diet. This is the same measure used on humans when their hunger is decreased because of disease or partial satiation.

Quite different is the situation after lesions in the hypothalamic satiation center. The effect of such a lesion is twofold. First, the chief (if not the only) chemical analyzer of the nutritive constituents of the blood is destroyed. Thus the brain is no longer informed about the nutritive needs of the organism, and in consequence the amount of food intake is no longer restrained by "blood satiation." On the other hand, since the appetite mechanism is not impaired, it takes over control of the food intake and even seems to be sensitized by the elimination of the satiation mechanism. Hence the hyperphagic animals become more "finicky" than normal ones, regulating their appetite almost exclusively by the palatability of the diet.

7. Preparatory protective unconditioned reflexes

Now we shall turn to the consideration of a preparatory activity somewhat different from the previous one—that concerned with protection from noxious agents. We shall begin our discussion with the analysis of preparatory defensive reflexes—that is, those whose consummatory phase consists in retraction. The preparatory phase of these reflexes serving to avoid the confrontation with a noxious agent, or at least provide a proper adjustment to its onset, is controlled by a state which we usually denote as *fear*.

If we consider fear a specific central process controlling the "fear reflex," we must analyze successively the stimuli eliciting it, the effects produced by it, and its central mechanism. In this chapter we shall discuss only those fear-eliciting stimuli which have an unconditioned character.

There is no doubt that most fear reflexes are closely correlated with pain. As a matter of fact, every living creature is *afraid* of pain, and a large part of its behavior is concerned with developing such preparatory activities as would prevent the occurrence of painful stimuli. It is, however, clear that preventing a noxious stimulus depends upon its anticipation, which is usually accomplished through conditioning. So the question arises, what is the unconditioned relation between pain and fear—that is, in which moment does fear arise as a *result* of a noxious stimulus and not as its anticipation?

In a preceding section we defined pain-producing stimuli as those which give rise to the defensive consummatory responses of the retractive character. The flexion reflex was a typical example. It is, however, well known that besides this somatic response, painful stimuli, particularly if they are strong, elicit a general autonomic reaction which, as we shall soon see, is characteristic of fear. Thus we may conclude that pain-producing stimuli have two aspects: one being "epicritic" and giving rise to a local adaptive response directly concerned with retraction; the other being "protopathic" and giving rise to a general adjustment of the organism to the emergency situation.

Although the consummatory retraction response to the painful stimulus and the fear response elicited by it are most often concomitant, it may be easily shown that they are largely independent of one another. First, the retraction response usually lasts as long as the operation of the painful stimulus, or at most a little longer, whereas the fear response considerably outlasts the stimulus, its gradual decay being a matter of minutes or even hours.* If the painful stimulus is weak, the fear response may be negligible or nonexistent but the consummatory response is still present. In some schizophrenic patients and after prefrontal lobotomies, strong painful stimuli, producing normal, or even increased, retraction response, do not elicit any perceivable fear response.[30] On the contrary, there exist purely protopathic pains which are accompanied by strong fear with no appreciable consummatory response (in heart attack, causalgia, and the like).

Although pain is an important source of fear, there are many fear responses, both in animals and in man, in which pain does not inter-

* The seeming contradiction to this statement is provided by the common experimental observation that if a short painful stimulus is administered routinely in a given situation (with or without being preceded by the conditioned stimulus), the fear response which precedes the painful stimulus ceases abruptly with its termination. This phenomenon is, however, produced entirely by the inhibitory conditioning mechanism, the animal being taught that after the stimulus is over it is safe from the danger for a number of minutes (cf. Chapter VI, Section 5).

vene either in the form of an actual releaser, or in the form of a reinforcing agent, as is the case in conditioned fear reflexes. In fact,
numerous observations of the behavior of animals in their normal
habitat as well as in special experiments indicate that innate fear reflexes may be elicited by the *signs* of a predator being nearby, namely,
by its sight, smell, or sound. These fear reactions are innate, certainly
being developed through natural selection, and have a true and pure
anticipatory character. The fear reactions observed in domestic birds
to the sight of a predatory bird, in a horse to the smell of a bear, in
small animals hearing the roar of a beast—all are illustrations of such
phenomena.

Human experience indicates that we also have many unconditioned
fear reflexes which are not necessarily based on painful sensations. In
children fear is easily evoked by strange-looking objects, particularly
if they are mobile. A strong and sudden noise, particularly a piercing
outcry of pain or horror by another person, regularly produces a
strong fear response. A mutilated and blood-stained human body elicits a horror which is perhaps unconditioned. Similarly, in both humans
and other primates strong fear is produced by snake-shaped moving
objects. The unconditioned fear reflex is also produced by looking
down from a high place. In most of these instances the fear-eliciting
stimuli are complex and require highly discriminative perceptive abilities of a given analyzer, which are probably acquired by perceptual
learning (cf. Chapter II).

The important problem is whether fear, like hunger, can be produced by humoral factors. In other words, do sufficiently strong
noxious stimuli elicit, as a part of their consummatory response, secretion of some hormone which directly activates the fear system?

Although we cannot give an unequivocal answer to this question,
it seems that the chemoreceptive mechanism in the production of fear,
in addition to other mechanisms, cannot be rejected. We know from
our own experience that sometimes we are in a prolonged state of
strong anxiety without any noticeable reason and are then highly sus-
ceptible to fears produced by some particular factors (cf. fear neuroses). Similarly, some small animals (for example, mice and rabbits)
which are usually exposed to the danger of being attacked by predators are constantly in the state of defensive alertness—that is, fear probably caused by humoral factors. If this hypothesis is confirmed, it
might be supposed that fear operates according to the principle of
positive feedback: the hormones produced as the effect of fear act on
the chemoreceptors of the fear center and contribute to its protracted
duration in the absence of stimuli which gave rise to it.

Whereas the problem of fear-provoking stimuli is, as we have seen, not clear, the same is not true of fear *effects*. Here, chiefly owing to the classical work of Cannon[31] and his collaborators, the problem was elucidated to a large extent and the results of his studies in this field are quoted in every textbook. There is, however, one point which was not emphasized by Cannon.

According to the biological protective role of fear in preservation of the individual, there are two ways to avoid a predator. The first is to mobilize the organism to *action*, to escape as quickly and efficiently as possible from its field of operation. It is, however, often much more profitable for the organism to keep as immobile as possible, in order not to be noticed by the predator, who usually pays attention only to moving objects (the "sham-death reflex," or "freezing" response). Accordingly, there are two lines of defense in animals: one may be called "active"; the other, "passive" defense.

The typical manifestations of the active defense are in some respects similar to those of hunger. First, there is the strong arousal of the motor behavioral system manifested in both motor restlessness (including vocalization) and increased muscular efficiency (a subject is capable of efforts he would not be capable of in a normal state). Second, there is the arousal of the sensory systems—the feeblest rustle and even the beating of one's own heart seem to be as loud as thunder. Finally, the most conspicuous manifestation of fear is the increased tonus of the sympathetic system: the pupils are dilated, the heart rate increased, the adrenal secretion augmented, the visceral vessels constricted, the muscular ones dilated, and so on. When for some reason the behavioral restlessness is precluded, increased muscular tonus and trembling occur.

On the contrary, the passive defensive UR follows a quite reverse pattern: the muscles are relaxed (the subject is paralyzed by fear), he cannot utter a sound (he is "mute" from fear), the blood pressure drops. Fainting from horror is undoubtedly one of the forms of the sham-death reflex.

The passive fear reflex is frequent among small animals who are the prey of predators (small birds, rodents). The freezing response of such animals is most usual and seems to appear when the danger is imminent and almost unescapable. Indeed, when the predator is very close, the best way of defense is to imitate death.

The autonomic symptoms of passive fear are not so systematically described as those of active fear. There is, however, some evidence indicating that passive fear may be accompanied by the increase of the parasympathetic tonus. Thus, cats in a state of fear display brady-cardia accompanied by exceeding calmness. Another parasympathetic symptom observed in passive fear is defecation and urination, occurring regularly in rats, mice, rabbits, and dogs. In some animals one of the two types of defensive reflexes clearly predominates; in others the reflexes are mixed, giving way to one or another depending on the actual situation with which the animal is confronted.

In unpublished experiments I exposed animals to very strong fear which followed the procedure of shooting at them from a sham gun which emitted bits of paper with great force, accompanied by a loud noise—then measured their blood pressures. In a dog each shot was followed by an increase of blood pressure; in rabbits, most frequently by a strong decrease, sometimes followed by a rise. A few animals died after several shots, owing to vascular collapse manifested by a critical fall of blood pressure.

Turning now to the analysis of the central mechanism of the fear UR, we should note that, beginning with the classical experiments of Hess[32] on hypothalamic stimulation, this mechanism has been intensively studied by numerous authors. There is clear evidence that the fear system, like the hunger system, consists of at least two levels: the lower one in the hypothalamus, and the higher in the limbic system (specifically in the amygdala). Stimulation of fear points in the hypothalamus (most frequently conducted in cats) produces a full picture of pure fear without the slightest signs of pain: the animal is clearly terrified, the pupils are maximally dilated, the heart rate increased; he is either exceedingly restless trying to escape or, on the contrary, frozen. Stimulation of definite points in the amygdala produces a similar picture. Lesions sustained in corresponding fields produce a decrease of fearfulness.[33]

As has been assumed in respect to the hunger system, we can state that the higher level of the fear system is concerned with conditioning of fear, as well as with eliciting fear reflexes, not by pain itself, but by those stimuli (particularly visual and auditory) which in phylogenesis become the signs of danger. In fact, amygdalectomized monkeys exhibit no fear of their natural enemies such as snakes,[34] and amygdalectomized wild rats exhibit no fear of such natural enemies as humans.

The problem arises as to whether the fear system, like the alimentary preparatory system, also has its antagonistic counterpart—that is, the system responsible for the state of *relief* occurring when fear is appeased.

The best argument to support this hypothesis would be provided by those experiments in which particular cerebral lesions would lead to the *increase* of fearfulness in the operated animals. Such evidence, however, is meager and not quite conclusive, because release of fear was not clearly separated from release of anger (see below). Another argument for the existence of the "relief center" is provided by the fact that the appeasement occurring after fear is conditionable (cf. Chapter VI, Section 5). Taking these data into account, we shall postulate that the defensive preparatory system, similar to the alimentary system, is composed of two reciprocal subsystems, the relief subsystem being activated when the fear-producing agents are terminated.

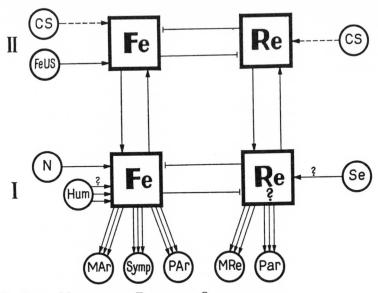

FIG. I-4. BLOCK MODEL OF THE FEAR-RELIEF SYSTEM

Fe, fear centers; Re, relief centers; Se, security stimulus; N, noxious stimulus; FeUS, unconditioned fear stimulus of non-noxious character. Other denotations as in Figure I-3.

Note that non-noxious fear stimuli are thought to act on the higher level of the fear system. Note also that the lower level of the relief system is considered uncertain.

Its biological role consists in counteracting the fear reflex when the situation is no longer dangerous. The block model of the preparatory defense system is represented in Figure I-4.

Now we shall turn to the description of the other protective preparatory activities—those connected with aggression. Whereas fear reflexes forestall the direct action of stimuli eliciting consummatory defensive responses, anger reflexes forestall the action of stimuli eliciting offensive responses. The fierce postures of a cat confronting a dog and of a monkey confronting a man are typical examples of anger reflexes.

Stimuli producing anger belong roughly to the same category as those producing fear, the response depending on the species (small and defenseless animals will display hardly any anger at a large predator), on the individual properties of the animal (a fearful animal will display fear in a situation in which a bellicose animal will display anger), and on the situation (the same stimulus will elicit anger when the animal is on its own territory and fear when it is on foreign ground).

The effects of anger, like those of fear, may be divided into somatic and autonomic effects. Somatic effects of anger are totally different from those of fear, so that there is no difficulty whatsoever in distinguishing them, not only in man, but also in animals. Although both responses involve the strong arousal of the motor behavioral system, quite different parts of the musculature take part in them. In anger, the face muscles play a dominant role (showing and gnashing the teeth, snorting); in fear, they do not. In some animals, particularly in primates, the fore limbs also take part in anger (striking movements in apes, clawing in cats, trampling in elephants); in fear, the major role falls on the hind limbs involved in rapid running.[35]

Analogous differences between fear and anger may be observed in autonomic responses. Although in both these states we observe the activation of the sympathetic system, the distribution of blood in the body is in each quite different. In man the face vessels are strongly dilated in anger (red face); in fear, they are constricted (paleness). The same is probably true about the upper limbs. It is certain that analogous differences could be found in animals by scrupulous examination of blood distribution and of other autonomic effects.

The central mechanism of anger is represented on at least two levels; in the hypothalamus, and in the limbic system. In fact, anger reactions can be easily evoked in cats by hypothalamic stimulation and by stimulation of the amygdala. Corresponding lesions, making the animals "tame" and calm, are particularly noticeable in ferocious animals (wild rats, wild cats).[36]

Another problem concerning the central mechanism of anger is again that of whether there exists a subsystem reciprocally related to the anger subsystem which is responsible for the *placidity* of the animal.

It seems that in respect to anger we have even more evidence of the existence of reciprocal centers than is true in respect to fear. In fact, numerous reports show that lesions sustained either in the hypothalamus or in the limbic brain "release" ferociousness to such a degree that animals which before the operation were tame later become totally unmanageable.[37] This indicates that the centers responsible for suppressing rage behavior have been destroyed.

One may ask whether the state of relief and that of placidity are represented by the same centers or by different ones. The fact that animals made ferocious by removal of the anger-suppressing areas do not become *ipso facto* more fearful seems to speak against the equality of these two centers.

To end these considerations on anger and aggression reflexes, it should be clearly understood that these differ radically from the seemingly similar phenomenon of the attack of a predator on its prey which was shown to be produced by electrical stimulation of the lateral hypothalamic nucleus.[38] It is clear that this latter response has nothing to do with the protective function of the organism, the prey being rather weak and in no way dangerous to the predator. This is a part of instinctive hunting behavior, and as such it belongs not to the protective but to the preservative activities of the organism.

8. Preparatory exploratory activity (searching reflexes)

As was emphasized in Section 5, most stimuli impinging upon receptive surfaces are not endowed with any specific biological role but serve only for the further adaptability of the organism to its surroundings. In order to fulfill this role, these stimuli must be perceived and recognized as precisely as possible, and for this purpose the category of consummatory reflexes, which we have called *targeting reflexes*, have been developed. It may, however, be foreseen that the behavior involved in responding to this kind of stimuli, which may be best called exploratory behavior, is by no means limited to the proper targeting of stimulus-objects which have already fallen upon the corresponding receptive surface. The organism is also able to search after these stimulus-objects when they are outside the receptive surface—in other words, to develop a special kind of preparatory behavior which fulfills this task. We shall call this type of behavior *searching behavior* or *searching reflexes*. The *spiritus movens* which controls searching behavior is called *curiosity*. We shall adopt this term, denoting by it the underlying physiological processes that govern searching behavior.

Now, let us analyze searching reflexes according to the same method as that applied to other basic activities of the organism.

As for the *stimuli* that evoke searching behavior the situation is far from being clear. Obviously, searching behavior serves many specific preparatory activities of the organism—for example, searching for food, searching a subject of the opposite sex, searching after the proper place for sleep. This type of behavior is, however, quite different from true exploratory behavior, since it implies looking for *definite* types of stimulus-objects, whereas exploratory activity is directed to *new* stimuli which for the time being are of no definite significance.

This is best substantiated by the fact that exploratory activity may be in operation when no other preparatory activities directed toward definite goals are present.

A prolonged absence of any variegated stimuli acting upon the receptive surfaces is known to be hardly endurable for the organism; thus these stimuli are almost as necessary for its well-being as is food or water. If this is true, we may assign exploratory behavior to the category of preservative activities, and in consequence look for some internal (humoral) factors which would regulate it. It may be tentatively postulated that neurons of all afferent systems are, in normal conditions, in an active state because they are "nourished" by the external stimuli impinging upon them. If these stimuli are lacking—that is, when there is a "hunger" for external stimulation—a hypothetical "exploration system" in the brain is thrown into action which tends to increase exploratory behavior and thus to restore a *sui generis* homeostasis of the sensory systems. It should be added that (as will be discussed in the next chapter) these external stimuli must arouse an interest in the subject either by their novelty or by being associated with some basic activities of the organism, because a repeatedly presented neutral stimulus becomes habituated and stops producing any exploratory reflexes.

In addition to this general, quasi-humoral mechanism of regulating exploratory activity, we may assume the existence of another mechanism analogous to the post-consummatory appetizing effect in alimentary activity: If a stimulus-object producing a targeting reflex is presented, and after a few moments the subject stops paying attention to it because of habituation, this immediately "whets his appetite" for new sensory experiences—that is, its cessation creates a stimulus for the searching reflex. In this way the searching reflexes in animals usually act in chains, each link of the chain being a stimulus for the next reflex. The systematic exploration of a new surrounding or a new object by vision and/or smell, so well known in rats, cats, and dogs, and by vision and touch in primates is a good illustration of these chains of searching and targeting reflexes. One cannot help comparing this alternating sequence of curiosity-targeting reflexes with a similar sequence of hunger-ingestive reflexes which is typical for the feeding behavior of primates.

It is clear that when the exploratory reflexes are wandering from one stimulus-object to another, they require the cessation of the targeting reflex directed to the first stimulus to allow the subject to turn attention to the next one. In the visual system, this cessation is brought about by a special cortical mechanism localized in the frontal eye area. In fact, lesions in this area in man produce a deficiency in overcoming the fixation and following reflexes, so that the patient is not able to divert his gaze from the object observed. For instance, in order to read, the subject has to move his finger along the line of type, and in this way, following the finger by his gaze, he moves his eyes from one word to another. There are probably similar targeting-overcoming mechanisms in other analyzers as well but to my knowledge they have not been subjected to any systematic analysis.

The *effects* of curiosity reflexes are characterized, as in hunger reflexes, by arousal of the motor behavioral system and, by definition, by strong arousal of afferent systems. The interesting manifestation of these effects is shown in experiments with "sensory deprivation" in which the subject is for a length of time exposed to maximally monotonous environmental stimuli. As a result, he experiences vivid images or even hallucinations of various modalities (cf. Chapter IV) and restlessness.[39] The state is amazingly similar to that produced by long-lasting hunger in a situation where food is unavailable.

The analogy between the hunger for food and the "hunger" for variegated external stimulus-objects even goes so far that in both instances we are dealing with particular appetites directed to particular types of stimuli. For example, there may be an increase of specific curiosity toward visual stimuli or auditory stimuli if the "sensory deprivation" has particularly affected the given modality. Accordingly, the visual curiosity may be fully satiated by a long series of variegated visual stimuli (the feeling we often experience in an art gallery), whereas the auditory curiosity, on the contrary, may be unsatisfied or vice versa.

Finally, the problem of the central mechanism governing the curiosity reflexes is still poorly understood. We do not know whether the controlling mechanism for curiosity is represented on the hypothalamic level, but we have good evidence of its existence on the cortical level. In fact, one of the striking effects of frontal lobotomy in man is precisely the decrease, or even loss, of curiosity with total preservation of targeting reflexes. This is, as a matter of fact, the chief feature which distinguishes a lobotomized patient from a normal (or even a psychotic) person and makes him so much like an automaton.

On the other hand, there are cases in which lobotomized patients manifest an exaggerated exploratory behavior and tend thoroughly to examine every object around them, switching their attention from one object to another.[40] This may be either due to the irritation of the exploratory system by a post-operative scar, or it may suggest the existence of a reciprocal system inhibiting the curiosity reflex.

Although analogous observations on animals are few and unsystematic, we occasionally see brain-lesioned animals which appear normal except that they do not display any "interest" in their surroundings or, on the contrary, animals whose exploratory behavior is strongly increased. I do not know of any systematic study of this problem.

To end our analysis of the preparatory exploratory behavior, it should be noted that the exploratory reflex is not the only type of response to biologically indifferent stimuli. It should be kept in mind that many such stimuli, particularly if they are presented for the first time, give rise to a fearlike reaction manifested by startle and sympathetic effects. These responses are strongly manifested, if the subject is timid, either individually or as a representative of a given species. It is very important not to confuse these fearlike reactions (which Pavlov called "orientation reactions") with the exploratory reactions, because both are controlled by quite different, and even antagonistic, mechanisms. In fact, when the exploring animal comes across a stimulus-object which for some reason or other elicits this fearlike "orientation reaction," its behavior is immediately changed. The exploratory behavior stops, and the animal either remains frozen for some time (passive fear reaction) or withdraws to a more familiar or safer place. Only after several repetitions of the given stimulus-object, at which time the fearlike orientation reaction undergoes extinction, does the curiosity response take place. Such shifting from one response to another is, in fact, often observed in children in whom a strange-looking object or person first evokes a manifest fear (crying and escape), then the orientation startle response, and eventually, when the latter is extinguished, true curiosity and searching responses are manifested.[41]

9. General properties of preparatory activities; the concepts of drive and emotion

As is clear from our foregoing considerations, the preparatory unconditioned activities of the organism, although differing in some details, nevertheless possess features which are characteristic for all of them. These are the following.

(1) Arousal of the motor behavioral system manifested in both behavioral hyperactivity and increased motor efficiency. Although the particular patterns of motor excitation are somewhat different in different activities, and their differences are further increased by individual and group experiences, the phenomenon is manifest in hunger, sexual preparatory activity, fear, anger, and curiosity. The only exception is perhaps the passive fear manifested in the sham-death reflex.

(2) Arousal of sensory systems enabling the animal to detect with

great precision the relevant stimuli of the external world. Again, it is certain that in different preparatory activities the arousal of different analyzers is particularly involved, but the phenomenon as such is seen in all of them.

(3) Increase of the tonus of the sympathetic system, most clearly manifested, although slightly differing in pattern, in active defense and aggression, but in all probability also present in other preparatory activities.

Whereas the precise mechanism of arousal of the motor behavioral system manifested in preparatory activities is not clear, the mechanism of arousal of afferent systems seems to be more apparent. The idea was first suggested by Jasper,[42] who has shown that unspecific thalamic nuclei ("thalamic reticular system") may transmit the facilitating effects from the lower levels of the emotive system to particular regions of the cortex. This would explain the diffuse, although not totally undiscriminative, projection of this system upon the cerebral cortex and its independence of the specific afferent systems.

The increase of sympathetic tonus is accomplished by means of the descending pathways running from the hypothalamus and the central gray matter (peduncular pathway).[43]

All the preparatory systems have their centers situated on at least two levels: in the hypothalamus, and in the limbic system. The hypothalamic centers are thought to control and coordinate chiefly the unconditioned performance of preparatory activities, the limbic areas, mainly to associate these activities with those neutral stimuli which happen to coincide with them and thus to mediate their conditioned reflex performance.

Further, we have good reason to assume that all these systems are composed of two parallel, reciprocally related subsystems, one giving rise to the given activity and the other one suppressing it. Thus, the hunger subsystem is reciprocally related with the satiation subsystem, the fear subsystem with the relief subsystem, and the anger subsystem with the placidity subsystem. Even the curiosity system seems to have its inhibitory counterpart which may be called indifference.

Finally, all preservative systems and probably also protective systems are endowed with intracentral chemoreceptors—that is, some of their afferent neurons develop their own receptors (most probably situated on their dendritic arborization) reacting to specific molecules contained in the surrounding fluid. The existence of such intracentral chemoreceptors can be considered experimentally demonstrated on the hypothalamic level of the hunger-satiation system and of the sexual system.[43a] It may be hypothesized in the fear-relief and anger-placidity system also.

A puzzling fact which can be easily accounted for in the framework of our present discussion is that, as stated by many investigators, the weak stimulation of a great variety of points both in the hypothalamus and in the limbic system gives rise to a rather uniform perceptual alertness, consisting of looking around, searching after something, pricking up the ears, sometimes sniffing. The pupils dilate and the EEG shows desynchronization. This gives the impression that the "orienting response" is widely represented throughout the brain and largely overlaps with points eliciting the above described preparatory activities. This inference is, however, not correct, because if we take into account the fact that sensory arousal is simply a general manifestation of all preparatory activities of the organism, the display of these searching or targeting responses is understandable as the first stage of these activities. In fact, if a stronger or more prolonged stimulation is administered, we find that this "orienting response" crystallizes in the form of fear, anger, or hunger.

Because of the enumerated common features of the basic activities of the organism and underlying functional systems, it seems reasonable to introduce a number of general terms which will unambiguously designate various aspects of the phenomena we are dealing with and the neural structures on which they depend.

The nervous processes controlling the basic preparatory activities, whether unconditioned or conditioned, guiding the organism to the accomplishment of the consummatory reflexes or guarding it from the operation of harmful agents will be called *drives;* the behavioral phenomena mediated by these processes will be referred to as *drive reflexes.* The proposed meaning of the term "drive" is in full harmony with its general usage, except that we tend to regard it (as many contemporary authors do) as a strictly physiological term. The subjective experiences corresponding to particular drives, familiar to us from introspection and supposed to be analogous in the higher animals, will be called *emotions.*

We have seen from our discussion that most drives—or perhaps all of them—have their physiological antipodes which are those states that arise when the given drive is satisfied—that is, the subject is satiated, the danger is removed, and so on. We have seen that these states are produced not merely by decrease of the excitability of drive centers but by bringing into action other centers reciprocally related to the former ones and thus exerting upon them an inhibitory effect. It seems reasonable to refer to the physiological aspects of these states as *antidrives.* They are connected with what Thorndike has called "satisfying state of affairs" and, as we shall see later, they are of utmost importance in the formation of acquired motor behavior. Concerning the term by which the psychological aspects of antidrives may be denoted, I propose to call them moods. In fact, it seems that with few exceptions such states as satisfaction after a good meal or after getting rid of a danger are commonly called moods—states in which there is nothing to be done. Pure sadness as a passive state when one is resigned and reconciled with ill fate, although far from being "satisfying," can be also placed in this category of experiences.

It is quite clear that the system controlling both drives and anti-drives differs both anatomically and functionally from that system which is responsible for the analysis of the external world (that is, perceptions) and for reacting to particular patterns of stimuli in a suitable way. Therefore we propose to call the system under discussion the *emotive* or *motivational* system; the system that is concerned with particular perceptions and specific behavioral acts, the *cognitive* or *gnostic* system.

The differences between the two systems will be made clearer in the course of our further considerations. At this point, however, let us indicate the most salient distinctions between them.

(1) The emotive and cognitive systems are subserved by two distinct central nervous structures. The cognitive system operates through what is generally called the specific division of the brain—the division of more or less strict localization and where the pathways leading from the receptors to the centers and from the centers to the effectors have an orderly topographical arrangement. Here are specific thalamic nuclei, both projective and associative, and the neocortex, both projective and associative. We shall refer to all these parts of the brain as the *cognitive brain*. On the other hand, the emotive system operates through what is generally referred to as the unspecific division of the brain; here the principle of topographical arrangements is less strictly binding and sometimes seems to be lacking. It is represented by the reticular system, the hypothalamus, the intralaminar thalamic nuclei, and the rhinencephalon (limbic system). We shall refer to all these parts of the brain as the *emotive brain*.[44]

(2) The receptive surfaces of the cognitive system are composed of more or less highly elaborated receptors, distributed on the surface of the body and its recesses, as well as in the muscles and joints. The simultaneous and successive patterns of stimulation of these receptors in all possible combinations most precisely and delicately control the patterns of motor responses.

On the other hand, the receptive side of the emotive system is quite different. First, as indicated earlier, the intracentral chemoreceptive surface in the hypothalamus plays a most important role in eliciting preservative drive reflexes and possibly an auxiliary role in protective drive reflexes. Second, in those instances when exteroceptive stimuli serve to elicit drive reflexes, this is accomplished by their "protopathic" (emotionally tinted) aspect, different anatomically and functionally from their "epicritic" aspect in cognitive reflexes. In fact, there is much evidence to show that every afferent system is equipped by collaterals, or even by separate peripheral pathways, conveying direct information through the reticular formation to the lower or higher level of the emotive brain. Hence, action potentials of stimuli of various modalities can be recorded in the reticular formation, hypothalamus, and limbic system. It will be convenient for our further discussion to use the term *emotive analyzer*, denoting by it the afferent side of all drive and antidrive reflexes.

It should be added, however, that the cognitive aspects of stimuli mediated by the neocortex also play a role in eliciting particular drive reflexes. In fact, some visual stimuli evoking innate hunting behavior, fear responses, or sexual responses are perhaps too complex to be conveyed by the more primitive protopathic system and require the mediation of the cognitive part of the visual analyzer. In this respect the role of these stimuli is similar to that of conditioned drive stimuli, which by definition have a purely cognitive character.

(3) Lesions sustained in the cognitive brain, in both animals and humans, give a quite different type of symptoms from those sustained in the emotive brain. The former ones, depending on their localization, concern some particular cognitive functions on a particular level of their complexity. The subject is incapacitated in a definite manner and can be even highly incapacitated if the lesion is large or its localization is crucial; but his whole "personality," which is based on the integrity of the emotive brain, is intact. On the other hand, lesions sustained in the emotive brain do not affect cognitive capacities and the cognitive store of the subject (unless they are blocked by emotive disturbances), but give rise to clearly emotive symptoms which may totally change the subject's "personality." Changes in aggressiveness, fearfulness, sexual behavior, social relations, and the like are most striking after such lesions.

(4) Accordingly, electrical stimulation of the cognitive brain and the emotive brain, in both humans and animals, produces quite different effects. Stimulation of the neocortex produces in humans either sensations of various modalities or movements, depending on the localization, but these sensations are usually devoid of any emotional character. The same is true of stimulation of homologous cortical areas in animals. On the other hand, stimulation of the emotive brain gives rise to clear emotional experiences accompanied by pronounced autonomic responses. The self-stimulation procedure to be discussed in a later chapter reveals that whereas stimulation of the cognitive

brain is motivationally neutral, stimulation of the emotive brain has a strong motivational value, either positive or negative.[45]

10. Interrelations between drive reflexes and consummatory reflexes

We now approach one of the most controversial problems of the physiology of drives—that of the relation between drives and the corresponding consummatory acts. Since this relation is somewhat different in preservative and protective activities, we shall discuss this problem for each separately. As a model representing preservative activity, we shall again use food intake.

The influence of the hunger reflex upon the consummatory food reflex is relatively clear. As stated before, the hunger drive produces sensory arousal, which is directed particularly to the gustatory and olfactory analyzers, and motor arousal, concerning particularly the masticatory muscles. Consequently, when food is brought into the mouth, the vigor of the masticatory movements depends on the strength of the hunger drive. Similar is the influence of the hunger drive upon salivation.[46]

The reverse relation—the influence of the consummatory reflex upon the hunger drive—is, however, not so obvious. The question may be raised as to whether the consummatory act increases the existing hunger, leaves it unchanged, or causes its diminution. To answer this question, let us see what happens to the effects of hunger in the course of the consummatory ingestive response.

As far as the general motor excitement is concerned, it is a common fact that a hungry animal calms down immediately when he obtains his food and becomes totally absorbed in the act of eating. A good illustration is provided by observing human sucklings: the excited and tense infant calms down immediately when his lips touch the nipple; his muscles relax, and his face expresses satisfaction and bliss. But if the nipple is withdrawn, the previous state of excitement and tension returns. Exactly the same may be seen in hungry dogs in the experimental situation before they have been habituated to the procedure of intermittent feeding. In short, we can ascertain that arousal of the motor behavioral system is abolished or at least diminished during the act of eating long before the state of satiation is reached.

We can see too that the second sign of hunger—the arousal of the sensory system—is also decreased. In a state of hunger, the subject is alert and pays attention to the slightest changes in the environment; during eating, his perceptual responsiveness is diminished. This is clearly seen again in dogs; when absorbed by eating, they hardly react to external stimuli, unless these stimuli are strong enough to inhibit the consummatory reaction. This diminution is less manifest in those animals in which feeding is intermittent, as in primates.

It may be argued that both these effects are not due to the suppression of the hunger drive itself during the act of eating but simply to "draining off" the motor and sensory arousal and directing them into specific channels. The act of eating and the taste stimulus may inhibit other motor responses and other targeting reflexes, leaving the intensity of the hunger drive unchanged. If so, it would be expected that the other effect of hunger—the contractions of the stomach which have no relation to the somato-motor and -sensory functions—should be unchanged or even increased at the beginning of the act of eating.

The experiments concerning this point were repeatedly performed on animals with the gastric fistula and gave unequivocal results. Pavlov in his classic study on the digestive glands had already written: "Spontaneous stomach contractions can be discontinued either psychically, if a dog is excited by food, or better if sham-feeding is performed (in an oesophagotomized dog)."[46a] This problem was thereafter carefully investigated by Boldyreff[46b] and other authors[46c] with identical effects: placing the food in the animal's mouth immediately produced the relaxation of the stomach and the cessation of hunger contractions (cf. Figure VI-1, p. 274, below).

Another important experiment concerning this point was performed on man by Carlson,[47] who studied in great detail the behavior of the stomach of the famous patient Fred Vlcek with the gastric fistula. This man was fed in such a way that the food normally masticated by the patient was placed in a syringe and introduced into the stomach through the fistula. This involved no discomfort, and the patient adjusted completely to this condition. The hunger contractions could be examined by recording the pressure of a balloon inserted into the stomach, or even by direct observation of the stomach through the fistula.

When during the state of hunger manifested by regular and pronounced stomach contractions food was put into the mouth, the contractions were immediately inhibited; this inhibition lasted as long as food was in the mouth. When the food was removed and the mouth rinsed with warm water, the gastric contractions reappeared, sometimes with increased intensity. They could be also inhibited by a taste stimulus provided by a piece of sugar or sugar solution.

When the subject was asked to make chewing movements with no food in the mouth, no inhibition of hunger contractions ensued. If the subject was asked to chew a neutral substance (for example, paraffin), inhibition of the contractions was only partial and the stomach quickly "escaped" from inhibition, even though chewing was continued with uniform vigor.

These observations leave no doubt that the taste stimulus giving rise to the alimentary consummatory reaction inhibits during its operation the hunger contractions of the stomach, and its cessation leads to their reappearance, sometimes with rebound.

And so we must reach the conclusion that during the consummatory food response the hunger drive itself is temporarily inhibited, to be restored with rebound after the response is over, unless food has been presented *ad libitum* and the subject becomes completely satiated. A diagram of the relations between the hunger drive UR and food UR is presented in Figure I-5a.*

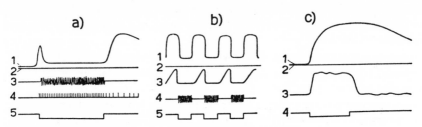

FIG. I-5. DIAGRAM OF THE RELATIONS BETWEEN DRIVE UR AND CONSUMMATORY UR

a) Relation between hunger reflex and food reflex in a continuous eating act: 1, the actual level of hunger (hypothetical); 2, its baseline; 3, mastication; 4, salivation; 5, food in the mouth.

b) Relation between hunger reflex and food reflex in an intermittent eating act: 1, the actual level of hunger; 2, its base-line; 3, instrumental motor acts procuring food intake; 4, mastication; 5, food in the mouth.

c) Relation between fear reflex and defensive flexion reflex: 1, the actual level of fear (hypothetical); 2, its baseline; 3, flexion of the leg; 4, its electrical stimulation.

Note that in (a) there is an initial increase of the level of hunger due to conditioning when the subject notices the portion of food and takes it into the mouth.

The thesis that the hunger drive is inhibited during the act of eating (which will be further substantiated in later chapters) may seem paradoxical to many readers. Resistance to its acceptance may be due to the fact that our manner of eating, in contradistinction to that of many other animals, is not *continuous* but intermittent. We put a morsel of food into the mouth by hand or special utensils (fork, spoon, chopsticks), this act being an instrumental response driven by hunger, chew and swallow, then take the next morsel, and so on. Thus, supposing that hunger *is* suppressed by the food in the mouth, it is immediately released with rebound after the morsel is eaten. In consequence, the periods of activation and inhibition of the hunger drive follow each other alternately in quick succession, thus giving no opportunity for reliable self-observation (Figure I-5b). By making the following sim-

* It should be noted that the idea of the inhibitory effect of the consummatory food reflex upon the hunger drive reflex was first advanced by S. Soltysik, to whom I owe much in the clarification of my thoughts in this field.

ple introspective experiment upon ourselves, we can, however, easily detect the phenomenon under discussion.

We are all acquainted with the experience of eating small and tasty bits of food one after the other—almonds, dates, olives, and the like. Since we cannot be easily satiated with this kind of nibbling, it usually happens that we simply cannot stop eating them, since each morsel irrepressibly causes us to take another one. This is due, of course, to the fact that the hunger drive is strongly increased after ingesting each morsel. In order to terminate this compulsory sequence of eating acts, we decide to take a handful of the dainties and we put away the rest of them. We are certain that this measure will be effective and that our desire to take more of them is finally terminated. But as soon as the ingestion of the portion is over, we again feel the irresistible desire to take another morsel. This desire will gradually vanish if we are able to resist the temptation for some time, showing that the rebound after the consummatory act was the chief cause of this specific hunger drive.

Another reason for the reluctance to accept the hypothesis of an inhibitory effect of the taste of food upon the hunger drive is that the process of inhibition involved is different from that inhibition which occurs during the state of satiation (see Section 11, below). The chief difference between the two states seems to be that in a state of satiation inhibition of the hunger center is long-lasting, but during the act of eating it operates against the background of strong excitation of the hunger system. Consequently, interruptions in eating immediately produce increased hunger as a rebound, being again appeased by a continuation of eating. Of course, when the hunger drive is very strong, its suppression by the act of eating is far from complete. In such a state a subject devours food with great speed and greediness, taking into the mouth new morsels of food before the previous ones are swallowed. Exactly the same picture may be observed in very hungry dogs. Thus, a too strong hunger, instead of facilitating the consummatory reaction, on the contrary disturbs its regular course.

Our assumption of the inhibitory effect of the taste of food upon drive is further substantiated by the congruence between the specificity of the hunger drive and the corresponding type of food. In a preceding section it was indicated that, depending on the needs of the organism at a given moment, hunger may be specifically directed to a given kind of food in preference to others. If the appropriate food is presented to the animal, it completely satisfies the given kind of hunger by producing its optimal inhibition during eating and the optimal rebound afterward. On the contrary, if the inappropriate food is presented, the satisfaction is less complete because of the poorer inhibition of the particular hunger. If we masticate a completely tasteless substance, as chewing gum, inhibition of hunger occurs hardly at all.

Thus, definite kinds of hunger are closely related to definite tastes and fit one another as a key to an appropriate lock. Of course, this congruence is not absolute, because a very hungry subject stops being finicky and consumes the food that is available at the given moment.

Exactly the same relation may be found between the curiosity drive manifested by the searching reflexes and the consummatory targeting reflexes. As a model of these relations, consider visual exploratory behavior. On the one hand, the visual searching reflexes consisting in scanning the surroundings facilitate the fixation reflex if for some reason a given stimulus-object has drawn the attention of the subject. On the other hand, when the fixation reflex is in operation, the searching reflex is actively inhibited. As stated above (see Section 8), this inhibition must be overcome by a special mechanism in order to restore the searching activity or to switch attention to another stimulus-object.

It should be emphasized that the conclusions we have reached on the basis of our analysis of the relations between the preparatory and consummatory reflexes in the preservative activities of the organisms are in full agreement with the observations on instinctive behavior made by ethologists.[48] It has been shown that successive innate stages of the animal's sexual activity are linked in such a way that each following stage produces a "negative feedback" of the preceding stage precluding its continuation or repetition, if the drive has been fully satisfied. The same is true of hunting behavior versus ingestion of food.

The essential problem arises as to whether the same kind of relations between the preparatory and consummatory reflexes is also obeyed in protective activities. Of course, just as is true of preservative activities, the fear drive or anger drive facilitates the defensive or aggressive consummatory response respectively. However, the analogy does not hold for the reverse relation—that is, the effect exerted by the consummatory defensive reflex upon the fear or anger reflex.

As was explained in Section 7, above, the noxious stimulus during its operation usually has a dual effect; it elicits a particular consummatory response specific for the stimulus applied *and* the general fear response. Thus, the fear drive is in full operation not only after the termination of the noxious stimulus but also during its action (Figure I-5c). In other words, we admit an essential physiological difference between "attractive" stimuli, producing the preservative consummatory response, and "aversive" stimuli, producing the protective consummatory response. We shall see later that this very difference accounts for a quite different function of both these categories of stimuli in instrumental conditioning.

To sum up our considerations, we offer the following statements.

(1) Every drive reflex, connected with either preservative or protective activity, produces a facilitation of the corresponding consummatory reflex.

(2) Whereas the preservative consummatory reflex during its action exerts an inhibitory effect upon the drive reflex, the defensive consummatory reflex does not.

(3) After the consummatory UR is terminated, the appropriate drive UR is in operation. In preservative reflexes it is released by the aftereffect of the consummatory US, but in the defensive reflexes it outlasts the operation of this US.

11. The problem of antidrives

As follows from our preceding considerations, the affective aspect of an animal's activity involves two diametrically opposite states: drives, and antidrives. Whereas the chief property of drives is in principle a general motor mobilization, the chief property of antidrives is motor demobilization and quiet. There is no doubt that although the general pattern of all drives is much the same, and sometimes they may be even indiscernible by superficial observation (cf. the crying baby), they *are* qualitatively different because each is satisfiable by a different antidrive.

The problem arises as to whether the same is true of antidrives. In our previous considerations we discussed the satiation produced by appeasing hunger, the relief produced by getting rid of fear, and the placidity produced by appeasing anger. We could add here sexual satiation, sleep satiation, and so on. One can ask whether all these states are represented by one common antidrive pool or whether they are separate, each being attached to the corresponding drive.

There are numerous arguments which favor the thesis of separate antidrives, each attached to the corresponding drive. Perhaps the most convincing argument in favor of this assumption is provided by Olds' experiments on self-stimulation, to be discussed in a later chapter. Olds has shown that the "satisfying state of affairs" produced by stimulation of particular points in the emotive brain is not anonymous but, rather, is connected with particular drives; this was evidenced by the fact that changes in the hunger drive or sexual drive affect in different ways the reinforcing value of particular self-rewarding points.[49] Further, there is no doubt that the fear antidrive produced by escaping from danger does not necessarily lead to the hunger antidrive, or vice versa, as it would if these two states depended on the same physiological process.

Another important problem concerning the structure of the antidrive systems is whether a given drive system can have only one antidrive counterpart. This problem does not exist in respect to protective activities, because here the appropriate antidrive mechanism simply goes into operation when for various reasons the subject stops being frightened or angry.

The situation is, however, not so simple in respect to the preservative activities, because there we encounter two (and, as it will be seen later, three) different aspects of the antidrive operation. One of these aspects is due to satiation in respect to a given drive—for example, after obtaining a needed kind of food in a needed quantity. But, as we have seen in the preceding section, the very consummatory act is also a state of temporary satisfaction of drive (one would say, a rather dynamic and phasic state), and we have good reasons to believe that it is connected with drive inhibition. Consequently, the question arises as to whether the antidrive produced by the consummatory reflex and that produced by the state of satiation represent one and the same phenomenon depending on one and the same antidrive system, or two different phenomena depending on different systems.

On the one hand, it could be assumed that the taste stimulus which, as we remember, immediately stops the hunger contractions of the stomach, may do so through the activation of the satiation center which momentarily counteracts the strongly activated hunger center and temporarily produces its partial inhibition. This mechanism, in contradistinction to true satiation, would not be "tonic" but "phasic," being in a dynamic balance with the strongly activated hunger center and producing its rebound excitation whenever the taste stimulus is discontinued.

The difficulty in accepting this hypothesis is that it would imply the abolition of the drive-inhibiting effect of food ingestion after a ventromedial hypothalamic lesion. We might expect that after this lesion the act of eating would not suppress hunger, and consequently, as will be explained later, the instrumental conditioning would be abolished. As is well known, this is certainly not true (cf. Figure I-7).

On the other hand, it might be assumed that the antidrive mechanism activated during ingestion of food is more intimately connected with the hunger drive, and the units involved in it are simply scattered among the hunger-drive units in the lateral hypothalamus. In other words, the lateral hypothalamus would be the center controlling *both the hunger drive when the animal wants food and the hunger antidrive when it receives it.* Of course, the units representing both systems would be reciprocally interrelated.

This hypothesis seems to be physiologically sound, because we now have much evidence to show that in other analyzers, belonging to the cognitive systems, reciprocally related units are closely intermixed. In fact, the so-called on-units and off-units have been detected in all the analyzers so far examined by the micro-electrode methods, and they are present on various levels of each afferent axis (see Chapter II).

The acceptance of this hypothesis seems to be not only physiologically reasonable but also workable, enabling us to explain a number of functional properties of the alimentary system, particularly the proper role of the lateral hypothalamus.

First, let us assume that, similar to other receptive systems, the gustatory receptors are divided into on-receptors and off-receptors, and the units of higher levels, into the on-food-taste units and off-food-taste units—the former being activated when the food is in the mouth, and the latter, when the bolus is swallowed. Now let us further assume that the messages conveying the taste of food and its aftereffect are transmitted not only to the cognitive system—through the ventral posteromedial nucleus of the thalamus to the gustatory area of the cortex—but also to the emotive system—to the lateral hypothalamus and the limbic brain. The former messages can be properly denoted as epicritic and the latter as protopathic. We assume that the on-food-taste impulses activate the anti-hunger units in the lateral hypothalamus (which may be more properly called off-hunger units) and inhibit the on-hunger units, whereas the off-food-taste impulses on the contrary activate the on-hunger units and inhibit the off-hunger units (Figure I-6a).

According to the present view, the hypothalamic hunger center, in contradistinction to the satiation center controlled mainly by humoral factors, is chiefly (or perhaps fully) controlled by the protopathic taste sensations activating particular types of off-hunger units when a given food is in the mouth or the corresponding on-hunger units when it is swallowed. The influence of the satiation center upon the hunger center may be assumed to consist only in regulating the *general level of excitability* of particular types of its units corresponding to specific kinds of nutritive substances. The activation of the satiation center by humoral factors decreases the excitability of the hunger center, whereas its inactivation by the lack of these factors produces the release effect (cf. Figure I-2). Moreover, it may be assumed that the inhibitory influence of the satiation center upon the hunger center equally affects on-hunger units and off-hunger units (cf. Figure I-6a). This assumption allows us to understand that when a subject is satiated, not only is the hunger drive (either to a particular food, or to food in general) decreased or abolished but *pari passu* there is a decrease or abolition of the satisfaction of this drive when food is taken into the mouth. On the contrary, when the hunger center is released from the inhibitory influence of the satiation center, not only is the appetite for a given food increased but *pari passu* is increased the satisfaction (the pleasure) produced by its taste. Similarly, we can easily understand why it is that when the ventromedial hypothalamus is destroyed the main regulating power of the food intake depends on the protopathic properties of the taste stimuli.

Furthermore, the acceptance of our hypothesis makes clear another important phenomenon, which has so far been unexplainable, namely,

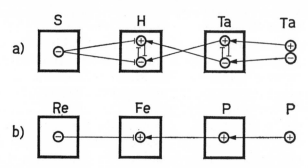

Fig. I-6. Relations between Drive and Antidrive Units in Hunger and Fear

a) Hunger-satiation system. S, satiation center; H, hunger center with on-drive units (+) and off-drive units (−); Ta, taste receptors and taste lower center with on (+) and off (−) units. →, excitatory connections; —|, inhibitory connections.

On-food-taste units activate off-hunger units, whereas off-food-taste units activate on-hunger units. Satiation units inhibit both on-hunger units and off-hunger units. Only protopathic pathways of taste are drawn, and the hunger mechanism for one nutritive substance is indicated.

b) Fear-relief system. Re, relief center with off-fear units; Fe, fear center with only on-fear units; P, pain receptors and pain lower center.

The fear center is homogeneous, reacting directly to the protopathic aspect of pain stimuli.

that stimulation of the lateral hypothalamus may have two contradictory effects: on the one hand, it increases the hunger drive, making the animal hyperexcited; on the other hand, it can be strongly satisfying by providing a self-rewarding effect on the instrumental conditioning.[50] Moreover, it has been shown that lesions sustained in, or procaine injected into the ventromedial hypothalamus significantly increases the self-rewarding effect of stimulation of the lateral hypothalamus precisely because of the removal of the suppressing effect of the former structure upon the latter one (Figure I-7).

The explanation of these facts is that short stimulation of the lateral hypothalamus activates for the most part the off-hunger units, which probably have a shorter latency and/or a lower threshold; a more prolonged stimulation of this nucleus recruits the on-hunger units, possessing a longer latency and/or a higher threshold. When an animal is satiated, the excitability of both off-hunger units and on-hunger units is decreased; hence the self-rewarding effect of stimulation is diminished. It may be added that the cessation of the self-rewarding stimulation produces by rebound the activation of on-hunger units,

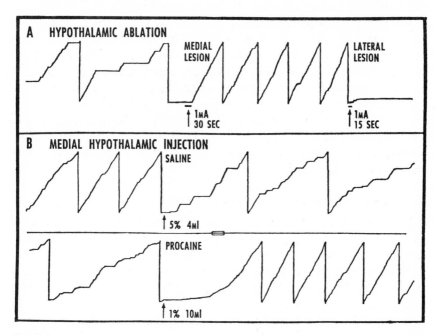

FIG. I-7

Representative cumulative-recorder records showing the changes in lateral hypothalamic self-stimulation rate produced by experimental influence of the hypothalamus. A, Acceleration of self-stimulation caused by destruction of both ventromedial regions. B, Inhibition of self-stimulation by chemical excitation of both ventromedial regions, and subsequent disinhibition of self-stimulation by anesthetization of these regions. (B. G. Hoebel and P. Teitelbaum, in *Science*, 35 [1962]: 375–77.)

and in consequence the animal is likely to perform the next instrumental response. This effect will be discussed in more detail in Chapter IX (p. 399).

Our concept of the mixed character of the hunger center and its comprising both on- and off-units may throw some light on the difference between the functional organization of the hunger drive system and fear (and anger) drive system. If we assume that the fear drive center is not heterogeneous but homogeneous, possessing only on-units activated by the protopathic aspect of pain stimuli, the essential difference in the effects of food and pain upon corresponding drives becomes understandable (cf. Figures I-5 and I-6).

The last point for consideration in the present context concerns a seemingly paradoxical phenomenon known mainly from human experience but existing also in higher animals which seems to contradict the rules outlined above—the phenomenon of joy.

Joy is experienced when some positive goal is attained, and therefore it certainly cannot be classified as drive but as antidrive, and the strong agitation (laughing, "jumping for joy") should be considered as a *sui generis* consummatory response. In fact, although joy is manifested by motor excitement, it has a quite different character from that encountered in drives. There is no tension in it and no striving to reach a goal. It may be considered a kind of release phenomenon, of discharging accumulated energy, but of course these definitions explain nothing and, as a matter of fact, we do not know why humans or animals rejoice loudly and not quietly.

12. Interrelations between various emotive states

What remains for discussion in the present chapter is a survey of relations between heterogeneous drives and antidrives, in order to detect their alliances and antagonisms. We do not intend to give here a complete analysis of this subject, but only to present briefly a general outline of the mutual relations existing between particular emotive states.

Perhaps the most conspicuous antagonism between heterogeneous drives is that manifested between the preservative and protective drives. If we place on one side the preservative drives (hunger drive, sexual drive, curiosity drive) and on the other the fear drive, we can assert that the latter drive is strongly antagonistic to the others. There is much evidence, based both on the human experience and on experimental data, to show that the appearance of strong fear immediately and completely inhibits hunger as well as sexual drive and curiosity. The reverse relation seems also to be true, but it is not so clear, because strong protective activity due to a state of emergency obviously dominates over the preservative activities. After all, preservative activities *can* be postponed to a later moment, but a state of emergency requires immediate action.

Less clear is the antagonism between the preservative activities and the anger drive. It is well known that in humans strong hunger may release angry behavior, and it was found that in dogs anger directed at an enemy may increase hunger.[51]

Further, there is an evident antagonism between the fear drive and the anger drive which is best manifested in human experience in the condition of fight. Strong anger totally suppresses fear, increases courage, and even inhibits reaction to pain. On the contrary, strong fear totally abolishes the possibility of aggressive behavior. Since both these drives are elicited by the same stimuli, it is clear that when they are moderate they may be easily interchangeable, as we can often observe in fights between animals or between humans.

It seems that the relations between various preservative drives are also in principle antagonistic to each other to a greater or lesser extent.

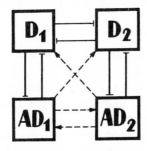

Fig. I-8. Relations between Particular Drives and between Drives and Antidrives

D_1, D_2, centers of particular drives; AD_1, AD_2, centers of corresponding antidrives. —⊣, inhibitory connections; →, excitatory connections. Heavy lines, strong connections; thin lines, weaker connections; broken lines, probable facilitatory connections.

Note that there are strong reciprocal relations between drives and corresponding antidrives, antagonistic relations of various intensities between heterogeneous drives, and weak facilitatory relations (or, perhaps, full neutrality) between antidrives and heterogeneous drives, as well as between heterogeneous antidrives.

For instance, strong hunger inhibits the sexual drive as well as curiosity; sexual drive inhibits hunger and curiosity; and the same is true of curiosity in respect to hunger. However, the satisfaction of each of these drives—the operation of the corresponding antidrives—facilitates the onset of other drives. Thus, moderate satiation may lead to facilitation of the sexual drive or curiosity, and the same is true of the antidrives arising after the satisfaction of the protective drives. In fact, after aggression is past, both the hunger drive and the sexual drive may be facilitated. Examples of this can be seen in the behavior of soldiers after having won a battle. The same *mutatis mutandis* is true after full relief following fear drive, at least in respect to hunger.

It may be concluded that the general principle of the interrelations between various drives and antidrives is as follows.

All the drives, whether preservative or protective, are usually antagonistic to each other, which seems to be biologically reasonable since the pursuit of a certain goal is in general incompatible with the pursuit of another goal. But the satisfaction of a certain drive which produces the state of the corresponding antidrive opens the gate for other drives to occur (we mean here the preservative drives) according to the actual needs of the organism. Further, whereas particular drives are, with few exceptions, antagonistic to each other, antidrives, on the contrary, seem to be allied. The block model representing all these relations in an oversimplified form is presented in Figure I-8.

13. Summary and conclusions

The basic activities of the organism—that is, those activities upon which the whole complex acquired animal behavior is superimposed—can be divided in respect to their biological roles into preservative and protective activities, and in respect to their particular stages into preparatory and consummatory activities.

Preservative activities lead to the preservation of the individuals by providing them with the necessary materials, by ridding them of waste materials, and by replenishing their vital capacities. They lead to the preservation of species by copulation and raising the progeny. Protective activities, on the other hand, are thrown into operation when the individual is subjected to a noxious agent or to its danger, and are directed toward getting rid of them. The protective activities take the form of retreat from the operation of a noxious stimulus or its danger (defense), of its rejection, or of destruction of its source (aggression).

Innate consummatory activities, both preservative and protective, are generally referred to as unconditioned reflexes (URs). They are in operation when the stimulus eliciting a given activity is presented and the organism reacts to it in the appropriate way. Thus, the food in the mouth elicits the ingestive or food UR (mastication, salivation, swallowing); the filled bladder elicits the urination UR; the intromission of the penis into the vagina elicits the copulatory UR; the presence of a "neutral" stimulus in the receptive field elicits the targeting UR; the noxious stimulus to the foot elicits the flexion UR; the foreign body in the trachea elicits the coughing UR; squeezing the tail elicits the aggressive UR—to give the most typical examples of each sort of consummatory activities.

Preparatory activities occur when the stimulus eliciting the consummatory UR is not present and must be provided, as is true in preservative activities, or has to be forestalled, as in protective activities.

Preparatory activities possess either the particular, more or less rigid, innate patterns of behavior (they are then called instincts), or they possess only the general patterns which are then modeled and specialized according to the individual animal's experience.

The controlling mechanisms of the preparatory activities are called *drives*, and their psychological counterparts are called *emotions*. Thus, the alimentary preparatory activity is controlled by the hunger drive; the sexual preparatory activity, by the sexual drive; the preparatory activity for targeting reflexes, by the curiosity drive; the protective preparatory activities, by fear drive for retreat reflexes and anger drive for aggressive reflexes.

The unconditioned drive-producing stimuli belong mainly to two categories. On the one hand, there are special humoral stimuli acting directly on the neurons (perhaps the dendrites) of the corresponding drive centers (intracentral chemoreceptors). Such stimuli are certainly in operation in producing most preservative drives. The question of whether they also elicit protective drives is still open. On the other hand, all drives, both preservative and protective, are elicited by specific protopathic stimuli—those which produce the corresponding consummatory reflexes. Whereas protective drive reflexes are evoked by actual operation of these stimuli, preservative drive reflexes are evoked by their cessation.

The effects of almost all drives are: motor hyperactivity (which we call arousal of the motor behavioral system); increased motor efficiency; arousal of particular afferent systems, probably mediated by the unspecific thalamic nuclei; and increased tonus of the sympathetic system.

Drives are controlled by the part of the brain which we call the "emotive system" (in contradistinction to the cognitive system). Its centers are situated on two levels: in the hypothalamus, and in the limbic system; the latter is thought to be involved in conditioning of drives.

When a given drive is satisfied by the corresponding consummatory response or the avoidance of a noxious stimulus, the state antagonistic to it arises, which corresponds to Thorndike's "satisfying state of affairs." We have called this state the "antidrive," and its psychological counterpart the "mood." Accordingly, we have the following antidrives: alimentary antidrive (satiation), sexual antidrive (sexual satisfaction), curiosity antidrive (indifference), fear antidrive (relief), and anger antidrive (placidity).

The organization of the drive-controlling systems is somewhat different in preservative and protective drives. In the hunger-satiation system, being the representative of the preservative drive systems, the satiation center is controlled by humoral stimuli, its activation producing the suppression of the hunger center and its inactivation producing the release of that center. Therefore, the satiation center regulates the *excitability* of the hunger center, or rather its particular groups of units corresponding to particular nutritive substances. The hunger center is assumed to be composed of on-hunger units of particular kinds and, reciprocally related with them, off-hunger units. The off-hunger units are activated by particular taste stimuli, whereas the on-hunger units are activated by the taste off-elements thrown into operation when the taste stimulus is discontinued.

This dual character probably does not exist in the protective drive systems, where the drive-producing stimuli, which are partially identical with the protective consummatory stimuli directly elicit the appropriate drive.

The interrelations between various drives and between drives and antidrives obey, in principle, the following rules:

(1) There is a mutual antagonism between each drive and a corresponding antidrive.

(2) Different drives, whether preservative or protective, are in mutual antagonistic relations—that is, when a particular drive is in operation, it tends to inhibit all other drives if none of them is stronger than the active one.

(3) If a given drive is satisfied and the antidrive comes into operation, it may facilitate the operation of other drives if the relevant stimuli eliciting them are present.

The drives and antidrives represent two sides of the energizing mechanisms of animal behavior, the former compelling the organism to do something for the sake of its preservation, and the latter allowing the organism to become calm or to be concerned with the consummatory activity, when the goal aimed by the drive is attained. Accordingly, they play the decisive role in modeling an animal's adaptive behavior in his individual life, since the drives enable the animal to find the means for achieving the necessary goals, whether supplying the necessary materials for life, getting rid of waste materials, or avoiding the noxious agents; the appropriate antidrives signal that these goals have been achieved. Thus, whereas drive activity is characterized by stress and tensions, the antidrive is characterized by relief and relaxation.

References to Chapter I

1.   J. Konorski. 1948. *Conditioned Reflexes and Neuron Organization.* Cambridge: Cambridge University Press.

———. 1950. Mechanisms of learning. In *Physiological Mechanisms in Animal Behaviour*, pp. 409–31. Symp. Soc. Exp. Biol., No. 4.

2. I. P. Pavlov. 1940. *Conditioned Reflexes: An Investigation of the Physiological Activity of the Cerebral Cortex.* Translated and edited by G. V. Anrep. London: Oxford University Press.

3. C. S. Sherrington. 1917. Reflexes elicitable in the cat from pinna, vibrissae, and jaws. *J. Physiol.* (London), 51: 404–31.

4. I. P. Pavlov. 1910. *The Work of the Digestive Glands.* 2d English ed. Translated by W. H. Thompson. London: C. Griffin.

5. S. C. Wang. 1943. Localization of the salivatory center in the medulla of the cat. *J. Neurophysiol.*, 6: 195–202.

6. B. P. Babkin and I. M. Buren. 1955. Mechanism and cortical representation of the feeding patterns. *Arch. Neurol. Psychiat.* (Chicago), 66: 1–19.

B. Żernicki and G. Santibanez. 1961. The effects of ablations of "alimentary area" of the cerebral cortex on salivary conditioned and unconditioned reflexes in dogs. *Acta Biol. Exp. Vars.*, 21: 163–76.

7. F. R. Miller and C. S. Sherrington. 1916. Some observations on the bucco-pharyngeal stage of reflex deglutition in the cat. *Quart. J. Exp. Physiol.*, 9: 147–86.

8. C. S. Sherrington. 1947. *The Integrative Action of the Nervous System.* 2d ed. Cambridge: Cambridge University Press.

9. L. J. O'Kelly and L. C. Steckle. 1939. A note on long enduring emotional responses in the rat. *J. Psychol.*, 8: 125–31.

R. E. Ulrich and N. H. Azrin. 1962. Reflexive fighting in response to aversive stimulation. *J. Exp. Analysis Behav.*, 5: 511–20.

10. J. M. Sprague and T. H. Meikle, Jr. 1965. The role of the superior colliculus in visually guided behavior. *Expl. Neurol.*, 11: 115–46.

11. H. Klüver. 1942. Functional significance of the geniculo-striate system. In H. Klüver, ed., *Visual Mechanisms*, pp. 253–99. Lancaster, Pa.: J. Cattell.

B. Dreher, P. L. Marchiafava, and B. Żernicki. 1965. Studies on the visual fixation reflex. II. The neural mechanism of the fixation reflex in normal and pretrigeminal cats. *Acta Biol. Exp. Vars.*, 25: 207–17.

12. W. D. Neff, J. F. Fisher, I. T. Diamond, and M. Yela. 1956. Role of auditory cortex in discrimination requiring localization of sound in space. *J. Neurophysiol.*, 19: 500–512.

G. Szwejkowska and L. Stępień. Unpublished experiments.

13. W. Baust and G. Berlucchi. 1964. Reflex response to clicks of cat's tensor tympani during sleep and wakefulness and the influence thereon of the auditory cortex. *Arch. Ital. Biol.*, 102: 686–712.

14. W. B. Cannon. 1929. *Bodily Changes in Pain, Hunger, Fear and Rage.* New York and London: Appleton-Century.

15. M. J. Grossman and I. F. Stein. 1948. Vagotomy and the hunger-producing action of insulin in man. *J. Appl. Physiol.*, 1: 263–69.

16. J. Mayer. 1955. Regulation of energy intake and the body weight: The glucostatic theory and the lipostatic hypothesis. *Ann. N. Y. Acad. Sci.*, 63: 15–43.
     B. K. Anand. 1961. Nervous regulation of food intake. *Physiol. Rev.*, 41: 677–708.

17. C. P. Richter. 1942. Total self regulatory functions in animals and human beings. *Harvey Lect.*, 38: 63–103.

18. B. Żernicki and J. Ekel. 1959. Elaboration and mutual relations between alimentary and water instrumental conditioned reflexes in dogs. *Acta Biol. Exp. Vars.*, 19: 313–25.

18*a*. И. С. Цитович. 1911. О присхождении натуральных условных рефлексов. (On the origin of natural conditioned reflexes.) Doctoral dissertation, St. Petersburg.

18*b*. F. P. Gault. Personal communication.

19. Ситуационные условные рефлексы у собак в норме и патологии. 1964. (Environmental conditioned reflexes in dogs in norm and pathology.) Сост.: П. С. Купалов, О. Н. Воеводина, В. Д. Волкова, И. В. Малюкова, А. Т. Селиванова, В. И. Сыренский, М. М. Хананашвили, Г. А. Шичко. Leningrad: Izdat. "Meditsina."

20. А. Д. Слоним. 1961. Основы общей экологической физиологии млекопитающих. Т. I. (Foundations of general ecological physiology of mammals.) Moscow and Leningrad: Izdat. Akad. Nauk SSSR.

21. W. Wyrwicka. Unpublished observations.

22. W. Wyrwicka and C. Dobrzecka. 1960. Relationship between feeding and satiation centers of the hypothalamus. *Science*, 132: 805–6.

23. P. Teitelbaum and A. N. Epstein. 1962. The lateral hypothalamic syndrome. Recovery of feeding and drinking after lateral hypothalamic lesions. *Psychol. Rev.*, 69: 74–90.

24. P. Teitelbaum. 1955. Sensory control of hypothalamic hyperphagia. *J. Comp. Physiol. Psychol.*, 48: 156–63.

25. M. K. Lewińska. 1967. Changes in eating and drinking produced by partial amygdalar lesions in cat. *Bull. Acad. Pol. Sci., Ser. sci. biol.*, 15 (in press).

26. E. Fonberg and J. M. R. Delgado. 1961. Avoidance and alimentary reactions during amygdala stimulation. *J. Neurophysiol.*, 24: 651–64.

27. E. Fonberg. 1966. Aphagia produced by destruction of the dorsomedial amygdala in dogs. *Bull. Acad. Pol. Sci. Ser. sci. biol.*, 14: 719–22.

28. B. K. Anand, S. Dua, B. Singh. 1961. Electrical activity of the hypothalamic "Feeding centres" under the effect of changes in blood chemistry. *Electroenceph. Clin. Neurophysiol.*, 13: 54–59.

29. A. N. Epstein and P. Teitelbaum. 1962. Lateral hypothalamic control of insulin-induced feeding. In *22d International Congress of Physiological Sciences, Leiden, September 10–17, 1962*, Vol. II, Abstr. No. 361. Amsterdam: Excerpta Medica Found. Internat. Congr. Ser. No. 48.

30. N. N. Traugott. Personal communication.

31. W. B. Cannon. 1929 (see note 14 above).

32. W. R. Hess. 1957. *The Functional Organization of the Diencephalon.* New York and London: Grune & Stratton.

33. H. Ursin and B. R. Kaada. 1960. Functional localization within the amygdaloid complex in the cat. *Electroenceph. Clin. Neurophysiol.*, 12: 1–20.

    H. Ursin. 1965. The effect of amygdaloid lesions on flight and defense behavior in cats. *Exp. Neurol.*, 11: 61–79.

34. H. Klüver and P. C. Bucy. 1939. Preliminary analysis of functions of the temporal lobes in monkeys. *Arch Neurol. Psychiat.* (Chicago), 42: 979–1000.

35. Charles Darwin. 1872. *The Expression of the Emotions in Man and Animals.* London: John Murray.

36. H. Ursin and B. R. Kaada. 1960 (see note 33 above).

    H. Ursin. 1965 (see note 33 above).

37. E. A. Spiegel, H. R. Miller, and M. J. Oppenheimer. 1940. Forebrain and rage reactions. *J. Neurophysiol.*, 3: 538–48.

    S. Brutkowski, E. Fonberg, and E. Mempel. 1961. Angry behaviour in dogs following bilateral lesions in the genual portion of the rostral cingulate gyrus. *Acta Biol. Exp. Vars.*, 21: 199–205.

38. M. Wasman and J. P. Flynn. 1962. Directed attack elicited from hypothalamus. *Arch. Neurol.* (Chicago), 6: 220–27.

    R. R. Hutchinson and J. W. Renfrew. 1966. Stalking attack and eating behaviors elicited from the same sites in the hypothalamus. *J. Comp. Physiol. Psychol.*, 61: 360–67.

39. D. E. Berlyne. 1960. *Conflict, Arousal, and Curiosity.* New York: McGraw-Hill.

40. H. E. Rosvold. Personal communication.

41. C. Bühler, H. Hetzer, and F. Mabel. 1928. Die Affektwirksamkeit von Fremheitseindrücken im ersten Lebensjahr. *Z. Psychol.*, Abt. 1, 107: 30–49. (Cited by D. E. Berlyne, note 39 above.)

42. H. H. Jasper. 1949. Diffuse projection systems: The integrative action of the thalamic reticular system. *Electroenceph. Clin. Neurophysiol.*, 1: 405–20.

    ———. 1954. Functional properties of the thalamic reticular system. In *Brain Mechanisms and Consciousness*, pp. 374–401. Oxford: Blackwell Sci. Publ.

    R. Jung. 1958. Coordination of specific and nonspecific afferent impulses at single neurons of the visual cortex. In H. H. Jasper et al., eds., *Reticular Formation of the Brain*, pp. 423–34. Boston: Little, Brown & Co.

43. V. C. Abrahams, S. M. Hilton, and A. Zbrożyna. 1960. Active muscle vasodilatation produced by stimulation of the brain stem: Its significance in the defence reaction. *J. Physiol.* (London), 154: 491–513.

43*a*. R. A. Gorski and R. E. Whalen, eds. 1966. *Brain and Behavior.* Vol. III: *The Brain and Gonadal Function.* Berkeley and Los Angeles: University of California Press. UCLA Forum Med. Sci. No. 3.

44. J. W. Papez. 1937. A proposed mechanism of emotion. *Arch. Neurol. Psychiat.* (Chicago), 38: 725–43.

45. J. Olds. 1956. A preliminary mapping of electrical reinforcing effects in the rat brain. *J. Comp. Physiol. Psychol.* 49: 281–85.

46. С. Ь. Хазен. 1908. О соотношении размеров безусловного и условного слюно-отделительных рефлексов. (On the interrelation of the size of unconditioned and conditioned salivary reflexes.) Doctoral dissertation. St. Petersburg.

46*a*. I. P. Pavlov. 1910 (see note 4 above).

46*b*. В. Н. Болдырев. 1904. Периодическая работа пищеварительного аппарата при пустом желудке. (Periodic work of the digestive apparatus with the empty stomach.) Doctoral dissertation, St. Petersburg.

46*c*. С. И. Гальперин. 1960. Нейро-гуморальные регуляции у позвоночных животных. (Neuro-humoral regulations in vertebrates.) Moscow: Izdat. "Vysšaja Škola."

47. A. J. Carlson. 1916. *The Control of Hunger in Health and Disease.* Chicago: University of Chicago Press.

48. N. Tinbergen. 1955. *The Study of Instinct.* Oxford: Clarendon Press.

49. J. Olds. 1958. Effects of hunger and male sex hormone on self-stimulation of the brain. *J. Comp. Physiol. Psychol.*, 51: 320–24.

50. D. L. Margules and J. Olds. 1962. Identical "feeding" and "rewarding" systems in the lateral hypothalamus of rats. *Science*, 135: 374–75.

   B. G. Hoebel and P. Teitelbaum. 1962. Hypothalamic control of feeding and self-stimulation. *Science*, 135: 375–76.

51. P. T. Young. 1943. *Emotion in Man and Animal.* New York: Wiley.

   I. P. Pavlov and M. K. Petrova. 1928. Analysis of some complex reflexes in dog. Relative strength of centers. In *Lectures on Conditioned Reflexes.* New York: International.

CHAPTER II

GENERAL PHYSIOLOGY
OF PERCEPTION

1. Introductory remarks

In the preceding chapter we made a general survey of the modes of functioning of the basic (innate) activities of the nervous system which insure the adaptation of the organism to the external world. These activities are, however, not sufficient for the preservation of higher animals and their well-being, because the organisms need to possess not only the mechanisms for adaptation but also those involving adaptability. Accordingly, the relatively rigid forms of the basic activities of the organisms have to be enriched and modulated through other mechanisms by means of which the adaptation of the organisms is permanently changed and perfected. This occurs, roughly speaking, by the continuous accumulation of incoming information sorted out in particular ways, by its storage, and by associations of messages arriving through different channels. Needless to say, in all these processes the information generated by the executive organs themselves—the so-called servo-mechanisms, or feedback, shaping and perfecting the efferent outflow—plays no less important role than the information obtained from the external world.

The most reasonable way of undertaking the task of systematic exposition of the principles of integrative action of the brain is, first, to see how the information provided by receptors is worked out and stored in nervous centers; then we should determine how various messages coming from different sources are combined and associated; last, we should consider how these messages are utilized by the executive organs. In the present chapter we shall deal with the general principles of handling information by the afferent systems, whereas in the next chapter we shall see how these principles operate within particular analyzers.

2. The general rules of the functioning of afferent systems

The experimental work of recent years, in which action potentials obtained from stimulation of particular receptive surfaces were recorded on various levels of afferent systems, either by macro-electrodes or more recently by micro-electrodes from single nerve cells, has substantially increased our understanding of the modes of functioning of these systems. In this section we shall try to present very briefly the general rules governing the functions of afferent systems as they may be inferred from electrophysiological studies concerning various analyzers.

(1) Each analyzer is built in the form of an n-storied (n-level) construction, the basement of which is represented by a particular receptive surface, and the top by that story in which the journey of messages sent from the receptors is terminated. Each level of the construction is composed of the aggregate of nerve cells whose axons run to the next higher level, except the top level whose axons are sent outside the given analyzer. We shall denote each such aggregate as the *afferent field* (or center, or area) of a given analyzer. We shall call the nerve cells involved in receiving particular messages from the lower levels or the basement the *units* of a given field.

The connections between the consecutive levels of each analyzer are arranged according to the *divergence-convergence principle,* the divergence generally being predominant (the relations between the basement and the first order level are not taken into account). In consequence the higher the level, the larger the number of units of which it is composed (Figure II-1).

(2) In some systems the connections between the succeeding levels have a precise topical arrangement: the level k is roughly a projection (in geometrical sense) of the level k-1, and so on down to level one. However, in some other systems this precise topical arrangement is not present. In some instances the k-1-level is twice or even thrice represented in the k-level (the so-called sensory areas I, II, and following), each representation having a different type of topical arrangement.

(3) The units of a particular level of a given analyzer either are connected with the units of the higher level of that analyzer or their axons run to other parts of the nervous system. We shall call the units of the first type *transit units;* the units of the second type, *exit units.* We shall not consider the problem of whether the transit units and the

exit units are separate or whether they may perform a dual role sending collaterals both to the higher level of the system and to other centers.

If an afferent field possesses only units sending their axons to the higher level of the given system, it will be called *transit field;* if it also possesses the units whose axons leave the system, it will be called *transit-exit field.* By definition, the highest level of each afferent system includes only exit units and therefore represents the pure *exit field* (Fig. II-2).

Exit units of the lower levels of each analyzer represent the last link in the afferent parts of various unconditioned reflex-arcs described in

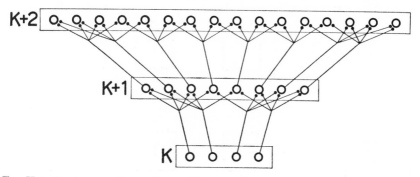

FIG. II-1. DIVERGENCE-CONVERGENCE PRINCIPLE IN AFFERENT SYSTEMS

Particular levels (K, K + 1, K + 2) are denoted by quadrangles, their units by circles, synaptic contacts by points. In this scheme the ratio of divergence is 1:4, that of convergence 1:2.

the preceding chapter, such as targeting reflexes to neutral stimuli, defensive reflexes to noxious stimuli, or alimentary reflexes to taste stimuli. On the other hand, exit units of the highest level of an analyzer, send their axons to the highest levels of other analyzers and form the anatomical substrate of the associative function of the nervous system (cf. Chapter IV).

As will become more apparent in our further discussion, the transit units play an intermediary role in elaborating the information *within* the given afferent system, whereas the exit units play a role in utilization of this information for various activities of the organism. Because of this rather essential difference in the physiological role of both types of units, we shall call the function of the transit units on all levels of the given analyzer the *receptive function* and the units concerned, the *receptive units;* we shall call the function of the exit units the *perceptive function* and the units concerned, the *perceptive units.* This is in agreement with current usage of these terms, since by perception, in contradistinction to reception, we mean that form of the afferent activity which takes part in associative processes and behavior of the animal.

(4) In every afferent system there is an important part of exit units which subserve the reflexes controlling its own activity (*recurrent reflexes*). There are at least two main types of these reflexes.

The first type is the one we have called targeting reflexes. Their function consists in adjusting lower levels of a given afferent system and the effectors related to the corresponding receptive organs for the best reception of the appropriate sensory input. The exit units giving

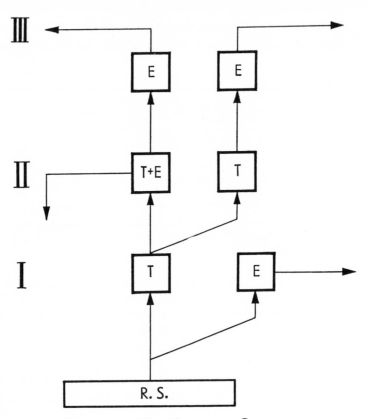

Fig. II-2. Block Model of the Main Features of Organization of Afferent Systems

R.S., receptive surface. I, II, III, successive levels of the system. T, transit fields; T + E, transit-exit field; E, exit fields. Vertical ascending arrows denote transit pathways; horizontal arrows denote exit pathways.

Exit field in level I denotes a field starting an unconditioned reflex-arc. In level II the exit pathway subserving the recurrent reflexes is indicated (arrow down). Level III is the top level of the given afferent system from which associative pathways to other afferent systems are shown.

rise to targeting reflexes are situated on various levels of afferent systems, but they are particularly well represented in the projective areas of the cerebral cortex (see Chapter I, Section 5).

The second type of recurrent reflexes is the one that, in contrast to the first type, suppresses the sensory input by closing the "gates" of a given afferent system (both in the afferent relay stations and on the periphery). These reflexes play an essential role in the phenomena of habituation and will be discussed in detail in Section 10, below.

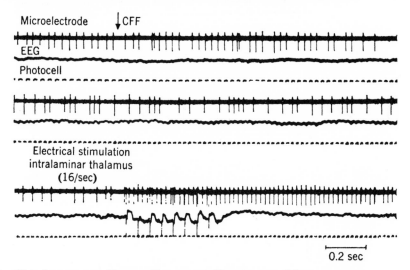

FIG. II-3. INCREASE IN FLICKER FREQUENCY DRIVING OF A NEURON IN THE VISUAL CORTEX PRODUCED BY INTRALAMINAR THALAMIC STIMULATION

Flicker at rising frequency gives regular neuronal discharges up to 18 per second (first record). At frequencies of 19 to 41 per second, the neuron can no longer respond to each flash and shows interruptions in firing. After a brief series of pulses (16 per second) in the intralaminar thalamus, the neuron follows the high-flicker frequency (third record). (From R. Jung, Neuronal integration in the visual cortex and its significance for visual information, in *Sensory Communication*, ed. W. Rosenblith [New York and London: M.I.T. Press and Wiley, 1961].)

(5) The units of particular levels (perhaps all levels) of afferent systems are not only activated by the corresponding sensory input whose messages are conveyed by the "specific" pathways but are also under the influence of the ascending "unspecific" system whose messages are conveyed through the unspecific thalamic nuclei to the large regions of the cortex. This phenomenon is illustrated in Figure II-3. As shown in Chapter I, Section 9, this system is a part of the emotive system, and its role is to facilitate (or inhibit) particular analyzers under the influence of particular drives. It is assumed that whereas

specific sensory input is transmitted through the axosomatic synapses, the unspecific input is conveyed by axodendritic synapses. As we shall see in our further discussion, the facilitatory effects exerted by the unspecific system upon the given afferent system play an important role in cognitive processes, being indispensable to perception and learning.

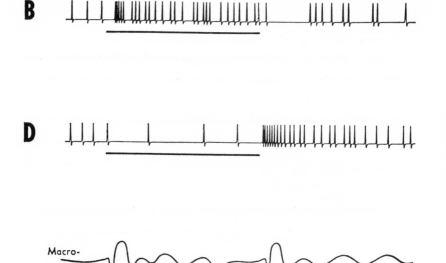

FIG. II-4. ON-UNITS AND OFF-UNITS IN THE VISUAL CORTEX
OF CAT (SEMISCHEMATIC)

B, on-unit; D, off-unit. Other explanations in text. (From R. Jung, Excitation, inhibition and coordination of cortical neurons, *Exper. Cell Res.*, 5 [Suppl. 1958]: 262–71. Simplified.)

(6) In particular fields of some (or all) afferent systems there are units which are activated by the onset of particular agents impinging upon the corresponding receptive surface (on-effect), and units which are activated by the termination of the operation of those agents (off-effect). The former units are called on-units; the latter, off-units (Figure II-4). The corresponding on-units and off-units are in reciprocal relations—the stronger the excitation of the former units, the stronger the inhibition of the latter, and vice versa.

The reciprocal relations between particular units exist not only in respect to the presence and absence of a given stimulus but also in respect to two opposite stimuli—for instance, the passive changes of limb postures in opposite directions (Figure II-5).

(7) In most instances the same units which are excited by the onset of a given agent continue to be active during its further operation; those units which are excited by the termination of an agent are still active during its absence (cf. Figure II-4). Usually the intensity of excitation of a unit, measured by the rate of its discharges, decreases

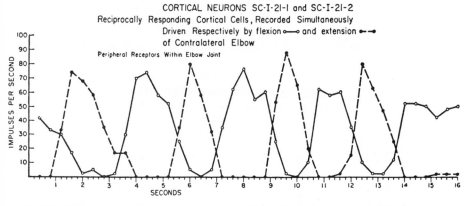

CORTICAL NEURONS SC-I-2I-I and SC-I-2I-2
Reciprocally Responding Cortical Cells, Recorded Simultaneously
Driven Respectively by flexion o——o and extension •——•
of Contralateral Elbow

FIG. II-5. RECIPROCAL RELATIONS BETWEEN TWO UNITS IN SOMATO-SENSORY CORTEX RESPONDING TO FLEXION AND EXTENSION OF ELBOW, RESPECTIVELY

(From V. B. Mountcastle, Modality and topographic properties of single neurons of cat's somatic sensory cortex, *J. Neurophysiol.*, 20 [1957]: 408–34.)

with continuation of a stimulus, attaining a definite steady state—the phenomenon referred to as adaptation (Figure II-6). The strength of adaptation, measured by the decrement of discharges with continuation of a stimulus, depends on the properties of a given unit and the kind of stimulus.

It follows from this thesis that the lasting *absence* of stimulation of a given afferent field may involve a continuous discharging of off-units (or at least some of them), which stops when some agent impinges upon this field. This discharging is usually referred to as "spontaneous." It shows that the absence of any external input upon the receptive surface is also a *stimulus* in physiological sense—that is it is a source of information about the character of the environment, no less important than information provided by various stimulus-patterns. We propose the hypothesis that the continuous activation of off-units, similarly to the continuous activation of on-units, takes place when a given afferent field is under the facilitatory influence of the unspecific

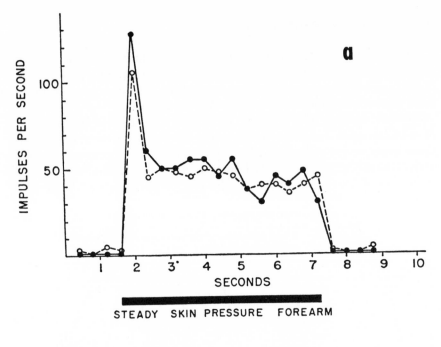

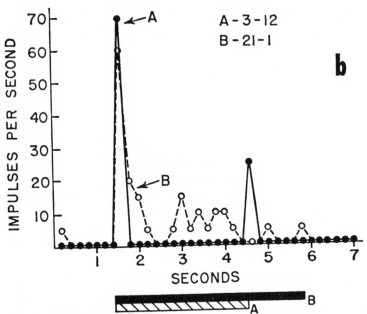

Fig. II-6. Adaptation of an On-unit in Somato-Sensory Cortex to Steady Skin Pressure

In (a) two identical stimuli were delivered 10 minutes apart. Other explanations in text. Note partial adaptation in (a) and nearly total adaptation in (b). (From V. B. Mountcastle and T. P. S. Powell, Neural mechanisms subserving cutaneous sensibility, with special reference to the role of afferent inhibition in sensory perception and discrimination, *Bull. J. Hopkins Hosp.*, 105 [1959]: 201–32.)

system. This assumption will help us to understand some phenomena encountered in conditioning (Chapter VII, Section 5).

(8) In certain afferent fields the activation of a unit by stimulation of a corresponding spot on the receptive surface may be totally suppressed if another spot lying in the vicinity is simultaneously stimulated (Figure II-7). This phenomenon is referred to as *lateral inhibition*. It is assumed to be due to inhibitory connections existing between the adjacent units within the particular afferent fields (Figure II-8).

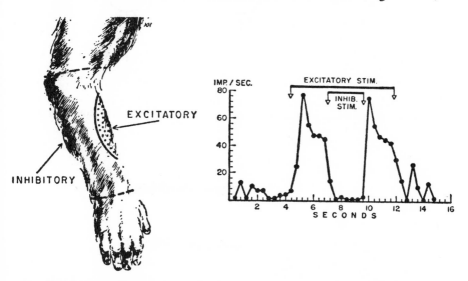

FIG. II-7. LATERAL INHIBITION IN THE SOMATO-SENSORY CORTEX IN MONKEY

The excitatory receptive field in respect to a given unit in the somato-sensory area is surrounded by the inhibitory receptive field in respect to this unit. The response of the unit is shown on the right. (From Mountcastle and Powell, *op. cit.*, Fig. II-6 above.)

As we shall see later, the higher the level of a given afferent field, the larger the scope of lateral inhibition.

(9) For each unit in a given afferent field of a given analyzer there is a stimulus (that is, a pattern of excitation of particular receptors), or a set of stimuli, which produces its optimal response in the sense of maximal rate of impulse discharge. Such a stimulus will be called the *adequate stimulus* for a given unit (Figure II-9).

(10) The higher the level of the given afferent system, the more complex and refined the adequate stimuli to which the units of this level react. This important rule has been determined with great precision by Hubel and Wiesel[1] for the visual analyzer, but it may be reasonably assumed to operate in other analyzers as well.

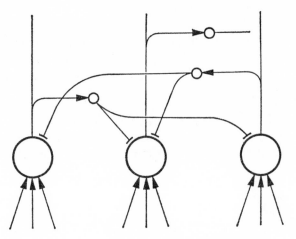

FIG. II-8. SCHEMATIC REPRESENTATION OF LATERAL INHIBITION

Large circles, units of a given level. Small circles, "Renshaw cells" mediating the inhibitory processes. →, excitatory connections; ⊣, inhibitory connections.

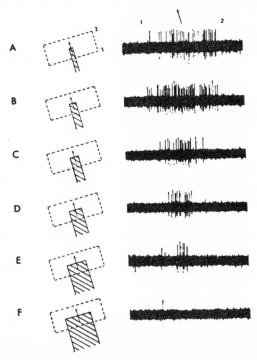

FIG. II-9. ADEQUATE STIMULUS FOR A UNIT IN VISUAL AREA III IN CAT

It is seen that the "tongue" in B gives the best response of the unit. (From D. H. Hubel and T. N. Wiesel, Receptive fields and functional architecture in two nonstriate visual areas [18 and 19] of the cat, *J. Neurophysiol.*, 28 [1965]: 229–89.)

As follows from the work of Hubel and Wiesel, the adequate stimuli for units situated in the lateral geniculate body (afferent field of the third order) are represented by small *spots* (light, dark, or colored) of a definite optimal diameter (Figure II-10*a*).

In recording responses from the units of the afferent field of the fourth order (visual projective area of the cortex, area 17), it turns out that here the adequate stimuli are provided by straight *lines*, of indefinite length but of quite definite orientations from horizontal to vertical. These lines are usually situated in specific places of the visual receptive field ("simple" units), but sometimes the whole set of lines of the given orientation within the larger area may be represented by the given unit ("complex" units). The lines represented by the units of the striate cortex are of three kinds: dark bars, light bars ("slits"), and edges separating dark and light planes (Figure II-10*b*).

In the visual fields of still higher orders (area 18 and 19 or, better, visual areas II and III, as proposed by Hubel and Wiesel), we see that the units there react to still more complex patterns: bidirectional edges ("corners"), dark or light bars of definite width limited on one end ("tongues") or two ends (let us call them "rods") ("hypercomplex" units) (Figure II-10*c*). Again, some units react to these more complex shapes only when they are situated in the given place of the retina; whereas others are not strictly location-bound, and react to the whole set of similar shapes within a definite area.

As it was assumed by Hubel and Wiesel, the units of the higher levels of the visual afferent system are formed by the *convergence* of appropriate units of the lower levels. In other words, a unit of the highest level represents a top of a pyramid whose basement consists of receptive organs. Since the same receptors and the same units of lower levels take part in different combinations in various pyramids, the number of pyramids may exceed the number of units of the lower levels. It should be emphasized that among the units of the lower level converging upon a given unit of the higher level both the on-units and off-units play an equal role—that is, the pattern of an adequate stimulus fitting the given unit of the higher level is composed from both the presence of certain elements and absence of others.

3. The concept of gnostic units

It may be observed that stimulus-patterns that are adequate for activating the units of particular levels of the visual afferent system, although certainly complicated from the point of view of a neurophysiologist who is concerned with their analysis, are nevertheless most simple and primitive in comparison with those patterns which a subject, whether a human or an animal, actually perceives and reacts to. In fact, we per-

FIG. II-10. VARIOUS TYPES OF STIMULUS-PATTERNS ADEQUATE FOR PARTICULAR
LEVELS OF THE VISUAL AFFERENT SYSTEM

a) Stimulus-patterns adequate for units of lateral geniculate body.
b) Stimulus-patterns adequate for units of visual projective area.
c) Stimulus-patterns adequate for units of visual paraprojective area.

ceive people, human faces, animals, small objects from nearby, large objects from afar; and there is no doubt whatsoever that cats and monkeys (which were the subjects of Hubel and Wiesel's experiments) have roughly the same perceptions, judging from their behavioral responses. However, neither humans nor animals notice lines, edges, corners, "tongues," or "rods," which were the adequate stimuli for the units so far investigated. We *are* indeed able deliberately to separate these elements from the whole objects seen by us, but this process is based on the analysis of the visual pattern of these objects and not on their more primitive immediate perception. Thus, although the above elements of the objects perceived certainly do exist in our (and animals') visual reception, we normally pay no attention to them or do not realize their existence.

Even more clear is the situation in respect to perceptions in other analyzers, because here their secondary analysis aiming at isolation of the elements involved is often totally impossible. We are unable to resolve the sound of the voice of a given person into the spectrum of its acoustic elements, although we recognize it without any difficulty. An illiterate man is unable to resolve the sound of a word into its phonemes, and none of us can resolve a spoken word into its kinesthetic elements. The taste of a given dish is recognized as such, not by its analysis, and the same is even more true of olfactory stimuli. In fact, one of the reasons for the foundation of Gestalt psychology was the realization that our perceptions are not formed through the summation of simple sensations, as was claimed by associationistic psychology of the nineteenth century.

Now the crucial problem arises why it is so.

It may be supposed that particular units of the so-called associative areas of the cortex become interconnected in various ways, forming what Hebb has called cell assemblies corresponding to particular perceptions.[2] These connections, according to Hebb, are so well established and multidirectional that it is sufficient to put into action one unit in order to activate the whole assembly.

But, having at our disposal the recent data derived from Hubel and Wiesel's experiments, we can extrapolate their findings and explain the origin of perceptions according to the same principles which were found to operate on the lower levels of the afferent systems. In other words, we can assume that perceptions experienced in humans' and animals' lives, are represented not by the *assemblies* of units but by *single* units in the highest levels of particular analyzers. We shall call these levels *gnostic areas* and the units responsible for particular perceptions, *gnostic units.*

According to this hypothesis, there is an essential difference between the role played by gnostic areas and that played by transit areas. Whereas the role of the transit units consists in *integrating* the elements of receptions into more and more complex patterns constituting the raw material for the gnostic units, the latter units represent the *biologically meaningful* stimulus-patterns which are used in associative processes and behavior of the organisms. It follows from this analysis that once the task of a given transit afferent field is fulfilled—that is, this field has transmitted the stimulus-patterns represented in its units to the afferent field of the higher order—these stimulus-patterns no longer participate as separate items in the further information processing, since they are amalgamated into the whole and thus completely lose their individuality. A unit of the higher order representing some integrated stimulus-pattern does not "know" from which components it is synthesized. Thus, we come to the solution of the vexing antinomy contained in Gestalt psychology, according to which, on the one hand, the perceptions are *certainly* composed of the simple elements provided by particular receptors of the given receptive surface, but, on the other hand, these elements are totally lost in our perceptions, since we have no realization of which elements they are composed. Even if we do perceive some simple patterns, represented in the lower level of the given analyzer—such as the geometric contours in the visual analyzer or tones in the auditory analyzer—it is not because we return to these lower levels utilizing the corresponding units but because we form the special perceptive units in the highest level; in other words, their simplicity is only apparent, and they are, in fact, even more sophisticated because they do not belong to the natural repertory of our perceptive experiences.

The more developed the given analyzer and the more complex the stimulus-patterns represented in its gnostic units, the higher the ladder of transit fields mediating the final result. The same principle certainly operates in phylogeny: the more developed the brain of a given species, the more levels the particular analyzer possesses. Consequently, the development of the cerebral cortex is accomplished not by the extension of the primary projective areas, which remain relatively constant in various animals, but by superimposing upon them (in the functional sense) the new levels of cortical integration and perhaps by their extension.

There is so far no direct electrophysiological evidence that perceptions are really represented by the units of gnostic areas. We have, however, a great bulk of indirect evidence which comes from psychological considerations, from neuroanatomical and neuropathological findings and from the effects of brain stimulation in waking human subjects. We shall survey now all these sources of evidence.

4. Psychological evidence of the existence of gnostic units

It should be once more recalled that according to our concept perceptive units and perceptive processes are not defined by the level of their integration and their complexity but rather by their functional role—namely, by their involvement in the associative processes guiding behavioral responses. Whereas the perceptive processes controlled by the lower levels of afferent systems were discussed in the preceding chapter, in the present chapter we shall be concerned chiefly with much more elaborated perceptions, such as those that constitute the main part of human experiences.

The selection of human beings as the principal subjects for our present analysis of perceptive processes is dictated by the fact that the access to our own perceptions is much more direct than to those in other animals. Whereas in the latter the existence of a given type of perception can be verified only indirectly, on the basis of their responses observed in special tests, our knowledge of human perceptions is based on our own introspection and detailed verbal reports presented by other subjects. Therefore, the considerations of this chapter, as well as of the three following ones, will be based mainly on human experience; the experimental material and observations on animals will be presented in a latter part of this book.

At the beginning of our analysis it should be emphasized that we shall be concerned here with only one form of perceptions—those occurring by paying attention to a definite, *already known* stimulus-object* and recognizing it *at once* without any special examination. The typical examples of such phenomena are: recognizing a familiar face immediately on looking at it, an object of everyday use, a familiar voice after hearing only one word, a familiar odor of something after one breath, the position of a limb, when one pays attention to it, and the like. We shall call such perceptions *unitary perceptions*, in contradistinction to complex perceptions which occur when we scrutinize a given object by shifting our attention from one of its elements to another.

It is clear that unitary perception, according to the above definition, can be experienced when, and only when, the appropriate gnostic unit

* By the term "stimulus-object" (S-O) we denote any event of the external world which acts on the receptors and gives rise to the unitary perception. The word "stimulus" reflects its action on the afferent part of the nervous system; the word "object" indicates that the stimulus is not elementary or partial but involves a pattern corresponding to the definite thing or event perceived. To give some examples, by stimulus-objects we shall denote: visual presentation of a pencil, an apple, a face, a word; somesthetic presentation of a rough material, or a pencil; gustatory presentation of a piece of apple; auditory presentation of a whir of a motor, or a human voice, or a spoken word, etc.

(or rather a number of equivalent units, see Section 7, below) is already formed in a gnostic area of a given afferent system. Thus gnostic areas may be considered as *files* of gnostic units representing all unitary perceptions established in a given subject.

Furthermore, it should be explained at once that we shall be dealing now with "pure" unitary perceptions—that is, we shall "strip" them in our analysis of all associations. Although in many instances we cannot avoid these associations—for example when seeing an object we immediately realize its use or name, this realization is *not indispensable* for the occurrence of the unitary perception. This thesis may be proved by observations from everyday life, by special experiments, using artificial stimulus-patterns, in which new perceptions devoid of any "meaning" are established, and by observations of patients with cortical lesions. To give only a few examples of this kind of loss of associations, we know from our own experience that we can see a face or hear a familiar voice without having at the moment any idea about whom it belongs to. We can see a well-known person and fail to recall his name. Similarly, a subject suffering from amnestic aphasia perceives an object presented to him without being able to recall its name, which in normal persons comes immediately to their minds. A patient suffering from "sensory" aphasia hears a word, recognizes it (that is, discerns it from the nonsense "words"), but fails to tell what it denotes.

Let us turn now to the analysis of unitary perceptions in order to see how their properties fit our hypothesis concerning their anatomical and physiological basis.

(1) The first property of unitary perceptions is that they are immediately preceded by, and closely related to, corresponding targeting reflexes. The first act which occurs when a stimulus-object impinges upon a given receptive surface is to focus our attention upon it and to adjust our receptive apparatus for its best reception. Only after this process is accomplished, does the recognition of the stimulus-object follow. This shows that not all stimuli falling upon our receptive surface are perceived, but only those which for some reason have elicited the targeting reflexes.

As discussed in Chapter I, the targeting reflexes are preceded by the exploratory drive or other drives producing the unspecific facilitation (arousal) of the given afferent system. We have good reasons to believe that this facilitatory influence is necessary for the activation of appropriate gnostic units—that is, for the act of recognition of a given stimulus-object.

(2) The next property, already mentioned, is the *integrity* of unitary perceptions—that is, their occurrence as single events. There are rather rare instances when we hesitate as to which category a given

stimulus-pattern should be classified in, but even then the alternatives do not mix, but rather follow one another in quick succession (compare the ambiguous figures largely used in psychological testing). In other instances we do not recognize a stimulus-object at first glance because it is entangled in other patterns; this may happen when a visual object is presented against a patchy background, or a familiar sound is heard in a noisy environment. But, again, if after some delay the stimulus is recognized, this occurs as an immediate experience and the pattern is grasped as a whole.

(3) Another important feature of unitary perceptions is the *complementary character* of their elements. According to our concept, the elements of which a given unitary perception is composed mutually complement each other because the units of the lower level representing those elements converge upon the corresponding gnostic unit. This is best shown by the fact that if one element of a given stimulus-pattern is missing, or replaced by a different one, or a new element is added to it, then one of two things may happen. Either the change will not be noticed at all—the presented pattern will be accepted by the corresponding gnostic unit in spite of its small alteration—or the deformation of the pattern will be enough to prevent its recognition. Then the pattern will not be acknowledged as belonging to our perceptive file but be considered a completely new pattern.

There are many examples from our everyday life illustrating this principle. On the one hand, we often fail to recognize a familiar face in a new headgear, when the beard is added or removed, or spectacles are put on, or, on the contrary, taken off. Similarly we fail to recognize a sound of a word if only one phoneme is changed, or subtracted, or added. On the other hand, it often happens that when reading words we do not notice an omission or change of a letter, an experience familiar to everybody reading proofs.

It may also happen that an object *is* recognized, but that "something" seems to be changed in it. This occurs when owing to a corresponding association we expect that a given stimulus-object and not another should appear in a given situation. A typical example is the sight of a well-known person with some change in his face or dress. The failure of realizing at once *what* has changed in the appearance of the person again clearly shows that the particular elements do not participate as such in our perception.

(4) The *relevance of particular elements* and irrelevance of other ones is another property of unitary perceptions. It is easy to observe that not *all* elements of a stimulus-object projected on the receptive surface are necessary for its recognition. In fact, a sketch of a face of a person made by only a few lines may represent the original so well that

everyone recognizes it without any hesitation—that is, the sketch activates gnostic units representing that face in spite of its sketchiness
(Figure II-11). The same is true when we see a pattern indistinctly
because of bad illumination. These facts remind us of the ethological
evidence that much simplified models of a predator or a subject of the
opposite sex may be substituted for the original[3] (Figure II-12). They
indicate that in our own perceptions, exactly as in those of animals,
there are the *essential* elements whose lack or change totally destroys
the perception and the *irrelevant* ones which play only a minor role, or
no role at all, in establishing a given perceptive unit. Which elements
are essential and which ones irrelevant for the given perception can be
found only by special experimentation similar to that carried out by
ethologists.

FIG. II-11. SKETCHES OF FACES OF KNOWN PERSONS

The principle of selectivity of relevant elements of perceptions can
again be easily deduced from our concept, and moreover it makes this
concept much more acceptable. In fact, we see that it is not true that a
great multitude of elements of the stimulus-pattern and an infinite
number of its details take part in the formation of a given gnostic
unit. This would be inadmissible because it would require an unbelievable number of units and their connections; further, this would be inadmissible from the biological point of view because too great selectivity of gnostic units would be highly maladaptive. As a matter of
fact, the integration of the afferent input consists as much of the convergence of features which are inherent in the given stimulus-object
as of sorting out those features which for some reason seem to be
irrelevant or even misleading.

(5) Another general feature of unitary perceptions is their *dis-
tortive character* in regard to the pattern provided by the appropriate

receptive surface. It is particularly evident in the visual analyzer. As we shall see in the next chapter, gnostic units do not faithfully reproduce the size of the visual stimulus-object, as it is projected on the retina, but correct it according to its standard. The same is true about the depth of a picture, its shades, colors, and many other features. All these distortions of visual patterns projected on the retina, which are

FIG. II-12. BIRD MODELS FOR TESTING REACTIONS OF VARIOUS BIRDS TO BIRDS OF PREY

The movement of the models is upward. Those marked (+) release escape responses.

Note that the chief characteristic of the predator is his short and thick "neck," other properties are irrelevant. (From N. Tinbergen, *The Study of Instincts* [Oxford: Clarendon Press, 1955].)

referred to in psychological textbooks as constancy principle, are explained by the fact that a gnostic unit represents a standard for the given stimulus-object and therefore bends the actual reception to this standard without regard to the photographic accuracy of the picture.

(6) The next important property of unitary perceptions is their *categorization*. This subject will be dealt with in detail in the following chapter, but in the present context we should like to state in general that unitary perceptions within each analyzer are divided into categories, the *principio divisionis* being based chiefly on the differences in *kinds of elements* of which they are composed. For example, we have in the visual analyzer separate categories of perceptions representing human faces, human figures, animals, small palpable objects, letters of the alphabet, and so on. Similarly, in the acoustic analyzer, we have separate categories of perceptions representing known sounds of the environment, words, or melodies. In the somatic analyzer, we can discern the category representing textures of objects touched, their shapes, positions of our limbs, and the like.

The categorization of unitary perceptions concerns not only particular *types* of stimulus-objects but also their particular *aspects*. Take, for example, the categories of perceptions involved in hearing human speech. We can pay attention either to the *words* uttered by other persons, that is to *what* is said, or to their *voices*, that is to *who* is speaking. In the first instance, unitary perceptions represent particular words heard, irrespective of who utters them; in the second instance unitary perceptions represent the voices of particular persons, irrespective of their contents. The same is true of perceptions representing particular *melodies* played on any instrument versus perceptions representing sounds of particular musical instruments irrespective of the melody played. Thus, our perceptions are able to *extract* from a given stimulus-object a particular feature with total neglect of other features.

As will be shown in Section 5 below, and documented in Chapter III, the categorization of perceptions has its physiological and anatomical counterpart in the organization of gnostic areas, in which every category of stimulus-object is represented by a separate field.

(7) The final important property of unitary perceptions is the mutual *antagonism* between some of them.

As mentioned earlier, the elements taking part in a given unitary perception are never antagonistic; on the contrary, they are complementary, resulting in the integrative character of the unitary perception. This is due to the convergence of units of the lower level representing these elements, upon the gnostic units representing the given perception.

Quite different, however, is the situation in respect to the relations *between* particular unitary perceptions. According to our common introspective experience—unfortunately not supported by many relevant experimental data—the antagonism between unitary perceptions seems to be strongest within the same category. If we try to recognize the faces of several persons with whom we are confronted, we have to shift our attention from one face to another and can hardly do so with one glance unless they form a known *group* representing a single unitary perception. Similarly, we can recognize particular words if we hear them in sequence, but not if they are heard simultaneously, even if each is uttered in a quite different pitch (see Chapter III).

Whereas antagonism between unitary perceptions of the same category is obvious, it is less pronounced in respect to unitary perceptions belonging to different categories within the same analyzer, and even less so in respect to perceptions from different afferent systems. For example, we can easily listen at the same time to the melody of a song and its words because the respective perceptions belong to different categories. Similarly, we can listen to music or conversation and at the same time eat, because of the lack of antagonism between gustatory and acoustic perceptions. Even more convincing evidence of the lack of antagonism between perceptions of different modalities is provided by the general practice of driving an automobile. Although the visual attention of a driver is concentrated on the road ahead, he can at the same time listen to the radio, converse with a companion, smoke a cigarette, in other words experience perceptions from other analyzers without any effect on driving.

It is true that sometimes the antagonism between two heterogenic sets of perceptions does arise. A driver in a difficult situation may stop listening to a conversation; a hungry person may become totally absorbed in eating; or he may become so absorbed in music that he will stop eating. In these examples, however, the antagonism between the two activities does not directly concern perceptions but *emotions* produced by these perceptions. In fact, if the perception of one modality evokes a strong emotion (for example, fear of an accident), then the emotion evoked by other perceptions (enjoying music or conversation) is completely inhibited and the subject stops paying attention to the irrelevant stimulus-objects.

The antagonism between perceptions belonging to the same category accounts for another important fact—that of retroactive or proactive inhibition. In fact, if we perceive in close succession a series of stimulus-objects of the same category, these objects manifest a strong tendency to compete in producing recent memory traces: the trace left by the first unitary perception tends to be obliterated by the following perception, or on the contrary to prevent the latter perception from occurring. Again, we have good evidence to show that perceptions within the same category have the strongest tendency to produce retroactive inhibition. For example, our immediate memory span is known to be increased when the items concerned belong to various categories.

The mechanism of antagonistic relations between gnostic units of the same category seems to be due to the existence, within the gnostic fields, of powerful lateral inhibition owing to which the activation of a unit representing one stimulus-object tends to suppress other units representing different stimulus-objects.

5. Neurological evidence of the existence of gnostic units

Looking at the general anatomical organization of the cerebral cortex, we may observe that the "projective" areas and "associative" areas have quite different intercortical connections. Whereas the former areas (being mainly the transit areas, according to our terminology) send their axons only to the adjacent areas still belonging to the given analyzer, the latter, called exit areas, send their axons to various parts of the cortex through the long associative pathways.[4] It is reasonable to assume that in these areas, which constitute the highest levels of the particular analyzers, the gnostic units are situated which represent those stimulus-patterns which are utilized by the nervous system for its integrative activity.

Even more informative are the data obtained from clinical observations of patients with lesions in particular parts of the cerebral cortex. Leaving the detailed description of these observations for the next chapter we shall present here their general characteristics.

There is a large body of evidence to show that lesions in the projective transit areas of the cortex produce quite different deficits in the higher nervous activity of the patients from those sustained in the gnostic areas.

Lesions in the projective cortical areas give rise to pronounced deficits in the *sensations* of stimuli of the given modality. These deficits usually have a clearly topical character if the lesion is not too extensive. This is most clearly manifested in the effects of lesions sustained in the somatic and visual projective areas. After lesions in the somatic area, the tactile and joint sensitivity of a given part of the body contralateral to the lesion is impaired—the feeling of touch is obscured, and the patient does not know the position of the affected limb. After lesions in the visual area, the chief symptom is hemianopia, the localization of which depends again on the site of the injury. We can assume that in both instances a part of the cortical transit units of the given analyzer is destroyed, and that therefore the messages from the corresponding receptive surface cannot reach the gnostic area.

On the other hand, lesions sustained in the gnostic fields have a quite different character. The sensation as such is preserved, and the patient correctly apprehends the site of the stimulus. Careful examination reveals, however, that certain categories of perceptions are lost: for instance the subject fails to recognize faces of well-known persons (prosopagnosia), although he is able easily to recognize other objects; or he fails to recognize letters of the alphabet (alexic agnosia); or he fails to recognize by touch the objects held in hand (astereognosia), and so on. It should be emphasized that the high selectivity of agnostic symptoms produced by limited lesions of the cortex seemed so bizarre and puzzling to many students who knew them only from reports that even now some of these students are skeptical about the very existence of the symptoms. From our point of view, however, this selectivity is entirely understandable, since it substantiates the thesis that particular gnostic fields represent particular categories of perceptions.

No less interesting and important are the data obtained by Penfield and his co-workers[5] by electrical stimulation of the cortex during neurosurgical operations in unanesthetized patients. These data seem to be in full harmony with those obtained after cortical lesions.

When electrical stimulation is administered to the projective areas of the cortex, the patient experiences crude and primitive sensations localized on a definite site of the receptive surface. Thus, stimulation of the somatic area provokes sensations described by the patient as "numbness" or "tingling" of the strictly localized places on the surface of the body. Stimulation of the visual area gives rise to seeing spots, lights of various colors, stars, diamonds, disks, sometimes long marks which have no resemblance whatever to objects perceived in normal life and which are considered by patients as "unreal."

Entirely different, however, are the experiences of patients in whom the areas which we call gnostic areas are stimulated. As will be explained in the following chapters, when the stimulated area is not affected by the disease, it is considered "silent"—that is, the subject feels nothing during its stimulation. If, however, stimulation is applied to those subjects in whom the epileptogenic focus is in this area, some patients experience most vivid perceptions (hallucinations) of episodes of their life which are deeply rooted in their memory. The most reasonable explanation of these phenomena lies in the assumption that stimulation affects particular gnostic units which for some reasons became hyperexcitable.

Analogous phenomena are observed in .epileptic patients in the periods just preceding seizures—during the so-called epileptic aura. Again depending on localization of the irritating focus, the subject experiences either some simple and crude sensations analogous to those described above, when the focus lies in a projective area, or stereotyped complex hallucinations which represent the recollections of some previous happenings, when the focus lies in a gnostic area.

6. The problem of the formation of gnostic units

As we have seen in our previous discussion, the very existence of gnostic units seems to be well documented, although its direct evidence is still lacking. Quite different however, is the situation concerning the problem of how the gnostic units and the gnostic fields are formed. In this area our knowledge is nearly nil, and therefore we propose only tentative hypotheses which can be inferred from our previous considerations and which seem to be in agreement with psychological and neurophysiological facts.

As has been shown in experiments by Hubel and Wiesel,[6] the functional organization of the projective visual area is innate. Newborn kittens without any visual experience possess ready-made units identical with those of the adult cats. The situation must, however, be quite different in respect to the *gnostic* units, since they are formed by experience and thus constitute a product of a particular type of *learning processes.*

In an earlier monograph,[7] we put forward a hypothesis that learning consists in transformation of *potential* connections established in ontogeny between two groups of neurons into *actual* connections. The neurons of the group transmitting impulses to the other group have been called *transmittent* neurons; those receiving the impulses from the first group, *recipient* neurons. We assumed that this transformation occurs by an increase of the transmissibility of synaptic contacts linking the axon terminals of the first group with the perikaryons of the second group of neurons. We disregard here the problem of the intimate nature of this increase of transmissibility, assuming that it may have either micro-morphological character (identical with growth) or biochemical character, or both.

Accepting the existence of potential connections between particular groups of neurons, we do not mean that these connections are completely impassable for impulses delivered by the transmittent group. As will be seen in our further discussion, we have good reasons to believe that if the excitability of the recipient neurons is increased, the potential connections may become temporarily actual. A large body of facts, denoted by Ukhtomski as "dominance"[8] and by other authors as pseudo-conditioning, can be explained by this very mechanism.

Whatever the intimate mechanism of the learning process, it seems that the formation of actual connections is not a momentary process occurring during, or immediately after, the excitation of neurons concerned. There is some evidence that the process usually called "consolidation" of memory traces occurs gradually and that it may be disrupted by unfavorable conditions occurring some time after the learning session.[9] We merely mention this fact without intending to enter into a more detailed discussion, in view of extremely contradictory and debatable experimental evidence concerning it (see Chapter XII).

We further assume that the learning processes occur when, and only when, the recipient neurons are under the joint operation of "specific" impulses delivered by the transmittent neurons and "unspecific" impulses delivered by the emotive system. In other words, we believe that the transformation of potential connections into actual connections takes place only if the recipient neurons are in a state of arousal produced by axodendritic synapses activated by the drive centers.

Although this assumption is so far not documented by direct electrophysiological evidence, it is supported by a great body of behavioral facts which will be discussed in later chapters. Recent experimental findings, showing that the anodal polarization of the recipient neurons facilitates the learning processes, may have a direct bearing upon this problem.[10]

Let us proceed now to the elucidation of the problem of how the above principles operate in the establishment of new gnostic units when a new stimulus-pattern impinges upon the corresponding receptive surface. It should be said in advance that our discussion of this subject will be greatly simplified and schematic. In fact, our only purpose is to give a general outline of a possible solution of this problem. The more detailed theory of the formation of gnostic units in particular analyzers requires a much more thorough analysis and it will be undertaken elsewhere.[11]

A diagram representing our model of the formation of new gnostic units is represented in Figure II-13. As seen in this figure, the transit field T, just preceding the given gnostic field G, is composed of n units $t_1, t_2, t_3, t_4, \ldots t_n$. The gnostic field G is composed of m units $g_1, g_2, g_3, \ldots g_m$, m being much larger than n because the divergence is assumed to be stronger than convergence. On each gnostic unit g_k of the G level there converge, in average, p units of the T level, p being smaller than n.

Thus we have the following sets of T level units subordinated to the particular G level units:

$$t_{g11}, \; t_{g12}, \; t_{g13}, \; \ldots \; t_{g1p} \; (=) g_1$$

$$t_{g21}, \; t_{g22}, \; t_{g23}, \; \ldots \; t_{g2p} \; (=) g_2$$

$$t_{g31}, \; t_{g32}, \; t_{g33}, \; \ldots \; t_{g3p} \; (=) g_3$$

$$\cdots\cdots\cdots\cdots\cdots\cdots\cdots\cdots$$

$$t_{gm1}, \; t_{gm2}, \; t_{gm3}, \; \ldots \; t_{gmp} (=) g_m.$$

Each particular unit t is obviously represented in many rows, since the product mp is much larger than the total number of these units n.

Let us assume now that each stimulus-pattern to be represented by a corresponding unit of field G is composed of an equal number of elements q, represented in field T, q being smaller than p.*

Assume that a subject has already some experience with stimulus-patterns which can be represented in the given gnostic field, that is, he has already developed gnostic units representing some of these patterns. These units may be called *actual* gnostic units, in contradistinction to those units which are still unengaged and which will be called *potential* gnostic units.

Now let us assume that the given gnostic field is under the action of the emotive system—that is, the subject, being under the influence of a particular drive (say curiosity drive), pays attention to the given category of stimuli, developing corresponding searching reflexes. If a definite stimulus-pattern is then presented, it momentarily evokes a strong targeting reflex mediated by the lower levels of the system owing to which the subject adjusts his afferent apparatus so as to "grasp" the stimulus in the optimal way. If the stimulus-pattern is already known—that is, it has a representation in the file of the gnostic field—the corresponding unit of the G level will be activated by actual connections established between particular units of the T level and that unit.

If, however, the pattern is new, then something quite different will happen. First, the arousal of the gnostic field as a whole will be still increased, owing to the strong orientation reaction "what is it?" described in the previous chapter. Second, the units of the T level activated by the elements of the new pattern will transmit messages to the G level and will find such unengaged units on which *all* the elements of the pattern converge. Owing to the arousal of these units produced

---

* Unfortunately the author is not able to solve a mathematical problem of what should be the relation between m, n, p, and q which would warrant a high probability of the subordination of each set of q elements of the T level to at least one unit of the G level.

by the emotive system, the potential synaptic connections will be transformed into actual connections, and the new actual gnostic units will be established. In consequence, whenever the same pattern will be presented again, it will activate the same set of units, because they now represent the corresponding unitary perception in the file of that gnostic field.

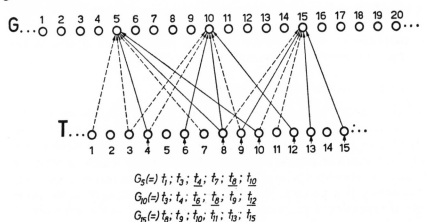

$$G_5(=) t_1; t_3; \underline{t_4}; t_7; \underline{t_8}; t_{10}$$
$$G_{10}(=) t_3; t_4; \underline{t_6}; \underline{t_8}; t_9; \underline{t_{12}}$$
$$G_{15}(=) \underline{t_8}; \underline{t_9}; t_{10}; t_{11}; \underline{t_{13}}; \underline{t_{15}}$$

FIG. II-13. THE ABSTRACT DIAGRAM OF THE FORMATION OF NEW GNOSTIC UNIT

T, last transit field; G, gnostic field. Units in each field are denoted by numbers. It is assumed that each gnostic unit accepts axons from 6 transit units ($p = 6$). For the sake of example three such gnostic units (g_5, g_{10}, and g_{15}) are shown. It is further assumed that each stimulus-object is composed of three and only three elements, represented in the transit field ($q = 3$). Thus the object composed of elements t_4, t_8, t_{10} can engage the gnostic unit G_5, the object composed of elements t_6, t_8, t_{12} can engage the gnostic unit G_{10}, and the object composed of elements t_9, t_{13}, t_{15} can engage the gnostic unit G_{15}. Connections actually operating in perception of a given object are denoted by continuous lines; those which are not in operation, by interrupted lines. The formula of composition of each of the three gnostic units selected is presented below, the actual transit units participating in perception of the given object are underlined.

Note that the same transit units may send axons to different gnostic units (divergence), and participate in different perceptions.

Since according to our assumption the number of elements q composing a given stimulus-pattern is smaller than the number of T level units p converging upon the given gnostic unit, this unit may be attacked by the messages originating from stimulus-patterns other than that which has already occupied this unit. Thus the problem arises as to how the gnostic unit behaves in respect to these new intruders trying to take it into their possession.

In accordance with similar phenomena occurring in the nervous system and even outside it,* we propose the hypothesis that once a potential gnostic unit has been occupied by the particular stimulus-pattern and thus transformed into the actual gnostic unit, it becomes *resistant* to any new stimulus-patterns, even if they potentially fit that unit. In other words we postulate that the new stimulus-patterns can contend only for those units in the gnostic field which are still unengaged, whereas those which have been already transformed into actual gnostic units are inaccessible to them. We shall call this phenomenon the principle of *immunization* of actual gnostic units against being occupied by other stimulus-patterns.

7. The redundancy of units in the gnostic field

As follows from these considerations, each unitary perception may be represented in a given gnostic field not by a single gnostic unit but by a number of them, because, if in a state of arousal of that field a new stimulus-pattern is presented, all unengaged units which potentially include its elements are capable of becoming the actual gnostic units representing that pattern. We shall refer to this property as the principle of *redundancy* of gnostic units; we shall refer to the assembly of units representing the same stimulus-pattern as the *set* of gnostic units (Figure II-14).

The sets of units representing various unitary perceptions are by no means equally large. Here we shall discuss the chief factors which determine the size of particular sets.

First, it may be assumed that in a young organism each presentation of a new stimulus-pattern should lead to the formation of a larger set of gnostic units than in the older. This is because, quite apart from the possible decrease of the plasticity of the nervous system with age, in young subjects the number of potential gnostic units largely prevails over the number of actual units, whereas when the subject acquires more experience in the given category of stimuli, this relation gradually shifts to the predominance of actual gnostic units. In consequence, when a given stimulus-pattern is presented to a very young subject (in whom the appropriate gnostic field has already developed) all the units which potentially include the whole assortment of its elements are available for being involved and occupied by this pattern. Later, however, some of the units which could be involved in representing a new stimulus-pattern have been already engaged in representing another pattern, and, according to the principle of immunization discussed in

---

* We have here in mind the resistance of innervated muscle fibers to accept new nerve fibers, or the resistance of the ovum to accept new spermatozoa after it has been already impregnated.

the previous section, they are not available. Thus, with aging, the gnostic fields have fewer free units to be employed in representing new stimulus-patterns.

Second, the number of gnostic units set up with each presentation of a stimulus-pattern may be thought to depend on the degree of arousal of the gnostic field involved in the respective perception. If the perception took place against the background of strong attention evoked by corresponding emotion, it may be anticipated that it will be represented by a larger set of gnostic units than an analogous perception experienced in a state close to indifference.

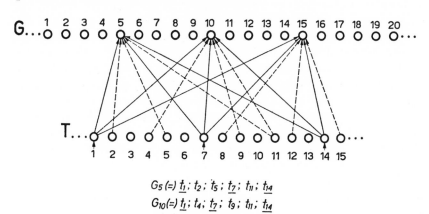

$$G_5 (=) \underline{t_1}; t_2; t_5; \underline{t_7}; t_{11}; t_{14}$$
$$G_{10}(=) \underline{t_1}; t_4; \underline{t_7}; t_9; t_{11}; t_{14}$$
$$G_{15}(=) \underline{t_1}; \underline{t_7}; t_8; t_{12}; t_{14}; t_{15}$$

Fig. II-14. The Diagrammatic Representation of the Redundancy Principle

All denotations as in Figure II-13.

Here all three selected gnostic units represent the perception of the same stimulus-object composed of elements reflected in transit units t_1, t_7, and t_{14}.

Third, it may be assumed that if the presentation of a given stimulus-pattern is repeated, the messages not only reach those gnostic units which have been already occupied by it in its first presentation, but in addition new identical gnostic units may be formed from those free units which potentially represented that pattern but have for some reason not yet been engaged. Thus, repeated presentation of a stimulus-pattern may lead to a further increase of the number of gnostic units representing it, although this increase is slowed down at least for two reasons: first, the frequent presentation of the same stimulus arouses less and less "interest" in it; and, second, free units which potentially represent that pattern become less and less numerous.

By means of these considerations we come to the important conclusion that although the repetition of a given stimulus-pattern may increase the set of gnostic units by which it is represented, this process is insignificant and clearly has an asymptotic character.

Finally, the formation of gnostic units depends largely on what happens *after* the presentation of the given stimulus-object. If during some period after its termination different stimulus-objects of the same category are presented, they may easily suppress the process of consolidating a given perception. This phenomenon, well known under the name of retroactive inhibition, has a strong deteriorating effect upon the formation of new gnostic units.

After a stimulus-pattern has been presented and its perception undergone consolidation, its recognition does not seem to depend very much on the number of gnostic units by which it is represented. A strong representation of the stimulus-pattern may at the most somewhat influence the latency of its recognition and how easily it is recognizable in unfavorable conditions (for example, when attention is poor or the background is noisy). It may, however, be foreseen that the number of gnostic units plays an essential role in the preservation of unitary perceptions after damage to the cerebral tissue. In fact, if, owing to old age or some pathological process, the cortical cells of a given field degenerate or are destroyed, it is obvious that those memories which are poorly represented within this field should be much more prone to obliteration than those which are copiously represented.

Many clinical observations strikingly confirm this conclusion. Typical mental changes which occur in senility or in general encephalopathies (for example, in Pick's disease) consist in the preservation of early memories and obliteration of those which have been acquired later. Moreover, as was often reported by old persons, memories of childhood become even more vivid than they were before, owing undoubtedly to the absence of competitive influence of more recent and currently utilized memories.

A similar selectivity in preservation of memorized material is also observed after focal lesions affecting particular gnostic fields. As will be shown in the following chapters, in particular forms of agnosias (when the given gnostic function is reduced but not abolished) those memories which were acquired early, or are in common usage, or have strong emotional overtones are better preserved than those which were not strongly consolidated. The scantiness of gnostic units representing the category of perceptions affected by a given type of agnosia explains also why the responses of patients to the corresponding tests are extremely unstable and unpredictable. In fact these responses change, not only from one test session to another, but also within the same session, largely depending on the emotional state of a patient. When he is in a favorable mood and encouraged by the examiner, his responses may be remarkably good, whereas in a state of fatigue or stress he may fail completely. We shall discuss this problem in more detail in Chapter IV, Section 10.

8. Perception of similar patterns and the problem of discrimination

In the two preceding sections we were concerned with the problem of the formation of new gnostic units if an entirely new stimulus-object is perceived which does not resemble any of the already known objects. Hence the impression of the novelty experienced by the presentation of this object, the physiological counterpart of which is assumed to be that it does not fit any existing gnostic unit; in consequence, it gives rise to the orientation reaction and to the increase of arousal in the given analyzer.

Now we shall discuss another, more complex process of the formation of gnostic units which comes into operation when a stimulus-pattern similar to that already known, and originally indistinguishable from it, is presented and life conditions require its discrimination.

At the beginning of these considerations we should emphasize that a sharp boundary must be drawn between two quite different, although often confused phenomena which we shall refer to respectively as *discrimination* of stimulus-objects, and their *differentiation*. We shall call discrimination a purely *perceptive process*, even not necessarily involving different associations or different responses established to each discriminated stimulus-object. On the other hand, by differentiation we shall denote, in agreement with the Pavlovian usage of the word, the *utilization* of discriminated stimuli for different responses of the organism. Whereas differentiation obviously presumes the discriminability of the two stimuli used, the converse is not necessarily true. In fact, as we shall see in Chapter X, the animal may excellently discriminate two stimulus-objects but not be able to utilize this knowledge for the given differentiation task.[12]

Whereas emphasizing the basic distinction between discrimination and differentiation, we do not in the least deny the close interrelations between the two phenomena, as will be clearly seen throughout our further discussion. The point is that since perceptions are in the service of associations and behavioral acts, appropriate gnostic units are to a large extent developed and shaped according to their requirement. Accordingly, as we shall soon see, if discrimination between two similar stimulus-objects occurs, this usually happens because it is *needed* —that is, the differences between these objects are utilized in the subject's behavior.

In the present section we shall deal with the analysis of discrimination—the phenomenon occurring on the perceptive level; the problem of differentiation involving the utilization of the discriminated stimulus-object will be discussed in later chapters (VII, X).

Let us assume that after a set of gnostic units representing a given stimulus-pattern has been established, another pattern is presented which differs from the preceding one in a few elements. The following possibilities may be then encountered.

First, the change of only one element may make the pattern unrecognizable because it will no longer fit the corresponding gnostic units. For instance, if we are confronted with a given letter of the alphabet, we can easily see that either the change of an essential element, or its omission, or the addition of a supernumerary element will totally change the meaning of the symbol (Figure II-15a). The same is true if one phoneme of a spoken word is changed, added, or omitted.

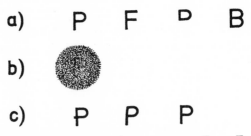

Fig. II-15. Various Consequences of Alterations of Some Elements of a Stimulus-Pattern

a) The pattern P is changed in one of its essential elements; in consequence, a quite new pattern arises.

b) The pattern P is seen in a dim light.

c) The pattern P is changed in some irrelevant elements; in consequence that pattern is preserved, unless a special discrimination training is carried out.

In the light of our preceding discussion, the explanation of this phenomenon is obvious. Omission of a given on-element means its substitution by the reciprocal off-element; on the contrary, addition of an on-element means its substitution for the reciprocal off-element. Thus, each change of the pattern means a replacement of one of its elements by a new element, and in consequence a new pattern does not fit the given gnostic units.

Second, the given pattern may be presented under unfavorable perceptive conditions. This happens, for instance, when a known visual stimulus-object is seen in a dim light or a known sound is subdued or presented in noisy surroundings. Then the corresponding gnostic units will be less strongly excited than in normal conditions, and in consequence the pattern may also be unrecognized if the stimulation is subliminal or recognized after a longer latency (Figure II-15*b*).

Finally, a new stimulus-pattern may be similar to that already known but differ only in those elements which are not taken into account by the appropriate units (Figure II-15*c*). Then the difference between the two patterns will not be perceived, and the new pattern will be immediately accepted by the units representing the old pattern.

Let us consider the further course of events when both these stimuli are repeatedly presented in unpredictable order. If two stimulus-patterns are neutral or have exactly the same consequences (for example, they signal the same US), there is hardly any opportunity for the respective perceptions to undergo any changes. The subject will simply not pay attention to the different properties of each pattern, and in consequence the gnostic units representing them will remain the same.

Assume, however, that each of the patterns *has* different consequences, as for instance, in regular Pavlovian differentiation. Then the double meaning of each perception will produce a conflicting situation, which in turn will increase the general arousal and particularly the arousal in the analyzer involved. In consequence the attention toward both stimuli will be increased, and the entirely *new* sets of perceptive units will be formed, each representing the appropriate pattern and reflecting its specific elements. Since, however, the old set of units representing the cruder properties of both stimuli will remain, it follows that each of these stimuli will be now represented by two sets of units; one reflecting those features which are common to both of them, and the other one reflecting the specific features which distinguish them (Figure II-16).

Thus we come to the important conclusion that discrimination of two stimulus-patterns which originally were perceived as identical *does not occur by transformation of the gnostic units concerned but through developing new units in addition to the old ones.*

The double representation of the discriminated stimuli explains the possibility of their analysis—that is, the perception of both their common character and their specificity—the fact which seemingly contradicts the principle of the integrity of unitary perceptions. For instance, hearing a voice of a known person we can recognize whether it is masculine or feminine and, further, we can recognize its individual character. Each of these two aspects of perception of the voice is a different unitary perception: one formed on the basis of units representing masculine and feminine voices in general, and the other on the basis of units representing voices of particular persons.

In summary, we see that although discrimination and differentiation are separate phenomena, the process of discrimination is guided largely by differentiation; in fact, the necessity to differentiate the two stimulus-patterns by the formation of different associations for each of them forces the subject to develop the discriminatory learning along the lines presented above. It should, however, be noted that once the discrimination is established and new sets of gnostic units are formed, their further fate does not depend on whether they are needed or not or for what purpose they are needed. In fact, our capacity to discriminate the given stimulus-objects, once established under the pressure of a definite demand, remains in spite of the fact that either it is now

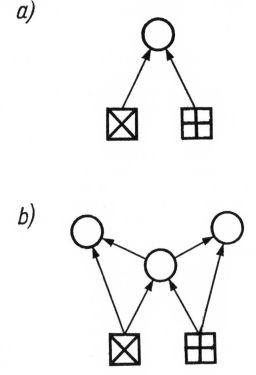

Fig. II-16. A Diagram of the Process of Discrimination of Two Similar Stimulus-Patterns

a, before discrimination; *b*, after discrimination. The common elements of both patterns are denoted by squares; the specific elements, by × and + respectively; gnostic units, by circles.

In *a* gnostic units are formed only to the common elements of two patterns and therefore they are indistinguishable. In *b* new gnostic units are formed representing both the common and the specific elements of the two patterns.

utilized for quite different purposes (cf., for instance, reversal learning) or it does not even play any role in life.

9. The problem of the formation of new gnostic fields

As seen from our preceding considerations, most stimulus-objects we deal with in life are represented not by one set of gnostic units but by two or more different sets; the set of more crude units representing the *general* properties of the given type of objects, and the set of units representing more *particular* properties characteristic only for some of them or even for one individual. Thus, we have gnostic units representing automobiles in general, those which represent cars of different makes, and those representing our own car; similarly, we have gnostic units representing small birds in general, and those representing each species of birds, particularly if we are ornithologists; we have units representing leaves in general, and those representing particular shapes of leaves, especially if we are interested in botany; and we have units representing human faces in general, faces belonging to particular groups of persons (males or females, children or grown up persons), and faces of our acquaintances.

The above conclusion seems to throw some light on the problem of the formation and organization of gnostic fields in general. We are very reluctant to discuss in detail this problem because of a complete lack at the present moment of any conclusive information about it. We can say that gnostic fields have potential connections with the corresponding fields of the lower order, and that some of these connections become actual according to the individual experiences of the organism. We do not, however, know whether these potential connections are prearranged in a particular manner according to the phylogenetic experience of a given species or whether they leave complete freedom as to the further development of gnostic fields, even under the influence of most improbable stimulus-patterns.

On the basis of the preceding considerations it seems safe to assume that gnostic fields have a *hierarchical structure*—that, similarly to the structure of afferent systems, as a whole, they are composed of superimposed levels. The details of this hierarchical structure depend fully on the individual experiences of a given subject or the collective experiences of subjects belonging to a definite social group. We must leave open the question of whether such a higher level of gnosis becomes represented in a separate anatomical field, or whether it is inserted into the corresponding lower level.

Let us assume now that a subject has a *crude* gnosis of a certain category of stimulus-objects—such as faces of another race, sounds of

a foreign language, or tastes of various kinds of wine—and he is not
interested in their individual details because they do not play any role
in his life. Assume, further, that his life conditions have changed in
such a way that the individual differences of these stimulus-objects
do become very important to him—for example, he moves to a country
in which most persons belong to another race, speak another language,
or drink much wine. At first the subject has a difficult time, because
he can no longer rely on his earlier crude gnostic units but must develop new, much more specific ones. If he is confronted at once with
many new stimulus-objects of a given category, he is of course completely lost because he cannot distinguish any of them. Gradually,
however, he begins to perceive differences between the particular
stimulus-objects of the new category and to identify more and more
of them. This occurs by learning to pay attention to those elements of
the stimulus-objects which he did not notice before; these elements
now play a substantial role in those gnostic units which he has developed. After much practice our subject becomes so familiar with the
given category of stimulus-objects that when confronted with an
entirely new specimen he is *at once* able to ascertain that it is not
included in his file; he develops a pertinent orientation reaction, grasps
a new object as a whole, and soon forms appropriate gnostic units
without any special process of discrimination. This phenomenon is
usually called "learning sets" and is often observed in both humans
and animals.[13]

The double (or multiple) representation of the stimulus-objects
of the given category also has its interesting neuropathological aspect;
if owing to a particular lesion in a given gnostic area the ability to
perceive particular stimulus-objects is abolished, the ability to perceive the category to which they belong may be preserved. Thus, a
prosopagnosic patient who fails to recognize particular faces knows
that they are faces; a patient who suffers from audioverbal agnosia
does not recognize particular words but does discriminate them from
other sounds. This shows that crude units representing the whole category of given stimulus-patterns without going into their details may
be preserved although units representing particular patterns of that
category are abolished. This fact would suggest that the former units
may be localized in a different cortical field than the latter ones.

Another, probably different, way of forming new gnostic fields (in
the anatomical, or at least in the functional, sense) occurs when the
gnostic units already formed constitute elements of more complex
stimulus-patterns which play a substantial role in the individual life.
Then it may be assumed that new "complex" units are formed according to the same principles as those found by Hubel and Wiesel. A

good example of such development is provided by learning to read and write in those languages in which pronunciation of words is closely related to spelling. At first, each letter constitutes a separate stimulus-pattern represented in the corresponding gnostic field of either the visual or the kinesthetic analyzer. Eventually, particular letters are integrated into words (seen or written), and it can be reasonably assumed that the most frequently employed words are represented in particular "complex" gnostic units separate from those representing particular letters. The relevant evidence will be presented in the next chapter.

In summary, gnostic areas of the cortex are in a state of continuous development, both in respect to the formation of new gnostic units in the already established gnostic fields and in respect to the setting up of new fields, representing new categories of stimulus-patterns. This development is most pronounced in the early period of life and then gradually decreases, to become nearly abolished in late senility.

10. The problem of habituation

As has been pointed out in the preceding chapter, the so-called neutral stimuli elicit at their first presentations a complex type of reflex denoted as orientation reflex. It is composed of the following elements: (1) targeting reflex, consisting in adjusting the afferent system to the reception of the stimulus; (2) autonomic responses, mostly of the sympaticomimetic nature; (3) desynchronization of the EEG, either general or limited to the given analyzer.

When a stimulus is repeatedly presented without being followed by any arousal-producing consequences, these effects are gradually attenuated and some of them may be eventually totally abolished. This phenomenon, originally denoted by Pavlov as "extinction of orientation reaction," is now usually called "habituation."

In spite of numerous experimental studies devoted to the phenomenon of habituation, its physiological mechanism remains obscure. It is generally accepted that this phenomenon represents some rather primitive form of plastic change and that it is due to an inhibitory process; there is, however, no agreement as to which part of the orientation reflex is influenced by inhibition and why this process comes into being.

We have good evidence that in the phenomenon of habituation the perceptive functions of the organism are directly involved. In fact, according to our own introspective experience, habituation means that we "lose interest" in the repeatedly presented stimulus-object and stop paying attention to it. This observation is in agreement with the fact that the amplitude of cortical potentials evoked by a stimulus tends to decrease with its frequent repetition. Yet this decrease does not occur when a subject is *urged* to pay attention to the stimulus—for instance, by the procedure of conditioning (Figure II-17).

Thus, we see that the problem of habituation is intimately connected with the topic of the present chapter, and we should try to explain it on the basis of our concept on the mechanism of perceptual processes.

A new stimulus-object eliciting an orientation reaction is *ipso facto* not yet represented in the gnostic files of the corresponding analyzer; the joint operation of the targeting reflex and of the part of the unspecific system particularly concerned with the given analyzer serve

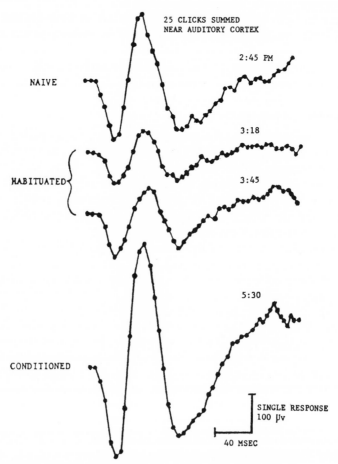

Fig. II-17. Average Evoked Response to a Click Recorded from the Temporal Lobe of the Monkey

(R. Galambos and G. C. Sheatz, in *Amer. J. Physiol.*, 203 [1962]: 174.)

to introduce that stimulus-object into the files of the appropriate gnostic field by establishing a new set of gnostic units.

On the other hand, if a stimulus-object is no longer novel—that is, if it is already represented in the appropriate gnostic field—its fate may be twofold.

For one thing, the stimulus-object may from the very beginning be accompanied by a drive-producing agent eliciting activation of the arousal system. Then, by way of classical conditioning (cf. Chapter VI), this stimulus will also produce the same arousal, and in consequence the targeting reflex elicited by it, accompanied by other signs of the orientation reaction, will be preserved.

For another thing it may happen that a stimulus-object registered in the files of the gnostic system does not coincide with any emotogenic factor—that is, it is of no importance to the well-being of the subject. Then, from the biological point of view, some mechanism should be developed which is directed to the suppression of the orientation reaction elicited by this stimulus; otherwise a subject would be doomed to permanently paying attention to innumerable phenomena occurring in his surroundings and inside his body which have no significance whatsoever in his life. This suppressing mechanism does in fact exist, and its action is manifested by habituation.

We propose a hypothesis that the *suppressing mechanism leading to habituation is intrinsic to the gnostic units themselves.* In other words, we assume that there exists a type of reflex which is elicited by already known stimulus-objects, mediated by the corresponding gnostic units, and producing the inhibitory effect upon the afferent messages directed to those units. We shall call this type of reflex the *inhibitory perceptive recurrent reflex.*

This reflex is in operation whenever it is not overcome and suppressed by the opposite mechanism generated by the arousal system. In all probability its effector is the inhibitory part of the unspecific system which suppresses the facilitatory part of that system and thus prevents the development of the orientation reflex, canceling it at its very outset (Figure II-18). This suppressing influence may be exerted upon that part of the unspecific inhibitory system which deals exclusively with the given analyzer—then habituation will have a strictly selective character leaving the subject alert in all other respects; or it may be exerted upon the whole system—then the subject will experience boredom and somnolence.[14]

This concept of the mechanism of habituation, however paradoxical it may seem at first glance, is in full conformity with the existing facts. Since the same stimulus-object is the source of either a positive unspecific effect facilitating the targeting reflex and giving rise to perception, or an inhibitory effect suppressing both these processes, it is clear that an unstable balance exists between these two effects. If for some reason the arousal of a given afferent system is increased, as happens under the influence of stimulant drugs or any emotogenic factor, then a subject well-habituated to a given stimulus will manifest a full orientation reaction. Conversely, tranquilizing drugs make the subject apathetic and decrease his orientation reactions.*

Another fact fully explained by our concept is that habituation has a highly selective character;[15] in fact, if a stimulus somewhat different from that which has been subjected to habituation is presented, it immediately evokes a full-size orientation response. This is because this stimulus does not fit the gnostic units established by the preceding stimulus; hence the inhibitory perceptive reentering reflex cannot be elicited. Moreover, if immediately after the operation of the latter stimulus; hence the inhibitory perceptive recurrent reflex cannot be elicited. Moreover, if immediately after the operation of the latter by the new stimulus.

Still another fact which can be interpreted by our concept is that after the orientation reflex to a given stimulus became extinguished, it may reappear when the subject is drowsy.[16] In fact, according to our own subjective experience, drowsiness produces a decrease of our perceptual capacity; hence a previously presented stimulus may be not immediately recognized as familiar, and in consequence it will give rise to the orientation reaction accompanied by arousal.

Finally, our concept explains the ubiquitous character of the phenomenon of habituation. In contrast to some early views that habituation does not occur in decorticated animals, we know now that it may take place on any level of the nervous system.[17] Whenever we deal with perceptions in the broader sense of the word (as functions of

---

* Here is a striking example of dishabituation due to emotion taken from experiments on humans (E. M. Glaser, *The Physiological Basis of Habituation* [London: Oxford University Press, 1966], p. 40): "It was intended to demonstrate habituation at a meeting of the Physiological Society, and a student doing an advanced course in physiology had agreed to be the subject for this demonstration. One of his hands had been habituated to immersions at 4° C. and 47° C., and 24 hours before the demonstration he showed an almost complete absence of responses of the blood pressure and heart rate to immersing his hand at either of those temperatures. The demonstration was held in a lecture room and the volunteer was inevitably aware of the people there, although he sat with his back to them and was unaware of the readings. He was a little nervous and he was interested in those present. When he immersed his hand in hot and cold water he produced responses which were indistinguishable from those at the beginning of the experiment before habituation had taken place. Forty-eight hours after the demonstration he was again tested in the usual laboratory and with only the experimenters present. The responses from the hand that had been repeatedly cooled and warmed were almost absent and indistinguishable from those observed 24 hours before the demonstration."

exit units giving rise to definite behavioral acts), even in their crudest and most primitive forms, we encounter the mechanism of habituation, which is not superimposed on the structures responsible for the orientation reflex but depends on these very structures. This seems a likely explanation of the fact that even after extensive removal of the auditory cortical area, habituation to auditory stimuli (tones) is not only preserved but retains to some degree its selective character.[18] It may be assumed that in this instance the perception of auditory stimuli occurs on the level of inferior colliculi which have a powerful exit mechanism providing targeting responses to these stimuli. Since this

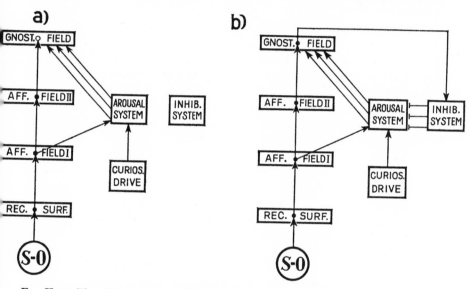

Fig. II-18. The Hypothetical Mechanism of Habituation

a) The operation of a *new* stimulus-object. The stimulus activates successively: particular elements of the receptive surface, particular units of the first order receptive field, particular units of the second order receptive field and hence the messages converge on some potential gnostic units (small white circle). Units of the first order receptive field (or of another central structure) fire to the unspecific arousal system which increases the excitability of the gnostic field. The joint action of the specific and unspecific impulses upon this field enables the formation of appropriate gnostic units.

b) The operation of the *known* stimulus-object. The original course of events is the same as in (a). The messages from the specific and unspecific systems reach the appropriate gnostic units and produce the perception of the stimulus-object. These gnostic units send impulses to the unspecific inhibitory system (or rather its part), which suppresses the corresponding part of the arousal system, and in this way the perception of the stimulus-object is momentarily stopped. In consequence, the flow of impulses from the gnostic units to the inhibitory system ceases and another perception instigated by the curiosity drive can take place.

structure has a precise tonotopic organization,[19] it is clear that different tones are represented there by different units.

If we take into account the fact that inhibition of the orientation reflex has a highly selective character and does not affect even those stimuli which differ slightly from the habituated one, it must be inferred that the latter stimulus is recognized every time it is presented. In other words, we assume that this stimulus elicits a short targeting reflex which is just sufficient for its recognition and for sending messages to the unspecific inhibitory system. Incidentally, this is another proof of the momentary character of unitary perceptions which may be provoked after a very short act of attention as an all-or-none phenomenon.

Ending our discussion we should notice that a complete and consistent habituation to a given stimulus-pattern should be considered an experimental artifact, rarely encountered in normal life of man and animals. Most stimulus-objects belonging to our surroundings have an ambiguous character—that is, they have sometimes a behavioral significance and sometimes not. In the first case they do attract our attention and do not display any habituation, in the second we neglect them completely, taking almost no notice of them. To show the universality of this dual attitude toward the known stimulus-objects of any modality, here are some examples. We are fully habituated to small objects on our desk, but dishabituation occurs whenever some of them are needed for our work. We are fully habituated to the ticking of a clock in our room, but this habituation is abolished whenever we check whether the clock did not stop. Finally, we are fully habituated to various postures of our body and limbs, since they have been experienced by us thousands of times; nevertheless we pay attention to each of these postures whenever it is utilized as a point of departure for some voluntary movement or the end-product of a movement relevant in a given situation.

11. Summary and conclusions

Each afferent system (analyzer) is built in a hierarchical manner, its higher levels being functionally superimposed on the lower levels and receiving from them messages ultimately originating on the receptive surfaces. Each level of afferent systems is composed of *units*—that is, neurons receiving particular messages from lower levels or from a given receptive surface. In some (or all) afferent systems this hierarchy may ramify, giving rise to more than one higher order afferent field.

The relations between consecutive levels are based on the convergence-divergence principle. Since each level possesses more units than the preceding one, divergent connections outnumber convergent connections. Owing to the convergence principle, the units of higher levels represent more complex sensory patterns than those of lower levels.

The afferent units may be divided into: *transit units*, which carry the messages received from units of the lower level to units of the higher level; *exit units*, which send messages outside the given analyzer to other parts of the brain; and probably transit-exit units of a mixed nature. The levels composed of only transit units are called *transit levels*; those composed of only exit units are *exit levels*; and those which have both types of units, *transit-exit levels*. By definition the highest level of a given analyzer is a purely exit level.

The function of transit units is called the *receptive* function; that of the exit units, the *perceptive* function. Accordingly, we denote by perceptions those sensory inputs which are engaged in associative or behavioral activity of the organism. The higher the level of the given exit (or perceptive) unit, the more complex the sensory pattern represented by it and the more complex associative functions this unit possesses.

One of the important types of exit units is that giving rise to the perceptive recurrent reflexes, ensuring the regulation of the sensory input on the lower levels (including receptive surfaces and effectors connected with them) by positive or negative feedback. The positive feedback is secured by facilitation of a perceptive process due to the targeting reflexes (increase of attention); the negative feedback is secured by suppression of a perceptive process due to the perceptive inhibitory reflex (decrease of attention).

We are concerned in this chapter only with the perceptive processes depending on the activity of the highest levels of afferent systems, usually referred to as "associative areas of the cerebral cortex." We call the units in these areas *perceptive*, or *gnostic units*; the areas themselves, *gnostic areas*.

By definition, each unit of a gnostic area represents a complex sensory pattern obtained by convergence of receptive units of lower levels (representing its elements). A perception which gives rise to the activation of a gnostic unit is called a *unitary perception*.

Accordingly we denote by unitary perception an act of recognition of a known stimulus-pattern which occurs instantaneously in a nonanalytical way as a single act of attention. A unitary perception arises when a known stimulus-pattern impinges upon the receptive surface of a given analyzer and elicits the appropriate targeting reflex directing the attention of the subject to that pattern. Perceptions arising as an effect of scrutinizing the stimulus-pattern and resolving it into elements are complex perceptions based on associations.

Unitary perceptions, in contrast to complex perceptions, obey the following principles:

(1) The principle of immediateness—occurrence of the perception as a single act of attention.

(2) The principle of integrity, analogous to the chemical integrity of molecules.

(3) The principle of complementarity of elements taking part in unitary perceptions.

(4) The principle of model perception—the essential character of some of its elements versus the irrelevance of the other ones.

(5) The amendment principle—the deformation of a sensory pattern projected on the receptive surface, approximating it to the standard stimulus-object.

(6) The principle of categorization of unitary perceptions.

(7) The principle of interunitary antagonism, manifest among the perceptions of the same category and depending on lateral inhibition.

All these properties can be easily deduced from our concept that gnostic units are the anatomical and functional substrate of unitary perceptions. It should be particularly emphasized that our concept satisfactorily resolves the annoying antinomy between the associationistic psychology stressing that perceptions are *composed* of elementary sensations, and Gestalt psychology stressing that perceptions should be considered unitary and unresolvable processes. The solution is that although perceptions *are* composed of elementary events called sensations, we do not—and sometimes even cannot—isolate them in our sensory experiences, because they are merged in the perceptive units which alone take part in the integrative processes handling the messages obtained from the periphery. To paraphrase the famous expression of Jackson that the brain "thinks" in movements and not in muscular contractions, we can say that the brain "thinks" in objects perceived and not in their elements. As a matter of fact, both these truths are the expression of the same general principle.

Both the psychological and neuropathological evidence indicate that unitary perceptions within a given analyzer are divided into particular categories, each category being represented by a part of the corresponding gnostic area, called the *gnostic field*. Thus the topography of gnostic areas is organized not according to the topical organization of the receptive surface, as in projective areas, but according to the qualities of unitary perceptions. Injury sustained in a given gnostic field gives rise to the development of a specific form of agnosia, in which perceptions of a given category are selectively impaired whereas perceptions of other categories within the same analyzer are preserved.

The categorization of perceptions of particular analyzers will be the subject of the next chapter.

In contradistinction to the receptive and perceptive units in the lower levels of afferent systems, which are built according to the innate patterns of neural organization, perceptive units in the gnostic areas are developed in the individual life of the subject in accordance with his experiences. The process of the formation of gnostic units to new stimulus-patterns encountered by a subject occurs in the following way.

It is assumed that in each gnostic field there are potential gnostic units—units which are linked with the units of the lower level by potential and not actual connections. If a new stimulus-pattern is presented, the messages from the lower level arrive at those gnostic units on which the axons of the corresponding units of that level converge. Simultaneously, this stimulus-pattern elicits an orientation reflex whose effect is, among other things, to create a state of arousal within the corresponding analyzer. This state of arousal is a necessary prerequisite for the transformation of the potential connections converging upon the given units into actual connections—that is, it makes possible the formation of the actual gnostic unit representing the given pattern.

The inference resulting from this hypothesis is that each stimulus-pattern perceived by a subject is represented not by one gnostic unit only but by a set of equivalent units—those which constitute the points of convergence for the elements of the given pattern (the principle of redundancy). The number of gnostic units in each set depends mainly on the following factors: (1) the period of life in which a given unitary perception was acquired; the earlier the period, the larger the set; (2) the intensity of arousal at the moment of presentation of the stimulus-pattern; (3) to some extent the number of presentations of the stimulus-pattern; (4) the lack of coinciding presentations of stimulus-patterns of the same category. The selectivity in preservation of certain unitary perceptions and abolition of others after partial destructions of a given gnostic field (because of senility, encephalopathies, or focal injuries) is explained by the principle of redundancy.

If a new stimulus-pattern is presented which is similar to that already represented in the given gnostic field, the following possible situations can result.

(1) The new stimulus-pattern differs from the old one in an essential element. Then the pattern is not identified with the old pattern; if it has some meaning for the subject, the new set of gnostic units will be established for it.

(2) The new stimulus-pattern differs from the old one in those elements which have not been included in the perception; consequently,

it seems to be identical with the old pattern. If, however, this new pattern has a different associative significance from the previous one, the process of discrimination takes place. It consists in the formation of separate sets of gnostic units for each pattern, which embody those elements in which they differ, in addition to the old set of units representing only their common properties. Then the subject is able to perceive both the common features of the two objects and the particular features characteristic of each of them.

On the basis of this discrimination process, the new categories of perceptions may be developed in the subject's gnosis represented by new gnostic fields, either in the functional sense or even in the anatomical sense.

When a given stimulus-pattern is repeatedly presented without coinciding with any emotogenic agent, habituation occurs—that is, the orientation reaction elicited by it subsides to a greater or lesser degree. It is suggested that habituation is intrinsically implied in the formation of gnostic units. In other words, the existence of a specific type of reflex—called *inhibitory perceptive recurrent reflex*—is postulated; it is elicited by the known stimulus-patterns, mediated by the gnostic units, and results in excitation of the appropriate part of the inhibitory unspecific system. This, in turn, suppresses the facilitatory effect of the arousal system upon the given perceptive process, canceling its development at the outset.

If a "neutral" stimulus is accompanied by an emotogenic factor, it produces arousal by way of classical conditioning, and in consequence the inhibitory perceptive recurrent reflex is silenced. In this way there occurs a selection between those stimulus-patterns which have acquired a definite significance in life due to associations with emotogenic factors and those which remain "neutral," not being followed by any significant consequences. It should be indicated, however, that whereas in experimental conditions these two groups of stimuli are usually sharply separated from one another, in normal life the same stimuli are completely "neutral" in some instances and most significant in others.

References to Chapter II

1. D. H. Hubel and T. N. Wiesel. 1959. Receptive fields of single neurones in the cat's striate cortex. *J. Physiol.* (London), 148: 574–91.
    ———. 1961. Integrative action in the cat's lateral geniculate body. *Ibid.*, 155: 385–98.
    ———. 1962. Receptive fields, binocular interaction and functional architecture in the cat's visual cortex. *Ibid.*, 160: 106–54.

————. 1965. Receptive fields and functional architecture in two non-striate visual areas (18 and 19) of the cat. *J. Neurophysiol.,* 28: 229–89.

2. D. C. Hebb. 1949. *The Organization of Behavior: A Neuropsychological Theory.* New York: Wiley.

3. N. Tinbergen. 1955. *The Study of Instinct.* Oxford: Clarendon Press.

4. W. S. McCulloch. 1944. The functional organization of the cerebral cortex. *Physiol. Rev.,* 24: 390–407.
   N. Geschwind. 1965. Disconnexion syndromes in animals and man. *Brain,* 88: 237–96.

5. W. Penfield and T. Rasmussen. 1950. *The Cerebral Cortex of Man.* New York: Macmillan.

6. D. H. Hubel and T. N. Wiesel. 1963. Receptive fields of cells in striate cortex of very young, visually inexperienced kittens. *J. Neurophysiol.,* 26: 994–1002.

7. J. Konorski. 1948. *Conditioned Reflexes and Neuron Organization.* Chap. 5. Cambridge: Cambridge University Press.

8. А. А. Ухтомский. 1926. К вопросу условий возбуждения в доминанте. (Concerning the condition of excitation in dominance.) *Nov. Refl. Fiziol. Nerv. Sist.,* 2:3–15.

9. S. E. Glickman. 1961. Perseverative neural processes and consolidation of the memory trace. *Psychol. Bull.,* 58: 218–33.

10. V. S. Rusinov. 1953. An electrophysiological analysis of the connecting function in the cerebral cortex in the presence of a dominant region area. In *19th International Physiological Congress, Montreal, 1953: Abstracts of Communications,* pp. 719–20.
    F. Morrell. 1961. Effect of anodal polarization on the firing pattern of single cortical cells. *Ann. N.Y. Acad. Sci.,* 92: 860–76.
    D. J. Albert. 1966. The effects of polarizing currents on the consolidation of learning. *Neuropsychologia,* 4: 65–77.

11. R. Gawroński and J. Konorski. In preparation.

12. The distinction between the two phenomena has been discussed in detail in the paper:
    J. Konorski. 1962. The role of central factors in differentiation. In 22d International Congress of Physiological Sciences, Leiden, September 10–17, Vol. III, 318–29. Amsterdam: Excerpta Medica Found. Internat. Congr. ser. No. 49.

13. H. F. Harlow. 1949. The formation of learning sets. *Psychol. Rev.,* 56: 51–65.

14. It should be noted that a concept very similar to that proposed here was put forward by E. N. Sokolov (1960, see note 15 below) and documented by a number of his experimental results.

15. S. Sharpless and H. Jasper. 1956. Habituation of the arousal reaction. *Brain,* 79: 655–80.

E. N. Sokolov. 1960. Neuronal models and the orienting reflex. In M. A. B. Brazier, ed., *The Central Nervous System and Behavior: Transactions of the Third Conference, Feb. 21–24, 1960, Princeton*, pp. 187–276. New York: J. Macy, Jr., Found.

16. E. N. Sokolov. 1960 (see note 15 above).

17. R. Hernández-Peón and H. Brust-Carmona. 1961. Functional role of subcortical structures in habituation and conditioning. In *Brain Mechanisms and Learning: A Symposium Organized by the Council for International Organizations of Medical Sciences*, pp. 393–412. Oxford: Blackwell Sci. Publ.

W. Kozak and R. Westerman. 1966. Basic patterns of plastic change in the mammalian nervous system. In *Nervous and Hormonal Mechanisms of Integration: Symposia of the Society for Experimental Biology*, 20: 509–44. Cambridge: University Press.

J. S. Buchwald, E. S. Halas, and S. Schramm. 1965. Progressive changes in efferent unit responses to repeated cutaneous stimulation in spinal cats. *J. Neurophysiol.*, 28: 200–215.

18. S. Sharpless and H. Jasper. 1956. Habituation of the arousal reaction. *Brain*, 79: 655–80.

19. J. E. Rose, D. D. Greenwood, J. M. Goldberg, and J. E. Hind. 1963. Some discharge characteristics of single neurons in the inferior colliculus of the cat. I. Tono-topical organization, relation of spikecounts to tone intensity, and firing patterns of single elements. *J. Neurophysiol.*, 26: 294–341.

CHAPTER III

CATEGORIES OF PERCEPTIONS
IN PARTICULAR ANALYZERS

1. Introductory remarks

In the preceding chapter it was shown that by extrapolation of the Hubel and Wiesel experimental data to still higher levels of afferent systems it is possible to advance a new physiological theory of perceptions which seems to explain satisfactorily a large bulk of the pertinent facts based both on psychological observations in normal subjects and neurological observations in brain-damaged patients. The theory claims that the unitary perceptions—that is, those psychological phenomena in which a subject immediately recognizes a known stimulus-object by a single act of attention—are represented in the gnostic areas of the cerebral cortex in the form of separate units which we have called perceptive or gnostic units. In consequence, the gnostic areas of particular analyzers constitute the *sui generis files* of all perceptions of a given modality representing all the stimulus-objects with which the subject is acquainted. The more developed and sophisticated the given analyzer, the more refined and complex the patterns represented in its gnostic department.

It has been shown that the organization of gnostic areas is based on the principle of categorization—each area being divided into a number of gnostic fields, representing particular categories of stimulus-patterns of the given modality. This categorization principle is supported by the following facts.

(1) The antagonism between unitary perceptions is the strongest in

respect to stimulus-patterns of the same category, which implies that the gnostic units representing these patterns are clustered in one field.

(2) The stimulus-patterns of the same category are composed of definite kinds of elements, different for particular categories; hence their tendency to topical polarization seems probable.

(3) The stimulus-patterns of the same category form associations with definite stimulus-patterns of other modalities; hence again their clustering seems likely.

(4) The neurological evidence clearly shows that limited cortical lesions in the gnostic regions produce the abolition of particular categories of perceptions, leaving other categories of the same afferent system practically unaffected.

On the basis of these criteria, an attempt can be made to categorize the unitary perceptions of each analyzer and to characterize briefly each of these categories. Furthermore, dealing with particular perceptions and their categories within each analyzer, we find it possible to substantiate more strongly than in the preceding chapter all the essential properties of unitary perceptions and to show that the physiological theory we have adopted for their interpretation is indeed based on firm factual evidence.

As stated in the Introduction, we shall not be very much concerned in our present discussion with the problems of topography of particular gnostic fields within the gnostic areas. Neither the precise localization of these areas nor their particular subdivisions are fully understood, and the literature provides us with many contradictory data. With the present methods at our disposal, we are still far from the solution of the topographical problems, the more so that in all probability the topography of gnostic fields is different in different subjects. Furthermore, in the present discussion we shall distinguish certain categories of perceptions on the basis of purely psychological evidence with no relevant data concerning the gnostic fields which form their anatomical representation. In such instances even the very existence of these fields is purely hypothetical, and we cannot be certain whether they occupy separate parts of the gnostic areas or are included within the fields, representing other categories. Therefore, the analysis in this chapter is purely functional, but we hope that it may help promote studies concerning the anatomical organization of the areas involved in gnostic functions.*

* In order to help the reader follow our discussion on the categories of unitary perceptions and their associations, we shall refer to them by definite symbols. Thus the particular modalities will be represented as follows: V, vision; A, audition; S, somesthesis; K, kinesthesis; Ol, olfaction; La, vestibular perceptions; E, emotional perceptions. The categories of perceptions will be represented by the symbol of the analyzer and the symbol of the given category. The same symbols will apply to the corresponding afferent systems and hypothetical gnostic fields.

2. Categories of unitary perceptions in visual analyzer (V)

It is important to realize that the visual system is composed of three subsystems playing quite different roles in the life of the organism and probably possessing quite different functional and anatomical organization. These subsystems are as follows.

(1) The system concerned with general illumination (light versus darkness): V-Il.

(2) The system concerned with the spatial relations between the organism and the environment and between various parts of the environment: V-Sp.

(3) The system concerned with the patterns and colors of the objects of the external world: V-P.

It is clear that although the general illumination of the environment above a certain level is the prerequisite for the proper functioning of two other subsystems, the perception of light and darkness as such and their various gradations is a quite independent function which operates also with eyes closed. It may be assumed that this system is phylogenetically the oldest one and its function is most primitive. This means that the exit units of this system are situated on the relatively low levels of the visual analyzer.

The illumination system plays a significant role in two basic activities of the organism: in sleep-vigilance activity, and in protective activity.

In most organisms sleep-vigilance activity is determined to a large extent by the illumination system: in many diurnal animals darkness is one of the main stimuli producing sleep, whereas in nocturnal animals darkness produces wakefulness and daylight produces sleep.

The second activity controlled by illumination is connected with the security of the organism. In many small animals (for example, frogs) the sudden shadowing of the large part of the visual field, such as occurs with the approach of a large predator, elicits fear and flight.

Unfortunately, we do not know the organization of the illumination system, of how many levels it is composed, and where the corresponding afferent fields are situated.

The second system—the one concerned with spatial relations between the subject and his environment and between various parts of this environment (V-Sp)—is highly elaborated in both man and many animals. As will be shown in a later chapter, this system operates in close correlation with the system of kinesthetic-spatial relations (K-Sp) and with the vestibular system (La), having bidirectional associations with each.

Although precise knowledge concerning the functional properties of gnostic units of this system is lacking, we can assume that they are concerned with the following types of unitary perceptions: (1) the relations between objects and ourselves—for example, the distance of the object and its position in the vertical and horizontal plane; (2) the distances and relations between the objects—for example, the relation of above, below, beside, near, remote, and the like. It is clear that some of these unitary perceptions are reciprocal to each other (for example, left and right), whereas other ones are not (for example, direction and distance). It is also clear that in the gnostic units representing spatial relations the properties of objects involved—their shape, color, and so on—play no role. In fact, we can be completely unfamiliar with the objects we are confronted with and nevertheless precisely determine their spatial relations.

For the sake of clarity we should add that the perceptions of spatial relations we are concerned with here are unitary—that is, the objects observed are situated in our visual field and the evaluation of their spatial relation is momentary. More complex processes occur when the objects are separated by some distance and, in order to appreciate their interrelations, we have to transfer our gaze from one to another, a process involving oculomotor responses and their kinesthesis. Although undoubtedly these complex spatial perceptions are closely related to the former ones and probably require their integrity, they are based on more complex mechanisms involving the interplay between unitary perceptions and oculomotor responses.

We have clear neurological evidence that the gnosis of spatial relations has its separate field in the visual gnostic area. In fact many clinical cases are described in which lesions in the rostral part of the occipital region give rise to the syndrome of visuo-spatial agnosia. The corresponding lesions are usually placed in the right hemisphere, probably because the spatial gnosis is loosely connected with verbal gnosis, which is chiefly represented in the dominant, generally left, hemisphere. In fact, our visual orientation in space can easily function without verbalization, and our visual images of spatial relations are rarely associated with words.

It is also worthwhile mentioning that stimulation of some points in the right occipital region in waking patients leads to bizarre distortions of visual space relations; epileptic seizures localized in this region may give similar symptoms.[1]

Although tests to reveal visuo-spatial agnosia usually do not deal directly with the unitary *perceptions* of spatial relations, they are nevertheless very informative. They tend to show the loss of images (rather than perceptions) of spatial relations with which a patient was well acquainted before the disease. Usually the patient is asked: to indicate on a contour map of his country the location of the largest cities, rivers, mountains; to draw a map of the part of the city in which he lives; to make a sketch of his apartment or the ward in which he lies, and so on. By these tests it is discovered that the patient with visuo-spatial agnosia has no idea of the spatial relations of the items concerned, although the items themselves are well known to him. Thus, a patient, formerly a taxi driver, living permanently in Warsaw was unable to sketch the center of the city, drawing the streets in false directions and not knowing which streets are parallel and which intersect. The fact that he did not recognize his own blunders on the map shows that his deficit was due to visual agnosia of spatial relations and not to a failure to reproduce these relations by hand (which is the effect of a different disorder). He also failed to describe verbally the relations between the streets; he could, however, easily name the particular streets and describe their peculiarities.

Another patient who was formerly a highly educated clerk suffered from no less severe visuo-spatial agnosia, being completely unable to grasp any spatial relations between objects seen. On the contour map of Poland he failed to show the location of any well-known cities or the neighboring countries. Nor could he draw a clock or tell whether a cow's horns are nearer the head or the tail. In spite of these most dramatic disturbances of evaluating spatial relations, he had not the slightest difficulty in recognizing and naming human faces, objects, and letters of the alphabet. His lexis was so good that he could read a printed text aloud. A more detailed examination of lexis revealed, however, some disorders due to visuo-spatial agnosia which will be discussed later.*

The gnosis of spatial relations is highly developed in many species of animals, particularly in those in which the spatial orientation is indispensable for their survival. It is, however, not clear whether the visual orientation in space plays as an important role in animals as it does in humans. The fact that lesions sustained in the parieto-occipital junction strongly affect space orientation in rats and cats,[2] as revealed by the maze performance tests, indicates that the visual afferent system shares considerably in this function.

The most highly developed visual system, at least in primates, is that concerned with pattern vision (V-P). We list here the main categories of perceptions of stimulus-patterns represented in the corresponding gnostic area of the visual cortex, and briefly describe their character-

---

* All cases reported in this book which are based on our own observations were studied in the Department of Neurosurgery of the Polish Academy of Sciences in cooperation with: E. Mempel, Jadwiga Srebrzyńska, L. Stępień and S. Żarski.

istics based on relevant psychological data and neurological observations.

(1) *Small manipulable objects of everyday living* (V-MO, Figure III-1a). The common features of these objects are: (a) they have sharply defined contours consisting of straight or oval edges; (b) they are movable—that is they are not associated with a given background; (c) they are seen not only from varying distances (a feature to be discussed later) but also from different sides, and therefore they are represented not only by equivalent gnostic units but also by units corresponding to different patterns; (d) their units form strong bidirectional connections with the corresponding gnostic units of the somatic analyzer representing the somesthetic unitary perceptions provided by holding the corresponding objects in hand (S-MO).

A separate group of visual stimulus-objects probably belonging to the same category is composed of larger objects which can neither be visually perceived at one glance (unless from a distance), nor handled as a whole (Figure III-1b). It may be assumed that these objects are represented by different units when they are viewed as a whole in a picture or from some distance and when they are viewed by scrutinizing each of their parts separately. Then they give rise to the complex perceptions represented by separate sets of gnostic units closely interconnected in the form of Hebb's "cell assemblies."[3]

We have good neurological evidence that perceptions of manipulable objects are represented in a separate gnostic field. Many clinical cases were reported in which the visual perceptions of inanimate objects were selectively impaired, whereas other visual perceptions remained almost intact. The following example demonstrates such disorder (Hécaen and Ajuriaguerra).[4]

The patient perfectly recognized his visitors before they began to speak. Asked to describe the appearance of various persons of the clinical staff he did so precisely, indicating the particular features of each. He recognized pictures of animals fairly well, correctly naming an elephant and a lion and describing a goat as "ce sont des petit cochons de la race des chats, mais pas des chats." But he failed completely to recognize inanimate objects. Seeing a picture of an airplane, he said: "Ça c'est un dessin, ça ne me revient pas"; about a table: "Ça représente . . . qu'est-ce que ça peut représenter?"; a car: "Je ne me rappelle pas; je ne vois pas ce que ça peut être." Remarkably, however, if the patient took the object in hand, he immediately knew what it was. For example, he was shown an ashtray. "Ça c'est pour voir, ça se met à côté et on regarde au travers"; later: "c'est rond, sur les côtés il y a des formes pour resserrer les objectifs." After he took the object in hand, he said: "Ah, c'est un appareil pour prendre de la cendre."

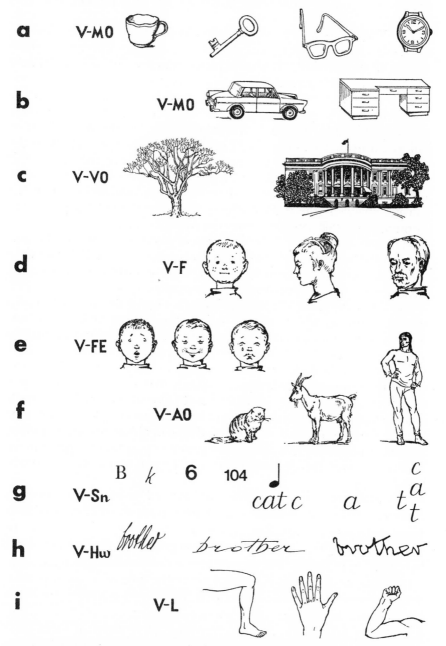

FIG. III-1. PARTICULAR CATEGORIES OF VISUAL STIMULUS-OBJECTS
PROBABLY REPRESENTED IN DIFFERENT GNOSTIC FIELDS

a, small manipulable objects; b, larger partially manipulable objects; c, non-manipulable objects; d, human faces; e, emotional facial expressions; f, animated objects; g, signs; h, handwriting; i, positions of limbs.

(2) *Non-manipulable objects perceived only by vision* (V-VO, Figure III-1c). The objects of this category clearly differ from those discussed above. First, they are usually unmovable and are closely related to the background against which they are seen; in fact the same stimulus-pattern presented against an unusual background may be completely unrecognizable. Another characteristic feature of these stimulus-objects is that they are strongly related to the vertical axis of our visual field: when the object is inverted, it does not represent the same unitary perception, and even if it is eventually recognized this occurs through the mental operation of its inversion. Finally, these objects are usually characterized by having no associations with the somatic analyzer—the feature which is perhaps the most important in distinguishing this category from the previous one.

We have distinguished the category of visual non-manipulable objects on the basis of purely psychological considerations. Whether they are represented in the anatomically separate gnostic field is not clear because of the lack of relevant documentation.

(3) *Human faces* (V-F, Figure III-1d). One of the first meaningful stimulus-patterns which appears before the eyes of an infant is undoubtedly the human face. It reappears again and again and quickly becomes associated with many other perceptions, visual, tactile, olfactory, and emotional. Therefore, according to what we know about the formation of gnostic units, we may assume that a powerful set of units representing human faces in general is developed. Gradually different faces acquire different meaning and become associated with different events: the baby learns to distinguish the faces of his mother, his father, and other persons. Thus, the extensive category of unitary perceptions concerned with recognition of familiar human faces must be established.

The category of unitary perceptions elicited by particular faces is in many respects highly specific and different from all other categories of visual perceptions. First, the human face is a *sui generis matrix* composed always of the same kinds of elements situated in the same places but differing in details. The change of one detail makes a face unrecognizable, either as a face in general or as the face of a given person. Second, faces always "belong" to given persons—that is, they are closely associated with other visual stimulus-patterns of particular human figures. Finally, gnostic units representing perceptions of faces form numerous powerful connections with particular categories of gnostic units of other analyzers and also with perceptive units of the emotive system.

Thus it becomes clear that unitary perceptions of faces must have a strong representation in a separate gnostic field whose destruction must lead to the abolition of the capacity to distinguish particular faces. Clinical observations completely confirm this conclusion, and there are numerous reports demonstrating the corresponding kind of agnosia—generally called prosopagnosia. Some relevant examples follow.

In a paper of Hécaen et al.[5] a patient is described who was completely unable to recognize the faces of familiar persons, even of his own wife, but he immediately recognized them when he heard their voices. He also could recognize a person (or his photograph) when he saw the entire figure or some additional cues. For instance, he was able to recognize the portrait of Louis XIV "à cause de la perruque"; he failed to recognize the face of Napoleon, but he did so easily when the entire figure was shown. He described his deficit in the following way: "Je vois très bien les détails de votre visage, votre bouche, votre nez, mais c'est comme flou, c'est comme un oubli de physionomie . . . je ne suis plus physionomiste du tout."

Another informative report on a patient in whom the facial agnosia was a major symptom was presented by Cole and Perez-Cruet.[6] Here are some fragments of their report:

When approached, he gazed at the person's face and moved his head in various directions in a puzzled manner. He stated that he first looked at the chin, and mouth, then carefully inspected the sides of the face, nose, eyes, and fore-head but according to his own statement "could not put it all together." At times he commented on the person's body contour, clothes, specific facial features, scars, eyeglasses, coloring, etc., and used this, occasionally with success, to identify the person in front of him. . . . This disability prevented visual recognition of those who were familiar to him including his wife. . . . When he looked into the mirror he stated that his own face appeared blurred and strange to him. [But,] he was able to recognize facial expressions mimicking anger and surprise. . . . There was no difficulty in pointing to objects, whether single or in groups, or pictures of those objects, when the examiner named them: nor was there difficulty in naming the objects or pictures when the examiner pointed to them. . . . He was able to state accurately the colors of common objects and claimed to be able to revisualize colors and shades. . . . Dreaming was reported as unchanged and stereoscopic vision was normal.

It should be noted that facial expressions belong to a different category of stimulus-patterns (V-FE, Figure III-1e) and are usually well preserved in prosopagnosic patients.

Much scantier is our knowledge concerning the unitary perceptions representing human figures and familiar animals (V-AO, Figure III-1f). The important property of these stimulus-objects is that they are mobile and certainly the nature of their movements constitutes an element facilitating their perceptions. In fact, a given person is often recognized from a distance on the basis of his gait or other manners.

Another feature of animate objects is provided by their smooth contours without jagged edges. As indicated above, agnosia for inanimate objects does not affect animate objects, and facial agnosia does not affect entire human silhouettes.

(4) *Letters of the alphabet, numbers, short words, and other signs* (V-Sn, Figure III-1g). Whereas all the categories of unitary perceptions described above are by no means peculiar to human beings—but are certainly present in other primates, and some of them (V-Il, V-Sp, V-VO), in other animals too—the category now under discussion is primarily human, because it is directly involved in speech and kindred phenomena designed as symbolic processes. Nevertheless, as far as the perceptive aspect of these stimulus-patterns is concerned, there is no principal difference between unitary perceptions of signs and other unitary perceptions of the visual system.

Let us characterize briefly the main features of stimulus-patterns representing signs, using for this purpose printed letters of the Latin alphabet. First, these letters are composed of specific combinations of a few elements such as straight and curved lines of different orientations. Second, the letters as a whole are always spatially oriented, in both vertical and horizontal dimensions. Third, each letter is associated with the particular articulate sound (or phoneme) and with a kinesthetic pattern representing its reproduction in writing.

As explained in the preceding chapter, we have good reason to believe that short sequences of letters, such as those occurring in frequently encountered syllables or words, also form gnostic units and in consequence are perceived as a whole without being decomposed into particular elements. It is interesting to note that such compound patterns of letters, in order to form unitary perceptions, must have a quite definite spatial arrangement—namely, their elements must appear in a definite direction—in Indo-European languages from left to right—and must follow one another in close succession. In fact, a well-known word written vertically and not horizontally or with widely spaced letters is not accepted by us as a unitary perception.

We have much evidence that visual stimulus-patterns representing signs possess a separate gnostic field. In fact, injuries sustained in the occipital region of the cortex may produce a selective deficit in recognizing letters and words but preserve other forms of visual gnosis. This syndrome is called alexic agnosia; it differs from another syndrome in which signs are recognized as visual patterns, but their associations with corresponding phonemes (auditory or kinesthetic) are impaired (alexic aphasia). This syndrome will be discussed in Chapter V.

The following description of alexic agnosia is based on six cases described in detail by Alajouanine *et al.*[7]

In most reported cases the gnosis of letters was not totally abolished, because some of them could be recognized. However, similar letters, such as P and R, D and O, and M and N were confused, and letters rarely used were not recognized at all. On the other hand, the alexic syndrome was most clearly manifested when the subjects were requested to read words. They either failed completely to do so or spoke quite different words.

Those patients in whom the gnosis of letters was preserved were able to read by syllabifying. They were also able to *write* the dictated text or write spontaneously; however, copying was impossible.

It is interesting to note that the patients were able immediately to recognize familiar handwriting. This fact shows that unitary perceptions of particular handwritings (V-Hw, Figure III-1*b*) belong to a separate category of perceptions, represented in a different gnostic field.

The above data are in full harmony with our considerations in the preceding chapter. Since the gnostic units representing words or rarely used letters are thought to be less numerous than those representing common letters, the probability of their abolition is greater; consequently, reading words was much more impaired than reading particular letters. Therefore, a subject had to return to the early period of lexis based on syllabifying each word. The preserved writing ability under the guidance of hearing words or verbalizing them is again understandable, because writing depends on the kinesthetic gnostic area which was not affected in these patients. On the other hand, writing by copying the seen words was not possible because the perception of the corresponding stimulus-patterns was abolished. Later (Chapters IV and V) we shall discuss the states in which, on the contrary, only writing by copying is preserved, whereas writing at dictation or spontaneously is impossible.

Further to emphasize the specificity of the above syndrome, we shall show a different and in some ways opposite deficit in reading which we observed in the patient discussed who was suffering from severe visuo-spatial agnosia.

As indicated above (see p. 115), this patient was able to read known words fairly well. However, when he was asked to spell them, he failed completely. He was also totally unable to read nonsensical words. When a word was presented to him in which one letter was changed, he usually did not notice the difference and read the word as if it were written correctly. For example, seeing the word "okilary" he read it as "okulary" (in Polish, spectacles) not being able to discover that one letter was changed. When more letters were changed, he failed completely to read the word.

This case shows that, as should be expected, analytical reading in normally educated persons involves spatial orientation and therefore is impossible when the subject suffers from a heavy visuo-spatial agnosia. On the other hand, his correct reading of well-known words clearly shows that the visual patterns of these words are integrated and grasped as unitary perceptions. Thus, a patient suffering from visuo-spatial agnosia is capable of reading known (but only known) words but cannot spell them; on the contrary, a patient suffering from minor alexic agnosia fails to read words (both known and unknown) as entities but can more easily read them by spelling them.

Incidentally, this analysis shows how careful we should be in evaluating various types of agnosias (and other central nervous impairments) and how important it is to apply suitable methods for disentangling and elucidating particular symptoms.

(5) *Visual perceptions of particular postures of our limbs and their movements* (V-L, Figure III-1*i*). The newborn child learns very early to observe those parts of his body which are within his visual field—particularly the hands and legs—and the changes in their posture due to movements. Therefore, we have good reason to believe that the corresponding visual pictures form a particular category of unitary perceptions, especially since they establish specific associations with somesthetic (S-L) and kinesthetic (K-L) unitary perceptions involved in the corresponding postures and movements. In the normal life of adults this category of gnosis does not play an important role because of the high development of proprioceptive gnosis, both somesthetic and kinesthetic; however, if because of an injury (for example, deafferentiation) these sources of information about the limbs are lacking, the visual control of our movements greatly increases in importance. This is true of various kinds of ataxia in which precise postures and/or movements of limbs are impossible without visual control.

The reader will certainly notice that we have omitted from our discussion the important part of the visual system concerned with color vision. We have done so deliberately in order not to complicate our analysis by describing a system which is poorly understood. After all, black-and-white film shows us that nearly all the visual events of the external world *can* be represented by black-and-white visual dimension; if we were all Daltonists, as some animals are, our vision would be deprived of much of its esthetic values, but our visual information would not be greatly impaired.

It is very probable that color vision has its special cortical field, since we know of a separate syndrome called color agnosia in which the external world is deprived of all colors for a patient. We are not certain whether this is a true agnosia or whether all colors are represented in some transit area from which they are distributed to particular gnostic units, tinting the patterns in a particular way. Especially interesting in this context is the fact that in many unitary perceptions of objects, colors do not belong to the essential elements of the patterns, since nearly every visual object *can* be recognized when it is reproduced only in black and white.

To end this survey of various visual gnostic fields, let us discuss briefly the problem of their localization. On the basis of the data of Hubel and Wiesel concerning the properties of units in areas 18 and 19[8] and the effects of stimulation of these areas in conscious patients,[9] it may be concluded that these areas still belong to the transit areas representing elements of perceptions but not perceptions themselves. In consequence, the gnostic visual fields must be situated still further rostrally and laterally, encroaching upon temporal cortex (areas 37 and 22?) and parietal cortex (area 39 and posterior part of area 7, see Figure III-12, below).

In fact, stimulation of the posterior temporal cortex in conscious epileptic patients gives rise to visual hallucinations usually representing persons and their faces,[10] which would suggest that the V-F gnostic field is situated in this region. The remaining visual gnostic fields are probably situated more dorsally, on the border of the occipital and parietal lobes. It may be assumed that the V-MO field and the S-MO field are close together, so as to establish the shortest mutual connections. The visuo-spatial gnostic field must also be situated so as to have the shortest connections with the vestibular analyzer, probably in the parietal lobe, and the kinesthetic gnostic field in the dorsolateral frontal region.

In monkeys, the gnostic visual area seems to be localized in the inferotemporal cortex, as judged from numerous experimental results in which ablations of this region produced impairment of visual discrimination.[11]

The problem of laterality of the particular visual gnostic fields remains unsolved. Most probably the laterality follows the rule that those cognitive functions which are involved in speech are represented in the so-called dominant hemisphere, whereas those which are not are represented in the non-dominant hemisphere. Accordingly, the gnostic field for signs (V-Sn) is probably located in the dominant hemisphere; that concerned with spatial relations (V-Sp) in the non-dominant. The V-MO gnostic field may be represented in both.

3. General properties of visual gnosis

After presenting a survey of the main categories of visual perceptions, we should like to return to the problems discussed in the preceding chapter and show how the rules presented and discussed there in general terms can be applied to visual gnosis.

It has already been indicated that visual unitary perceptions are not the most convenient models of their unitary character, because in most instances we can easily apprehend not only the integrated stimulus-patterns but also their elements which are included in our visual gnosis. Only in relatively rare instances are we in situations where the given visual "Gestalt" is irresolvable, as in recognizing handwriting or silhouettes.

On the other hand, we can give innumerable instances of the principle of virtual independence of unitary perceptions from the exact picture of the object projected on the retina. This principle, referred to as the *constancy* of perceptions, was thoroughly studied in respect to shape and size of objects observed.[12] Let us analyze in more detail the rule of size constancy—that is, the apparent preservation of the sizes of objects irrespective of their distance from the eye. To give a typical example, if I compare a tree in front of my window situated at some (not remote) distance and the flowers in the pot inside my room, I *perceive* the tree as much taller than the flowers in spite of the fact that its reflection on the retina may be the same or even smaller.

Another well-known example of size constancy is that persons on the television screen seem to us of "normal" size and we never experience an awkward feeling that they are pygmies. Similarly, we see persons and objects in a film as being of "normal" size, whether we are sitting near (but not too near) or far (but not very far) from the screen.

The principle of size constancy can also be demonstrated in a striking manner by a very simple experiment illustrating the so-called Emert's effect. In the picture for studying afterimages (Fig. III-2), fix the red sign "RED" at a distance of 16 inches for thirty-five seconds. Then, transfer your eyes to the gray square and move the entire picture to a distance of 32 inches or bring it nearer to a distance of 8 inches. You will see that when the figure is at a distance of 32 inches, the afterimage of the sign will become very large, whereas if it is at a distance of 8 inches it becomes very small. The explanation of this phenomenon is simple. Of course the size of the afterimage on the retina as well as in our projective area is always the same. However, when we compare it with the sign "RED," which we perceive as *constant* irrespective of distance, in the first instance we see the afterimage as increased, and in the second, decreased. In other words, we do not perceive the change of the angular dimension of the sign, when moving the picture farther away or bringing it closer.

All these phenomena can be explained by assuming that various objects are represented in our perceptive file as possessing a definite *standard* size. A fly has a size of a typical fly, a man of a typical man, and a tree of a typical tree. Therefore, in spite of the *real* differences of the size of the given visual patterns on the retina and in the projective area, the gnostic fields neglect these differences and introduce the others, based on the standard relations of absolute sizes between particular objects. It should be stressed that this sort of "illusion" is a result of our visual *experience* and is not due to our abstract *knowledge* of the size of objects. In fact, sun and moon are never seen by us as colossal in spite of our knowing their true dimensions.

In summary, our visual perceptions of known objects rarely correspond to the real angular dimensions of their pictures on the retina, because in the units of our visual gnostic area only their standard size is represented and this size is imposed upon our visual sensations. We can call this phenomenon a corrective illusion, since here the distortion of the "true" visual pattern leads to a more adequate estimation of a real object.

It should be emphasized, however, that the above principle operates only within some narrow limits of the distance of objects. When we see a tree far on the horizon the mechanism of the corrective illusion stops working and the tree appears very small, because it forms another unitary perception; then we identify it with closer trees only on the basis of our associative and not perceptual experience. In this connection, here are some data presented in an article by Turnbull concerning his observations on a pygmy tribe in Africa.[13]

A young and intelligent guide of Turnbull was a member of a tribe living in dense forests, and was for the first time in his life brought by an automobile into an open field. When he saw buffalo from a distance he asked the name of those insects. When he was told that they were buffalo, he refused categorically to believe it and thought that he was being ridiculed. When the automobile approached and the size of the figures increased in his eyes, he thought that this was witchcraft and he was very frightened. He had the same difficulties when he saw from a distance a fishing boat with several persons on board. He could not believe that this was a boat but thought it was a piece of wood. On the other hand, he had no difficulty identifying objects (persons, birds, branches) from a distance of a few yards.

Let us turn now to the documentation of the antagonistic relations between the visual unitary perceptions of the same category. The best method to demonstrate such relations seems to be provided by presenting different stimulus-patterns to each eye in a stereoscope. In that situation eye rivalry causes that either this or that stimulus-pattern is seen, or even the mosaic of both, but the patterns almost never merge into one whole. However, the conditions of the experiments performed to illustrate this rule did not fulfill our requirements, since the stimuli presented (colored planes, geometrical patterns, or human faces unknown to the subject) did not represent the unitary perceptions in our sense. Therefore the relevant data are scarce. In an experiment of Engel[14] two faces, one normal and one upside down, were shown and, as expected by our concept, only the normal face was seen. In another experiment of Engel, one of the faces presented was by chance known to the subject, and again this face dominated over the unknown face.

More reliable are the casual self-observations by subjects who are accustomed to look through the monocular microscope and have learned to do so with the other eye open. It is a common experience that in that situation we can switch our attention either to the image in the microscope or to the objects at the side of the microscope (for example, a drawing of the preparation), but are totally unable to observe both at the same time.

The stereoscopic method would probably be excellent for studying the interrelations between various unitary perceptions and detecting when they are and when they are not antagonistic. It would be interesting also to determine whether presenting to both eyes complementary figures (for example, to one eye a face without a nose, and to the other a nose alone) would cause the mergence of both and the appearance of a coherent visual pattern.*

Another test proving the existence of interperceptual antagonism involves the so-called ambiguous figures. The cube test, the staircase test, and—most sophisticated of all—"my wife versus my mother-in-law" or "my husband and my father-in-law" are typical illustrations of this rule.

Let us analyze the latter test (Figure III-3). The same visual pattern represents two different faces depending on "how" one looks at it. If we look at the picture for the first time, we immediately see one of the faces without going into details and analyzing what we see. Then, it is

---

* C. M. Graham ("Visual Perception," in *Handbook of Experimental Psychology*, edited by S. S. Stevens, New York, London, 1951, p. 894) reports that under "certain circumstances the figure of a fence presented to one eye and a figure of a pony presented to the other results in the report of a pony jumping over the fence." This is a typical case of mutual complementation of two unitary perceptions which are not antagonistic to each other. Our own pilot stereoscopic experiments on the perception of faces of known persons gave results fully confirming our expectations.

nearly impossible for us to see the other face, no matter how hard we try or how much we are prompted by another person—"Look, here is the mouth, here is the nose. . . ." We cannot integrate these details into a new whole, because the face we do see suppresses the new perception. Then suddenly we do perceive the second face, but at the same time the perception of the first face vanishes completely. Again, we experience the same resistance when we try to reevoke the first face.

Fig. III-3. Equivocal Stimulus Pattern

"My wife and my mother-in-law." (E. G. Boring, *The Physical Dimensions of Consciousness* [New York: Century, 1933].)

4. Categories of unitary perceptions in the acoustic analyzer (A)

The general structure of the auditory gnosis in man differs essentially from that of the visual gnosis. Whereas vision is the chief channel of information about the events of the external world, and its role in speech function is limited to a rather recent acquisition in the form of lexis, the opposite is true of audition: here the relatively primitive auditory gnosis, consisting in recognizing various sounds of the external world, is really insignificant; perhaps, if we were in some way deprived of them (leaving speech unaffected), this would bring us some relief in our noisy age. On the other hand, the most essential function of the auditory analyzer in man is that of hearing human speech. As a matter of fact, the auditory gnosis of human speech is a basis of our social relations, and in this respect the auditory analyzer is much more important than the visual analyzer. In fact, persons who are deprived of vision from birth, being thus cut off from the main source of information about the external world, are socially better adapted than persons who have been deaf from birth and cut off from hearing human speech. It follows that in man the gnostic apparatus of hearing speech is highly developed; the fact that its localization is unilateral, which undoubtedly is a great oversight on the part of nature, is of great advantage for its investigation.

According to psychological and neurological evidence, unitary auditory perceptions can be divided into the following categories: (1) various sounds of the external world (A-Sd); (2) speaking voices of particular persons (A-Vo); (3) particular sounds representing the elements of human speech (words and short phrases (A-W); (4) melodies (A-M). We shall separately consider each of these categories as follows.

(1) Unitary perceptions representing the known sounds of the external world (A-Sd) can be divided into several groups: (a) sounds produced by man-made things, such as bells, motors, whistles or musical instruments; (b) natural sounds such as those produced by wind, thunder, sea; (c) sounds produced by animals; (d) emotional expressions of animals and men, such as screaming, moaning, whining, laughing.

There is no evidence whether all these groups are represented by a common gnostic field or whether they are anatomically separated. Such a separation seems probable, in view of the fact that the last groups (b), (c), (d), above, were most important for primitive man. This problem may be studied systematically by applying special ethological tests that present typical samples of each group of sounds and examining their effects in normal and brain-lesioned persons.

The sounds produced by definite objects and animals form strong associations with visual stimulus-objects representing their sources. On the other hand, sounds expressing emotions are chiefly connected with the emotive system.

(2) A special category of auditory perceptions, probably subserved by a separate gnostic field, is concerned with various vocal characteristics of human speech (A-Vo). We all recognize the "voices" of our acquaintances immediately, even after hearing one word, without seeing the person; a new human voice, not belonging to our file of voices, elicits an orientation reaction until it is included into our register. Here we have a far-reaching analogy with the visual gnosis of human faces: just as the features of individual human faces belong to another category of visual perceptions than facial expressions determined by emotions, so individual human voices belong to an entirely different cate-

gory of auditory perceptions than do emotionally induced intonations of speech. As will be discussed in Chapter V, there are precise mutual associations between individual human voices and individual human faces, suggesting that the two corresponding fields might be situated in close proximity.

(3) We turn now to the discussion of the main category of auditory perceptions in man, which is much more elaborated than the preceding ones and also much better known from both the psychological and the neuropathological points of view—auditory speech perceptions subserved by the auditory gnostic field, commonly called auditory speech area (A-W).

We have a great body of psychological evidence supported by neuropathological data that auditory unitary perceptions of speech are represented by *words* or short phrases. This is because from his earliest period of life a child learns to perceive the sounds of entire words and has no opportunity to hear the sounds of individual letters. Only later, in the period of learning to read, does he decompose the words into letters (phonemes), and only then are these sounds included in the file of unitary perceptions. Such a stage certainly does not exist at all in illiterate persons. We shall call the auditory unitary perceptions of speech *audioverbal perceptions;* the corresponding gnostic units, *audioverbal units.*

The audioverbal unitary perceptions have almost exactly the same properties as unitary visual perceptions. They follow the all-or-none principle, being either recognized as a whole or not recognized at all. Their recognition is most often followed by associations with other perceptions, because words usually have a definite "meaning." We can, however, be familiar also with meaningless "words,"* or we may temporarily forget the meaning of a given word; in these instances we have a pure auditory recognition of the word pattern without any associations.

Since in different languages different elements are essential for the formation of audioverbal gnostic units, discrimination and recognition of words is the best in our mother tongue. For instance, the English language possesses more vowels than the Polish language; in consequence, various shades of vowels indistinguishable for my own ear are quite distinct for somebody to whom English is the mother language. Since a word is the unitary perception, the change of one vowel modifies the *whole* word and may make it unrecognizable. For exam-

---

* For the sake of convenience, but against the accepted tradition, we shall use the term "word" to denote auditory patterns of wordlike character, irrespective of whether they have any meaning. Otherwise we would fall into confusion, because an English word would not be a word for a subject not knowing English or, for that matter, for an English-speaking patient suffering from sensory aphasia.

ple, the words "destruction" and "distraction," or "Russian" and "ration," which sound quite different for English-speaking persons, have hardly any difference for me and I can easily substitute one word for another. Similarly many Japanese, in whose language the difference between the sound of l and r does not exist, cannot distinguish between "light" and "right" or "fry" and "fly" and use these pairs indicriminately. For English-speaking persons and for me too these words are quite distinct, and it would never come to our minds that they have something in common.

Furthermore, if a word is transfigured either by bad pronunciation or by another dialect, what usually happens is that either one recognizes the word as the same word and does not notice any difference—in that case, the proper units respond to it in spite of its transfiguration—or one does not recognize it at all. Both these cases are quite familiar to me in connection with my English. It often happens that my Anglo-Saxon colleagues do not understand a word spoken by me, although to my mind I pronounce it quite correctly, and, what is even more noticeable, I do not see *any* difference between my pronunciation and theirs, unless it is specially pointed out to me. Only rarely do we recognize the word and recognize that it is pronounced oddly; this usually occurs when we are already acquainted with the given pronunciation and have got used to it.

The principle of antagonism between particular audioverbal perceptions is even more manifest than between visual perceptions of the same category, because two auditory stimuli can be presented at exactly the same time. If we hear simultaneously two words uttered by different persons, we recognize only that one on which we concentrate our attention. On the other hand, the antagonism between auditory perceptions of different categories seems to be much less pronounced or may even be absent. We are able, for instance, to recognize at the same time the words we are listening to and the voice of the person speaking, or to recognize at the same time the melody of a song and its words.

Since the audioverbal gnostic field is situated exclusively in the dominant hemisphere, and the effects of lesions in this field are most conspicuous, there are many reports of cases of audioverbal agnosia—the so-called verbal deafness. The chief characteristic of this type of disorder is that a subject does not recognize the sounds of speech but has no difficulty recognizing other sounds. Those patients in whom the verbal deafness is not combined with amnestic aphasia (cf. Chapter V)—and who consequently are able to report on their own deficit—complain that they hear a sort of indistinct murmuring instead of clear speech. If the deficit is less pronounced, the subjects have difficulty in

Fig. III-2. Manifestation of the Size-Constancy Principle

Stare at the dot in the center of the letter E at the left while counting slowly to 35. Then look directly at the dot in the center of the gray square, right, simultaneously bringing the book nearer or farther from the eyes. The after-image will become smaller or larger, respectively. (D. O. Hebb, *A Textbook of Psychology* [Philadelphia and London: W. B. Saunders Co., 1958], Fig. 11.)

discerning similar words or in following rapid speech. If they have to repeat words, they display severe paraphasias. Analogous paragraphias they display when writing under dictation, while the copying is unimpaired (that is, the syndrome is just the reverse to that of alexic agnosia).

Here is the example of a typical, relatively mild word deafness, taken from a paper of Stoliarova-Kabielianskaja.[15]

Comprehension of speech was strongly impaired in this patient. When he did not understand a word, he often repeated a similarly sounding word and then indicated the object named. For instance, hearing the word "nogot" (in Russian, "nail"), he repeated "nogi" ("legs") and pointed to his legs. Hearing "oossy" ("mustache"), he said "volossy" ("hair") and pointed to his hair. He also failed to notice distortions in spoken words. Both in the spontaneous speech and in repetition he displayed many paraphasias. Naming of objects seen was preserved, but again the word was uttered with paraphasias. He was never conscious of his errors in speech and did not try to correct himself. Copying a text was unimpaired, but in spontaneous writing many paragraphias were observed.

As we shall see in Chapter V, audioverbal agnosia differs from "sensory" aphasia, where the recognition of words is unimpaired (which may be tested by the request to repeat them) but their comprehension is abolished, and from "central" aphasia, where again the recognition of words is preserved (which may be proved by their comprehension), but they cannot be repeated. In these two forms of aphasia not the gnostic field itself, but its connections with gnostic fields of other analyzers are severed.

(4) To end this survey of auditory perceptions, let us mention briefly those concerned with melodies (A-M). Since this type of auditory gnosis does not play any indispensable role in our everyday life, we shall not deal with it to any extent. This type is represented by a gnostic field separate from the audioverbal field, and even situated at some distance from it, because usually the audioverbal agnosia is not accompanied by melody agnosia (or amusia), and vice versa.

The problem of localization of auditory gnostic fields is no less obscure than that of visual fields. Area 41 on the border of the sylvian fissure is considered a projective (transit) acoustic area. Below it is area 42 (paraprojective), and below that, in the middle temporal convolution, is the gnostic area 22. Somewhere in these regions, in the dominant hemisphere, the audioverbal field is situated. Further down (in areas 21 and 20), close to the visual gnostic field V-F, are fields representing human voices (A-Vo) and melodies (A-M), judging from the fact that stimulation of this region in epileptic patients produces corresponding hallucinations. The fields representing other sounds (A-Sd) are not known. They are probably situated in the non-dominant hemisphere or in both.

5. Unitary perceptions in olfactory (Ol) and vestibular (La) analyzers

Since vestibular and olfactory gnosis are much less developed in humans than the auditory and visual gnosis, and they play a relatively insignificant role in associative functions, we shall comment only briefly on their main properties.

There is no doubt that known odors often encountered in everyday life—such as those of particular foods, flowers, excrements—are unitary perceptions, and as such are represented by corresponding units in the olfactory gnostic field. The associations formed between the olfactory analyzer and other analyzers are partly cognitive (particularly in blind persons, for whom smell substitutes largely for vision) and partly emotive. In fact, odors play an important role in our emotional life, being strongly reflexogenic for both appetitive and aversive drive reflexes.

In animals with poor vision (such as dogs) the olfactory gnosis is better developed and refined than in man; consequently, we may assume that these animals have large olfactory gnostic fields representing all kinds of odors with which they are acquainted. In fact, if a dog meets an unknown person on his own territory, to whom he does not display any hostility, he immediately throws into operation the olfactory searching-targeting reflexes (as the effect of curiosity drive) and inspects this person by smell as we do it by vision. Thus, a dog recognizes various known persons, and perhaps inanimate objects too, chiefly by smell, which in these animals is probably closely associated with vision.

Even less may be said about the vestibular analyzer. Its gnostic apparatus provides information concerning the posture of the head in relation to the vertical axis and turns of the head in various directions. This information, in conjunction with postural, kinesthetic, and visual informations, contributes to our orientation in space and, more precisely, to the relation of our body to the environment. The vestibular perceptions elicit chiefly eye reflexes, postural neck reflexes, and postural trunk and limb reflexes, which were studied by Magnus in his classical work.[16]

6. Categories of unitary perceptions in the somesthetic and gustatory analyzers (S)

By somesthetic analyzer we denote that afferent system which is concerned with sensations originating on the surface of the body (mouth included), in joints, and in internal organs.

Among the receptors dealing with sensations from the surface of the body, we distinguish tactile receptors, pressure receptors, pain receptors, and temperature receptors. It will be convenient to include here also the gustatory receptors, because they act in close cooperation with other surface receptors in the mouth. The afferent system dealing with all these submodalities of sensations will be called somesthetic exteroceptive system (S-ES).

Among joint receptors we shall discuss only those which provide information on postures of the limbs and body, and shall not speak on articular pain receptors. The afferent system concerned with articular postural receptors will be referred to as the *somesthetic proprioceptive system* (S-PS), in contradistinction to the *kinesthetic proprioceptive system* (K-PS) providing information on movements, to be discussed in Section 7, below). Thus, according to Sherrington's usage, the term "proprioception" denotes both kinesthesis and postural somesthesis—that is, all the perceptions involved in movements and postures of the limbs.

We shall omit from our discussion the interoceptive afferent system dealing with sensations from internal organs, since that system plays only a minor role in somatic gnosis.

Among various categories of somesthetic perceptions, we shall specify the following ones which play an important role in associative functions and whose existence is documented by neurological observations.

(1) Perceptions of limb postures (somesthetic proprioceptive gnosis, S-L).

(2) Perceptions of textures of objects touched, including pain and temperature (textural gnosis, S-T).

(3) Perceptions of shapes of small manipulable objects (stereognosis, S-MO).

(4) Perceptions of tastes (gustatory gnosis, S-G).

(5) Perceptions of mouth postures involved in speech (oral gnosis, S-Or).

(1) *Perceptions of limb postures* (S-L). This is probably one of the earliest categories of somatic gnosis developed after birth. An infant has a continuous inflow of information from all joints and, by directing attention to particular postures (through the somatic targeting reflexes), he integrates the messages from several joints so as to perceive a posture of the limb concerned.

We assume that the general "feeling" of particular parts of the body which we experience whenever we direct our attention to a given limb derives from the somesthetic proprioceptive system. Moreover, this system is responsible for our "body scheme"—for the realization of the relations between various parts of the body, their shape, size, and so on.

In consequence, when the somatic gnostic field storing all this information is impaired, the patient experiences such peculiar somatic disorders as the feeling of the total absence of the limb (asomatognosia), the feeling that it belongs to somebody else, the feeling that it has changed in size and so forth.[17] The fact that these disorders affect usually only one limb on the side contralateral to the lesion shows that the corresponding gnostic fields have strictly topical arrangement.

The purely gnostic character of the syndrome in question is documented by the fact that lesions in the projective somesthetic area leading to a great impairment of the postural and tactile sensations are generally not accompanied by asomatognosia. It should be also noted that amputation of a limb does not lead to the feeling of its absence but, on the contrary, to the explicit sensation of its presence, the symptom referred to as the phantom limb. Thus we see that the deprivation of the sense of a limb is produced only by the damage of those gnostic units which are responsible for its somesthetic perception.

(2) *Perceptions of textures of objects touched* (S-T). The objects of the external world we deal with in our life are characterized by their "macrostructure," which is chiefly perceived by the visual system (unless the subject is blind) and their "microstructure" or texture, whose perception is accomplished by exteroceptive somesthesis. Here belong such properties of objects as: smoothness versus roughness, porosity, softness versus hardness, elasticity versus plasticity, dryness versus moistness, sliminess, coldness versus warmth. Here also belongs the sharpness of an object or its strong pressure producing localized pain, either of the pinprick or pinching type. Most receptors for the corresponding sensations are situated in the inner parts of the digits of the hand; this part of the human body represents the chief receptive organ for textural gnosis. In those animals in which hands are not developed, and also in human infants, the organ utilized for this type of gnosis is the mouth.

The above textural features of objects we handle in our everyday life are so common and so unchanging that we pay hardly any attention to them. However, if we would think for a moment of all the objects we handle in dressing, washing, eating, and in our everyday work, we may realize how many textures we recognize and identify and, in consequence, how many perceptive units we have at our disposal in the appropriate gnostic field of the somesthetic analyzer.

Agnosia concerning textural stimulus-patterns was described in detail by Delay,[18] who termed it "ahylognosia."

(3) *Somesthetic perceptions of shapes of small manipulable objects* (S-MO). Another category of somesthetic perceptions is provided by

the "macrostructural" properties of objects. If we take into our hand a well-known object, we can immediately recognize it, showing that we possess a somesthetic gnosis (stereognosis) integrating the separate features of that object into one unitary perception. Since our main channel of information about the shapes of objects is provided by the visual analyzer, and, as was stated in a preceding section, a powerful gnostic system is developed to cope with this information, we can ask whether the recognition of handled objects does not occur by association. However, neurological observations show that it is not necessarily so, since a subject with severe visual agnosia, who fails completely to recognize a given object by vision, recognizes it immediately if he takes it into his hand (cf. p. 116).

Similarly to the gnosis of textures, stereognosis also depends chiefly on the receptors in the hand. As shown by appropriate clinical data, stereognosis is based exclusively on somesthetic sensations, whereas kinesthesis does not play any role in it. In fact, we have often observed that patients with injuries in front of the central sulcus, who have severe paresis of the hand, easily recognize objects if we passively bend their palm and fingers around them. On the other hand, patients with parietal lesions can skillfully and precisely palpate an object (with covered eyes) but nevertheless do not have the slightest idea of its shape.

The gnostic units responsible for stereognosis are situated in the parietal region behind the somatic projective area for the hand. Lesions in this region produce a syndrome called astereognosia or amorphognosia. There is some evidence that stereognosis consists of two stages. First, the elementary properties of a given object, such as its shape and hardness, are integrated, and then the tactile perception of the whole object emerges from it. These relations are well illustrated in the following fragment from a protocol of examination of a patient with a lesion in the left parietal lobe (Ajuriaguerra and Hécaen[19]). The patient was asked to recognize the objects given him in the right and left hands.

	Main gauche	Main droite
Stylo	Stylo	C'est oblong, c'est froid, une aspérité
Boîte d'allumettes	Boîte d'allumettes	Un objet de moyenne grosseur, rectangulaire, peu épais, c'est du bois
Pipe	Pipe	Une grosseur, puis c'est long, rond . . . une pipe
Clef	Clef	C'est un objet long, rond, un cercle vide, du métal (longue hésitation), une clef.

It is clear from this examination that objects taken by the left—un-affected—hand are recognized immediately; those taken by the right hand are first characterized by their tactile and stereognostic elements, and only then may the conclusion be reached—or not—as to their identity.

This informative protocol shows that we have here again an example of a two-level gnosis, similar to that encountered in the visual analyzer for human faces or words. Since, according to other observations, the primitive type of somesthetic agnosia, which is perhaps partly identical with textural agnosia, is always contaminated by the deficits of sensation, it may be conjectured that the corresponding gnostic field lies either just behind the somatic projective area or within this area itself—that is, that some of its units are exit units and possess perceptive character.

As mentioned above, the gnostic function of the hand, which in normal persons has an important, but only limited significance for the cognition of the external world, acquires a crucial importance in blind persons. This fact throws some light on the problem raised in the preceding chapter concerning the potentialities and "creative power" of the afferent systems in respect to the formation of new gnostic fields (or at least gnostic categories) which never exist in normal persons. We know that blind persons are able not only to integrate keenly their tactile sensations but, moreover, they learn to recognize by touch relief letters either in Braille or in the ordinary alphabet and in this way to "read" with amazing dexterity. What is even more amazing is the fact that deaf-blind persons can learn to "hear" the speech of others by palpation of the speaker's larynx. Imagine how many extremely fine and delicate perceptive units must be formed in the somatic gnostic field in order to cope with this task!

(4) *Perceptions of tastes* (S-G). Since the mouth constitutes a gate through which all nourishment enters the organism, its receptive surface must be organized in such a way as to discern edible substances from inedible ones and then to distinguish among various edible substances. To fulfill this function a great number of chemical receptors are situated on the tongue, excitable by various elementary tastes. The mixed messages conveying various attributes of food—its taste, texture, and temperature—reach the projective area of the cortex localized in man in the posterior part of the Rolandic operculum above the circular sulcus. The sparse but unequivocal neuropathological evidence seems to indicate that the part of the insula closely adjacent to the projective area represents the gnostic gustatory area.[20] This is in keeping with the fact that the insular region, insignificant in animals, grows in the human brain to a considerable magnitude.

It may be assumed that the gnostic gustatory system in animals is poor, judging from the great monotony of their natural diet. Therefore we think that the perceptive area in animals is only slightly separated from the projective area and may be even totally included in it. This would explain the curious and unexpected fact that, as found in experiments on animals, many neurons in this area are plurimodal.[21] According to our present concept, we would suspect that these very neurons integrate various sensory aspects of food.

In contradistinction to that in other species, the gustatory gnostic system in humans is highly developed, as can be judged from the innumerable different kinds of food civilized man eats. In consequence, our culinary experience led to the formation of numerous sets of perceptive gustatory units representing various foods in our menu. Although the core of each unitary perception is made up of taste elements and their various combinations, the other aspects of food (such as odor, texture, and even temperature) also play a significant role in the gustatory patterns. Indeed, the same food prepared in different ways (in large morsels, small morsels, or minced; dry or moist; soft or crisp; cold or hot; and so on) can have different tastes and in consequence be represented by different gnostic units.

The gustatory unitary perceptions have exactly the same properties as those of other analyzers. They are psychologically indecomposable, recognizable at the first mouthful, and may be radically changed even by a slight modification of only one ingredient (as, for instance, adding salt, sugar, or pepper).

It should be stressed that the gnostic aspect of taste is quite independent of its attractive or aversive character, which remains under the control of the hunger drive system and selects meals best adjusted to the unconditioned and conditioned specific hunger reflexes (cf. Chapter I, Section 6). Precisely as the elementary tastes remain the same irrespective of hunger or satiation (although sensitivity to each undergoes some changes), so it is with complex tastes. Thus, we recognize the taste of a given food whether we like it or not or whether at the given moment it arouses our appetite or we are satiated with it.

Incidentally, the same is true of other categories of perceptions. The visual perception of a given face, the auditory perception of a voice, or the name of a given person is almost completely independent of our emotional attitude, which may change to a large extent. This is because the gnostic character of a stimulus-pattern and its emotional character are quite distinct, reflecting the functional and anatomical separateness of the cognitive and emotive brain. The phenomenological unity of both these aspects, which is so prominent in our subjective experience, is due to strong associative bonds bidirectionally linking the given gnostic units with the appropriate emotive units.

(5) *Perceptions of mouth postures involved in speech* (S-Or). In humans the receptive apparatus in the mouth has not only gustatory significance but it is also involved in speech function. Although speech is subserved mainly by the kinesthetic analyzer (to be discussed in Section 7 below), nevertheless the somesthetic analyzer also plays a significant role in that function, as substantiated by the appropriate neuropathological evidence. The point is that pronunciation of each phoneme is determined not only by the kinesthesis of particular movements of the lips, tongue, and soft palate but also by postures of these parts of the mouth. These oral postures, although highly complex and refined, form unitary perceptions characteristic for each phoneme. Those perceptions which are characteristic for our mother tongue and which we learned in childhood are of course very stable, whereas those we have acquired later when learning foreign languages are much less perfect and stabilized.

The gnostic field in which the corresponding gnostic units are formed is localized in the parietal operculum of the dominant hemisphere behind the projective somesthetic area for the mouth. Lesions in this field produce distinct and easily recognizable symptoms which consist in the failure to take a correct oral posture for producing a given sound. In consequence, the words pronounced by the patient are strongly distorted and usually unintelligible. The patient is wholly aware of his deficit, because his auditory feedback gives him clear information about his distorted speech. He tries to correct himself by pronouncing the same word many times in different ways, but all his attempts are in vain.

This syndrome has been studied in great detail by Luria.[22] Accordingly, we shall refer to it as *somesthetic* or *Luria aphasia,* as the counterpart to kinesthetic or *Broca aphasia,* produced by lesions in the analogous area of the kinesthetic analyzer (see Section 8, below). However, the proper term for this kind of disorder is *oral agnosia,* because it affects the gnostic units representing postures of the oral cavity. In agreement with this view is the fact that, as was convincingly shown by Luria, lesions in the parietal operculum affect not only oral postures involved in speech but also all other oral postures, such as various positions of the tongue, lips, or cheeks.

All somesthetic gnostic fields except the gustatory, are localized in the parietal lobe caudally to the postcentral gyrus (areas 5 and 7). They preserve in principle the somatotopic organization characteristic for the projective area. Accordingly, the gnostic oral field (S-Or) is situated in the operculum parietale, the somatognostic fields (S-L) are probably distributed along the corresponding projective fields, and the textural and stereognostic fields (S-T and S-MO) are localized on the dorsolateral aspect of the parietal cortex as the caudal extension of the somesthetic hand area. As mentioned above, the S-MO field is probably adjacent to the V-MO field. The gustatory gnostic field is situated below the projective mouth somesthetic area in the upper part of the insula.

As far as the laterality of the somesthetic gnosis is concerned, it is well known that oral somesthesis is represented in the dominant hemisphere, and the somatognosis of particular limbs is represented in the corresponding contralateral fields. Other categories of somatognosis are localized either in one hemisphere or in both.

7. Central organization of the kinesthetic analyzer (K)

While we were speaking of exteroceptive and joint-proprioceptive perceptions we were on the firm ground of basic facts and ideas, because the afferent systems involved are fairly well known and the principles of transmitting the messages in consecutive levels of each system are fairly well understood. The stimulus-patterns, whether provided by the external world or originating in the postures of the limbs, can be manipulated from outside the body, and the task of the nervous system is to elaborate and utilize them in the proper way.

Quite different is the situation in respect to *kinesthesis*, the afferent system which sends information to the higher nervous centers not about those events which have happened outside or inside the body but about those which are produced by the central nervous system itself— that is, active movements. This is why the kinesthesis is often referred to as sensory feedback, because it informs the central nervous system of the results of its own activity.

The first fundamental problem which arises is whether kinesthetic gnosis exists as a separate afferent system or whether the information about movements reaches the cerebral cortex through other afferent channels, primarily through joint proprioception. Although nineteenth-century physiologists and psychologists had no doubt about the separate existence of the sense of position, the sense of movement, and the sense of effort,[23] this distinction somehow became blurred in our own times. We now find a number of authoritative opinions that the sensations of movement are transmitted through the joint-proprioceptive system and that the muscular receptors serve only for the reflex coordination of motor acts by the spino-cerebellar mechanisms. These opinions seem to be based on data obtained from experiments showing that the joint receptors do send messages to the cortex concerning the changes in the postures of limbs and that passive movements of joints in opposite directions give rise to the opposite effects in reciprocally related neurons.[24] However, we should notice that these data are nothing else but the application of the general principles of adaptation and reciprocity of afferent units, which principles operate in all other afferent systems. In fact, it is obvious that the subject pays attention to the changes of the postures of the limbs induced either passively or by active movements rather than to their steady states, and also that he perceives changes of posture in the opposite direction in a different manner. Therefore, to conclude that these messages should constitute the source of information about active movements seems to me entirely unwarranted.

In our further discussion we shall try to show that this concept is incorrect and that the kinesthetic afferent system originating from muscular and tendon receptors is the system informing the cerebral cortex of the movements performed by the organism. In short, we shall propose here a theory of kinesthetic gnosis which will be further developed in the succeeding chapters and which will account for the origin of skilled movements and their performance.

First, let us realize clearly that the kinesthetic afferent system differs significantly from the other afferent systems, not only because of its feedback role with respect to the motor activity of the organism but even more because it involves the distinct ways of transmitting the messages obtained from the peripheral receptive organs.

As we saw in the preceding sections, in all other analyzers physical or chemical events impinging upon the receptors are "encoded" in the form of nerve impulses and as such transmitted to the higher levels of the given analyzer. The role of each level is to "reshuffle" elementary messages and to integrate them into various more complex patterns. In other words, what the higher levels of afferent systems do is to select from the innumerable elements of the given stimulus-objects only those elements which when integrated provide cues for particular activities of the organism.

In the kinesthetic analyzer, something quite different happens. Here the receptors provide information only about the *tensions* of muscles, whereas the cerebral cortex is mainly interested in their *movements*. In consequence, a specific mechanism had to be developed—that of *inferring* the kind of the performed movements from the tensions recorded by particular muscular receptors.

It is well known that the muscle receptors are divided into two types: one disposed in parallel with the contractile elements (spindles), and the other disposed in series with them (tendon organs) (Figure III-4). In the consequence of this arrangement various functional states of a muscle are accompanied by appropriate functional states of each of these types of receptors. Thus passive stretching of the muscle produces acceleration of the discharge in both types of receptors proportional to the strength of tension; pure isometric contraction of the muscle produces acceleration of the discharge of tendon organs and deceleration of the discharge of spindles; contraction against the constant resistance (for instance, when lifting a weight) produces also a deceleration of the spindle discharge with the tendon organ activity unchanged, and so on. In this way each type of muscular contraction (isometric, isotonic, under different resistances, under changing resistances, and so on) is followed by a particular combination of functional states of spindles and tendon organs. To generalize, there is a strict correspondence between the behavior of muscular receptors on

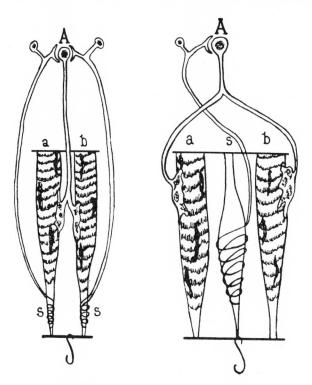

Fig. III-4

Left: A diagram showing the mechanical conditions obtaining when muscle end-organs (s) are disposed "in series" with the tension-supporting elements. In these circumstances tension, whether active or passive, will affect the end-organs indiscriminately. a and b, skeletal muscle fibers; A, anterior horn cell.

Right: A diagram showing the mechanical conditions obtaining when a muscle end-organ is arranged "in parallel" with the tension-supporting elements. a and b, skeletal muscle fibers; s, afferent end-organ associated with a fiber running parallel with (a) and (b) (an intrafusal fiber); A, anterior horn cell.

(J. F. Fulton and J. Pi-suner, in *Amer. J. Physiol.* 83 [1928]: 554–62.)

the one hand and the strength and character of muscular contractions on the other.

In keeping with this specific character of the kinesthetic analyzer, we shall expect it to be composed of two consecutive segments: one of which *translates* the language of muscular and tendon stretch receptors into the language of muscular contractions, the other *integrates* proprioception of elementary contractions into proprioception of complex movements. This is exactly how the kinesthetic analyzer is built. The messages from stretch receptors traveling via the spino-cerebellar pathways reach the cerebellar cortex; hence the other messages traveling via the cerebellar nuclei and the thalamus reach the "motor" cortex. It is reasonable to suggest that this translation mechanism is situated in the cerebellar cortex—in other words, messages from the periphery enter the cerebellum as those telling about the muscular tensions, but leave that organ as those representing muscular contractions. In this way we can look upon the cerebellar cortex as a true *receptive surface* for elementary movements where the "receptors" are represented by granule cells, whereas the role of ganglion cells, integrating the messages arriving from the periphery and delivering them to the brain, is played by Purkinje cells.

Adopting this point of view, we may see immediately that the kinesthetic analyzer—that is, the afferent system whose peripheral end is represented by the cerebellar cortex—does not differ in its anatomical organization from other afferent systems and in particular from the somesthetic analyzer. In fact, the messages sent by the Purkinje cells arrive in the cerebellar nuclei, which correspond to the Goll and Burdach nuclei of the somesthetic system. From these relay stations the somesthetic and kinesthetic messages run to the two adjacent ventrobasal nuclei of the thalamus—namely, the *nucleus ventralis posterolateralis* and the *nucleus ventralis lateralis*—and these nuclei transmit the relevant information to the adjacent areas of the projective cortex: the somesthetic area in the postcentral gyrus and the kinesthetic area in the precentral gyrus. The latter area is a nearly perfect mirror image of the former one, since the representations of somesthesis and kinesthesis of particular parts of the body lie opposite each other on the two banks of the central sulcus.

As was explained in the preceding section, just behind the projective somesthetic area is the gnostic somesthetic area (5 and 7), which is concerned with the perceptions of complex stimulus-patterns whose elements are represented in the projective area. Analogously, just *in front* of the kinesthetic projective area is the kinesthetic gnostic area (called premotor area, or area 6), which is concerned with perceptions of complex movements whose elements are represented in the "motor" projective area. The block diagram of both systems is presented in Figure III-5.*

The important point which emerges from this discussion is that the kinesthetic system, in contradistinction to the joint-somesthetic system, is not only concerned with the evaluation of the displacement of the limb but also with the effort of muscles, independently of whether or

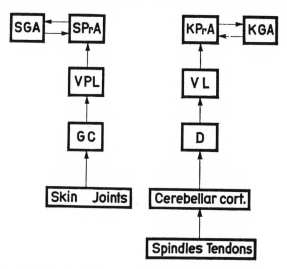

FIG. III-5. BLOCK MODELS OF SOMESTHETIC AND KINESTHETIC
AFFERENT SYSTEMS (SIMPLIFIED)

Left, somesthetic afferent system: GC, Goll and Burdach nuclei; VPL, ventral postero-lateral thalamic nucleus; SPrA, somesthetic projective area; SGA, somesthetic gnostic area.

Right, kinesthetic afferent system: D, dentate cerebellar nucleus; VL, nucleus ventralis lateralis thalami; KPrA, kinesthetic projective area; KGA, kinesthetic gnostic area (nucleus ruber is omitted for the sake of simplicity).

Note the clear symmetry between the two systems except for the peripheral segment of the kinesthetic afferent system.

not the displacement took place. In fact, many of our "movements" are purely isometric—as, for instance, the tonic sustaining of a heavy object—and here the evaluation of the effort put into this function and the precise adjustment of this effort to the weight of the object are exclusively the problems of kinesthesis.

* In recent times it has been found that there is a direct projection of muscle afferents to the sensorimotor cortex through the posterior funiculi and the ventral posterolateral thalamic nucleus (O. Oscarson and I. Rosén, Short-latency projections to the cat's cerebral cortex from skin and muscle afferents in the contralateral forelimb, *J. Physiol.*, 182 (1966): 164–84). It was hypothesized that these very afferent pathways "are used in the integration of movements elicited from the cortex." According to our concept the direct pathways running from the muscular stretch receptors to the cerebral cortex,

Since non-isometric motor acts are perceived by information provided by both joint receptors and muscle receptors, it follows that somesthetic and kinesthetic proprioception can partly substitute for each other and share the responsibility for the accurate performance of skillful movements. Depending on the character of these movements, either articular somesthesis or kinesthesis may play a major role: if the task requires a precise and continuous posture of the limbs, independently of the muscular effort—as for instance, when we hold a parcel in our hands—then of course articular proprioception is indispensable. (I knew, for instance, a patient in whom the very first symptom of a parietal tumor consisted in dropping parcels she was carrying in her affected hand.) On the other hand, if the task requires a precise measuring of effort—for instance, when we must carefully adjust two frail objects so as not to break them—then the kinesthetic sensations play a dominant role.

In Table III-1 we present various examples of situations in which either somesthetic or kinesthetic proprioception provides a dominant feedback.

TABLE III-1

Type of Task	Involvement of Somesthesis and/or Kinesthesis		
Passive displacement of limb	+		−
Active displacement of limb	+	or	+
Task requiring exact posture of limb	+		−
Task requiring exact effort	−		+
Continuous posture of limb without muscular effort	+		−
Continuous posture of limb requiring effort	+	and	+
Quick, purposeful movement	+	and	+

If our hypothesis of the functional organization of the kinesthetic afferent system is correct, we should expect that removing the cerebellum, or severing the pathways connecting this organ with the cortex would lead to the total loss of the kinesthetic sensations with total preservation of the somesthetic ones. As shown by clinical observations and experiments on animals, this is indeed true: the major cerebellar symptoms, such as the dysmetria which can take a form of either hypermetry or hypometry, the dynamic tremor manifested chiefly at the termination of purposeful movements, adiadochokinesis, and

---

bypassing the cerebellum, simply convey the information about the *tensions* of the muscles concerned exactly in the same way as the pathways running from the joint receptors convey the information about the *postures* of the limbs. Both these sources of information are certainly most useful for the performance of skillful movements and, even more, for the evaluation of their end-effects. We do not think, however, that they can play any *direct* role in the patterning of these movements, since this function is fulfilled by the kinesthetic analyzer in the strict sense of the word, and mediated by the cerebellum.

others, can be easily understood as due to the lack of kinesthetic feedback of the performed movements. Incidentally, this is why symptoms produced by cerebellar lesions are often referred to as cerebellar *ataxia*, although it is always stressed that they radically differ from ataxias produced by injuries in the somesthetic afferent system.

The mechanism of the formation of gnostic units within the kinesthetic gnostic fields is exactly the same as that in other analyzers. In a newborn infant who is not in sleep, the motor behavioral system is almost permanently aroused under the influence of various drives, such as curiosity (in respect to its own body and environment), fear, or hunger. Chaotic movements performed by the child send messages to the kinesthetic system, and some particular configurations of these which are found to be successful (see Chapter IX) establish gnostic units in the particular kinesthetic fields. In this way some simple kinesthetic patterns are acquired, such as putting the hand or fingers into the mouth, flexing and extending the arms and legs, or grasping small objects. Gradually these patterns are integrated into more complex ones, when the child learns to manipulate his own postures and available objects. The further acquisition of the kinesthetic gnosis comes at a later age, when a great number of skillful movements are trained, and thus more and more units are established in the particular kinesthetic gnostic fields representing and integrating all appropriate motor patterns.

As we remember from the description of other afferent systems, these are furnished with two powerful auxiliary mechanisms whose aim is to secure the best perception of the stimulus-objects impinging upon the corresponding receptive surfaces. One of these mechanisms is concerned with mobilizing the particular analyzers which may be useful for the given activity of the organism by general arousal produced by the corresponding drive. This is the basis of what we have called searching reflexes. The other mechanism is concerned with concentrating upon particular stimulus-objects which are relevant for the given activity by adjusting the receptors and higher afferent centers for their best reception. This is what we have called the targeting reflex.

Exactly the same two mechanisms exist also in kinesthesis, and the efferent system by which they operate is the γ system. In the last two decades it has become known that the role of the γ system—that is, the efferent pathways innervating the intrafusal muscles—is to sensitize spindle receptors and in this way to increase the precision of information provided by them to the cerebellum.[25] It is further known that the γ system may be activated in two ways: either as the effect of general arousal produced by drives—in that case all the γ motoneurons are activated through the reticulo-spinal pathways—or as the effect of local activation of those γ motoneurons which supply muscles contracted in the given motor act through cortico-spinal, or cortico-rubro-spinal pathways. Whereas the first mechanism prepares the organism for any muscular activity, the second one prepares it for a particular motor act and as such has all the attributes of the kinesthetic targeting reflex. In fact, the subjective side of this mechanism consists in paying attention to the limb to be moved, the act accompanying both the intention of the movement and its accomplishment.

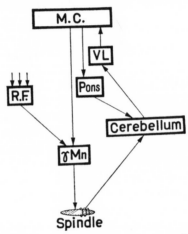

FIG. III-6. A BLOCK MODEL OF THE CENTRAL CONTROL OF KINESTHETIC FEEDBACK

R.F., reticular formation; γ Mn, gamma motoneuron; VL, ventro-lateral thalamic nucleus; M.C., motor (kinesthetic) cortex.

Note that gamma motoneurons are under the influence of the reticular formation ("searching reflex") and the motor cortex ("targeting reflex") and that the motor cortex exerts its influence both upon spindles and upon the cerebellum.

However, it should be realized that the γ efferent mechanism is probably not the only mechanism of kinesthetic targeting reflexes. We should remember that the proper kinesthetic receptive surface representing movements is in the cerebellar cortex. Therefore we have good reasons to assume that the projective kinesthetic area in the cerebral cortex exerts its controlling influence upon this "receptive surface," just as other projective areas do so in respect to other receptive surfaces (cf. Chapter I, Section 5). This is effectuated by cortico-cerebellar pathways running either via *pons*, or via *nucleus ruber*, or via both.

The block model of the central control of kinesthetic perceptions, both in "preparatory" activity (through reticulo-spinal pathways) and "consummatory" activity (through cortico-spinal and cortico-cerebellar pathways), is represented in Figure III-6.

To end this section, it should be noted that the efferent output just described is of course not the only output originating in the kinesthetic projective area. The most powerful and admittedly the most important descending pathways are those which link the cerebral cortex, directly or indirectly, not with γ motoneurons but with α motoneurons and which thus control the motor activity of the organism. The existence of these descending pathways caused the kinesthetic aspect of the precentral cortical area to be cast into shadow and its "motor" aspect to gain the main attention of scientists. The role of this efferent system in motor behavior will be discussed in the next chapter.

8. Categories of kinesthetic unitary perceptions

As emphasized in the last section, the kinesthetic perceptions, being generated by active movements and not produced by external agents, cannot be tested in the same manner as exteroceptive perceptions. Therefore, we must find another way to deal with kinesthetic gnosis, utilizing for this purpose not the peripheral channels but, rather, the associative channels to bring about the activation of the corresponding units. As will be explained in the next chapter, the evidence for the existence of kinesthetic gnostic units is provided by the ability to perform movements whose elements are integrated in those units. In consequence, undertaking the task of categorization of the kinesthetic gnosis, we shall not resort to the method of recognition, as we did in the previous sections, but to the method of proving whether a given integrated movement can be performed. The ability to perform integrated movements constituting unitary behavioral acts is called *praxis*.

According to this criterion, we can specify the following most important categories of kinesthetic gnosis.

(1) The kinesthetic hand gnosis responsible for the performance of particular skillful movements of the hand (hand praxis, K-H).

(2) The kinesthetic body gnosis responsible for various patterns of particular skillful movements of the body and legs (body praxis, K-B).

(3) The kinesthetic mouth gnosis responsible for the performance of skillful movements of the mouth, used particularly in speech (mouth speech praxis, K-W).

(4) The kinesthetic gnosis of spatial relations responsible for the appreciation of distances and directions on the basis of locomotor behavior (K-Sp).

Let us discuss each of these categories of kinesthetic gnosis in succession.

(1) *The kinesthetic gnosis of the hand and fingers* (K-H). This gnosis, highly developed in primates, belongs to those types of gnosis of which we are not aware because we do not notice the multitude of

habitual unitary motor acts we routinely perform in our everyday practice. Therefore, let us specify some typical unitary behavioral acts performed under the guidance of corresponding kinesthetic units in the sequence of their occurrence during the day.

Activities performed during washing: soaping various parts of the body (each part is soaped in a particular way), manipulating with the sponge, drying oneself with the towel (again note that drying each part of the body requires different movements).

Particular phases of dressing.

Manipulations during the consumption of food: cutting bread, cutting meat on the plate, pouring coffee into the cup, mixing sugar in it, taking food by spoon or fork, and so on.

Manipulating a key in a lock, cleaning eyeglasses, lighting a match, lighting a cigarette, and so on.

Moreover, there are many different unitary behavioral acts connected with every profession. Quite different is the repertory of these acts performed by a farmer, a carpenter, a locksmith, a barber, a tailor, a surgeon, a general practitioner of medicine, a pianist, a violinist. As a matter of fact, a large part of the training for any profession consists in learning not only *what* to do in the given circumstances but also *how* to do it; and a good practice, sometimes requiring a long period of training, consists in nothing but establishing many kinesthetic units necessary for a given task.

A special type of praxis is involved in writing (graphia), where particular letters and their most common sequences (our own signature included) make up corresponding gnostic units.

The unitary character of particular motor acts is evidenced by their smooth and routine course, by lack of realization of elements of which they are composed (without special analysis), and by strong antagonism between different acts. It is hardly possible to perform at the same time two different behavioral acts, not only with one hand (which may be technically impossible), but each with a different hand. I am, for instance, unable to shave with my right hand and at the same time to lather my face with the left, although each of these activities in quick succession can be easily performed.

It is generally agreed that the kinesthetic gnostic area responsible for hand praxis is in front of the motor (projective) area for hand in the dorsal lateral part of area 6 of the dominant hemisphere. Lesions in this region produce apractic syndrome usually for both hands without any signs of paresis. It is claimed that graphia has its own separate gnostic field, since its impairment (agraphia) occurs independently of other apractic symptoms. The apractic syndrome in monkeys after ablations of area 6 was described in the classic work of Jacobsen.[26] This syndrome consisted in the inability to perform specific skillful hand movements learned before the operation.

(2) *The kinesthetic body gnosis* (K-B). This type of gnosis is of course more poorly developed than that of the hand, because in everyday life the complex motor acts of the body are not learned. In many persons sitting down, getting up, lying down, turning from one side to another in a lying position are nearly all the performances depending on bodily kinesthesis. Quite different, however, is the situation in persons specially trained in particular bodily skills; gymnastics, acrobatics, football playing, dancing, swimming, and the like. In each of these skills particular complex motor coordinations of the body and limbs are represented in the corresponding gnostic units. According to the general topography of the kinesthetic gnostic area, it is to be expected that the body gnostic field is situated in the dorsal and dorsomedial surface of the cortex in front of the corresponding "motor" representations for the body and legs.

(3) *The kinesthetic gnosis involved in speech* (K-W). In the preceding section it was indicated that somesthetic oral perceptions, both articular and tactile, play an important role in speech, because the proper setting of the oral cavity is indispensable for the correct pronunciation of phonemes. The role of somesthetic gnostic field, however, is here only auxiliary, because the proper speech units are situated in a special gnostic field belonging to the kinesthetic analyzer. This is to be expected, because pronunciation of words is a complex muscular activity, and therefore the delicate coordination of the elementary movements of tongue, lips, soft palate, and jaws taking part in it makes speech possible. The so-called speech motor area, which we consider the *kinesthetic gnostic speech field*, was discovered a hundred years ago by Broca by a postmortem examination of two clinical cases of what was later called "motor aphasia" or "aphasia of Broca." According to the results of this examination, the cortical region responsible for speech function was found to be situated in the frontal operculum of the dominant hemisphere. This localization of the "speech area" seems to be understandable in view of the fact that it is in the vicinity of the kinesthetic projective area of mouth.

The formation of speech in children occurs in a way similar to that described above for the formation of skilled movements. When a child is about nine months old, it begins to babble—to utter some chaotic sounds as a manifestation of the arousal of the motor behavioral system. Probably at that time some primitive type of kinesthetic mouth gnosis is formed, represented either in the oral motor projective area itself or in that part of the frontal opercular region which separates the projective area from the proper speech area.

Then, owing to the existence of the connections linking the acoustic gnostic area with the kinesthetic gnostic area (to be discussed in Chapter V), the child learns to repeat sounds he hears and in this way articulate speech is developed. Since the child hears *words* which form gnostic units in the audioverbal field, the same thing occurs in the word-kinesthetic field, where the kinesthetic perceptions of spoken words become represented by particular gnostic units.

We have a large body of psychological and neurological evidence that words and short phrases are in fact represented by word-kinesthetic units. First, pronounced words form unitary events and cannot be resolved into their elements. Only much later, when the child learns to read and to write in the Indo-European languages, does he become acquainted with the letters as separate gnostic events and learns to decompose the words into them.

Even more convincing are the observations made on patients suffering from word-kinesthetic agnosia ("motor aphasia") due to an injury in the so-called motor speech area. If the deficit is partial and is not contaminated by anarthria (see below), the patient's speech is very scanty (telegraphic), sometimes even reduced to only a few words, but those words he *has* preserved are pronounced correctly. Other words cannot be pronounced at all, or are uttered rarely, even if the patient hears them and tries to repeat them.

The analysis of speech impairment in patients suffering from word-kinesthetic agnosia shows that this impairment strictly follows the principle of redundancy discussed in the preceding chapter. In fact, if a patient has preserved only a few words, they are those which were acquired in early life, or those which have been in permanent usage, or those which are strongly loaded emotionally. Similarly, if a patient speaks several languages, the words of his native language are usually better preserved than those of the languages acquired later. Incidentally, it should be noted that simple phonemes or the names of letters do not usually belong to the repertory of words preserved in an aphasic patient, although from the "technical" point of view they seem to be the most easily pronounced.

The principle of redundancy is clearly manifested not only in word-kinesthetic agnosia but also in the decreasing ability with age to acquire new words. Whereas in childhood the acquisition of new words is instantaneous and occurs as one-trial learning, it later becomes less and less easy, and in old age it may be practically impossible. Some old persons cannot memorize any new name, unless it can be decomposed into words which are already in the subject's verbal repertory.

Word-kinesthetic agnosia should be clearly distinguished from a kindred disorder, by which it is sometimes contaminated—anarthria. In this disorder a patient is able to speak fluently, but each phoneme is uttered indistinctly and is sometimes totally unintelligible. Anarthria is said to be caused by injury of the projective area representing the mouth movements or its descending pathways. The question may be raised as to whether anarthric symptoms are also due to a form of kinesthetic mouth agnosia concerning some primitive laryngo-oral coordinations that are the prerequisite of articulate speech.

Another form of the mouth gnosis is that involved in kinesthetic patterns of melodies (K-M). It is particularly well developed in singers and is of course closely connected with the corresponding auditory gnosis (A-M). There is no doubt that the kinesthetic melody field is completely separated from the word-kinesthetic field, since in most cases a complete "motor aphasia" is accompanied by no deficit in the capacity to reproduce melodies. It is very probable that the modulations of voice occurring in normal speech are represented in the same gnostic field as that subserving singing. In fact, in subjects suffering from "motor aphasia" the intonation of speech is usually preserved, and is even exaggerated, since the patient tries in this way to compensate for his deficit in verbalization.

According to what we know about the distribution of functions between the dominant and non-dominant hemisphere, it may be supposed that the kinesthetic melody field is localized in the non-dominant hemisphere or in both hemispheres.

(4) *Kinesthetic gnosis of spatial relations* (K-Sp). In previous sections we briefly discussed the visuo-spatial gnosis (V-Sp) and the vestibulo-spatial gnosis (La) based on the function of visual and vestibular analyzers respectively. It may, however, be easily imagined that these two gnostic categories do not exhaust our gnosis of spatial relations of the external world. In fact, if we were allowed to be only passive observers of the surroundings without any possibility of moving in it (as it is with monkeys immobilized in special seats for chronic neurophysiological experiments), our knowledge of the external world would be very limited. This is because the distances and directions of various objects of our surroundings in respect to our body are estimated mainly by our locomotor behavior. As will be discussed in detail in Chapter V, the kinesthetic gnosis of this behavior is in a continuous interplay with the visuo-spatial and vestibular gnosis concerning our position in the surrounding world. Just as before performing a known skilled hand movement we have a program based on our previous experience represented in our corresponding hand-kinesthetic units, so before moving from one known place to another we have an analogous program in our locomotor kinesthetic units. Similarly, just as our skillful motor acts are usually terminated by the visual or tactile perceptions of their expected results, so the locomotor acts are

terminated by visual perceptions of the new place we intended to reach.

It is not easy to conceive what are the unitary perceptions of our locomotor kinesthetic gnosis, but the following comments may be helpful in understanding their nature.

First, it is clear that the locomotor kinesthetic gnosis is not concerned with the technicalities of the movements involved in locomotion, for instance, with the number of steps needed to cover a certain distance, the type of motion utilized to cover it (walking or running), and so on. In experiments with rats this thesis is documented by the fact that when a given maze is mastered, the rat traverses it in many ways, depending on the possibilities: for example, by running, creeping, or swimming.[26a] In other words, the gnosis of locomotor acts has an *abstract* character representing the very essence of active moving in space but not the method of doing so.

Second, it seems that, similar to the character of gnostic units in other gnostic fields, the spatio-kinesthetic units represent some short segments of our locomotor behavior, which nevertheless have an integrated and complete character. To give a simple example, my own locomotor kinesthetic units in respect to my apartment represent moving from one room to another, to particular parts of each room, going out to the staircase, and so on. In some behavioral acts only single sets of units intervene, as in such actions as going to bed, going to the cupboard for food; in others we have to do with the sequences of activation of various sets of units, as when we go for a walk in familiar surroundings.

Third, it is clear that the spatial-kinesthetic gnosis can to a large extent be compensated for by the visual gnosis, especially in respect to unitary locomotor acts. For instance, when I move in a well-known place (for example, my apartment), the lack of the kinesthetic program can be easily compensated for by the visual cues that are the landmarks in my itinerary to the goal and the visual perception of the goal itself. Therefore, it seems that the effects of lesions in the prefrontal areas in animals and man (see below), which appear to be completely compensated for, may prove to become evident in the absence of visual cues. Unfortunately, we have only sparse documentation of this important inference.

Since the ordinary behavior of human beings, both normal and with frontal lesions, does not provide a clear picture of the kinesthetic-spatial gnosis, because of the great role of visual gnosis which may substitute it, we must resort to experiments with animals for more precise information on this matter.

Let us describe in some detail a series of experiments on rats by Dabrowska which are particularly illustrative in this respect.[27]

The experiments were performed on rats under food reinforcement in a four-unit-quadruple-choice apparatus represented in Figure III-7. After preliminary training in which all doors were open, the animals were trained to follow a particular itinerary, since in each unit only one door was unlocked. When this task has been mastered and the rats had made six errorless runs, the itinerary was changed and the rats were trained again until they made six errorless runs. The series were repeated many times. It turned out that the rats solved the problem faster and faster, and eventually only two or three runs were needed for an errorless performance (Figure III-8). It was clear that the rats had gradually acquired the capacity of integrating the complex task into a unitary zigzag-like motor act which could be mastered after a few presentations of the kinesthetic stimulus-pattern. This conclusion was strongly supported by the fact that if in some of the

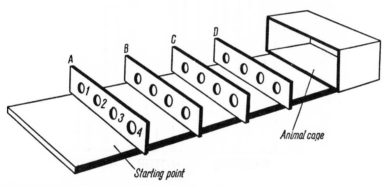

Fig. III-7. Four-Unit-Quadruple-Choice Apparatus

A, B, C, D—partitions; 1, 2, 3, 4—doors. (J. Dąbrowska, in *Acta Biol. Exper.*, 23 [1963]: 11–24.

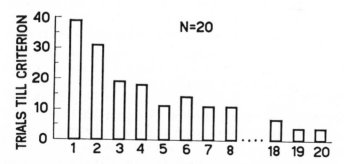

Fig. III-8. The Increasing Rate of Learning of Succeeding Tasks in Four-Unit-Quadruple-Choice Apparatus

Abscissae, serial numbers of succeeding tasks, ordinates, trials till criterion. (After J. Dąbrowska, in *Acta Biol. Exper.*, 19 [1959]: 105–21.)

consecutive reversals only one door (even the last one) was changed, while the others remained the same, the rats nevertheless committed errors in unchanged units too, as though the whole pattern of the run had been altered.

Quite different was the performance of rats which before training were subjected to bilateral prefrontal lesions. (Figure III-9). Whereas the first training was similar to that of the normal animals, it appeared that in the next reversal trainings the prefrontal rats did not improve, each of the succeeding tasks being mastered at the same rate as the first one. The conclusion could be reached that the prefrontal rats were not capable of integrating their performance into a unitary

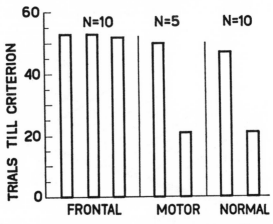

Fig. III-9. Failure of Prefrontal Rats to Increase Their Rate of Learning in Succeeding Tasks in Four-Unit-Quadruple-Choice Apparatus

(Dąbrowska's experiments.)

act and that they had to learn the proper way in each unit separately. This conclusion is supported by the curious fact that if in the reversal training only a door in the last unit was changed, the prefrontals were superior to the normals. Whereas the normal rats learned the whole task anew, committing errors in unchanged units too, the reversal training in the prefrontals was limited only to the last unit.

No less informative were the experiments by Łukaszewska[28] in which the reverse T maze presented in Figure III-10 was used. The rats were taught to retrieve a piece of food at the end of the stem of the maze and then immediately to return to the arm from which they started. Five trials were given each day, and the place of the starting cage was changed on the third trial of each experimental session; the following session began with the cage at the place where it was at the end of the preceding session.

Five groups of rats were run: normal rats, normal but blinded rats, normal rats trained in the maze in which one arm was white and another one black, rats with prefrontal lesions, and blinded rats with prefrontal lesions.

The results of these experiments, presented in Figure III-11, are quite clear. First, it was established that additional visual cues disturbed the correct return reaction, increasing the tendency to approach that arm from which the animal started in the preceding trial; on the contrary, blinding the animals improved their performance. This shows that the return reaction in rats is based on the kinesthetic gnosis, whereas learning to return along the previously used pathway is based chiefly on the visual gnosis. Second, in keeping with this, it was found that prefrontal lesions which destroyed the spatial-kinesthetic gnosis

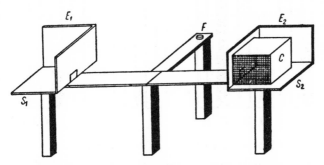

FIG. III-10. REVERSE T-MAZE USED FOR STUDYING RETURN RESPONSES

S_1, S_2, starting platforms; E_1, E_2, screens; C, starting cage; F, bowl with cake. (I. Łukaszewska, in *Acta Biol. Exper.*, 23 [1963]: 249–56.)

strongly impaired the return reaction, this impairment being again stronger in seeing rats than in blinded ones.

Another test of the effect of prefrontal lesions on spatial-kinesthetic gnosis in animals is that involving delayed responses. It will be discussed in Chapter XII devoted to the problems of recent memory.

Now the problem of prime importance arises as to whether the prefrontal symptoms encountered in humans can be attributed to the same defect as that described in animals.

There is no doubt that some of the prefrontal symptoms are to a great extent similar to, if not identical with, those described above in animals. The impairment of orientation in space is often observed after extensive prefrontal lesions. It was also emphasized that this impairment is particularly clear in darkness.[29]

In a recent experimental work it has been shown that prefrontal patients, both with and without vision, are particularly deficient in maze learning[30]—a symptom very similar to that found in rats in the experiments reported above. It is worthwhile to notice that the impairment in orientation in space is much more pronounced after right prefrontal lesions than after left ones. This is in good agreement with the fact that orientation in space, both visual and kinesthetic, does not need much verbalization.

It seems, however, that the defect of programing motor acts displayed by patients with prefrontal lesions does not apply only to spatio-kinesthetic tasks. As was shown by Luria,[31] lesions sustained in

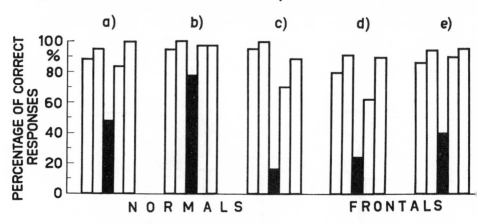

Fig. III-11. Return Responses in Various Groups of Rats

Each five-column block represents the average responses of all sessions in all animals of a given group (about 100 sessions). In each session in the first two trials the cage was in the same place as in the last three trials in the preceding session. In the third trial (black column) the place of the cage was changed. The lower the black column, the greater the tendency to repeat the return response performed in the preceding trials.

a, normals; b, normals but blind; c, normals in black-white T-maze; d, prefrontals; e, prefrontals but blind.

Note that visual cues and/or prefrontal lesions increase the tendency to repeat the previous return run and thus hamper the correct return response.

the left prefrontal area produce an impairment of transformation of verbal instructions into motor acts. For instance, if patients are required to react by a particular movement to particular stimuli according to a verbal instruction, they fail to do so, although they are able correctly to repeat the instruction. Only if the task is learned by way of normal instrumental training, do they easily master it, unless it requires a permanent kinesthetic programing.*

* This applies, for instance, to such a task as reacting by prolonged bulb pressing to a short signal, and by short bulb pressing to a long signal. Since this task requires a permanent programing of movement in order to oppose the natural tendency of contrary responding, prefrontal patients dramatically fail in their performance, although they perfectly understand the given task (cf. M. Maruszewski—see Luria [31]).

Another test revealing the impairment of motor programing was used by Brenda Milner.[32] Subjects were required to sort cards according to definite successive instructions. Prefrontal patients performed this test with great difficulty, tending to persevere in the principle used in the preceding sorting in spite of a change of instruction. The author noticed that there is no correlation between performance in the sorting test and that in the maze test, the former being impaired after lesions of the left prefrontal area, the latter, after lesions of the right. This would show that programing of movements based on speech depends mainly on the left prefrontal area.

Finally, according to recent data obtained by our group,[33] patients with left (but not right) prefrontal lesions have great difficulties in performing arithmetic operations involving keeping in mind several principles to be applied at different times.

In summary, it seems that in the prefrontal area of the cerebral cortex some specific gnostic fields are situated which have to do with higher forms of the organization of behavior in the absence of other cues dictating the appropriate motor responses. These forms fall into at least two categories. The first category is concerned with programing spatio-kinesthetic motor acts involved in our locomotor behavior. It is well represented not only in humans (in the non-dominant hemisphere) but also in nomadic animals living in a complex terrain. The second category, characteristic mostly of humans, is concerned with organization of higher forms of behavior of non-spatial but manipulatory character. It is represented in the dominant hemisphere, being probably closely connected with speech.

9. Perceptions of emotional states

As indicated in Chapter I, the emotive part of the brain controlling the drive and antidrive reflexes possesses its own afferent system composed of several levels situated in various segments of the neural axis. For the sake of simplicity we are interested here in two of them: the hypothalamus, and the limbic brain. Whereas the exit units of the former subserve the innate drive and antidrive reflexes, the limbic brain plays chiefly the associative role, receiving connections from, and transmitting connections to, the gnostic fields of other analyzers.

The emotive system receives its afferent input from two main sources: from receptors of various modalities belonging to other analyzers and reaching that system probably through the reticular formation, and from specific intracentral chemoreceptors situated in dendritic arborizations of hypothalamic neurons. To the first category belong painful stimuli, loud noises producing fear, pleasant or unpleasant odors, tastes of various nutritive substances and so on. To the second category belong humoral factors regulating the hunger drive or sexual drive.

Particular sets of perceptive units of the emotive brain represent particular emotional states, such as being hungry, satiated, curious, sleepy, afraid, angry, sad. Each drive and antidrive is thought to have its own set of perceptive units remaining in antagonistic or agonistic relations with other sets of units of the emotive analyzer. The mutual relations between various drives and antidrives were discussed in Chapter I, Section 12.

From the psychological point of view, the experience of each emotion or drive has all the attributes of unitary perception. In fact, it is always experienced as a unitary mental event—is momentarily recognizable and indecomposable. Since perceptive units of the highest level of the emotive system form powerful associations with most of the gnostic fields (to be described in Chapter V), the particular emotions and moods are rarely experienced as isolated emotive states without any cognitive component. Although the experience of pure fear, or pure anger, or pure sorrow are certainly familiar to everyone ("I have quite forgotten what I am worried about" said a nervous lady in a well-known Polish novel), nevertheless we are usually afraid *of* something, angry *at* someone, sorry *because of* something, and so on.

The problem of localization of particular sets of emotive units is still poorly understood. Whereas some studies stress the discrete localization of particular sets of units (cf. the different localizations of fear units and anger units in the amygdala),[34] others claim that they cannot be topographically separated. It may be assumed that the perceptive units of particular emotions *can* be partly intermixed, and therefore that their specificity may be detected by pharmacological and biochemical methods rather than by neurosurgery.*

It should be emphasized that, according to ample clinical and experimental evidence, the orbital areas of the prefrontal region in primates must be considered a part of the emotive brain. On the one hand, these areas control the antidrive reflexes, as judged by the fact that damage to these areas leads to disinhibitory symptoms, such as increased irritability, sexuality, voracity.[35] (The relevant experimental

---

* Here is a striking example of the selectivity of triggering different drives by application of different active substances to the same locus in the emotive brain:

"One animal [rat] has been found that consistently responds to injection of carbachol by drinking, to injection of noradrenalin by eating, and to injection of a soluble steroid by building nests. All three chemicals have been applied to the same rhinencephalic locus at the junction of the area of the diagonal band of Broca and the medial preoptic region, and all three effects are specific with respect to the chemical or chemical family implicated." (A. E. Fisher and J. W. Coury, Cholinergic tracing of a central neural circuit underlying the thirst drive, *Science*, 138 [1962]: 691–93.)

material on animals will be discussed in Chapter X.) On the other hand, as shown by the effects of prefrontal lobotomies, the "higher emotions"—such as curiosity, esthetic feelings, social drives—are impaired after these operations, indicating that their representation is situated somewhere in the emotive part of the prefrontal region.

10. Summary and conclusions

In the present chapter we were concerned with the systematic presentation of particular categories of unitary perceptions in each analyzer. Our classification was based on the following: (1) psychological evidence based chiefly on antagonistic relations between perceptions of the same category; (2) developmental evidence; (3) differences of elements in particular categories of perceptions; (4) differences of associations with perceptions of other analyzers; (5) neuropathological evidence of the existence of discrete gnostic fields for particular categories.

Here we specify once more the main categories of perceptions in each analyzer, with an indication of the type of agnosia resulting from the injury in the appropriate gnostic field.

Visual analyzer (V)

Gnosis	Agnosia
A. General illumination (V-Il)	?
B. Spatial relations (V-Sp)	Visuo-spatial agnosia
C. Patterns (V-P)	
(1) Manipulable objects (V-MO)	Visual object agnosia
(2) Nonmanipulable objects (V-VO)	?
(3) Human faces (V-F)	Prosopagnosia
(4) Their expressions (V-FE)	?
(5) Animate objects (V-AO)	?
(6) Signs (V-Sn)	Alexic agnosia
(7) Handwritings (V-Hw)	?
(8) Postures of limbs (V-L)	?

Acoustic analyzer (A)

(1) Sounds of the external world (A-Sd)	Non-verbal sound agnosia
(2) Human voices (A-Vo)	?
(3) Words (A-W)	Audioverbal agnosia (word deafness)
(4) Melodies (A-M)	Amusia

Olfactory analyzer (Ol)

(1) Smells	?

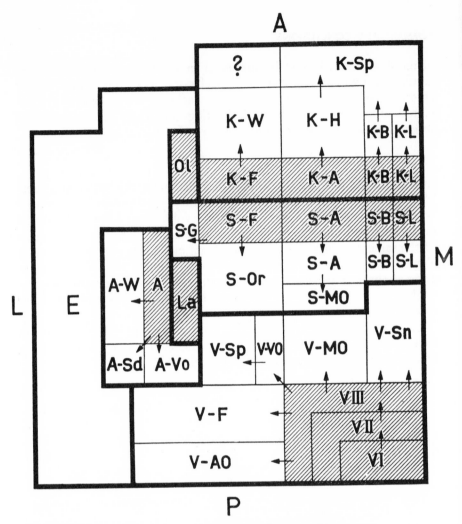

Fig. III-12. Conceptual Map of the Human Cerebral Cortex of
Left Hemisphere (Left) and the Cytoarchitectonic Map of
That Hemisphere According to Brodmann (Right)

Symbols: A, P, L, M, outside the figure denote the anterior, posterior, lateral (and latero-basal) and medial sides of the cortex. Projective transit fields are hatched; gnostic (exit) fields are plain. The boundaries of particular analyzers are drawn by thick lines; the boundaries of particular fields by thin lines. Arrows denote connections between transit and gnostic fields.

The projective and gnostic fields of the conceptual chart are tentatively related to the cytoarchitectonic fields of the Brodmann chart.

Visual analyzer (V): VI, VII, VIII, transit visual fields (areas 17, 18, 19 respectively); V-Sn, signvisual field (area 7b); V-MO, visual field for small manipulable objects (7b); V-VO, visual field for large purely visual objects (39); V-Sp, visual field for spatial relations (39, right hemisphere); V-F, visual field for faces (37); V-AO, visual field for animated objects (37).

Auditory analyzer (A): A, projective auditory field (41, 42); A-W, audioverbal field (22); A-Sd, auditory field for various sounds (22, right hemisphere); A-Vo, auditory field for human voices (21).

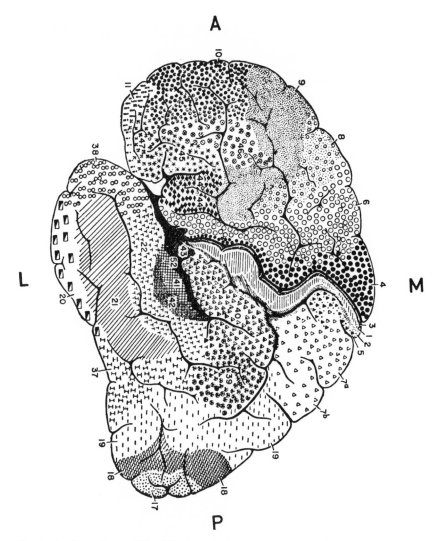

Somesthetic analyzer (S): S-F, S-A, S-B, S-L, projective somesthetic fields for face, arm, body and leg, respectively (3, 1, 2); S-Or, oralsomesthetic field (40); S-A, S-B, S-L, gnostic somesthetic fields for arm, body and leg, respectively (5, 7a); S-MO, somesthetic field for small manipulable objects (7a); S-G, gustatory field (43).

Kinesthetic analyzer (K): K-F, K-A, K-B, K-L, projective kinesthetic fields for face, arm, body and leg, respectively (4); K-W, wordkinesthetic field (44, 45); K-H, handkinesthetic field (6); K-B, K-L, gnostic kinesthetic fields for body and leg, respectively (6); K-Sp, kinesthetic field for spatial relations (9, right hemisphere); La, vestibular analyzer (not known); Ol, olfactory analyzer (not seen on Brodmann's map); E, emotional analyzer (not seen on Brodmann's map).

Note that for the sake of simplicity *all* the gnostic fields have been put in the left hemisphere, although in reality some of them are situated in the right hemisphere. Note also that our conceptual brain map is unfolded so as to show the latero-basal aspect of the cortex (not seen in Brodmann's map). The medial part of the emotive brain is not shown.

Vestibular analyzer (La)

Gnosis   Agnosia

(1) Positions and movements of head   ?

Somesthetic analyzer (S)

A. Exteroceptive systems (S-ES)
    (1) Textures (S-T)   Ahylognosia
    (2) Shapes of objects (S-MO)   Astereognosia
    (3) Taste (S-G)   ?
B. Proprioceptive system (S-PS)
    (1) Postures of limbs (S-L)   Asomatognosia
    (2) Postures of mouth (S-Or)   Postural oral agnosia (Luria aphasia)

Kinesthetic analyzer (K)

(1) Hand movements (K-H)   Apraxia and agraphia
(2) Body movements (K-B)   Body apraxia
(3) Oral movements in speech   Word-kinesthetic agnosia
    (K-W)   (Broca aphasia)
(4) Oral movements in singing   ?
    (K-M)
(5) Locomotor behavior (K-Sp)   Prefrontal syndrome
(6) Complex behavioral acts   Prefrontal syndrome

Emotive analyzer

(1) Particular emotional states   ?

Whereas our analysis concerning exteroceptive and postural somesthetic gnosis was based on the recognition of stimulus-patterns reflected in particular unitary perceptions, in the analysis of kinesthetic gnosis this approach was impossible and we had to specify particular gnostic units and their categories, not on the basis of unitary perceptions, but on the basis of unitary behavioral acts.

In Figure III-12 we present two representations of the human cerebral cortex. One is Brodmann's map indicating the projective and "associative" fields distinguished by this author. The other is the "conceptual" chart deduced from the discussion in this chapter. Although the relation between the two figures is roughly the same as that between the realistic portrait of a person and his cubistic image, nevertheless we can easily see that the two figures are not very remote from each other.

The conceptual chart will provide a basis for our further analysis of the functions of the brain concerning the connections between gnostic fields of particular analyzers. This task will be undertaken in Chapter V.

References to Chapter III

1. W. Penfield and H. Jasper. 1954. *Epilepsy and the Functional Anatomy of the Human Brain.* 1st ed. London: J. & A. Churchill.

2. I. Krechevsky. 1935. Brain mechanisms and "hypotheses." *J. Comp. Psychol.,* 19: 425–62.

    J. M. Warren, H. B. Warren, and K. Akert. 1961. Umweg learning by cats with lesions in the prestriate cortex. *J. Comp. Physiol. Psychol.,* 54: 629–32.

    J. Dąbrowska. Unpublished experiments.

3. D. C. Hebb. 1949. *The Organization of Behavior: A Neuropsychological Theory.* New York: Wiley.

4. H. Hécaen and J. de Ajuriaguerra. 1956. Agnosie visuelle pour les objets inanimés par lésion unilatérale gauche. *Rev. Neurol.,* 94: 222–33.

5. H. Hécaen, J. de Ajuriaguerra, C. Magiset, and R. Angelergues. 1952. Agnosie des physionomies. *Encéphale,* 41: 322–60.

6. M. Cole and J. Perez-Cruet. 1964. Prosopagnosia. *Neuropsychologia,* 2: 237–46.

7. T. Alajouanine, F. Lhermitte, and B. de Ribaucourt-Ducarne. 1960. Les alexies agnosiques et aphasiques. In T. Alajouanine, ed., *Les grandes activités du lobe occipital,* pp. 235–60. Paris: Masson.

8. D. H. Hubel and T. N. Wiesel. 1965. Receptive fields and functional architecture in two nonstriate visual areas (18 and 19) of the cat. *J. Neurophysiol.,* 28: 229–89.

9. W. Penfield and T. Rasmussen. 1950. *The Cerebral Cortex of Man.* New York: Macmillan.

10. *Ibid.*

11. K. H. Pribram and M. Mishkin. 1955. Simultaneous and successive visual discrimination by monkeys with inferotemporal lesions. *J. Comp. Physiol. Psychol.,* 48: 198–202.

12. J. J. Gibson. 1950. *The Perception of the Visual World.* Cambridge, Mass.: Riverside Press.

13. G. M. Turnbull. 1961. Some observations regarding the experiences and behavior of the Bambuti Pygmies. *Am. J. Psychol.,* 74: 304–8.

14. E. Engel. 1956. The role of content in binocular resolution. *Am. J. Psychol.,* 69: 87–91.

15. Д. Г. Столярова-Кабелянская. 1961. Клинические и патофизиологические различия между корковой и транскортикальной сенсорной афазией. (Clinical and pathophysiological differences between cortical and transcortical aphasia.) In Вопросы клиники и патофизиологии афазий. Ред. Е. В. Шмидт и Р. А. Ткачев, pp. 24–57. Moscow: Medgiz.

16. R. Magnus. 1924. *Körperstellung.* Berlin: Springer.

17. See many interesting details of this syndrome in:
    M. Critchley. 1953. *The Parietal Lobes*. London: E. Arnold.
18. J. P. L. Delay. 1935. *Les astéréognosies: Pathologie du toucher. Clinique, physiologie, topographie*. Paris: Masson.
19. J. de Ajuriaguerra and H. Hécaen. 1960. *Le cortex cérébral: Étude neuro-psychopathologique*. 2d ed. Paris: Masson.
20. W. Penfield and H. Jasper. 1954. See note 1 above.
21. S. Landgren. 1957. Convergence of tactile, thermal, and gustatory impulses on single cortical cells. *Acta Physiol. Scand.*, 40: 210–21.
22. А. Р. Лурия. 1947. Травматическая афазия. Клиника, семиотика и востановительная терапия. (*Traumatic aphasia. Clinics, semiology and rehabilitation therapeutics.*) Moscow: Izdat. Akad. Med. Nauk USSR.
    ———. 1962. Высшие корковые функции человека и их нарушения при локальных поражениях мозга. (Higher cortical functions in man and their disturbances in local brain lesions.) Moscow: Izd. Moskovskogo Univ.
23. W. Wundt. 1910. *Grundzüge der physiologischen Psychologie*. Bd. 2, 6 Aufl. Leipzig.
    W. Nagel, 1905. *Handbuch der Physiologie des Menschen: Physiologie der Sinne*. Brunswick.
    M. Foster. 1891. *A Textbook of Physiology*. Book III. 5th ed. London.
24. V. B. Mountcastle and T. P. S. Powell. 1959. Central nervous mechanisms subserving position sense and kinesthesis. *Bull. Johns Hopkins Hosp.*, 105: 173–200.
25. L. Leksell. 1945. The action potential and excitatory effects of the small ventral root fibers to skeletal muscle. *Acta Physiol. Scand.*, 10 (Suppl. No. 31): 1–84.
    S. W. Kuffler, C. C. Hunt, and J. P. Quilliam. 1951. Function of medullated small-nerve fibers in mammalian ventral roots; efferent muscle spindle innervation. *J. Neurophysiol.*, 14: 29–54.
    R. Granit. 1955. *Receptors and Sensory Perception: A Discussion of Aims, Means, and Results of Electrophysiological Research into the Process of Reception*. New Haven: Yale University Press.
26. C. F. Jacobsen. 1932. Influence of motor and premotor area lesions upon the retention of skilled movements in monkeys and chimpanzees. *Res. Publ. Ass. Nerv. Ment. Dis.,* 13: 225–47.
26a. K. S. Lashley and J. Ball. 1929. Spinal conduction and kinesthetic sensitivity in the maze habit. *J. Comp. Psychol.*, 9: 71–105.
27. J. Dąbrowska. 1959. Kinaesthetic tasks in relearning albino rats. *Acta Biol. Exp. Vars.*, 19: 105–21.
    ———. 1963. An analysis of reversal learning in relation to the pattern of reversal in rats. *Ibid.*, 23: 11–24.

————. 1964. Reversal learning in frontal rats. *Ibid.*, 24: 19–26.

J. Dąbrowska. 1967. Reversal learning in relation to the pattern maze alterations in frontal rats. *Acta Biol. Exp. Vars.*, 27 (in press).

28. I. Łukaszewska. 1961. A study of returning behaviour of white rats on elevated maze. *Acta Biol. Exp. Vars.*, 21: 253–65.

————. 1962. Return reaction versus one trial learning. *Ibid.*, 22: 23–30.

————. 1964. The effect of intra-maze visual cues on return reaction in rats. *Ibid.*, 24: 153–59.

————. Unpublished experiments.

29. P. Marie and P. Béhague. 1919. Syndrome de désorientation dans l'espace consécutif aux plaies profondes du lobe frontal. *Rev. Neurol.*, 26: 3–14.

30. B. Milner. 1965. Visually-guided maze learning in man: effects of bilateral hippocampal, bilateral frontal, and unilateral cerebral lesions. *Neuropsychologia*, 3: 317–38.

S. Corkin. 1965. Tactually-guided maze learning in man: effects of unilateral cortical excisions and bilateral hippocampal lesions. *Neuropsychologia*, 3: 339–51.

31. А. Р. Лурия. 1963. Мозг человека и психические процессы. Т. I. (The human brain and mental processes), pp. 430–53. Moscow: Izd. Akad. Pedag. Nauk RSFSR.

A. R. Luria and E. D. Homskaya. 1964. Disturbances in the regulative role of speech with frontal lobe lesions. In J. M. Warren and K. Akert, eds., *The Frontal Granular Cortex and Behavior*, pp. 353–71. New York: McGraw-Hill.

32. B. Milner. 1964. Some effects of frontal lobectomy in man. In J. M. Warren and K. Akert, eds., *The Frontal Granular Cortex and Behavior*, pp. 313–34. New York: McGraw-Hill.

33. J. Subczyński. 1961. Zaburzenia odtwarzania złożonych ciągów liczbowych w ogniskowych uszkodzeniach mózgu. (Disorders of reproduction of compound numerical sequences in focal lesions of the brain.) *Rozpr. Wydz. Nauk Med. PAN.*, R. 6, T. 2: 181–201. Polish with English summary.

T. Pilipowska and J. Szumska. 1967. Analiza zaburzeń rachowania w przypadkach ogniskowych uszkodzeń płatów czołowych. (Disorders of calculation after prefrontal lesions in man.) *Rozpr. Wydz. Nauk Med. PAN.* Polish, in preparation.

34. H. Ursin and B. R. Kaada. 1960. Functional localization within the amygdaloid complex in the cat. *Electroenceph. Clin. Neurophysiol.*, 12: 1–20.

35. H. F. Jarvie. 1954. Frontal lobe wounds causing disinhibition. (A study of six cases.) *J. Neurol. Neurosurg. Psychiat.*, 17: 14–32.

CHAPTER **IV**

GENERAL PHYSIOLOGY OF ASSOCIATIONS

1. Introductory remarks

From discussions in the two preceding chapters it is clear that the role of perceptions is to provide the brain with the accurate and relevant information about environmental events and those which take place within the organism itself. We have seen that the organization of the afferent systems assures the best possible fulfillment of this role. This is because the gnostic fields represent the highly selective picture of the external world—a picture which depicts the essence of the current events more faithfully and deeply than does their rather superficial and photographic reflection provided by our receptors, biased by a momentary and constantly changing viewpoint.

Receiving and consolidating perceptions in our gnostic files is, however, only a first step in the integrative action of the brain. What happens further is association of perceptions caused by their synchronous occurrence and finally their utilization for behavioral acts. This will be the subject of the remaining parts of the present study.

To avoid terminological confusion, we shall use the term "association" to describe the relation between stimuli, perceptions, or images, and the term "connection" (meaning actual connection) to denote the relation between corresponding units. In other words, "association" will have rather a psychological or, more generally, functional meaning, whereas "connection" will refer to the anatomical substrate.

The problem of the formation of new functional connections between neurons of particular parts of the brain was discussed in Chapter II (Section 6). It was stated there that, according to our concept, the prerequisite for the formation of such connections, which we call actual connections, is the existence of potential connections between the corresponding neurons—the anatomical pathways leading from the transmittent to the recipient neurons. In the formation of unitary perceptions these actual connections are established between receptive units of the transit fields and potential perceptive units of the gnostic fields to which the receptive units converge. The indispensable condition for the actualization of these connections is that the recipient units should be in a state of arousal produced by the axodendritic connections leading from the unspecific facilitatory system (Figure IV-1a).

Slightly different is the situation in the formation of actual connections between the units of particular gnostic fields, occurring in the associative processes. Here both the transmittent and the recipient gnostic units must be synchronously excited through the axosomatic connections leading to them from the receptive units of the lower afferent fields. This excitation should occur under the facilitatory influence of the unspecific arousing system exerted upon both the transmittent and the recipient gnostic units, the influence indispensable both for perception of corresponding stimulus-patterns and for the formation of actual connections between these units (Figure IV-1b).

One can speculate whether this difference between conditions in which actual connections are established in the formation of perceptions and of associations is essential and what its origin is. In the formation of associations, the excitation of the recipient units from the periphery is indispensable for providing the proper *address* for messages originating in the transmittent units; in the formation of perceptions, this special addressing device is not necessary, since the formation of actual connections is ensured by the convergence of transmittent units on the particular recipient unit (compare Figures IV-1b with IV-1a). It may be noted, however, that this dichotomy of rules governing the formation of actual connections in the genesis of perceptions and associations respectively could be totally avoided if we would accept the alternative view that the associative processes are based on the same principles as perceptive processes. In fact, we can assume that the associative process is due to the formation of new gnostic units combining the stimulus-patterns provided by each of the synchronous perceptions. In other words, we would admit the existence of plurimodal gnostic fields whose units would be the points of convergence of gnostic units of particular analyzers (Figure IV-1c).

This theory of explaining associations by convergence of messages on the units of the "associative" areas (now in the literal sense of this word) has been proposed by Fessard and Gastaut[1] on the basis of

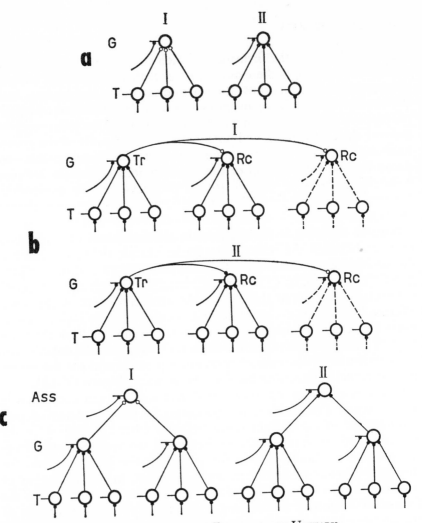

FIG. IV-1. PROBABLE MECHANISMS OF THE FORMATION OF UNITARY PERCEPTIONS (a) AND ASSOCIATIONS (b, c)

Neurons are denoted by circles (soma) with dashes (dendrite). Their axons terminate by white knobs (potential connections), or by black knobs (actual connections). Continuous lines denote those connections which are actually activated; interrupted lines denote those which are not activated. T, transit level; G, gnostic level; Ass, in (c), associative level. Tr, transmittent unit; Rc, recipient unit. Axons on the left of each gnostic unit ending on its dendrite denote unspecific afferents indispensable for the formation of a plastic change. I, the original state; II, the state after the formation of a plastic change.

a) The formation of a gnostic unit; in I there are potential connections between transit units and the corresponding gnostic unit; in II these connections are transformed into actual connections.

b) The formation of association. Of two recipient units only the left one is activated from the periphery and therefore actual connection is formed only with this unit.

c) The formation of association according to the convergence theory. Note that the assumed mechanism of the formation of association is exactly the same as that of the formation of a gnostic unit.

electrophysiological evidence indicating the existence of polivalent neurons in those areas. Although its acceptance for our discussion is tempting, we prefer to resist this temptation and to follow a more beaten (and perhaps safer) track of connectionistic approach to the phenomena of associations. The point is that the acceptance of the convergence concept of associations would require the assumption of a number of highly speculative hypotheses to account for their complex properties, which are easily and naturally explained from the connectionistic point of view. This would introduce into our work too much arbitrariness in dealing with the integrative nervous processes, which we would like to avoid. If in the future convincing evidence will be found in favor of the convergence theory of associations, then the whole problem of the physiological mechanism of their properties must be reconsidered.

To return to our subject, let us call attention to the fact that, according to the basic neurophysiological principles, associations, like connections, are always unidirectional—that is, the existence of association leading from the unitary perception A to the unitary perception B does not imply that association leading from B to A also exists. The two processes are independent of each other, and so the problem arises of what criteria determine the direction of association of two coincident perceptions if between the sets of gnostic units representing perceptions A and B potential connections exist in both directions.

To begin with, it is clear that if perception A is *always* accompanied by perception B, but perception B often operates without A, then association leading from A to B is readily established and firm, whereas association leading from B to A may be either weak or absent. For instance, if the voice of a given person (perception A) is nearly always accompanied by seeing this person (perception B), but the reverse is only seldom true, we may expect that association leading from voice to sight will be much better established than the reverse association.

Second, the temporal sequence of coincident perceptions seems to play an important role in determining the direction of associations. In fact, the extensive experimental material in the field of classical conditioning (being a special case of association) indicates that if two perceptions operate in the overlapping sequence, association is formed in the direction from the leading perception to the following one and not in the opposite direction ("forward association" versus "backward association"). We shall discuss this problem in detail in the chapter concerned with classical conditioning (Chapter VI, Section 8).

Although, according to our connectionistic theory of associations, the formation of associations and the formation of unitary perceptions occur in different ways, the basic properties of the two processes are much the same. Associations, like perceptions, are more readily formed in young subjects than in old ones, in the state of emotional arousal than in the state of indifference, and they depend to some extent on the number of pairings of two stimulus-objects. The "stronger" the associations between the given stimulus-objects, the more resistant they are to detrimental agents, such as senility or brain injury. In other words, associations, like perceptions, obey the principle of redundancy.

When between two sets of gnostic units A and B actual connections A → B have been formed, the recipient set of units B may be activated in two ways: either from the periphery through afferent pathways, or from the transmittent set of units A through associative pathways. Thus the question should be asked as to whether the activation of the given set of gnostic units in either of these two ways is identical or different, from the physiological and psychological point of view. It may be easily seen that there is an essential *psychological* difference between these two events, because each gives rise to a distinct mental experience: whereas the activation of a set of gnostic units through the afferent pathway produces the experience of *perception* of a stimulus-object concerned, the activation of this set of units through associative pathways usually produces the experience of its *image*. And so we are confronted with an important problem of what is the *physiological* difference between these two phenomena, which would account for their introspective specificity.

2. Physiological basis of images

First, it should be noted that the psychological distinction between the two experiences—perception and image—is essential and cannot be reduced to the mere quantitative difference. In fact, we can experience an extremely vivid image, either visual or auditory, of a certain event (especially if it has occurred in a state of high arousal) without any tendency to convert this image into hallucination (quasi-perception, see below), and we can experience a dim perception (for example, of a visual object seen in a mist, or a feeble sound) without any tendency to convert it into an image.

It seems that the chief psychological difference between perceptions and images is that whereas *perceptions* are usually attributed to definite events occurring *in the external world, images* are thought to occur "*inside our mind.*" This difference is most conspicuous in the visual analyzer. Visual perceptions are always projected to those places in which the stimulus-object operates or seems to operate. Even in those instances in which stimulus-objects arise in our eye (as in the phenomenon of "*mouches volantes*") or on our retina (as in the phenomenon of the "afterimage"), these stimuli are not perceived as occurring in the place of their origin but are seen somewhere *before* us. As far as *mouches volantes* are concerned, at first we even have the impression that they are in fact before us and we try to brush them off, until we realize that this is in vain.

On the other hand, visual images are clearly devoid of this attribute. This fact is most obvious when we visualize those objects which are not related to any particular place in space because their location is changeable. For instance, when I imagine a face of a familiar person, or a candle, or a book, I most often "see" these objects isolated before my eyes but without any externalization. Somewhat different is our experience when the familiar object is related to a definite place—for example, the armchair in my apartment. Then I visualize it in its own place (even if it is behind me), but again the realization of its location occurs in my mind.

As far as auditory experiences are concerned, the situation is roughly the same. Auditory perceptions are projected to those places of the outer world where they seem to originate. Those sounds which do not have any particular localization—for example, thunder—are nevertheless clearly perceived as occurring outside us. Even buzzing in our own ears may be located in the outside world or in the ear, but again not in our minds, as it is with auditory images.*

It seems that these introspective differences between perceptions and images are closely related to their physiological differences. As explained in earlier chapters, the operation of each afferent system is inherently connected with targeting reflexes whose function consists in adjusting the receptive organ for the optimal reception of the given stimulus. These reflexes are thrown into action when a stimulus-object activates some units in the *projective* area of the cerebral cortex, and they are indispensable for the occurrence of unitary perceptions (cf. Chapter II, Section 4).

There is clear evidence that targeting reflexes are not elicited by images. Even when a visual image is accompanied by turning the eyes

* How much proper localization of the buzzing in our ears is a matter of experience is shown by the following episode which happened to me. After a long journey in a noisy airplane I came to a hotel in a foreign city and realized that there was a clear, monotonous sound in my room. I was certain that it came from the bathroom, until, by moving from place to place, I realized that the sound originated in my own ears.

It is worthwhile to quote in this context an anecdote which seems to be pertinent. A master asks the servant to find out where the ringing noise that keeps him awake is coming from. "Sir," answers the servant, "I am sorry to say that it comes from *my ears*."

in the direction where its object is visualized to be, this is not due to the targeting reflex but to the searching reflex, of an entirely different character and depending on different nervous structures. Therefore, we assume that precisely these targeting reflexes, faithfully driven by, and dependent upon, external stimulus-objects, give our perceptions the mark of "reality" of which images are devoid.

On the basis of these considerations, it is reasonable to suggest the following physiological hypothesis concerning the difference between perceptions and images. We shall assume that a subject experiences a perception whenever the gnostic units are activated *in concomitance* with the activation of corresponding projective units giving rise to the

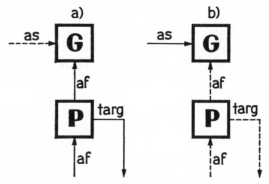

FIG. IV-2. PHYSIOLOGICAL MECHANISM OF PERCEPTION AND IMAGE

G, gnostic level; P, projective level; af, afferent pathways; as, associative pathways; targ, efferent pathway for targeting reflex. Pathways actually activated are denoted by continuous lines; pathways not activated, by interrupted lines.

  a) Functional organization of unitary perception.
  b) Functional organization of image.

targeting reflex, whereas he experiences an image whenever the gnostic units are activated *in the absence* of activation of corresponding projective units. In other words, we assume that externalization of our perceptions is precisely conferred on them by activation of the projective level of a given afferent system (Figure IV-2).

If this hypothesis is correct, we can anticipate that if a subject has lost his sensory input by damage to the appropriate receptive surface or afferent pathways up to the projective area after his gnosis has been formed, his images are intact, although perceptions no longer are possible. On the contrary, in those subjects in whom only a gnostic field representing some category of perceptions has been damaged, the images of corresponding stimulus-objects are lost, although the sensory input including targeting reflexes is unimpaired.

Many observations strikingly confirm these conclusions. Below we give some illustrative examples.

A good example of the preservation of visual gnosis after losing sight is provided by the famous case of Skorokhodova, who became blind and deaf at the age of five. By special training she learned to speak, to typewrite, to read Braille, and to get information from other persons through tactile dactylology. She graduated in psychology and wrote an interesting monograph about her condition.[2]

According to her report, Skorokhodova not only preserved some visual images of the early period of her life but she was able to form new visual images either on the basis of tactile perceptions or even on the basis of verbal descriptions reported to her by other persons or read in a book. She also had vivid dreams.

Below we give some extracts of her self-observations:

Of course I do not imagine a whole group of objects at once, but each of them in succession: a chair, a table, a wardrobe, a bed, etc. I visualize them . . . in their natural size, and those objects I know I visualize not partially, e.g., first one foot of a chair, then the other one, then the back. No, a familiar thing I imagine at once, as a whole in its natural size. It is different when I would inspect [sic] a part of an unfamiliar or unusual object. Not knowing it as a whole I would imagine only that part which I would touch by hands. For instance, if I were requested to touch one end of, say, the horn of a stag and were asked: "Do you imagine the branched horns of this animal and the whole stag?" I would answer without doubt "no." However, when touching the border of my bed, I can say that I visualize the whole bed.

No less convincing is another famous case: Ludwig van Beethoven, who wrote and performed on the piano his Ninth Symphony and many other works when he was totally deaf.

Quite similar is the situation in respect to those subjects who lost their sight by lesions in the projective area of the cortex. An excellent description of such a case is given by Nielsen.[3] "A man had embolia into the calcarine area of both sides. He immediately saw a million stars, as he describes it, and from that time he was totally blind, but was able at all times to revisualize anything he had formerly seen, and he was able to give visual descriptions, including colors of all his past memories."

On the other hand, patients suffering from particular types of agnosia clearly ascertain that they have lost not only perceptions produced by the corresponding stimulus-objects but also their images.

For illustration, we cite after Critchley[4] a dramatic description by a subject who suddenly developed a heavy visual agnosia, probably in consequence of a hemorrhage. This was a patient of Charcot, who asked him to report his self-observations in a letter. Here are fragments of this letter.

Comme je vous l'ai dit, je possédais une grande facilité de me représenter intérieurement les personnes qui m'intéressaient, les couleurs et les objets de toute nature, en un mot tout ce qui se reflète dans l'oeil.

Permettez-moi de vous faire observer que je me servais de cette faculté dans mes études: Je lisais ce que je voulais apprendre et en fermant les yeux je revoyais clairement les lettres dans leurs plus grands détails: il en était ainsi pour la physionomie des personnes, des pays et villes que j'avais visités dans mes longs voyages, et, comme je vous le disais plus haut, de tout objet qui avait été aperçu par mes yeux.

Tout d'un coup cette vision intérieure a absolument disparu. Aujourd'hui même, avec la meilleure volonté, je ne peux pas me représenter intérieurement les traits de mes enfants, de ma femme, ou de n'importe quel objet me servant journellement. Donc, étant établi que j'ai absolument perdu la vision intérieure, vous comprenez facilement que mes impressions sont changées d'une façon absolue.

Le sens de la représentation intérieure me manquant absolument, mes rêves se sont également modifiés. Aujourd'hui, je rêve seulement paroles, tandis que je possédais auparavant, dans mes rêves, la perception visuelle.

Comme conclusion, je vous prie de remarquer que je suis obligé aujourd'hui de me dire les choses que je veux retenir dans ma mémoire, pendant que j'avais auparavant seulement à les photographier par la vue.

Thus we see that, in agreement with our concept, lesions of particular afferent systems sustained in all transit levels including the projective area of the cortex produce abolition of the appropriate sensory input but leave the images proper to the given system unaffected. On the contrary, lesions sustained in the gnostic area of a given analyzer do not affect the sensory input, but they make impossible both its integration in the form of perceptions and its reproduction in the form of images.

3. Physiological basis of hallucinations

As is well known, in some particular cases activation of gnostic units by way of association leads to experiences which *are* projected to the external world and thus have all properties of perceptions, although they are not bound to any actual stimulus-objects. We denote such phenomena as hallucinations; our task is to discover in which conditions they appear and what their physiological mechanism is.

At the beginning of our analysis of hallucinations, it should be noted that we do not include in this category the phenomena discussed in Chapter II in which stimulation of the projective area of particular analyzers produces "perceptions" of tingling in the given limb, stars in part of the visual field, or buzzing. As explained before, the projective area must be considered as a part of afferent pathway *outside* the area where the perceptions are organized, and in consequence its stimulation should legitimately produce external sensations similar to those produced by stimulation of the lower levels of the afferent system.

In order to understand the mechanism of "true" hallucinations, we must accept an assumption that the units of the gnostic areas not only receive fibers from the units of the projective areas but also send fibers to these units. Although this assumption is based on definite neuronographic evidence,[5] the existence of these connections is not generally

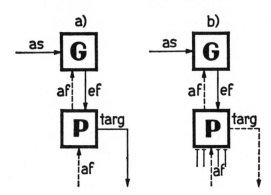

Fig. IV-3. Physiological Mechanism of Hallucination

Denotations as in Figure IV-2.
a) Functional organization of hallucination.
b) Functional organization of image in which the tendency to hallucination is overcome.

In (a) the efferent pathway from G to P (ef) is shown, which is responsible for the occurrence of hallucination. In (b) there are shown inhibitory afferent pathways in respect to a given stimulus-pattern which suppress the effect of the efferent pathway from G to P. If the excitation delivered from G to P is very strong, then it takes an upper hand over these inhibitory messages and hallucination can break through.

accepted. We should, however, keep in mind that since the very localization of particular gnostic fields is not clearly identified, the negative anatomical evidence cannot be considered conclusive.

Thus, if a given set of gnostic units is activated by association, the impulses from those units *can* run to the projective area, and, as we assume, to those units which are activated by the corresponding stimulus-object. Since activation of the receptive units of this area gives rise to the corresponding targeting reflex, it follows that the conditions for the appearance of perception-like experiences—hallucinations—are thus fulfilled (Figure IV-3a).

But, if such is the case, the question is bound to arise as to why hallucinations do not always occur in associative processes but are rather exceptional and far from being typical.

The answer to this question can be only tentative. In general it may be supposed that the backward connections leading from the gnostic units to the corresponding projective units are poorly developed and are therefore thrown into activity only in particular conditions. It is worthwhile to specify these conditions in order to understand better the mechanism of hallucinations.

To begin, it may be reasonably assumed that the sensory input provided by the receptors, even if it is monotonous and does not give rise to any perceptions, nevertheless activates the receptive units in the projective area of the cortex and therefore keeps away the messages arriving from the gnostic area which are incompatible with them (Figure IV-3b). For instance, if we keep our eyes closed, we "see" darkness, because the off-units of the projective area are activated and they exert a strong reciprocal inhibition on those units which should be excited by the active units of the gnostic area. The same is true of the auditory analyzer. Even if there are no sounds coming from the periphery, the off-units of the projective area representing silence are activated and inhibit the messages from the auditory gnostic area representing particular auditory images. We may, however, expect that if the units of the projective area are really idle, the conditions favorable for hallucinatory experiences may arise.

There are many reasons to believe that the mechanism of normal sleep (but not narcosis!) consists, among other things, in the cutting off of the sensory input by inhibition of some relay stations of the afferent systems. In consequence, neither on- nor off-messages from the periphery (or rather, few of them) reach the cerebral cortex, and therefore the images produced by associations may take the form of hallucinations. This is the mechanism of dreaming.

In good agreement with the proposed explanation of dreams is the well-established fact that dreaming is accompanied by desynchronization of EEG and by rapid eye movements.[5a] In fact, vivid visual hallucinations produced by emotional states (cf. Chapter V, Section 2) lead to an arousal of the visual gnostic area manifested by high frequency–low voltage cortical activity. On the other hand, the messages produced in the visual gnostic area flowing "downward" to the visual projective area activate the units controlling the targeting reflexes which give a pseudo-perceptional, hallucinatory character to the appropriate experiences. For this reason dreaming and rapid eye movements are closely correlated with each other.

It may be also expected that if a given afferent system is for a long time deprived of any varied stimulation, and the monotonous sensory input is subjected to strong habituation, then true hallucinations may arise. Although special experiments with "sensory deprivation" have not provided any unequivocal data in this respect, probably because a subject submitted to a strong perceptual "hunger" (cf. Chapter I, Section 8) is able to supply himself various auditory and visual stimuli, there are cases in which true hallucinations seem to arise in this condition. For instance, Schwertschlager reported that when his eyes were tightly bandaged for a length of time because of a retinal hemorrhage, he experienced clear visual hallucinations having a "real corporeal character."[6]

A somewhat different mechanism of hallucinations is in operation in some pathological states involving strong emotional excitement. It may be assumed that in such states particular sets of gnostic units are so strongly excited through associations with the emotional system (cf. Chapter V), that the impulses fired by them break through to the projective area and take an upper hand over the messages coming from the periphery. This is what usually occurs in delirium states, when a patient who is fully concentrated on his delusions projects them to the external world.

An analogous mechanism of hallucinations is encountered in patients suffering from focal epilepsy of the visual or auditory gnostic areas. According to numerous observations by Penfield,[7] both in the epileptic aura and when the exposed cortex was stimulated during operation, patients experienced hallucinations which they compared to dreams. On the other hand, stimulation of the same gnostic areas in non-epileptic patients was without effect. Similarly, interesting stereognostic hallucinations are encountered in subjects with parietal lesions, undoubtedly because of the irritative foci in the impaired region. In these cases "the patient has a feeling as if something were lying in the palm of one hand. The feeling may be so vivid that the patient can go on to describe the size, shape, texture and temperature of the object, and he may be astonished to find later that the hand is really empty."[8]

The explanation of these facts is that when a given gnostic area is in a state of increased excitability owing to some irritative focus (which is clearly seen in the EEG record), the activated units of this field discharge strongly into the corresponding projective area, suppressing the input from the periphery and causing hallucinatory effects. On the other hand, in a normal gnostic field the activation of units elicited by electrical stimulation should produce images which cannot be distinguished by the patient from those experienced by him in the natural manner.

In summary, we may reach the conclusion that the mechanism producing hallucinations is built into our brains, but it can be thrown into operation only in some exceptional conditions. This seems to be biologically understandable, because if we took all our visual and auditory images for perceptions, our adaptation to the external world would be extremely inadequate.

But, as it follows from our analysis the distinction between perceptions and images can be developed only in those afferent systems in which the projective area and the gnostic area are separated. In those analyzers in which the projective units play also the role of perceptive units, exactly the same units are excited both from the periphery and by way of association. Since the units concerned cannot discern where the excitation comes from, it could be anticipated that their excitation by association would give rise to the same process as their excitation from periphery—that is, the hallucination will appear instead of the image (Figure IV-4).

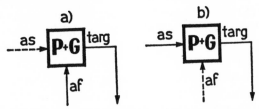

Fig. IV-4. Mechanism of Hallucination in a Primitive Afferent System

Denotations as in Figure IV-2.
a) Functional organization of perception.
b) Functional organization of association involving hallucination.

The observed facts strikingly confirm this anticipation.

As stated in the preceding chapter, the exteroceptive somesthetic gnosis of the body, except for the hands and the mouth, is poorly developed, because no complicated patterns are represented by its units. Therefore, the units of the projective sensory area represent not only the elementary sensations of stimuli acting on the skin but also their perceptions utilized in the associative activity of the brain. In consequence, excitation of these units by association should give rise, not to images, but to hallucinations.

As an example, imagine that we are sitting in a crowded room and beside us sits a man in dirty clothes who is incessantly scratching himself. Of course, by association we have a visual image of being invaded by fleas, but at the same time we feel real, and not imaginary, itching on various places of our bodies. Thus, a flea on our own body or a flea on the body of our neighbor gives us exactly the same somesthetic sensation.

Similarly, if a sensitive person witnesses, for example, another person's finger being cut, he will undoubtedly suffer *actual pain* in his own finger (and not its image), in clear contradistinction to the visual image of the accident, which although vivid is hardly converted into hallucination.

Expressive descriptions of this sort of hallucinations are given by Ribot.[9] "A student, says Gratiolet, playfully struck his companion's outstretched finger with the handle of a scalpel. The latter felt a pain so acute that he thought the instrument had pierced his finger to the bone. . . . A butcher remained hanging by one arm from a hook, he uttered frightful cries, and complained that he was suffering cruelly, while all the time the hook had only penetrated his clothes, and the arm was uninjured."

Further examples illustrating the same principle of hallucinations replacing images in those afferent systems in which gnostic areas are not clearly separated from the projective areas will be given in the next chapter, when we shall be dealing with the analysis of particular associations.

The important conclusion which may be drawn from our analysis is that hallucination should be considered *a phylogenetically earlier associative phenomenon than image.* Accordingly, it could be expected that hallucinations arise in animals to a much larger extent than in humans and that within those analyzers in which humans experience predominantly images, animals may experience hallucinations.

Since some readers will be reluctant to attribute to animals such mental experiences as hallucinations on the grounds that they are unverifiable (although for that matter the same applies to perception), we should recall that, according to our concept, "hallucination" has not only psychological but also physiological meaning. By "hallucination" we denote the activation of a given set of gnostic units by way of association accompanied by the targeting reflex toward the nonoperating stimulus. Since in our present state of experimental techniques it is still difficult to identify the action potentials corresponding to activation of the given set of gnostic units (except when they are "labeled"; see below), we must base our judgment chiefly on the occurrence of the targeting reflex and/or other behavioral responses characteristic for the given stimulus.

Although the class of phenomena which may be suspected as due to hallucinations in animals has never been systematically investigated in CR experiments, some casual observations, mostly unpublished, seem to suggest that these phenomena are common. Here are some relevant examples from my own experimental practice.

A dog trained in avoidance conditioning was taught to lift his foreleg in response to a buzzer on the side wall of a sound-proof CR chamber, to avoid the introduction of acid into his mouth. When the instrumental responses occurred only to the sound of the buzzer and not in the intertrial intervals, it nevertheless occasionally happened that suddenly the dog intently turned his head toward the buzzer and lifted his foreleg. This behavior was indistinguishable from that produced by a true sound of the buzzer, and could suggest that the animal actually had the auditory hallucination of it.[10] Here the activation of the corresponding gnostic units was elicited through associations established between the experimental situation and the auditory stimulus. As will be shown in later chapters, we have good objective evidence that such an association is in fact set up.

Another observation concerns analogous episodes in the course of alimentary conditioning. Here again in intertrial intervals a dog occasionally suddenly turns his head to the source of the CS, then to the feeder and salivates as copiously as in the presence of the CS.

We have recently observed a dog who was trained under food reinforcement to lift his right foreleg and put it on the feeder in response to a tactile stimulus applied to the distal part of that leg. Thereafter the somatosensory cortical field representing that leg was removed. The conditioned reflex disappeared after this operation, but it spontaneously recovered, although weaker than before surgery, as tested by the resistance to extinction.[11] Several months after surgery, however, a new phenomenon was observed—in the intertrial intervals the animal occasionally looked suddenly at his right forepaw, then placed his leg on the feeder and intently looked at the feeding place. This behavior was exactly the same as the reaction to the conditioned stimulus. We may assume that the scar formed in the operated area irritated the remaining sensory representation of the leg, giving rise to hallucination of the tactile stimulus.[12]

Finally, observation of the behavior of well-trained dogs in a CR chamber in response to conditioned stimuli also seems to suggest that animals then experience true hallucinations of the unconditioned stimuli. For instance, in response to a CS signaling the introduction of acid into his mouth, the animal reacts exactly in the same way as he does to the US itself (vigorous mouthing movements and salivation); in response to a CS signaling an air-puff into his ear he performs as vigorous shaking movements as he does to the US.

Perhaps some results obtained in electrophysiological experiments on waking animals may allow us to attribute them to hallucinations. It has been found, for instance, that if an acoustic continuous stimulus is repeatedly paired with flickering light, producing rhythmic evoked potentials in the occipital area, the same rhythm is often (although not regularly) observed in that area in response to the sound[13] and sometimes even in the intertrial intervals. It may be assumed that this rather capricious but distinct phenomenon is the manifestation of visual hallucination of flickering produced by the sound.

4. Properties of unitary images

Since the physiological mechanism of images, as far as their gnostic aspect is concerned, is the same as that of perceptions, it can be expected that the chief attributes of perceptions discussed in the preceding chapters hold true in respect to images. Moreover, it may be foreseen that since images represent a pure form of activation of gnostic units without its contamination by activation of the projective units, these attributes will be manifested even more clearly than in perceptions.

We shall discuss here two of the properties of unitary images: their integrity, and their mutual antagonisms.

The integrative character of unitary experiences is seen in images even more clearly than in perceptions. In fact, whereas visual or auditory perceptions are usually complex, being composed of a number of unitary perceptions which are either simultaneous (if there is no antagonism between them) or occur in quick succession, images are usually unitary, their unity and purity being indeed amazing. According to my own experience, I can easily evoke a pure image of the handwriting of a known person without imagining any particular words. It is clear that this cannot occur in perception, because seeing *what* is written and *how* it is written is practically inseparable. Similarly, when I am tired I have auditory images of speaking voices of other persons without "hearing" what they say, not because the words are blurred or indistinct, but simply because they do not take part in my imagery. Again such separation in perception is hardly possible.

Further, since images, in contradistinction to perceptions, are evoked in the absence of the appropriate stimulus-object, they may inform us about a given gnostic event in those cases where the perception was unique and unrepeatable.

Take a case of being a witness to some tragic event—for example a fatal accident on the street. Everyone knows from his experience that its perception becomes firmly consolidated in his memory, and the respective image can be repeatedly evoked, even after a long time, always in the same form—for instance a blood-stained dead man lying on the pavement. The image may become with the lapse of time less and less vivid (see below), but the picture is always the same, being as stable as if we had a photograph in our mind.

The same applies to auditory images. If we witnessed a tragic event and heard a piercing cry of pain or fear, its auditory image would persist for a long time, and could be evoked by association always as the same cry, as if it were fixed on a tape recorder.

Mutual antagonism between unitary images or images and perceptions follows the same rules as those of the antagonism between perceptions. Since (as will be discussed in Section 5, below) the strength of images varies within wide limits, it follows that among various competing unitary images the strongest takes the upper hand and inhibits all others.

A good illustration of the competition between various images may be provided by the following common experience. Suppose that I have seen a dramatic event which strongly occupies my visual imagination. I go to bed, but the obsessive image keeps me awake and totally suppresses all other images. Then, in order to get rid of it, I take a novel and start to read. If my obsessive image is strong, reading is completely unsuccessful; although perceptions of the words read are normal, since they belong to the category not antagonistic to the obsessive image, I do not know *what* I read—that is, my visual images, normally evoked by words, are inhibited by the image of the experienced event. If, however, the image of the event is not potent, the images represented by the words read will become dominant and I shall be able to get rid of the obsessive image and concentrate on the text of the book. But, alas, as soon as I lay the book aside and turn out the light, the obsessive image returns and again suppresses all others, reinstating the whole cycle of events. In this example the delicate interplay between various antagonistic images is most instructive.

Since the activation of gnostic units produced by actual stimulus-objects are generally stronger than their activation through associations, an actual perception usually suppresses all images antagonistic to it. Thus, looking intently at a picture, we cannot at the same time visualize another picture of a kindred subject; or, hearing one voice, we cannot at the same time have an image of the voice of another person. However, looking at a picture, we *can* at the same time "hear" in our imagination a voice of someone who explains its subject; or, hearing a person speaking, we easily visualize the subject of his story. This is because the gnostic units belonging to various categories are not antagonistic to each other.

Although actual perceptions usually dominate over images, this is not a general rule. If the activation of a particular set of gnostic units produced by association is strong, as happens under strong emotional excitement, then it can easily overshadow the activation of a competing set of units brought forth by the actual stimulus-object. For instance, we do not hear people speaking by radio when we are strongly absorbed by our own thoughts which involve auditory verbal images. Unfortunately, this is a rare case, and in most instances the loud voice transmitted by radio of our neighbors makes our own mental work simply impossible.

5. The strength of unitary images

If a set of gnostic units is activated by a known stimulus-object giving rise to the unitary perception, the strength of this activation is relatively stable; on the other hand, if the activation of gnostic units is produced by association, it is released from the stabilizing factor provided by the sensory input. As a result, whereas fluctuations of the strength of perceptions (the stimulus-object being constant), depending on the actual excitability of gnostic units involved, are (except in extreme cases) relatively small, fluctuations of the strength of images are most conspicuous. We have here a full analogy with the relations encountered in classical conditioning which is nothing but a particular case of association: whereas the *unconditioned* response produced by the actual operation (that is, perception) of the corresponding unconditioned stimulus is relatively stable and unchanging, the *conditioned* response produced by the conditioned stimulus by way of association is incomparably more variable, depending on numerous factors.

In this section we shall discuss the main factors influencing the strength of unitary images, basing our considerations chiefly on introspective data. We shall resume this discussion in Chapter VI, where the evaluation of the activation of gnostic units will be based on another index—that of an overt response established by conditioning.

In Chapter II it was indicated that the formation of gnostic units is largely dependent on the arousal of the concerned afferent system produced by a given emotional state. The same factor determines to a large degree the intensity of activation of these units by association after they have been established. Thus, as indicated above, when we have witnessed a tragic incident, its clear and vivid picture (visual and/or auditory) stays for a long time obsessively in our mind and absorbs us completely. Thereafter, when the emotional state caused by the accident is gradually attenuated, at the same time the associative activation of the gnostic units concerned will also become weaker, causing the appropriate images to become fainter and fainter.

Such is roughly the course of events following a single episode producing fear, horror, anger, or the like. Quite different is the situation when we are dealing with emotional states subserving the preservative reflexes, such as hunger or sexual drive. These emotional states cyclically return, not as an echo of a past event, but whenever the given drive is in operation. Thus, if we are hungry, the first thing to appear is the image of a table set with a meal toward which our appetite is directed. Under the influence of strong hunger the visual or auditory images connected with food may be converted into illusions or even hallucinations, according to the mechanism discussed in a preceding section. The analogous facts are easily observed under a strong and unfulfilled sexual drive, when a person to whom our drive is directed, or an indefinite person of the opposite sex, appears vividly, and sometimes even obsessively, in our visual imagination. Such visual images stop completely when our drive is satiated and even if we try we cannot voluntarily evoke them.

The vividness of images depends, however, not only on the specific drives associated with them, but also on a general state of arousal caused, for instance, by caffeine or amphetamine. We feel then that our mind is more clear, that our thoughts are more lucid, which is merely the result of the increased vividness of our images.

The next category of factors determining the vividness of our images is provided by the strength of connections established between the two sets of gnostic units participating in a given association. For instance, when we palpate some familiar object, we immediately experience its visual image; when we write a sign (for example, a letter of the alphabet) with eyes closed or in darkness, we immediately visualize what we have written. Similarly, some persons when reading experience vivid auditory images of the words read. All these images are clear and are unfailingly evocable by associations, because of the strong connections established between the corresponding sets of gnostic units.

This infallibility does not, however, hold equally true of all associations. For instance, looking at an apple, I may or may not imagine its taste, depending chiefly on whether I am hungry. Hearing someone on the telephone, I may or may not actually imagine his appearance, again depending on how much I am interested in that person and whether the perception of other persons I may be looking at inhibits the image. Walking in the street, I may or may not actually imagine what I shall see around the corner, depending on whether I am interested. In general, among many associations emanating from the given perception, only those to which our attention is directed at a given moment become actualized. Speaking physiologically, we can say that among many sets of gnostic units which are recipient to a given transmittent set, only those are activated which for particular reasons are in a state of increased excitability. Thus we come to the third category of factors determining the vividness of our images—the excitability of the recipient set of units at the moment of activation of the transmittent set of units.

The problem under consideration will be resumed in Chapter VI, Section 7, when we shall discuss the factors determining the magnitude of classical conditioned reflexes.

The next important problem requiring our consideration is that of the actual mechanisms determining the intensity of images. It is reasonable to assume that the strength of a given image experienced by a subject is in proportion to the intensity of activation of the corresponding set of units. As was shown earlier this depends on the strength of activation of transmittent units firing to the given set, on the number of connections linking the two sets, and on the level of excitability of the recipient set. On the other hand, the size of the recipient set of units seems not to play an essential role in the intensity of the image represented by this set. In fact, we have no clear evidence that the old experiences represented in the appropriate gnostic areas by large sets of units *ipso facto* give rise to more vivid images than those represented by small sets.

6. Interrelations between perceptions and associations

Since, according to our discussion, a given set of gnostic units may be activated either by the appropriate perception or by association, it is clear that if these two sources of excitation are operating at the same time they should give rise to the summation of their respective effects. In this section we shall analyze the rules of this summating mechanism in more detail.

In the normal condition, when a unitary perception is evoked by a fully adequate stimulus, the activation of appropriate gnostic units is maximal, and therefore the messages arriving at them by association are almost totally occluded (in the Sherringtonian sense of the term). The only effect of the associative impulses may be manifested by the shortened latency of recognition of the stimulus-object (see Section 7, below). If, however, a stimulus-object is presented in unfavorable conditions, so that its recognition is to a greater or lesser extent attenuated, the importance of the associative messages at once becomes apparent. Let us recall that, as stated in Chapter II (Section 8), in this condition the convergence of afferent impulses from the proximate transit field upon the appropriate set of gnostic units is not complete because of the lack of some elements normally participating in a given perception. In consequence, the messages arriving at these units either stimulate them subliminally—then the recognition of the given stimulus-object does not occur—or they produce the appropriate perception after a prolonged latency. If at the same time the messages reach the same units by the associative route, they will summate with the perceptual messages and produce a normal unitary perception.

There are numerous examples illustrating such conditions. If we see an indistinct silhouette of an approaching person, we may immediately recognize him if we expect his arrival. If we read an indistinct text of an old manuscript, we recognize the words much better if we know its subject matter. If we hear a speech blurred by background noise, by distance, or by unclear radio reception, we easily recognize the words we expect to hear and hardly recognize those which we do not anticipate. We immediately recognize a faint odor of burning if we see smoke or fire. According to the general rules of summation, the more abundant and precise the associative messages reaching the given gnostic unit, the poorer and more inadequate the perceptive messages can be. It should be noted, however, that as long as there are messages arriving at the gnostic field from the receptive surface, the resulting experience will take always the form of *perception* and not of *image;* this is because the actual stimulus-pattern, whatever its distinctiveness, elicits the appropriate targeting reflex, which is a sufficient condition for experiencing perception.

In the preceding paragraph we dealt with the situation in which the messages provided by perception and association impinge upon a set of gnostic units actually representing the given stimulus-object. It may, however, happen that the incomplete stimulus-pattern subliminally activates a number of sets of gnostic units and that the given association selects the set of units which represents, not the actual stimulus-object, but another one. In such a case our perception will be misleading—the phenomenon which is denoted as *illusion.*

Following are some typical examples of illusions.

We walk in a forest in the night and are afraid of bandits. In such a situation each bush of an appropriate shape is perceived as a kneeling man with a gun, and if the branches of a bush are stirred by the wind we see the bandit changing his position. Or else, we walk in a crowded street looking for a girl with whom we made an appointment; when the time of the date is passing and we grow more and more impatient, we perceive the silhouette of our acquaintance in many similar girls seen from the distance. Again, if we are in a city about to be bombarded, we easily take the slamming of a door for an explosion. Or else, a subject afflicted by *Beziehungswahn* will easily hear his own name pronounced or abuses directed to him in the indistinct voices of strangers.

To end these considerations, let us remember that the above summation of messages reaching a gnostic unit by perception and association (that is, through axosomatic synapses) is quite different from the summation of perceptive or associative messages on the one side and impulses impinging upon a given gnostic field from the nonspecific system. In the former, we have a true summation of *information* flowing to the gnostic units through different channels of the cognitive system; in the latter, we have *sensitization* of these units to the messages received, without procuring any information other than that obtained from the cognitive sources.

7. Methods of the study of associations

As seen from our previous discussion, the introspective method is most informative in studying the properties of unitary images (and, consequently, of the gnostic units representing them), and it can provide much important and precise material which may be verified and corroborated by other methods. This method cannot, however, be considered fully satisfactory, because it fails to give us complete information about all the associations which are formed in us or in other persons.

As pointed out in the preceding section, evocation of a given image by association is not always reproducible, particularly when we try to do so in a special experimental condition. It was stressed that the existence of connections between two sets of units of various gnostic fields does not imply that the unitary perception activating the given set will by association activate supraliminally (in the psychological or physiological sense) the other set, giving rise to the corresponding image and/or autonomic or motor response. We have shown that only a limited number of associations are unfailing in producing the corresponding images. In many cases they are not. We see, for instance, many persons in our surroundings, and hardly ever experience actual images of their voices or, even less, their handwriting, although certainly we do possess the corresponding associations. As a matter of fact, each stimulus-object is associated in our minds with a host of other stimulus-objects, but we actually select in each particular case only some of them, depending on which gnostic units are predisposed to being supraliminally excited at a given moment. Therefore, we should have other, more reliable methods for detecting the existence of associations in those cases in which they are not proved by actual evocation of the corresponding images.

One of these methods may be called the *substitution method*, and it consists simply in observing the effect of replacing the expected perception by a quite different one.

For example, suppose that we present to a subject a familiar person and then by some trick (for instance, in the dubbing experiment) this person begins to speak with another's voice. Although the subject might not have actually imagined the voice of the person seen, nevertheless hearing the strange voice (perhaps even very familiar to him), he will certainly experience a strong surprise or even shock, because the voice is not congruent with the association he has established between the appearance and the voice of the given person. Similarly, by putting on earphones connected with a special apparatus, we can hear our own speech delayed, which produces a curious and distressing effect, showing how strong our associations are between speaking and immediately hearing what we have said.

Many similar experiments can be performed by utilizing some ingenious tricks. We can, for instance, offer a person a savory beefsteak which will have the taste of cake, or vice versa; we can present a typical-looking cushion made of lead, or dumbbells made of papier-mâché, and so on. We can also deprive an object of some attribute. This recently happened to me in the course of a CR experimental session carried out in a sound-proof, radio-equipped chamber. When by mistake the transmitter was not turned on, I saw a dog barking vehemently without emitting any sound. The incongruence of this picture taught me how strong the association is in my mind between the appearance of a barking dog and hearing his voice. I would not have been less shocked if I had heard the dog barking loudly with his mouth closed.

To sum up, we see that by presenting a given stimulus-object in combination with a new stimulus-object instead of that which usually accompanies it, we may detect the existence of associations which are not necessarily revealed by actual images.

It may be noted that this substitution method for testing associations can be easily applied in animals, since the surprise caused by a change in the normal sequence of stimuli gives rise to a very conspicuous and unmistakable orientation reaction, consisting in startle, slight motor excitement, staring at the substituting stimulus (even if it is not novel for the animal), and disturbance of its normal effect—for example, in conditioning procedure. Unfortunately, this method has been so far only occasionally applied in animals, chiefly because of the lack of interest in this problem.

Another objective method of detecting associations, similar to the previous one, may be called the *expectation method*. The appropriate experimental procedure may run, for instance, in the following way. We repeatedly present in a given situation a number of known stimulus-objects and measure the minimal time required for their recognition. In another situation we present in the same way another set of known stimulus-objects. Then in the test trials we present in one situation some stimulus-objects belonging to the other situation. We may anticipate that the minimal time for recognition of the tested stimuli will be prolonged because the subject does not expect them to occur in the given situation. This shows that between the given situation and the objects presented against its background, the associations are established which subliminally activate the corresponding gnostic units. In a later chapter we shall give convincing evidence that analogous associations are formed in animals.

A third objective method of studying associations consists in using behavioral responses as indicators of the activation of certain gnostic or emotional units. If a set of units having such an overt sign of being activated becomes a recipient set, then the association may be proved by the appearance of this sign in response to the activation of the transmittent units. As is well known, the method of classical conditioning is based precisely on this principle. In the next section of this chapter we shall utilize this method for the analysis of kinesthetic gnosis.

The method of classical conditioning is sometimes used for detecting associations between neutral stimuli according to the following procedure: first, two neutral stimuli, S_1 and S_2, are repeatedly presented in close sequence. Then, stimulus S_2 is combined with stimulus S_3, displaying some overt response. After stimulus S_2 has acquired the capacity of eliciting this response due to conditioning, stimulus S_1 is again presented. If it now produces the same response, this means that stimuli S_1 and S_2 have indeed become associated.

The above method has sometimes been used for detection of the existence of associations between neutral stimuli in animals.[14] However precise and reliable this method is in respect to positive results, its sensitivity is certainly below that of the previous methods. In fact, the negative result does not imply the absence of association between S_1 and S_2, since this association may not be strong enough to produce the effect of S_3 in response to the action of S_1, especially since these stimuli never did actually coincide.

Finally, the existence of associations can be verified by electrophysiological methods—namely, by recording action potentials through macro- or micro-electrodes from the recipient cortical field when the transmittent field is excited. This method was originated by Durup and Fessard,[15] who have shown that if a sound is repeatedly paired in humans in overlapping sequence with a light producing desynchronization of EEG record in the occipital cortex, then the former stimulus eventually produces the same response. Similar data were obtained thereafter in many other studies by using a variety of animals and by pairing various stimuli. It is clear that this method leads in principle to the manifestation of associations between the neutral stimuli which do not evoke any clear overt responses.

In summary, it may be seen that several methods of detecting the existence of associations may substitute or supplement the direct introspective method based on ascertaining the occurrence of particular images in particular situations. As stated before, this introspective method, similar to other methods, has both advantages and drawbacks, being very useful in some instances and inadequate in others.

8. Kinesthetic images and their relation to movements

In the preceding chapter it was emphasized that the kinesthetic analyzer differs from other analyzers, not only in respect to its more complex anatomical structure involving two-stage information processing (muscle receptors–cerebellum and cerebellum–cerebral cortex), but also in respect to its physiological role. Whereas all other analyzers provide information of the phenomena which occur outside the central nervous system and independently of its proper activity, compelling that system to react to them in one way or another, the role of kinesthetic analyzer is quite the reverse: the animal performs movements produced by the activity of the appropriate nervous centers, and the kinesthetic receptors provide feedback information that these movements have indeed been executed. This essential difference results in the function of the kinesthetic analyzer being different from that of other analyzers, although, as we shall see, it is based on the same general principles.

Let us return briefly to the formation of kinesthetic gnostic units and take typewriting as a convenient model for our analysis. Assume that a subject has already established a set of simple visual-motor responses consisting in finding a key denoting a particular letter and pressing it with the appropriate finger. Since typing common syllables and words requires definite sequences of pressing movements, the kinesthetic perceptions arising by pressing particular keys become integrated and represented by gnostic units of a higher order than those representing single pressings. Thus a new gnostic field (in the functional or anatomical sense) is formed in which motor sequences involved in each commonly used word or syllable are represented by particular sets of units. In the same way all other kinesthetic gnostic units, more usual for our everyday behavior, are formed (Figure IV-5).

It is, however, important to realize that once the gnostic kinesthetic units representing particular behavioral acts have been established, the role of these units changes radically, because now they begin to function independently of the sensory input to which they owe their formation. To continue with our example, when typewriting is performed under the guidance of acoustic or visual perceptions or appropriate images, the gnostic units representing kinesthetic typing patterns of particular words are activated by association *before* the word is typed, and the motor performance is the result of this activation.

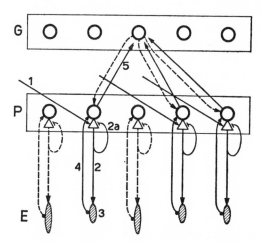

Fig. IV-5. Model of the Formation of Kinesthetic Gnostic Unit

G, kinesthetic gnostic field; P, kinesthetic (motor) projective field; E, effectors (muscles). Circles in G and P denote perceptive and receptive units, respectively; triangles in P denote pyramidal cells; thin spindles in E denote relaxed muscle fibers, thick spindles denote contracted muscle fibers. Arrows (→) touching a unit denote excitatory synaptic contacts; arrows not touching a unit denote potential excitatory contacts; stopped lines (—|) denote inhibitory synaptic contacts. Continuous lines denote actually operating connections; interrupted lines denote inactive connections.

The course of events: 1, impulses elicited by reflex reach particular pyramidal cells in the projective area; 2, descending impulses reach muscle fibers (2a, Renshaw loop inhibits the pyramidal cell after its excitation); 3, contraction of muscles; 4, ascending impulses (via cerebellum) reach the receptive kinesthetic units in the projective area; 5, impulses arrive at the potential gnostic unit through pathways converging upon that unit and transform it into the actual gnostic unit.

And so we come to the important conclusion that after a given integrated motor act (generally called purposeful or voluntary act) has been established, the corresponding kinesthetic gnostic units are activated through associative ways and transmit the orders for its performance to the executive centers. In other words, the kinesthetic gnostic units play the role of *programing* devices of behavioral acts which a subject has acquired by appropriate practice.

Now, the problem of first importance arises as to the physiological mechanism of this downward stream of messages leading *from* the kinesthetic gnostic units *to* the executive organs.

We think that we can give a reasonable solution of this problem on the basis of our general ideas concerning the functional organization of afferent systems.

As assumed in Section 3 of this chapter, connections between the projective areas of the cerebral cortex and the gnostic areas superimposed upon them are bidirectional: on the one hand, elementary units of the former area converge upon the gnostic units of the latter area; on the other hand, these units send back their axons to the corresponding units of the projective area. It was also stated (Chapter III, Section 7) that although *all* the projective areas are equipped with exit units which subserve the corresponding targeting reflexes, this exit unit system is particularly powerful in the kinesthetic projective area, from which every elementary movement of the body can be elicited.

As far as exteroceptive analyzers are concerned, the downward connections leading from the gnostic areas to the projective areas are rarely used in normal conditions, since the latter areas are kept permanently busy receiving the stream of information from the receptors and thus suppressing the messages from the higher levels (cf. Figure IV-3b). The situation is, however, quite different in the kinesthetic analyzer, since here the whole afferent input to the projective area is a feedback of movements which have been programed in a particular gnostic field of this analyzer. In consequence, at the moment when a given movement is by way of association programed in the appropriate gnostic field, the corresponding part of the projective area is *silent* and can receive the messages arriving from that field. These messages are transmitted to the efferent neurons (chiefly pyramidal cells) which send them to the motoneurons and muscles.

Thus, we see that the integrated patterns of the motor acts, which have been established in the gnostic units by kinesthetic receptors, are now reproduced by association, are disintegrated into their elements, and in this form are transmitted to the effector organs. This course of events is diagrammatically represented in Figure IV-6.

We can ask an important question: Why is the movement once initiated by way of association not performed perpetually, taking into account that the kinesthetic messages from muscles participating in that movement are sent upward and reach the same gnostic units? The most probable answer to this question is that pyramidal cells are endowed with a powerful inhibitory loop, analogous to that attached to motoneurons (Renshaw cells), whose role is precisely to preclude perpetuation of a movement initiated in the kinesthetic units[16] (3a in Figure IV-6). It may be assumed that an analogous loop is attached to the kinesthetic gnostic units, precluding the reactivation of the projective area and in this way safeguarding the unitary character of the programed movement.

The proposed mechanism of voluntary movements seems to be in full agreement with, and largely supported by, both our psychological everyday experience and clinical observations.

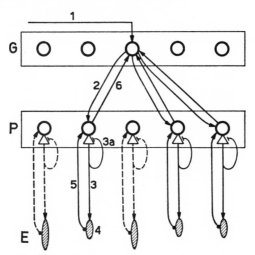

FIG. IV-6. MODEL OF ACTIVATION OF KINESTHETIC GNOSTIC UNIT BY ASSOCIATION

All denotations as in Figure IV-5.

1, Impulses from another gnostic field activate the kinesthetic gnostic unit; 2, impulses running to the projective area activate the corresponding receptive units which excite the pyramidal nerve-cells; 3, descending impulses reach muscle fibers, while impulses (3a) running through Renshaw loop inhibit the activated pyramidal cell; 4, contraction of muscle; 5, ascending impulses (via cerebellum) activate the receptive units in the projective area; 6, impulses running through converging connections to the kinesthetic gnostic unit reactivate this unit. The repetition of the same cycle of events is precluded by inhibitory Renshaw loop attached to the pyramidal cell (3a), and possibly to the gnostic unit itself (not indicated).

As far as the psychological evidence is concerned, we know that imagining a certain movement leads either to its overt performance or at least to its latent performance, manifested by the EMG record. The idea that the image of a movement is an agent eliciting that movement was clearly stated by James,[17] who called this phenomenon "ideo-motor action," and who provided extensive evidence to show that it is true. It is worthwhile to cite some of his own statements concerning this problem:

An anticipatory image, then, of sensorial consequences of a movement plus (at certain occasions) the fiat that these consequences shall become actual, is the only psychic state which introspection lets us discern as the forerunner of our voluntary act (*op. cit.* p. 501).

Sometimes a bare idea is sufficient, but sometimes an additional conscious element, in the shape of a fiat, a mandate or express consent has to intervene and precede the movement. The cases without a fiat constitute the more fundamental, because the more simple, variety (*op. cit.* p. 522).

We may then lay it down for certain that every representation of a movement awakens in some degree the actual movement which is its object; and awakens it in a maximum degree whenever it is not kept from so doing by an antagonistic representation present simultaneously to the mind (*op. cit.* p. 526).

These quotations show how clearly James saw the mechanism of voluntary movements, a mechanism at which he had arrived on the basis of astute introspection. It is most encouraging to know that we have come to exactly the same concept by quite different considerations—namely, through the physiological analysis of these movements.

No less conclusive seems to be the neurological evidence based either on the effects of injuries of the cortex or of its stimulation in unanesthetized subjects.

It is well known that lesions in the motor (projective kinesthetic) area of the cortex produce impairment of the *performance* of the voluntary movements programed in the gnostic area but do *not* abolish their plan. In fact, there is no doubt that a patient *has in mind* the movement he has to perform, tries to perform it, but is helpless or nearly so because his executive mechanism is damaged. Moreover since his peripheral feedback is normal, he knows that the joints did not change their posture, as required by the program, and in consequence he increases his mental effort to put the muscles into action exactly in the same way as one does when the movement encounters a resistance. The co-movements of the unaffected limb often observed in such cases are the manifestation of the mental effort of the patient expended in the fruitless attempt to perform the movement with the paralyzed limb. In those cases in which after a lapse of time the impairment is compensated, the motor patterns are *ipso facto* restored, and the subject does not need to learn them anew.

It is also noticeable that when particular elementary movements are elicited by stimulation of the corresponding points of the exposed motor cortex during a neurosurgical operation, they are *never* considered by the patient as true voluntary movements produced by himself but as being imparted to him independently of his will. In this respect the sensation is exactly the same as that experienced when a peripheral nerve or a muscle is artificially stimulated. This foreignness of the movement elicited by stimulation of the motor cortex is again explained by the fact that it is not programed in the gnostic kinesthetic field but produced by executive centers.

Further, according to our concept it could be expected that if a subject has a paralyzed limb caused to an injury in the descending pathways (for example, *capsula interna*), and concomitantly, because of the extension of lesion, he is deprived of the somesthetic proprioceptive sensations from that limb, he should not be aware of his paralysis. This is because he has correctly programed the movement by the kinesthetic gnostic field, has sent messages for its execution, and has no contrary information that the order was not fulfilled. In consequence, he should have a hallucination of the performance of the movement based on the same mechanism as hallucinations in exteroceptive analyzers discussed in Section 3, above (cf. Figure IV-3*a*).

As is well known, this conclusion is correct. There are patients with severe paresis or paralysis who deny its existence, asserting that they *are* quite capable of moving the affected limb. The symptom is often described by neurologists as "anosognosia."[18] In most cases it is only transient, because the visual feedback indicating that the limb does not move substitutes for the lack of proprioceptive feedback and teaches the patient that his feeling of movement is misleading.

On the other hand, quite different are the symptoms observed in those cases in which lesions are situated in front of the motor area and affect particular gnostic kinesthetic fields. As shown in the preceding chapter, the effects of such lesions (apraxias) consist in the impairment of *programing* of a given category of movements. In these cases the patient *can* perform a definite motor act, but he does not know *how* to perform it because of the destruction of the appropriate gnostic units. Thus, a patient who suffers from kinesthetic hand-agnosia and who was before the lesion a skilled typist has completely lost this ability and returned to his original method of pressing each key separately under the guidance of vision.[19] Similarly, a patient who suffers from kinesthetic word agnosia ("motor aphasia") is unable to speak, not because of the impairment of motor oral functions, but because his programing of speech patterns is destroyed. Consequently, in contradistinction to an anarthric patient, he is unable to *think* in words—his *internal* speech is lost, as can be shown by appropriate tests (see Section 9, below).

The important conclusion which can be inferred from our concept is that when a set of gnostic units representing a definite kinesthetic pattern has already been established, it can be thrown into operation through the associative way independently of the sensory input from the limb concerned. In other words, a given movement can be programed and executed even if the kinesthetic feedback is impaired or abolished. This is why a subject who has sustained a cerebellar operation does not lose either the programing of purposeful movements or the ability for their execution. The impairment concerns only the precision of a movement and its smooth character, because sensory feedback is indeed necessary in the course of the performance of motor acts, particularly when they are complex and serial. In this respect the kinesthetic gnosis does not differ at all from the auditory or visual gnosis. A subject who has lost his sight after the visual gnostic fields have been established, largely utilizes his visual imagery in spite of the absence of visual perception; a man who grew deaf as an adult utilizes his auditory images in spite of the absence of acoustic perception; in the same way a man who has lost kinesthetic input after the corresponding gnostic fields have been developed is able to utilize his kinesthetic images for performing those behavioral acts which he had learned before the injury. In all these subjects gnostic imperfection due to the lack of corresponding perceptions prevents their regulating behavior by the influx of information from the receptors, but does not prevent their utilizing gnosis as a programing device. This concept seems to be most important in our understanding and evaluation of the difference between those subjects who have lost the given modality of perceptions after the appropriate gnostic units had already been formed and those whose deficit occurred immediately after birth and whose gnosis had no opportunity to be developed.

To end our considerations concerning the mechanisms of voluntary movements, we shall return to the problem of the anatomy of the kinesthetic system and answer the question of the functional significance of the powerful descending pathways leading from the cerebral cortex to the cerebellum.

Of course the existence of these pathways should be compared to the efferent pathways proper to every analyzer, whose task is to control the sensory input by regulating its intensity and to subserve the targeting reflexes. It is, however, clear that such a descending controlling mechanism has a particular importance in the kinesthetic analyzer. In fact, the cerebellar cortex, being a true receptive surface of that analyzer, should be precisely informed about each movement which has been ordered by the programing centers. It seems probable that, since the messages from the cortex carrying information about the *program* of a movement reach the cerebellum slightly before the messages reaching this organ from muscles and carrying information about the *performance* of that movement, comparison of these informations has a first-rate significance for the motor behavior of the organism. In fact, if these two sets of messages are not congruent the cerebral cortex should immediately be informed and appropriately change the pattern of movement.

Assume, for instance, that we are placed in a medium which offers a resistance to our movements different from that in normal condition. This occurs when our body is immersed in water or when we perform movements partly in water and partly above its surface. When we put a limb out of water, we have a strange feeling that it has become unusually heavy, whereas when we submerge it, it seems unusually light (this will be also our feeling when we travel to the moon). In such situations the messages sent to the executive organs commanding the performance of a definite movement will certainly be false, and they will not fit those sent from the periphery to the cerebellum. The incongruence of the two sets of information will be immediately recorded by that organ, and the messages for the appropriate correction will be dispatched to the cortex.

Since not only the movements originating in the kinesthetic analyzer are regulated by the cerebellum, but also those involved in targeting reflexes and depending on other afferent systems, it is obvious that not only the kinesthetic area is bidirectionally connected with the cerebellum, but also the cortical areas representing somesthetic, visual, and auditory systems. In fact, the computation of the *programing* of a movement involved, say, in a visual targeting reflex, consisting in turning the head and eyes toward a given stimulus-object, with the actual *performance* of that movement, as verified by grasping that object by the foveal vision, is again of first importance for the animal's well-being. Hence the conclusion that exteroceptive stimuli, as well as, although to a lesser extent than, kinesthetic stimuli, should be represented in the cerebellum—a fact which has puzzled many investigators concerned with the problems of cerebellar functions.

9. Programing of motor acts with and without their execution

As we saw in the preceding section, James' solution of the problem concerning the *psychological* mechanism of voluntary movements was that the image of a movement is a sufficient condition for its execution, whereas the mental "fiat," "mandate," or "express consent" does not usually appear in our introspection and is thrown into action only in some special cases. According to James' view, if the image of a movement is *not* followed by its performance, this is due only to the fact that it is "kept from so doing by an antagonistic representation presented simultaneously to the mind."

Let us see whether James' statement is true also from the physiological point of view.

In Chapter XI, where we shall discuss in detail the mechanism of the instrumental motor acts in animals on the basis of the relevant experimental material, we shall see that their performance is due to a joint operation of cognitive associations and drives. Moreover, it will be shown that the stronger the associative bond between the stimulus and the motor response, the smaller amount of emotive arousal is needed for the elicitation of that response.

We think that this rule, which, as we have seen in our previous discussion, is also observed in all associative processes, may be extrapolated to the human motor behavior—that so-called voluntary movements are motivationally determined in the same way as instrumental responses in animals. Accordingly, we think that the "fiat" proposed by James, consisting precisely in the motivational aspect of the performance of a movement, is indispensable for *every* motor act produced by association independently of whether it is or is not introspectively detectable.

Incidentally, it should be added that, just as it is true in respect to other analyzers (cf. Section 5), this "fiat" is already included in the very act of the *intention* of a movement and not in its performance. Precisely as we do not imagine the taste of food when we are not hungry or sexual episodes when we do not experience the sexual drive, so we do not imagine a movement when there is no emotional motivation facilitating it. As stated before, the strength of this emotional motivation necessary for the performance of the movement is inversely related to the strength of associative bond between the actually operating stimuli and the kinesthesis of that movement.

Following is a simple example illustrating this situation.

Suppose that we are in the habit of arising punctually at a given hour and do it every morning. The association between the moment of our arising (checked by a watch) and the kinesthesis of this act is so strong that we perform this act almost "automatically," hardly realizing its motivation. If, however, our intention is inhibited by some antagonistic factors, such as a cold room, rheumatic pains, or simply sleepiness, then, depending on the situation, either the behavioral act of getting up will not be performed and we shall remain in bed, or the motivation will be increased (and in effect clearly realized: for example, "I shall be late for work" or "I shall miss the train") and the motor act will be accomplished. Incidentally, the situation is exactly the same as that encountered in experiments on rats who have to reach a feeder by passing through an electrified corridor.

The situation is, however, more complex in respect to oral kinesthesis involved in speech. As is well known, speech plays a double role in our lives. On the one hand, it is a behavioral act, being the main source of interhuman communication and as such analogous to all other behavioral acts described above (so-called "expressive speech"). On the other hand, as we know from self-observation, we are endowed with the capacity of "internal speech" or "verbal thinking," whose output is directed, not to the effectors, but to other parts of the cognitive system. Thus, the important problem arises as to the intimate mechanism of internal speech and why, in contradistinction to other instances of the activation of kinesthetic gnostic units discussed above, internal speech is not followed by the performance of motor acts, as is the case with expressive speech.

We are not in a position to present an unequivocal solution to this problem, but we should like to offer tentatively two hypotheses which may account for verbal thinking.

To begin with, it is generally assumed that when a child has just learned to speak, he utters everything he "has in his mind"—that is, the activation of his verbal gnostic units is immediately transmitted to the efferent neurons, as is true of other parts of kinesthetic gnosis. But growing older, a person gradually learns to "hide his thoughts"— that is, to inhibit the overt motor acts produced by activation of kinesthetic verbal units. In this way internal speech is thought to develop.

It is often argued that internal speech is *due* to the minute muscular contractions of the mouth shown by electromyographical records. This view, however, seems to be erroneous, since even total paralysis of muscles involved in speech, produced by central or peripheral lesions, does not affect internal speech.

The proposed inhibitory theory of internalization of speech is in agreement with a number of facts observed both in normal subjects and in psychiatric patients. For instance, we may observe that whereas in normal conditions we hardly ever speak aloud when we are alone, our internal speech becomes externalized when we are in a state of strong arousal. Hence the loud emotional utterances produced when we are in a rage or frightened, and the entire speeches we deliver aloud when we imagine our adversary before us. Sometimes when we perform some complex reasoning involving a strong mental effort, we have also a tendency to utter our ideas. Similarly, in certain cases of schizophrenia the patient continuously "speaks forward"—the symptom denoted as *"Vorbeireden"*; the same is sometimes observed in senile persons. Finally, the fact that our internal speech *is* usually accompanied by minor muscular contractions of the mouth may be explained as the result of their incomplete inhibition.

It seems possible, however, to explain the internalization of speech by a quite different mechanism, considering it not as a secondary event due to inhibition, but as a primary event, parallel to, but not derived from, external speech.

It is worth noting that our switching from external speech for the use of interpersonal communication to internal speech for our own use occurs extremely smoothly, and we hardly ever substitute one for the other. Incidentally, there are persons who have a strong tendency to speak aloud and who use their pet animals as listeners. In others, the tendency not to speak prevails, and they must make a mental effort to compel themselves to communicate their thoughts to others.

Now it may be supposed that the immediate device which switches external speech (aloud or in a whisper) to internal speech, and vice versa, depends simply on the *posture of our mouth and glottis*. For instance, when writing these words I notice that with my mouth tightly closed, I write under the control of internal speech only; if, however, I keep my mouth half open I immediately begin to make the corresponding movements with my mouth. I wonder whether other persons have the same experience. Thus, we assume that when the mouth-closing muscles are relaxed and the vocal cords are constricted, the activation of word-kinesthetic units leads to loud speech; when the mouth-closing muscles are relaxed and the vocal cords are relaxed, whispered speech ensues; when mouth-closing muscles are contracted, our speech is internal. These postures of glottis and mouth are to a large extent associated with particular external and mental situations, and in this way speech can easily be switched from one type to the other as the effect of a *sui generis* instrumental conditioned reflex. Thus, participating in a social meeting, we speak aloud when our speech is directed to everyone, we whisper when we have something to say to our neighbor, and we think verbally if our thoughts are destined for ourselves.

To repeat, we propose that the postures of the mouth and glottis represent those behavioral acts which are nicely adjusted by conditioning to particular social and mental situations, whereas the type of speech (internal, whisper or external) is a direct effect of these postures.

It seems that the proposed concept applies not only to our verbal behavior but also to all other types of kinesthetic gnosis. If, for instance, lying in our beds in the morning we plan our behavioral acts (locomotor and/or manipulatory) we must perform during the day, we may have their clear images in our minds without any tendency to their realization, simply because our actual posture is incompatible with them. Similarly, we may observe that it is much easier for us to abstain from a highly motivated movement when our actual posture does not allow us to perform it, than when we are on the verge of its performance. As a matter of fact, many persons, in order to resist the temptation of doing something inappropriate, try beforehand to create a situation in which the corresponding motor act would be handicapped. Ulysses, who ordered his colleagues to tie him to the mast of his ship in order to prevent him from visiting the Sirens, may be considered as the most drastic example of such a situation.

Returning to our further analysis of the internal speech, we can infer that a lesion sustained to the word-kinesthetic gnostic field producing "motor aphasia," in contradistinction to a lesion in the projective mouth area producing anarthria, affects not only external but also internal verbalization. Since such a patient is *ipso facto* unable to inform us of his status, we have to resort to indirect proofs. For illustration we shall present a case which, owing to the localization of the lesion, was particularly instructive.

A female patient, age forty-two, was hit on the head by an ax, the injury affecting almost exactly the left frontal opercular region. As a result, the patient completely lost her speech but had no impairment of hand praxis.

One month after the accident the patient was in a generally good state, very cooperative and alert. She was able to care for herself, in dressing, eating, and so on. No hand apraxia or agraphia was observed.

Spontaneous speech was impossible. She uttered only a few words—"yes," "no," "here," "Jesus"—pronouncing them without any anarthric distortions. When trying to speak, she utilized these words in various sequences giving them vivid intonations. After some time the vocabulary of the patient was somewhat increased and included such words and phrases as: "mister," "do you know?" "isn't it?" "it seems to me"; her speech still consisted in repeating these words and phrases in various combinations. She was of course perfectly aware that these did not represent what she wanted to say, and she repeatedly manifested her impatience and distress about it. Her mimicry was fully preserved; by making various grimaces, she tried to convey her feelings and thoughts.

Naming was impossible, although she always indicated the usage of objects presented to her. Her responses consisted only in uttering words of her repertory. Repetition of words heard was also impossible; sometimes she succeeded in repeating some vowels. On the other hand, singing without words was totally preserved. Comprehension was fairly good, but she was able to perform only one task of a few tasks ordered.

Copying of written words was preserved; however writing under dictation, or after showing her objects, was impossible. The only thing she was able to write without copying was her signature or the sequence of digits when the first few were already written.

For our present consideration, the most important feature of this patient was that of her total failure to write words when she heard them and/or the corresponding object was shown to her, in contradistinction to the ease with which she wrote them when copying, or when she had to write some well-known sequence of signs. This failure was due to the fact that writing words under dictation or as an expression of one's own thoughts is preceded by their *internal verbalization*, which in this patient was abolished. The lack of internal speech explains also why the patient, having unimpaired comprehension of speech, failed to perform more than one task. We know from our own experience that when we have to perform only one task, we do it directly in response to the auditory order; but having two tasks to perform, we verbalize them in our internal speech and then perform the second one on the basis of its reverbalization.

10. General pathology of associations

When the pathway between two gnostic fields is damaged, the connections which have been formed between the units of these fields are reduced or abolished. In consequence the appropriate associative processes are to a greater or lesser extent disturbed. In humans these disorders are best manifested in those associations which are involved in speech. Perhaps the most illustrative material in this respect is provided by cases of pure amnestic aphasia not contaminated by "motor" aphasia (word-kinesthetic agnosia). As will be shown in Chapter V, Section 5, this form of aphasia is due to the damage of the connections linking the visual gnostic area (V) with the word-kinesthetic gnostic field (K-W). As a result of this damage the patient has difficulty in naming objects either perceived or imagined.

Below we list the most important and common characteristics of defects of speech manifested in these patients.

(1) The disorders of naming have a dynamic character—that is, the responses of the patient are usually unstable. He is able to name a given object properly, and then fail to do so a few minutes later, or vice versa. Similarly, the general level of his naming performance may change considerably from one test session to another, depending on his emotional state, fatigue, good or bad feeling, etc.

(2) Other things being equal, the probability of a good verbal response depends on how common the object is, how strong its emotional taint, and how early in life its name was learned.

(3) The response-latency in naming objects is usually longer in aphasics than in normal subjects, and this depends again on how common the given word is.

(4) If several common objects are shown to the patient and he has to name them in quick succession as the examiner repeatedly points to them in random order, his responses deteriorate very rapidly.

(5) When a patient with amnestic aphasia fails to give a proper re-

sponse to the object shown to him, he either may give no response at all (saying, for instance, "I don't know") or he may give a *wrong* response. In the latter instance the patient commonly utters the name of an object *belonging to the same category* as the object pointed to him.

(6) Some patients with amnestic aphasia display a perseverative tendency in naming objects. For instance, if a patient has named correctly the first object shown to him, and then we point to another object of the same category, he may repeat the previous name. Or the patient exhibits an obsessive tendency to name many objects shown to him by one definite name.

Below we present an extract of the examination of a patient suffering from relatively pure amnestic aphasia who had a strong tendency to give any response, whether it was good, or bad.

Objects Shown to Patient	Responses by Patient
handkerchief	handkerchief
pen	cigarette
cigarette	cigarette
spectacles	cig ...
coin	coin
key	cigarette, no

Interval

coin	coin
cigarette	cigarette
handkerchief	handkerchief
watch	coin
pencil	cigarette
spectacles	coin, no coin
purse	such a coin
key	cigarette
watch	coin

Interval

picture of a pig	pig
picture of a cart	cart
picture of a mouse	little pig

It should be stressed that comprehension of words heard and their repetition were in this patient almost unimpaired, and that when the examiner prompted him by saying the beginning of the word, he immediately was able to give the full name.

The enumerated characteristics of the disorders of associations observed in amnestic aphasia are also seen after impairment of other associative systems. For instance, if we take a patient with impairment of comprehension of words heard due to the damage of connections between the audioverbal gnostic field (A-W) and visual gnostic area (Chapter V, Section 2), we again notice the dynamic character of the disorder, the prolonged latency of the responses, the detrimental effect of trials given in quick succession, the categorial character of errors and the tendency to perseveration.

How can these disorders be explained in the framework of our concept?

First, it should be observed that all the symptoms listed above may be divided into two groups. In the first group we include those symptoms which simply manifest the impairment of the given sort of connections, such as: the failure to give any response, the prolonged latency of the response, and its dependence on the familiarity of the object and/or its emotional significance. These symptoms may be explained by the redundancy principle, assuming that the more numerous the connections between the two sets of units, the greater the probability of their preservation. The fact that in a state of moderate arousal the responses of the patient improve is explained by the unspecific facilitation of the recipient gnostic units.

The second group of symptoms includes those in which *wrong* responses appear instead of the correct ones. The question may be asked what the mechanism of the occurrence of these wrong responses is.

In order to explain this mechanism we must take into account the following two properties of the higher nervous activity. The first property, which will be discussed in detail in Chapter XII, is that if a set of gnostic units is activated by perception or association, this activation produces a more or less prolonged facilitatory after-effect in these units. This after-effect is assumed to be due to the reverberating circuits attached to the gnostic units and thrown into operation by their excitation. The second property relevant for our discussion concerns the structure of the gnostic units representing the discriminated stimulus-patterns (cf. Chapter II, Sections 8 and 9). It should be remembered that these patterns are doubly represented in the gnostic areas—by more "crude" units representing the general properties of the whole category of the given patterns and by "fine" units corresponding to individual properties of particular patterns (cf. Figure II-16).

Having in mind these two principles we can easily understand both the occurrence of erroneous responses in aphasic patients and their main characteristics. Take for our analysis again the wrong naming in amnestic aphasia. Each object of the external world to be named is represented in the visual gnostic area by categorial units and individual units. Since the categorial units participate in *each* perception of the stimulus-objects of a given category, they send their axons to *all* the word-kinesthetic units representing the names of these objects. On the other hand, the sets of individual-object units send axons to the word-kinesthetic units representing their individual names (Fig. IV-7*a*).

After the injury sustained to the pathways linking the gnostic visual area with the kinesthetic speech field the axons of categorial units are less affected than the axons of individual-object units because they are much more numerous. In consequence, when an object belonging to a given category is presented, the messages originating from the individual-object units may fail to reach the appropriate word-kinesthetic units, but the messages originating from the categorial units will certainly reach a number of word-kinesthetic units representing the names of the objects of the given category. In consequence, the patient will either fail to utter any name, if the activation of these units is subliminal, or he will utter that name within the scope of a given category of objects which happened to be facilitated by previous experiences (Figure IV-7*b*). Accordingly, he may utter a name which he said before, making a perseverative error; or he may say the name of a similar object possessing some emotional significance (such as coin or cigarette); or he may say the name of a similar object, which is better known to him; for instance, he will say nut instead of acorn, frog instead of lizard, or parrot instead of owl. It should be added that since in these patients comprehension of speech may be completely preserved, the subject pronouncing a given name is frequently aware of his mistake. Hence the following types of responses are most common: (a picture of lizard is shown) "how it is called, I learned it in biology, this is not a *frog*, I cannot say"; (rabbit) "*cat*, no *cat*, but similar to a *cat*"; (bear) "it is wild, I forgot, *woolf*, no this is no *woolf*, something different."*

It should be emphasized that although erroneous responses are most conspicuous and abundant when the given associative system is impaired, they may be also present in the normal condition, or on the borderline between normalcy and pathology. Thus if somebody calls one person by the name of another person for emotional reasons, or if an old person speaking about meals regularly confuses their names (fully recognizing his lapses), these facts are explainable by the same mechanisms as those discussed above.

Thus our interpretation of erroneous responses in aphasic patients can be applied to a large range of phenomena in the associative functions. To sum up, it may be said that if a stimulus-object playing a transmittent role in a given association is represented in the appropriate

* All these examples are taken from a recent monograph by M. Maruszewski, *Aphasia, the Problems of Theory and Therapy* (Warsaw, 1966) (in Polish).

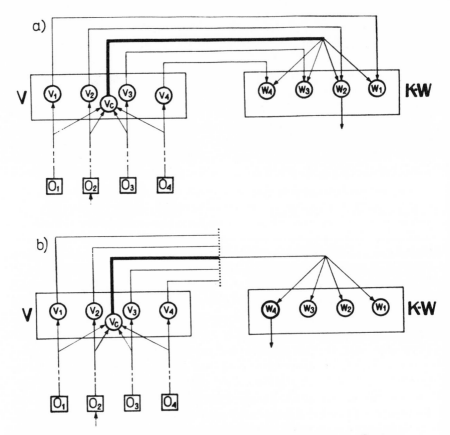

Fig. IV-7. Schema Representing Connections between Visual Gnostic
Area and Word-Kinesthetic Gnostic Field (a) and the
Result of Their Damage (b)

V, visual gnostic area; K-W, word-kinesthetic gnostic field. O_1, O_2, O_3, O_4, four visual objects of a given category; v_1, v_2, v_3, v_4, corresponding individual visual units; w_1, w_2, w_3, w_4, corresponding word-kinesthetic units; v_c, categorial visual unit.

In (a) connections between individual visual units and corresponding word-kinesthetic units are shown by thin lines; connections between categorial visual unit and *all* word-kinesthetic units representing the names of the objects of a given category are shown by a thick line to emphasize their great quantity. The object shown (O_2) is named correctly.

In (b) injury (dotted line) is sustained in the pathway linking V with K-W. For the sake of simplicity it is assumed that all the individual connections are destroyed, whereas categorial connections are partially preserved. In consequence, the verbal response depends on the temporary increase of excitability of the given word-kinesthetic unit (thick circle). Therefore, the presentation of object O_2 activates the word-kinesthetic unit w_4 instead of w_2 and produces a wrong verbal response.

gnostic area by both categorial and individual sets of units, then the messages reaching the recipient gnostic field may be misled and delivered to those units which for some reason are in a state of raised excitability. The stronger the connections between the individual-object units of the transmittent gnostic field and the units of the recipient gnostic field, the more stable the associations and the smaller the probability of a mistake; on the contrary, the stronger the dominance of the categorial units over the individual-object units, or the stronger the excitability of a particular set of recipient units, the more probable is the erroneous response.

11. Summary and conclusions

Whereas in the two preceding chapters we dealt with activation of gnostic units obtained through the stimulation of receptors, this chapter was concerned with activation of these units by association. Whereas excitation of gnostic units by messages coming from the periphery gives rise to unitary perceptions, excitation of those units by association usually leads to the occurrence of images. This psychological difference between the two phenomena was explained by the difference in their physiological organization. It was pointed out that unitary perceptions arise when the messages coming from the lower parts of the afferent system to the projective area elicit the targeting reflex adjusting the sensory organs to the optimal reception of a given stimulus-object. This reflex gives to the experience the mark of externalization and reality of which the image is devoid. Thus, it was assumed that we have the experience of perception whenever the gnostic units are excited together with the corresponding projective units, whereas we have the experience of image whenever the gnostic units are excited separately.

It may be deduced from this hypothesis that lesions sustained on any level of the afferent axis, including the projective area, lead to the loss of perceptions but leave images unimpaired, if these lesions occurred after the development of the gnostic area. On the other hand, lesions sustained in the gnostic fields do not affect reception of the stimulus-objects, but render both perceptions and images of the given category impossible. The observed facts confirm this deduction.

The next problem which had to be solved was that of the origin of hallucinations—that is, those experiences which arise by association but nevertheless have the psychological quality of perceptions. It was assumed that in these cases the excitation of the gnostic units through association is transmitted to the projective area by the pathways running downward from the gnostic area, causing both areas to be jointly activated. This downward excitation of the projective area does not occur in a normal condition, because this area is constantly busy with receiving messages from the periphery, blocking those messages which come from the gnostic area. Thus the conclusion is reached that hallucinations occur when the projective area is totally idled by being cut off from any sensory input. This indeed happens in deep sleep, giving rise to dreams, during long-lasting sensory deprivation, and in delirious states when the subject is in a power of strong endogenous excitement inhibiting all afferent input.

Another type of hallucination may arise in those afferent systems in which gnosis is poorly developed and in consequence the perceptive units are represented by the same neurons as projective units. This happens, for instance, in the somesthetic analyzer and gives rise to the formation of hallucinations of itching or pain when the respective units are excited by association.

It may be inferred from this analysis that the occurrence of hallucinations in the normal life of animals is more usual than in man, since the gnostic fields of the former are more poorly developed. In fact, close observation of dogs in a variety of experiments suggests that this may be true. In particular, it may be conjectured that in classical conditioning the well-established CS evokes the hallucination of the US rather than its image.

The strength of images may vary within a wide range, depending on the abundance of the connections between the transmittent and recipient set of units, on the intensity of excitation of transmittent units, and on the strength of arousal of a given gnostic field. In other respects unitary images obey the same rules as those for unitary perceptions, in particular the principle of integrity and the principle of antagonism between images represented by the gnostic units of the same field.

When the same gnostic unit is subjected to the bombardment by impulses reaching it through perceptive ways and associative ways, the summation of the two volleys occurs. The following particular cases of this summation may take place.

(1) The stimulus-pattern eliciting a given unitary perception is fully adequate, and therefore, it is recognized completely with minimal latency; then the associative messages can add nothing to the activation of the unit (Sherringtonian occlusion).

(2) The stimulus-pattern acting on the receptive surface is defective, and therefore the convergence of the messages coming from the periphery upon the given gnostic unit is not complete; in that case the impulses arriving at that unit by associative ways are no longer

occluded and may contribute significantly to the recognition of the stimulus-object.

(3) The stimulus-pattern acting on the receptive surface is defective, but the associations are misleading; in that case a subject will perceive, not a true object or phenomenon, but another one which also fits this pattern. As the result the phenomenon called illusion will take place.

In humans the simplest method of detecting associations is by introspection, when the perception of a stimulus-object represented by the transmittent set of gnostic units gives rise to the image of a stimulus-object represented by the recipient set of gnostic units. This method is, however, not sensitive enough, because in many situations the existing associations may fail to be revealed in this way. Two other experimental methods are proposed which seem to be more reliable in this respect; the substitution method, when the recipient stimulus-object is substituted by another, and the reaction of surprise is observed; the expectation method, in which the latency of perceptions of associated and non-associated stimulus-patterns is compared. Other methods detecting associations are based on conditioning procedure and on labeled evoked potential procedure; they have, however, the same, or even lesser, sensitivity than the introspective method.

The function of the kinesthetic gnostic area differs from that of other gnostic areas in that whereas the role of the latter consists in perception and transmission of messages to other gnostic areas, the main role of the former area is the programing of skillful (voluntary) movements performed by the organism. This role is accomplished as follows: the messages arriving from other gnostic fields reach a given set of kinesthetic gnostic units when these are facilitated by the emotive system, and are delivered to the projective units; hence the messages are sent through descending pathways to the muscles. This process occurs because at the moment when the gnostic kinesthetic units are activated the corresponding projective units are inactive.

This concept finds its confirmation in a number of psychological and neurological facts. In this context, of particular importance is the old concept put forward by James, stating that the chief, if not the only, source of voluntary movements is provided by their images (ideo-motor action). On the other hand, the neurological data show that whereas an injury to the kinesthetic projective area does not abolish the program of a voluntary motor act, an injury to the gnostic kinesthetic area does. When the injury affects the motor descending system, it produces a paralysis which is noticed by the patient, since his sensory feedback from the affected limb is preserved; when, however, this injury is combined with that affecting the sensory input, the paralysis fails to be noticed by the patient (except by vision), because he has no information whether the orders sent from the programing units were fulfilled (anosognosia).

Along with the messages sent from the cortex to the executive organs for fulfillment, a copy of these messages is sent to the cerebellum. In this way the cerebellum receives information about both the program of the movement dictated by the gnostic kinesthetic units and its fulfillment by effectors. If the two messages are not congruent, the cerebellum sends orders to the cortex requiring the correction of the program.

As a rule the associative activation of a given set of kinesthetic gnostic units leads *ipso facto* to the performance of the movement concerned. There are, however, numerous instances in which activation of gnostic units does not lead to the overt motor act. The most conspicuous instance of this kind is provided by so-called internal speech or verbal thinking.

A discussion of the difference between expressive speech (in which a subject performs the appropriate mouth movements) and internal speech (in which he only thinks in words without their utterance) leads to two hypotheses: first, that internal speech is developed from expressive speech by inhibition of overt motor acts, second, that different postures of mouth and glottis are the determining factors of loud speech, whispering, or verbal thinking.

An injury sustained to the word-kinesthetic gnostic area, in contradistinction to an injury sustained to the corresponding projective area, produces the impairment not only of expressive speech but also of verbal thinking. A proof of this impairment is that whereas copying of a written (or printed) text is unimpaired, writing under dictation or spontaneous writing is impossible, because it requires internal verbalization.

When the pathways linking two gnostic fields are damaged, the corresponding associative processes are either totally abolished or disturbed. This disturbance is manifested by partial loss of associative responses, by their prolonged latencies, and/or by substituting the wrong responses for the correct ones with the tendency to perseveration. These symptoms are explained by reference to the redundancy principle and by the assumption that categorial gnostic units have more numerous connections with the recipient units than individual-object gnostic units.

In the next chapter particular connections between various gnostic fields established in humans owing to their common experiences will be described.

References to Chapter IV

1. A. Fessard and H. Gastaut. 1958. Correlations neurophysiologiques de la formation des réflexes conditionnels. In M. A. Fessard, H. Gastaut, A. N. Leontiev, G. de Montpellier, and H. Pieron, eds., *Le conditionnement et l'apprentissage*, pp. 15–90. Paris: Presses Universitaires.

2. О. И. Скороходова. 1954. Как я воспринимаю и представляю окружающий мир. (How I perceive and imagine the external world.) Moscow: Izd. Akad. Pedag. Nauk RSFSR.

3. J. M. Nielsen. 1951. In discussion in L. A. Jeffress, ed., *Cerebral Mechanisms in Behavior*, pp. 183–93. New York: Wiley.

4. M. Critchley. 1955. *The Parietal Lobes*, pp. 311–12. London: Arnold.

5. G. H. von Bonin, H. W. Garol, and W. S. McCulloch. 1942. The functional organization of the occipital lobe. In H. Klüver, ed., *Visual Mechanisms*, pp. 165–92. Lancaster, Pa.: Cattell.
   P. Bailey, G. H. von Bonin, H. W. Garol, and W. S. McCulloch. 1943. Functional organization of temporal lobe of monkey (*Macaca mulatta*) and chimpanzee (*Pan satyrus*). *J. Neurophysiol.*, 6: 121–28.

5a. W. Dement and N. Kleitman. 1957. Cyclic variations of EEG during sleep and their relation to eye movements, body motility and dreaming. *Electroenceph. Clin. Neurophysiol.*, 9: 673–90.

6. T. V. Moore. 1939. *Cognitive Psychology*. Philadelphia: J. B. Lippincott.

7. W. Penfield and H. Jasper. 1954. *Epilepsy and the Functional Anatomy of the Human Brain*. London: J. & A. Churchill.

8. M. Critchley. 1955 (see note 4 above), p. 91.

9. Th. Ribot. 1911. *The Psychology of the Emotions*, p. 143. New York: Walter Scott Publishing Co.

10. Ю. Конорски и С. Миллер. 1936. Условные рефлексы 'двигательного анализатора. (Conditioned reflexes of the motor analyzer.) *Trudy Fiziol. Lab. I. P. Pavlova*, 6: 119–278. English summary, pp. 285–88.

11. C. Dobrzecka, B. Sychowa, and J. Konorski. 1965. The effects of lesions within the sensory-motor cortex upon instrumental response to the "specific tactile stimulus." *Acta Biol. Exp. Vars.*, 25: 91–106.

12. C. Dobrzecka and J. Konorski. Unpublished observations.

13. F. Morrell and H. H. Jasper. 1956. Electrographic studies of the formation of temporary connections in the brain. *Electroenceph. Clin. Neurophysiol.*, 8: 201–15.

14. И. О. Нарбутович и Н. А. Подкопаев. 1936. Условный рефлекс как ассоциация. (The conditioned reflex as association.) *Trudy Fiziol. Lab. I. P. Pavlova*, 6 (No. 2): 5–24. English summary, pp. 243–44.
   W. J. Brogden. 1939. Sensory preconditioning. *J. Exp. Psychol.*, 25: 323–32.
   See also *Hilgard and Marquis' Conditioning and Learning*. 1961. Revised by G. A. Kimble. 2d ed., New York: Appleton-Century-Crofts.

15. G. Durup and A. Fessard. 1935. L'electroencephalogramme de l'homme. *Année Psychol.*, 36: 1–32.
16. C. G. Phillips. 1956. Intracellular records from Betz cells in the cat. *Quart. J. Exp. Physiol.*, 41: 58–69.

   D. P. Purpura and H. Grundfest. 1956. Nature of dendritic potentials and synaptic mechanisms in cerebral cortex of cat. *J. Neurophysiol.*, 19: 573–95.

   K. Kubota, H. Sakata, K. Takahashi, and M. Uno. 1965. Location of the recurrent inhibitory synapse on cat pyramidal tract cell. *Proc. Japan Acad.*, 41: 195–97.
17. W. James. 1950. *The Principles of Psychology.* Vol. II, chap. 26. New York: Dover.
18. M. Critchley. 1955 (see note 4 above), chap. 8.
19. A. R. Luria. Personal communication.

CHAPTER V

A SURVEY OF THE MAIN ASSOCIATIONS
IN MAN AND ANIMALS

1. Introductory remarks

It should be realized that in the present period of the development of behavioral sciences there prevails a certain approach to the phenomena of animal and human behavior which is now deeply rooted and often considered as the only scientific approach to this subject. It has two main characteristics; it is experimental, and it is artificial. The artificial nature of the approach is manifested by the fact that the stimuli we choose for our investigation and/or the motor responses we require that the subject perform never happen in ordinary life. On the afferent side, the dog in his normal life never has to expect food when he hears strange sounds originating in places not contiguous to the source of food, never has to discriminate between two pure tones, one signaling the food and the other not; the rat never has to jump in the Lashley apparatus, choosing the door with the triangle and disregarding that with the circle; and so on. On the efferent side, the dog never has to work to obtain food by lifting his hindleg; the cat, by pseudo-scratching or pseudo-licking his anus; and the rat, by continuously pressing the bar under the most sophisticated schedules of reinforcement.

The origin of this approach may be easily determined. It stems from that moment when Pavlov first used the metronome as a food CS, substituting it for the natural CS consisting in the presentation of food and when Thorndike forced cats to scratch in order to be released from a cage.

As is well known, this line of research grew immensely in the course of this century; the artificial character of the tasks required of animals, and also of human subjects, became, as a matter of fact, its main property and privilege.

Not detracting anything from the great merits of this line of research (which is largely represented in the second part of this book), we think it is proper to give a thought to whether it is the only reasonable approach to the problems of behavior. After all, we should not forget that animals' and humans' nervous systems grew in phylogeny and ontogeny under the continuous pressure of the surrounding world which carved them in such a way as to make them best adjusted. In consequence, if we substitute artificial factors to act upon the organism for those which really and constantly act upon it, we may lose something very substantial which can contribute largely to understanding the functioning of that organism. Therefore, it seems that the time is ripe for us to become again more "naturalistic," and, in addition to having the animals trained by inventing new agents to influence them and new responses to be performed by them, to observe also in which ways natural life *has* already trained an animal or man and which mechanisms were developed for this purpose.

We have already done this in the preceding chapters, in which we were concerned with the physiological analysis of perceptions and images—not those which were artificially instilled upon the subject, but those which the subject already has in his repertory. We shall follow the same track in the present chapter, and we shall see which are the associations developed in man and animals under the influence of the agents of the external world operating according to the laws of nature, and not according to those laws which we ourselves have instituted in the experimental chamber, and which cease to be obeyed outside this limited space.

As in the preceding chapters, the main subject of our analysis will be the man brought up in our contemporary civilization, because the associations formed in his life are without any doubt best known to us. In fact, we have the opportunity to observe ourselves and our fellows during our whole life, whereas other species are observed only by some of us in artificial conditions and during the time of our professional duties.

It has to be admitted that the chief, or perhaps the only, anatomical substrate for interperceptual associations of higher order are provided by the associative fibers connecting various parts of the cerebral cortex. We do not know whether any role is played by the interthalamic connections, and therefore we have to leave this question open. As far as the cortical associative bundles are concerned they have been studied by both anatomical and physiological (chiefly neuronographical) methods. Of course, it would be tempting to try to superimpose those purely functional *associations* we shall discuss in this chapter on the canvas of actually existing anatomical *connections* linking particular areas of the cortex. We will, however, resist this temptation for the following reasons. First, the anatomical evidence concerning intercortical connections is still highly spurious and often contradictory; it is also certainly not complete. Second, as pointed out in the preceding chapters, the localization of various gnostic areas is also far from being exactly known, and various methods of their study give contradictory results. This being so, we feel that such an adjustment of the psychological data presented below to the spurious anatomical evidence would be rather futile and arbitrary. Only in those cases in which the evidence of the correspondence between two sets of data seems to be convincing shall we turn our attention to it.

The large part of our considerations will be concerned with those associations which play a substantial role in human speech. In effect this chapter will give a broad and general outline of the physiological mechanisms involved in this important, and purely human, associative function. In order to avoid possible misunderstandings, we must stress that we do not enter into the immense, and sometimes controversial, literature concerning speech disorders or to any comparisons of our conclusions with those of other authors. We simply follow our own way ensuing from our concepts, and the fact that many authors (but of course not all) have similar if not identical views which are based on their own materials makes the documentation of our view more substantial. It should, however, be realized that in spite of thousands of cases of various forms of aphasia described in the literature, this field of investigation still remains shaky and uncertain for at least three reasons. First, lesions of the brain, whether traumatic, vascular, or due to tumors, are always complex, and their localization obviously does not correspond to strict limits of functional areas. Second, the methods of examination of patients are widely divergent, mostly casual and not rigorous; therefore they often do not provide the proper documentation for drawing definite conclusions concerning the character of a speech disorder in particular cases. Third, we have good reasons to believe that functional organization of various aspects of speech may vary widely in different persons, depending on the innate developmental properties of various brains and the methods by which the given verbal function is acquired. To give an illustrative example: acquisition of reading faculty is accomplished by learning to read entire words as entities in some languages and by learning to form words from letters in others; some persons grasp the meaning of the written word directly from its visual pattern, whereas others do so by the intermediary of internal, or even external, speech, still others, by the intermediary of its auditory image, or by mixing all these methods in various proportions. In consequence, the symptomatology of alexic aphasia may be totally different in various patients even after exactly the same lesions, depending on which mechanism of reading was in operation in the given case. Another example: since I began to learn English as an adult, by reading English texts, my understanding of the spoken language often occurs through visualizing written words. In consequence, if I should develop visual agnosia, my comprehension of spoken English would be certainly much impaired, and nobody would understand why.

As will be seen from further discussion, we shall return here to the old line of thinking, called contemptuously "diagram-making" and severely criticized by later authors. We are not at all convinced by this criticism; we believe that if diagrams proposed by the pioneers of aphasiology are inaccurate or misleading, because of their inadequate information, this does not mean that diagram-making as such should be rejected, but only that improved diagrams should be used. It is quite possible that our own diagrams of connections responsible for speech are also inaccurate, as evidenced by the fact that many times we are unable on their basis to understand the particular symptomatology of a given case. This is because both our knowledge of the gnostic areas involved in speech is still unsatisfactory and the connections between them may be different from those we suggest. What we do claim, however, is that our general approach to aphasiology is sound and that pursuing this line will contribute both to understanding the speech mechanisms and to finding proper ways for their compensation in case of disorders of these mechanisms.*

Our discussion on speech and its disorders is limited to the most primitive and basic functions, and we do not go into any complicated problems which would require many arbitrary suppositions. Therefore, we deliberately omit here the discussion of such problems as the mechanisms of calculation, abstraction, and the like. We deal only with concrete speech on the most primitive level of its development.

Considering each group of associations, we shall separately discuss those associations which are not involved in speech function and those which are involved in it. The first type of association is in many cases proper not only to humans but also to animals; the second type is characteristic only for humans. For the sake of brevity, we shall call

---

* The same line of approach to the problems of aphasia has been recently assumed by N. Geschwind, who considers speech disorders as due to disconnection syndromes (N. Geschwind, Disconnection syndromes in animals and man, *Brain*, 88 [1966]: 237–96).

the first type "non-verbal associations" and the second type, "verbal associations."

If in preliminary training, connections are firmly established leading from a set of units A to a set of units B, and from units B to units C, then it is nearly certain that this pathway will be utilized when connections from A to C are being established. In other words, A-C connections will run, not directly, but by way of the intermediary of B units. This principle plays an important role in the development of speech, and some interesting and bizarre phenomena can be explained by reference to it. It seems that it has a general application to the formation of all associations, but direct evidence on this issue is still lacking.

Our survey of human associations is not complete, even if all the "artificial" types or those developing only in some particular groups of persons are deliberately omitted. Our aim was rather to show a number of those associations developed in humans which, although established outside the conditioned reflex chamber and not submitted to rigorous training in the CR experiments, nevertheless provide rich material enabling us to understand the architecture of integrative activity of the brain. The problem will be undertaken again in the following chapters, in which the considerations will be based on experimental material allowing us further to elucidate the formation of associations, their properties and the rules of their transformations.

2. Associations directed to the visual analyzer

As was emphasized earlier, the visual analyzer provides us with most of the information on the external world. Since meaningful patterns representing various stimulus-objects are rather complex and highly variegated, a rich gnostic system has been developed around the projective cortical area, whereas this area itself was degraded to a transit station supplying elements to be integrated in the higher levels of the visual analyzer. In consequence, according to our concept proposed in the preceding chapter, the associative activation of the gnostic units of this analyzer has normally the psychological aspect of images, whereas visual hallucinations are produced in normal life rather exceptionally in a state of complete idleness of the projective zone because of its blocking in the lower levels of the afferent axis.

According to the discussion in Chapter III, the following main visual gnostic fields can be specified: (1) the gnostic field representing the visual perceptions of particular limbs of our own body and their positions (V-L); (2) the gnostic field representing visual perceptions of small manipulable objects (V-MO); (3) the gnostic field representing those objects which are perceived only or mainly by vision (V-

VO); (4) the gnostic field representing human faces (V-F); (5) the gnostic field representing visual signs (letters of the alphabet, numbers, and words) (V-Sn); (6) the gnostic field representing visual aspects of spatial relations (V-Sp).

The main associations leading from other afferent systems to the enumerated fields are represented in Plate I. Following is a list of these with comments.

A. Non-verbal associations

(1) *The stereognostic-visual associations* (S-MO → V-MO). Since many small objects of the external world are both handled and seen, strong connections leading from the somesthetic gnostic field of the hand to the visual gnostic field for such objects are formed in the individual human life and probably also in primates. Owing to these connections, the activation of the somesthetic gnostic units produced by touching a familiar object without seeing it leads immediately to its visualization. As pointed out earlier, this happens also in blind persons, if their visual gnosis was developed before the loss of sight.

As for the anatomy of connections involved in these associations, these connections are perhaps included in the superior occipito-frontal fasciculus, which, among other things, joins the dorso-lateral parietal region with the dorso-lateral occipital area.

(2) *Somesthetic-visual limb associations* (S-L → V-L). Since the positions of our limbs—particularly hands and fingers—are perceived both by articular proprioception and by vision, strong connections between corresponding gnostic units are established in our (and primate) life. As a result, when our eyes are closed we can clearly visualize the position of each limb, and the images are particularly vivid in respect to the position of our hands and fingers.

The strength of the association between somatic perception of the position of the limb and its visual image is convincingly demonstrated by the substitution method applied long ago by Stratton.[1] This author for a number of days wore spectacles whose lenses reversed vision of the external world upside down and from left to right. He noticed that "as regards the parts of the body, their pre-experimental representation often invaded the region directly in sight. Arms and legs in full view were given a double position. Beside the position and relation in which they were actually seen, there was always in the mental background, in intimate connection with muscular and tactual sensations, the older representation of these parts. As soon as my eyes were closed or directed elsewhere, this older representation gathered strength and was the dominant image."

Subsequently, this visual image of the pre-experimental position of the limbs became more dim and eventually was substituted by their visualization harmonizing with the new visual experience. It is difficult to find a better example of a conflict between the visual image of the limb evoked by association and its actual perception.

The associations now under discussion are formed in early childhood when the infant begins to manipulate with his limbs and observe them. It is interesting to note that according to my experience I have a clear visual image of the position of my toes when, for instance, I make their dorso-flexion, although I do not think that I have had much opportunity to see it for some time. Thus, the association established in my childhood has survived in spite of its rare utilization in maturity. On the contrary, I have no visual images of the positions and movements of my tongue within my mouth, because the appropriate somato-visual associations have never been established; but I can clearly visualize my own tongue stretched outside the mouth, since I have occasionally seen it in a mirror.

(3) *Kinesthetic-visual associations concerning manipulable objects and signs* (K-H → V-MO and K-H → V-Sn). When we manipulate objects under the guidance of vision, we always see the effect of our manipulation—the act of cutting a lemon leads to its transformation into slices; the act of tying a necktie leads to the visual perception of a knot, and so forth. In consequence, the connections are formed between particular kinesthetic units representing various skilled motor acts and visual units representing the effects of these acts. Accordingly, when performing such an action without seeing it, we can clearly visualize its result. As will be seen later, these associations take part in the interplay between kinesthesis and vision securing our visually guided skilled motor behavior.

A particular type of this sort of association is represented in writing. Since the act of writing implies the coincidence (or, to be more exact, an overlapping sequence) of the kinesthetic perception of the motor act involved in drawing signs and seeing these signs written on the paper, strong associations are formed between the two perceptions. As a result, drawing a sign in the air with a finger with our eyes closed, or even imagining such drawing, immediately evokes in us a vivid visual image of the same sign.

It may be assumed that analogous connections have also been formed between the kinesthesis of the motor acts and the visual effect of the displacement of the limb (K-H → V-L). We cannot, however, be sure of the existence of such direct connections, because it is more probable that they are established by the intermediary of the so-mesthetic gnostic field for limb postures (K-H → S-L → V-L).

(4) *Auditory-visual associations* (A-Sd → V-MO, A-Sd → V-VO,

A-Vo → V-F). There is a large category of events in the external world in which visual perceptions are more or less closely related to auditory perceptions. The most typical examples are: seeing a bell and hearing its ringing; seeing an automobile and hearing its motor; seeing a dog and hearing his bark; and last, but not least, seeing a person and hearing his voice. Accordingly, strong connections (running probably in an inferior longitudinal bundle) have been formed in our life between the auditory gnostic units representing various sounds (A-Sd) or human voices (A-Vo) and visual gnostic units representing the objects which give rise to these sounds, and particularly those aspects of the objects which are closely connected with them (for example, the visual picture of a barking dog or a speaking person).

The associations discussed now give rise to curious effects, particularly in our age of radio, which enables us frequently to hear many persons without seeing them. When I am listening to radio and hear the voice of a person whom I know by sight, I immediately visualize this person. On the other hand, when I listen to a voice known to me only by radio, this voice may be familiar to me and easily recognizable, but no visual images emerge when I hear it.

The associations we are discussing now are probably present not only in man but also in animals. In fact, it is easy to prove that if a dog is called by his master who is out of his sight and if after responding to the call he finds another person, he becomes restless and looks for his master. A lion hearing his mate roaring from a distance probably visualizes his partner when looking for her.

(5) *Labyrinthine-spatiovisual* (LA → V-Sp) *and spatiokinesthetic-spatiovisual* (K-Sp → V-Sp) *associations.* It has been recently shown by Beritoff[2] that labyrinthine afferent system plays an important role, in both humans and other species, in orientation in space, side by side with the visual afferent system. In fact, when the eyes are covered and the labyrinths are destroyed, both humans and animals cannot solve even the easiest spatial tests, such as finding a place which was previously frequented or following along a curved route along which the subject was guided before.

Whereas the labyrinthine perceptions play a chief role when our turns to right or to left are accomplished passively, as happens when we travel in a vehicle we are not driving, the kinesthetic perceptions from the eyes, head, and body play a major part in our locomotor behavior in maze-like situations. In consequence, associations between these three afferent systems are formed which render it possible for one of these systems to be substituted by the others. Here we shall give only a few examples to show the existence of associations linking the labyrinthine and kinesthetic perceptions on the one hand with the visual perceptions on the other.

Suppose that I am traveling by train, starting my journey from the city where I live. Even if I do not look out through the window, I have a clear spatiovisual image of the station left *behind* me. If at some station the engine is transferred to the other end of the train, so that it now goes backward, I have the irrepressible image that I am returning home, and I clearly "see" the station with its surroundings as being before me. In fact, it is impossible for me to imagine it as being behind. On the contrary, if the train makes a large loop, unperceivable by my labyrinthine sensation, so that I *know* now that I am returning home, it is again impossible for me to imagine that this is so, and I cannot absolutely visualize the station as being before me. This feeling is most distressing, and the discomfort ends only when near the station I perceive one detail of the familiar landscape. Then suddenly all things return to their normal places and my directional illusion is gone.

This example shows that our spatiovisual imagination is strongly in the grip of the labyrinthine perception and cannot be changed voluntarily, but only if some visual cue helps us "find ourselves" in the proper place.

As far as the spatiokinesthetic-spatiovisual associations are concerned, it can be easily demonstrated that the phenomenon generally referred to as "stability of the external world" is based on these associations. In fact, when we are moving our eyes, or our head, or our whole body around and accordingly we see different parts of our environment, we have a strong feeling that *we* are moving around while the external world is immobile. This is what von Holst has denoted as "*Reafferenz-Prinzip.*"[3] But, whenever the position of our eyes or body changes without our actively taking part in it, the stability of the external world is no longer experienced. This happens when we push our eyeball with a finger—then the external objects "jump over" immediately in the opposite direction—or when we see the external world from the window of a quickly moving train—then the environment runs off in the opposite direction.

Extremely interesting and informative is still another condition in which the environment becomes mobile in spite of the fact that we perform *active* movements of the eyes or head. This is when we wear glasses distorting our visual field. This phenomenon was first noticed by Stratton,[4] who observed that when he put on glasses inverting his visual field, the first thing which happened was that the visual world stopped being stable: "When I moved my head or body so that my sight swept over the scene, the movement was not felt to be solely in the observer, as in normal vision, but was referred both to the observer and to objects beyond."

The explanation of this fact is obvious: since the movements of the eyes or head did not produce those changes in the visual field which were associated with them, but the opposite ones, the changes actually observed were experienced as caused by the motion of the surroundings. Only gradually, when the new associations between the movements and the changes of the visual field had become established, did the external world again become stable, because the changes occurring in it were those which had been expected. Again, we have here a striking example of the operation of the substitution method in detecting associations.

Incidentally, it should be emphasized that in the kinesthetic-spatio-visual association the decisive role is played, not by the *feedback* of the eye movement performed, but by the very programing of that movement in the kinesthetic gnostic field. This is documented by the well-known fact that if the voluntary movement of the eye is not executed because of the paralysis of eye muscles, the subject has the impression that the environment moves in the direction of the intended movement. This is again due to the fact that according to well-established associations, he should see not the scene in front of him but that in the direction of his intended glance.

It is easy to show that all our visual orientation in space is due to an interplay between our visual and proprioceptive afferent systems, the kinesthesis of eye movements here playing a decisive role. For instance, I am sitting with closed eyes at my desk facing the balcony. I can very easily visualize the furniture and pictures on the walls on my left and right sides. But when I imagine the left side of the room, I turn my eyes to the left, and when I imagine the right side, I turn my eyes to the right. I have tried very often to "look" (with my eyes closed) at the left side of the room and visualize its right side, but I was unsuccessful. The same is true when I try to visualize that part of the city (streets, houses, buses) which is on the left or on the right side of me. Again the indispensable condition for this is to turn my eyes, even insignificantly, in the proper direction. It would be well if psychologists performed special experiments to prove this phenomenon.*

The situation is a little different when I try to reproduce a long chain of visual images—say, to imagine that I leave my apartment and go for a walk. I successively imagine that I go to the door, open it, go out, close the door, go down the staircase, open and close the front door of the house, turn left, go along the street to the main street, see it by my eyes of mind, with all its traffic, go right in the direction of

---

* The only relevant experimental evidence I know is that provided by G. H. Deckert,[5] who has shown that while imagining the oscillating pendulum we indeed make movements of our eyes to left and to right.

the cinema, see the cinema, and so on. It may be assumed that this chain of mental events is due to the interplay between the images of the scenery visualized in front of me and *kinesthetic* images of my behavioral acts, such as leaving my apartment, going down the staircase, opening and closing the door, and turns on the street. The latter images are certainly not visual, since I do not possess them in my visual gnostic file, because I never see *myself* doing all these things.

Thus, we come to the important conclusion that the chains of visual images involved in our locomotor behavior occur by the alternation of visual images and kinesthetic images and/or kinesthetic perception of eye movements, according to the formula $K_1 \rightarrow V_1 \rightarrow K_2 \rightarrow V_2 \rightarrow K_3 \rightarrow V_3. \ldots$ Whether we are able to establish associations between successive visual images without this alternation is rather doubtful, in view of the fact that these images are mutually antagonistic and do not overlap.

Since the alternating imaginary sequence of the kinesthetic and visual images requires the presence of spatiovisual gnosis as well as spatiokinesthetic gnosis, it follows that both corresponding gnostic fields must be preserved in order that this sequence could occur. The fact that in spatiovisual agnosia such imaginary sequences fail to occur was repeatedly ascertained by us: a patient suffering from that agnosia cannot describe how he finds his way to familiar streets or how the rooms in his house are arranged. We should expect that the same is true in spatiokinesthetic agnosia caused by prefrontal lesions; however, I am not aware of any studies concerning this problem.

To end these considerations, we should put the question whether the associations linking the kinesthetic and labyrinthine perceptions with visual perceptions play the same role in orientation in space in animals as they play in man. There is no doubt that this is true. Experiments on space orientation were performed in great detail on rats. The classical works of Tolman[6] and his associates have clearly indicated that a rat, after being acquainted with a given maze, has a clear map of it in his visual gnosis. Judging from his behavior, we can safely assume that when turning to a succeeding alley the animal visualizes whether it is blind or open, or whether it is long or short, or in which direction the next turn is to be expected. No less outspoken in this respect are the studies of Maier[7] on "reasoning" in rats. In familiar surroundings these animals are able to find their way to food from any place where they are put. The works of Beritoff have already been mentioned above.

(6) *Emotional-visual association* ($E \rightarrow$ V-MO, $E \rightarrow$ V-VO, $E \rightarrow$ V-F). So far we have spoken of the connections leading to the visual gnostic fields from gnostic fields of other analyzers. We must remember, however, that, besides the gnostic afferent systems conveying in-

formation from the receptors situated in various strategic points of the organism, there exists also the emotional afferent system conveying information about those states which control the general dispositions of the subject and determine the broad lines of his behavior. It has already been noted that emotional perceptions also make associations with gnostic perceptions, these associations being particularly strong because they are established under intensive arousal produced by the emotions involved.

It may be easily realized that the associations linking various emotional states with visual perceptions play an important role in the life of animals and man. These associations lead to the production of vivid visual images of all those stimulus-objects which coincide with given emotions. Thus, since hunger is associated with all visual perceptions coinciding with feeding, when we are hungry, we experience vivid images of the place of our meals or our favorite foods. It has already been stressed that since in normal persons appetite is highly selective, depending on the needs of the organism and conditioned factors, so our images are also selective and determined by the character of our hunger drive. For instance, a girl who suffered from hypoglycemic crises told me that whenever she experiences them "candies always fly before her eyes."

Not less vivid are the visual images evoked by the sexual drive which concern persons of the opposite sex (individual or typical) and various events connected with sexual experiences. Again, we are here dealing with highly selective images depending on some general sexual affinities or concrete affinities established by conditioning toward particular persons.

As stated before, particularly strong visual images with an obsessive character are produced by protective drives such as fear, horror, or disgust. The images of some abhorrent incidents or mutilations, of a sudden attack of an enemy, of confronting a snake, and the like are here typical. The common fact that after experiencing such incidents persons have a tendency to report on them again and again to anyone who is willing to listen is caused by strong visual images which they experience again and again.

It is often claimed that when a person is in mortal danger his whole life appears before his eyes. A good description of such an episode is reported by Stratton (quoted after Young).[8] It concerns the experiences of an aviator when his airplane was temporarily out of control. Here are fragments of his account:

During this fall I re-lived more events of my life than I can well enumerate. These were in an orderly series, very distinct, and I cannot recall that anything was out of its place. . . .

It was when I [age three and a half] had to stay home when my mother had to leave me and teach school for a while. . . .

Next I [age four] was playing under a grape-arbor in the back yard of my grandmother's. In throwing things at the little chicks, I accidentally killed one of them. Then I buried it feeling very sorry over what I had done. . . .

Another [age nine] was a very cold night in Kansas City when we . . . got stalled on the street cars because the snow was so heavy.

Swimming in the icy lake at midnight, as the result of dare [a detailed report of this episode follows].

As seen from this account, these events were clearly connected with anxiety or sorrow. Although this is not explicitly shown in other events accounted by the subject, we assume that this is the very mechanism of the "rapid survey of one's life." By association with a strong fear, all the situations which are emotionally similar appear before the subject's eyes, and their vividness is due to the strength of the emotion actually experienced.

It may be reasonably assumed that the mechanism of dreams is based on these emotional-visual associations. According to our view, the nature of deep sleep is that a subject is cut off from nearly all the sensory input owing to inhibition of relay stations leading to the gnostic fields of particular analyzers (the phenomenon quite distinct from that of "sensory deprivation"), and cut off from the most part of the motor output owing to activation of the inhibitory reticular system. This does not imply, however, that the central nervous processes are inactivated (as in anesthesia) or generally inhibited. On the contrary, intense intrinsic activity, mainly emotional, is going on in the brain, largely released from the actual sensory input and thrown into operation by the reverberating neuronal circuits. Thus, all the undercurrent emotions, which in the waking state are suppressed by the mental processes driven by the events of the external world and their associations come to the surface and by association activate those sets of gnostic units connected with the appropriate emotional units. The fact that this associative activation of gnostic units takes the form of hallucinations and not images was explained earlier (Chapter IV, Section 3) as due to blocking of the sensory input of a given analyzer and leaving room for its activation from the appropriate gnostic fields.

Among various analyzers whose gnostic units are connected with emotional units, the visual analyzer is perhaps the outstanding, at least in man, because it provides us with most of the information about the external world. Accordingly, in humans, visual dreams are of most common occurrence and represent the episodes of our life associated with our overt or undercurrent emotions. Thus, when we are very hungry, we dream of excellent meals; when we are under sexual drive, we have erotic dreams; when we are in a state of anxiety, we dream of passing the examination.

We may reasonably assume that visual images produced by emotional-visual associations are proper, not only to humans, but also to higher animals. Thus a dog probably experiences images of other dogs when he is in a state of heat, of meat when he is hungry, or of a lighted lamp when this stimulus became a signal heralding an emotional event in the CR experiment. Convincing evidence of the appearance of such images in dogs was provided by Beritoff.[9] When, for instance, an animal had been offered food and then carried away before he had finished his portion of food, he infallibly returned to that place if he was allowed to do so. This is certainly because he has preserved a visual image of the food left in the bowl. When observing dogs during sleep we cannot resist the impression that they experience occasionally very vivid dreams based on emotional states.

B. VERBAL ASSOCIATIONS

The only associations involved in speech function which are directed to the visual analyzer are those linking the words heard (A-W) with the visual stimulus-objects designated by them. These associations lead to almost all visual gnostic fields. In fact, sounds representing words designate small manipulable objects through associations A-W → V-MO; larger objects known only by sight through associations A-W → V-VO; faces or persons whose names we know (A-W → V-F); signs of letters and words (A-W → V-Sn); and visual spatial relations designated by such words as below, above, beside, near, far (A-W → V-Sp). All these associations provide a main basis for what is called *comprehension* of speech heard. It is true that not all stimulus-objects are perceived through the visual analyzer, and therefore some words, such as those designating tastes, textures, our own limbs, actions, sounds, are comprehended by associations with other perceptions. Yet, most words designating concrete objects or actions have associations with corresponding visual perceptions.

It is interesting to consider the types of visual images we experience when we hear various words. If we hear a word designating a particular object, such as the name of a familiar person, we visualize this person, because the sound activates by association the set of visual gnostic units representing him. If, however, we hear a word designating a whole class of objects—chair, watch, automobile, horse—we have either an image of some concrete object the gnostic units of which were at the moment subliminally activated for some special reason (for example, my own watch, a horse I saw yesterday on the meadow), or a crude

PLATES I–V

image representing the whole category of perceptions about which we spoke in the preceding chapter.

We should remember, however, that even when a word heard does not at a given moment evoke any visual image of an object designated by it, this does not mean that the appropriate association is not established. We have other methods of manifesting its existence, particularly the substitution method (cf. Chapter IV, Section 7).

Since the audioverbal gnostic field is localized only in the dominant hemisphere and is not close to the visual gnostic fields for objects, it may easily occur that the connections between the two fields can be damaged without serious lesions in these fields themselves. Then a patient will not suffer from audioverbal agnosia—that is, he will be able normally to recognize the sounds of speech; nor will he suffer from visual agnosia—that is, he will be able to recognize visually various objects and know their significance. He will, however, be unable to establish any associations between words which he hears and visual stimulus-objects which are designated by them. Such a deficit is usually called sensory or auditory aphasia. We call it *auditory-visual aphasia,* to indicate the connections affected.

The usual method of testing such patients is as follows. First, it should be verified that the subject has neither audioverbal agnosia (by asking him to repeat the words heard) nor visual agnosia (by asking him to name objects or at least to show what is their significance). Then, we offer him several well-known objects, and pronounce the name of one of them, asking him (by gestures) to point at the object designated by the word. Whereas normal persons will immediately point to the corresponding object, patients suffering from auditory-visual aphasia will not do so. In severe cases they will be unable to identify any object, either refusing to do so or simply giving chance responses. In milder cases, subjects are able to point to a correct object but do so after hesitation, and become easily confused if the trials are given in quick succession. It is remarkable that the patients usually cannot learn to give proper responses when the same tests are repeated; on the contrary, they may react better at the beginning of the examination and be totally confused at the end of it.

If a subject is able to speak coherently enough to explain his deficit, he complains that words lose any meaning for him, as if they were pronounced in a foreign language. He is, however, able to discern between those words which are familiar to him and pure neologisms, which is impossible in a patient suffering from audioverbal agnosia.

An excellent description of patients with a relatively pure form of auditory-visual aphasia, without agnostic symptoms, is given in a paper of Stoliarova-Kabelianskaja,[10] from which we present the following data relevant for our considerations.

The four patients described were able to discern speech-sounds (phonemes), even those which are similar as "ba-pa," "da-ta," "va-fa," "paba-bapa." They also easily recognized when a word was distorted. When, for instance, the patient heard the meaningless word "leezdok," he said: "leezdok? I do not know that. Leestock (a sheet of paper)— this is different, this I know, this has some sense." They were able to repeat fairly well both familiar words and neologisms. Some of them could write (with some errors) under dictation. Their spontaneous speech was relatively normal without paraphasias, and they could fairly well name objects shown to them. All this showed that they had neither auditory nor visual agnosia.

On the other hand, they failed nearly completely to understand speech or even individual words. Following are some examples. The patient is asked to indicate the collar. "How? Collar? What is it? I don't know, I don't remember." Another patient is asked to indicate the floor. "Floor? Where is the floor?" He points to a window. Another patient is asked to indicate the floor. "Floor, floor, floor. This is the wall; no, it is after all the floor (he indicates the wall). Is it not? Well, maybe it is this (indicates the ceiling). Is it not? Floor, floor; oh, excuse me, it is here" (he has pointed at the floor after about two minutes).

In one of these patients it was found post mortem that "pathways (in the left hemisphere) leading from area 22 and from the Heschl convolution in their upper parts are preserved, whereas the pathways leading from the second temporal convolution to the occipital region are totally destroyed."

Here is another fragment of the examination of a patient observed by us, a man of fifty-one, who had thrombosis of a terminal branch of the arteria cerebri media and developed a "pure" auditory-visual (and auditory-somatic to a lesser degree) aphasia. His other speech performances will be described later; here we shall concentrate only on the description of his comprehension of speech heard.

When several objects of everyday usage were placed before him, and he had to point to those named by the examiner, his performance turned out to be strongly impaired. For instance, the examiner said "spoon." "This is in some sense spoon (shows pencil)—a spoon for writing." "Watch." "Let us say that this is watch" (correct). "Comb." "Comb, comb, this is in some sense a comb" (takes a bunch of keys) "one comb, second, third, many combs." "Matches." He pointed to the mirror, and said, "In some sense these are matches." In all his answers he hesitated and was never sure of their correctness, and it was clear that they were quite haphazard. On the other hand, his performance was significantly better when he could read the name of the object or was requested to write it.

The symptomatology of these patients is clearly different from that described in Chapter III, Section 4, in which because of audioverbal agnosia the subjects failed to discern similar phonemes or words and were unable to repeat them.

To end these considerations, it should be stressed once more that the faculty of comprehension is based, not only on audioverbal-visual associations, but also on associations linking words heard with stimuli of other modalities. Therefore, if we find that a patient understands the words designating parts of his body, or actions, or even small manipulable objects, much better than he does purely visual objects (colors, letters, or remote objects), this should mean that the connections between the audioverbal gnostic field and other than visual gnostic fields were not damaged. The reverse relations may also exist (see below).

Further, as emphasized in the preceding chapters, the principle of redundancy is, in the impairments under discussion, in full operation and explains why common words, acquired in childhood or with emotional overtones are better understood than those used infrequently and/or acquired only recently.

3. Associations directed to the auditory analyzer

As indicated in Chapter III, the auditory gnosis can be divided into three main categories: that representing various sounds of the external world (A-Sd), that representing various voices and intonations of human speech (A-Vo), and that representing words heard (A-W). Following are the main connections directed to these fields from other analyzers (Plate II).

A. Non-verbal associations

(1) *Visual-auditory associations* (V-MO → A-Sd, V-VO → A-Sd, V-F → A-Vo). We have clear psychological evidence that visual perceptions of objects emitting sounds, and in particular those perceptions which catch the very moment in which a sound is produced (a speaking person, a barking dog, a ringing bell) give rise to auditory images. The strict correspondence between the sight of a person (particularly of the face) and his voice was noted before.

(2) *Emotional-auditory associations* (E → A-Sd, E → A-Vo). Other connections leading to the gnostic fields of sounds and voices originate in the emotional units. Examples illustrating the corresponding associations are: images of sounds involved in preparation of a meal when we are hungry, or obsessive images of a shrill cry evoked in a state of fear or horror.

B. Verbal associations

(1) *Word-kinesthetic–audioverbal associations* (K-W → A-W). These associations are based on the connections leading from the kinesthetic speech field, situated in the frontal operculum (Broca center), to the auditory speech field. As explained in the preceding chapter (Section 8), the units of the kinesthetic speech field are activated either when we are speaking aloud or when we are thinking in words—in our "internal speech." When a child begins to speak, his speech is accompanied by auditory feedback, because of which strong connections leading from the kinesthetic speech field to the auditory speech field are formed. These connections have a clear point-to-point correspondence—that is, each set of units in the kinesthetic field has its counterpart in a particular set of units in the auditory field.

The existence of these connections can be easily detected by introspection. When we are speaking aloud, this is of course not possible, because auditory perception of the word heard occludes its auditory image. During verbal thinking, however, the auditory images of our speech become quite distinct. The experiment is particularly successful when we recite in our minds some favorite poem or rehearse in mind a speech we are going to make. The word-kinesthetic–audioverbal associations are also clearly manifested during writing. As will be shown in a later section, writing a word is preceded by its internal verbalization, which is transmitted to the audioverbal gnostic field and gives rise to its auditory image.

In the auditory images of words produced by internal speech we generally "hear" our own voice but not always. If, for instance, I heard my favorite poem being recited by a good actor, then when I later recited it in my mind I would clearly hear in my imagination *his* voice and not my own. This also happens sometimes during my writing, when I am in a state of mental fatigue. I then hear, not my own voice pronouncing the words, but the voice of one of my acquaintances. This image of another voice is rather distressing, and I must then stop my work. Similarly, if we read a speech delivered by a person with whose voice we are familiar, we hear *his* voice and intonation underlying the text.

We assume that the anatomical substrate of word-kinesthetic–audioverbal connections is provided by the arcuate bundle precisely linking the frontal operculum with the first and second temporal convolutions (see Section 5).

(2) *Audioverbal-sound associations* (A-W → A-Sd). There are words which designate definite sounds: ringing, thunder, barking, and so on. Hence, when we hear the corresponding word and we understand it, this means that we are able to imagine the sound designated by

it. Thus a rather small category of these associations represents a special case of comprehension of speech.

(3) *Visual-audioverbal associations* (V-MO → A-W, V-VO → A-W, V-F → A-W). We may easily observe that when seeing a familiar object we can reproduce in thought the auditory image of its name. The problem arises, however, whether this occurs through the direct connections linking the visual gnostic fields with the audioverbal field, or whether we first pronounce the name of the object in our internal speech, owing to the direct visual–word-kinesthetic connections, and only then "hear it in our mind," owing to the kinesthetic-auditory connections discussed above.

It seems that we cannot give an unequivocal answer to this question by a pure psychological analysis. There is, however, no doubt that patients suffering from "motor" aphasia who have lost totally their internal speech are, nevertheless, quite able after seeing the object to evoke the auditory image of its name. This is proved as follows: We show an object to a patient and, when he tries in vain to name it, we suggest a false name. The patient at once protests vigorously, thus indicating that he does not have that word in his auditory imagination. On the contrary, when we suggest the right name, the patient immediately approves with great satisfaction. Observing the behavior of a subject, one has an irresistible impression that he has a clear auditory image of the proper name of the object seen (owing to the fact that the visual-audioverbal associations are intact) and that he tries in vain to transmit it to word-kinesthesis. The great importance of these associations in normal speech will be discussed in a later section.

(4) *Intrinsic audioverbal associations* (A-W → A-W). When we listen to a known text (for example, to recitation of a poem) and the speaker makes a mistake, we immediately notice it. This shows that the audioverbal images belonging to the memorized sequences of words form in our auditory speech field associations among themselves, so that the given auditory image evokes the next one and so on. The significance of these associations will be discussed later.

4. Associations directed to the somesthetic analyzer

As shown in our discussion on associations directed to the visual analyzer, its function in primates is partially correlated with the somesthetic analyzer, since both of them are chiefly concerned with the analysis of objects of the external world. Whereas the visual analyzer gets information about these objects when they are at some distance from the subject, the somesthetic analyzer (including the gustatory sense) is concerned with those objects which come in close contact with the organism. Since the usual course of events is such that many objects are first seen and only then touched or tasted, it could be predicted, according to the principle of forward associations, that the chief bulk of connections leads from the visual gnostic fields to the somesthetic fields. This is actually the case. Whereas somesthetic-visual associations are, as we saw, designed to grasp by visual image what has already been grasped by somesthetic perceptions and, as such, have more clinical interest than vital significance (except in blind persons), associations leading in the opposite direction are much more important: they allow the subject to *foresee* the immediate properties of an object when it comes in contact with the surface of the body. This is true of both the tactile and the gustatory aspects of the objects.

According to the discussion of somesthetic gnosis presented in Chapter III, we can distinguish the following gnostic fields of the somesthetic analyzer (Plate III): (1) the gnostic field representing the postures of particular parts of the body (S-L); (2) the gnostic field representing manipulable objects recognized by palpation (S-MO); (3) the gnostic field representing tegumental sensations of skin (S-T), such as localized pain, itching, recognition of textures, pressures; (4) the gustatory gnostic field (S-G); (5) the gnostic field representing oral postures in pronouncing phonemes (S-Or). For the sake of convenience, we shall also include in this section: (6) the labyrinthine gnostic field (La), and (7) the olfactory gnostic field (Ol). It should be recalled that part of the tegumental gnosis and perhaps the labyrinthine gnosis are represented in the projective fields themselves, and therefore activation of the corresponding units by association gives rise to hallucinations rather than to images.

A. Non-verbal associations

(1) *Visual-stereognostic associations* (V-MO → S-MO). These associations link the visual aspects of small manipulable objects with their somesthetic aspects (stereognosis). The severance of the corresponding connections should lead to the failure to identify objects perceived by vision and by palpation.

(2) *Visual-tegumental associations* (V-MO → S-T). This is a large category of associations which enables the subject to foresee the sensory aspects of the surface of objects available by touch on the basis of their visual aspects. In fact, dealing with familiar objects we discern by vision whether they are rough or smooth, concave or convex, soft or hard, light or heavy, and we experience a definite surprise if our anticipation turns out to be wrong. When the object is such that its touch causes pain or itching, then the corresponding experience produced by association is particularly vivid and, because of its primitive character, gives rise to hallucinaton. If I see a sharp knife approaching my body,

it is very probably that I shall experience hallucination of pain, especially if I had been cut by such a knife not long ago. The sensation of itching when seeing body insects was commented upon in an earlier chapter.

(3) *Visual-somesthetic postural associations* (V-L → S-L). These link the visual aspect of a posture of the limb with its somesthetic aspect. Of course, in normal condition it is impossible to reveal the existence of these associations, because the somesthetic perception of the posture of the limb closely accompanies its visual perception. We can, however, do so by putting distorting glasses on our eyes, which would disrupt the close relation between both these experiences (substitution method).

(4) *Visual-gustatory associations* (V-MO → S-G). It is a general experience that when we are hungry and see the meal we are about to eat, we have a vivid gustatory image of that meal. As will be seen in the next chapter, it is the image of food and not hunger which forces us to salivate. Similarly, if we see somebody eating a lemon, we have a clear image (or even hallucination) of a sour taste in our own mouth, and again this image makes us salivate.

Since gustatory images (or hallucinations) produced by associations give rise to the same overt response as gustatory perceptions produced by food or acid, this sort of associations had a scientific career of its own, having been called a conditioned reflex and having been exploited in hundreds of papers concerned with the objective study of associative processes. These phenomena will be dealt with in detail in the next chapter.

Of course, not only natural visual stimuli can be associated with gustatory perceptions, but, as we know from special experiments, any other stimuli or their traces. But since we are concerned here only with typical associations formed in normal human life, we shall not include these others in our list.

(5) *Visual-olfactory associations* (V-MO → Ol, V-VO → Ol). These are produced by those visual stimulus-objects which are characterized by some odors such as those of flowers, soaps, excrements, trees, gardens. Seeing these objects may evoke images, or even hallucinations, of the respective odors.

(6) *Spatial visual-labyrinthine associations* (V-Sp → La). These associations are to be expected if we take into account a close cooperation between the two afferent systems discussed in a previous section. The relevant example may be provided by the common experience observed during train journeys. Since during the journey we are accustomed to the fact that the backward motion of the surroundings means that the train is moving forward, we often experience a strange sensa-

tion when our train is stopped and we see a train on a parallel track move in the opposite direction. We are quite certain then that it is our train which has started to move, and we notice our mistake only when we look through the opposite window and see that the surroundings are immobile. This experience has a character of hallucination because of the rather primitive nature of the vestibular gnosis.

(7) *Kinesthetic-somesthetic hand associations* (K-H → S-L, K-H → S-MO, K-H → S-T). Since almost every motor act performed by a subject leads to a change of the posture of the limb involved in it, the kinesthetic perception of a movement becomes closely associated with the somesthetic perception of its result provided by the articular gnosis (K-H → S-L). Besides, motor behavioral acts usually lead to other somesthetic sensations, such as the perception of texture (when the movement leads to the contact with some object) (K-H → S-T) or the perception of the shape of the object touched (K-H → S-MO). Since all these somesthetic perceptions usually constitute the feedback of a motor act providing information about its correctness and elicit corrective movements if necessary, the kinesthetic-somesthetic interplay fulfills an important role in all our somesthetically guided behavior. We shall deal with this interplay in the next section.

In our normal life the somesthetic feedback of every motor act exactly fits its expectation, and therefore we hardly notice its existence. If, however, for some reason this does not happen, we can immediately observe that something is wrong (substitution method). Following are some illustrative examples.

Suppose that I take part in a mountain excursion and am climbing with a heavy rucksack. Of course, my muscular effort exerted at each step becomes accurately adjusted to my burden and the slope of the terrain. If after some hours of such climbing I hand over the rucksack to a companion, I experience a clear sensation of springing up with each step, because the muscular effort I apply to raise my body now turns out to be too energetic for this aim, since my own weight has been diminished. Another sort of such overshooting may be produced if I am asked to lift repeatedly, with my eyes closed, some heavy object (for example, an iron dumbbell) and then the iron object is replaced by a wooden one. Such facts show that my muscular effort is closely adjusted, according to my experience, to a given postural effect, and therefore a change of the effectiveness of my effort leads to a different effect.

Another type of evidence of the mechanisms we are concerned with is provided by pathological cases of patients with lesions in the post-central cortical area. As is well known, these patients exhibit a strong impairment, or even total loss, of postural sensation. If a finger or a wrist is flexed or extended passively, they fail (with their eyes covered) to tell the position of the limb. When, however, they make the flexion or extension movement by themselves, their appreciation of the position is correct, unless we have changed it passively in the meantime. This result is explained by the fact that kinesthesis of the performed movement, which is fully preserved in these patients, evokes a somesthetic (or perhaps also visual) image of a resulting posture.

(8) *Emotional-textural associations* (E → S-T). The obsessive preservation of tactile experiences which have occurred in the presence of strong emotional excitement is fairly common. Usually it takes a form of hallucination. It often happens that when we have touched an object evoking a strong disgust (for example, excrement), we experience a need to wash our hands again and again because we feel that they are dirty. Lady Macbeth continuously making the movements of washing her hands after touching the bloodstained sword by which her husband killed Duncan is a classical example of this mechanism.

Another phenomenon explainable by reference to the emotional-somesthetic associations is that of intractable pain produced by neuralgia or causalgia. Such a pain, after long duration, becomes totally independent of corresponding peripheral irritation, since we cannot annihilate it by any operation dissecting the afferent pathways (rhizotomy, splanchnotomy, chordotomy, and so on). The cure may be provided by sensory cortical topectomy or by frontal lobotomy.

The explanation of this intractable pain on the basis of our concept is as follows. The exceedingly strong and continuous pain produced by a causalgic peripheral focus is easily associated with the emotional state of fear. In consequence, the pain becomes centrally induced, since the vicious circle (to be described later) is formed between the two experiences: the fear of the imminent pain evokes this pain, and when it is evoked it increases the state of fear. This explanation is in good agreement with the positive effect of frontal lobotomy, which divides the connections between the sensory field (in the cortex or thalamus) in which the pain-perceptive units are situated with the emotive field in which the fear-perceptive units are situated. Thus, the vicious circle is severed, and even if the patient is experiencing pain (which happens when the source is still in the periphery), it is not amplified by the central emotional factors.

(9) *Emotional–limb-somesthetic associations* (E → S-L). In normal life these associations are rarely detectable for the simple reason that the postural gnosis is permanently under the control of corresponding perceptions giving information about the actual position of each limb. Good evidence of the existence of these associations is, however, provided by the phenomenon of "phantom limb." As explained in Chapter

III, after the limb has been amputated, the subject still feels its existence, owing to the fact that the somesthetic gnostic field of the "bodily scheme" is intact. More detailed examination of subjects who have lost a limb in the state of full consciousness in an accident reveals that the phantom posture of that limb is exactly the same as it was at the very moment of the accident. Thus, a soldier who lost the arm when he was firing the rifle feels his phantom arm lifted and extended; a man whose bent finger was cut by a saw feels his phantom finger to be in flexion.

This curious fact may be explained by assuming that the horror accompanying the accident becomes strongly associated with the actual position of the limb involved in this accident; the feeling of this position cannot be removed by other postural perceptions of that limb, since the corresponding receptive surface no longer exists.

(10) *Emotional-gustatory associations* (E → S-G). These associations are fairly common in our lives, and are in operation under the alimentary drives. Thus, if we are hungry, we may experience the gustatory images of the meals we desire to have; on the contrary, if we experience a strong aversive drive because of eating some distasteful substance, we often cannot get rid of the image or even hallucination of the taste of that substance.

(11) *Emotional-olfactory associations* (E → Ol). The existence of these associations is again easily detectable under the operation of various drives. To give the most common examples, let us remember the images or hallucinations of an odor of tasty food experienced when we are hungry, of an odor of the perfume used by a lady to whom we are attracted, or of an odor of loathsome substances to which we felt strong detestation.

Following is a vivid description of olfactory hallucinations of detestable smell reported by Ribot.

I had been to the hospital, to see my friend B., who was suffering from the cancer of the face. . . . When he spoke it was necessary to come quite close in order to hear what he said, and thus, in spite of the antiseptic dressings, an acrid, fetid odor forced itself on one's nostrils. . . . I was to go again to see him—I had promised to do so: but this prospect was intensely repugnant to me. While walking in a part of Paris, where neither space, nor fresh air was wanting I reproached myself silently for not having gone to see the poor patient. . . . At this very moment I perceived, as though I had been close to him, the same acrid odor, recognizable as that of the cancerous tumor—so suddenly that I instinctively held my sleeve to my nose in order to see whether I had not brought away the smell in my clothes. This, however, was immediately succeeded by the reflection that I had not been to the hospital for five days, and that, moreover, I was not wearing the same overcoat as on the occasion of my visit.[11]

B. Verbal associations

Verbal associations directed to the somesthetic analyzer deal, first of all, with comprehension of the names of those stimulus-objects which are either totally or predominantly perceived not by vision but by somesthesis. Here belong:

(1) *Audioverbal-somatotextural associations* (A-W → S-T). Since most textures—such as hardness versus softness, or roughness versus smoothness—are perceived by somesthetic gnosis, we can a priori infer that comprehension of the names of all these modalities is based on connections established between audioverbal gnostic units and corresponding somesthetic gnostic units. In consequence, lesions affecting the relevant pathways would lead to auditory-somesthetic aphasia —an aphasia in which only comprehension of the names of textural stimulus-objects should be affected. I do not find in the literature any reliable reports of such cases, perhaps because the proper tests examining this faculty have not been used. I had the opportunity to see a patient who had a lesion in the parietal region; she was certainly unable to understand the names of textures she touched by her hand (see below). More attention should be given to this aspect of "sensory aphasia" in examining the aphatic patients.

(2) *Audioverbal-gustatory associations* (A-W → S-G). Exactly the same is true of comprehension of the names of stimulus-objects perceived by gustation, such as saltiness, bitterness, and so on. The audioverbal gnostic units form connections with appropriate gustatory units which account for comprehension of the corresponding names. The pathophysiological evidence of these connections is lacking.

(3) *Audioverbal–limb-somesthetic associations* (A-W → S-L). As indicated in Chapter III, somesthetic gnosis of particular parts of the body involving the feeling of their existence and position is developed early in ontogenesis and is independent of, and possibly even earlier than, their visual gnosis, particularly if these parts are not, or rarely, seen in ourselves. In consequence, it may be again inferred that when audioverbal gnostic units are formed to designate particular parts of our own body, the appropriate connections are formed between the audioverbal gnostic units and the limb-somesthetic gnostic units. The evidence that this is indeed true is provided by extensive pathological material. When in routine tests for examination of comprehension of aphasic patients we compare comprehension of names representing visual objects with those representing parts of the body, we are struck by the discrepancies between these seemingly identical faculties. We have seen patients with parietal lesions who were able to point to every visual object whose name they heard but failed to do so when they had

to indicate parts of their own body. To show that their "body scheme" itself was not affected, they were requested to point at parts of their own bodies indicated by the examiner on another person or vice versa. The patients performed this task without difficulty.

Following is a case in which the discrepancy between comprehension of the names of visual objects and somesthetic objects was particularly manifest. (This case has already been described in the previous chapter.)

A lady was hit by an ax so that the opercular part of the frontal and parietal lobe was severely damaged with no impairment of the upper parts of these lobes. In consequence, her expressive speech was practically lost, although her understanding of the speech of others was apparently quite normal, and she vividly and adequately reacted to everything she was told.

A more detailed examination of her comprehension of speech by special tests revealed that comprehension of the names of visual objects was indeed nearly perfect. She selected, without any difficulty or hesitation, pictures corresponding to names she heard; she could easily point out details of a landscape and parts of an automobile shown her in a picture. In contradistinction, she was amazingly helpless in indicating parts of her own body, even her leg or arm. She hesitated, reflected, corrected herself, but was obviously not sure even when her response was right, which was rather rare. Her bad performance concerned not only pointing at parts of her own body but also those of the examiner and those in a picture. When the picture of a goat was shown her she had no difficulty in pointing at horns and hoofs, but hesitated when pointing at legs and belly. When, however, the task consisted in pointing out on herself parts of the human body indicated in the picture, or vice versa, she performed correctly. She was also able to indicate without hesitation what was wrong in a picture of a face or body in which some part was missing.

She failed to indicate which of two objects was rough or smooth, or soft or hard, although she noticed the differences in texture and her stereognosis was perfect. The impression was that the names of various textures had simply lost any sense for her. On the other hand, she did understand the terms "hot" and "cold" or the names of various tastes.

(4) *Word-kinesthetic–oral-somesthetic associations* (K-W → S-Or). Still another kind of verbal associations in which the somesthetic analyzer is involved comprises those linking kinesthetic verbal gnosis with somesthetic oral gnosis. The pronunciation of a phoneme is accompanied by a specific setting of the mouth. In consequence, connections between word-kinesthetic gnostic units situated in the Broca area

and oral-somesthetic gnostic units situated in the Luria area are formed. These connections supply the speech feedback parallel to that represented by word-kinesthetic–audioverbal connections. Its importance may be proved by a strong impairment of speech when the oral-somesthetic gnostic field is damaged. It may be assumed that, just as most skilled movements of the hand are performed by the interplay between the postural gnosis and kinesthetic gnosis, so is the case in our skilled movements of the mouth involved in normal speech.

5. Associations directed to the kinesthetic analyzer

As pointed out in the preceding chapter, the functional role of the kinesthetic analyzer is quite different from that of other analyzers, because it is not concerned with the analysis of stimulus-objects, which are provided from outside the nervous system, but rather with the programing of behavioral acts according to the messages which are provided to the kinesthetic gnostic units by associative pathways. In consequence, the associative pathways leading to the kinesthetic gnostic fields from other analyzers should be more abundant than those leading to other gnostic fields, since, as a matter of fact, here the shaping of human behavior, including expressive speech, is accomplished.

We have divided the gnostic area of the kinesthetic analyzer into three main fields: (1) the gnostic field for skilled movements of the body, and especially of the hand (K-H) (leaving out the others, for the sake of simplicity); (2) the gnostic field for locomotor behavior in space (K-Sp); (3) the gnostic field for speech (K-W). As before, we shall discuss separately those associations which are not involved in speech—most of them being common to both man and higher animals—and those which participate in verbal behavior (Plate IV).

A. NON-VERBAL ASSOCIATIONS

(1) *Visual–hand–kinesthetic associations* (V-MO → K-H, V-L → K-H). Most skilled motor acts performed by the hand are controlled by vision in greater or lesser degree. In some of these, somesthesis can substitute for vision—as in shaving, opening a door with a key, cutting bread, and so on. In others, the participation of vision is indispensable, as is the case when the motor acts are guided *only* by sight—for instance, when we grasp by hand objects we are confronted with, or copy a drawing we are looking at. Since the visual situation achieved by a motor act usually leads to the performance of the next motor act, our visually guided motor behavior consists in the interplay between the visual and kinesthetic gnostic units according to the formula:

$$\boxed{V_1 \rightarrow K\text{-}H_1} \rightarrow r_1 \rightarrow \boxed{V_2 \rightarrow K\text{-}H_2} \rightarrow r_2, \text{ and so on}.$$

A special case of a visual-motor interplay is represented by writing. Here the visual cues help us to write more distinctly, to keep the proper distances between successive words and successive lines, and also to place the words along a horizontal line; but the act of writing itself may occur without vision.

Since, as stated in Section 2, the kinesthetic perceptions evoke visual images (owing to the existence of kinesthetic-visual connections, K-H → V-MO and K-H → V-L, see Plate I), we may ask whether these images play any role in the sequential movements performed in the absence of the visual control—that is, whether and to what extent the visualization of the effect of a given motor act controls the performance of the successive act when vision is not present.

Although it is difficult to answer this question, it seems that the role of visual images in the performance of chain motor acts is limited. This may be deduced from the fact that people suffering from alexic agnosia who cannot visualize letters and words are able to write fluently, either spontaneously or under dictation, although they cannot read what they have written. The same may be true of other sequential motor acts performed by hand.

The visual–hand-kinesthetic associations play an important role in reproduction by hand of all types of visual stimulus-objects. Drawing from models perceived or visualized is a typical manifestation of the existence of such associations. There is much clinical evidence that the connections involved in these functions are localized in the non-dominant hemisphere, since lesions sustained in that hemisphere produce a dramatic impairment of drawing from nature or of other types of copying—the symptom referred to as "constructional apraxia."[12] This symptom is even more conspicuous since it occurs in right-handed people who occasionally do not notice their defect until it is shown to them. We observed, for instance, a highly competent technician who, after excision of a large tumor in the temporo-parieto-occipital region in the right hemisphere, to his great amazement failed completely to draw a bicycle or an automobile.

(2) *Somesthetic–hand-kinesthetic associations* (S-L → K-H, S-MO → K-H). In the preceding section we said that articular and tactile perceptions provide a feedback for a motor act, informing about its success or failure (especially in those cases in which vision is not involved), and accordingly they send messages to correct this act or to perform the following one. The best example of such a kinesthetic-somesthetic interplay is provided by the act of mastication of food or of drying oneself with a towel after a bath. On the other hand, it should be realized that in *routine* motor acts the kinesthetic programing of movements is sufficient for their skillful execution, without any

somesthetic feedback, if the visual feedback is in operation. This fact is evidenced by observing patients with lesions of the somesthetic area for the right hand. Although both the articular and tactile sensations in these subjects are strongly impaired or lost, and they are neither able to appreciate the posture of the affected hand, nor to recognize objects held in it, they remain exceedingly skillful in their motor performances. We have seen a number of patients with severe impairment of somesthesis who performed, with the corrective help of vision, all routine activities (including writing) without any difficulty. One female patient with extensive parietal lesion was able to crochet with the same skill as before the operation.

(3) *Emotional–hand-kinesthetic associations* (E → K-H). As shown in the preceding sections of this chapter, emotions can form associations with perceptions of each analyzer and evoke images or hallucinations of the corresponding stimulus-objects. The same principle is in operation in association between emotions and kinesthetic perceptions. But whereas the existence of emotional-visual or emotional-auditory associations can be detected only by introspection, at least in the present state of our neurophysiological methods, the existence of emotional-kinesthetic associations is manifested by the motor acts corresponding to the given kinesthetic images.

Since, as we shall see in subsequent chapters, a great part of motor behavior in animals is the result of the emotional-kinesthetic associations, these associations, in contradistinction to the emotional-exteroceptive ones, yield themselves to precise objective investigation in special experiments. Thus, in this field we are confronted with the same favorable situation which we have encountered in associations leading to gustatory experiences manifested by the overt salivary effects. Whereas the experimental study of the latter associations in animals has opened up a large field of research, called "classical conditioning," the emotional-kinesthetic associations have opened up another large field of research, called "instrumental conditioning." This being so, we shall postpone the further discussion of these associations to later chapters, in which they will be analyzed under rigorous experimental conditions.

(4) *Spatiovisual-spatiokinesthetic associations* (V-Sp → K-Sp). These associations are no less important in human life than those leading in the opposite direction from the kinesthetic to the visual analyzer (see Section 2, above). This may be evidenced by the following examples.

When we see a distance or a height we must leap over, we precisely adjust the program of the motor act we have to perform, so as to land on the proper place; as a matter of fact, a large part of training in sports consists in establishing such precise visual-kinesthetic associations. Similarly, when we have to go through a low passage, we bend our bodies so as not to bump our heads against its ceiling. All these associations are undoubtedly even better developed in animals who live in a complex terrain (jungle or mountains) requiring permanent visual-kinesthetic adjustments and in those who hunt prey and seize it in one leap.

The most important and common field of spatial visual-kinesthetic associations is, however, manifested in our locomotor behavior guided by visual spatial cues. Usually knowing the location of objects in space by our visual experience, we can utilize this knowledge for reaching or avoiding these objects. Thus, if I have a visual image of the place in which a given object is situated (for example, a book on a shelf in another room), this image produces the programing and execution of a definite sequence of movements directed to achieve the goal.

This mechanism of visually guided locomotor behavior is so powerful that sometimes it is based on even more complex associations. Let us suppose that we have to find a house in a district of the city with which we are not familiar. We may look at a map and, having the visual model of this district, can find the given place. But we may also hear from other persons a description of the route to that house; on this basis we are able to form a visual image of the route, crude in details, but exact in spatial relations, which allows us to program accordingly our locomotor behavior.

An illustrative experiment showing the operation of visual-kinesthetic associations by the way of substitution method is demonstrated in Stratton's paper concerning the reversal of the visual field by special glasses.[13] The subject (the author himself) in the first days of the experiment had insuperable difficulties in his locomotor behavior if it was guided by vision. It was much easier to him to move in a well-known space with eyes closed because of the absence of the misleading visual perceptions of his own movements. Similar experiments performed with the use of prismatic glasses were often repeated with the same results.

As noted in a preceding section, visual-kinesthetic gnostic interplay plays a most important role in human locomotor behavior, and it is no less (perhaps even better) developed in many animals, especially those who live in large and variegated terrains. The ability of animals to display roundabout responses is of course one typical manifestation of visual-kinesthetic spatial associations.

B. VERBAL ASSOCIATIONS

(1) *Audioverbal–word-kinesthetic associations* (A-W → K-W). These associations are essential for the development of speech in nor-

mal (not deaf) humans. In children, at the age of about nine months, there develops a "spontaneous" motor activity of the mouth and larynx named "babbling." It is originally not related to the auditory system, as documented by the fact that it appears also in deaf children. The normal child, however, hears its own babbling, and therefore, as indicated in an earlier section, the connections are formed between the kinesthetic vocal units and corresponding auditory units. We assume that in these connections, not the proper speech kinesthetic field, but, rather, the intermediary zone lying between the kinesthetic projective area for mouth and the Broca area is engaged.

Then, in the next stage of development, a particular type of reflex activity is established which may be called physiological echolalia or *parroting reflex*. It. consists in the tendency to repeat sounds articulated by other persons. Since the child usually hears *words*, it learns to repeat them—that is, the actual connections leading from the audioverbal units to the newly formed word-kinesthetic units are developed, these units being situated in the proper kinesthetic speech field. Thus the "vocabulary" of the child is gradually increased, although at that time the words may be still fully devoid of any designating significance, because the connections with other analyzers have not yet been established.

The parroting reflex, which is very prominent in early life, gradually decreases—the echolalic tendency diminishes and eventually disappears. This is certainly due to inhibition, because in many instances this reflex is released. For one thing, we can always voluntarily repeat a word heard when, for instance, we are asked to do so. For another, if we have to memorize some complex verbal orders, or difficult names, or several telephone numbers, we automatically repeat them either aloud or in our internal speech. It is also worthwhile noting that in some schizophrenic patients the echolalic tendency is totally disinhibited; the patient, against his own will, repeats everything he hears, even if the words are obscene and he is much distressed in doing so.

The parroting reflex is not the only manifestation of audioverbal–word-kinesthetic associations. At a later age, when a person learns to talk with others, many verbal responses are directly elicited by the audioverbal stimuli without the intervention of other analyzers. This is the case when we "automatically" answer routine questions (such as those concerning the multiplication table) or we continue the automatized verbal sequence (a poem) began by another person. The fact that when asked a question in one language (of several we know) we have a strong tendency to answer it in *the same* language and not in another one, even if we know the latter better, is again a manifestation of the connections between the auditory and kinesthetic verbal fields.

We have good evidence that the anatomical substrate of auditory-kinesthetic connections involved in speech are represented by the *fasciculus arcuatus* of the dominant hemisphere linking the posterior parts of the temporal lobe with the frontal cortex (Figure V-1). First, it may be shown that lesions sustained in the region where this fascicle runs give rise to the form of aphasia which may be easily explained as due to a division of auditory-kinesthetic connections (see below). Second, if we closely examine the map of long associative fascicles in the cortex of the chimpanzee, we can see that in spite of the great similarity of the whole arrangement of these fascicles with those found in man, the arcuate fascicle is lacking in this animal. This may be why the chimpanzee is unable to develop even a most primitive "language," in spite of the fact that its larynx has the same anatomy as that in man. In fact, Hayes[14] tried to teach a young chimpanzee to utter words but was almost totally unsuccessful, although the animal lived with the Hayes's nearly from birth, was very intelligent, and understood a great deal of human speech. The absence of the parroting reflex in apes is even more amazing when we realize that this very reflex is highly developed in many birds whose songs are learned by imitating their companions in early life.[15]

Lesions sustained in the posterior part of the first temporal gyrus and/or in the white substance beneath the supramarginal gyrus give rise to a special type of aphasia—called "conduction" or "central" aphasia—of which the chief symptom is the strong impairment of repetition of words heard, although comprehension of these words (based on audioverbal-visual associations) is preserved. We call this type of aphasia *auditory-verbal aphasia*.[16]

As will be shown below, we have good reason to believe that we can divide all men into two groups in respect to their mechanism of naming: in one group, naming is based on the direct connections leading from the visual analyzer (and other analyzers too) to the kinesthetic speech area; in the other, this faculty is mediated by the audio-verbal gnostic field. If auditory-verbal aphasia develops in subjects belonging to the former group, both descriptive speech and naming are only slightly impaired, whereas if it affects subjects belonging to the latter group, these functions are much more impaired, and a tendency to paraphasias and agrammatisms is observed. When such a patient fails to name a certain object he cannot be helped by prompting him with the beginning of the word, because of his inability of repetition.

Although patients suffering from pure auditory-verbal aphasia have no impairment in comprehension of speech heard, they fail to cope properly with a comprehension test if several orders are given to them

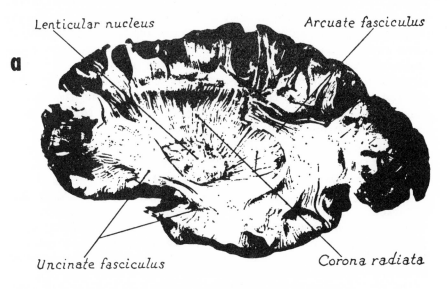

Lenticular nucleus

Arcuate fasciculus

a

Uncinate fasciculus

Corona radiata

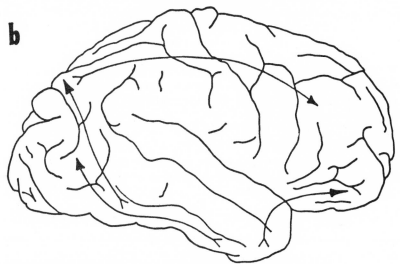

b

Fig. V-1. The Arcuate Fascicle in the Brain of Man (a) and Its Absence in the Brain of Chimpanzee (b)

(a) From O. S. Strong and A. Elwyn, *Human Neuroanatomy* (Baltimore: Williams & Wilkins, 1943).

(b) From P. Bailey, G. von Bonin, H. W. Garol, and W. S. McCulloch, in *J. Neurophysiol.*, 6 (1943): 129–34.

in quick succession or if several objects named by the examiner are to be pointed to. It is, however, easy to see that this deficit is not due to the impairment of comprehension but to the impairment of repetition of the words heard; in fact, in order to fulfill several orders given in advance, we always have to repeat them in our minds in order to preserve them in our short-term memory. In order to overcome this obstacle, one of our patients resorted to the trick of spotting the objects named by a quick glance as soon as he heard the name. In this way he was able successfully to fulfill the test even with several items.

Below we give some extracts of a report by Stengel and Patch[17] concerning a typical case of the auditory-verbal aphasia.

This female patient, age fifty-five, had been a clerk.

The patient did not look ill and her behavior in hospital was normal. She was able to dress and take her food without help. . . . Repetition of words spoken to her was grossly disturbed. . . . While her ability to name objects, and to understand, improved steadily in the course of the year following the onset of her illness, her disability in regard to the repetition of spoken language improved only slightly. . . .

28.8.50: (How are you?) As soon as I get up I get that pain, not pain. (Pain?) Not in—I can't say. It does not hurt, it just feels funny. (Speech?) I think this is a bit better. . . . Repetition of words spoken to her: (table) tangent, t, a, b, i,—(neck) notch,—(thumb) r, u, it's wrong. . . .

30.8.50: (Table) scondel, I can't,—(hospital) po, po, poscital. . . .

Postmortem: The white matter of the left supra-marginal and angular gyri, of the posterior third of the superior temporal gyrus . . . were largely replaced by linear scars stained with hemosiderin. . . .

In another patient described in the same paper repetition was as bad as in the previous case, but in addition

naming of objects was impaired. The patient either attempted to state the use of the object, or he produced paraphasias, or he did both. . . . Spontaneous speech was characterized by . . . frequent paraphasias with paragrammatism. . . . The patient had no difficulty in understanding simple questions and orders. . . . Reading was surprisingly good with only occasional distortions of words. He used to read the newspaper with good understanding.

The analysis of the symptoms of these two patients shows that in the first case the direct mechanism of speech prevailed, and therefore naming and spontaneous speech were not strongly impaired. In the second case there was a predominance of auditorily mediated speech; hence naming and spontaneous speech were affected. This, however, did not concern reading, which is usually based on direct visual-kinesthetic associations (see below).

(2) *Visual–word–kinesthetic associations* (V-L → K-W, V-MO →

K-W, V-VO → K-W, V-F → K-W, W-Sn → K-W, V-Sp → K-W). These extremely important associations form a basis for the function of naming. When we perceive or imagine an object, a face of a known person, a letter or a word, or a given spatial relation between objects, messages are sent from the respective visual gnostic fields to the corresponding sets of kinesthetic speech units; thus, we can pronounce aloud or in our minds the appropriate names. These associations are so strong that in many cases we pronounce in our minds the name of an object perceived quite automatically, and we cannot help doing so even if it is superfluous.

There arises a most important problem as to whether the connections linking the visual gnostic area with the word-kinesthetic field are direct (V → K-W), or whether they run through the audioverbal gnostic field (V → A-W → K-W). Since, as earlier indicated, we have good evidence of the existence of both visual-audioverbal and audioverbal–word-kinesthetic connections, it follows that naming mediated by the audioverbal field is certainly possible. If so, we should ask whether this is the only mechanism of naming, or whether we have evidence of the direct pathway linking the visual gnostic field with the speech field.

It is clear that the answer to this question cannot be based on purely psychological evidence. When we say the name of some object in our mind, we experience the auditory image of the corresponding word; but we cannot realize whether this word is imagined *before* its internal verbalization, owing to the V → A-W connections, or *after* its verbalization, owing to the K-W → A-W connections. In other words, we cannot know whether we have pronounced (in mind) the word because we heard it beforehand in our imagination or, on the contrary, we heard the word because we mentally pronounced it.

The important evidence suggesting that the direct connections between the visual gnostic area and the word-kinesthetic field *can* exist is brought forth by the fact that persons deaf from birth *are* able to learn to talk and their speech does not much differ from that of normal persons. This indicates that the direct potential connections between the two fields do exist in the human brain; we cannot, however, be sure whether they are *utilized* in those persons who have their hearing intact.

In order to answer this question, we must turn to the pathological material and see whether the disruption of the auditorily mediated pathway leading from the visual analyzer to the word-kinesthetic field destroys the naming function.

After studying the literature of the subject and the appropriate clinical cases, we came to the conclusion that naming of visual objects may either be mediated by the audioverbal gnostic field or it may occur with total neglecting of the auditory mediation, and that various persons, for reasons which will be discussed below, utilize predominantly either the direct visual-kinesthetic pathway, or the visual-auditory-kinesthetic pathway, or both, depending on which categories of objects are named.

Patients whose lesions are situated in the temporal lobe and do not impinge on the temporo-occipito-parietal junction can be divided into two groups. In one group, the audioverbal symptoms, consisting in the impairment of either comprehension, or repetition, or both, are accompanied by a clearly manifested amnestic aphasia; the patient is unable to name objects shown to him, and prompting by pronouncing the beginning of the word does not help him, because he cannot repeat what he has heard. What is very interesting in such patients is the fact that the naming of letters and numbers is, as a rule, totally preserved, and even reading is possible; this shows that in many persons naming letters is not accomplished by the mechanism involving the audioverbal gnosis.

In another group of patients, however, analogous lesions, producing also a strong auditory-visual aphasia (disability of comprehension) or auditory-verbal aphasia (disability of repetition) do not seriously affect either naming or spontaneous speech. These patients speak quite fluently, without much agrammatism, are able to express their thoughts in writing, although they do not understand anything they are told and/or they cannot repeat the words heard. The difference between the two groups is indeed striking, although no difference in localization of lesions accounts for it.

We shall describe here a very illustrative case of a patient recently examined by us, who after a thrombosis of a small branch of the *arteria cerebri media* had developed a severe auditory-visual ("sensory") aphasia. A severe impairment of his comprehension of speech heard was reported on p. 228; now we shall describe and analyze his other performances. His spontaneous speech was not much impaired; it was fluent, coherent, and rather logorrhoeic, although extremely poor in nouns. The naming of small objects presented to him was nearly nil, as was his comprehension of the words heard. For instance:

Object Pointed Out to Him	His Response
mirror	I know this, this is. . . .
pencil	I know, this is for writing.
comb	I know this; its name is. . . .
finger	These are my hands, one hand.
mouth	This is my . . . not hand . . . my body.
ear	This is my head, my head composed of two parts.

In contradistinction to this bad performance, the naming of letters was perfect, and the patient was able to read relatively fluently. He was also able to name correctly and without hesitation the actions performed in front of him; for instance; "Now you get up. Now you sit down. You walk. You run. You put your hand into (hesitation) your pocket. You raise your hands."

He writes under dictation without any errors. He is also able to repeat without difficulty words heard as well as short sequences.

The results of this examination indicate that in this case we had to do with a severe impairment of connections between the audioverbal gnostic field and visual gnostic area (and, perhaps, somatic gnostic area). Therefore, the patient's comprehension of nouns heard was dramatically affected. Along with this was impairment of the naming of objects pointed out to him, showing that this function was accomplished via the audioverbal gnostic field. On the other hand, the naming of letters was not affected, because it occurred through direct visual-kinesthetic connections. Most interesting was his ability to name human actions. Perhaps when seeing these actions he imagined himself doing them, and their naming occurred through direct body-kinesthetic–word-kinesthetic connections (see below). His writing under dictation occurred through the unaffected audioverbal–hand-kinesthetic connections.

In contradistinction to patients in whom naming is impaired because of a lesion along the visual-auditory-kinesthetic pathways (that is, a lesion affecting either visual-auditory connections, as in the quoted case, or audioverbal gnostic field, or audioverbal–word-kinesthetic connections), there is another category of patients, with lesions affecting the white matter beneath the angular gyrus, who manifest a "pure" visual-verbal (amnestic) aphasia. Comprehension and repetition are normal in these patients, but they have great difficulty in naming objects seen, although in most cases they are able to describe their usage—"This is for cutting" (knife). "This is for writing" (pen). "This is for smoking" (cigarette). When we prompt them by uttering the beginning of the word, they immediately reproduce the whole word. Their speech is characteristic in that it consists almost exclusively of verbs and not of nouns. Interestingly enough, in contradistinction to the patients of the preceding group, the naming of letters seems to be even more impaired in them than the naming of objects, and therefore they are not able to read (alexic aphasia).

To sum up, we can reach the conclusion that the naming of visual objects (and similarly of stimulus-objects of other analyzers) can be developed in two ways. First, since in the development of speech the audioverbal–word-kinesthetic connections are formed which are responsible for the faculty of repetition, the nominative function of speech is developed by adding to it the visual-audioverbal segment, according to the principle which was stated in the first section. Hence, the function of naming is mediated by the audioverbal field—that is, the subject must first imagine the sound of a word in order to pronounce it. Second, this function can develop independently of the audioverbal field by utilizing the potential connections linking the visual gnostic area with the word-kinesthetic field, which is already formed owing to the parroting reflex. We shall call the first of these two mechanisms "the auditorily mediated speech mechanism"; the second, "the direct speech mechanism." Depending on the mechanism of speech proper to a given subject, the given cortical lesion may produce a different effect. It should be stressed, however, that even in those persons whose speech has developed according to the auditorily mediated mechanism, the naming of letters (and digits) is established by the direct mechanism. This may be due to the fact that when a child learns to read, letters are not yet represented in his audioverbal field, and therefore the formation of direct connections between sign units and word-kinesthetic units is easier than the formation of connections via the audioverbal units.

If our hypothesis is true, it may be assumed that compensation of speech, which occurs after some time (with the help of logopedia), occurs by involving the mechanism which is not impaired. Thus, when a patient has developed amnestic aphasia because of a lesion in the region of the angular gyrus, he can learn to name objects by involving the auditorily mediated mechanism; this is not difficult, since his faculty of repetition is intact. More difficult is the reeducaton of aphasic patients with lesions in the auditory region, but here a subject can learn to name objects with the aid of his unimpaired reading faculty.

What are the factors that determine by which of the two mechanisms the child learns to speak? It may be assumed that in those children in which the period of parroting well precedes the period of naming the auditorily mediated mechanism of naming is predominant, since the new function becomes simply attached to the one already firmly established. On the contrary, when both functions, parroting and naming, develop *pari passu*, the direct mechanism of naming prevails.

Since it is indubitable that speech based on the direct visual-kinesthetic pathways is superior to that mediated by auditory word images, it follows that special instructions should be given educationists to teach children to name objects *as soon as* they begin to imitate human voices. Judging from the material with which I am acquainted, I think that in persons from sophisticated milieus temporal lesions affecting comprehension do not lead to amnestic aphasia, whereas in persons from rural districts it does. The fact that in sophisticated milieus children are *taught* to name objects whereas among peasants they are rather left to themselves may account for this difference.

(3) *Limb-somesthetic–word-kinesthetic associations* (S-L→K-W). It has been frequently observed that in nearly all cases of amnestic aphasia there is no exact parallelism between the impairment of naming objects seen and naming the parts of the body. There are cases in which visual objects are named much better than the parts of the body or vice versa. This discrepancy sometimes has even a bizarre character, because when we show a patient a picture of an animal and ask him to name the parts of its body, he easily names those parts which are absent in man (such as the tail or the horns) but has difficulty in naming the eye, ear, or even leg. It is also known that such an amnestic aphasia concerning the parts of the body, as opposed to aphasia concerning visual objects, is caused by lesions situated in the dorsal parts of the parietal lobe of the dominant hemisphere.

It must be stressed that this type of aphasia should not be confused with autotopagnosia (discussed in Chapter III). In fact, a patient is able to identify a limb on another person (or in a picture) with his own limb but simply fails to name it.

The explanation of this kind of aphasia is that the naming of the parts of our own body is based, not on the visual analyzer, but on the somesthetic analyzer—on that field where the particular limbs or their parts are represented (S-L in our schemes). The connections formed between limb somesthetic gnostic units and corresponding word-kinesthetic units are so strong that visual perceptions or images of the parts of the body are linked with these word units, not directly, but by the intermediary of the somesthetic gnostic field (V-L → S-L → K-W). Hence, the subject with an impairment of S-L → K-W connections fails to name the parts of his body even if he perceives them by sight.

(4) *Hand-kinesthetic–word-kinesthetic associations* (K-H → K-W). This is a type of association which, to my knowledge, has not been discussed in the literature. If we assume that the gnostic hand-kinesthetic area is responsible for kinesthetic gnosis of skilled actions, we should conclude that their naming occurs on the basis of the connections established between the sets of units representing them and corresponding word-kinesthetic units. The same is true of body-kinesthetic gnostic units involved in changing body positions and leg movements. This would explain the curious fact that patients with heavy amnestic aphasia concerning the naming of visual objects are able to name the verbs representing their usage and also to name movements of the body (cf. p. 249). In consequence, as said before,

the speech of such patients consists mainly of verbs whereas nouns are nearly absent.

Here are typical extracts of such a speech. A patient is asked to describe his work (he was the chief of a workshop): "I went around, whether all in order. Each to his work, this went to his, other to other, I must beforehand show to each, then I go, then one rides to work farther."[18] The patient described above (p. 248), who is rather logor-rhoeic, explains his deficit of naming by saying: "This is, professor, because nobody tells me what it is, and since nobody tells me I cannot say."

On the contrary, if a lesion is situated in the gnostic kinesthetic area itself affecting the connections between gnostic field for hand and for mouth, then the patient is able to pronounce names of objects but fails to use verbs. This is what is usually called the "telegraphic style." Here is an illustrative example of such type of speech.[19] A soldier describes the story of his injury: "Now, front, now attack, now ex-plosion, now nothing, now operation, now splinter, speech, speech, speech." Another patient we observed, suffering from a frontal menin-gioma, describes in this way a picture of a family: "Mother, schoolgirl, dog"; the rural picture: "Haymaking, indeed, haymaking, tractor, rye, women." Note the precise usage of the nouns pronounced.

We assume that, exactly as parts of one's own body are named owing to the limb-somesthetic–word-kinesthetic connections, even if these parts are perceived by vision, the same is true of naming the actions: when we perceive some familiar action performed by an-other person, which is also proper to ourselves, we name it because of the indirect associations leading from its visual perception via its kinesthetic image to the image of a corresponding word.

It should be stressed that whereas the amnestic aphasia for visual objects may occur in an almost pure form, because the distance be-tween the two areas concerned is great, the pure amnestic aphasia for actions is hardly possible and must be contaminated either by kines-thetic hand agnosia (apraxia), or by kinesthetic word agnosia ("motor aphasia"), or by both. Nevertheless, the essence of the telegraphic style and the lack of fluency of speech in such patients can be easily attributed to their failure to name the actions represented by verbs.

(5) *Emotional–word-kinesthetic associations* (E → K-W). It is well known that various emotions are associated with particular verbal expressions, such as: fear or horror with the exclamation "Jesus Christ!" strong desire with "Oh, God!" anger with "Go to hell!"

Since the connections leading from the emotional units to other fields are always very strong because of strong arousal which accom-panies their operation, it is clear that they are particularly resistant to damage, and even in severe cases of kinesthetic aphasia they remain unimpaired. This is why some authors believed that such exclamations did not depend on the speech area proper but on the symmetrical area in the non-dominant hemisphere.

(6) *Word-kinesthetic–word-kinesthetic associations* (K-W → K-W). To end this list of connections converging on the word-kinesthetic field, we should turn attention to a very important category, which may be called the intrinsic connections of that field. Normal speech not only consists of descriptions of perceptions and images provided by other analyzers, but the words are also strongly interconnected, forming more or less automatized verbal sequences. Ample pathological evidence shows that in most cases these verbal sequences (such as counting from one to ten, enumerating the days of the week, saying prayers) are extremely resistant to cortical injuries, and, in particular—contrary to our expectation—they may not depend on the auditory feedback. In fact, all our patients with auditory-verbal aphasia, manifested by the total loss of repetition, were amazingly skillful in reciting such well-established automatized verbal sequences.

These data seem to indicate that the programing of these sequences is founded within the word-kinesthetic field, and lesions in this area destroy not only many (or some) of the corresponding units but also their interconnections. Another alternative would be that these sequences depend on some area closely related to, but not identical with, the proper word-kinesthetic field.

Following is a description of a clear case of total abolition of automatized verbal sequences.[20] A girl of ten was operated upon because of an angioma of the left carotid artery. After the surgery she suddenly lost consciousness and thereafter developed a right hemiplegia and total aphasia due to an emboly in one of the large brain arteries.

She was forcibly trained in speech for two years. There were no savings from the preoperative period, and she had to learn to speak from the very beginning.

At the time of her examination (two years after the surgery) she had a heavy hemiparesis of the right limbs. She spoke slowly and without any fluency. In tests for repetition, comprehension, and naming she was good, but her automatized verbal sequences were very poor. Before the operation she had known by heart many nursery rhymes, prayers, and the like. There was no recovery of any of these memories, and she had great difficulty in learning verbal sequences anew. She was unable to recite any verse, and she made errors in enumerating weekdays and months. The chief characteristic of her spontaneous or descriptive speech was precisely that it was not sufficiently automatized.

It must be assumed that in this patient all the gnostic fields engaged in speech—and in particular the word-kinesthetic field—had to be developed anew in the right hemisphere. Its deficiency was manifested by the fact that although naming as such had been reestablished, the more difficult function of the formation of interkinesthetic associations was strongly handicapped.

If our concept—that the intrinsic mechanism of automatized verbal sequences depends on the word-kinesthetic gnostic field is true—then the reproduction of these sequences should be a good test for separating true kinesthetic aphasia from anarthria or from those disorders in which pronunciation of primitive phonemes originally used in babbling is affected. Here we can quote an illustrative case of a man who lost his expressive speech because of a tumor in the frontal operculum. After surgery he could utter only one syllable. Then his vocabulary was gradually enriched, but the words he uttered were so distorted that sometimes they were hardly recognizable. Nevertheless, with this distorted language he could express himself well, and, according to all available evidence (good writing, repeating a long series of words), his internal speech was preserved.

Automatized verbal sequences are not only manifested in "automatic" production of well-memorized material, but they are largely involved in our normal speech. We have in mind here grammatical forms of words (even more strongly emphasized in those languages, like Latin, which have more flexible nouns and verbs than is true in English), compelling us to say: "I read" but "he reads"; or "one pencil" but "two pencils" and so on. Again, although agrammatisms occur in some patients whose auditory speech area is impaired, showing that they may depend on the loss of auditory feedback, this is far from being the general rule. We can cite, both from our own material and from the literature, cases of auditory-verbal or auditory-visual aphasia or even audioverbal agnosia in which fluency and correctness of speech was fairly well preserved. This shows that the auditory control is not necessarily involved in that aspect of language, but probably occurs only in those subjects in whom the auditorily mediated mechanism of speech prevails over the direct mechanism.

Further evidence showing the strong ties between particular groups of words can be provided by the following simple experiment. Ask a subject to tell a short story in succession in two languages which he knows very well. Then, ask him to tell the same story in such a way that the words from each of these languages would be pronounced in alternating sequence. The utmost difficulty, or even unfeasibility, in performing this task lies in the fact that the words of the same language are strongly associated among themselves but not with words of the other language (except, of course, in professional interpreters). This is why it is so difficult to translate immediately a given word into another language, even if both languages are familiar to us. If the word designates a definite stimulus-object we usually visualize that object and only then name it. If, however, the word is abstract or the proper shade of meaning should be expressed, an immediate answer is never forthcoming, even if we have to translate the word into our own language.

(7) *Word-kinesthetic–hand-kinesthetic associations* (K-W → K-H). To end this list of verbal associations involving the kinesthetic analyzer, we turn attention to those associations which are involved in controlling handwriting.

Our handwriting generally occurs as the effect of: (1) copying, (2) dictation, or (3) our own speech (external or internal).

Writing by copying is accomplished by the straight sign-visual–hand-kinesthetic associations (V-Sn → K-H) not involving any other speech areas. This is best documented by the fact that patients with severe impairment of either auditory speech area or kinesthetic word area (or their interconnections), who have great difficulties in naming and/or comprehension of speech, are strikingly unimpaired in copying words seen, either in print or written. On the contrary, copying is impaired in cases of alexia (sign-visual agnosia).

On the other hand, writing by dictation is totally lost in cases of audioverbal agnosia, auditory-verbal aphasia, or word-kinesthetic agnosia (Broca aphasia)—that is, when one of the links of the audio-verbal–word-kinesthetic connections (A-W → K-W) is damaged.

Spontaneous writing through internal or external verbalization is also not possible in Broca aphasia, but it is possible in those cases of audioverbal agnosia or auditory-verbal aphasia which are not accompanied by abolition of naming.

All these facts clearly show that the only link through which handwriting (but not copying) is accomplished is the *word-kinesthetic field*—in other words, that in order to write a word spontaneously or under dictation, we must first verbalize it.

It is interesting to note that in those languages in which spelling faithfully reflects pronunciation, writing is incorrect in those cases in which pronunciation is disturbed. This is highly characteristic of patients suffering from oral-somesthetic agnosia produced by lesions in the parietal operculum. When writing words they make errors strictly corresponding to those made in their pronunciation. For instance, if a patient says in Polish "kod" instead of "kot" ("cat") he will certainly write "kod"; then, seeing the word written, he may correct his error under the visual feedback. This shows that the word-kinesthetic field functions in close synergy with the oral-somesthetic field in shaping the patterns of pronounced (and thought) words. All these relations are diagrammatically presented in Figure V-2.

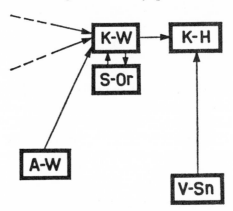

FIG. V-2. ASSOCIATIONS CONTROLLING HANDWRITING

K-W, word-kinesthetic field; S-Or, oral-somesthetic field; K-H, handwriting field; A-W, audioverbal field; V-Sn, sign-visual field.

Note that handwriting controlled by dictation or by various images is mediated by verbalization, while writing controlled by copying does not need verbalization.

6. Associations directed to the emotive analyzer

This subject has already been mentioned in Chapter I, and will be considered in detail in Chapter VI. In this section we shall specify only those connections leading to the emotional field which are regularly developed in human life and discuss some of their properties (Plate V).

A. NONVERBAL ASSOCIATIONS

(1) *Visual-emotional associations* (V-MO → E, V-VO → E, V-F → E). A great variety of visual stimulus-objects which commonly accompany particular emotions enter into associations with them. Thus, the hunger drive in a not oversatiated subject will appear when he is brought to a situation where he regularly obtains food—when he sees a table set, and various dishes being consumed by others. The sexual drive is aroused by seeing naked or half-naked persons of the opposite sex, or their pictures—a circumstance constituting a great part of the social life in our culture. On the other hand, the horrible scenes we have witnessed, the threatening gestures directed against us, or the sight of abominable creatures elicit horror, fear, or disgust. A wide

range of various emotions, such as love, attachment, respect, fear, hatred, disgust, is elicited by the sight of faces of persons we are acquainted with (V-F → E). Similarly, the expressions of human faces (menacing, angry, gentle, horrified) easily elicit in us appropriate emotions.

In this brief survey we may observe that whereas some of these associations have a purely acquired character and are based exclusively on our experience, this is not true of others. Why is it that the sight of terrible mutilations or of a bloodstained person evokes horror, whereas other transfigurations may evoke laughter? Does the sight of a naked person of the opposite sex evoke the sexual drive without any preceding sexual experiences? These problems have been discussed in Chapter I, where we came to the conclusion that these stimuli comprise some elements which elicit appropriate drives on the hereditary basis.

(2) *Auditory-emotional associations* (A-Vo → E, A-Sd → E). Here we have to do with such auditory stimuli as various types of speech intonation (gentle, menacing, angry), piercing cries, various types of roars, strange murmurs, and many, many others which elicit appropriate emotions. Again, some sounds (like piercing cries) are probably inbornly associated with the given emotion, whereas others are purely conditioned. The same is true of various intonations of human voices.

(3) *Somesthetic-emotional associations* (S-T → E). It is well known that tactile stimuli are associated, either innately or by way of conditioning, with many emotions both attractive and aversive. For example, sexual emotions are elicited by the touch of the body of a person of the opposite sex; disgust, by the touch of a greasy substance; or fear, by pain-producing stimuli.

(4) *Gustatory-emotional associations* (S-G → E). The taste of savory meals may increase or produce the attractive emotion of hunger, whereas the taste of certain inedible substances may produce aversive emotions like disgust or fear.

(5) *Olfactory-emotional associations* (Ol → E). The emotogenic significance of various odors, either innate or acquired, is so familiar that no examples are needed. Since olfaction plays a rather limited gnostic role in human life, the chief domain of its operation is in establishing associations with various emotions.

(6) *Labyrinthine-emotional associations* (La → E). Vestibular perceptions, depending on their character or strength, can facilitate either sleep when they are gentle or fear when they are abrupt (loss of balance).

B. Verbal associations

Whereas nonverbal associations between various stimulus-objects and emotions are abundant, direct associations between words (deprived of their intonations) and emotions are scarce. This does not contradict the truism that words are strong emotogenic factors, and that even one word may produce a heart attack or an outburst of immense joy. In fact, by words (heard or read) we can produce any kind of emotion whose intensity will be no less strong than that produced by other factors. If, however, we analyze the mechanism of the emotogenic character of words, we can easily come to the conclusion that their operation is indirect—they produce the images (chiefly visual) of given situations or objects which are associated with particular emotions (A-W → V-MO → E, A-W → V-VO → E, and so on). The existence of direct associations of words with emotions without this intermediary link is rather doubtful.

Comparing the diagram representing the connections directed toward the emotional field with diagrams representing the connections leading from that field to other analyzers, we may observe that all of them are strictly bidirectional. This means that if a given stimulus-object elicits by association a definite emotion, this emotion will also elicit the image of the same stimulus-object. For instance, if the visual perception of a given food gave rise to a strong appetite for it, hunger aroused by other factors will be likely to evoke the image of that food. Analogous examples can be given in respect to sexual emotions, fear, anger, and so on.

This bidirectional character of connections linking the emotional units with gnostic units, combined with the long-lasting and inert character of emotions, discussed in Chapter I, leads to a peculiar phenomenon based on the positive feedback which may be called *emotional avalanche*. Let us explain this phenomenon by giving the following typical example. Suppose that we have recently experienced a dramatic accident, and after it is over try to have some rest or go to sleep. Since, however, the given emotional state, although in a much attenuated degree, is still in operation, it easily evokes through E → V connections the image of the accident. This, in turn, through the V → E connections makes the emotion more intense, and this intensified emotion leads to the strengthening of the corresponding visual image. Thus, in a few minutes the emotion rises to the same intensity as at the time of the accident itself, and we find that we are unable to get rid of it without the help of a strong tranquilizer. Such an emotional avalanche is certainly familiar to everyone, and may concern any emotion—sexual drive, anger, despair, fear, and so on.

There is no doubt that many psychiatric cases of long-lasting extreme aggressiveness, pathological anxiety, or depression are due to this mechanism of emotional avalanche. The fact that, even after the appeasement of the hyperemotional state by the tranquilizing drug, this avalanche immediately regenerates when the drug is no longer effective, is easy to understand if we take into account its self-augmenting mechanism. Therefore, the only possibility of annihilating this state is either to eradicate the given emotion by psychotherapy or, if it is impossible, to sever the reverberating circuit leading to its regeneration. This latter is probably provided by prefrontal lobotomy, after which the patient is still able to experience various emotional states, but they lose their self-regenerating character.

A special case of the emotional avalanche is provided by the phenomenon of "intractable pain." As was previously noted, this condition arises after a long-lasting severe pain and consists in its becoming totally independent of the original source evoking it. This is because the frequent attacks of insufferable pain become bilaterally associated with the fear of the pain; as a result, fear elicits pain by way of association, whereas this pain in turn increases fear. The complete cure of this state by frontal lobotomy was commented upon in Section 4.

Since all emotional states may arise either by specific stimuli eliciting them or by way of association, we may ask whether unconditioned emotions and conditioned emotions differ in our introspection, giving rise to subjective experiences of perceptions and images respectively, or whether they are always represented by the same qualitative experience. Taking into account that the emotive brain belongs to the most primitive afferent systems, we should expect that the second alternative is true.

This is precisely what we find by analyzing our own emotions. We do not differentiate at all those emotions which are produced by specific factors serving for their unconditioned elicitation and those which are produced by way of association. Fear is exactly the same experience irrespective of whether it has been elicited by severe pain, or by a conditioned signal heralding it, or even by hearing the information that pain is imminent. We do not even properly realize whether and to what degree the given drive (for example, hunger) is produced by such internal factors as the composition of the blood, or by the stimuli to which it was conditioned. Here the utilization of the word "hallucination" for the associative origin of a drive is rather unusual, because the drive always operates in the same way irrespective of its origin.

It should be recalled that many years ago a bitter argument arose about the problem of whether the *memory of emotions* exists.[21] It seems that precisely as with many arguments concerning principles, this one may also be reduced to a purely terminological quarrel. If by memory we understand the fact that a given experience may be called forth by way of association, then the answer to this question is certainly positive. In fact, by presentation of a stimulus which was associated with fear a long time ago we can elicit this same emotion, which may be as vivid as it was before. For instance, in my own experience, hearing the characteristic sound of a diving airplane elicits fear in me even now, twenty-five years after the bombardment of Warsaw. If, however, by memory we understand the elicitation of *images*, and not actual perceptions, then the memory of emotions does not exist, since emotions are always actual, irrespective of the way in which they are produced. It is worthwhile to cite in this context the following passage of the reminiscences of Sully-Prudhomme communicated to Ribot.[22]

When I remember the emotions aroused in me by the entry of the Germans into Paris after our last defeats, I find it impossible not to experience this same emotion afresh, simultaneously and indivisibly, while the mnemonic image of the Paris of that day remains in my memory very distinct from any actual perception . . . I am almost inclined to ask myself if every *recollection of feeling does not take on the character of a hallucination.* (Italics by Ribot.)

It is the only passage in the literature I know in which emotion experienced as an effect of conditioning *is* called hallucination, as for that matter it should be.

7. Summary and conclusions

The present chapter was concerned with a general survey and evaluation of associations normally formed in the life of human beings in the present condition of their existence. The information about these associations comes mainly from two sources: from self-observation of one's own typical mental experiences, and from observation and examination of patients with various injuries of the brain.

All the bulk of associations established in normal human life may be divided into two groups: associations involving speech in all its aspects (verbal associations), and associations not involving speech (non-verbal associations). Whereas the former group is certainly inherent only to homo sapiens, the latter is present also in many other species, depending on which gnostic fields are developed in them.

A. NON-VERBAL ASSOCIATIONS

The most important non-verbal associations are the following:

(1) *Mutual associations established between the visual analyzer and*

the somesthetic (including vestibular and olfactory) analyzer. Here belong: (a) bidirectional associations between the tactile (stereognostic) aspects of small manipulable objects and their visual aspects; (b) associations between the visual aspects of manipulable objects and their textural, gustatory, and olfactory aspects; (c) associations between the position of a limb and its visual aspect, and (d) bidirectional associations between spatial relations perceived by labyrinth and vision.

(2) *Mutual associations established between visual and auditory analyzers.* Here belong bidirectional associations between the visual aspects of sound-producing objects and their auditory aspects. A special highly developed group is represented by associations between human faces and sounds of human voices.

(3) *Mutual associations established between visual and kinesthetic analyzers.* Here belong: (a) bidirectional associations between the visual aspects of objects and kinesthetic patterns of their manipulation; these associations are involved in the mutual interplay between the corresponding gnostic fields, being the basis of visually guided skillful movements; (b) bidirectional associations between the visual aspect of spatial relations and kinesthetic patterns of locomotion including head and eye movements; again, the mutual interplay between the corresponding gnostic fields is the basis for visually guided locomotor behavior or its images.

(4) *Mutual associations established between somesthetic and kinesthetic analyzers.* Here belong bidirectional associations between somesthetic aspects of objects and limb positions and kinesthetic patterns of motor acts performed on their basis. This is the basis of somesthetically guided behavior, which plays a dominant role in blind persons or in those activities which are not visually perceived (for example, mastication).

(5) *Mutual associations between all the analyzers and emotional states.* All these associations are bidirectional; if the given emotion is not satisfied, it may give rise to its avalanche facilitation.

B. VERBAL ASSOCIATIONS

The most important verbal associations are the following:

(1) *Mutual associations established between the auditory aspect of speech and the kinesthetic aspect of speech.* These associations provide a basis for the development of language in normal (not deaf) persons. They are originally formed on the one hand on the basis of the auditory feedback provided by the inarticulate and later articulate speech, and on the other hand on the basis of parroting reflexes.

(2) *Associations established between the auditory aspect of speech and stimulus-objects of various analyzers (visual, somesthetic, kin-*

esthetic, and auditory). These are the basis for the comprehension of human speech.

(3) *Associations established between stimulus-objects of various analyzers (visual, somesthetic, kinesthetic, auditory) and the kinesthetic aspect of speech.* These are the basis for the denotative function of speech.

(4) *Intrinsic associations established between words heard.* These are the basis for auditory verbal sequences. Analogous associations are formed for tones in music.

(5) *Intrinsic associations established between words pronounced.* These are responsible for the recitation of automatized verbal sequences, for fluency in speech, and for grammatical quality.

Damage to the connections linking the audioverbal gnostic field with the word-kinesthetic field gives rise to "conduction" aphasia, which we call auditory-verbal aphasia. Its most prominent symptom is the impairment of repetition of words heard.

Damage to the connections linking the audioverbal gnostic field with gnostic fields of other analyzers gives rise to the "auditory" (or "sensory") aphasia, which we call auditory-visual, auditory-somesthetic, or auditory-kinesthetic aphasia. Its main symptom is the impairment of comprehension of words heard.

Damage to the connections linking the gnostic fields of various analyzers with the gnostic field of word-kinesthesis gives rise to the "nominal" or "amnestic" aphasia, which we call visual-verbal, somesthetic-verbal or kinesthetic-verbal aphasia respectively. Its main symptom is the impairment of naming of stimulus-objects perceived or imagined.

On the basis of the pathological material, it is assumed that the connections linking the gnostic fields of various analyzers with the word-kinesthetic gnostic field may run either directly to that field, or through the mediation of the audioverbal gnostic field, depending on (1) individual differences between persons (due probably to different ways of the development of speech), and (2) on the categories of stimulus-objects forming associations with words.

It has been indicated that among many various associations there are some which are distinguished from others by being manifested by overtly detectable responses of the subject. This happens either when the excitation of recipient gnostic units produces an inborn response or when it concerns the kinesthetic analyzer. These types of associations were labeled respectively as classical (type I) or instrumental (type II) conditioned reflexes, and were subjected to a detailed and extensive experimental investigation. The following chapters are concerned precisely with these types of associations.

References to Chapter V

1. G. M. Stratton. 1897. Vision without inversion of the retinal image. *Psychol. Rev.*, 4: 341–60.
2. J. S. Beritoff (Beritashvili). 1965. *Neural Mechanisms of Higher Vertebrate Behavior*. Translated and edited by W. T. Liberson. Boston: Little, Brown & Co.
3. E. von Holst. 1954. Relations between the central nervous system and the peripheral organs. *Brit. J. Anim. Behav.*, 2: 89–94.
4. G. M. Stratton (see note 1 above).
5. G. H. Deckert. 1964. Pursuit eye movements in the absence of a moving visual stimulus. *Science*, 143: 1192–93.
6. E. C. Tolman. 1932. *Purposive Behavior in Animals and Man*. New York: Appleton-Century.
   ———. 1948. Cognitive maps in rats and man. *Psychol. Rev.*, 55: 189–208.
7. N. R. F. Maier. 1929. Reasoning in white rats. *Comp. Psychol. Monogr.*, 6 (No. 3, Serial No. 29): 1–93.
8. P. T. Young. 1945. *Emotion in Man and Animal*, pp. 32–34. New York: Wiley.
9. I. S. Beritoff (Beritashvili). 1965 (see note 2 above).
10. Л. Г. Столярова-Кабелянская. 1961. Клинические и патофизиологические различия между корковой и транскортикальной сенсорной афазией. (Clinical and pathophysiological differences between cortical and transcortical sensory aphasia.) Вопросы клиники и патофизиологии афазий, pp. 24–57. Ред. Е. В. Шмидт и Р. А. Ткачев. Moscow: Medgiz.
11. T. Ribot. 1911. *The Psychology of Emotions*, p. 39. 2d ed. New York: Walter Scott.
12. M. Critchley. 1955. *The Parietal Lobes*, chap. 6. London: Arnold.
13. G. M. Stratton. 1897 (see note 1 above).
14. C. Hayes. 1952. *The Ape in Our House*. London: V. Gollancz.
15. W. H. Thorpe. 1961. *Bird-song: The Biology of Vocal Communication and Expression in Birds*. Cambridge: Cambridge University Press.
16. J. Konorski. 1961. Analiza patofizjologiczna różnych rodzajów zaburzeń mowy i próba ich klasyfikacji. (Pathophysiological analysis of various forms of speech disorders and an attempt at their classification.) *Rozpr. Wydz. Nauk Med. PAN.*, R. 6, T. 2: 9–32. English summary.
17. E. Stengel and J. C. L. Patch. 1955. "Central" aphasia associated with parietal symptoms. *Brain*, 78: 401–16.
18. B. Selecki and L. Stępień. 1961. Zaburzenia mowy w ogniskowych uszkodzeniach okolicy pogranicza płatów skroniowego, ciemieniowego i potylicznego dominującej półkuli mózgu. (Speech disorders produced by focal lesions of the junction of temporal, parietal and occipital lobes of the dominant cerebral hemisphere.) *Rozpr. Wydz. Nauk Med. PAN.*, R. 6, T. 2: 55–72. English summary.
19. А. Р. Лурия. 1962. Высшие корковые функции человека и их нарушения при локальных поражениях мозга. (Higher cortical

functions in man and their disturbances in local brain lesions.) Moscow: Moscow University.

20. E. Osetowska-Więckowska. 1955. Próba interpretacji patofizjologicznej wyników klinicznego badania afazji ruchowej. (An attempt of pathophysiological interpretation of clinical examination of motor aphasia.) *Neurologia, Neurochir. Psychiat. pol.*, 5: 605–21. English summary.

21. T. Ribot. 1911 (see note 11 above), chap. 11.

22. *Ibid.*, p. 154.

CHAPTER VI

CLASSICAL CONDITIONED REFLEX (TYPE I)

1. Introductory remarks

In the two preceding chapters an attempt was made to present some general rules of the formation of associations between perceptions, and to survey the most important associations established in human beings as a result of their everyday experiences. We have chosen humans and not animals for the study of this subject because, first, the information on associations is so far predominantly based on introspection and, second, because these phenomena are far more abundant and manifold in humans than in other animals, even primates. This does not mean, however, that associations cannot be successfully studied in animals too. On the contrary, there is a large and rewarding field of research in animal behavior concerned specifically with associations and throwing much light on some important aspects of these phenomena. This is the research concerning the so-called Pavlovian, or classical, or type I conditioning performed mainly on dogs.

It may be observed that the very procedure of classical conditioning fulfills all requirements which have been specified for the formation of associations, supplemented by an additional requirement—that the recipient stimulus (the stimulus activating recipient units in the given association) must produce a definite, observable response. As a result of the paired presentations of the transmittent and the recipient stimuli, actual connections are established between corresponding perceptive units; these connections are manifested by the transmittent stimulus acquiring the property of eliciting the response characteristic for the recipient stimulus. The whole phenomenon is called, after

Pavlov, the conditioned reflex (CR); the transmittent stimulus, after acquiring this new property, becomes a conditioned or conditional stimulus (CS). The recipient stimulus is now called a reinforcing stimulus or reinforcement of the CS or of the CR. Since an effective reinforcing stimulus has to produce a stable and regular response, the stimuli serving this role are commonly chosen from those agents which produce an ostensible inborn unconditioned reflex (UR).

Considering a classical CR as nothing else but a particular case of association in which the recipient stimulus produces an overt response, we may notice that the term "reinforcement" is rather misleading, the more so that it is burdened with many miscomprehensions. As a matter of fact, the expression "a CS is reinforced by the US" is tantamount to the expression "a CS is closely followed by the US" and the "reinforcing stimulus" is nothing else but the "recipient stimulus." The term "reinforcement" causes terminological confusion because it is used in different senses in the Pavlovian and Hullian systems, and because it is not clear whether it should be used when the recipient stimulus has no overt response but is detected only by the EEG records, as with rhythmic light.

Nevertheless, being aware of all these drawbacks of the term "reinforcement," we shall not abandon it in the present work. In spite of its ambiguity, this term is so widely used, and so convenient, that avoiding it would not help the reader to follow the text but, on the contrary, it would make it even less easily readable. Accepting the term and its usage, we should, however, clearly define its meaning and scope of application. We shall agree to use it only when the presentation of a stimulus called reinforcer either in the classical or instrumental procedure *leads to the establishment of a conditioned response to the transmittent stimulus and sustains this response after it is established.* Using this term, we shall remember that it has only an operational meaning and throws *no light whatsoever* on the physiological mechanisms of the phenomena described with its aid.

It is clear that the specific character of the reinforcing stimuli causes a substantial limitation of associations studied by the method of conditioning, only a small part of these phenomena being embraced by it. But, the advantage of the method is that with its help we are able to follow closely the formation of associations and their further fate, to examine their properties and the effects of various disturbing factors, and to analyze their central mechanisms with much more detail and precision than could possibly be done by introspection. In fact, whereas the introspective method is mainly descriptive, the CR method is mainly analytical, the conditioned response playing a role of a "tracer" allowing the association to be detected.

Before we finally adopt the thesis of identifying classical conditioning with association, another hypothesis should be explored—that conditioning occurs by establishing connections between the central representation of the CS and the center controlling the *efferent* output of the unconditioned reflex. To be more explicit, let us take, for example, a CR obtained by pairing the sound of a buzzer with the introduction of acid into the mouth of a dog. As the result of such training, in response to the CS the animal salivates and performs mouthing movements analogous to those performed in response to the US. We can either consider this fact as meaning that the connections have been formed between the auditory units for the buzzer and taste units for acid or that instead of, or besides, these connections the CS units have become directly connected with the centers of salivation and mouthing movements or, in general, with the efferent centers of the UR.

Although this latter hypothesis cannot be finally ruled out on the basis of the available evidence, there are facts which seem to contradict it. First of all, it should be noted that all transformations of CRs, such as their extinction or differentiation (see Chapter VII), are based on manipulating the pairing procedure of the CS and the US. If connections were really established between the CS units and the salivary and mouthing centers, the process of extinction would be inconceivable, since the coincidence of the CS with salivation and mouthing is not stopped by the withdrawal of the reinforcing stimulus.

Furthermore, introspective evidence seems also to speak in favor of the S-S (and not S-R) association in conditioning. Indeed, a CS reinforced by acid produces in human beings the image, or even the sensation, of sour taste in the mouth, a CS reinforced by the pinprick evokes the sensation of pain, and so on. As a matter of fact, the phenomena of suggestion are nothing but CRs produced by verbal or gestural CSs brought forth by the experimenter. The suggestion always provokes a vivid image of the USs, such as cold, heat, pain, or nauseating tastes, but it never appeals to their responses, such as shivering, sweating, withdrawal of the limb, or vomiting. The conclusion of this consideration is that since we have no convincing evidence to show the existence of conditioned connections directly linking the CS units with the effector center of the UR, we shall consider the classical CR phenomenon as due exclusively to the formation of the connections between the CS and US units and treat it as a typical, although experimentally privileged, case of interperceptive association.

2. The identity of conditioned and unconditioned response in classical conditioning

According to the purely associative concept of the mechanism of classical conditioning, the effects of the CS should consist only of those effects which are included in the UR. We know very well that in most cases this is true. In fact, the whole procedure of conditioning is based on pairing the stimulus to be conditioned with the US and expecting, and then recording, one of the effects of the latter stimulus (salivation, withdrawal of the leg, cardiovascular effects, and so on) to appear in response to the CS. It occasionally happens, however, that in the course of classical conditioning some other responses are elicited by the CS which do not belong to the repertory of the effects produced by the US. Here we give some examples of such discrepancies between the effects produced by the CS and the US with an attempt to make their analysis.

We may often observe that, in food conditioning, various dogs behave in different ways during the CS-US interval: some of them become immobile whereas others display a strong motor excitement. The explanation of this difference is that immobility reflects the posture taken during the consummatory food UR, whereas motor excitement is the manifestation of the hunger drive. Since the same stimulus may become either a consummatory or a drive CS, depending on the experimental conditions (see Section 4 below), it may produce a response mimicking this or that unconditioned response.

Another discrepancy puzzling to students of classical conditioning is that concerning the heart rate response in defensive CRs. Whereas an electric shock used as a reinforcing US always produces acceleration of the heart rate, the CS may produce either its acceleration or deceleration, depending on the experimental procedure and/or the species of animals.[1] Although the explanation of this phenomenon is not quite clear, it probably has something to do with two different fear responses discussed in Chapter I (Section 7). Whereas one type of response consists of motor excitement and increased sympathetic tonus, the other type consists of immobilization and increased parasympathetic tonus. Depending on which conditioned fear response is developed in the given instance, we may observe the preponderance of this or that effect.

A different mechanism of the discrepancy between the effects of the CS and the US in classical conditioning is in operation when occasionally some "parasitic" instrumental responses are formed which are quite different from, and even antagonistic to, the proper classical conditioned response. Following are some examples illustrating this point.

At the beginning of food conditioning it often happens that the dog turns toward the source of the CS as the result of the targeting response. Since this response is followed by presentation of food, it easily becomes instrumentally conditioned and is stabilized in spite of the fact that it may be antagonistic to the motor response directed to the feeding place. This conclusion is supported by the fact that the CSs reinforced by harmful stimuli, not only stop producing this response, but, on the contrary, often elicit the response of turning away from the CS.

A similar unintentional formation of the instrumental response occasionally takes place in classical defensive conditioning. If a neutral stimulus is reinforced by a shock administered to the paw, this stimulus very soon starts to elicit the classical conditioned response of flexion of the leg. But in the next stage of training, this conditioned flexion is paired with shock, and therefore, according to the principles of instrumental conditioning, the instrumental extension reflex may be formed, by which the classically conditioned flexion is suppressed. Since then again extension of the leg is followed by shock, eventually the instrumental responses are eliminated.

Let us turn now to the opposite irregularity in the formation of a classical CR—that of the absence of a certain effect which is a component part of the reinforcing UR. Here the most spectacular example is provided by the analysis of a food CR established by the usual Pavlovian method consisting in pairing the CS with presentation of food in a bowl moving into position. It may be argued that whereas the UR to the presentation of food consists of seizing, masticating and swallowing the food, and salivation, the only effect occurring during the CS-US interval is salivation.

The origin of this anomaly is not quite clear. On the one hand, it may be supposed that the masticatory reflex, similar to the swallowing reflex, being based on the somesthetic and not gustatory stimuli, occurs only in response to the actual stimulation of the appropriate reflexogenic zones in the mouth (cf. Chapter I, Section 3). On the other hand, it should be realized that the Pavlovian procedure of alimentary conditioning is not so simple as it seems at first glance. The point is that the CS is not followed directly by the US (food in the mouth) but by the *sight* of a bowl with food. This visual stimulus elicits a natural instrumental CR consisting in taking the food either by mouth (in some species) or by hand (in others). This CR, being inserted between the CS and US, may prevent the formation of the masticatory CR in response to the CS. The argument in favor of this supposition is that in those experiments in which the CS is immediately followed by the proper US, as with acid CRs, conditioned salivation is accompanied by vigorous mouthing movements, identical with those occurring in response to the US.*

To sum up, we assume that the true classical CR comprises by definition the same elements as the UR on which it is based. If some other motor or autonomic responses appear besides, or instead of, those proper to the UR, these responses have a different origin which should be clarified by special experiments. On the other hand, it is not clear whether all the effects of the UR are conditionable, since it is probable that some of them can be elicited only by specific stimuli and not by their substitutes.

3. Food conditioned reflex

In Chapter I it has been indicated that all the basic activities of organisms are composed of two different although closely interrelated components which have been called preparatory and consummatory reflexes. Whereas preparatory reflexes are controlled by the part of the brain referred to as the emotive or limbic system and depend on central mechanisms denoted as drives or emotions, consummatory reflexes are controlled by lower parts of the cognitive system and depend on particular innate reflex mechanisms. Accordingly, on the basis of each of these types of URs, the appropriate classical CRs can be formed which will be called drive CRs and consummatory CRs respectively.

It should be recalled also that the basic activities may be divided into preservative and protective activities, according to whether they are indispensable for the preservation of individuals or species in *all* natural conditions of life or whether they protect the organism against the action of harmful agents.

As a good model of preservative conditioned activity we may take into consideration alimentary CRs, especially since these very reflexes were utilized in most experimental studies. In fact, whereas we have at our disposal a meager number of studies concerning CRs based on sexual, evacuating, or soporific activities, the alimentary conditioned activity has been subjected to thorough and systematic investigation

---

* The answer to this question has recently been given in our laboratory by S. Sołtysik, Hanna Kieryłowicz and I. Divač. In two groups of dogs the alimentary CRs were established by reinforcing a CS, by either presenting the bowl with diluted milk (or water), or introducing this fluid directly into the mouth through a hole made in the cheek. It was found that whereas in the first instance the conditioned response consisted mainly of the posture of expectation, in the second instance the vigorous mouthing movements and even swallowing movements (!) were observed in response to the CS. As a matter of fact, the conditioned response was so similar to the unconditioned response that by observation of the behavior of the animal it was not possible to tell at which moment the fluid was introduced into the mouth.

for many years. It seems that CRs based on other preservative activities follow roughly the same principles as alimentary CRs.

We shall separately consider alimentary consummatory CRs, referred to as food CRs, and alimentary preparatory CRs, referred to as hunger CRs; thereafter we shall discuss their mutual interrelations.

The food CR is a product of association between a *stimulus of any modality* acting as a transmittent stimulus and a *gustatory stimulus* produced by a given sort of food put into the mouth acting as a recipient stimulus. The main indicator of the formation of this association used in experimental practice is the salivary response from a chronic fistula of the parotid or submaxillar gland. In consequence, the best food for a reinforcer is that which produces copious salivation—for instance, the powdered bread mixed with powdered dry meat slightly moistened with water. The stimuli used as CSs are those which are relatively neutral—that is, they do not produce any specific responses which would be antagonistic to the alimentary activity.

The best way to establish food CRs is to present a neutral stimulus and food in overlapping sequence with a very short (one second) CS-US interval. Only gradually is this interval protracted to from ten to twenty seconds, a period indispensable for recording the salivary conditioned response.

As stated in Chapter IV, the formation of association between two synchroneous perceptions may occur only against the background of nonspecific (axodendritic) facilitatory influence exerted upon the units of the recipient stimulus and provided by the appropriate drive. In food conditioning, this facilitatory factor ensuring the formation of the CR is procured by the hunger drive. The hunger drive elicits, among other things, arousal of the gustatory and olfactory analyzers, particularly of those units which represent taste and smell of the food pertinent to a particular kind of hunger—that is, a particular appetite. In this way it constitutes a proper emotive factor enabling the formation of the actual connections between the units representing the CS and those representing the food US. This is well documented by the fact that, according to common experimental practice, the food CR fails to be established if the dog is not hungry enough in the course of the training procedure. The precise evidence confirming these observations has been recently procured by de Bold, Miller and Jensen in their experiments in which water was introduced into the mouth of rats through an oral fistula.[2] The CR was measured by movements of the tongue toward the palate recorded by an electrical device. When a stimulus to be conditioned was followed by introduction of water while the animals were water-satiated, no CR was manifested when the animals were later tested while thirsty.

The hunger drive exerts its influence, not only upon the recipient units of the gustatory analyzer, but also upon the transmittent units representing the CS. The point is that the hunger drive produces arousal, not only in the analyzers directly connected with its action, but also in other analyzers, particularly in the auditory and the visual. On this basis connections are formed between the hunger drive units and those units which represent the given CS (emotional-visual and emotional-auditory associations described in the preceding chapter). In consequence, when an animal is under the influence of a hunger drive, presentation of the food CS elicits an increased attention directed to it, producing its better perception; this in turn increases the intensity of firing from the corresponding units to the units of the gustatory analyzer.

When an animal is under the influence of a sufficient hunger drive and is habituated to the environment and experimental procedure (for example, to the repetitive character of food intake separated by intertrial intervals, the specific character of the CSs used in experiments, and the particular method of food presentation), then the formation of the food CR is a very rapid process occurring within a few trials. It should, however, be realized that the whole setup in which the conditioning experiments are performed is so unusual for the dogs that adjustment to it may require a more or less prolonged period, depending on the individual qualities of the animal and its previous experiences. Therefore, competent conducting of the preliminary experiments, taking into account all these obstructing factors, largely determines the success of conditioning and the regularity of CRs.

When the food CR is firmly established, the animal's behavior on the stand and his salivary responses are amazingly regular and reliable. The motor response to the CS consists usually of the initial, short-lasting targeting reflex toward the source of the CS (being partly the parasitic instrumental response and partly the effect of E-CS association) followed by persistent gazing at the feeder and a state of complete immobility. Salivation is more or less copious, depending on the individual qualities of the animal and his actual state. The rate of salivation is either constant or increases toward the end of the CS-US interval.

In Chapter I we brought forth a large body of evidence that the alimentary consummatory UR elicits a state of hunger antidrive, manifested by, among other things, the attenuation of the motor excitement accompanying the hunger drive. We have every reason to believe that the same is true of a well-established consummatory CR. In other words, we suggest that *a well-established food CS, similar to the food US, calls forth the partial suppression of the hunger drive* and that the calmness of the animal during the operation of the CS is the manifestation of this very suppression.

Our thesis concerning the attenuation of the hunger drive during the operation of a well-established CS is strikingly supported by experiments of Galperin.[2a] This author has found that the food CS produces total inhibition of hunger contractions of the stomach in the oesophagotomized dogs, identical with that produced by the food in the mouth (Figure VI-1). It is worth mentioning that the CS signaling presentation of bones fails to produce this effect. In fact, bones in the mouth do not stimulate taste receptors and therefore they do not inhibit the hunger drive.

We quote a very informative description by Galperin of the behavior of one of his dogs:

The dog manifested during the experimental sessions a considerable restlessness: he climbed the feeder, bit the rubber tubes from the salivary capsule and often turned to the source of the CS. The behavior of the animal clearly showed a strong yearning for food. The record of the gastric movements showed very large oscillations of the periodic waves of the contractions of the stomach. During the operation of the auditory CS the animal immediately became quiet. . . . The periodic contractions of the gastric musculature came to a stop. . . . After the termination of the operation of the CS without reinforcement the restlessness returned and the periodic waves and their oscillations increased considerably.

The next problem to be discussed is that of the localization of the "center" of the US involved in classical conditioning. Since, according to our concept, we consider that this center is identical with the set of gnostic taste units representing the food offered to the animal as reinforcement, we should look for it first in the cerebral cortex.

Unfortunately, the localization of the cortical area for taste in the dog has so far not been systematically investigated. Judging from the analogy with the site of the taste area in other animals, we may assume that it is in the rostral part of the coronal gyrus and anterior composite gyrus. The effects of ablations of this field upon salivary CRs were studied in experiments performed by Travina and by Żernicki and Santibanez.[3]

It was found in these experiments that the cortical representation of the gustatory receptive surface is ipsilateral (the result obtained later for rats).[4] Accordingly, unilateral ablation of the taste area produced a dramatic impairment or abolition of salivary food CRs from the ipsilateral parotid gland and decrease of the salivary unconditioned response on that side. The CRs on the contralateral side were either unchanged or even increased. In Travina's experiments in which the

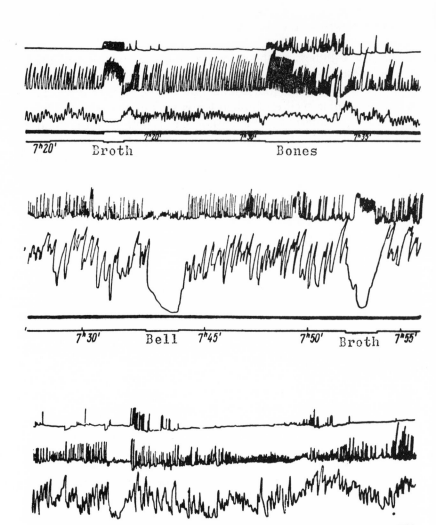

FIG. VI-1. EFFECT OF ALIMENTARY USs AND CSs ON HUNGER CONTRACTIONS OF THE STOMACH

First graph, from top to bottom: masticatory movements of mouth, respiration, stomach contractions, time-marker (not seen), presentation of food. On the left, broth; on the right, bones.

Second graph: respiration, stomach contractions, time-marker, presentation of the bell (CS) on the left (without reinforcement), and of broth on the right.

Third graph: masticatory movements, respiration, stomach contractions, time-marker, presentation of CSs. On the left, bell signaling presentation of broth; on the right, horn signaling presentation of bones.

(Galperin, see Reference 2a).

lesions were more extensive, the impairment lasted for several months; in experiments by Żernicki and Santibanez, it was less protracted, and an increase of salivary reflexes usually followed. After both unilateral and bilateral lesions, the hunger drive was not impaired.

Although the whole problem should be studied more thoroughly, the data obtained seem to confirm our hypothesis with one reservation —that the cortical taste field is probably not the only zone responsible for the food CRs, and that after its removal some other parts of the brain are responsible for this function.

4. Hunger conditioned reflex

Since we consider the hunger drive, like all other drives, a reflex function, it should be expected that it is conditionable—in other words, that it can be elicited, not only by the specific hunger-arousing stimuli, but also by neutral stimuli which coincide with them. The formation of the hunger CR is based on actual connections being established between the set of perceptive units representing the CS and the perceptive units representing the hunger drive. It should be remembered that according to our assumption the latter units are situated in the higher level of the hunger system localized probably in the amygdala.

The conditionability of the hunger drive has been occasionally questioned, because it was assumed that when a subject is wholly satiated he will not experience any hunger when placed in a situation in which he has repeatedly received tasty food. This statement seems, however, not quite true. We have often observed that when a dog had been fully satiated before the experimental session, and then placed on the experimental stand and given the type II CS, he immediately performed the trained movement (that is a sign of hunger drive, see Chapter IX) and often consumed a portion of food offered him. Thus, a strong hunger CS can produce hunger even in a state of satiation.

Furthermore, it should be realized that, according to the general principles of reflex activity, the occurrence of a given reflex, either innate or acquired, is possible when the nervous structures involved have at least a minimal level of excitability. Thus, if the hunger center of the subject is strongly inhibited by satiation, it is quite natural that the impulses impinging upon it from the CS units may not be sufficient to overcome that inhibitory process and activate this center. The hunger CR, like any CR, should be studied only at the appropriate level of excitability of the centers which take part in it.

Let us now analyze the formation of a hunger CR as it is manifested in experiments on a dog. A dog deprived of food for several hours is brought daily to a CR chamber where no smell of food is present and where nothing happens. After some time the animal is fully habituated to this situation—he is calm and occasionally falls asleep. One day a bowl with food is unexpectedly offered to the animal by some automatic device. The sight and smell of food will immediately evoke the hunger drive (partly unconditioned and partly conditioned) and as a result the dog will attack the food and take it into his mouth. If the portion of food is not very large, the hunger reflex, inhibited during the consummatory response, will return by rebound after its termination. The dog will become alert and look for more food. After this single trial the dog is removed and brought again to the chamber on the next day under the same degree of food deprivation. We shall see immediately the great change in his behavior as compared with previous days: the sleepiness and inactivity have vanished completely, and the animal is excited, sniffing around and manipulating at the device from which the food was presented. He will clearly develop a hunger CR to the experimental situation after only a single trial.

An interesting, and so far unanswered, question arises as to which period of the operation of the hunger drive is more important as the reinforcing factor: whether the short moment of seeing and smelling food *before* the consummatory response, or the longer period of rebound hunger *after* this response is over. Occasional observations show that the after-consummatory hunger drive does play a positive role in the formation of a hunger CR. This is manifested by the fact that, when the portions of food offered to the dog during experimental sessions are frequent and small, this reflex is more pronounced than when they are larger and separated by longer intervals. The role of hunger immediately preceding the consummatory response should be analyzed by special experiments.

Similar is the course of events if offering food is preceded by a short-lasting, sporadic stimulus. After a few repetitions of such pairing, the sporadic stimulus will clearly provoke the hunger CR even earlier than any salivation will appear in response to it. More evidence confirming this point will be presented in Chapter IX, on the basis of experiments with instrumental conditioning. Hence, the conclusion may be reached that pairing an external stimulus with food presentation leads first to the formation of a *hunger* CR, and only afterward, with appropriate training procedure, is it gradually transformed into a *food* CR. This result may be easily inferred from the fact that since the hunger drive involves a direct excitation of the unspecific system, it is a source of arousal which is immediately utilized for the formation of the CS → drive association. The formation of the food CR occurs only as the second stage of alimentary conditioning, since it requires the "blessing" of the hunger drive. The relations between the two CRs are diagrammatically represented in Figure VI-2.

According to the principles of classical conditioning, the effects of the hunger CR are exactly the same as those of the hunger UR. In response to the hunger CS we observe the arousal of the motor behavioral system manifested by general motor excitement and vocalization and the arousal of sensory system manifested by increased searching behavior—sniffing, exploring the surroundings, and so on. As shown by Galperin (cf. Figure VI-1) the hunger CR involves hunger contractions of the stomach. As will be shown in Chapter IX (Section 4), salivation does not belong to the repertory of hunger drive reflexes; when it appears, it is the result of the admixture of the food CR.

Although the alimentary conditioning usually begins with the formation of the hunger CR, the further fate of this conditioning depends on many procedural factors. It should be realized that whereas food intake is a "phasic" process, beginning and terminating abruptly, the hunger drive is usually a "tonic" and prolonged process. Consequently, whereas the optimal food CSs are represented by those agents which immediately precede presentation of food, the optimal hunger CSs are represented by agents of a more continuous character, such as the whole feeding situation. Another agent which plays the role of a hunger CS in normal life is the time at which the subject is usually fed. This CS will be discussed in a later section.

To sum up, we come to the conclusion that ordinary alimentary CR training consists of two separate, although closely interconnected, series of events. First, connections are formed between the gnostic units representing the experimental situation and those representing the hunger drive. These connections give rise to the *hunger CR*, its effects consisting of restlessness, increased sensitivity to external and taste stimuli and the hunger contractions of the stomach. Second, connections are formed between the gnostic units representing the CS and the units representing the taste of the food used as reinforcement. These connections give rise to the *food CR*, consisting of salivation and inhibition of the hunger contractions of the stomach. In contrast to the restlessness of the animal produced by the hunger CS, the food CS produces nearly total immobilization accompanied by looking intently at the feeder.

Although, as indicated above, the hunger CR is mainly produced by the experimental situation connected with feeding, and the food CR is mainly produced by the sporadic stimulus immediately preceding the presentation of food, nevertheless both these stimuli—particularly the latter—may elicit a mixed response, alternately increasing the hunger CR and producing the food CR. The preponderance of the food or hunger CR in response to the sporadic stimulus largely depends on both the experimental procedure and the character of the animal.

If we follow the procedure developed in Pavlov's laboratories, according to which the CS-US intervals are short at the beginning of training and the portions of food presented at each trial are rather substantial (requiring about one minute to be consumed), then the food CR usually dominates over the hunger CR. The animal, even if restless in the intervals (being under domination of the hunger CR), immediately calms down at the onset of the CS, stares at the feeder, and displays a steady and abundant salivary response. This is because the CS is followed immediately by the consummatory food response, and is separated from the postconsummatory hunger reflex by a

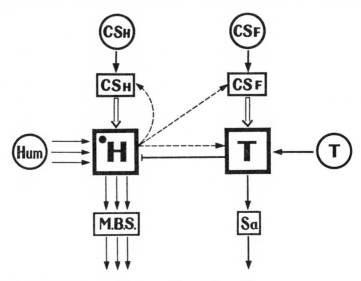

Fig. VI-2. Block Model of Hunger CR and Food CR and Their Interrelations

Squares and quadrangles denote centers; circles denote stimuli. Continuous line arrows, inborn excitatory connections; broken line arrows, inborn facilitatory connections; double-line arrows, conditioned connections; continuous stopped line, inborn inhibitory connection. Point inside the square denotes logical product of connections.

H, hunger system; M.B.S., motor behavioral system; Hum, humoral stimuli; CS_H, hunger CS.

T, food gustatory system; Sa, salivation; CS_F, food CS.

On the left, hunger CR is shown. Hunger center is activated by the joint operation of humoral factors and CS. Its activation produces arousal of motor behavioral system and arousal of taste analyzer and of analyzers of CS_H and CS_F.

On the right, consummatory food CR is shown. Gustatory food US (T) or CS_F produces salivation; both these stimuli produce inhibition of the hunger drive system.

long period of eating. If, however, the portions of food are small (requiring a few seconds to be consumed) and/or the CS-US intervals are from the beginning of training long, then the conditions are more favorable for the establishment of the hunger CR in response to the CS; dogs who are moderately tranquil in the intertrial intervals become extremely excited when the CS is presented. This is because a long CS-US interval precludes the formation of a strong bond between the CS and food, while the short act of eating brings the CS nearer to the postconsummatory increase of hunger. Generally, both hunger CRs and food CRs are best preserved when the dog is still hungry at the termination of the experimental session, because then no satiety CR is developed (see below).

It is quite natural that even in those dogs which, because of their voraciousness, display a strong hunger CR in the presence of the CS at the beginning of training, with more prolonged training, the food CR eventually takes the upper hand. In fact, since in classical conditioning the CS *always* precedes the presentation of food, and since this sequence takes place for hundreds of trials quite independently of what the animal does during the CS-US interval, the strong CS-US associations tend to prevail and determine the behavior of the animal in response to the CS. The hunger CR becomes inhibited by the strong conditioned excitation of the taste units in exactly the same way as it does when the food is already present in the animal's mouth.

If the CR experiments are conducted in a stereotyped manner with constant (and sufficiently long) intertrial intervals, then the further course of events is often the following. Since during the intertrial intervals food is never presented, a strong antidrive CR develops in them (see Chapter VII); the dog becomes more and more calm and apathetic and often falls asleep, becoming alert just before the time of the CS. Sometimes the sleepiness becomes so strong and the animal is so "bored" with the monotonous experimental condition that he fails to pay attention to the onset of the CS and even refuses to take offered food because of the strong suppression of the hunger drive. This whole course of events was denoted by Pavlov as "extinction with reinforcement,"[5] and led him to express the view that every stimulus, when repeated over a long time, eventually becomes an "inhibitory" stimulus. The only role of food reinforcement was assumed to be that for some reason it delayed this inevitable process. This view, which was obviously incorrect, was abandoned at a later period, but the fact itself remained unexplained.[6]

Since the deterioration of food CRs with their frequent repetition was a *sui generis* plague in Pavlov's laboratories, many remedies were proposed to cope with it. One of the measures was to abandon completely the whole set of CSs so far used and to introduce a new set. This measure proved to be effective, at least for some time. Another, even more effective, remedy was to establish fine differentiation—that is, to introduce a stimulus similar to one of the CSs used and not to reinforce it by food. The change in the animal's state was often nearly immediate: he became alert, his indifference vanished, and his vivid reactions to CSs, both motor and salivary, recovered, occasionally becoming even higher than originally.[7] In some experiments it was noted that the presentation of the differential (unreinforced) CS at the beginning of the experimental session was sufficient to keep the animal alert and reacting well throughout its course.

The explanation of the effectiveness of these measures is quite clear. As already stated, the routine performance of the CR experiments according to Pavlov's procedure, favoring the formation of the classical food CRs, gradually reduces, and occasionally abolishes, the hunger CRs. In order to restore them, we have either to change the CSs so far utilized or to break the inevitability of food presentation. In fact, if the well-established classical food CS is unexpectedly not reinforced, it immediately releases the hunger reflex which facilitates CRs in the following trials. The effect of regular presentation of a differentiated CS is that the classical CR to the original CS is not impaired by occasional non-reinforcement, but it is facilitated by the increase of hunger drive produced in the non-reinforced trials.

To end our discussion of hunger CRs, it should be noted that, according to some casual observations, the state of satiation is also conditionable. In fact, if a dog is brought to a CR chamber immediately after being fed *ad libitum*, a kind of satiation CR is established. It is manifested by the diminished food CRs in the next session or in a few following sessions. In this context the experiments of Fonberg and Delgado should be mentioned.[8] In these it was possible to establish a permanent aversive CR to some kind of food if consuming of that food was combined with stimulation of the amygdaloid complex in which the higher level of the satiation center seems to be situated.

5. Defensive conditioned reflexes

As shown in Chapter I (Section 10), in the defensive activity of the organisms the relation between the preparatory and consummatory reflexes is different from that encountered in the alimentary activity. In the latter, the consummatory food reflex is accompanied by the antidrive reflex which suppresses the hunger reflex, appeasing the animal during the act of eating; in the defensive activity, the noxious stimulus elicits *pari passu* the phasic consummatory response and the tonic fear response outlasting the operation of that stimulus (cf. Figure I-5c, p. 46). In consequence, the corresponding *conditioned* reflexes are not in antagonistic relation as in alimentary CRs but may be in operation simultaneously.

Let us start our discussion of defensive CRs with the reflex most common in experimental practice—that reinforced by an electric shock administered to the paw. When a neutral stimulus is paired with the shock, two kinds of connections are established: (1) the gnostic units representing the neutral stimulus form connections with somatic gnostic units representing the pinprick pain at the given place on the skin, and (2) the same gnostic units form connections with the units of the higher level of the emotive system, representing the fear drive. The former connections are responsible for the occurrence of the shock CR consisting in retracting the leg subjected to stimulation; the latter connections are responsible for the occurrence of the fear CR occurring either in the form of motor arousal and sympathetic outflow (Figure VI-3) or, on the contrary, in the form of freezing.

Although both the shock CR and the fear CR are reinforced by the same agent, their concomitance is far from being absolute. On the one hand, the noxious agent, as a fear-producing stimulus, gives rise to the arousal of the structures involved in conditioning, and therefore the connections between the CS units and the fear drive units are established almost immediately; moreover, since the fear UR has a "tonic" character, not only the sporadic stimulus just preceding the administration of the shock but the whole experimental situation becomes the fear CS. On the other hand, the connections between the CS units and the pinprick units responsible for the shock CR are established only in the next stage against the background of arousal produced by the state of fear; since the shock UR has a "phasic" character, the shock CR is stimulus-bound, being elicited only by the sporadic CS.

These theoretical considerations are fully confirmed by the relevant experimental evidence. Whereas the fear CR manifested by the increase of the heart rate is formed usually as one-trial learning and "spreads" over the whole experimental situation, the shock CR manifested by leg flexion is established later and occurs only in response to a sporadic CS.[9]

Since pain is the main emotogenic factor cementing the consummatory shock CR, the formation of the latter reflex depends largely on the strength of fear produced by the reinforcing agent. If the shock is very weak (but still producing flexion of the leg), the CR may fail to appear because of insufficient fear or, if present, it may be very irregular. When the shock is moderate, the CR is regular and the animal is quiet and matter of fact. Further increase of the shock will make the animal uneasy in the intertrial intervals, and the motor conditioned responses will be prompt and vigorous. If, however, the noxious stimulus is very strong, the animal will become highly excited throughout the experimental session (or, on the contrary, frozen), and then the isolated flexion reflex may fail to appear because

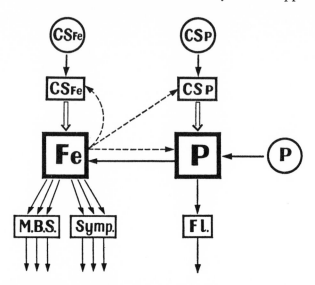

FIG. VI-3. BLOCK MODEL OF FEAR CR AND SHOCK-TO-THE-PAW CR

General denotations as in Figure VI-2.

Fe, fear system; M.B.S., motor behavioral system; Symp., sympathetic system; CS_{Fe}, fear CS.

P, nociceptive system; Fl., flexion of the leg; CS_P, shock CS.

On the left, the fear CR is shown. Fear center is activated either by the noxious US (P) or by the CS. Its activation produces arousal of motor behavioral system, sympathetic outflow and arousal of analyzers of somesthesis (pain), of CS_{Fe} and CS_P.

On the right, the consummatory shock CR is shown. Nociceptive US or CS produces flexion of the leg; both of them produce also activation of the fear system.

of the overwhelming fear disrupting the normal course of the cognitive associative processes.

Since the gnostic units representing the pinprick pain are situated in the somesthetic area of the cortex, it may be inferred that the removal of this area would lead to the abolition of the specific shock CR with total preservation of the fear CR. The experiments by Mettler et al.[10] seem to confirm this deduction. These authors have found that after removal of the neocortex in dogs the formation and preservation of the fear CR consisting in general restlessness is unimpaired, but the shock CR is permanently abolished. It remains to be determined which cortical areas are particularly responsible for this defect.

Irrespective of on which level of the somesthetic analyzer the exit units responsible for the specific pinprick reflex are situated, the appropriate gnosis involved in this sensation is relatively primitive. Hence the conclusion may be drawn that most probably a CS eliciting the shock CR tends to produce a hallucination of the pinprick sensation instead of its image. Incidentally, it should be noted that in analogous experiments performed in humans, sensitive persons often assert that they felt the pin-prick sensation in those trials in which shock was not being administered.

An important extension of the defensive conditioning method based on electric shock reinforcement was introduced in dogs by Corson et al.[11] In this method the antidiuretic response was utilized as the index of the fear CR. After repeated pairing of a tone with an electric shock to the paw, it turned out that whereas the motor defense response was strictly stimulus-bound, the antidiuretic response was elicited by the whole experimental situation and was manifested throughout the experimental session. Further, it was found that in some dogs in which the fear reflex became particularly strong (resistance to entering the CR chamber) both the unconditioned and conditioned antidiuretic responses were suppressed by catecholamines inhibiting release of the vasopressin. This shows that we have here two forms of fear responses possessing different autonomic and humoral organization.

Another well-known method of experimentation with defensive CRs similar to the previous one is that based on an air-puff into the eye used as reinforcement.[12] This method is widely used in both animals and man. Since the corresponding US is very weakly emotogenic, the subject is not much aroused during the experimental session, and hence the CS elicits a strictly local response of blinking. In consequence, the CR is hardly ever firmly established, rarely reaching a 100 per cent performance, and easily deteriorates if the CS-US interval is somewhat protracted.

Many studies performed on dogs in Pavlov's laboratories were concerned with the acid CR in which the introduction of a solution of acid (most often hydrochloric acid) was used as reinforcement. This CR has turned out to be very useful, since it has the same indicator as the food CR—salivation—whereas the UR is not preservative but protective, being completely independent of the hunger drive.

The relations between the consummatory CR and drive CR are here the same as in previous defensive CRs. Thus, if the acid is highly diluted, the acid CR cannot be established, although the US itself may evoke a conspicuous salivary response. Evidently this failure is caused by the fact that the fear drive elicited by the US is too weak. On the other hand, when the acid solution is strong and causes an injury to the mucous membrane, the animal becomes restless and salivation is suppressed. Evidently, in this case too, the proper balance between the fear CR and the acid CR must be found in order to obtain a regular and reliable conditioned response to the CS.

The gnostic field for the acid US is the same as that representing the food US—the cortical taste area. In fact, the removal of that area in dogs strongly impairs the salivary acid CR.[13] Although both the acid US and the food US are represented by the same gnostic field, different sets of gnostic units are responsible for each of these stimuli. In fact, if in the same animal both acid and food CRs are established to different CSs, they are practically independent of one another. There is a slight facilitatory effect exerted by the stronger CR upon the weaker one, but this effect is due to the peripheral mechanism of post-excitatory potentiation, which is particularly strong and long-lasting in salivary glands.[14]

Quite different is still another defensive CR procedure proposed by Estes and Skinner,[15] popularly called "conditioned emotional response" (CER). The experiments are performed on rats. In the preliminary training the animals are taught to press a lever for food under variable intervals of reinforcement in order to keep them hungry throughout the experimental session. Then several times in each session a sporadic stimulus is given which after a few minutes is followed by an electric shock administered through the floor of the compartment. After a few such trials a strong fear CR is established to the stimulus, manifested by freezing, excitement, defecation, urination, panting, and so on. Since the fear drive inhibits the hunger drive under which the lever pressing is performed, these responses are suppressed during the action of the CS, the degree of this suppression being the measure of the intensity of the defensive CR. Since in this experimental procedure the CS-US interval is much longer than in the previous ones, the defensive CR consists mainly of the fear response, whereas the conditioned shock response is practically absent.

Finally, it must be noted that, as should have been expected, fear without any admixture of pain can also be easily conditioned. The evidence is supplied by numerous experiments in which a neutral stimulus is reinforced by the fear-producing stimulation of the hypothalamus or amygdala. As a result of this procedure, the "pure" fear

CR not contaminated by pain CR appears in response to the neutral stimulus. It is manifested either by the autonomic response or by an instrumental avoidance CR easily developed on the basis of the fear-producing stimulation.

To sum up, we see that all defensive CRs used in experimental practice can be analyzed and their properties can be understood if we accept the premise that they are composed of two relatively independent CRs: the fear drive CR, and the consummatory CR (shock CR, acid CR, air-puff CR, and so on). The first CR is established by linking the CS units of the given analyzer with the fear units of the limbic system, and thus it is a common component of all defensive CRs. On the other hand, the consummatory CR is established by linking the CS units with the US units specific to the given reinforcement. The properties of each particular defensive CR depend on the relations between the strength of these two CRs. Although the consummatory CR is always "fed" by the fear CR, there is an optimal level of the strength of the latter reflex for the preservation and effective performance of the former reflex.

To end our considerations on defensive CRs, it should be noted that exactly as in alimentary reflexes, here too not only the fear drive reflex but also the fear antidrive reflex (that is, the relief reflex) is conditionable. The clear experimental evidence of this fact was produced by Segundo et al.,[16] who have shown that if a neutral stimulus (tone) precedes the *termination* of a subcutaneous shock stimulation of the leg, it produces the behavioral appeasement of the animal, accompanied by a clear diminution of action potentials elicited by shocks (Figure VI-4). As indicated in Chapter I (Section 7), this fact has a theoretical significance because it supports the view that relief is produced, not by a mere cessation of the fear drive, but by throwing into operation the fear antidrive system.

Another important phenomenon, easily explainable by the reference to the fear antidrive center, is the evolution of the UR produced by the shock in the course of the defensive CR training. As already stated, when a shock is administered to the paw for the first time, it produces a vigorous fear response, considerably outlasting the operation of the shock. This response becomes shorter and shorter with further training, and eventually it disappears altogether. The stage is then reached at which the CS produces a more or less pronounced fear CR (particularly strong when the CS is long-lasting), which is immediately cut short after the termination of the shock. The animal calms down because the shock (or its termination when it lasts for some time) now becomes a fear antidrive CS, since it is regularly followed by a period of total security. This calmness gradually subsides during the intertrial interval as the time for the next CS-US trial approaches.

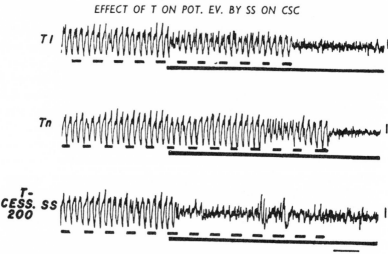

Fig. VI-4. Effect of Tone on Potentials Evoked by a Rhythmic Noxious Stimulus (SS) in the Contralateral Sensory Cortex of Cat

Interrupted line, rhythmic noxious stimulus; continuous line, tone. T1, first presentation of tone at the end of SS; decrease of rhythmic waves produced by shocks due to the novelty of the stimulus.

Tn, after habituation tone does not produce any visible response.

T-Cess., after 200 pairings tone produces a clear cessation of rhythmic activity.

(After J. P. Segundo, C. Galeano, J. A. Sommer-Smith, and J. A. Roig, in *Brain Mechanisms and Learning* [Oxford, 1961], pp. 265–91.)

6. Associations between neutral stimuli involved in conditioning experiments ("sensory preconditioning")

Since the attention of the investigators in CR experiments has concentrated almost exclusively upon the CS-US associations, other events regularly occurring during the experimental sessions have frequently remained unnoticed, although the latter constitute an important part of the conditioning procedure. These are the mutual associations established between various stimuli that take part in the procedure but do not belong to the class of USs.

As noted in Chapter IV, the associations between "neutral" stimuli—those which do not produce any constant overt response—can be studied in animals only indirectly by the method of substitution or by subsequent conditioning of the recipient stimulus. Since these methods are rather tedious and not very reliable, and the problem has never been subjected to any systematic investigation, we have only fragmentary information about the existence of these associations. Here we shall present some of the data, which, although not systematically collected, seem to be indubitable.

(1) If a stimulus is repeatedly presented in a given situation, with or without reinforcement, it is certain that the animal expects its presentation in that situation. If experiments are performed in two different situations (call them I and II) and in each of them another set of CSs is presented, the presentation of CSs belonging to situation I in situation II, or vice versa, is immediately noticed by the animal, since the "foreign" stimulus produces the clear orientation response. This response is manifested by a slight startle or "amazement," by the lack or delay of the conditioned response if it is a positive CS, or by disinhibition of the response if it is the differentiated CS.[17] This shows that actual connections are formed that link the gnostic units representing the situation and those representing the stimulus presented in it. The energizing factor cementing these connections remains to be explained: whether the arousal produced by the stimulus itself is sufficient (curiosity drive), or whether the connections are "fed" by the drive which forms the background of the given experiment.

(2) When in CR experiments compound stimuli are used composed of two elements always presented in the same succession, the change of sequence or the substitution of the second element by another stimulus also used in that situation never goes unnoticed by the animal. A particularly frequent observation of this kind is this: Suppose that stimuli S_1, S_2, and S_3 are positive CSs, and the successive compound S_0S_1 is presented without reinforcement and is differentiated from S_1 presented alone. If in a test trial S_0 is followed, not by S_1, but by S_2 or S_3, this makes a great difference to the dog. The stimulus elicits a clear orientation reaction, and the inhibitory response is disinhibited. This shows that the animal *knows* that S_0 should be followed by S_1 and is astonished if the other stimulus is substituted for it.

(3) In some of our experiments (reported in Chapter IX) two auditory stimuli—the sound of the metronome and the sound of the buzzer—were presented to dogs from the front and from behind respectively. It turned out that when the places of the stimuli were reversed, the animals noticed the difference and displayed a more or less pronounced orientation response. This again shows that the animals developed associations between the quality of the stimulus and its direction—that they knew that the sound of the metronome should come from the front and that of the buzzer from behind.

(4) The formation of associations between the neutral stimuli was

also proved by the method of subsequent conditioning of the recipient stimulus and the transfer of the conditioned response to the transmittent stimulus (cf. Chapter IV, Section 7).[18]

In this context it is appropriate to make a comment concerning the intersensory associations formed in the secondary conditioning procedure. It is well known from Pavlov's early findings that if a stimulus is paired with a firmly established CS (not reinforced at those occasions by US), it may become a "secondary" or second order CS although it was never paired with the reinforcing US itself. It may be shown that the formation of the secondary CR occurs in two ways: (1) the gnostic units representing the secondary CS become connected with the primary CS units and through them activate the US units, and (2) since the secondary CS coincides with activation of the US units brought about by the primary CS, direct association between the secondary CS and the US is also formed. In fact, there is experimental evidence that the secondary CR is not changed when the CR to the primary CS is transformed into the heterogeneous CR.[19]

On the other hand, when a compound composed of the secondary CS and primary CS is repeatedly presented without reinforcement, this compound becomes inhibitory in regard to the given UR (the so-called conditioned inhibition). In this case the association between the two elements of the compound remains unchanged, whereas that linking the secondary CS with the US becomes inhibited.

(5) Finally, the most dramatic examples of the intersensory associations combined with drive-sensory associations are those reported in Chapter IV (Section 3). It was observed that after the CR (alimentary or defensive) was established, there were episodes in the course of a session when the animal suddenly turned his head to the source of the CS, fixed his gaze on the device, and displayed a normal conditioned reaction as if the stimulus were actually in operation. The impression is bound to arise that the animal experienced a true hallucination of the CS. It may be thought that the vividness of this experience is due to the fact that two lines of connections are here in operation: the one linking the gnostic units representing the situation with those representing the CS, and the other linking the drive units with the CS units. Of course, the stronger the drive, the more clear the image or hallucination of the CS.

7. The magnitude of classical conditioned reflexes

In this section we shall deal with the problem of the factors which determine the magnitude of the classical CRs. We shall base our analysis chiefly on consummatory CRs, especially on the food CRs, on which the relevant data are most abundant. However, since the data concerning the shock CRs, air-puff CRs, and some drive CRs, although more scarce, are in full agreement with the former ones, we can reasonably accept that the rules we shall present here are general and apply to all sorts of classical CRs. It may be added that, as will be later explained, these rules are pertinent also to instrumental CRs.

We shall take into consideration CRs that are already firmly established and have achieved a practically steady level. There are then three factors (partly overlapping) that determine the magnitude of the CRs: (1) the strength of arousal, both specific and general; (2) the intensity of the US; and (3) the intensity of the CS. We shall discuss each of these factors separately.

(1) The effect of arousal on the magnitude of CRs is no less prominent than it is on their formation. The increase of hunger, up to a limit, produces an increase of food CRs, whereas satiation has an opposite effect.[19a] Furthermore, when the hunger drive is reduced by such extraneous factors as illness, fear, or sexual drive, the CRs are immediately affected. The same applies to the defensive shock CRs. If the fear drive is increased at the beginning of a session by "priming" the animal with a strong shock, the CRs are increased on that day; the administration of chlorpromazine has an opposite effect.

The same effects are produced by increase or decrease of general arousal caused by increase or decrease of sensory input. Thus increased illumination of the CR chamber, or the white noise during the experimental session, improves the dog's CR activity. On the contrary, monotony in the experimental procedure and total silence in the CR chamber are frequently deleterious for the CRs. The reason for all these effects is obvious: the nonspecific excitation of the units involved in conditioning is prerequisite to both the formation of S-S connections and their proper functioning.

(2) The effect of the strength of the US on the magnitude of the CR is also well known from the experimental practice concerning food CRs, acid CRs and shock CRs. It is explained by the assumption that the more intense the activation of the US units during the conditioning training the stronger the corresponding CS-US association and in consequence the larger the conditioned response.

A special case of the influence of the reinforcing agent upon the magnitude of the CR is provided by the amount of food presented in alimentary conditioning.[20]

If a usual portion of about fifty grams of meat and cracker powder presented in CR training is gradually reduced to twenty, ten, or five grams, the salivary conditioned response decreases and may eventually drop to zero. Sometimes the animals become neurotic in the course of this procedure and refuse to take small portions of food at all. On the contrary, increasing the portions above fifty grams does not produce any increase in the magnitude of the CR. Similarly, if two CSs are reinforced by two different portions of food respectively—for instance, fifty grams and twenty grams—that stimulus which signals the bigger portion will· elicit a larger CR. Thus the CR is to a certain degree precisely adjusted to the amount of food offered as reinforcement.

The explanation of this phenomenon is the following. If the portions of food presented to the animal are so small that the act of eating lasts for only a few seconds and the intertrial intervals are long, the CS becomes a signal, not only of the onset of the US, but also of its termination. In consequence, the CR is a result of two opposite responses and its magnitude is decreased. Hence, there is a tendency for the animals to develop an experimental neurosis, if the amount of food reinforcement has been drastically reduced. On the contrary, if the portion of food is so large that the act of eating lasts half a minute or so, the cessation of the US is more delayed and this ambiguity of the CS does not appear.

(3) Finally, we shall turn to a discussion of the dependence of the magnitude of the CR on the intensity and quality of the CS, formulated long ago by Pavlov as the "principle of strength of the CS effects."[20a] This important principle is unobservable in some experimental procedures—namely, those in which short CS-US intervals are given, or experiments are carried out under too strong a drive. In such conditions the differences between the effects of various CSs are not seen, simply because all CSs produce maximal effects. In experiments with classical food CRs the principle of strength is most clearly manifested when the CS-US interval is between ten and twenty seconds and the hunger of the animal is moderate. When the animal is more hungry, the responses may be equalized on the maximal level for all CSs; when he is satiated, they all may be reduced to the zero level.

Extensive experience with salivary CRs has led to the establishment of the following rules determining the relation between the character of the CS and the magnitude of the conditioned response.

(a) Other things being equal, the greater the physical strength of the CS (measured in decibels, candles, pressure, and the like), the larger the conditioned response to it.

(b) "Rough" CSs (that is, of irregularly changing intensity) produce a larger CR effect than monotonous CSs, and intermittent CSs produce a larger effect than continuous CSs. The higher the frequency of the intermittent stimulus, the stronger its effect.

(c) Auditory stimuli (tones, buzzers, and so on) usually produce stronger CR effects than visual stimuli (lamps) and tactile stimuli (rhythmic touch of the body).

(d) Very strong auditory stimuli produce a lower effect than strong ones, at least in alimentary CRs.

(e) According to my own experience, CSs closely related in space with the US produce a larger effect than more remote CSs (contiguity principle).

The above rules depend on several factors.

First, the dependence of the response of a nerve cell upon the intensity of the input is one of the general principles of the operation of the nervous system, confirmed by micro-electrode techniques for a wide range of cortical neurons in all projective areas. Another no less universal principle is that of adaptation. According to this principle, both the receptors and the nerve cells usually react most strongly to the onset of a continuous stimulus; thereafter the response rapidly diminishes and becomes stabilized at a certain level, depending again on the strength of the stimulus (cf. Chapter II, Section 2).

Whereas the dependence of the neuronal response on the strength of the stimulus directly explains the first of our rules, the tendency to adaptation of that response accounts for the second rule, which asserts the greater physiological strength of the "rough" and intermittent stimuli over the monotonous and continuous ones.

Second, it is worth pointing out that, according to the extensive experimental evidence of the Pavlov school, there is a close correlation between the strength of the effect of a given CS and the strength of the orientation reaction elicited by that stimulus before it became conditioned (as measured by the inhibitory effect exerted by the tested stimulus upon an already established CR). Since the orientation reaction is a direct result of arousal, we can conclude that the principle of strength of the CS effects depends also on that very factor. It may be assumed that the conspicuous difference between the strength of the effects of the auditory CSs and visual CSs used in CR experiments (rule c) is due to the different degrees of arousal produced by them.

Rule d, according to which in food CRs very strong auditory CSs elicit a reduced effect in comparison with the strong ones, is due to the fact that these stimuli give rise to the unconditioned fear reaction antagonistic to the alimentary reaction. It should be remembered that Pavlov interpreted this fact by reference to the unfortunate concept of "top-inhibition," discussed in detail and dismissed in my previous monograph.[21]

Finally, rule e, stating the dependence of the strength of the CS effect on its spatial proximity to the corresponding US, may be explained by a stronger or weaker similarity of targeting reflexes evoked by each of these stimuli.

The existence of so many factors influencing the size of a conditioned response accounts for the fact that even in well-established CRs these responses may vary considerably from day to day and from trial to trial. Below we give some typical examples of these variations. In most dogs the alimentary CRs tend to decrease toward the end of the session, sometimes even very steeply, chiefly as a result of the decrease of the hunger drive. On the contrary, the acid CRs tend to rise during the session as the result of increasing sensitization to the acid solution. The presentation of an inhibitory CS may have either the enhancing or the suppressing effect upon a CR, depending on whether it increases or decreases the hunger drive. Finally, there are "good dogs" who display reliable and regular conditioned responses (they usually behave very matter-of-factly throughout the session) and "bad dogs" in whom salivation is irregular and unpredictable. (These latter are often discarded for this very reason.) The utmost unpredictability of the responses is often a symptom of a neurotic state.

8. The role of CS-US sequence in classical conditioning

In the ordinary conditioning procedure a stimulus to be conditioned and a reinforcing stimulus are applied in overlapping sequence in such a way that the former stimulus always precedes the latter one. Most probably such a procedure has been adopted for intuitive reasons, taking into account the biological role of the CS as an agent "anticipating" the advent of an unconditioned agent.* The problem of the possibility of the formation of the CR with the reverse stimulus sequence ("backward conditioning") arose much later, chiefly for theoretical reasons. Although much experimentation has been performed to elucidate this problem, it remains so far unsolved.

Let us try to approach this problem on the basis of our concept concerning the formation of associations.

We assume that the indispensable condition for the formation of every association is that impulses from the set of transmittent units reach the set of recipient units at exactly the same time that the latter are activated from the other source. Since the strongest excitation of

---

* It should be noted that the anticipatory character of a classical CS, which is considered by many psychologists to play an essential role in conditioning, is strongly overstated. There are indeed many instances in which, because of the repeated sequential character of two paired stimuli, the antecedent stimulus "anticipates" the occurrence of the subsequent one. This situation is, however, far from being general. When we see a person consuming a lemon, we salivate copiously in spite of the fact that we do not anticipate that it will be introduced into our mouth. Similarly, when we experience considerable fear while reading a good detective story, we do not anticipate any noxious stimulus to be inflicted on us. According to our view, "anticipation" (whatever this term denotes) may be a by-product of an associative process, but it is by no means inherently connected with it.

the given unit falls at the beginning of its stimulation, the optimal moment for establishing the synaptic connections is when the impulses generated by the transmittent units arrive at the recipient units precisely at the onset of the operation of the US.

The same holds true for the best moment of the operation of the CS. When this stimulus is thrown into action, it elicits a much more intense firing of impulses than later. Therefore, in order to have a good conditioning, the US should follow the onset of the CS as closely as possible. In the defensive consummatory CRs, the optimal CS-US interval has been found to amount to a few hundred milliseconds.[22]

Quite different, however, is the situation when the onset of a neutral stimulus strictly coincides with the onset of the US or when it begins to operate *after* the onset of the latter stimulus. There is a large body of evidence that in such a condition a CR cannot be established at all or that the positive effect is most uncertain and evanescent. This negative result concerns both the alimentary and defensive CRs.[23]

The explanation of this negative result is not clear. As far as the alimentary CR is concerned, it may be noted that, according to our concept, the act of eating inhibits the hunger drive, and in consequence the association between the neutral stimulus and the taste stimulus cannot be established. This explanation, however, cannot be applied to the unconditionability of defensive reflexes in the same condition, since we have no reason to believe that the fear drive is suppressed during the operation of a noxious stimulus.

The problem is even more puzzling if we take into account that in both humans and animals the formation of associations between the neutral stimuli seems to be possible if they act synchronously, provided that the two sets of units are not mutually antagonistic. A good example of such associations was presented above, when we found that localization of a stimulus-object is easily associated with its quality, although both these perceptions are precisely simultaneous.

Let us turn now to still another procedure, in which a neutral stimulus is applied *after the termination* of the US. Some authors claim that in such a condition a very feeble and unstable CR is established to the neutral stimulus.

Much information on the nature of this controversial phenomenon has recently been provided by the experiments performed independently by Varga and Pressman, and by Lelord.[24] These authors have found that if two stimuli are applied in the experimental situation in a random order, one never coinciding with the other, they also have a tendency to become mutually connected.

Varga and Pressman, in experiments performed on dogs, made use of two almost neutral stimuli: S_1 was a passive flexion of the hindleg which produced inhibition of the EMG potentials of the extensor muscles in that leg; S_2 was a light air puff into the eye eliciting blinking. If these two stimuli were presented in overlapping sequence, S_1 being the leading stimulus, a stable and regular CR was established to it, and as result this stimulus elicited eyelid response. If S_2 was leading, the stable CR to it was established consisting of inhibition of the EMG. In addition, however, in both cases the backward connections were occasionally manifested: in the test trials in which each stimulus was presented separately, the air puff following the passive movement produced the inhibition of EMG; the passive movement following the air puff produced eyelid response. These responses were irregular, and tended to disappear in the course of training. It has, however, been shown in other dogs that if the same two stimuli were applied separately in random order, and never coincided with each other, it occasionally happened that each stimulus produced, in addition to its own response, the response of the other one. Statistically the occurrence of these "conditioned responses" was as frequent as in "backward conditioning."

How are these facts to be explained?

As has been indicated in an earlier section of this chapter, the repeated presentation of a given stimulus in a given situation leads to the formation of an association between the two corresponding perceptions, and in effect the image or hallucination of that stimulus has a tendency to emerge when the animal is brought into that situation.

Suppose that several times the "image" of stimulus S_1 was followed immediately by S_2. This was enough to establish connections between the corresponding units; in consequence, when S_1 was *actually* presented, it evoked the response proper to S_2. Since, however, the actual S_1 was never followed by S_2, the connections $S_1 \rightarrow$ no S_2 began to dominate, and the CR was in the long run doomed to extinction (cf. Chapter VII).

This explanation, which is of course only tentative, allows us to understand why the CR obtained by the mere "coexistence" of two stimuli in the same situation is so unpredictable, irregular, and evanescent. Moreover, our hypothesis may be submitted to experimental testing by applying a labeled stimulus, consisting of flickering light, as one of the two separately presented stimuli. As shown by Yoshii,[25] application of such a stimulus leads, after some time, to the appearance in the EEG record of "spontaneous" rhythmic potentials corresponding to the flickering light whenever the animal is brought to the experimental situation. If every burst of such "spontaneous" rhythmic potentials corresponding to the image of the flickering light is reinforced by the US, then, according to our hypothesis, the CR to the flickering light should be established, although the actual stimulus had never been followed by the US.

To end this discussion, we should like to stress that we cannot exclude the operation of other mechanisms accounting for "backward conditioning." For instance, in the first stages of training, presentation of food or electric shock is regularly followed by an increase of the respective drive. Therefore, the neutral stimulus coinciding with this drive may easily become conditioned to it in spite of the non-reinforcement by the US. It should also be pointed out that if two neutral stimuli have never been paired, and consequently the corresponding gnostic units are linked by only potential connections, these connections *can* become temporarily functional if the units concerned are in a state of strong arousal (cf. Chapter II, p. 86). Such a phenomenon, called "dominance" or pseudo-conditioning, is indeed often observed, and we should be careful not to mistake it for true conditioning.

9. The problem of localization of classical conditioned reflex

In the preceding chapter, when dealing with associations established in human beings in the course of their normal life, we assumed that these associations occur between cortical gnostic fields of particular analyzers. Although we have no convincing evidence that this is always so, the great body of clinical data shows that in fact the cerebral cortex in humans plays a leading role both in perceptions of stimulus-objects normally encountered in our life and in their associations. This conclusion may be also inferred from the fact that these perceptions have in most instances a rather complex character requiring a great deal of analysis, which certainly occurs in the cortical parts of particular analyzers. However, the question may be asked whether the associations, involving more crude and general properties of the stimulus-objects impinging upon animals' receptors, are accomplished also by the cerebral cortex or whether the subcortical structures are sufficient to deal with them. The answer to this question may be obviously given, in the first place, on the basis of CR experiments performed on decorticated animals.

The problem of conditioning in decorticated animals has its long and rather stormy history, because of the great authority of Pavlov, who strongly supported the idea that the cerebral cortex is *the* organ of, and for, conditioning. However, beginning with the early work on this problem, it became clear that decorticated animals are capable of establishing some CRs, although not all experiments were successful in this respect. It seems that the first author to whom we owe the systematic study of this problem was Zeleny in the Pavlov laboratory, who contrary to the belief of his master, claimed that various types of classical conditioning are preserved in decorticated animals.[26] Subsequently many other authors confirmed his findings.[27]

According to vast experimental evidence collected more recently by a number of authors on various animals and by various methods, we may reach the following conclusions concerning the conditionability of animals deprived of the cerebral cortex.[28]

If dogs or cats are subjected to bilateral lesions in which the whole neocortex is removed and basal ganglia are not affected, these animals preserve clear orientation responses to stimuli of various modalities. Although these responses may be absent immediately after the surgery, they are restored within several weeks. Defensive CRs established beforehand disappear after the operation, but they can be retrained (or perhaps they are spontaneously restored) and new CRs can be formed. The general characteristic of these reflexes is that—to put it in terms of our concept—the consummatory shock CR is lost but the fear drive CR is certainly preserved and even seems to be unimpaired: in response to a defensive CS, the animal displays strong excitement, sometimes with vocalization, changes in respiration and the heart rate. Crude differentiation between dissimilar stimuli is also possible.

As far as the alimentary CRs are concerned, the results were roughly the same. In response to a food CS, animals displayed motor excitement of a type of searching behavior, sometimes licking the lips, and increase of the heart rate. If a dish of food was always put in the same place in the cage, the animals learned to approach this place after a relatively short time. Here again the hunger drive CR was much better manifested than the consummatory food CR.

Similar data were obtained when the neocortex was not entirely removed but lesions were sustained in particular analyzers. Again it is generally agreed that, even after extensive neocortical lesions affecting the whole projective and paraprojective auditory area, animals do react to the auditory stimuli and are able to establish positive CRs to these stimuli. Differentiation of sounds, however, particularly if they are complex, is impaired or even abolished.[29] Extensive cortical lesions sustained in the visual analyzer abolish pattern vision but do not affect CRs to changes of general illumination.[30] As stated above, lesions in the cortical taste area strongly affect the food taste reflexes (both conditioned and unconditioned), but again after some time they are recovered.

To sum up, there is abundant evidence to show: (1) that perceptions of stimuli of various analyzers are preserved after neocortical lesions; and (2) that, on the basis of these perceptions, associations with other analyzers, documented by the formation of classical CRs, are also formed. In other words, both the gnostic function and the associative function can occur beyond the neocortex; these functions are, however concerned only with crude aspects of stimulus-objects and not with their detailed analysis.

The problem arises as to whether we are able to identify those structures which are responsible for this crude gnosis operating in the absence of the neocortex. Although this problem is far from being solved, we propose the tentative hypothesis that this role is played in the first place by the basal ganglia (striate body).

The basal ganglia certainly belong to the least understood brain structures, in spite of the fact that numerous investigations of their functions have been conducted. Their study is complicated by the fact that they are permeated by many pathways which are not necessarily connected with them functionally but which are concomitantly damaged by lesions sustained in these structures. In any event, confusion in the analysis of the function of the basal ganglia lies, not in the fact that it is difficult to discover any symptoms after lesions, but, on the contrary, that the symptoms are so manifold and variable.

Observations by members of our laboratory[31] seem to suggest that one of the prominent symptoms of some (but not all) striatal lesions is the lack of any targeting response to external stimuli. The animal behaves as if he did not hear the acoustic stimulus or did not see the visual stimulus; hence, the disappearance of CRs established before surgery with practically complete preservation of URs. One has the impression that the basal ganglia represent a large multi-analyzatory system, probably as much topographically organized as the cortex, which is concerned with more crude and less sophisticated aspects of external (and proprioceptive) stimuli and more primitive responses to them. The close anatomical relation between this system and the limbic system is explained by the fact that most stimuli normally involved in drive CRs do not require a highly elaborated gnostic function. In other words, we tentatively propose a hypothesis to the effect that whereas purely gnostic associations are effectuated mainly between particular gnostic fields of the cortex, the CS-drive associations are mainly (but certainly not exclusively) effectuated between the basal ganglia and the limbic system. This is why neodecorticated animals are strongly incapacitated in their gnostic functions because they do not discriminate visual or auditory *patterns* of the stimuli presented, whereas animals with striatal lesions have a more fundamental deficit because they do not react to the very occurrence of these stimuli. The proposed concept will be further developed in Chapter XI, where we shall show that there is an analogous difference between the effects of neocortical and striatal lesions in motor activities of the organisms.

If we assume that the neocortex has more to do with the gnostic side of CRs (in both their CS and their US link), whereas the basal ganglia have more to do with the emotive side of CRs, then it is clear that both these structures are necessary to the normal occurrence of conditioned responses, different types of disorder being produced by lesions in each. The role of the basal ganglia seems also to depend on the species of animal, being less prominent in higher animals, in which some of their functions are taken over by the cortex.

10. The role of classical conditioning in human life

Since CRs are simply special instances of associations in which the recipient stimulus evokes an overt response, it is obvious that human life is as full of these kinds of phenomena as of other associations. Whereas the repertory of associations regularly encountered in human life was presented in the preceding chapter, let us here make a short survey of typically encountered human CRs and subject them to an analysis similar to that given in earlier sections of this chapter.

Human CRs may be divided into two categories: those which are developed in *every* person, because they are an immanent part of human life; and those which have been developed only in particular circumstances, owing to special experiences of an individual or a whole group. Most of the defensive CRs belong to this second category, and it does not seem useful to dwell upon them, simply because they do not necessarily belong to the repertory of experiences of every reader of this book. Therefore, let us concentrate upon the first category of human CRs and discuss those whose analysis seems to us particularly instructive; these are the CRs involved in feeding and in sleep.

Feeding. Human beings belong to that rare group of mammals which have their meals regularly distributed and concentrated at particular times of the day. Both the time of meals and the situations where they take place, although widely varying among nations and social groups, are amazingly constant and even rigid within the same group. This constancy, which seems so natural to us, is primarily due to classical conditioning. The individual who has his meals at definite times of the day and in definite situations develops a hunger CR to those times and situations, which causes him to repeat the meals on the following days at the same time and place. This in turn more strongly fixes the alimentary CRs and makes feeding habits more and more rigid. Further, the development of these habits in whole groups of persons produces temporo-spatial arrangements, such as preparing meals at definite times and serving them in definite places, which again imposes rigorous limits for feeding, further consolidating the corresponding CRs.

It is interesting to analyze the relations and interplay between the two basic CRs connected with feeding—the hunger CR, and the food CR—as they manifest themselves in human life.

The hunger CR is chiefly determined by the time factor—that is, by the remoteness from the last meal. The evidence that this factor largely acts as a conditioned and not unconditioned stimulus is based on the fact that appearance of hunger totally depends on our daily stereotype and is precisely adjusted to it. We feel hungry just before our usual meal times, whenever in the day they occur, and whatever are the intervals between them. If food is not provided at the usual time, the hunger usually disappears (again demonstrating its conditioned nature), only to reappear at approximately the time of the next meal.

These hunger CRs are not only adjusted to the times of meals but also to their quantities and character. Although, as indicated in Chapter I, both the amount of food ingested at any given meal and its quality (assuming that all sorts of food are available) depend on the intensity of the unconditioned hunger drive, and its selectivity is related to the wants of the organism, nevertheless both these aspects of hunger depend to a large extent on conditioning. If we are accustomed to having a light meal at a given time, the intensity of the hunger CR is adjusted accordingly and we feel uncomfortable if a substantial meal is offered. On the contrary, if a given meal is usually heavy, consisting of a number of dishes, we are unsatisfied if the meal is light. Again, if, for instance, we are accustomed to a breakfast of coffee, toast, eggs, and jam and, instead, we are served soup and meat, we display an aversive reaction to this change because our conditioned hunger drive is directed at the moment to a different type of food. We simply feel then that we are given inedible substances, although a few hours later we shall consume the same kind of food with great appetite.

Whereas our hunger CRs are first and foremost established to time and much less to external stimuli, the food CRs are, on the contrary, almost exclusively dependent on exteroceptive stimuli closely preceding the act of eating, particularly on the visual environment of our meals. We do not salivate when we get up from our desk after finishing our work in the office, put on our coat, and go to our usual restaurant, although we may experience at that time a very strong hunger drive. But when we arrive at the place, sit down at our usual table, pick up the napkin, and study the menu, then salivation begins, a sign that the food CR is in its full operation.

It is worth mentioning that the food CR manifested by salivation can also appear in a situation quite distinct from that connected with feeding. If, for instance, we are sitting in a company of bons vivants who with gusto describe various meals, we soon notice that we begin to salivate copiously. This is because the vivid images of food evoked by activation of corresponding gnostic units through connections leading from audioverbal units can substitute for the corresponding perceptions; in this way we provide ourselves with the food CS by pure imagination.

The relations between the hunger CR and food CR in human beings follow the same rules as those described in animals. Persons whose feeding stereotype is strictly observed (for example, in boarding houses) and who are generally overfed rarely experience true hunger, and the stimuli which cause them to come to meals have a different (for example, social) character. Nevertheless, the strong food CSs to which they are exposed when sitting at a well-laden table—and especially the first morsels of tasty food—cause the hunger drive to appear; to their great amazement, they are able to consume the whole meal with great appetite and satisfaction. This follows the rule "L'appétit vient en mangeant."

On the contrary, if a person experiences a very strong and even unbearable hunger drive which compels him to go to a restaurant, and then he sits down at a well-laden table, the strong CSs signaling that the food will soon be served appease his hunger.

Just as the hunger drive is easily conditionable, so is satiation, especially oversatiation. It is a common experience that when we are overfed with a particular food or in a particular place, both this food and place may subsequently evoke an aversion as far as feeding is concerned, because they have a tendency to produce a conditioned satiation and suppress the appetite.

Sleep. It should be stressed that unconditioned sleep activity, like alimentary and defensive activities, has a dual aspect. We should clearly distinguish between the *sleep drive*—the *desire* to fall asleep, which we call the somnolence UR, and *actual sleep*—the sleep UR. Whereas the somnolence UR is elicited chiefly by a lack of sleep for a prolonged period of time, the sleep UR is produced by such external stimuli as a lying or half-lying position, relaxation of the antigravitational muscles, monotony of the environment, and softness of the bed we are lying upon.

It is easy to observe that, as in alimentary activity, both somnolence and sleep are easily conditionable and are subject to the same rules as hunger drive and feeding.

Somnolence CRs are generally established to time, according to our daily stereotype of going to sleep. Those persons who are accustomed to sleep in the afternoon become somnolent at that time and are unhappy when the situation prevents them from doing so. But, if this nap has been prevented on the given day, the sleepiness dissipates, again showing its conditioned character. If this happens repeatedly day after day, the drowsiness not reinforced by sleep ceases to appear, according to the principle of extinction of the CRs. Most persons become drowsy at night, being accustomed to go to sleep then, but those who have a nocturnal occupation are, on the contrary, fresh and alert at that time and become sleepy in the morning.

On the other hand, our sleep CR is established to those stimuli which usually accompany falling asleep, such as our bedroom, our own bed and bed-clothes, a definite position we take before sleep, reading a book, listening to the radio, smoking a cigarette. This is because the gnostic units representing corresponding perceptions form connections with the units representing the above enumerated hypnogenic stimuli. It is well known that if the situation in which we are accustomed to sleep is radically changed, we are unable to fall asleep unless we are exceedingly somnolent. In such a condition, a strong unconditioned somnolence produced by a prolonged lack of sleep, compelling us to fall asleep even in an unfamiliar situation, conditions this situation to sleep, because then the connections are established between the corresponding gnostic units and the hypnogenic units.

The question may be asked as to how the somnolence CRs and sleep CRs can be established, in view of the fact that both these states are apparently opposite to the state of arousal.

The answer to this question is that, as we have stressed before, the formation of associations is not necessarily based on the *general* arousal of the nervous system (which seems to be rather a physiological artifact obtained in an artificial experimental condition) but on the *partial* arousal selectively affecting certain structures and leaving the others in the shade. In keeping with this, we do not agree that somnolence is a less active state than any other drive. On the contrary, a sleepy animal looks actively for some place to fall asleep, just as the hungry animal looks for food, and certainly he is very alert to all those stimuli which suit this aim. Therefore, somnolence is as good for activating the associations involved in sleep CR as hunger is for activating the associations involved in the food CR.

We have given above a short ethological survey of two important CR activities in human beings in order to clarify the general role of preservative classical conditioning in life. The main conclusion which may be made from our analysis is that both the preparatory activity and the consummatory activity are unconditioned and regulated in the first approximation by "needs" of the organism communicated to the corresponding nervous centers, chiefly by chemoreceptors distributed both in the periphery and within the central nervous system itself. However, a more precise regulation of these activities is provided by conditioning, which, although not so potent as to change their general amount, is able to distribute them in time and space so as to adjust them to the individual or collective conditions of life.

Another large field of CR phenomena in human beings is involved in their social behavior; therefore we propose to call them *social CRs*. Since social environment constitutes the essential part of human "habitat" from birth to death, it obviously provides the greatest number of external stimuli shaping human life. Without going into all details of interhuman relations, we should like to draw attention to only one important aspect of these relations closely connected with our present discussion.

Every person, child or adult, develops in respect to other persons with whom he is in a permanent contact a whole range of different and highly specific emotional attitudes which are clearly based on the principle of classical conditioning. The formation of these emotional CRs is as follows. For a given subject (call him S) *behavioral acts* of other persons (P_1, P_2, P_3 . . .) with whom he is in touch may be considered as *sui generis* USs eliciting various emotional and consummatory URs. For instance, person P_1 was repeatedly aggressive to our subject, abusing him and/or inflicting harm upon him; person P_2 was repeatedly kind and tender to S; person P_3 was the partner in sexual intercourse; P_4 released S from a danger (true or imaginary), thus appeasing his anxiety; P_5 tried to be mischievous to S but failed completely, leaving S with the feeling of victory. Accordingly, behavior of P_1 elicited in S the fear UR or the anger UR; P_2 produced in S affection; P_3 elicited sexual drive and sexual consummatory UR; P_4 provided S with a feeling of relief; P_5 elicited in him contempt. Usually, various behavioral acts of a given person produce a number of emotional URs, either allied (affection and sexual drive) or sometimes partly antagonistic (affection and fear).[32]

In consequence, according to the principles of classical conditioning, a given person—that is, his sight, voice, or image—becomes a typical conditioned stimulus, eliciting corresponding emotional CRs —such as the conditioned fear reflex, affection reflex, sexual drive CR, relief CR. It may be noted that these social CRs have properties amazingly similar to those of classical CRs established in experimental animals during various conditioning procedures. This fact will be clearly demonstrated in the next chapter, when we discuss transformations of CRs due to a change of the reinforcing agent paired with a given CS.

Still another type of classical conditioning playing an important role in human behavior is that connected with words heard or read. As discussed at length in the preceding chapter, words are strongly associated with stimulus-objects designated by them, producing their images or even hallucinations. If these stimulus-objects are associated with emotional or consummatory USs, the typical second-order CRs are elicited by words.

Here are some examples: if we are in a company of persons talking about tasty food, we may notice that very soon this talk produces in us a hunger CR and/or food CR; if we read a novel describing sexual episodes, the images evoked by words read may produce in us the sexual CR; if we read a novel full of dreadful events, the appropriate images produce the fear CR.

The same principle of verbal conditioning is in operation in a kindred class of phenomena, denoted as suggestions. If, for instance, we convincingly persuade a subject that the room he has just entered is very cold, he may experience the hallucination of being cold and display shivering. Similarly, if we persuade a subject that there was a worm in the food he has just eaten, he will display nausea and vomiting. If we persuade him that he is sleepy, that his eyelids are heavy, he may actually fall asleep.

The susceptibility to suggestion varies among persons, depending on, among other things, their emotionality and the strength of associations between words and emotions. Further, the acceptance of a given suggestion depends largely on the emotional attitude of the subject caused by his actual drives. Thus, it is much easier to persuade a subject that a bush in a dark forest is a lurking bandit when he is in fear than when he is in a merry and lighthearted mood. Similarly, it is easier to persuade him that the odor he experiences is the odor of food if he is hungry than if he is satiated. Here we have clear examples of the summation of excitation of US units by joint operation of a weak CS and a weak US. It is needless to say that the essence of this mechanism is exactly the same as that involved in the summation of excitation of gnostic units by perception and association, described in detail in Chapter IV.

11. Summary and conclusions

According to the ideas developed in the present chapter, the classical conditioning is merely the formation of associations between neutral stimuli and biologically important stimuli—those which give rise to overt, unconditioned responses. Since in these conditions the neutral stimulus acquires the capacity of eliciting the same response as the US, the properties of associations can be studied in an objective and relatively precise way. Thus, by definition, the classical CR comprises only those effects which are elicited by the reinforcing agent; it is, however, not clear whether all the effects of the US or only some of them are conditionable.

Since most of the basic activities of organisms are composed of preparatory (drive) reflexes and consummatory reflexes, the same is true of the corresponding CRs. Thus, the alimentary CRs can be divided into hunger CRs and food CRs, defensive CRs can be divided into fear CRs and pain CRs, and so on.

The hunger CR is based on the connections established between perceptive units representing the CS and those representing the hunger drive and situated in the higher level of the emotive system. On the other hand, the food CR is based on the connections established between the CS units and particular taste units. The chief indicator of the hunger CR is motor restlessness, which turns into a particular instrumental response if instrumental training is devised (see Chapter IX). The chief indicator of the food CR is salivation from the salivary gland fistula.

Whereas the energizing factor for the formation of the hunger CR is provided by the hunger UR, the energizing factor for the formation of the food CR is provided by the already established hunger CR, producing arousal both in the gnostic field of the CS and in the gustatory gnostic field.

Since the food US elicits, besides its specific unconditioned response, the antidrive reflex, partly suppressing the hunger reflex during its action, the same is true of its substitute, the food CS. In consequence, the food CS and the hunger CS are usually represented by different stimulus-objects; the hunger CS is normally represented by the situation in which the animal is fed and/or the usual time of feeding, whereas the food CS is represented by the sporadic stimulus immediately preceding the food US. Often, however, the two CRs are interwoven, substituting for each other in the presence of the same CS. If a neutral stimulus is regularly reinforced by presentation of food with a short CS-US interval, the food CR elicited by it strongly prevails over the hunger CR, even to the point where the animal will reluctantly take food in its presence because of the lack of the hunger drive. If, however, this stimulus is occasionally non-reinforced by food, or if another stimulus similar to the CS is repeatedly presented without reinforcement, the hunger drive will increase. To generalize, it may be said that the *certainty* of the arrival of food or of any other attractive US, in the presence of the corresponding CS, tends to appease the drive concerned and to make the subject relatively indifferent to achieving the goal; the *uncertainty*, on the contrary, incites the drive and makes the goal more desirable. As a matter of fact, the whole ritual of courting, so largely displayed by both animals and humans, the essence of which consists in making the partner not immediately available, has no other biological role but to increase the sexual drive and thus to facilitate the sexual consummatory response. The problem of the relation between the sexual drive and the availability of the sexual goal was analyzed in great detail by Proust[33] in his monumental work.

As far as the defensive CRs are concerned, the situation is slightly different, because here the reinforcing noxious stimulus produces both the fear UR and the consummatory defensive UR. Accordingly, the two corresponding CRs overlap to a higher degree than in alimentary CRs. However, here too the long-lasting stimuli, such as the experimental situation, elicit mainly (or even exclusively) the fear CR, whereas short-lasting stimuli closely preceding the noxious US elicit

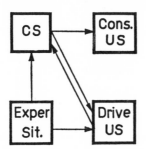

FIG. VI-5. MAIN RELATIONS BETWEEN THE CS, EXPERIMENTAL SITUATION, CONSUMMATORY US, AND DRIVE US

also the consummatory CR. The stronger the fear component comprised in a given defensive CR, the more stable and vigorous the conditioned consummatory response, unless the fear CR is so strong that it produces a disrupting effect upon the corresponding CS-US associations.

The regular conditioning procedure leads, not only to the formation of associations directed from the experimental situation and sporadic CSs to a drive US and a consummatory US, respectively, but also to other types of associations: (1) those from the experimental situation to the CS, and (2) those from the drive US to the CS (Figure VI-5). Owing to these associations, the excitability of the CS units is strongly enhanced in the experimental situation. This is why the same CS presented beyond this situation may produce a weaker conditioned effect or even no effect at all.

The magnitude of the classical CR depends on the strength of arousal of the gnostic fields which are involved in conditioning, on the strength of the reinforcing agent, and on the character of the CS.

Ample experimental evidence has shown that the conditioned response elicited by a given CS is larger when the stimulus is more intense, when it is not monotonous, and when it is contiguous to the US. In dogs the auditory CSs are more effective than the visual CSs. All these facts may be explained on the basis of general properties of excitability of neurons and the influence of arousal.

The best timing procedure for the formation of a CR is when the CS precedes the US in overlapping sequence. The problem as to why the simultaneous presentation of the CS and US does not lead to the formation of the CR is not clear. If two stimuli are presented at random order in the same situation, weak associations are formed between them. Probably, "backward conditioning" is a particular instance of this phenomenon.

The effects of lesions affecting particular cortical areas or the whole neocortex indicate that although the damage sustained to these structures impairs the perceptual capacity of the CSs and USs involved in conditioning, it does not destroy the conditioning capacity as such. We propose the hypothesis that perceptions of stimulus-objects in their crude form are accomplished by the basal ganglia which represent a more primitive multi-analyzatory system chiefly concerned with establishing connections with the emotive brain and thus subserving mainly the drive CRs. This is why large neocortical lesions may be detrimental to particular consummatory CRs but do not destroy drive CRs.

Experimental data concerning classical conditioning in animals throw light on the analogous phenomena observed in human beings. The classical CRs playing an important role in the normal human life are the following: (1) hunger CRs and food CRs; (2) drive and consummatory CRs connected with other preservative activities (sex, sleep, defecation); (3) social CRs in which the behavioral acts performed by other persons toward a subject play the role of USs and the persons themselves become the appropriate CSs; and (4) CRs to words heard or read which by producing images of the situations represented by them elicit the appropriate conditioned responses. The phenomena denoted as suggestions are based on this mechanism.

References to Chapter VI

1. D. Zeaman, G. Deane, and N. Wegner. 1954. Amplitude and latency characteristics of the conditioned heart response. *J. Psychol.*, 38: 235–50.

K. Jaworska. 1959. The effect of removal of the cerebellum on the conditioned reflex activity in birds and mammals. Doctoral dissertation, Leningrad.

W. H. Gantt. 1960. Cardiovascular component of the conditional reflex to pain, food and other stimuli. *Physiol. Rev.*, 40 (Suppl. No. 4): 266–91.

K. Jaworska, M. Kowalska, and S. Sołtysik. 1962. Studies on the aversive classical conditioning. 1. Acquisition and differentiation of motor and cardiac conditioned classical defensive reflexes in dogs. *Acta Biol. Exp. Vars.*, 22 (No. 2): 23–34.

H. G. Santibanez, M. A. Saavedra, and S. Middleton. 1963. Cardiac and respiratory concomitants in classical defensive conditioning in cats. *Acta Biol. Exp. Vars.*, 23: 165–70.

2. R. C. de Bold, N. E. Miller, and D. D. Jensen. 1965. Effect of strength of drive determined by a new technique for appetitive classical conditioning of rats. *J. Comp. Physiol. Psychol.*, 59: 102-8.

2a. С. И. Гальпéрин. 1960. Нейро-гуморáльные регуляции у позвоночных животных. (Neuro-humoral regulations in vertebrates.) Moscow: Izdat. "Visshaia Shkola."

3. А. А. Травина. 1956. Влияние удаления различных участков коры головного мозга на пищевые и кислотные условные рефлексы. (Effects of selective brain lesions on the alimentary and acid conditioned reflexes.) *Ezhegodnik Inst. Exp. Med. A. M. N. SSSR.*, pp. 44–46.

B. Żernicki and H. G. Santibanez. 1961. The effects of ablations of "alimentary area" of the cerebral cortex on salivary conditioned and unconditioned reflexes in dogs. *Acta Biol. Exp. Vars.*, 21: 163–76.

4. R. M. Benjamin. 1963. Some thalamic and cortical mechanisms of taste. In Y. Zotterman, ed., *Olfaction and Taste: Proceedings of the First International Symposium held at the Wenner-Gren Center, Stockholm, September 1962*, pp. 309–29. Oxford: Pergamon Press.

5. I. P. Pavlov. 1927. *Conditioned Reflexes*. Translated and edited by G. V. Anrep. Chap. 14. London: Oxford University Press.

6. For discussion on this problem see:
J. Konorski. 1948. *Conditioned Reflexes and Neuron Organization*. Cambridge: Cambridge University Press.

7. I. P. Pavlov. 1927 (see note 5 above).
H. S. Terrace. 1966. Discrimination learning and the concept of inhibition. In typescript.

8. E. Fonberg and I. M. R. Delgado. 1961. Avoidance and alimentary reactions during amygdala stimulation. *J. Neurophysiol.*, 24: 651–64.

9. W. H. Gantt. 1960 (see note 1 above).
K. Jaworska, M. Kowalska, and S. Sołtysik. 1962 (see note 1 above).
J. E. O. Newton and W. H. Gantt. 1966. One-trial cardiac conditioning in dogs. *Conditional Reflex*, 1:251–165.

10. E. Culler and F. A. Mettler. 1934. Conditioned behavior in a decorticate dog. *J. Comp. Psychol.*, 18: 291–303.
E. F. Girden, F. A. Mettler, G. Finch, and E. Culler. 1936. Conditioned responses in a decorticate dog to acoustic, thermal, and tactile stimulation. *J. Comp. Psychol.*, 21: 367–85.

11. S. A. Corson, E. O'Leary Corson, and B. Pasamanick. 1963. Neuroendocrine factors in conditioned and unconditioned renal responses. In *Proceedings of the Second International Congress of Nephrology, Prague, 1963*, pp. 530–34. Amsterdam: Excerpta Medica Found. Internat. Congr. ser. No. 78.
12. E. R. Hilgard and D. G. Marquis. 1940. *Conditioning and Learning*, chap. 2. New York: Appleton-Century-Crofts.
13. A. A. Travina. 1956 (see note 3 above).
    B. Żernicki and H. G. Santibanez. 1961 (see note 3 above).
14. J. Bruner and W. Kozak. 1954. Zjawisko długotrwałych sladów pobudzenia efektora w ślinowych odruchach bezwarunkowych. (The phenomenon of long-lasting traces of excitation of the effector in salivary conditioned reflexes.) *Acta Physiol. Pol.*, 5: 107–8.
    M. Czarnecka and S. Sołtysik. 1962. "Augmented secretion" in unconditioned salivary reflexes in dog. *Acta Biol. Exp. Vars.*, 22: 15–21.
15. W. K. Estes and B. F. Skinner. 1941. Some quantitative properties of anxiety. *J. Exp. Psychol.*, 29: 390–400.
16. J. P. Segundo, C. Galeano, J. A. Sommer-Smith, and J. A. Roig. 1961. Behavioural and EEG effects of tones "reinforced" by cessation of painful stimuli. In J. F. Delafresnaye, ed., *Brain Mechanisms and Learning*, pp. 265–91. Oxford: Blackwell Sci. Publ.
17. W. Wyrwicka. 1958. Studies on the effects of the conditioned stimulus applied against various experimental backgrounds. *Acta Biol. Exp. Vars.*, 18: 175–93.
18. И. О. Нарбутович и Н. А. Подкопаев. 1936. Усолвный рефлекс как ассоциация. (The conditioned reflex as association.) *Trudy Fiziol. Lab. I. P. Pavlova*, 6 (No. 2): 5–25. English summary, pp. 243–44.
    W. J. Brogden. 1939. Sensory pre-conditioning. *J. Exp. Psychol.*, 25: 323–32.
19. A. A. Lindberg. 1932. The report of Wednesday meeting of 2 November 1932. In *Pavlovskie Sredy. Protokoly i stenogrammy fiziol. besed*, T. 1: 240. Moscow-Leningrad: Izd. Akad. Nauk SSSR.
19a Ф. П. Майоров. 1954. История учения об условных рефлексах (The history of the studies on conditioned reflexes). Moscow-Leningrad: Izdat. Akad. Nauk SSSR.
20. С. В. Клещов. 1936. О зависимости величины пищевых условных рефлексов от количества безусловного подкрепления. (On the dependence of the value of alimentary conditioned reflexes on the size of the unconditioned reinforcement.) *Trudy Fiziol. Lab. I. P. Pavlova*, 6 (No. 2): 27–53. English summary, pp. 237–39.
20a F. P. Maiorov. 1954 (see note 19a above).
21. J. Konorski. 1948 (see note 6 above), chap. 3.
22. E. R. Hilgard and D. G. Marquis. 1961. *Conditioning and Learning*. Revised by G. A. Kimble. 2d ed. Chapter 6. New York: Appleton-Century-Crofts.
23. I. P. Pavlov. 1927 (see note 5 above), pp. 27–28.

Б. И. Пакович. 1960. К вопросу об условиях образования оборони-тельно-двигательных условных рефлексов. (Concerning conditions for the formation of defensive-motor conditioned reflexes.) In: Центральные и периферические механизмы двигательной деятельности животных. Сборник докладов международного симпозиума Польша, 1958г. Pp. 86–123. Moscow: Izdat. Akad. Nauk SSSR.

24. M. Y. Varga and J. M. Pressman. 1963. Some forms of relationship between two temporarily connected motor reflexes. In E. Gutman, ed., *Central and Peripheral Mechanisms of Motor Function: Proceedings of the Conference held at Liblice near Prague, May 15–21, 1961*, pp. 279–84. Prague: Publ. House of the Czechoslovak Acad. Sci.

G. Lelord. 1966. Étude EEG chez l'animal et chez l'homme d'un mode d'association spécifique, distinct du conditionnement classique, l'acquisition libre. *Acta Biol. Exp. Vars.*, 27: 379-405.

25. N. Yoshii and W. J. Hockaday. 1958. Conditioning of frequency characteristic repetitive electro-encephalographic response with intermittent photic stimulation. *Electroenceph. Clin. Neurophysiol.*, 10: 487–502.

26. Г. П. Зеленый. 1930. Результаты удаления мозговых полушарий. (The results of the removal of cerebral hemispheres.) *Mediko-biol. Zh.*, 1–2: 3–18.

S. S. Poltyreff and G. P. Zeliony. 1930. Grosshirnrinde und Assoziationsfunktion. *Z. Biol.*, 90: 157–60.

S. S. Poltyreff and A. Alexejeff. 1936. Über die Möglichkeit der Bildung bedingter Reflexe bei Hunden mit extirpirten Hirnrinde von der Hemisphäre gegenüberliegenden Körperoberfläche aus. *Z. Biol.*, 97: 297–305.

Г. П. Зеленый и Б. И. Кадиков. 1938. Условные рефлексы у собаки после экстирпации мозговой коры. (Conditioned reflexes in dogs after removal of the cerebral cortex.) *Eksp. Medicina*, 3: 31–34.

27. E. Culler and F. A. Mettler. 1934 (see note 10 above).

E. P. Girden, F. A. Mettler, G. Finch, and E. Culler. 1936 (see note 10 above).

J. ten Cate. 1934. Akustische und optische Reaktionen der Katzen nach teilweisen und totalen Extirpationen des Neopalliums. *Arch. Néerl. Physiol.*, 19: 191.

R. B. Bromiley. 1948. Conditioned responses in a dog after removal of neocortex. *J. Comp. Physiol. Psychol.*, 41: 102–10.

28. Н. Ю. Беленков. 1965. Условный рефлекс и подкорковые образования мозга. (Conditioned reflex and subcortical structures of the brain.) Moscow: Izdat. "Medicina."

29. W. D. Neff. 1961. Neural mechanisms of auditory discrimination. In W. A. Rosenblith, ed., *Sensory Communication*, pp. 259–78. New York: M.I.T. Press and Wiley.

30. J. Orbach. 1959. "Functions" of striate cortex and the problem of mass action. *Psychol. Bull.*, 56: 271–92.

31. С. Солтысик. 1960. Влияние повреждения головы хвостатого тела на
     двигательные условные рефлексы (II типа). (Effects of lesions
     on the head of caudate nucleus on conditioned reflexes in dogs.) In:
     Центральные и периферические механизмы двигательной
     деятельности животных. Сборник докладов международного
     симпозиума Польша, 1958г. Pp. 300–309. Moscow: Izdat. Akad.
     Nauk SSSR.
     I. Stępień. Unpublished observations.
     R. Tarnecki. Unpublished observations.
32. For the analysis of various types of social emotional attitudes see:
     W. McDougall. 1924. *An Introduction to Social Psychology.* 24th ed. Lon-
     don: Methuen.
33. M. Proust. 1924. *A la recherche du temps perdu.* 44th ed. Paris: Editions
     de la Nouvelle Revue Française.

VII

"INTERNAL INHIBITION" AND TRANS-
FORMATION OF CLASSICAL CRs

1. Introductory remarks

The problem of internal inhibition is undoubtedly among the most controversial and debatable in the whole field of behavioral sciences. Of many reasons which are responsible for this state of affairs we shall discuss here only the most important.

On the one hand, since inhibition denotes a definite *neurophysiological* process, it is natural that psychologists concerned with animal behavior are reluctant to use this term, considering it as foreign to the framework of their concepts. On the other hand, in neurophysiology, the Sherringtonian era, when the occurrence of inhibition was *inferred* from the "behavioral" effects of a spinal or decerebrate preparation, is long past. At present a student of central nervous activity, being accustomed to observe directly the occurrence of inhibitory processes in individual neurons, is reluctant to speak of these processes unless he sees them on the oscilloscopic records. In consequence, *both* psychologists and physiologists tend, for different reasons, to renounce this term if it is applied to the phenomena of animal and human behavior.

Further, the term "inhibition," if used at all in behavioral sciences, was used in a sense conferred upon it by Pavlov and his school. As I tried to show in my previous monograph,[1] and as it seems now to be generally agreed, Pavlov's understanding of inhibition cannot be integrated with our modern physiological concepts. In consequence, if some students of animal behavior borrowed the term from Pavlovian theory, they did not bother to endow it with a clear physiological meaning and used it in a quite arbitrary sense (cf. Hull's use of the term.)[2]

It is clear that when approaching the behavioral responses of the organism from the physiological standpoint we cannot deliberately and a priori avoid the concept of inhibition, since it is unbelievable that a process so ubiquitous in the activity of the nervous system and so often encountered in analytical research of the brain function would not intervene in the integrative action of this organ. Therefore, it is even more important to have a clear idea of what this term precisely denotes and of the instances in which we are justified in making use of it in behavioral sciences.

In accordance with the meaning of the term "inhibition" in neurophysiology, we shall use it whenever *a definite response of the organism (either peripheral or intercentral) elicited by a given stimulus and mediated by a given process in the nervous system is decreased or abolished by another central process produced by another stimulus, or even by the same stimulus if its physiological role has been changed.* The last condition is the only one which is added to the usual meaning of the term, in order to include plastic changes occurring in the central nervous system. It is not necessary for our present discussion to adopt any definite current theory concerning the intimate mechanism of inhibitory processes: we are not concerned here with the problem of whether inhibition is due to the release of a special transmitter produced in inhibitory interneurons, or whether it is due to the activation of synapses of special kind, or depends on the definite localization of the synapses on the surface of the neuron. The only assumption we do require is that inhibition is a process antagonistic to excitation, and that the output of a neuron is determined by a sort of algebraic summation of excitatory and inhibitory inputs impinging upon it. In opposition to some analytical neurophysiologists, we are not afraid to "jump" from the evidence brought forth by direct studies of individual neurons in acute experiments to responses of the waking animal under nearly normal conditions. On the contrary, if the facts established in the analytical research on the neuronal level reflect the truly existing phenomena of the nervous function, as we strongly believe they do, then we are not only justified but even obliged to utilize them when dealing with the big assemblies of neurons constituting the functional units of the nervous activity.

2. A short outline of Pavlov's concept of inhibition

At the very beginning of his research on CRs, Pavlov came across two types of phenomena which, although totally distinct from each other, were considered by him to be manifestations of inhibitory processes occurring in the brain. One of these types he called external inhibition; the other, internal inhibition.[3]

By external inhibition Pavlov denoted a phenomenon consisting in a decrease of a given conditioned response under the influence of an extra stimulus acting before or during the operation of the CS. For instance, a stimulus eliciting an orientation reaction coinciding with the food CS dramatically reduces the conditioned response evoked by it. Even stronger is the depressive effect exerted upon the food CR by fear-producing stimuli. Pavlov was quite aware of the fact that inhibition of this kind is the same phenomenon as that encountered in the mutual interrelations between antagonistic unconditioned reflexes; therefore he also called external inhibition "unconditioned inhibition."

In contradistinction to external inhibition, internal inhibition (also called "conditioned inhibition" in the broader sense of this term) occurs when the CS gradually loses its conditioned effect because it is no longer reinforced by the US. Pavlov strongly advocated the view that the disappearance of the conditioned response due to this procedure depends on a special kind of inhibitory process, which he called "internal," because it developed within the given CR arc and did not operate from the other centers as is the case with external inhibition.

It should be remembered that Pavlov distinguished three varieties of internal inhibition, according to different experimental procedures involved: (1) extinction occurring when the given CS is not reinforced by the US; (2) differentiation occurring when a stimulus similar to the original CS, producing the conditioned response owing to generalization, is not reinforced by the US whereas the original CS is; and (3) inhibition of delay occurring when the CS-US interval is protracted and the animal learns to display the conditioned response shortly before the moment of reinforcement. For the sake of uniformity of terminology, we propose to denote by "extinction" any procedure leading to the decrease of the conditioned response by non-reinforcement, whether this procedure concerns the CS proper, the CS formed by generalization, or only the initial period of the CS-US interval. The CS which has partly or totally lost its conditioned effect owing to extinction (in the broader sense) was called by Pavlov an inhibitory CS, and it was assumed that such a stimulus elicits an inhibitory CR.

The properties of inhibitory CSs were subjected to careful and extensive investigations in Pavlov's laboratories, and many interesting, and occasionally unexpected, findings were discovered. It has been found, for instance, that repeated presentation of the inhibitory CS produces an inhibitory aftereffect on positive CSs, its strength being different in different conditions; sometimes such a procedure leads to somnolence and even deep sleep; if, however, the positive CS is applied immediately after the inhibitory CS, the increase of its effect is also possible, this phenomenon being called positive induction; extra-stimuli of moderate strength tend to "disinhibit" the inhibitory CR.

On the basis of these findings, Pavlov strove until the end of his life to establish a coherent theory of internal inhibition which would account for all the manifold facts discovered in this field. In the early 1920's, impressed by the experimental results showing that the strength of the inhibitory aftereffect depended on the proximity of the tested CS to the extinguished CS, Pavlov developed a theory which determined to a great extent his general view upon the mechanisms of cortical activity. According to this theory, it was assumed that the inhibitory process is localized in the "center" of the inhibitory CS. From this "point," the process of inhibition was thought to irradiate gradually over the whole analyzer (or even further, including the whole cortex), and then to concentrate to its point of departure. Whereas the irradiation of inhibition accounted for inhibitory aftereffects and sleep, its concentration accounted for positive induction. By analogy, Pavlov assumed that exactly the same mode of operation—irradiation over the cortex and concentration to the place of origin—was true of the excitatory processes. Irradiation and concentration of excitatory and inhibitory processes and their interactions were considered by Pavlov the main principles by which all animal and human behavior could be explained.

3. The concept of internal inhibition developed in my previous work

Internal inhibition was one of the most important problems dealt with in my previous monograph.[4] There I presented all the essential facts in this field collected by the Pavlov school, and on their basis developed a theory congruent with the general concepts of central nervous activity. Without discussing this subject in great detail, I find it necessary to give here a brief summary of my earlier ideas, since they will constitute the point of departure of our present consideration.

According to my previous concept of conditioning, the actual excitatory connections between the future CS center and the US center are formed if—and only if—impulses fired by the former center reach the latter center at the moment of *increase* of its excitation due to the *onset* of action of the US. Similarly, it was assumed that when impulses fired by the CS center reach the neurons of the US center at the moment of a *decrease* of their excitation, then, on the contrary, *inhibitory* connections are formed between these two centers. The most distinct situation in which such coincidence takes place is when the CS is put into operation during the act of eating and it signals the withdrawal of food. Then the excitation of the US center is drastically reduced, and the CS should produce a purely inhibitory effect. Therefore, I considered experiments of this kind to be a direct model of the inhibitory CR, which was thought of as a true counterpart of the excitatory CR.

Now the problem arises as to the course of events occurring when a firmly established CR is subjected to extinction because the corresponding CS is not reinforced by the US. Originally, the CS elicits excitation in the CS center, which sends impulses activating the US center. However, since the US does not follow the CS, excitation of the US center is rapidly diminished, and according to our principle, conditions are provided for inhibitory connections to be formed between the two centers. It was *not* supposed that the excitatory connections are *transformed* into the inhibitory ones, because this would be both against the neurophysiological evidence and also against many behavioral data showing that, in spite of extinction, the excitatory CR is not lost but only hidden. Therefore, it was assumed that in the course of extinction the inhibitory connections are being formed *side by side* with the totally preserved excitatory connections, so that the previously purely excitatory CR is transformed into an excitatory-inhibitory CR. The more inhibitory connections formed with each trial, the more the inhibitory processes counterbalance the excitatory ones, leading to a gradual decrease of the CR until the zero level is obtained.

According to our hypothesis concerning the development of inhibitory conditioned connections, the exact course of extinction of the unreinforced CR can be easily deduced. In the first extinction trial, the US center is strongly excited by the CS, and therefore the decrement of excitation when the US is not given is very great; in consequence, many inhibitory connections are formed. But in the second extinction trial, the excitation provided by the CS center is smaller because of the operation of recently established inhibitory connections, and so the decrease of this excitation is also proportionately smaller when the US is not given; hence the smaller increment of the inhibitory connections. The process of extinction stops when all excitatory connections are counterbalanced by inhibitory connections, so that no excitation of the US center occurs when the CS center is excited.

An important consequence, which followed from our concept, was that the numerous excitatory synapses formed between the CS and the US center when the corresponding CR has been established do not prevent the inhibitory synapses from being developed when the CR is extinguished; on the contrary, they facilitate their development because the stronger the excitatory CR, the stronger the inhibitory CR produced by the extinction training. Conversely, the "neutralization" of the excitatory connections by the inhibitory connections allows new excitatory connections to be formed when the conditioning training is repeated.

When the above theory of internal inhibition was formulated, only meager direct experimental evidence was at hand to support it. The theory seemed, however, to fit perfectly the large body of facts collected by the Pavlovian school in the field of internal inhibition and, moreover, was able to give satisfactory explanation to those facts which had been quite incomprehensible. Among other things, the exponential character of the curve of extinction often encountered in experimental studies seemed to speak in its favor. Other phenomena easily explained by the theory were: the specific character of inhibitory processes, and the great variety of complex interrelations between the inhibitory and excitatory CRs described by Pavlov under the terms of irradiation of excitatory and inhibitory processes, and mutual induction between them (cf. Chapter X of my earlier monograph).

It was quite natural that as soon as a new laboratory of higher nervous activity was instituted in Warsaw after the war, my first aim was to test the theory by special experiments which were considered crucial for its accuracy.

4. New experimental evidence on internal inhibition

Let us state clearly the major experimental deductions to be derived from the above theory of internal inhibition.

First, it had to be expected that the courses of extinction and restoration of a CR would be symmetrical, both of them having an exponential character.

Second, the repeated extinction and restoration of the CR would take the same course, because of the total "neutralization" of excitatory connections by inhibitory connections and vice versa.

Third, since the inhibitory connections were assumed to be "fed" by the decrease of excitation in the US center, the amount of these connections—that is, the strength of the inhibitory CR established to a given CS by its non-reinforcement—would be proportional to the strength of the excitatory CR from which it was derived. This should be true both of extinction of the original CSs of varying strength (according to the law of strength of CS effects) and of differentiation of similar stimuli of varying similarity to the original one.

Fourth, it was expected that if a neutral stimulus beyond the scope of generalization of the CS were repeatedly presented without being followed by the US, it would not acquire inhibitory properties in respect to this US. This means that its presentations, however numerous, would have no negative effect upon the succeeding conditioning process, if the stimulus began to be paired with the US.

In order to approach the above problem in a proper way, we decided to abandon the procedure of acute extinction commonly used in experimental practice and to substitute chronic extinction for it. This was done for the following reasons.

In acute extinction the CS is repeatedly presented without reinforcement in the same session until the conditioned response disappears. In this way the normal schedule of the experimental session is greatly disturbed and many factors beyond those we intend to study are in operation. The most important of these factors concerns the drastic changes of the drive level during the course of extinction—its increase in the first extinction trials and decrease in the last trials.

On the other hand, in chronic extinction the whole daily stereotype of experiments is left intact: the stimulus subjected to extinction is presented once or twice (in a partly randomized order) in each session among reinforced positive CSs. This allows us to watch day after day how the animal learns not to react to the non-reinforced CS and to compare the effect of the CS to be extinguished with that of the positive control stimulus. Exactly the same procedure is applied in the restoration of the CR by re-reinforcement of the extinguished stimulus.

To our great amazement, it was found that all the aforementioned predictions concerning the mechanism of inhibition were not fulfilled and that the rules of transformations of the excitatory CRs into inhibitory CRs and vice versa appeared to be quite different from those depicted above.

In our very first experiments of this kind, performed in dogs on food CRs, it appeared that the process of extinction and the process of restoration take a totally different course and are quite asymmetrical. Whereas the process of extinction is long and gradual, manifesting many fluctuations, the process of restoration is most rapid: in fact, a few re-reinforcements of the extinguished CS are enough completely to restore the CR to it (Figure VII-1). In other words, whereas the resistance to extinction of the firmly established CS is very strong, its resistance to restoration is, on the contrary, very weak. This result seems to indicate that, contrary to our expectation, the inhibitory process developed in the course of extinction cannot be strong, since it is almost totally overcome by only a few restoration trials.[5]

It could be assumed that the weakness of the inhibitory process developed during the extinction series was due to the fact that an attractive stimulus (food) was used as reinforcement, and therefore the positive CS was followed by a "satisfying state of affairs." In order to test this supposition, analogous experiments were performed with defensive CRs in which a CS was reinforced by an electric shock applied to the paw. As seen in Figure VII-2, the results of these experiments were quite similar to those obtained with food CRs: whereas the process of extinction of a defensive CR was long and gradual, the process of its restoration was very rapid.[6]

Another finding opposite to that anticipated by our theory was the following. A "neutral" stimulus was repeatedly presented without reinforcement in many sessions among positive CSs reinforced by food. Then the regular conditioning training of this stimulus was begun. It has been found that the formation of the CR to it was very protracted

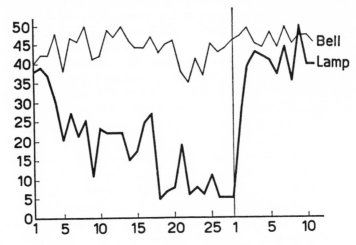

Fig. VII-1. An Example of Chronic Extinction and Restoration of Classical Food CR

Abscissae, experimental sessions (in each session one extinction trial); ordinates, conditioned salivation in arbitrary units. Vertical line denotes the beginning of restoration of the CR to lamp. Lamp is the extinguished CS; bell is the control CS just preceding the extinction trial.

Note that the process of extinction is slow and irregular, while restoration of the extinguished CR is immediate.

and deficient, in obvious contrast to the formation of CRs to new stimuli and to the restoration of CRs to the extinguished stimuli (Figure VII-3). The conditioned responses were small and characterized by a pronounced irregularity. In addition it was often observed that the dogs refused to take food offered them in the presence of these stimuli or consumed it slowly and reluctantly. Therefore, we may conclude that the stimulus, by being merely presented without reinforcement, acquires strong and permanent inhibitory properties manifested by its subsequent resistance to conditioning.[7] Similar results were obtained also by other authors.[8]

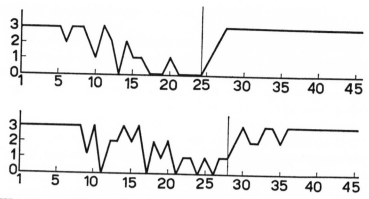

FIG. VII-2. CHRONIC EXTINCTION AND RESTORATION OF CLASSICAL DEFENSIVE CR

Abscissae, experimental sessions; ordinates, the number of positive responses to the extinguished and restored CS; in each session this CS was presented 3 times among positive CSs. The vertical line denotes the beginning of restoration of the CR. Each graph denotes the experimental series in one dog.

Note the slow and irregular course of extinction and much more rapid course of restoration of the CR.

(J. Konorski and G. Szwejkowska, in *Acta Biol. Exper.*, 16 [1952]: 91–94.)

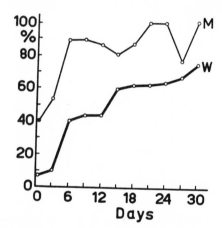

FIG. VII-3. THE FORMATION OF CLASSICAL FOOD CR TO A NEW STIMULUS (METRONOME) AND TO A STIMULUS REPEATEDLY PRESENTED WITHOUT FOOD REINFORCEMENT (WHISTLE)

Abscissae, experimental sessions; ordinates, conditioned salivation in percentage of a well-established CR.

Note that a new stimulus (M) elicits from the very beginning considerable salivation (pseudo-conditioning), rapidly attaining the level of the control CR, whereas the non-reinforced stimulus (W) originally elicits a negligible salivary response which very slowly increases when the stimulus is reinforced. The irregularity of the responses is not seen, because each point denotes the average of three sessions.

(J. Konorski and G. Szwejkowska, in *Acta Biol. Exper.*, 16 [1952]: 95–113.)

It was thought that the inhibitory character of a stimulus consistently presented without reinforcement may be revealed by another, more direct method—by combining it occasionally with a positive CS and testing whether the effect of the latter stimulus will be diminished. The experiments of this kind ran as follows.[9]

In two dogs the alimentary CRs were established to two stimuli: bell, and bubbling water (S_1 and S_2). Then two new stimuli were introduced: metronome and whistle (S_3 and S_4), which were never reinforced by food. The positive and negative stimuli were presented in random order.

After a lengthy training of this kind, in occasional crucial sessions one of the positive CSs was paired with one of the negative CSs, and the salivary effect was observed. As seen in Figure VII-4, in all trials in which such pairing was made, the salivary effect of the positive CS was decreased. On the other hand, the effect of pairing of two positive CSs ($S_1 + S_2$) was always fully positive, whereas the effect of pairing of two negative stimuli ($S_3 + S_4$) was fully negative. The same result was obtained when the unreinforced positive CS was closely followed by the negative stimulus; the salivary aftereffect of the positive CS was momentarily curtailed by the negative stimulus.

The problem immediately arose as to whether a stimulus repeatedly presented without any reinforcement becomes inhibitory to *all* kinds of CRs (defensive, sexual, and so on) or only to those which were displayed in a given drive situation. It should be noticed that the majority of experiments on conditioning are performed in a mono-drive situation—that is, when only CRs connected with one kind of reinforcement are elicited. In a later section it will be shown that an inhibitory stimulus trained in the alimentary situation—in a situation where only food is presented as a US—is inhibitory only in regard to the alimentary reflexes and not to other activities of the organism. This result may be also deduced theoretically on the basis of our concept concerning the mechanism of internal inhibition, to be presented in the next section.

A stimulus consistently presented without reinforcement in a situation in which a given unconditioned activity (alimentary, defensive, and so on) is displayed has been called a "primary inhibitory stimulus," whereas a stimulus which was previously a positive CS but has lost its conditioned response by extinction training has been called a "secondary inhibitory stimulus." We have seen that the properties of the primary and secondary inhibitory stimuli are quite different, as judged by their resistance to being conditioned. This fact clearly indicates that the "history of a stimulus" plays an important role in determining its actual properties.

The next problem to be solved was to clarify the properties of

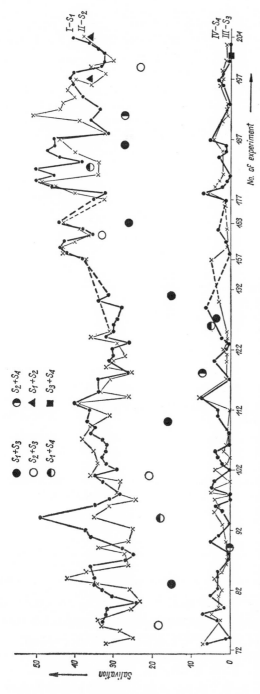

FIG. VII-4. THE SIMULTANEOUS PRESENTATION OF POSITIVE AND NEGATIVE CSs

Abscissae, experimental sessions; ordinates, salivation. S_1, S_2, positive CSs; S_3, S_4, negative CSs.

Note that the coincidence of positive and negative CSs produces a more or less diminished salivary effect in comparison with the effect of the CS alone; coincidence of two positive CSs gives a full salivary effect, whereas coincidence of two negative CSs gives no effect.

(G. Szwejkowska and J. Konorski, in *Acta Biol. Exper.*, 19 [1959]: 161–74.)

stimuli which also are not reinforced from the beginning of their application but are not quite "neutral," since they are within the scope of generalization of earlier established positive CSs. In order to accomplish this, after a food CR had been firmly established to stimulus S_1, stimuli S_2 and S_3 were introduced into experiments, stimulus S_2 being more similar to S_1 than S_3 (as judged by the strength of generalization). Both these stimuli were applied without reinforcement among positive trials, and their extinction course was studied. Thereafter they

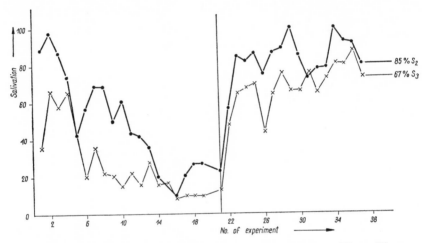

FIG. VII-5. EXTINCTION OF TWO STIMULI SIMILAR TO A POSITIVE CS AND THEIR TRANSFORMATION INTO POSITIVE CSs

Abscissae, experimental sessions; ordinates, salivation in percentage of the effect of the positive CS (S_1); vertical line denotes the beginning of positive conditioning.

Note the strong resistance to extinction of a CR to stimulus more similar to the positive CS (S_2) than to stimulus less similar (S_3), and the weaker resistance to conditioning of the former stimulus than of the latter one.

(G. Szwejkowska, in *Acta Biol. Exper.*, 19 [1959]: 151–59.)

were reinforced by food, so that we could examine their resistance to conditioning.[10]

A typical result of such experiments is presented in Figure VII-5. It is seen that the extinction of stimulus S_2, close to S_1, runs more slowly than the extinction of the more remote stimulus S_3 and is less complete. On the contrary, the rate of conditioning of stimulus S_2 is much faster than that of S_3 and approximates the rate of restoration of the original CS after its extinction. Thus it may be concluded that a non-reinforced stimulus situated on the periphery of the generalization field resembles the primary inhibitory stimulus, whereas a stimulus close to the original CS resembles the secondary inhibitory stimulus—that is, the original positive CS subjected to extinction.

A number of analogous experiments were performed in Pavlov's laboratories.[11] It was proved that when an inhibitory CR to the differentiated stimulus is firmly established, it manifests a strong resistance to positive conditioning: conditioned responses to the CS are poor and very irregular, and if such a transformed stimulus is subjected to acute extinction, the resistance to it is very weak (Figure VII-6).

Thus it became clear that the inhibitory CR is not established by the *decrease* of excitation in the US center following the operation of the CS, but rather by the *lack* of excitation in this center during its operation. Moreover, it was demonstrated that the kind of the primary training of a given stimulus, whether excitatory or inhibitory, determines its later properties: it is as difficult to transform an excitatory CS into an inhibitory one (resistance to extinction), as it is to transform a primarily inhibitory CS into an excitatory one (resistance to conditioning).

5. The mechanism of the "primary inhibitory conditioned reflex"

The main results of the experiments described in the preceding section may be summarized in the following way.

(1) If in an alimentary situation—a situation in which the animal receives food—a stimulus never accompanied by food is repeatedly presented, a special sort of inhibitory training occurs in which this stimulus becomes a signal of no food. The result of this training is recognized only indirectly in two ways: first, if later reinforced by food, the stimulus exhibits a great resistance to being conditioned; second, if it is combined with a positive alimentary CS, the effect of the latter is diminished.

(2) If a positive food CS is converted into a negative CS by non-reinforcement, it manifests a strong resistance to such a conversion (resistance to extinction); the result of this conversion is unstable, and the previous positive character of the stimulus may be easily revealed, as indicated by an extremely rapid restoration of the old CR.

Our aim now is to find out whether these facts can be accommodated to the framework of our concepts developed in the preceding chapters and what light they throw on the problems of internal inhibition.

It should be remembered that, according to our present concepts, the establishment of a classical food CR measured by salivation occurs because of the formation of synaptic connections between the CS units and the taste units for the given food. The formation of these connections and their functional state depend on the state of arousal existing

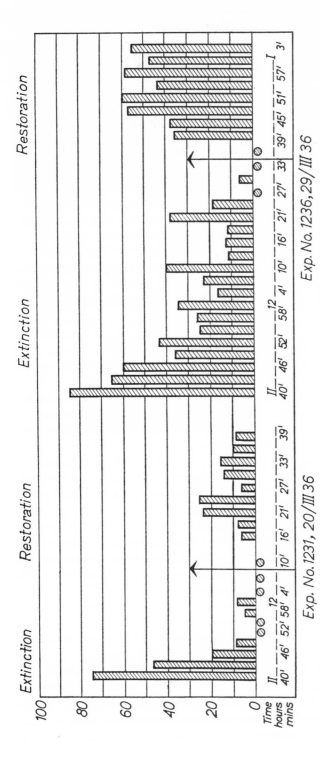

FIG. VII-6. ACUTE EXTINCTION AND RESTORATION OF AN ORIGINALLY NEGATIVE CS AND OF A PURELY POSITIVE CS

The left side of the graph represents acute extinction of the CR to a metronome 60 beats per minute, which was well trained as a negative CS differentiated from metronome 120 beats per minute; afterwards it was converted into a positive CS, which was achieved with great difficulty. Acute extinction of the CR to this stimulus is very prompt and its restoration very poor.

The right side of the graph represents extinction and restoration of the CR to a purely positive CS, bubbling. Resistance to extinction is here strong, while restoration is very prompt.

(V. V. Yakovleva, in *Trudy Fiziol. Lab. I. P. Pavlova*, 9 [1944]: 31–43.)

in the analyzers of the CS and the US. This arousal is brought about by excitation of the hunger units in the emotive system produced by joint operation of the humoral stimuli (such as lack of glucose in the blood) and of hunger CSs provided by the situation in which the animal receives food.

Let us analyze what happens when in the alimentary situation a given neutral stimulus is systematically not followed by food. We have strong reasons to believe that gnostic units of the stimulus become connected with *the taste units reacting to no food in the mouth*. These units, of course, are hardly excited in a situation unrelated to food, simply because their activation in that condition undergoes a total adaptation. In the alimentary situation, however, the taste of no food is repeatedly interspersed with the taste of food, which occurs each time that food *is* presented, and therefore its adaptation is impossible. Moreover, it may be suggested that the perception of no food in the mouth is sharpened and enhanced by the hunger drive exactly as it is with the taste of food. Thus, it may be assumed that the negative food CR is established to a given stimulus by the presence of the hunger drive in exactly the same way as is the positive food CR, and that in the absence of this drive it cannot be established at all, simply because the relevant US units (in this case the no-food units) are not activated. This would explain our supposition put forward in the previous section that the "primary inhibitory CS" (such as no-food CS in the alimentary situation or no-shock CS in the defensive situation) is not inhibitory in regard to all the activities which it does not signal but only to those which are elicited in the given situation.

The repeated presentation of the CS signaling no food soon leads to another effect. As explained in Chapter VI (Section 4), in the intertrial intervals (particularly when they are irregular and not very long) the animal displays a "tonic" hunger CR to the experimental situation, because time and again he receives food in that situation. During the operation of a primary no-food CS, however, there is a certainty (based on previous experience) that food will not be offered, and in consequence a new type of alimentary CR is established to it—the *hunger antidrive CR*. It is manifested by the striking fact that a voracious animal, who displays a strong motor excitement during the intertrial intervals due to the hunger drive CR, momentarily calms down when the primary no-food CS is presented.

Incidentally, it may be noticed that in such a situation two opposite CSs—a well-established food CS and a well-established no-food CS—produce, for different reasons, similar motor responses consisting in complete calmness. The food CS produces this effect because it gives rise to a strong consummatory food CR, inhibiting the hunger drive, whereas the no-food CS does so because of inhibition of drive by regular non-reinforcement. One may say that the certainty of obtaining food and the certainty of not obtaining it give rise to similar motor effects. Of course, as for the salivary response, it is in both cases diametrically opposite: the food CS elicits copious salivation, whereas the no-food CS elicits no salivation.

It was shown in Chapter I (Sections 10 and 11) that there are two different unconditioned hunger antidrive states, that produced by satiation, and that produced by the taste of food in the mouth, eliciting the consummatory reflex. It was assumed that both these states have different neural mechanisms: satiation is produced by the excitation (chiefly by humoral factors) of the hypothalamic satiety center, whereas the hunger antidrive brought forth by the taste of food is caused by excitation of corresponding antidrive units situated in the *hunger center itself* and reciprocally related to the hunger units (cf. Figure I-6). In Chapter VI (Section 3) it was shown that exactly the same antidrive state is produced, not only by the actual taste of food provided by the US, but also by its expectancy provided by the CS.

Now it turns out that we are confronted with a third hunger antidrive state, that provided by a CS heralding that during its action food will *not* be presented.

It seems to us that this third antidrive state is more akin to the satiation state than to the food-in-the-mouth state. The similarity to satiation is manifested by the behavior of a dog when quite unexpectedly food is offered in the presence of this no-food CS. In nearly all the animals the act of eating is either delayed for a few seconds, or the dog refuses to take food at all during the operation of the stimulus and starts eating only some time after its termination. The repeated pairing of food presentation with a no-food CS frequently leads to an experimental neurosis, a state commonly resulting from the conflict between two antagonistic drives. It should be also stressed that, as shown in the preceding section, the no-food CS is very resistant to food conditioning: in spite of numerous reinforcements of this stimulus by food, the CR remains undersized and erratic. The same is true of CRs elicited under the condition of partial satiation.

We should remember that, according to our assumption, all drive and antidrive CRs are formed through the intermediary of the higher level of the emotive brain, situated in the so-called limbic system. Accordingly, we may assume that whereas in the medial hypothalamus there is a hunger antidrive center which suppresses hunger on the basis of information provided by humoral factors, in the limbic system there exists another hunger antidrive center which suppresses hunger on the basis of conditionally acquired information to the effect that in a given situation food is unavailable. It seems that this inhibitory mechanism plays a most important role in the adaptation of the organism to its environment, because otherwise the animal would be condemned to display the hunger drive only under the control of humoral factors, instead of being free to engage in other activities. It seems that the artificial hunger antidrive CR elicited by a corresponding CS in the experimental situation is a good model of this important mechanism. In Chapter X (Section 6) we shall provide experimental evidence that such a center actually exists.

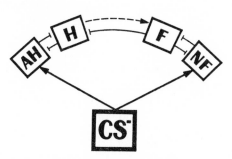

FIG. VII-7. MODEL OF AN ORIGINALLY NEGATIVE CS

CS⁻, center of the negative stimulus; AH, hunger antidrive center; H, hunger drive center; F, food taste units; NF, no-food taste units.

Continuous line arrows, excitatory connections; broken line arrow, facilitatory connection; stopped lines, inhibitory connections.

In view of our present concept, an important conclusion may be reached: that both the terms "internal inhibition" and "inhibitory CR" are not adequate and should be abandoned. The CR established by food non-reinforcement of a given stimulus is based on two *excitatory* CR arcs. One arc runs from the CS units to the no-food taste units which are reciprocally related to the food taste units. The other arc runs from the CS units to the units of hunger antidrive center situated in the higher level of the emotive brain and reciprocally related to the higher level hunger center (Figure VII-7). In consequence, the "inhibitory CR" is no more and no less inhibitory than the excitatory food CR, in which, on the contrary, the no-food taste units are reciprocally inhibited by the food taste units, and the antidrive center is inhibited by the hunger drive center. Just as we do not call the defensive CR an inhibitory CR, because the fear center inhibits the hunger center, so we have no reason to call the no-food CR inhibitory, because the hunger drive center is inhibited by the hunger antidrive center.

For the sake of convenience we shall call the CR reinforced by a given explicit US (as presentation of food, electric shock, etc.) a *posi-*

tive CR, and the respective CS, *positive* CS; the CR not reinforced by a definite US or, to be more exact, the CR reinforced by the withholding of the given US will be called a *negative* CR, and the respective CS, *negative* CS. It should be emphasized once more that these terms have a purely operational sense and that no difference in the nature of the respective phenomena is thereby claimed.

It should be clearly understood that introducing this drastic change into our concepts concerning negative CRs does not repudiate the very existence of inhibitory processes; what we do now is merely to stress that we do not have evidence of *inhibitory connections being formed* in the course of negative training, as was accepted in our previous work. What we do have the right to assume is that inhibitory interconnections established in ontogeny between antagonistic centers of the brain are *utilized* in any conditioning procedure, as they are in the unconditioned activity of the organism. Whether there is a possibility that new inhibitory connections are developed as the result of plastic changes is still an open question, but until this possibility is well documented we have no reason to admit it in analyzing the facts under consideration.

The problem arises as to whether the same relations are in operation in defensive CRs.

We remember that, according to our assumption, a defensive CR reinforced, for instance, by an electric shock to the paw is established by the formation of dual connections: those linking the CS units with the fear drive center, and those linking the CS units with somatic pinprick units. The former type of connections paves the way, so to speak, for the formation of the second type of connections.

Now, if a given stimulus operating in a fear drive situation is repeatedly not reinforced by the electric shock, the connections between its gnostic representation and no-shock units in the somatic analyzer are formed. In consequence, the operation of this stimulus gradually becomes a security signal—that is, in its presence the animal calms down because he is temporarily relieved from danger.

In Chapter I (Section 7) we have hypothesized the existence of the fear antidrive (or relief) system reciprocally connected with the fear drive system and thrown into operation when the latter is abated. It was further assumed that, not settling the problem of whether the relief center does exist on the hypothalamic level, its existence in the limbic brain may be postulated chiefly on the basis of the data in the field of conditioning (Chapter VI, Section 5). Although, unfortunately, we have no experimental material concerning the *primary* no-shock CSs analogous to the primary no-food CSs, the data on the secondary no-shock CSs transformed from the positive shock CSs are abundant.[12]

These data indicate that, after a repeated non-reinforcement of a shock CS, the animal not only stops performing the conditioned flexion response to it but also that, after a more prolonged training, his cardiac response and motor arousal significantly decrease (see Section 6, below). We can reasonably admit that this is due to the development of the fear antidrive CR based on the formation of connections linking the CS units with the units of the relief center.

6. The mechanism of transformations of positive conditioned reflexes into negative conditioned reflexes, and vice versa

After having become acquainted with the assumed mechanism of primary negative CRs as the antipodes of the primary positive CRs, we shall turn now to the analysis of their mutual transformations.

The types of phenomena to be explained are the following: (1) conversion of a positive CS into a negative CS by non-reinforcement—that is, extinction of a CR; (2) restoration of the positive character of the CS by its re-reinforcement; (3) conversion of a negative CS into a positive CS by its reinforcement; (4) restoration of the negative character of the CS by its non-reinforcement.

(1) Extinction of the positive CS (say, alimentary) is based on the substitution of the food reinforcement by no-food reinforcement carried out in the hunger drive situation. As indicated above, the no-food reinforcement means activation of the no-food taste units, which are in reciprocal relations with food taste units.

In the beginning of the extinction training, the strong excitation of the food taste units produced by the CS totally inhibits the no-food taste units, and consequently the formation of the CS → no-food connections is hindered. This is the explanation of the so-called resistance to extinction, which is more intense as the positive CR to the given CS is stronger.

It should be realized, however, that whereas during the presentation of the CS the food taste units are excited, the situation is radically changed when the food reinforcement is not offered in due time. First, this situation produces a vigorous orientation reaction (astonishment) to the novelty of the stimulus sequence. Then, the hunger drive, which has been so far greatly appeased by the smooth CS-US sequence, is at once aroused; the animal, to this point quiet and even a bit somnolent (cf. Chapter VI), becomes momentarily alert and begins to be agitated and sometimes to struggle for food.

Thus, under the condition of arousal produced by the increased hunger drive, the CS is accompanied by no food; therefore, the connections between the CS units and the no-food taste units can be formed. Since the old CS → food connections are by no means destroyed, the CS units are now connected with two reciprocally related sets of units: food taste, and no-food taste. The fact that excitation of food taste units produces inhibition of no-food taste units and vice versa makes the process of extinction irregular (cf. Figures VII-2, 3, and 5) and the conditioned response erratic, not only from trial to trial, but even within a particular trial. In fact, one often observes a staircase character of salivation to the CS under extinction, when salivation, zero at the beginning of a trial, rises steeply after a few seconds or, on the contrary, begins at a normal rate and then stops abruptly. One has the impression that the dog alternately expects food, visualizing the appearance of the full bowl, and then at once shifts to visualizing the empty bowl. As a matter of fact, this psychological speculation is nothing but the translation of the physiological events deduced from experimental observations into psychological language.

Incidentally, it may be noticed that our present theory of extinction gives a quite different prediction concerning its course than our previous theory, assuming the formation of inhibitory connections between the CS and the US centers side by side with the existing excitatory connections. According to the latter theory, the process of extinction should be smooth and regular as more and more inhibitory connections are formed between the CS center and the US center; according to our present theory, it *must* be irregular because of the antagonism between the two US centers involved in the process and alternative overweighing of the excitation of this or that center, causing the immanent instability of the system. This is due to the fact that, on the one hand, the fresh CS → no-food connections are still poorly consolidated and may be weakened overnight, and that, on the other hand, the increased hunger drive facilitates the food taste units, the excitation of which inhibits the no-food taste units.

Gradually the CS → no-food association takes an upper hand over the CS → food association, and salivation to the CS drops to zero or nearly so. This means that the food taste units are completely inhibited by the excitation of the no-food taste units and cannot be thrown into action in spite of the existence of connections linking them with the CS units.

Quite different, however, is the situation in regard to CS → hunger drive associations. As pointed out in the preceding chapter, the hunger CR (similar to any other drive CR) is much more inertial than the food CR and may be in operation when the latter reflex is totally absent. In fact, judged by the animal's behavior, the CS may still produce alertness and agitation (accompanied by the instrumental response if it is established) in spite of a total absence of salivation. Returning again for a moment to the psychological language, we may say that the animal still has a hope of getting food in the presence of the extinguished CS (since he remembers the period when he got it), in clear contradistinction to his reaction to the primarily negative CS, in the presence of which food was never offered him. This is why, when after the extinction training food is again offered to the animal in the presence of the CS, he never fails to take it at once, not manifesting any neurotic symptoms.

An important inference to be made from these considerations is that the process of extinction is, as a matter of fact, "fed" by the hunger drive. It follows that if the extinction procedure were conducted against the background of the hunger antidrive, the extinction would be ineffective, and the CR to the corresponding CS, elicited in the state of hunger, would be fully preserved.

Experiments supporting this inference have been performed, and ran in the following way.[13]

In dogs the conditioned inhibition procedure was applied in which a positive food CS S_1 was differentiated from the compound S_0S_1 presented in non-overlapping sequence. When the full differentiation was achieved, the presentation of the stimulus S_1 alone was discontinued and the compound S_0S_1 was presented a sufficient number of times to make sure that the extinction of S_1 (if acting alone) would occur. After this series the stimulus S_1 not preceded by S_0 was tested.

It was found that, in spite of many repetitions of S_1 without reinforcement when preceded by the conditioned inhibitor S_0, there was not the slightest sign of the extinction of the CR to the stimulus S_1 presented alone (Figure VII-8). On the other hand, when a similar repeated presentation of S_0S_1 without reinforcement was applied without the preceding differentiation training, the normal extinction of the CR to S_1 did occur.

It seems that these results are easily explainable in the framework of our present concept. The conditioned inhibitor S_0, never paired with food, elicits a strong negative CR, acting not only during its presentation but also after its cessation so as to cover stimulus S_1 following it. In this way the latter stimulus is, so to speak, *screened* by the conditioned hunger antidrive produced by S_0 and is, therefore, impervious to extinction, which does occur when this protection is not given. In another series of experiments[14] analogous screening was provided by a strong fear-producing stimulus immediately preceding the CS, which was in this compound not reinforced. In spite of many trials of this kind, the CR to the CS acting alone was preserved, again because a fear-producing stimulus induced the hunger antidrive, in whose presence the extinction could not be established.

When the extinguished CS is repeatedly presented over a long period of time among positive CSs, it may eventually be transformed into a hunger antidrive CS—that is, the animal will stop expecting food in response to it. This process, however, although theoretically possible, hardly ever occurred in our own experiments. In fact, even after a hundred or more extinction trials, the recovery of the positive CR was nearly immediate, showing that the hunger drive was in full operation during the action of the extinguished CS. Of course, if we are concerned with the extinction, not of the original CR, but of the CR

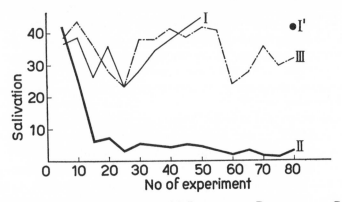

FIG. VII-8. LACK OF EXTINCTION OF A CS REPEATEDLY PRESENTED IN CONCOMITANCE WITH A CONDITIONED INHIBITOR.

Abscissae, experimental sessions; ordinates, salivation in arbitrary units.

I, salivation to positive CS (S_1); II, salivation to a non-reinforced compound S_0S_1; III, salivation to a control positive CS (S_2).

During the first fifty experimental sessions differentiation is established between S_1 and S_0S_1. Thereafter stimulus S_1 is withdrawn and only S_0S_1 is presented among positive S_2 trials. After thirty sessions S_1 is again presented (point I'). No extinction of the CR to this stimulus has occurred.

(H. Chorążyna, in *Acta Biol. Exper.*, 22 [1962]: 5–13.)

produced by generalization, the hunger antidrive CR may be obtained much easier, particularly if the new stimulus is not very similar to the original CS.

Similar principles to those described in respect to alimentary CRs hold true also in respect to defensive CRs.[15] The chronic extinction of the CR to a given positive CS (either original or similar to it) goes through two stages. In the first stage, the shock CR is transformed into the no-shock CR, because the excitation of the recipient pinprick units gives way to the excitation of the reciprocally related to them no-pinprick units. As the result, the CS stops eliciting leg flexion. In the second stage, occurring after a more prolonged extinction training, dogs may develop also, to a certain degree, the fear antidrive CR manifested by the attenuation of the heart-rate response elicited by the positive CS. Again, this antidrive CR is easier obtainable if not the original shock CS but a stimulus similar to it is used (Figure VII-9).

(2) The course of events occurring during the restoration of the extinguished CR is exactly the reverse of that during extinction, except that the CS → food associations are already formed in the animal and have to be utilized anew. Since, as explained in the preceding paragraph, the hunger drive, occurring in the presence of the extinguished CS (provided that the extinction was not too much overtrained), is not abolished, few additional connections have to be formed between the CS units and the food taste units in order to overbalance the CS → no-food connections so far in operation. Again owing to the reciprocal relations between the two sets of units, the restoration of the positive CR occurs almost immediately, although some irregularities in its course usually do occur.

As we see from this analysis, the extinction of the CR does not lead to its *transformation* in the precise meaning of the word, but rather to the establishment of a new, opposite CR side by side with the old one. In consequence, two antagonistic CRs are actually formed to the CS, either this or that taking the upper hand.

The dual character of a CS which has undergone the extinction (and restoration) procedure explains another interesting fact frequently observed in Pavlov's laboratories. This is that when from time to time we carry out acute extinction sessions in which the CS is repeatedly presented without food reinforcement, the following peculiar fact is observed. The salivary responses in "normal" sessions are high, and the experiment runs quite regularly. It is enough, however, to present the CS once or twice without food reinforcement to cause the salivary response immediately to drop to zero. The dog after a single trial "knows" that in a given session no food will be paired with the CS and immediately adjusts to this condition.[16] Another good example of a dual character of a CS is provided when it is reinforced by food if presented alone but is not reinforced if preceded by a conditioned inhibitor.

(3) In contradistinction to the case discussed in (2), the elaboration of the positive CR to a primarily negative CS is much more difficult than the restoration of the extinguished CR and is never fully successful. The CR is irregular and usually smaller than that to the primarily positive CS. Experimental neuroses frequently develop during this training. The explanation of this fact is that, as shown in the preceding section, the CS units are in this case strongly connected both with the no-food taste units and with the hunger antidrive units (cf. Figure VII-7). In consequence, when the animal for the first time receives food in the presence of the CS, his hunger drive is so much

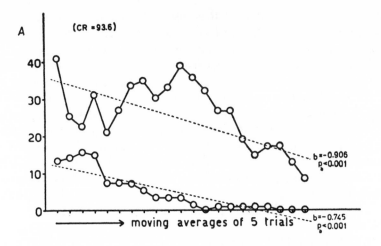

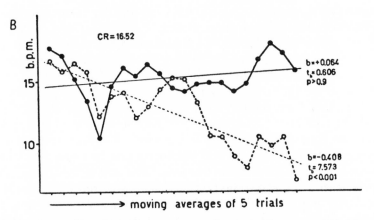

Fig. VII-9. Acute Two-Day Extinction of Classical Defensive CR (Average from Experiments on Seven Dogs)

A. Latencies of motor responses calculated by the formula $100(3-L)$, where L is latency in seconds (the duration of the CS was 3 seconds). Upper curve, the first extinction day; lower curve, the second extinction day.

B. Cardiac response measured as the difference between the mean pulse rate during the CS and the mean pre-CS pulse rate. Black circles, first day of extinction; white circles, second day of extinction.

Note prompt extinction of the motor response (flexion of the leg) and much slower extinction (only on the second day) of the cardiac response.

(K. Jaworska, M. Kowalska, and S. Sołtysik, in *Acta Biol. Exper.*, 22 [1962]: 102–13.)

inhibited that he either refuses to take it till the CS is terminated or takes it reluctantly. In the succeeding trials the situation gradually improves: the hunger antidrive elicited by the CS is substituted by the hunger drive, and this drive in turn facilitates the formation of connections between the CS units and the food taste units. Of course, since the old connections linking the CS units with antidrive units and no-food units remain intact, we have here another example of a dual character of the CS manifested by both the irregular course of the positive CR and its weak resistance to extinction.

(4) The prompt extinction of the positive CR to a CS converted from the originally negative CS is easily explained by the fact that in this case the connections CS → no-food are already present and the training requires only their strengthening in order to make them predominant over the CS → food connections. The analysis of that process is analogous to that of the restoration of the positive CR to the originally positive CS.

7. Transformations of heterogeneous conditioned reflexes

The discussion presented in the preceding sections made it clear that conversions of positive CSs into negative ones and vice versa—that is, extinction and restoration of CRs—are based on the same general principle as are transformations of any antagonistic heterogeneous CRs. The latter type of transformations, however, has one big advantage over the former one; this is that whereas the negative CR has no direct overt effect and therefore its presence has to be inferred indirectly (by its resistance to conditioning or combining it with a positive CR), both of the two heterogeneous CRs possess overt and measurable effects. Consequently, a new series of experiments was undertaken in which the alimentary CRs were transformed into the defensive ones and vice versa.[17]

The dogs were trained in two kinds of CRs: in response to certain stimuli (denoted as CS_F) food CRs were established, while to other ones (denoted as CS_D) defensive CRs were formed by reinforcing them with electric shock applied to the paw. The strength of the food CR was measured by the amount of salivation, whereas the strength of the shock CR was measured by the latency and height of leg flexion. In both series of experiments (performed separately in the same chamber) besides the positive CSs one negative (non-reinforced) CS was introduced. Thus, all in all we had four kinds of CSs: positive food CSs ($CS_F{}^+$); negative food CS ($CS_F{}^-$); positive defensive CSs ($CS_D{}^+$); and negative defensive CS ($CS_D{}^-$). Then both the positive and the negative CSs were converted into positive CSs of the other category:

$$CS_F^+ \text{ into } CS_D^+$$

$$CS_F^- \text{ into } CS_D^+$$

$$CS_D^+ \text{ into } CS_F^+$$

$$CS_D^- \text{ into } CS_F^+$$

The conversion of the stimuli was conducted in such a way that they were presented once daily among the original CSs of that category into which they had to be converted. Thus, the CS_F converted into CS_D was presented among CSs_D and vice versa.

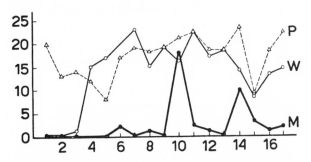

Fig. VII-10. Transformation of Alimentary into Defensive CRs

Abscissae, experimental sessions; ordinates, amplitude of defensive conditioned response (leg flexion) in millimeters of kymographic record. P, defensive response to rotor (original defensive CS); M, defensive response to metronome (original positive alimentary CS); W, defensive response to whistle (original negative alimentary CS).

Note the striking difference between the defensive CR to metronome and whistle.

(J. Konorski and G. Szwejkowska, in *Acta Biol. Exper.*, 17 [1956], 141–65.)

The main results of these experiments were as follows.

(1) The conversion of CS_F^+ into CS_D^+ was very difficult, and was practically not achieved in this series of experiments. Only when the intensified defensive training of CS_F^+ was undertaken by presenting the stimulus repeatedly day after day with shock reinforcement, was a regular defensive CR established to it. On the other hand, the conversion of CS_F^- into CS_D^+ was in the same condition very prompt, and after a few conversion trials its effect became similar to that of the original CS_D^+ (Figure VII-10).

(2) Analogously, the conversion of CS_D^+ into CS_F^+ was very difficult, and the salivary responses to it were small and irregular. On the other hand, the conversion of CS_D^- into CS_F^+ was much easier, and the salivary responses, although smaller than to the control CS_F^+, were

regular (Figure VII-11). It should be noted that although the whole series of experiments was conducted in the alimentary situation with no shocks administered, it was rather trying to the animals; although the dogs used for these experiments were calm and voracious, they became restless, and the salivary responses to the control $CS_F{}^+$ sometimes became erratic. Therefore, in order to avoid more serious disorders, the conversion trials occasionally had to be withdrawn for a few days until the CR activity of the dogs again became normal.

(3) When the converted stimuli were presented against their original background, they produced their original responses. Thus, the $CS_D{}^+$ converted into $CS_F{}^+$ produced the defensive response when pre-

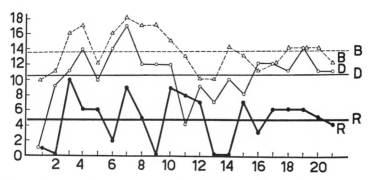

FIG. VII-11. TRANSFORMATION OF DEFENSIVE CRs INTO ALIMENTARY CRs

Abscissae, experimental sessions; ordinates, salivation in arbitrary units. B, salivary response to bell (original positive CS); R, salivary response to rattle (original positive defensive CS); D, salivary response to moving disk (original negative defensive CS).
Note the striking difference between the CR to rattle and disk.
(J. Konorski and G. Szwejkowska, in *Acta Biol. Exper.*, 17 [1956], 141–65.)

sented among the defensive CSs. This never happened when in the same condition the original $CS_D{}^-$ converted into $CS_F{}^+$ or the pure $CS_F{}^+$ was presented (Table VII-1).

Thus, we have clear evidence that the converted CSs acquired a dual character and that they formed associations with both USs: the alimentary and the defensive. Depending on the drive under which the stimulus was presented, it produced either the defensive or the alimentary response.

Turning to the discussion of these results, we should note that they fully confirm our previous conclusions concerning the transformations of CRs and make them even more explicit, because both CSs subjected to conversion have their overt effects. Therefore, we now must add only some brief comments to those made before.

The greater difficulty in the conversion of the food CS into the shock CS or vice versa, as compared with the conversion of a positive into a negative CS or vice versa, is due simply to the fact that the antagonism between hunger and fear is much stronger than that between the hunger drive and the hunger antidrive (cf. Chapter I). (Incidentally, this is not true of the USs used as reinforcements: the antagonism between the food taste and no-food taste is certainly more

TABLE VII-1

ALIMENTARY CSs TESTED AGAINST THE DEFENSIVE BACKGROUND
EXTRACTS FROM PARTICULAR PROTOCOLS

No. of Trial	Time (in Min.)	CS	CS-US Interval (in Sec.)	Defensive CR		Food CR	Rein-force-ment
				Latency (in Sec.)	Strength of Motor Response	Salivation in Scale Units	
7	23	Splash	10	4	++	13	Shock
8	26	Splash	10	8	++	8	Shock
9	29	Bell	10	—	—	43	Food
5	16	Splash	10	5	++	6	Shock
6	19	Splash	10	7	++	10	Shock
7	22	Rattle	10	5	+++	15	Food
5	14	Splash	10	6	++	0	Shock
6	17	Splash	10	5	+++	11	Shock
7	20	Disk	10	—	—	25	Food

Splash, defensive CS; bell, pure alimentary CS; rattle, alimentary CS transformed from positive defensive CS; disk, alimentary CS transformed from negative defensive CS.

Note that rattle produces strong defensive response and poor salivation, whereas bell and disk produce only alimentary response. Background salivation in this dog amounts to about 10 units in 10 seconds.

(J. Konorski and G. Szwejkowska, in *Acta Biol. Exper.*, 17 [1956]: 158.)

pronounced than that between the food taste and pinprick sensation, since the first pair belongs to the same perceptive field whereas the second pair does not.) In consequence, the conversion of the food CS into the shock CS or vice versa requires inhibition of the respective drive and its replacement by the antagonistic drive. Since, as stated before, the drive CRs are characterized by strong inertia, it is clear why the conversion of the conditioned significance of the corresponding CSs is so difficult. In order to make the task easier for the animals the shock CS converted into the food CS was presented in the food situation, whereas the food CS converted into the shock CS was presented in the shock situation. Thus, the dominant drive in the given situation helped to suppress the antagonistic drive. It seems that if we did not resort to this measure, the conversion would be more difficult or even impossible.

A special comment should be made concerning the transformation of *negative* CRs of one category into the *positive* CRs of the other category. Since the primary negative food CS does not elicit the hunger drive but the hunger antidrive, which is not antagonistic to the fear drive, the easy conversion of that CS into the defensive CS is quite understandable. Similarly, the primary negative shock CS is easily converted into the food CS, since it produces the fear antidrive, which is not antagonistic to the hunger drive. As noted in an earlier section, these results are significant for an additional reason—because they give clear evidence that the primary negative stimuli are negative (that is, inhibitory) only in relation to that drive reflex, or consummatory reflex, which was operating in a situation in which they were presented.

We have proved in our experiments, and explained why it is true, that the *formation* of a CR to a stimulus not hitherto associated with any other activities of the organism is much easier than its *transformation* from another CR antagonistic to the new one. The converted CS is handicapped in comparison to the pure CS because it has a dual character, and its previous conditioned significance may always hamper its new effect. However, the important problem arises as to whether the first associations established for the given CS are, other things being equal, more stable and stronger than the later associations established when the CS is paired with another US.

Although in our earlier paper[18] we claimed that "the principle of the primacy of first training" does exist, and we presented much evidence to support it, I do not think now that this evidence is indeed conclusive. First, in our own experiments the counter-training concerning a given stimulus was always less persistent than the original training, and we do not know what the result would be if both were really equal. Further, one should take into account that in many observations from everyday life supporting this principle the first training was conducted at an earlier age than the counter-training. As indicated in Chapter IV, the associations acquired earlier in life (beginning at some critical period) are more stable than those acquired later. Therefore, this problem must be left open until more reliable experimental evidence is provided.

To end this discussion on the transformation of CRs, we should draw attention to the fact that, as it can be inferred from our considerations, the term "transformation" is quite inadequate for defining the phenomena we were dealing with. If this term is applied in a purely phenomenological sense it may be accepted, but if it refers to the *mechanism* of the processes involved it is most misleading. In fact, we have proved that *no* transformations of connections occur in the reversal training, because what actually happens is the formation of new connections joining the CS units with a set of units representing another US. As a result, two CRs are established to the same CS with the relative dominance of the new reflex.

8. Transformations of classical conditioned reflexes in human beings

In the last section of Chapter VI, we discussed some typical and most important classical CRs established in human life. Now we should like to apply to human higher nervous processes the principles developed in the present chapter—those concerned with transformations of classical CRs, which occur when for some reasons the hitherto established associations no longer fit the requirements of the changed conditions of life.

As pointed out in the preceding chapter, a large category of classical CRs in humans is the "social CRs"—those reflexes in which other members of the community are classical CSs eliciting a great variety of emotional and consummatory conditioned responses. It should be noted, however, that human interrelations are by no means static, but on the contrary they are subjected to numerous alterations depending on the multitude of factors, such as maturation of either the subject (S) in whom conditioning is established or the persons (Ps) being CSs in regard to him, changes in the life situation of S or P, in their mutual relations due to these changes, and many others.

Not being able to deal in detail here with this extensive field of phenomena, we should like to cite a few life situations which will illustrate particular cases of transformations of social CRs in human beings.

Suppose that a female subject fell in love with a given male, married him, and the marriage has appeared to be successful. This means that the husband provides our subject with satisfaction of sexual drive and behaves in such a way as to evoke in her other attractive feelings, such as harmony, trust, feeling of security, gratitude for kindness. All these fragments of the behavior of the partner are the USs reinforcing the well-established appetitive CRs. In consequence, whenever the subject has actually to do with her partner or thinks about him in his absence, she experiences a compound of attractive emotions consisting of tenderness, affection, occasional sexual drive, and so on.

Suppose now that into this idyllic condition a harsh, jarring event intrudes. The husband may return drunk home and be rude and repulsive to the subject. Or he may be guilty of conjugal infidelity and our subject learns about it. Now, depending on the further course of events (something like various training procedures), different consequences may follow. We shall consider some of them.

It may happen that the disturbing episodes will become so frequent and the earlier tender behavior of the partner so rare (or absent) that a true and consistent counter-training will occur. A new attitude of bitterness, fear, and hatred may be established and may totally and permanently suppress the previous feelings with all kinds of behavioral (instrumental) consequences, which are beyond the scope of our analysis. In effect, the appetitive CRs elicited by the husband will be fully and irreversibly transformed into repulsive CRs. However, in spite of the fact that the old conditioned connections have hardly any opportunity now to be manifested, because of their total suppression by the new connections, they are not lost. This is proved by the fact that when the husband dies, our subject will certainly return to her old memories associated with him: his image will produce the old and for years not elicited CRs. It may even happen that these old conditioned connections will suppress the more recent ones and the subject will think of the deceased husband as tenderly as she did in the first period of their marriage. If not, then both types of CRs will appear in alternative sequence but never mixing.

Another course of events may be such that after a single unfortunate episode peace is restored and relations return to their previous form. Incidentally, it may even happen that the episode, if not very drastic, will have a positive effect upon the married life, increasing the sexual drive inhibited by the routine occurrence of the consummatory sexual reflexes. After a lapse of time the clash will be "forgotten," which means that the negative attitude formed owing to a single aversive reinforcement will become so suppressed by the appetitive CRs that the corresponding associations will have no chance to be manifested. There is, however, no doubt that they will not disappear, because if after a long time a similar episode occurs, the memories of the old episode will immediately revive in all their freshness.

Finally, it may happen that the episode of drunkenness or infidelity is not unique but may recur again and again, although in the meantime the behavior of the husband may be quite blameless. In that case most often the CS acquires a dual role, eliciting alternately the attractive or aversive CR with amazing rhythmicity. If you are by chance in the subject's confidence you can hear with amazing regularity two stories: one story is that this time she has had really enough; she hates him, will throw him out of the house, or go away, or kill him, or herself, depending on the temperament and situation; however, after a few days you will hear another story that he promised that this will never happen again, that he is *so* kind and tender, that she couldn't live without him, and so on. What is interesting is that these two attitudes are quite separate, and usually do not mix. There is no algebraic summation of the two CRs but rather the exclusive dominance of one of them.

As a matter of fact, I think that such dual CRs are very frequent in our relations with people and are rules rather than exceptions. In fact, it is very rare that people are uniform in their behavior toward others, being consistently either angels or devils. Most of us are both angels and devils, and each side of our nature—the pleasant, and unpleasant—may be manifested in various conditions, depending on humoral factors, or previous events, or both. Accordingly, most of us are not reliable and consistent reinforcers of social CRs established in other persons toward us, since we may be a source of different and quite opposite URs for them.

What is interesting in these alternating CRs this is the fact that if we are at the given moment under the influence of one CR (and the other is suppressed), not only do we experience a strong emotional attitude of the given kind (e.g. annoyance or affection) but also all images associated with that attitude emerge and we now remember all the previous situations when we were in the identical mood. In other words, not only do we perceive the actual situation evoking the given CR, but we also mobilize all the images of the earlier situations which are allied in their CS significance with the present one and consequently strengthen the given CR. This mechanism was explained in Chapter V as based on the connections leading from the set of units of the given drive to the gnostic units with which it was concomitantly excited.

It does not seem necessary to quote other examples of transformations of various CRs (or, in general, associations) occurring in human beings, since all of them follow roughly the same rules. These rules are: (1) the indestructibility of the old associations if they are firmly established; (2) their susceptibility to being suppressed by fresher associations established with the USs antagonistic to the old ones; and (3) their susceptibility to being restored or, rather, remanifested under suitable conditions.

9. Summary and conclusions

The considerations of this chapter show what a long distance we have traveled in the field under discussion, not only from the old Pavlovian concept of "internal inhibition," but also from the more modern version of this concept proposed by us in our previous study.

The Pavlovian concept was based on the assumption that internal inhibition is localized *in the center of the inhibitory CS*. Long ago it became clear, not only for us, but also for many other students concerned in this field (Anokhin, Asratian, Beritoff, and others)[19] that this point of view was untenable.

Another hypothesis, which seemed to fit experimental facts much better, was that the process of internal inhibition occurs *between the CS center and the US center*, owing to the formation of inhibitory synapses on the neurons of the latter center. In this way the inhibitory process involved in internal inhibition lost its anonymous, undirected, or—rather—multidirected character, and was thought to be as specific as the excitatory process involved in excitatory CRs.

This view was developed in great detail in my previous monograph, and did not seem to be in contradiction with the facts available at that time. But new experimental work undertaken in order to test this theory has thrown a serious doubt upon its correctness, because the facts obtained turned out to be in clear contradiction. The most important of these facts were the following.

(1) The clear asymmetry between the course of extinction of the CR and its restoration—that is, a much stronger resistance to extinction than the resistance to restoration of the CR.

(2) The much stronger resistance to conditioning of a "primary inhibitory stimulus" (a stimulus presented without reinforcement among other reinforced stimuli) than of a new stimulus or of a CS subjected previously to extinction.

(3) The strong resistance to transformation of a defensive CR into an alimentary CR and vice versa, and the similarity of the rules governing these transformations with the rules of transformations of the positive into negative CRs and vice versa.

(4) The preservation in a latent form of the old character of the CS after its conversion into the CS of the other kind.

(5) The utmost irregularity inherent in each transformation process.

These data made it necessary for us to revise our previous concept of internal inhibition and to look for another concept which would better fit the new evidence.

In the present chapter a new concept concerning the phenomena in question is advanced which, on the one hand, is consistent with the general ideas of brain functions presented in this book and, on the other hand, accounts for the experimental facts now at our disposal.

The present concept is based on the two following assumptions:

(1) When in a situation in which a given US is repeatedly presented—that is, in which a given drive is dominant—a "neutral"

stimulus is repeatedly presented without being followed by this US, then the gnostic units representing this stimulus form connections with the gnostic units representing the *lack of the US* and with the *antidrive* units. In this way the negative CR is established to that stimulus, being antagonistic to the positive CR established to the stimuli followed by the given US. This negative CR is formed under the sponsorship of the drive acting in the given situation.

(2) When a given CS being a signal of a given US is followed by a new US instead of the previous one, then the gnostic units of that CS form connections with the gnostic units of the new US and the corresponding drive units, leaving the old, previously established connections unaffected. Since the old and the new US units, as well as the old and the new drive units, are in reciprocal relations, that CR which is stronger in the given stage of training or in the given circumstances takes the upper hand and inhibits the other CR. Hence, even the relatively small overbalance of this or that reflex is sufficient for its complete dominance at the given moment.

It follows from these assumptions that the so-called extinction of a CR is nothing but the substitution of a new reinforcement for the old one (in that case no-US for US) and thus follows the general rules of "transformations" of CRs. These rules are as follows.

(1) Each "transformation" of a CR into the antagonistic one, whether alimentary-defensive CR transformation or positive-negative CR transformation, encounters a certain resistance owing to the fact that the formation of new connections leading from the CS units to the new US units and the new drive units is handicapped by strong excitation of the old US units and the old drive units elicited by that CS.

(2) On the contrary, the restoration of the previous CR is a much easier process, because the old connections on which this CR is built are already there and the reverse training consists only in establishing their relative dominance over the connections with the antagonistic units.

On the basis of these considerations, we come to the conclusion that neither the term "internal inhibition" (and its derivates "inhibitory CR" and "inhibitory CS") nor the term "transformation of CRs" is adequate for the denotation of the *mechanisms* involved in the corresponding processes. These terms can be used at most in a phenomenological sense. As far as "internal inhibition" is concerned, we have no clear evidence that new *inhibitory* connections are formed between two sets of units, because all the relevant cases of inhibition we have so far dealt with may be reasonably accounted for by the assumption that *excitatory* connections are formed between the transmittent set of units and the set of units reciprocally related to the recipient units (no-US units and antidrive units). In consequence, the "inhibitory CR" is no more and no less inhibitory than any other CR. Similarly, we have seen that the "transformation" of CRs is actually based on the formation of new connections joining the transmittent set of units with the new recipient set of units, whereas the old connections with the previous recipient set of units are not affected.

Getting rid of these two notions, as far as their explanatory value is concerned, much simplifies our understanding of all the relevant facts and provides us with a unitary theory of all the phenomena in the realm of classical conditioning. It remains to be seen whether the same principles are applicable also to the phenomena of instrumental conditioning. This problem will be dealt with in the following chapters.

10. Addendum: A mechanism of generalization and differentiation

One of the first achievements in the study of CRs was the discovery that if a given CR has been established to a particular stimulus, then all the stimuli similar to it—that is, possessing some common properties—are able to elicit the same conditioned response. This phenomenon was called by Pavlov "generalization of a CR." Numerous studies were performed both in Pavlov's and other behavioristic laboratories to show the existence of a gradient of generalization, according to which the more remote the given stimulus is in respect to the original CS, the less its reflexogenic capacity. This capacity was measured either directly by the strength of the conditional response or indirectly by its resistance to extinction.

If a given stimulus producing the conditioned response by generalization is repeatedly presented without reinforcement, whereas the original CS is reinforced, the process called "differentiation" occurs. Its result is that the secondary CS gradually loses its conditioned response whereas the original CS preserves it. The closer the secondary CS to the primary one, the more difficult or "finer" the differentiation, whereas the more remote the secondary CS, the easier or "cruder" is the differentiation. It should be remembered that, as stated in Section 4 (Figure VII-5), the more remote the differentiated stimulus from the original CS, the more it becomes similar to a primary negative CS, situated outside the generalization range of the positive CS.

The first attempt to account for the physiological mechanism of generalization and differentiation was given in my previous monograph.[20] According to that concept, each stimulus was assumed to be represented in the cerebral cortex by a *pool* of neurons activated by the operation of that stimulus. The stronger the stimulus, the more extensive the corresponding pool of neurons was assumed to be. The similarity of two stimuli was accounted for by the partial overlapping of the pools representing each of them, the stronger the similarity the more extensive this overlapping. Thus, the centers of the two differentiated stimuli were thought to be composed of three parts: (1) the subcenter a, particular only to the reinforced stimulus; (2) the subcenter b, belonging to both stimuli; and (3) the subcenter c, particular only to the unreinforced stimulus. The extent of each of these subcenters was assumed to depend on the strength of the corresponding stimuli and the degree of similarity between them.

From this simple assumption all the then known facts concerning both generalization and differentiation could be easily deduced. It was considered that the so-called conditioned inhibition, in which the CS alone is reinforced but the compound composed of the CI (conditioned inhibitor) and CS is not, provides a good model of the differentiation process, since in that case the subcenters b and c could be manipulated separately.

It seems that our present concepts of perceptions and conditioning allow us to go deeper into the mechanisms of generalization and differentiation and to deprive these processes of a certain oversimplicity which was characteristic of our previous ideas.

Let us remember that, as explained in Chapter II (Sections 8 and 9), two stimulus-objects can be considered: (1) identical, if they are addressed to the same set of gnostic units; (2) similar, if they are addressed to the set of units representing their common elements and to different sets representing their specific features; (3) dissimilar, if they are addressed to two different sets of units.

In this discussion we are concerned only with the second condition —that is, with a stage when the discrimination between two similar stimuli is already established and the animal has to learn that each of these stimuli should be associated with a different US (cf. Figure II-16, p. 96). It was assumed that in this stage the gnostic representation of these stimuli is composed of the set of units common to both of them (GU_s), and of the sets of units corresponding to each of the stimuli separately (GU_{s1} and GU_{s2}). And so we see that our present concept of central representation of the two differentiated stimuli is not very remote from the old one, except that instead of anonymous "pools of neurons" we introduce units possessing a definite meaning.

Let us see now how the process of differentiation occurs if, according to the usual Pavlovian procedure, the CR is first firmly established to the original CS (S_1), and only then another stimulus (S_2), similar to it, is introduced.

As was explained in Chapter II, we have good reasons to believe that in the original conditioning chiefly the crude elements of the CS take part, because, first, they are represented by a larger set of units, and, second, the more precise examination of the stimulus to be conditioned is not necessary for the given task. When stimulus S_2 is now presented for the first time, the animal perceives at once that it differs from stimulus S_1 and displays a more or less pronounced orientation reaction inhibiting to some extent the conditioned response which should be elicited by this stimulus because of generalization. This inhibition is documented by the fact that usually, with the repetition of the stimulus, along with habituation of the reaction to its novelty,

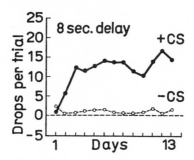

Fig. VII-12 Lack of Generalization of Positive and Negative CSs Simultaneously Introduced into Training

Abscissae, experimental sessions from the beginning of training; ordinates, salivation to CSs in drops (0 level means pre-CS salivation). CS+, tone 510 cps, CS−, tone 1,700 cps (or vice versa).

(G. D. Ellison, in *J. Comp. Physiol. Psychol.*, 57 [1964]: 373–80.)

the conditioned response increases in spite of the lack of reinforcement (cf. Figure VII-5). Only in the next stage does the conditioned response to S_2 gradually diminish. This occurs through the total reorganization of perceptive processes to both stimuli: Attention in regard to S_1 is shifted from its crude elements to its specific elements, represented by GU_{S1} units. In consequence, GU_{S1} units form connections with US units, whereas GU_{S2} units form connections with no-US units, and in this way full differentiation is established.

Quite different, however, is the situation when both differentiated stimuli, S_1 and S_2, are introduced into experiments *at the same time*. Although the evidence to that issue is scarce, it seems that in this case the generalization is very poor and the two stimuli behave as if they were entirely different[21] (Figure VII-12). The explanation of this result is that now the gnostic units GU_S, representing both stimuli, are of no use for training, since they form connections with both US and no-US units. In consequence, the animal from the very beginning of training pays attention only to the specific aspects of each stimulus and therefore, the separate connections $GU_{s1} \to GU_{US}$, and $GU_{s2} \to GU_{no-US}$ are formed at once.

Another important problem in the field of differentiation is that of the relation of strength of the positive and negative CSs taking part in this process.

This problem has been recently studied by Zielinski by the so-called CER method on rats.[22] Against the background of alimentary instrumental responding, the defensive CR was established to a white noise of a given intensity, and then a noise of different intensity, which was not reinforced by shock, was introduced.

The results of these experiments are represented in Figure VII–13. It is seen that, other conditions being equal, the differentiation of the two stimuli is much easier when the absolute strength of the positive CS is greater than the absolute strength of the negative CS. In other words, the generalization of a positive CR from the weaker CS to the stronger CS is manifested more strongly than the generalization from the stronger CS to the weaker one.

These results are very instructive, since they show the asymmetry of the US–no-US differentiation in respect to the relative strength of the presented CSs. This asymmetry is due to the fact that, of two differentiated CSs, the positive one is associated with drive producing the increase of arousal, whereas the negative CS is associated with antidrive producing the decrease of arousal. In consequence, a stronger stimulus, producing *per se* a stronger arousal, is better fitted to play the role of a positive CS, whereas a weaker stimulus, producing a weaker arousal, is better fitted to play the role of a negative CS.

In another experiment performed by Zieliński,[23] the food instrumental responding occurred against the noise background of a certain intensity, whereas the fear CR was established to either the decrease or the increase of that noise. Thereafter the opposite changes of noise intensity were tested.

The obtained results were most significant (Figure VII-14). First, it was found that the decrease of intensity of noise is a much weaker fear CS than the identical increase of noise. This confirms the general thesis that the absolute intensity of the CS plays an essential role for the strength of the conditioned response. Second, what is more important in the present context is the fact that there is *no* generalization between the increase and the decrease of the intensity of noise. This result strikingly confirms and extends, on the behavioral level of research, the concept of a discreteness of on- and off-receptive units in

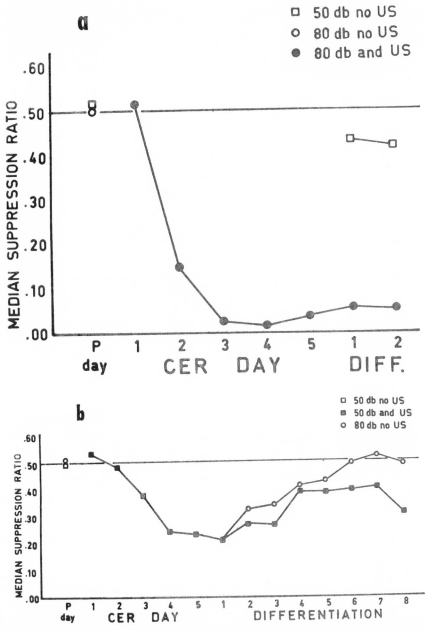

FIG. VII-13. THE ROLE OF INTENSITY OF THE CS IN GENERALIZATION OF DEFENSIVE
CRs IN CER PROCEDURE

a) The strong white noise is a positive CS; the weak one is a test stimulus.
b) The weak white noise is a positive CS; the strong one is a test stimulus.
Note the strong generalization of the CS in b and very weak generalization in a.
(K. Zieliński, in *Acta Biol. Exper.*, 25 [1965]: 317–35.)

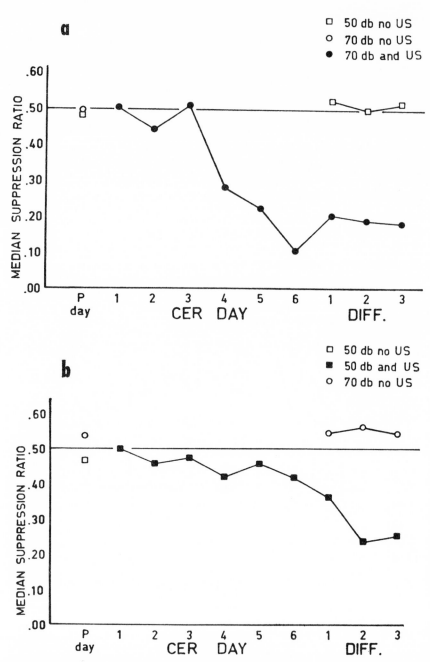

FIG. VII-14. LACK OF GENERALIZATION OF DEFENSIVE CRs TO THE REVERSE
DIRECTION OF AUDITORY STIMULI IN CER PROCEDURE

The background noise is 60 db. In *a* the noise of 70 db is a CS, and the noise
of 50 db is a test stimulus, in *b*, vice versa. Note the total lack of generalization
between the CS and the test stimulus.

(K. Zieliński, in *Acta Biol. Exper.*, 25 [1965]: 337–57.)

all analyzers, a concept inferred from electrophysiological studies (cf. Chapter II, Section 2). Moreover, it is shown that not only the onset and the termination of an external stimulus, but also the increase and decrease of a stable level of stimulation, are represented by different receptive (and perceptive) units. If we accept the fact that these two changes are treated by the nervous system as quite different events, it is clear that separate gnostic units are formed on their basis and therefore no differentiation process is needed to put them apart.

References to Chapter VII

1. J. Konorski. 1948. *Conditioned Reflexes and Neuron Organization*. Chap. 3. Cambridge: Cambridge University Press.
2. C. L. Hull. 1943. *Principles of Behavior: An Introduction to Behavior Theory*. New York: Appleton-Century.
3. I. P. Pavlov. 1927. *Conditioned Reflexes: An Investigation of the Physiological Activity of the cerebral cortex*. Translated and edited by G. V. Anrep. London: Oxford University Press.
4. J. Konorski. 1948 (see note 1 above), chaps. 2, 3, 9, and 10.
5. J. Konorski and G. Szwejkowska. 1950. Chronic extinction and restoration of conditioned reflexes. I. Extinction against the excitatory background. *Acta Biol. Exp. Vars.*, 15: 155–70.
6. ———. 1952a. Chronic extinction and restoration of conditioned reflexes. III. Defensive motor reflexes. *Ibid.*, 16: 91–94.
7. ———. 1952b. Chronic extinction and restoration of conditioned reflexes. IV. The dependence of the course of extinction and restoration of conditioned reflexes on the "history" of the conditioned stimulus. (The principle of the primacy of first training.) *Ibid.*, 16: 95–113.
8. Н. А. Костенецкая. 1949. Образование тормозных условных рефлексов на индиферентные раздражители. (Formation of inhibitory conditioned reflexes to indifferent stimuli.) *Trudy Fiziol. Lab. I. P. Pavlova*, 15: 124–37.
9. G. Szwejkowska and J. Konorski. 1959. The influence of the primary inhibitory stimulus upon the salivary effect of excitatory conditioned stimulus. *Acta Biol. Exp. Vars.*, 19: 161–74.
10. G. Szwejkowska. 1959. The transformation of differentiated inhibitory stimuli into positive conditioned stimuli. *Acta Biol. Exp. Vars.*, 19: 151–59.
11. For references see J. Konorski and G. Szwejkowska. 1952b (see note 7 above).
12. K. Jaworska, M. Kowalska, and S. Sołtysik. 1962. Studies on the aversive classical conditioning. 1. Acquisition and differentiation of motor and cardiac conditioned classical defensive reflexes in dog. *Acta Biol. Exp. Vars.*, 22 (No. 2): 23–34.
K. Jaworska and S. Sołtysik. 1962. Studies on the aversive classical conditioning. 3. Cardiac responses to conditioned and unconditioned defensive aversive stimuli. *Acta Biol. Exp. Vars.*, 22 (No. 3): 193–214.

13. H. Chorążyna. 1962. Some properties of conditioned inhibition. *Acta Biol. Exp. Vars.*, 22 (No. 1): 5–13.
14. J. Konorski and G. Szwejkowska. Unpublished experiments.
15. K. Jaworska, M. Kowalska, and S. Sołtysik. 1962 (see note 12 above).
16. I. P. Pavlov. 1927 (see note 3 above), chap. 9.
17. J. Konorski and G. Szwejkowska. 1956. Reciprocal transformations of heterogeneous conditioned reflexes. *Acta Biol. Exp. Vars.*, 17: 141–65.
18. J. Konorski and G. Szwejkowska. 1952*b* (see note 7 above).
19. J. Konorski. 1948 (see note 1 above), chap. 3.
20. *Ibid.*, chap. 9.
21. G. D. Ellison. 1964. Differential salivary conditioning to traces. *J. Comp. Physiol. Psychol.*, 57: 373–80.
22. K. Zieliński. 1965*a*. The influence of stimulus intensity on the efficacy of reinforcement in differentiation training. *Acta Biol. Exp. Vars.*, 25: 317–35.
23. ———. 1965*b*. The direction of change versus the absolute level of noise intensity as a cue in the CER situation. *Ibid.*, 25: 337–57.

CHAPTER VIII

INSTRUMENTAL CONDITIONED REFLEXES (TYPE II): EARLIER EXPERIMENTAL EVIDENCE AND CONCEPTS, 1928-39

1. Introductory remarks

If we make a most general survey of the acquired activity of both animals and man, we may come to the conclusion that this activity is built according to at least three principles. One principle, dealt with in great detail in the early chapters of this work (II and III), may be called the principle of integration of sensory input, or of the formation of perceptive units. This principle operates in its more primitive forms on the lower levels of the central afferent systems, but reaches its apogee in the gnostic fields of the cerebral cortex. The second principle, considered in Chapters IV–VII, is that of association, or of the formation of connections between various sets of perceptive units. The classical CR is a special instance of this principle. Finally, the third principle which will be dealt with in this and successive chapters is that of the ability of the organism to provide itself with new stimulus-objects and consequently new perceptions by performance of motor acts.

These three principles are presented in Figure VIII-1. As clearly seen in these diagrams, the difference between principle II and principle III is significant. In the former, the connection is established between the gnostic unit GU_1 activated by the relevant stimulus-object SO_1 and gnostic unit GU_2 activated by this very connection

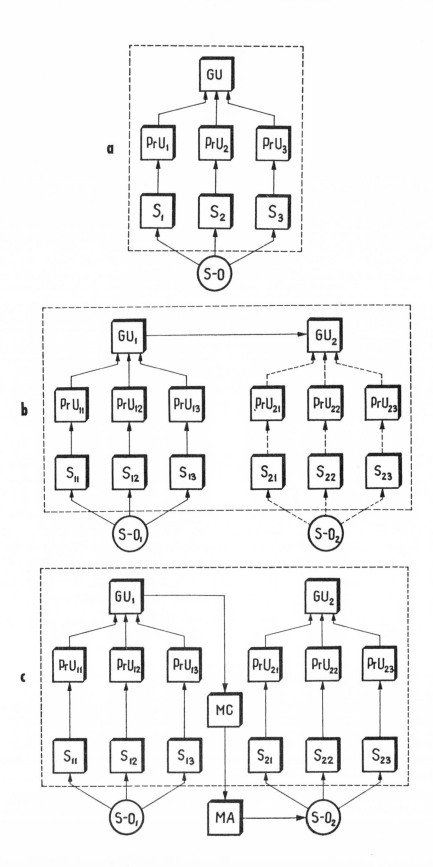

in the absence of the corresponding stimulus-object SO_2. In consequence, the activation of the unit GU_2 produces only the image and not the perception of this stimulus-object. On the other hand, according to principle III, the activation of the GU_2 is brought forth through the stimulus-object $S-O_2$ provided by the motor act MA, and therefore it takes a form of actual perception.

These three principles, although phenomenologically different are not necessarily irreducible to one another. As noted earlier (Chapter IV, Section 1), it is possible that the mode of operation of the second principle is the same as that of the first one and that it constitutes the extension of the first principle over the pluri-modality integration. Similarly, as shown in Chapter IV, Section 8, and will be further documented in later chapters, principle III may be considered as association between exteroceptive and kinesthetic gnostic units. Nonetheless it seems profitable to discuss each of these principles separately because they represent quite different classes of phenomena.

CRs occurring according to principle III—those in which a stimulus-object acquires the power to elicit a given motor act providing another stimulus-object or preventing it—constitute a new type of conditioning, originally called type II CR by Konorski and Miller,[1] and later called an instrumental CR by Hilgard and Marquis,[2] and an operant CR by Skinner.[3] Since the term instrumental CR is the one most frequently applied in the literature, we shall preferentially use this term as opposed to the classical CR, but we shall also resort to our original term CR type II as opposed to CR type I. This is because, as will be seen below, just as we need to distinguish between CR type I and CR type II, it is also indispensable to distinguish between CS type I and CS type II—that is, between those CSs which evoke classical and those which evoke instrumental conditioned responses. Since the term "instrumental CS" seems to be rather awkward, as possessing *contradictio in adjecto*, our original terminology may be profitable.

Fig. VIII-1. Diagram of Three Principles of Plasticity in Higher Nervous Functions

a) Principle I, integration of sensory input.
b) Principle II, intersensory association (including classical conditioning).
c) Principle III, instrumental conditioning.

S-O, stimulus-object; S_1, S_2, S_3, etc., its elements on the receptive surface; PrU_1, PrU_2, PrU_3, etc., receptive units in the projective area of the cortex; GU_1, GU_2, units representing the corresponding stimulus-objects in the gnostic area of the cortex; MC, motor center; MA, motor act.

Continuous arrows denote interneural connections (or causal bonds) active in the given moment; dashed arrows denote those interneural connections which are not active in the given moment.

We shall not enter now into the discussion of the problem of whether instrumental responses are represented only by motor acts, or whether they can be also recruited from autonomic reactions. This problem will be discussed later, when we shall deal with the mechanism of instrumental responding (Chapter XI, Section 6). Now it should be noted only that the main (or maybe exclusive) role of motor acts in type II conditioning seems to be comprehensible from the biological point of view. In fact, the essence of instrumental activity is *to change the relation of the organism to the external world*, either by changing its position in space (locomotor activity) or by influencing surrounding objects (manipulatory activity). It is clear that both these functions are accomplished by motor acts, whereas autonomic reactions play in them only an auxiliary role.

The history of the experimental work and theoretical concepts concerning instrumental conditioning has taken a rather peculiar course. On the one hand, since the time at which Miller and I embarked on the study of type II CRs, much experimental material has been gathered along this line and certain hypotheses to explain it have been developed by us and by our followers. On the other hand, the work on instrumental conditioning, or operant behavior, has quite independently and most extensively been carried out by American psychologists, and again innumerable facts have been found and many concepts proposed. Our own work, however, remained almost unknown to American authors, since our original papers appeared in Polish or Russian or in journals which were not widely circulated in America.

Our own work, in contradistinction to that performed in America, started under the influence of Pavlov's ideas and on the basis of experimental procedures used in his laboratories. When we realized that the mechanism of type II CRs cannot be reduced to that of Pavlovian CRs, we tried to set up, along the same lines as those followed by Pavlov, a model of the phenomena in which we were interested. Our aim was to interpret the mechanism of type II conditioning in much the same way as Pavlov did with respect to classical conditioning. In consequence, our studies, although conducted in the same general field as those carried out by American investigators, did not overlap with their research work; even now many facts which have been obtained by us are hardly known in American laboratories.

This being so, I think I am entitled to proceed in the following way. It seems that it would not be profitable to present here the history of the studies in instrumental conditioning developed in American psychology. First, I do not feel as competent in this matter as are those who know this development from their own immediate experience.

Second, such a survey is hardly needed, since there are excellent surveys of this kind and it would not be reasonable to add another one which would surely be inferior to those already available. On the other hand, it seems useful to present here the history of our own work and ideas, since they are hardly known to the American readers and since they constitute a basis on which our present concepts are developed. This will be the subject of the present chapter.

2. First experiments on type II conditioned reflexes

The starting point of our work was the realization that the paradigm of the Pavlovian CR does not suffice to account for all the acquired forms of animal behavior. In particular, it was easy to demonstrate that the vast and important class of phenomena called "habits" in American psychology does not fit into the framework of the Pavlovian CR. For one thing, whereas the paradigm of the classical CR is always the same whatever the reinforcing stimulus is, the motor acts involved in habit formation are "stamped in" or "stamped out," depending on whether the reinforcing stimulus is attractive or aversive. For another, whereas the Pavlovian conditioned response by definition closely imitates the unconditioned response to the reinforcing stimulus, the motor acts taking part in habits are, as a rule, quite different. And so our aim was to build an experimental CR model which would account for this new (in the Pavlovian field of research) aspect of behavior in the same way as the classical CR accounts for S-S association.

The solution to this problem was as follows. If an external stimulus S_E (either a continuous stimulus provided by the experimental situation or a sporadic stimulus used in the Pavlovian procedure) is occasionally accompanied by a movement M produced in any way and then followed by an attractive US (US^+) such as food, whereas the stimulus S_E without the movement M is not accompanied by the US, after a number of such trials S_E will begin to elicit the movement M. If S_E accompanied by M is followed by an aversive US (US^-), whereas S_E alone is not, then after a number of trials the performance of the movement M will be suppressed and thus the action of US^- avoided.

These two experiments may be represented in the paradigms shown in Table VIII-1.

The new CR consisting of eliciting the movement M by S_E in the first paradigm ($S_E \rightarrow M$) and suppressing it in the second paradigm ($S_E \rightarrow \sim M$) has been called type II CR, and the stimulus S_E acquiring this property type II CS.

It was important to design the appropriate CR experiments which would exemplify these paradigms.[4]

TABLE VIII-1

	Trial 1	Trial 2	Trial 3	Trial 4 · · · ·	Trial n
	S_E	S_E	S_E	S_E	S_E
1	S_x ↳M	S_x ↳M	—	S_x ↳M	↓ M
	US+	US+	—	US+	US+
	S_E	S_E	S_E	S_E	S_E
2	S_x ↳M	S_x ↳M	—	S_x ↳M	↓ ~M
	US−	US−	—	US−	—

In these paradigms S_E denotes an external stimulus (continuous or sporadic); S_x, an original factor provoking the movement M; ∼ M, suppression of the movement; US+ and US− attractive and aversive US respectively; →, elicits. Each column represents the sequence of events within each trial.

Experiment I. A dog is on the stand in a standard Pavlovian setup, and a band with electrodes is attached to his left hindleg. Every few minutes a tone is presented, and in a few seconds during its operation a light electric shock is administered to this leg; when the animal lifts his leg, food is presented. Now and again the tone is presented without the shock; since the animal does not raise the leg, food is not given. After a number of trials the animal starts to lift his hindleg "spontaneously" without the shock. He does so both in the presence of the tone and in the intervals. The movements in the presence of the tone are followed by presentations of food, whereas the movements during the intervals are not. Soon the intertrial movements disappear, and those in response to the tone remain.

Experiment II. Using the same dog, we attach a band to the left foreleg connected by a string and a series of pulleys to a point near the experimenter, so that by pulling the string he is able to raise the dog's leg (passive flexion). Every few minutes a lamp is lit in front of the dog, the passive flexion of the foreleg is accomplished, and food is presented. In some trials the light is not accompanied by passive flexion, and then food is not presented. After a few experimental sessions the animal starts to perform the movement of the left foreleg actively, both in the presence of the light and during the intervals. Since only the former movements are followed by food, the intertrial movements disappear and those to the light are established (Figure VIII-2).

Experiment III. Another dog placed in a similar setup is compelled by means of passive movements to lift his right foreleg and put it on a small board before him. Each such movement is followed by presentation of food. After a number of such trials the dog starts to perform this movement actively and soon does so with maximal frequency regulated by the amount of food offered to him. During the act of eating the movements are never performed (Figure VIII-3).

Experiment IV. The dog used in the first two experiments is placed in an empty compartment where he barks from time to time. Every few minutes the beating of a metronome is heard, and if the animal barks in its presence a piece of meat is dropped from the food container. Soon the animal starts to bark continuously in the experimental

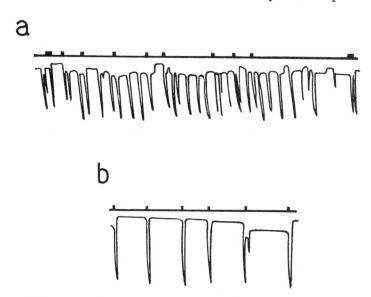

Fig. VIII-2. One of the First Records of Type II CRs

Upper graph: CS (lamp).
Lower graph: record of the movements of the left foreleg.
a) The movement is performed in the presence of the CS and in intervals.
b) The movement is performed only in response to the CS.
(Konorski and Miller, 1933 [see Ref. No. 4], p. 68.)

situation; but since barking during the intervals is not reinforced by food, the vocal reactions become limited only to the presence of the metronome.

In these experiments the trained movements were provoked in various ways. In Experiment IV the vocal reaction was originally elicited by some uncontrolled emotional factors (the animal being left alone in the empty compartment); in Experiment I it was produced reflexly by a weak noxious stimulus (shock → flexion of the leg); in Experiments II and III the source of the movement was passive flexion. Whatever the source of the movement, in each case it was transformed into an instrumental movement by food reinforcement according to paradigm I. In those cases in which the instrumental CR was established to a sporadic stimulus, it passed through the stage when it was elicited by the experimental situation and only afterward became limited to the presence of the CS. This point will be discussed later.

When the alimentary type II CR is established, its further fate depends fully on food reinforcement. This is illustrated by the following experiments.

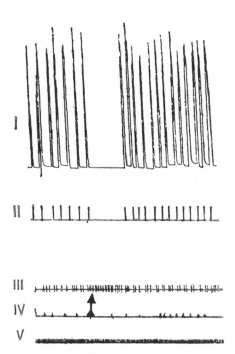

Fig. VIII-3. Alimentary Type II CR Established to the Experimental Situation

From top to bottom: movements of the foreleg, pressing the lever, salivation. Arrow denotes the increased portion of food.
(Konorski and Miller, 1933, p. 114.)

Experiment V. A dog was trained by the method of passive flexion to lift his hindleg in the experimental situation, each movement being reinforced by food. When the type II CR was firmly established, food was no longer presented. In the first stage the movements appeared at maximal frequency one after another, owing to the fact that their appearance was not interrupted by feeding. In the next stage, however, the bursts of leg flexion became interspersed by periods of no movement, which became more and more protracted, and eventually the animal stopped performing the movements altogether (Figure VIII-4).

Experiment VI (continuation of Experiment I). When the type II CR was firmly established to the tone (S_{E1}), another tone of higher frequency (S_{E2}) was introduced. Owing to generalization, at the very beginning it evoked the same response of lifting the left hindleg. However, its repeated presentation without food reinforcement led to the disappearance of the movement originally elicited by it, whereas the

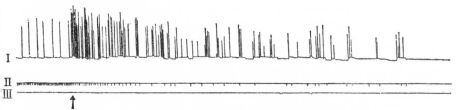

Fig. VIII-4. Extinction of the Type II CR to Experimental Situation

I, lifting of the hindleg; II, salivation in drops; III, arrow, the beginning of extinction.

Note that at the beginning of extinction the movements of the leg are very frequent and their amplitude is increased.

(Konorski and Miller, 1936 [see Ref. No. 5], p. 135.)

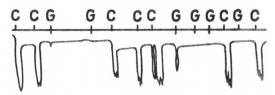

Fig. VIII-5. One of the First Records of Differentiation of Type II CR

C, positive tone; G, negative tone.
Below, lifting of the left hindleg.
(Konorski and Miller, 1933, p. 77.)

original tone continued to produce the motor response (Figure VIII-5).

Another series of experiments was performed by us later in Pavlov's laboratory in order to clarify the following point. According to Pavlov's supposition, the type II CR was established owing to the mere *association* between the external stimulus and the movement as proprioceptive stimulus, food playing only some vaguely determined facilitatory role. In consequence, Pavlov claimed that the motor CR would also be established if the S_E and M were paired in *every* trial and reinforced by food. To test this assumption the procedure suggested by Pavlov was applied in two dogs.[5]

Experiment VII. In a dog that had been previously trained in classical food CRs, a new stimulus—bubbling of water—was introduced. After a stimulus duration of ten seconds a passive flexion of the right foreleg (accomplished by pulling the string running through a system of pulleys to the paw) was added for five seconds and then food was given.

The results of the experiment were as follows. (1) After a few trials bubbling became a type I CS, as judged by a copious salivary response; (2) active movements appeared during the intertrial intervals in great quantity, but since these were not reinforced by food they soon disappeared; (3) in the period when the dog repeatedly lifted his right foreleg during the intervals, bubbling immediately suppressed them. Only when in the later training the trials were occasionally given in which bubbling alone without passive flexion and without food was presented, the animal began actively to perform the movement immediately after the CS and then in its presence.

Experiment VIII. Since it was suspected that bubbling as a strong stimulus "masked" the passive flexion, in another dog a very soft noise was used as the CS. The course of the sessions was the same as in Experiment VII. The soft noise produced an insignificant salivation, which increased only when the passive flexion of the leg was added. Very soon the active movements appeared in the intervals; they were not performed, however, in the presence of the noise until that stimulus was occasionally presented alone.

We proceed now to a description of our original experiments illustrating the second paradigm of type II CRs in which US⁻ was used.

Experiment IX. The dog used in Experiments I, II, and IV was used again for this experiment. A small tube was attached to his ear, enabling the experimenter to blow a short air puff into it. The right hindleg was passively flexed by dropping a weight attached to a string connected to the paw through a pulley. Each passive flexion was followed by an air puff into the ear. At the beginning of these experiments a weight of 0.5 kg. was sufficient to raise the animal's leg. Gradually this weight became ineffective and had to be replaced by heavier ones. Eventually even a weight of three kg. could not produce passive flexion. The leg became maximally extended and stiff throughout the experimental session; whereas the animal was fidgeting with the other three legs, this one was immobile as if it were fixed to the floor of the stand.

Experiment X. The same dog received small pieces of meat from the food container every few seconds. From time to time a buzzer was presented. When the animal seized food, which was continually presented to him, during its operation, he received a water puff on the mouth from an atomizer. After a few sessions the dog learned to abstain from taking food during the action of the buzzer. Usually he turned away from the bowl and remained in this position some time after the cessation of the stimulus.

Although the procedure in both these last experiments is different, their results exactly illustrate our second paradigm of type II CRs. In Experiment IX the S_E was a continuous stimulus (experimental situation), whereas in Experiment X it was a sporadic stimulus (buzzer). In the first experiment the movement was originally produced by passive flexion of the leg, and the effect of the type II CR consisted in the suppression of this movement through an active extension of the leg. In the second experiment the movement was provoked by the presentation of food and consisted in its seizure, whereas the effect of type II conditioning was the movement of turning away from the bowl.

Both these experiments show that the suppression of the provoked movement by an aversive US is accompanied by the antagonistic movement. This important fact will be discussed in detail later.

3. Original concept concerning type II conditioning

The two paradigms of type II CRs proposed by us and the first experiments confirming these paradigms enabled us to develop a theory concerning this type of conditioning and establish its interrelation with type I conditioning.[6]

It was clear that the performance of a movement M, provoked in any way, necessarily leads to the generation of a proprioceptive compound stimulus (S_{Pr}) sending messages to the brain about its occurrence and character. In consequence, when S_E combined with S_{Pr} is reinforced either by food or by a noxious stimulus, a classical CR (type I), either alimentary or defensive, has to be formed to this compound.

According to the rules of the formation of type II CRs, the stimulus S_E accompanied by M is reinforced, whereas S_E alone and the movement M alone are not reinforced. In other words, on the level of classical conditioning, a differentiation is established between the compound $S_E + S_{Pr}$, which is reinforced, and its components S_E and S_{Pr}, which are not reinforced when presented alone. In consequence, S_E and S_{Pr} acting alone become inhibitory (negative) CSs, whereas the compound composed of both of them is an excitatory (positive) CS. Experiments of some of Pavlov's co-workers[7] have, indeed, shown that such differentiation is possible with respect to exteroceptive stimuli.

Thus our two paradigms concerning type II CRs may now be reformulated as in the diagrams shown in Table VIII-2.

According to these paradigms, a type II CR is formed when a US is made contingent on a compound type I CS consisting of an exteroceptive stimulus and the proprioceptive stimulus generated by a certain movement. If the US signaled by this compound CS is attractive, the exteroceptive stimulus elicits the movement generating the proprioceptive stimulus and thus completes the compound CS. If, however, the US signaled by the compound CS is aversive, then the exteroceptive stimulus inhibits the movement generating the proprioceptive stimulus and thus prevents the compound CS from being completed and the US^- from being administered.

TABLE VIII-2

	Trial 1	Trial 2	Trial 3	Trial 4 · · · ·	Trial n
3	S_E $M-S_{Pr}$ $US^+\rightarrow UR$	S_E — —	— $M-S_{Pr}$ —	S_E $M-S_{Pr}$ $US^+\rightarrow UR$	S_E $M-S_{Pr}$ US^+
4	S_E $M-S_{Pr}$ $US^-\rightarrow UR$	S_E — —	— $M-S_{Pr}$ —	S_E $M-S_{Pr}$ $US^-\rightarrow UR$	S_E $\sim M$ —

S_E denotes exteroceptive stimulus; S_{Pr}, proprioceptive stimulus generated by movement M; —, generation; US^+ and US^-, attractive and aversive USs; UR, unconditioned response (or type I conditioned response); $\sim M$, movement M suppressed; →, elicitation. The type I compound CS is enclosed in a rectangle.

It will be seen that this concept fits perfectly the facts so far reported.

When the movement M is simply provoked in a given situation (as in Experiments III and IX) and reinforced by US^+ (Experiment III) or US^- (Experiment IX), S_{Pr} generated by this movement in compound with S_E provided by this situation becomes a type I CS signaling the US. When the US is attractive, the animal provides himself S_{Pr} and in consequence the US; when it is aversive, he prevents the occurrence of S_{Pr} and thus avoids the US.

When the compound $S_E + S_{Pr}$ is reinforced by US^+ (as in Experiments VII and VIII), and S_E alone is not given, then each of these stimuli becomes a type I CS on its own account (provided that they are not mutually masked): the stimulus S_E elicits salivation, and the movement M generating S_{Pr} appears in the experimental situation.

However, S_E does not elicit M, because the compound $S_E + S_{Pr}$ is not differentiated from its components, as was required in paradigm 3. When, however, $S_E + S_{Pr}$ is reinforced but S_E is not, then S_E does evoke M; but since S_{Pr} was not applied separately, as required by our paradigm, the movement M is actively performed in the intertrial intervals until the type I CR to the proprioceptive stimulus alone is extinguished. This explains the disappearance of the intertrial movements when the type II CR is already established.

Another fact easily explainable within the framework of our concept is that of extinction of type II CR when M is no longer reinforced by food (Experiment V). When the learned movement fails to be reinforced, first it appears very frequently (since it is not inhibited by the act of eating), being accompanied by copious salivation. Each performance of the movement means, however, another presentation of S_{Pr} without reinforcement. This necessarily leads to the extinction of the type I CR to the S_{Pr}, and this extinction causes the abolition of the movements generating this stimulus. Therefore, the more movements performed without reinforcement, the more readily they are extinguished.

Again, we know from Pavlovian experimental practice that when the CS subjected to extinction is not presented for a certain time, the CR to it tends to restore spontaneously. The same phenomenon is observed in extinction of the type II CR. The type I CR to the S_{Pr} being extinguished, the movement M fails to appear. However, its disappearance for some time means the non-presentation of the S_{Pr}; this leads to its spontaneous restoration and consequently to the reappearance of the movement as a visible sign of this restoration. However, the burst of unreinforced movements appearing after an interval shares the fate of its predecessors and is abolished even more rapidly and for a longer period, as extinction of the type I CR to the S_{Pr} becomes deeper. Of course, the reinforcement of the S_{Pr} leads to the restoration of the type II CR.

One can regard the extinction, or differentiation, of type II CR to a sporadic stimulus (Experiment VI) in exactly the same way. The non-reinforcement of the movement M elicited by the S_{E2} means the non-reinforcement of the compound $S_{E2} + S_{Pr}$ and the extinction of the type I CR to this compound. Consequently, stimulus S_{Pr} no longer forms with S_{E2} a compound type I CS, and this leads to the disappearance of the movement M in the presence of S_{E2}. Of course, the compound stimulus composed of S_{E1} and the same S_{Pr} may remain fully active, and therefore the movement M will be elicited by this stimulus.

To end these considerations, attention should be given to one more conclusion emerging from our concept which, as we shall later see, will be crucial for its acceptability. This is that utilization of a passive displacement of the limb has to be considered as *the* proper method for type II conditioning, because in this way the proprioceptive stimulus is directly provided. On the other hand, if the reflex motor act (for example, elicited by a shock) is used as a source of instrumental response, the proprioceptive stimulus is, so to speak, a by-product of the movement produced actively. We shall see in the next chapter that this viewpoint is completely wrong, since what chiefly matters in establishing a type II CR is just the active performance of the movement and not the passive displacement of the limb.

Taking the passive movement as the main source of an instrumental response, we realized that from the technical point of view the proprioceptive stimulus provided by this method is always contaminated by a cutaneous stimulus S_C produced by pressure on the limb exerted in the course of changing its position. As a result, the passive flexion produces a compound stimulus $S_C + S_{Pr}$. When this compound is reinforced by food, it may happen that stimulus S_C being stronger than S_{Pr} will mask it, and in consequence the type I CR will be established only to the cutaneous but not to the proprioceptive stimulus. In this case the instrumental CR will fail to be established in spite of the repeated reinforcement of the passive movement, because the animal will wait for the cutaneous pressure rather than actively lift his leg.

Therefore, when describing the method of passive movements in type II conditioning, we have always emphasized that in order to have a successful training the cutaneous component of the compound should be extinguished. According to our experience, the best way of achieving this aim is either to pull the leg upward with moderate strength throughout the operation of the S_E and wait until the dog raises the leg, or to tug this leg in the moments of fidgeting inducing the full-sized flexion. We called such movements "half-active movements" and considered their provocation as the best intermediary stage in establishing the type II CR.

To sum up this discussion concerning our first concept of type II conditioning, it may be seen how closely this phenomenon is related to type I conditioning. It may be said that, according to our view at that time, the type II CR arose always when the type I CS was a proprioceptive stimulus, and as such it could be either provided by the animal itself when the reinforcement was attractive or prevented when the reinforcement was aversive. This was considered a biological role of type II conditioning and a source of acquired adaptability of organisms to their environment. In this respect the type II CR was considered a physiological model of voluntary motor acts, not provided by the Pavlovian CRs. According to our concept, the essence of the voluntary or purposeful character of the motor acts lay precisely in their proprioceptive feedback, as the process should be called now. We thought that the inability of the organism to manipulate autonomic responses in an instrumental way depended on the fact that as a rule these responses were lacking this feedback and in consequence their performance was not reported to the brain and could not become the type I CS.

4. Interrelations between salivary and motor responses in type II conditioning

The fact that our studies on type II conditioning were incorporated into the Pavlovian type of experimentation on alimentary CRs provided the unique opportunity of studying in parallel the salivary effect of the type I CR and the motor effect of the type II CR so that we could closely examine their interrelations.

According to our concept presented in the previous section, close parallelism between the two responses should be expected, on the assumption that performance of the instrumental response is the sign of the alimentary classical CR having been established to the proprioceptive stimulus. This parallelism should be demonstrable in the following circumstances.

(1) When the passive flexion of the leg is reinforced by food, as soon as the salivary response appears—that is, the S_{Pr} becomes a type I CS—the animal should actively perform the same movement.

(2) Conversely, when the type II CR becomes extinguished by non-reinforcement, salivation should disappear at the same time.

(3) When the type II CR is established to a sporadic stimulus, the stimulus itself should not produce the salivary response, but this response should immediately follow the performance of the movement.

(4) In the differentiation of the type II CR to two similar stimuli by non-reinforcement of one of them, the decrease of motor and salivary response should take a parallel course.

Experiments testing the above relations were performed, and gave the following results.[8]

(1) *Experiment XI.* A band attached to the right hindleg of a dog was connected by a string and a system of pulleys with the experimenter's desk in the pre-chamber. Every few minutes three successive passive flexions of that leg (lasting a total of ten seconds) were executed, and then the food was immediately presented by putting into position the bowl with the meat and biscuit powder. Salivation and movements of the right hindleg were recorded. The results of this experiment are presented in Table VIII-3. It is seen that during the first four days, in which twenty-eight trials were given, the salivary CR to the passive flexion was either zero or very negligible and the active

movements of the leg did not appear. On the fifth day the salivary response to the triple passive flexion became regular, and on the same day the animal started to perform actively the movement of the leg. Since each active movement was reinforced by food, there was almost a continuous flow of salivation, and no further observation of the relation between the two responses was possible.

(2) *Experiment XII.* Even more conclusive are the experiments in which the instrumental response established to the experimental situation is extinguished by non-reinforcement, because here the conditioned salivation is not masked by the unconditioned one and may be closely followed. As seen in Figure VIII-4, the decrease of salivation

TABLE VIII-3

THE RELATION BETWEEN THE SALIVARY AND INSTRUMENTAL RESPONSE
DURING THE FORMATION OF TYPE II CR

Session	Number of Trials: Triple Passive Flexion+Food	Sum of Cond. Salivary Responses in All Trials in Scale Units	Maximal Salivary CR in Given Session	Comments
1	2	3	4	5
1..........	5	5	5	
2..........	8	0	0	
3..........	8	0	0	
4..........	7	14	5	
5..........	4	33	10	After four trials the active movements began to appear

SOURCE: Konorski and Miller, 1936 (see Ref. No. 5), p. 130.

runs nearly *pari passu* with the decrease of the motor response and both responses disappear nearly at the same time.

(3) In many experiments the relations between the salivary and motor responses were observed within the same trial. Unfortunately, no definite conclusions could be reached on the basis of our previous material as to the sequence of both responses. There were trials in which the salivary response closely followed the motor response; in other trials, however, salivation clearly preceded the performance of the trained movement. In some cases, especially in the course of extinction of the type II CR to a sporadic CS, this CS elicited only the motor act without salivation (see below).

(4) *Experiment XIII.* In order to follow closely the relation between salivary and motor response, differentiation of two similar

stimuli was carried out. Bubbling of water was a type II CS eliciting flexion of the right foreleg. It was presented six to eight times in each session. A bubbling of different pitch from another apparatus was introduced and presented without reinforcement twice daily among positive trials. The relation between salivary and motor response to both the positive and negative CSs was closely followed. As seen in Figure VIII-6, there was again a general parallelism between the two responses, but certainly it was not absolute. In some negative trials the motor response failed to appear, but salivation was still present; in others, the animal performed the trained movement but did not salivate.

To sum up, the conclusion may be reached that the parallelism between the type II conditioned response (motor act) and the type I conditioned response (salivation) was not as close as it should have been according to the predictions of the theory, and the lack of full coincidence in particular cases could not be satisfactorily explained. This problem will be reopened in Chapter IX.

5. Interrelations between type I and type II conditioned reflexes

It has been stated in a previous section that the type II CS cannot be a fully active type I CS, but it must be partly inhibitory. In this connection the problem was bound to arise as to what would be the effect of positive and negative type I CSs upon instrumental responses established after the type I CR training had been carried out. In one type of experiment the instrumental response was formed to the experimental situation, as was the case in Experiment III; in another type the instrumental response was formed to a sporadic stimulus, as was the case in Experiment II.

Following are examples for each of these types.

Experiment XIV. A classical alimentary CR was established in a dog to a bell and a metronome set at 120 beats per minute (M_{120}). A metronome set at 60 beats per minute (M_{60}) was differentiated by not reinforcing it by food. The isolated action of the CSs was always fifteen seconds. The bell and M_{120} elicited copious salivation, whereas to M_{60} salivation was negligible.

Then the experiments with classical CRs were discontinued, and the dog was trained to lift his hindleg in the experimental situation, each movement being reinforced by food. When the instrumental CR was quite regular and the animal performed the trained movement immediately after consuming the foregoing portion of food, the following tests were performed. For a few seconds food was not presented, and consequently the dog performed the trained movement with maxi-

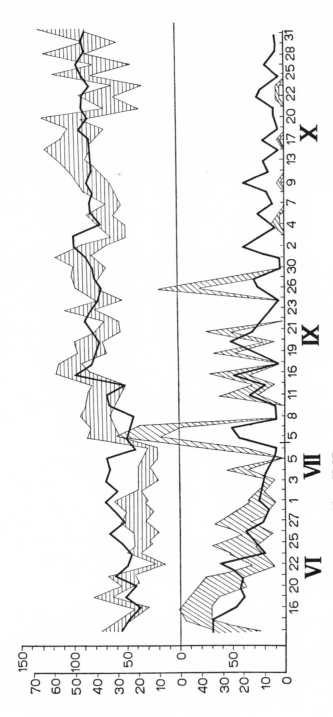

Fig. VIII-6. Differentiation of Type II CR

Upper graph: salivary and motor response to CS+.
Lower graph: salivary and motor response to CS−.
Abscissae: dates of sessions (break of experiments from July 5 to September 5). Ordinates: left scale, intensity of movements; right scale, salivation in arbitrary units.

Continuous lines, course of salivary responses to CS+ and CS−. The lower margin of each strip denotes the duration of motor response in seconds; the width of the strip denotes the amplitude of motor response in 0.5 cm. Each point denotes the average of responses for the given day.

Note that the responses to CS− gradually diminish, the salivary and motor responses taking an approximately parallel course.

mal frequency. Then either a positive type I CS (bell or M_{120}) or the inhibitory one (M_{60}) was presented. Each acted for fifteen seconds.

It was found that in response to the positive CS the dog immediately stopped performing the trained movement, looked at the feeder and salivated copiously. On the contrary, in response to the differentiated stimulus, salivation was much reduced but the movements of the leg continued to appear with maximal frequency (Figure VIII-7).

Experiment XV. A classical CR was established in a dog to a metronome (M_{100}), to a lamp, and to a rhythmic tactile stimulus on the

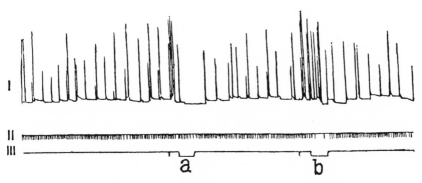

FIG. VIII-7. THE EFFECT OF TYPE I CS$^+$ AND CS$^-$ ON TYPE II CR ESTABLISHED IN THE EXPERIMENTAL SITUATION

I, movements of the hindleg; II, salivation; III, CS$^+$ (a) and CS$^-$ (b).

The animal repeatedly lifts his right hindleg, each movement being reinforced by food. Then (mark in line III) food is not presented for a few seconds and thereafter CS$^+$ (bell) is presented and lasts for 15 seconds. The dog momentarily stops performing the movement, waits for food, salivates copiously. The food is presented, CS$^+$ is terminated, and the type II responses are restored. Then again food is not given for a few seconds, and CS$^-$ (M_{60}) is presented. The movements are not stopped, but the salivation is much reduced.

(Konorski and Miller, 1936, p. 141.)

shoulder (TS$^+$). A tactile stimulus applied to the hip (TS$^-$) was differentiated by non-reinforcement. The CS-US interval was fifteen seconds, and the duration of the TS$^-$ was thirty seconds. Then the experiments with the classical CRs were discontinued, and an instrumental CR was established consisting of raising the right foreleg in response to bubbling (B). The reflex became regular, and its latency was a few seconds. Immediately after the performance of the movement food was presented.

Thereafter, in the same experimental sessions, type I CSs both positive (M_{160}, lamp, and TS$^+$) and negative (TS$^-$) were presented among the type II CSs (B). The CS-US interval for type I CSs was, as before, fifteen seconds; for type II CSs it was shorter, depending on the latency of the motor response.

The results of these experiments were quite clear (Table VIII-4). To the positive type I CSs the animal *never* performed the trained movement; he stood immobile looking at the food-tray throughout the CS-US interval and salivated copiously. On the contrary, in response to the negative type I CS, he performed many trained movements and the salivary response was sometimes disinhibited.

TABLE VIII-4

THE EFFECTS OF TYPE I CS+ AND CS- ON
TYPE II CONDITIONED RESPONSE

Session	Type I CS	Isolated Action of CS (in Secs.)	Conditioned Salivary Response	Instrumental Responses in Secs. of Action of CS	Reinforcement
1	2	3	4	5	6
1	$M_{100}+$	15	60	....	food
2	$M_{100}+$	15	55	....	food
	$M_{100}+$	15	45	....	food
	$M_{100}+$	15	50	....	food
3	$M_{100}+$	15	45	....	food
	$M_{100}+$	15	50	....	food
	TS+	15	55	....	food
	TS-	30	5	2, 6, 10, 20, 29	no food
4	TS+	15	50	....	food
	TS-	30	40+5	2-20 (6 times)	no food
5	TS+	15	30	....	food
6	TS+	15	45	....	food
	Lamp+	15	20	....	food
	TS-	30	15+10	7, 12	no food

SOURCE: Konorski and Miller, 1936, p. 168.

We have since performed many experiments in which both type I and type II CRs (the latter being established after the former ones) were given in the same sessions, and almost never did the animals perform the trained movement in response to the type I CS. This is even more remarkable if we take into account that in the presence of the type II CS the dog obtained food immediately after performing the trained movement, whereas in the presence of the type I CS he had to wait for food for at least fifteen seconds.

The situation, however, changes radically when the type I CS is not reinforced by food. This is illustrated by the following experiment.

Experiment XVI. In the dog described in Experiment XV the type I CS, M_{100}, was repeatedly presented without reinforcement (acute extinction). The animal started immediately to perform the trained movement in response to this stimulus, and did so in a number of consecutive trials (Figure VIII-8).

It was also observed that in the early period of the type II CR training the animals displayed a particular tendency to perform the learned movement immediately after the termination of the act of eating.

To sum up, we may conclude that whereas the fully active type I CS not only does not exhibit any tendency to provoke the type II conditioned response but exerts an inhibitory effect on its performance, the non-reinforced CS in the early period of extinction training, or the termination of the act of eating, has, on the contrary, the power to evoke this response.

These results seem to explain satisfactorily the fact brought forth in Experiments VII and VIII that simple pairing of the S_E with movement M reinforced by food fails to lead to the establishment of the instrumental CR to this stimulus. Since S_E is regularly reinforced by food, it becomes an active type I CS and as such it inhibits the type II CR which has in the meantime been established to the experimental situation owing to the reinforcement of the passive movements. On the other hand, if the CS is occasionally not reinforced, it becomes partly negative, or rather ambiguous, and this property allows it to elicit the type II conditioned response.

The problem arises as to what is the mechanism of this particular reflexogenic power of partly inhibitory alimentary CSs in respect to type II conditioned responses. We have given much attention to this problem in our earlier publications,[10] and we present here our considerations concerning this matter.

There is ample evidence collected by the Pavlov school to show that inhibitory (negative) CSs in their early stages of training have a number of peculiar properties which disappear when their inhibitory character is firmly established. First, in the presence of such a CS the animal is not calm and resigned, as he is in later stages of inhibitory training, but, on the contrary, he is alert and agitated. Second, such a stimulus is easily disinhibited by extra stimuli, whereas the well-established inhibitory CS is not. Third, as shown in numerous experiments at the Pavlov laboratories, the positive CS presented immediately after the inhibitory CS elicits an increased conditioned response, a phenomenon which was called positive induction. In this respect the experiments by Kalmykov are particularly instructive.[11]

Taking these facts into account, we came to the conclusion that the inhibitory CS in its early stage of development produces a state which

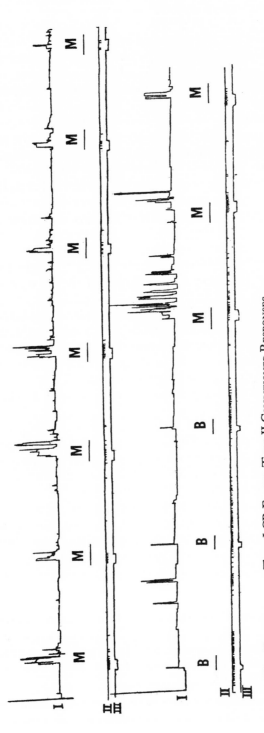

Fig. VIII-8. Extinction of Type I CR Elicits Type II Conditioned Responses

From top to bottom: I, movements of the right foreleg; II, salivation; III, CSs.

The session begins on the lower record. Three times type II CS (B) is given, the dog performs the trained movement (not high), and food is presented. Then type I CS (M) is repeatedly presented without food reinforcement. In the first extinction trial, the termination of the CS evokes long-lasting, intense type II conditioned response accompanied by copious salivation. With repetition of the CS both motor and salivary responses gradually diminish. (Konorski and Miller, 1936, p. 38.)

differs from that produced both by the positive CS and by the firmly established inhibitory CS. Whereas the positive CS produces a pure alimentary response resembling that elicited by the US itself, and the well-established inhibitory CS produces the inhibitory response, the early inhibitory CS gives rise to a conflict between the two, resulting in an entirely new state.

This state was assumed to be the "increased excitability of the alimentary center," identical with what would now be called the "increased hunger drive." We assumed that this state in turn caused a rise of excitability of the higher *motor* centers, activating in particular those centers which were in the given situation on the verge of being excited. These were precisely the centers of movements taking part in type II conditioning.

6. Two other varieties of type II conditioned reflexes

Our general concept concerning the mechanism of type II CRs discussed in the previous sections led to another important development of our experimental work concerning this type of conditioning.

In all our previous experiments (cf. paradigms 3 and 4) the compound of S_E and S_{Pr} was reinforced by the US, whereas the stimulus S_E alone was not. This led to the occurrence or suppression of the movement M generating S_{Pr} in the presence of S_E, depending on the attractive or aversive character of the US.

Now it can be observed that experiments of this type can be arranged in a reverse way; this occurs when the stimulus S_E presented alone is followed by the US, whereas this stimulus accompanied by the movement (and thus by S_{Pr}) is not. In other words, the proprioceptive stimulus does not signal the presentation of the US but, on the contrary, signals its absence.

The procedure, according to which a CS presented alone is reinforced by the US, whereas the CS accompanied by another stimulus is not, is well known in classical conditioning and many experiments have been performed along this line.[12] The suppression of the type I CR to the CS when accompanied by this additional stimulus has been called "conditioned inhibition" in a narrower sense of the word, and the stimulus canceling the positive meaning of the CS was referred to as "conditioned inhibitor." The only slight difference between the schedule proposed above and that regularly used in classical conditioning is that in the latter the conditioned inhibitor is always used either before or simultaneously with the CS whereas in ours it slightly succeeds the onset of the CS.

According to our rules concerning the formation of type II CRs, it should be expected that if the proprioceptive stimulus prevents the presentation of an attractive US, the animal will suppress the movement generating this stimulus, whereas if that stimulus prevents the presentation of an aversive US, the animal will on the contrary perform the corresponding movement and thus avoid the noxious stimulus. The paradigms illustrating these cases are presented in Table VIII-5.

TABLE VIII-5

	Trial 1	Trial 2	Trial 3 · · · ·	Trial n
5	S_E	$\boxed{\begin{array}{l}S_E\\M\!-\!S_{Pr}\end{array}}$	S_E	$\sim M \nearrow S_E$
	—		—	
	US+	—	US+	US+
6	S_E	$\boxed{\begin{array}{l}S_E\\M\!-\!S_{Pr}\end{array}}$	S_E	$M \nearrow \boxed{\begin{array}{l}S_E\\S_{Pr}\end{array}}$
	—		—	
	US−	—	US−	—

Denotations are the same as in the preceding paradigms.

Experiments were performed according to these paradigms, and following are their typical examples.[13]

A. EXPERIMENTS FOLLOWING PARADIGM 5

Experiment XVII. In a usual experimental set-up the classical alimentary CR was established to a metronome (M_{100}). The CS-US interval was fifteen seconds. Then in some trials the metronome was accompanied by passive flexion of the left foreleg, and in that case food was not presented. The unreinforced trials ran as follows. After five seconds of the operation of the M_{100} the passive flexion of the left foreleg was carried through by pulling a string attached to the paw by means of a system of pulleys; after five seconds pulling was discontinued, and then after another five seconds the metronome was discontinued. Since the string was connected with a dynamometer, the resistance of the animal to passive flexion could be measured.

In the first negative trials the passive flexion of the leg occurred with no resistance at all, since the animal was already accustomed to such procedures. Accordingly the strength of pulling amounted only to 0.5 kg. Then the strength of pulling was predetermined for each session; if the animal did not raise his leg at this strength, the food was presented; if he yielded, the food was not offered. It appeared that gradually the strength of pulling required to produce flexion of the leg had to be increased; eventually the maximal strength applied, amounting to 3 kg, was not enough to raise the animal's leg. When the dog was on the stand, the leg was stiff and immobile as if fixed to the floor. When pulling was successful and the animal yielded, salivation dropped immediately, showing that flexion of the leg had become a strong conditioned inhibitor.

In order to measure the strength of the pressure exerted by the dog on the floor by each leg, pneumatic platforms with Marey capsules underneath were placed on the stand. In this way the extension of the left foreleg could be recorded in detail (Figure VIII-9). As seen from this figure, at the onset of M_{100} the animal begins to extend his leg, pressing on the platform. When the leg is pulled upward, the pressure is naturally weakened; afterward, when pulling is discontinued, the pressure rises significantly until the end of the CS-US interval.

It may be easily seen that the formation of the type II CR consisting in extension of the leg to M_{100} follows closely the general rules concerning alimentary type II conditioning. M_{100} followed by passive flexion of the leg was not reinforced, and therefore it became partly inhibitory. Since M_{100} accompanied by the extension of the leg was reinforced by food, the animal learned to produce an active extension in response to this stimulus and in this way to secure the presentation of food. Thus, in the present experiments the extension of the leg became the necessary completion of the external stimulus to form a compound type I CS reinforced by food.

Although the origin of the trained movement was somewhat unusual, in every other respect this reflex did not differ from those described earlier in which the trained movement was flexion of the leg. This was shown by the following experiments.

Experiment XVIII. When the type II CR $M_{100} \rightarrow$ extension of the leg was firmly established, the type I CSs (the tactile stimulus and light) were applied. They elicited a normal salivary response, but the movement of extension was absent (Figure VIII-10).

Experiment XIX. The CR to M_{100} was acutely extinguished by repeated presentation of this stimulus in short intervals without food reinforcement. As seen in Figure VIII-11, both the salivary reaction and the extension of the leg gradually decreased and eventually disappeared. In this particular case salivation vanished earlier than the movement, a fact which again shows only a relative parallelism between the two responses. It may be observed that after the extension of the leg was extinguished small flexion movements (in the form of fidgeting) appeared. This fact is even more remarkable, since, as was said earlier, in all the other sessions of this series the left foreleg was immobile, particularly during the action of M_{100}.

Experiment XX. A new stimulus, M_{50}, was introduced and was not reinforced by food. Again it was observed that the salivary and motor

a

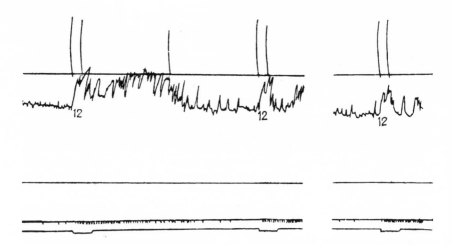

b

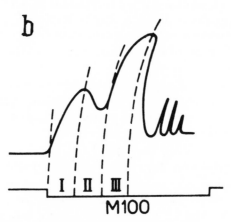

M100

Fɪɢ. VIII-9. Exᴛᴇɴsɪᴏɴ Tʏᴘᴇ II CR ɪɴ Rᴇsᴘᴏɴsᴇ ᴛᴏ M_{100}

a) Some illustrative records. From top to bottom: marks of CS-US interval, and also of the end of eating; the pressure of the left foreleg on the platform; the upward movements of the left foreleg; salivation; CS (M_{100}). The number beneath the pressure record denotes the strength of tugging the leg upward (12 scale units = 3 kg). During the CS-US interval regular strong pressing of the platform is seen. Note that during the act of eating the pressure of the platform is also increased, because the animal leans more firmly on the platform with both forelegs. Also note that the left foreleg is quite immobile both during trials and in intervals.

b) Schematic representation of the extension type II CR: I, active extension of the foreleg before pulling the string; II, pulling the string; III, pulling discontinued; then food is presented.

(Konorski and Miller, 1936, pp. 200, 201.)

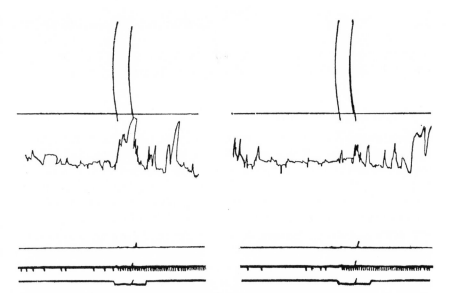

FIG. VIII-10. ABSENCE OF EXTENSION MOVEMENT TO TYPE I CS

From top to bottom: CS-US interval; record of pressing the platform by the left foreleg; movements of this leg upward; salivation; CS (mark in the middle denotes presentation of food).

On the left the type II CS (M_{100}) is presented for control; on the right the type I CS (lamp) is presented. Note that this stimulus does not elicit any extension movement of the left foreleg.

(Konorski and Miller, 1936, p. 204.)

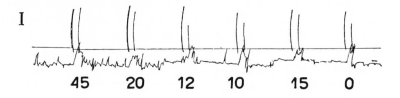

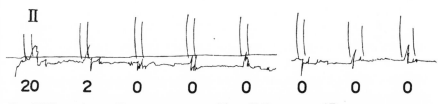

FIG. VIII-11. ACUTE EXTINCTION OF THE TYPE II EXTENSION CR

From top to bottom: duration of CS (M_{100}), record of pressure of the left foreleg on the platform; numbers denote salivation to the CS in scale units.

Note the gradual disappearance of extension movement; in some trials the fidgeting movements appear (downward deviation of the curve).

(Konorski and Miller, 1936, p. 208.)

responses to that stimulus decreased nearly *pari passu* and that at the end of differentiation M_{50} started to elicit movements of flexion instead of extension.

B. EXPERIMENTS FOLLOWING PARADIGM 6

Experiment XXI. In the dog used for our earliest experiments the classical defensive CR was established to a bell by reinforcing it by an air-puff into the ear through a small tube attached to the conch. In response to this US the animal displayed strong head-shaking movements with a tendency to bite objects near his head. After several trials the bell started to evoke the same response. Then in some trials the CS was accompanied by passive flexion of the right foreleg, and in those cases the air-puff was omitted. Very soon the animal started actively to perform the flexion of the right foreleg and thus to protect himself from the air-puff. The classical CR disappeared. The intertrial movements were very rare and soon totally disappeared.

In spite of the fact that with the formation of the type II CR bell → flexion the air-puff was not applied any more, this reflex turned out to be exceedingly stable and practically never failed to appear during many weeks.

It is, perhaps, interesting to mention parenthetically here that in the dog described above four different type II CRs were established in various periods of his CR career. First (cf. Experiment I), the animal was trained to perform the flexion of the left hindleg in response to a tone by means of food reinforcement. The origin of the movement was electrical shock administered to the paw. Then (cf. Experiment II) another alimentary type II CR was trained, consisting in lifting the left foreleg in response to the light. In this case, however, the movement was accomplished by passive flexion of the leg. Thereafter (cf. Experiment IX) the animal was trained to resist a passive flexion of the right hindleg, this flexion being reinforced by the air puff into the ear. Finally, in the present experiment, by means of passive flexion, the dog was taught to lift his right foreleg in response to the bell, this movement protecting him from the air puff into the ear.

Experiment XXII. An analogous experiment was performed later with an attempt to follow closely the formation of the type II CR and its relation to the salivary response.[14] For this purpose, the introduction of hydrochloric acid into the mouth of the dog was used as the reinforcing stimulus. Since it is rather a unique experiment of its kind, it will be reported here in some detail.

First, the classical acid CR had been established to a white noise (N). The CS-US interval was thirty seconds, and during that time salivation amounted to from sixty to eighty units on the scale (twelve to sixteen drops). Then, among positive CS-US trials, negative trials were given in which N was accompanied by the passive flexion of the right foreleg and no acid was introduced. The flexion was carried through by the method described above. It usually commenced on the fifteenth second of N and lasted for five seconds.

The whole course of the first four experimental sessions is represented in Table VIII-6. It can be seen that in the first negative trials the passive flexion causes a diminution of salivation, owing to the external

TABLE VIII-6

FORMATION OF THE AVOIDANCE TYPE II CR

No. of Session	No. of Trial	CS	Isolated Action of CS (in Sec.)	Passive Movement (in Sec. of CS)	Salivation during CS in 15-Sec. Periods	Active Movements (in Sec. of CS)	Reinforcement
1	2	3	4	5	6	7	8
1	1	N	15	....	37	....	Acid
	2	N	30	....	37 33	....	Acid
	3	N	30	....	40 43	....	Acid
	4	N	30	....	25 45	....	Acid
	5	N	30	15–20	40 25	....	....
	6	N	30	....	36 37	....	Acid
2	1	N	30	....	25 45	....	Acid
	2	N	30	....	43 42	....	Acid
	3	N	30	15–20	36 25	....	....
	4	N	30	....	30 33	....	Acid
	5	N	30	15–20	40 18	....	....
	6	N	30	....	25 25	....	Acid
	7	N	30	15–22	45 35	....	....
3	1	N	30	....	25 42	....	Acid
	2	N	30	....	38 50	....	Acid
	3	N	30	15–20	40 25	....	....
	4	N	30	....	30 40	....	Acid
	5	N	30	15–20	45 25	....	....
	6	N	30	15–20	23 15	....	....
	7	N	15	....	20	6	....
4	1	N	20	....	15/20 sec	5, 10, 15	....
	2	N	25	....	32/25 sec	7, 25	....
	3	N	20	....	10/20 sec	3, 6, 19	....
	4	N	15	....	0	2, 4, 6, 15	....
	5	N	15	....	1	3, 4, 7, 15	....
	6	N	15	....	0	7 times	....
	7	N	15	....	0	2, 5, 12, 14	....
	8	N	15	....	0	1, 2, 6, 12, 15	....
5	1	N	30	....	2/30 sec	10, 15, 22	....
	2	B	5	....	0/5 sec	....	Acid
	3	B	15	....	25	....	Acid
	4	B	15	....	45	4, 5, 10, 15	....
	5	B	15	....	28	6 times	....
	6	N	15	....	16	4 times	....
	7	N	15	....	0	1, 3, 9, 15	....

SOURCE: Konorski and Miller, 1936, pp. 224–27.

inhibition elicited by the orientation reaction to a new stimulus. However, in spite of the fact that passive flexion of the leg was repeated, the decrement of salivation in the second fifteen seconds of the CS remained unchanged. Taking into account many analogous observations on the formation of conditioned inhibition to exteroceptive stimuli, we may be certain that the lack of increase of salivary response in the second half of the CS accompanied by passive flexion was due to the transition of external into internal inhibition—that is, to the formation of an inhibitory (negative) type I CR to the compound $S_E + S_{Pr}$.

In the last trial of the third session, the dog for the first time actively raised his right foreleg on the sixth second of operation of the CS. The movement was very high, and, interestingly enough, the animal started to lick the lifted leg. Of course, acid was not introduced into the mouth.

On the fourth day the dog started to raise his leg from the very beginning of the session, and did so in all trials throughout the operation of the CS. It is noticeable that salivation was much reduced from the first trial and very quickly completely disappeared. There is no doubt that this rapid abolition of salivation cannot be due simply to extinction of the acid CR and that true conditioned inhibition to the compound $S_E + S_{Pr}$ took place.

Thus we may safely come to the conclusion that the formation of the defensive type II CR to N was truly connected, or at least coincided, with the formation of inhibitory (negative) type I CR to the compound of N and S_{Pr} generated by flexion.

The defensive type II CR established in this way again appeared very stable and needed practically no reinforcement. Also, as in the previous dog, intertrial movements were nearly absent from the very beginning of the experiments. The salivary type I CR originally established to the CS disappeared completely, but the occasional reinforcement of this stimulus (when the trained movement was not performed) immediately restored salivation for a few trials.

When the above-described defensive type II CR had been established, another stimulus, bubbling of water (B), was presented with acid reinforcement. In the first trial this stimulus elicited an orientation reaction with no defensive component. However, in the third trial it evoked numerous movements of the right foreleg accompanied by copious salivation (Table VIII-6, session 5).

Thus we see that immediately after a stimulus became the type I CS signaling the introduction of acid into the mouth, it began to elicit the avoidance response established to another stimulus without any special training.

The same was true when the classical acid CR was established to two different stimuli and then one was transformed into a type II CS. The presentation of the other stimulus produced the avoidance movement at once.

Whereas the transfer of the defensive type II CR to another CS reinforced by the same noxious US occurred immediately without exception, the effect of the US itself was not so clear. In some instances, the application of the US evoked a strong type II CR; however, in other instances, the CR was much weaker than that evoked by the CS. We had the impression that a strong motor unconditioned response to the US, such as head shaking in the case of the air-puff into the ear or mouthing movements in the case of introduction of acid, inhibited the instrumental response in greater or lesser degree. On the other hand, the remote action of the US was very conspicuous. The application of this stimulus at the beginning of a session, even without the CS, made the avoidance CR more vigorous throughout that session.

The above described properties of the defensive type II CRs seem to indicate that the actual type I CS signaling an aversive US plays the same role in regard to the defensive type II conditioning as the partially inhibitory type I CS plays in alimentary type II conditioning. This is the role of increasing the excitability of motor centers producing the activation of those centers which, owing to the preceding training were subliminally excited.

The most peculiar property of the defensive type II CR is its total preservation in spite of the fact that the CS to which it is established is never, or at least very rarely, reinforced by the aversive US. From the biological point of view, this phenomenon is fully understandable. Since the animal has learned that the performance of a given movement protects him from a harmful agent, he *should* perform that movement in the given situation without "verifying" whether this agent is still imminent. However, the physiological mechanism of the phenomenon is difficult to explain. This problem will be discussed in detail in the next chapters on the basis of new relevant experimental evidence.

7. The transfer of type II conditioned reflexes

In the previous sections of this chapter it has been shown that once a type II CR is established to a certain stimulus, the conditioned response may be easily elicited by other stimuli, although they are far beyond its range of generalization. These other stimuli must fulfill some particular conditions: in alimentary type II CRs, they should be partly inhibitory type I CSs; in defensive type II CRs, on the contrary, they should be actual type I CSs reinforced by the same US which served to establish the instrumental response.

Thus, having stated that the type II conditioned response is not "bound" to the stimulus to which it was established, we have approached a more general problem concerning the rules of the transfer, or rather of the interchange, of instrumental responses *between* various type II CSs, both homogeneous and heterogeneous in respect to the reinforcing agents. This problem was studied by us in great detail, and here we shall report the chief results of our research.

A. Interchange of instrumental responses in homogeneous CRs

In the beginning of our work on type II CRs, we came quite accidentally across the following facts, manifesting the easy interchangeability of two instrumental conditioned responses reinforced by the same US (food). Following are two original experiments illustrating these phenomena.[15]

Experiment XXIII. In a dog the alimentary type II CR was established consisting in barking in the presence of the sound of a metronome (Experiment IV). This CR was trained in the free-moving animal. Then the dog was put on the stand situated in the same room, and another type II CR was established consisting in lifting the left hindleg to the tone (Experiment I). When the dog was on the stand, the metronome was presented. The dog began immediately to lift the hindleg vigorously instead of barking, and started to bark only after the prolonged operation of this stimulus.

Experiment XXIV. Two alimentary type II CRs were established in a dog consisting in lifting the left hindleg to a tone and lifting the left foreleg to a light (Experiments I and II). During the training of each of these reflexes the band connected with the apparatus recording the movements was attached to the corresponding leg. After both CRs were established it was found that when the band was attached to the left hindleg, the animal raised this leg to both the tone and the lamp; when the band was attached the left foreleg, only that leg was raised to both stimuli. If the band was put on the legs still "unused," no movements appeared in response to the CSs. If, however, the bands were attached to both left legs the animal did not show any sign of discriminative responses, and usually performed both trained movements in quick succession in every trial.

Analogous experiments to that just described were routinely repeated by us with the same results. Very illustrative in this respect is the following experiment.

Experiment XXV. In the dog described in Experiment XV an alimentary type II CR was established, consisting in raising the right foreleg in response to bubbling (B). Thereafter the animal was trained to extend the left foreleg in response to the metronome (M_{100}). When the band was attached to the left foreleg, B was presented. The animal immediately performed a clear movement of extension of this leg, exactly the same as he used to perform to M_{100}. Since food was not offered to the dog (because the movement was "incorrect"), the extension lasted for about one minute (Figure VIII-12). It should be remembered that the type I CSs (TS^+ and light) did not produce this movement (cf. Figure VIII-10).

All these experiments show that the interchange of instrumental responses occurs quite independently of whether the movements are similar, opposite, or quite different from one another. A given type

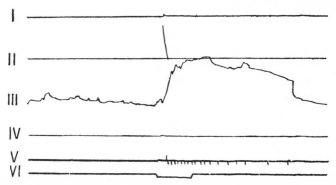

FIG. VIII-12. TRANSFER OF THE EXTENSION RESPONSE TO ANOTHER TYPE II CS ELICITING LIFTING OF THE RIGHT FORELEG

I, lifting of the right foreleg; II, mark of the onset of CS; III, extension of the left foreleg; IV, lifting of the left foreleg; V, salivation; VI, duration of CS (it is not reinforced by food).

Note the strong and long-lasting extension of the left foreleg instead of lifting the right foreleg.

(Konorski and Miller, 1936, p. 205.)

II CS may elicit any of the homogeneous type II CRs; conversely, a given instrumental response may be elicited by any of the type II CSs reinforced by the same US.

Of course the problem arises of whether it is possible, by appropriate discriminative training, to teach the animal in the same condition to perform two different movements to two CSs under the same reinforcement. According to our more recent experiments, which will be described in a later chapter, it appears that the difficulty of this task depends greatly on the character of the CSs used in the discriminative learning.

B. Interchange of instrumental responses
   in heterogeneous CRs

This problem was dealt with in great detail in a special paper.[16] Here we shall briefly present our main results.

We were chiefly concerned with the interrelations between the alimentary and defensive CRs. Our routine method was that an alimentary type II CR consisting of lifting one leg (movement M_A) was established to one stimulus (S_A), whereas a defensive type II CR consisting of lifting another leg (movement M_D) was formed by the avoidance method to another stimulus (S_D). The aversive US on which this CR was based was either an air puff into the ear or introduction of acid into the mouth. The bands connected with the recording apparatus were put on both legs.

First, it was observed that the situation here was quite distinct from that encountered in the case of homogeneous CRs. The two instrumental responses M_A and M_D could be established quite independently of each other, and no interchange between them was observed. This interchange could be occasionally provoked by special procedures which were thoroughly studied.

(1) When after a series of experimental sessions in which only alimentary CRs were given the S_D was presented, the animal might first perform the alimentary movement M_A and only then in the same trial switch to the proper defensive movement S_D (see Table VIII-7, protocol I). Similarly, if the S_A was given after a series of purely defensive experiments, it might first produce the movement M_D; but then alimentary movements would immediately appear. The general conclusion has been reached that one of the factors determining which movement would be performed to a given stimulus was the unconditioned background against which it was presented. If the alimentary background prevailed, the first movement to the S_D could be alimentary; and vice versa, against the defensive background, the first movement to appear to the S_A could be defensive. But these "erroneous" responses were far from being the rule, and we had a dog who never committed them in his whole CR career however hard we tried to induce him to do so (Table VIII-7, protocol II).

To sum up, two instrumental CRs, the defensive and the alimentary, could be given in the same experimental session, and no serious interchanges of responses would take place.

(2) We could observe the interchange of alimentary and defensive instrumental movements on special occasions when the dog was strongly agitated. When we carried out a very deep acute extinction of the alimentary type II CR, it happened that, after the alimentary movement was already extinguished and the dog continued to be rest-

less, the defensive movement emerged. Similarly, when we prolonged the action of the S_D for many seconds, then the defensive movement gradually subsided, but the animal began to perform the movement trained as the alimentary one (Figure VIII-13). These facts will be commented upon further in a later chapter.

The general conclusions reached on the basis of all our experimental material concerning the transfer phenomena of type II CRs were the

TABLE VIII-7

TRANSFER OF HETEROGENEOUS TYPE II CRs

Min. of Session	CS	Character of CS	Isolated Action of CS	Cond. Saliva- tion	Alim. Movement	Defen. Movement	Rein- force- ment
1	2	3	4	5	6	7	8
			Protocol I				
1	Lamp	Alim. type I	15"	16	. . . . . .	. . . . . .	Food
5	Metr.	Alim. type I	15"	35	. . . . . .	. . . . . .	Food
10	Bub.	Alim. type II	2"	0	1"	. . . . . .	Food
14	Bell	Defen. type II	13"	8	3"	7", 10", 13"	. . . . . .
18	Tact.	Alim. type I	15"	33	. . . . . .	. . . . . .	Food
22	Metr.	Alim. type I	15"	25	1"	. . . . . .	Food
26	Lamp	Alim. type I	15"	26	. . . . . .	. . . . . .	Food
			Protocol II				
2	Metr.	Alim. type I	15"	13	1 time	. . . . . .	Food
6	Bell	Alim. type II	15"	34	4 times	. . . . . .	Food
10	Tact.	Alim. type I	15"	26	. . . . . .	. . . . . .	Food
14½	Bell	Alim. type II	15"	31	6 times	. . . . . .	Food
18	Tone	Defen. type II	5"	5	. . . . . .	2 times	. . . . . .
20	Tone	Defen. type II	7"	0	. . . . . .	3 times	. . . . . .
22½	Tone	Defen. type II	3"	0	. . . . . .	1 time	. . . . . .
24½	Bell	Alim. type II	15"	24	5 times	. . . . . .	Food

SOURCE: Konorski, 1939, pp. 22, 25.
In protocol I the defensive type II CS presented after alimentary CSs elicits at first the alimentary instrumental movement. Such a transfer does not happen in protocol II taken from another dog.

following. We could distinguish: the "determining stimuli," which did not elicit any trained movement but which *predisposed* the animal to perform a particular movement; and the "releasing stimuli," which *elicited* that movement. The determining stimuli were usually continuous and were represented by the given experimental situation or the band attached to the leg taking part in type II conditioning. The alimentary or defensive background, depending on which CSs and USs were hitherto presented, was also considered as a determining

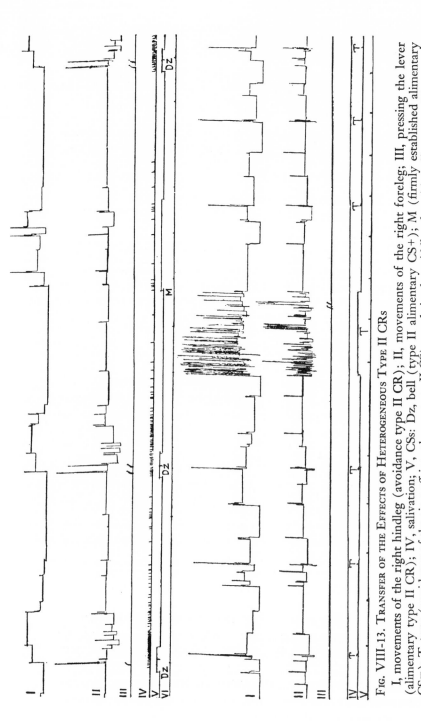

Fig. VIII-13. Transfer of the Effects of Heterogeneous Type II CRs

I, movements of the right hindleg (avoidance type II CR); II, movements of the right foreleg; III, pressing the lever (alimentary type II CR); IV, salivation; V, CSs: Dz, bell (type II alimentary CS+); M (firmly established alimentary CS−); T, tone (avoidance of the air-puff into the ear type II CS); mark in the middle of positive alimentary CS, presentation of food; VI, time in minutes.

Upper record: bell evokes salivary and alimentary type II conditioned response. Prolongation till 120 seconds of the operation of M evokes the avoidance movement of the hindleg.

Lower record: the tone normally evokes the movement of the hindleg; however, when it is prolonged for 120 seconds, movements of the foreleg with lever-pressing occur.

Small deviations of the record of movements are due to fidgeting and changing position.

stimulus. On the other hand, the "releasing stimuli" were represented by the sporadic stimuli possessing reflexogenic power in respect to type II CRs. Here belonged all the proper type II CSs eliciting both attractive and aversive type II CRs as well as partly inhibitory type I food CSs and actual aversive CSs and USs. It was thought that the boundary between the determining and releasing stimuli was not absolute, because the determining continuous stimulus might be at the same time a releasing stimulus (as is the case in type II CR established to the experimental situation) and, vice versa, the sporadic stimulus might not only release the movement but also determine which one was to be elicited.

8. Summary and conclusions

In this chapter the experimental work performed in the interwar period by Miller and me on type II conditioning has been presented. By type II CRs we have called those CRs in which the movement is performed in response to a given stimulus, because by its performance the animal procures an attractive US such as food (US$^+$) or avoids an aversive US such as the introduction of acid into the mouth or an air puff into the ear (US$^-$).

We have specified four varieties of experimental procedures by which type II CRs are obtained. They are as follows.

(1) If an external stimulus S_E accompanied by a movement M is reinforced by US$^+$ whereas S_E alone is not, then the animal learns to perform this movement in the presence of the external stimulus ($S_E \rightarrow M$).

(2) If an external stimulus S_E accompanied by a movement M is reinforced by US$^-$ whereas S_E alone is not, then the animal learns to resist the provocation of this movement by performing the antagonistic movement ($S_E \rightarrow \sim M$).

(3) If an external stimulus S_E is reinforced by US$^+$ whereas S_E accompanied by movement M is not, then the animal learns to resist the provocation of this movement by performing the antagonistic movement ($S_E \rightarrow \sim M$).

(4) If an external stimulus S_E is reinforced by US$^-$ whereas S_E accompanied by M is not, then the animal learns to perform this movement in the presence of the external stimulus ($S_E \rightarrow M$).

According to our earlier views, the movement taking part in type II conditioning could be provided in a number of ways: it could be evoked reflexly as a result of a motor UR; it could be "spontaneous" —that is, evoked by some uncontrolled agents; or it could occur through a passive displacement of the limb or the body. In all these cases the course of establishing type II CR was supposed to be the same.

Since the type II CRs take a different course, depending on whether the reinforcing agent is attractive or aversive, we shall consider these two classes of reflexes separately.

Type II CRs based on attractive reinforcing stimuli (appetitive type II CRs). For the study of these reflexes, food reinforcement was utilized according to the procedure specified in the first or third variety. Although in the first variety the trained movement is the same as that provoked by the experimenter, and in the third it is opposite to it, the properties of the established type II CRs are the same.

The alimentary type II CR once established fully depends on food reinforcement. If not reinforced, it is extinguished; if reinforced in the presence of one stimulus and not in the presence of a similar one, it is differentiated.

If we compare the interrelations between the salivary (type I) and the motor (type II) response in the course of extinction or differentiation, we come to the conclusion that either they run approximately *pari passu*—that is, salivation to the CS disappears more or less simultaneously with the disappearance of the motor response—or considerable discrepancies occur between their course.

When the type II CR is established to a given stimulus, it may be elicited by other stimuli which were never combined with the trained movements. These stimuli are: (1) inhibitory (negative) type I CSs not very firmly established; and (2) other alimentary type II CSs trained to evoke other motor acts. On the contrary, type I positive CSs and the US itself (food in the mouth) not only do not elicit the type II conditioned response but, on the contrary, tend to suppress that response.

If several alimentary type II CRs are established to different stimuli, they will interchange, unless each of them is given in the presence of a different continuous facilitatory stimulus. Such facilitatory stimuli are provided by the experimental situation or by the band attached to the leg taking part in the given motor act. These are "determining stimuli," because they determine which of several type II conditioned responses will be elicited at the given moment. On the other hand, the sporadic stimulus may be called the "releasing stimulus," because it may elicit any alimentary type II conditioned response designated by the determining stimulus.

Type II CRs based on aversive reinforcing stimuli (defensive type II CRs). For establishing these reflexes an air-puff into the ear or introduction of acid into the mouth was utilized. They can be established according to the procedure specified in the second and fourth variety. Whereas in the second variety the trained movement is antagonistic to that provoked by the experimenter, in the fourth variety it is the same movement. However, the general properties of the reflexes established according to both these procedures are the same.

The defensive type II CRs are not followed by the aversive US. This stimulus is presented only when the type II conditioned response is not performed. Since in a well-established defensive type II CR the motor response is stable and appears to every presentation of the CS, such a reflex is practically unextinguishable (or undifferentiable), unless special measures described in a later chapter are applied. In this respect the defensive type II CR differs both from the alimentary type II CR and from any type I CR, whether alimentary or defensive.

If a defensive type II CR is established to a certain stimulus, the conditioned response may be produced by other stimuli which were not combined with that response. A type I CS reinforced by the same aversive US which was used for the establishment of the type II CR will unfailingly elicit the type II conditioned response. The US itself is not so reliable in this respect. Still less reliable (but nevertheless effective) are type I CSs reinforced by other aversive USs or other USs themselves (see Chapter X).

Concerning the mechanism of type II CRs, the following concept was proposed.

The formation of the type II CR was thought to be based on the formation of type I CR to the proprioceptive stimulus S_{Pr} generated by the provoked movement. If S_{Pr} becomes an indispensable complement to an external stimulus S_E to form a type I compound CS signaling food, then S_E will elicit the movement M generating this S_{Pr}. The same occurs when S_{Pr} is a conditioned inhibitor in respect to the type I CS signaling an aversive US. On the contrary, when S_{Pr} is a component of a type I compound signaling an aversive US or a conditioned inhibitor with respect to a type I CS signaling food, then S_E will elicit the movement antagonistic to that generating S_{Pr}.

It should be emphasized that the above concept can satisfactorily account only for the "operational" rules of the formation and appearance of type II CRs, but it does not solve the problem of why it is that in the circumstances just specified the reflex is established. The solution of this problem was attempted in our earlier publications,[17] but all these attempts proved to be unsatisfactory. It seems, however, that at the present time, on the basis of new experimental evidence obtained in our laboratory and new progress in our knowledge of the functioning of the brain, the problem of the mechanism of type II conditioning can be properly solved, at least in some of its aspects. The following chapters of this book will deal with this subject.

References to Chapter VIII

1. S. Miller and J. Konorski. 1928. Sur une forme particulière des réflexes conditionnels. *C.R. Séanc. Soc. Biol.*, 99: 1155–58.
2. E. R. Hilgard and D. G. Marquis. 1940. *Conditioning and Learning*. New York: Appleton-Century-Crofts.
3. B. F. Skinner. 1938. *The Behavior of Organisms*. New York: Appleton-Century.
4. J. Konorski and S. Miller. 1933. *Podstawy fizjologicznej teorii ruchów nabytych: Ruchowe odruchy warunkowe*. (Les principes fondamentaux de la théorie physiologique des mouvements acquis: Les réflexes conditionnels moteurs.) Warsaw-Lvov, Książnica Atlas TNSW. French summary.
5. Ю. Конорски и С. Миллер. 1936. Условные рефлексы двигательного анализатора. (Conditioned reflexes of the motor analyzer.) *Trudy Fiziol. Lab. I. P. Pavlova*, 6 (No. 1): 119–278. English summary, pp. 285–88.
6. J. Konorski and S. Miller. 1933 (see note 4 above).
7. I. P. Pavlov. 1927. *Conditioned Reflexes: An Investigation of the Physiological Activity of the Cerebral Cortex*. Translated and edited by G. V. Anrep. Chap. 8. Cambridge: Cambridge University Press.
8. J. Konorski and S. Miller. 1936 (see note 5 above).
9. ———. 1930. Méthode d'examen de l'analysateur moteur par les réactions salivomotrices. *C.R. Séanc. Soc. Biol.*, 104: 907–10.
   ———. 1933 (see note 4 above).
   ———. 1936 (see note 5 above).
10. ———. 1933 (see note 4 above).
    J. Konorski. 1948. *Conditioned Reflexes and Neuron Organization*. Cambridge: Cambridge University Press.
11. I. P. Pavlov. 1927 (see note 7 above), chap. 11.
12. *Ibid.*, chap. 5.
13. J. Konorski and S. Miller. 1936 (see note 5 above).
14. *Ibid.*
15. S. Miller and J. Konorski. 1928. Le phénomène de la généralisation motrice. *C.R. Séanc. Soc. Biol.*, 99: 1158.
    J. Konorski and S. Miller. 1933 (see note 4 above).
16. J. Konorski. 1939. O zmienności ruchowych reakcji warunkowych. Zasady, przełączania korowego. (Sur la variabilité des réactions conditionnelles motrices.) *Przegl. Fizjol. Ruchu*, 9: 1–51. French summary.
17. ———. 1948 (see note 10 above).

CHAPTER IX

TYPE II CONDITIONED REFLEX
AND DRIVE

1. Introductory remarks

As may be seen from the preceding chapter, our concept of type II conditioning, based on the early experiments performed by Miller and myself in the interwar period, consisted of two rather independent but mutually complementary ideas. According to one of them, the formation and existence of the type II CR were based on the proprioceptive stimulus (generated by the provoked movement) being either a positive or inhibitory type I CS in regard to the US used in a given type II conditioning. According to the second idea, there were certain categories of type I CSs which were thought to be reflexogenic in respect to type II conditioned responses: these were partly inhibitory food CSs and fully active aversive CSs.

It may be observed that both these ideas were unsatisfactory as explanatory principles accounting for the mechanism of type II conditioning. The first idea was rather teleological. It gave precise rules determining whether and when a given exteroceptive stimulus would elicit a given instrumental response, but it did not answer the question of why it would do so. On the other hand, the second idea attempted to answer this very question but was too vague and indefinite properly to fulfill this role.

As we look back now and survey the state of affairs concerning the second idea from the viewpoint of our contemporary knowledge, we can honestly admit that the problem in question was at that time simply unsolvable because we were lacking some essential information on the physiological mechanisms of unconditioned reflexes. It seems, however, that since that time the situation has changed radically, and we are now in a position to provide a satisfactory explanation of the peculiar reflexogenic power of certain type I CSs in respect to instrumental responses.

It should be remembered that at the time Pavlov proposed his concept of unconditioned reflexes as higher order innate nervous activities responsible for preservation of both the individual organism and species, the knowledge of the functional role of the hypothalamus and the limbic brain was still non-existent. Led by some sound intuition, supported by the observation of decorticated animals, Pavlov attributed these activities to the "subcortical centers," not specifying which structures were involved here. His analysis of the "alimentary center"[1] (fully hypothetical at that time), carried out on the basis of an analogy with the then much better known respiratory center, was highly ingenious and penetrating.

On the basis of his experimental work on classical conditioning, Pavlov was aware from the very beginning of the two different aspects of the activity of the alimentary system, one being involved in hunger and the other one in consummatory function—that is, the act of eating. He realized that the level of hunger was chiefly dependent on humoral factors—the presence or absence of some substances in the blood—in much the same way as respiration was regulated by the content of carbon dioxide in the blood. Not being aware of the special anatomical system subserving this function, he attributed various intensities of hunger to various levels of excitability of the unique alimentary center. This concept could be easily extended to the defensive URs, in which the state of fear could be considered as an increase in the excitability of definite subcortical centers subserving these reflexes.

The revolution of ideas on the organization of UR centers was brought about by Hess, Papez, Anand and Brobeck, and many other authors who have substantially clarified the functional role of the hypothalamus and the limbic system.[2] To put it briefly, this revolution consisted in realizing that all states denoted as drives—hunger, thirst, fear, and the like—have their own special centers in these structures, being practically independent of the "consummatory" URs and their particular centers localized in quite different regions of the brain.

This problem has been discussed in detail in Chapter I of this book. In Chapter VI we could ascertain what a great impact this revolution had on our understanding of classical, purely Pavlovian CRs. It was shown there that each classical CR is composed of two "reflex arcs": one running from the CS units to the US units of the corresponding gnostic fields; the other, from the CS units to the corresponding units of the limbic system. Accordingly, the former CR has been called a consummatory CR; the latter, a drive (or emotional) CR. It has been shown that although in many instances both these CRs are elicited by the same CS, this is not always true: the short-lasting stimuli closely preceding the consummatory US usually become consummatory CSs, whereas long-lasting stimuli are more likely to become drive CSs.

The second, no less important, revolution which occurred at nearly the same time was connected with the name of Magoun and his co-workers and was concerned with the discovery of the unspecific arousing system.[3] Of particular importance for our present context was the discovery of the *ascending* arousing system by Moruzzi and Magoun.[4] Again, this finding provided direct neurophysiological evidence for activation of large parts of the CNS and of the cerebral cortex in particular. Thus, the general activation of the motor centers, playing such an important role in our experiments on type II conditioning, has gained a natural basis.

In this chapter we shall see what impact these new ideas have on our understanding of the mechanism and structure of type II CR.

2. The role of drive and arousal in type II conditioning

When it was realized that the state we referred to as "increased excitability of the UR center" is in fact excitation of definite structures in the diencephalon, the solution of the problem which puzzled us for so long became immediately evident. As stated in Chapter I, one of the major effects of the excitation of drive centers is the arousal of afferent systems on the one hand and the arousal of the central motor behavioral system on the other. This is why the animal in a state of drive is motorically alert or even very agitated. When excitation of the particular drive center coincides with the excitation of the motor center controlling the performance of a *given* movement, the conditions are fulfilled for the association between the two to be formed. It should be remembered here that, according to our previous considerations (Chapter IV), we have assumed that in such an association the afferent part and not the efferent part of the motor act is involved—namely, the kinesthetic units determining the pattern of a given movement.

Let us now analyze in more detail the whole process occurring in establishing the type II CR.

Suppose that a fasting dog is brought to a certain situation and given food there. As shown in Chapter VI, the type I hunger CR is immediately established to this situation. Owing to this CR, when the animal is again brought to the same place, he will manifest the signs of hunger and in particular motor agitation.

Suppose now that against such a background the animal performs, either "spontaneously" or in response to certain stimuli, a series of movements M_1, M_2, M_3, and so on, and that only the movement M_n is followed by presentation of food. Since the central motor behavioral system is in a state of arousal, any of these movements may become associated with the hunger drive. However, all those movements which do not interrupt this drive and in consequence do not suppress the motor arousal are subjected to retroactive inhibition produced by the successive movements. Quite different, however, is the situation in respect to the movement immediately preceding the presentation of food. As explained in Chapters I and VI, the taste of food immediately produces the hunger antidrive inhibiting the hunger drive, and therefore only the last movement is followed by motor relaxation. If a given movement is repeatedly followed by food and other movements are not, then connections between the hunger center and central representation of that movement will be formed; in consequence, when the animal is hungry, he will perform this very movement.

As is clear from the data presented in the preceding chapter, the movement established as an instrumental response may be either originally produced as a "spontaneous" movement—that is, with no clearly known eliciting stimulus—or as a reflex movement elicited by a particular stimulus applied by the experimenter. In the first situation we have to do with the so-called trial-and-error learning, whereas in the second situation a procedure which may be denoted as "evoked movement learning" is used.*

Similar reasoning may be applied in respect to type II defensive CRs. Suppose that a stimulus S_E is followed by an aversive US, say by an airpuff into the ear. After a few pairings, the S_E becomes the fear type I CS—that is, it evokes a conditioned fear drive. The animal is restless in the presence of S_E and successively performs a number of movements. If a definite movement, whether performed "spontaneously" or provoked by a definite stimulus, is followed by the cessation of S_E, the fear drive is momentarily reduced or abolished. Again the conditions arise for the consolidation of association between the fear drive and the given movement, whereas associations between that drive and other movements cannot be formed because of retroactive inhibition.

* The circumstance that the behavioristic experiments on instrumental conditioning dealt exclusively with the trial-and-error procedure weighed heavily upon the theoretical approach to this field of investigation. Since it was assumed that before the instrumental training the animal occasionally performs the movement used as instrumental response (the so-called free operant), it was inferred that this training consists, as a matter of fact, in mere "increase of probability" of the performance of that movement (cf. B. F. Skinner, *The Behavior of Organisms*, New York: Appleton-Century 1938). The large body of evidence provided by the evoked movement procedure in instrumental conditioning makes this approach inadmissible.

In this way we come to our first, simplest model representing the type II CRs, both for appetitive and defensive reflexes (Figure IX-1). As seen from our diagrams, the only difference between the two reflex arcs is that in appetitive CRs the drive is inhibited by the stimulus eliciting the consummatory response whereas in aversive CRs it is stopped by the cessation of the fear CS. In both these cases, however, the trained movement leads to a substitution of drive by the corresponding antidrive.

The proposed model implies: (1) that the formation of an instrumental CR occurs only when the animal is under the action of drive; (2) that the trained movement should be followed by drive reduction; (3) that the elicitation of the already formed instrumental response occurs only in the presence of the corresponding drive, its intensity being proportional to the strength of drive; and (4) that satisfaction of drive is accompanied by the cessation of trained movement.

We shall discuss each of these theses separately.

The dependence of the *formation* of the type II CR on drive action is substantiated by innumerable observations emerging from the routine practice of instrumental conditioning. It is well known that a defensive type II CR cannot be established if the animal is not in fear, and that an alimentary type II CR fails to be formed when the animal is not hungry. A modern version of hedonistic approach, according to which the pleasure of the "rewarding" stimulus and not the drive itself is the *spiritus movens* of instrumental conditioning, was disproved in our earlier discussion (Chapter I), where it was stated that this very pleasure is nothing but drive satisfaction (antidrive) and therefore cannot exist without drive. In other words, according to our concept, both pleasure and annoyance are not the inherent properties of corresponding perceptions, but they depend on the effect exerted by a given stimulus upon drive.

The recent experimental technique of implanting electrodes into various parts of the emotive brain has allowed us to approach this problem experimentally, because it became possible to switch on a given drive artificially by direct stimulation of the drive center.

The appropriate experiments were performed by Wyrwicka et al.[5] on naïve goats with electrodes implanted in the hypothalamic hunger center. The animals were completely satiated before each experimental session. In procedure I, after the goat was brought to the experimental situation, the hypothalamus was stimulated, the foreleg of the animal was passively lifted, and food was offered. After the consummation of food the stimulation was discontinued, to be repeated in a few minutes. In procedure II, first the foreleg was passively lifted and thereafter stimulation of the hypothalamus and food reinforcement was given.

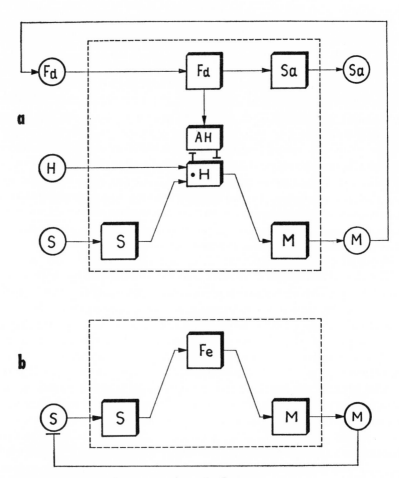

FIG. IX-1. FIRST BLOCK MODEL OF TYPE II CR ARC

Circles, peripheral structures (receptors and effectors); squares, central structures.

Arrows denote positive causal connections (within the CNS, excitatory connections); stopped lines denote negative causal connections (within the CNS, inhibitory connections); point within the square denotes logical product.

S, receptor and center of the CS; H, receptor and center of hunger drive; AH, center of hunger antidrive; Fe, center of fear drive; Fd, receptor and center of food intake; M, center and effector of instrumental motor act; Sa, center and effector of salivation.

a) Block model of alimentary type II CR.

b) Block model of defensive type II CR. The fear antidrive center is not indicated because the cessation of CS is sufficient to reduce the fear drive.

It appeared that whereas in procedure I the animals very promptly learned to flex the leg when the lateral hypothalamus was stimulated and performed this movement when they were naturally hungry, they did not do so when procedure II was applied: here, in spite of numerous pairings of the passive movement with feeding, the instrumental CR failed to be established. Thus, we have clear evidence that if a movement is provoked in a no-drive situation it is not instrumentalized in spite of the fact that it is "rewarded" by food in a drive situation.

It seems reasonable in this context to explain the mechanism of the formation of instrumental CRs by the so-called self-stimulation procedure introduced by Olds and Milner.[6] According to our concept, stimulation of those points in the emotive brain which produce the "reward" effect is connected with activation of the antidrive units—that is, it leads to satisfaction of a certain drive. The cessation of this stimulation should produce a rebound drive effect which is responsible for the performance of those movements which are followed by stimulation. This concept (similar to that put forward by Deutsch[7]) explains the fact that, in spite of the great intensity of the instrumental CR reinforced by self-stimulation, its disappearance due to non-reinforcement is extremely rapid because it depends on the prompt subsiding of the corresponding drive.[8] Of course, "priming" the animal by giving stimulation "gratis" immediately restores the trained movement.*

On the contrary, stimulation of "self-punishing" points produces activation of the drive units; this is why the animal develops an escape-conditioned response when this stimulation is given.[9] The dual character of many points whose stimulation is first "rewarding" and then "punishing" is due to the fact that in some emotive systems the drive on-units and drive off-units are intermingled (cf. Figure I-6, p. 52).

The second thesis, that the trained instrumental movement has to be followed by *drive reduction* or drive inhibition (being probably tantamount to antidrive), is no less obvious from all relevant observations. Therefore we should here discuss only those facts which apparently contradict this thesis.

One of these facts is that in many experimental procedures (for example, maze learning) food reinforcement is provided, not after the performance of a single movement, but after a *series* of movements, which

* The excellent confirmation of this concept has been recently provided by the experiments of C. R. Gallistel, Motivation effects in self-stimulation, *J. Comp. Physiol. Psychol.*, 62 (1966): 95–101. This author found that the instrumental response consisting in running through a corridor for obtaining positive brain stimulation depends on the intervals between trials. The shorter the interval the more vigorous the response. Increasing the strength of stimulation produces a stronger instrumental response in the next trial.

have to follow one another in a definite sequence (a "chain" type II CR). When the animal has mastered the given sequential task, all movements of the series except the last one certainly do not terminate the drive; otherwise the successive movements could not occur.

Let us analyze the simple chain type II CR in which in the presence of the CS the animal has to perform two movements in succession, M_1 and M_2. According to our unpublished experiments on monkeys, at the beginning of training the animal exhibits a strong tendency to perform only the movement M_2 preceding food reinforcement. Since, however, this movement is not followed by food, it becomes partly extinguished and the movement M_1 appears. This movement again does not lead to food; but if then, under the still lasting drive, the animal performs the movement M_2, it obtains food. This again leads to a tendency to perform only movement M_2, and the whole cycle of events is repeated. Such a situation may either last permanently—the animal will then always perform the sequence M_2 M_1 M_2—or eventually the association between M_1 and M_2 will be formed and these movements will fuse into a single motor act (cf. Chapter IV).

If the particular movements are separated by exteroceptive stimuli representing so-called secondary reinforcements (according to the schedule $\boxed{CS_1 \rightarrow M_1} \rightarrow \boxed{CS_2 \rightarrow M_2} \rightarrow F$), then of course their fusion is not possible. In that case, however, the formation of direct connections between CSs and corresponding movements discussed in Chapter X will help to establish a type II chain reflex.

Another point which requires a comment in our present discussion is that of training the animals (rats) to perform an instrumental movement by intragastric injection of food.[10] Since this procedure obviously does not involve the hunger antidrive produced by the taste of food, the question may be raised as to what sort of satisfaction of the hunger drive is here in operation.

It is difficult to answer this question without further experimentation. A hint at the solution of the problem is given by Teitelbaum's observation that after a lesion sustained in the ventromedial hypothalamic nucleus (satiation center) the animals fail to learn this task, unless at the same time they receive small amounts of a tasty substance (for example, saccharin) by mouth. This indicates that the antidrive center involved is the satiation center which receives information about intragastric food injection either directly from the stomach or indirectly by humoral ways (cf. Chapter I).*

---

* The drive-reduction theory of instrumental conditioning and, more generally, of instrumental behavior is often disproved by the argument that in both humans and animals instrumental responses are established or elicited in the absence of a final con-

The third thesis, according to which the performance of an instrumental response is under the control of a drive to which it has been established, will be the subject of our further discussion. To quote here some obvious facts substantiating this thesis we shall mention the control of the instrumental response by humoral factors or drugs increasing the corresponding drive, by artificial stimulation of the drive center,[12] or suppression of that response by antagonistic drives (as in the so-called CER method).

To turn now to those facts which seem to contradict this thesis, the results of Fonberg's experiment should be discussed.[13] Fonberg has found that if an avoidance CR is established by the method described in the preceding chapter (that is, by reinforcing a CS alone with an aversive US, and non-reinforcing it when accompanied by a given movement), then the transfer of the instrumental response to the operation of the US is usually surprisingly small. Since it is assumed that the actual operation of a noxious stimulus elicits fear, it is not clear why the

---

summatory response. For instance, male rats learn to go to the compartment containing a female in heat without being allowed to copulate.[11] These facts led to a view that drive induction rather than drive reduction serves as a reinforcing agent.

It seems that these facts do not contradict our version of the drive-reduction theory, simply because according to our view the term "consummatory response" does not denote only the final biological component of a given unconditioned activity, such as swallowing in the alimentary reflexes or ejaculation in sexual reflexes. The drive reflexes of higher organisms, and particularly of man, are not limited to those which tend to satisfy these elementary needs. For instance, in interhuman relations we regularly observe drives directed to merely meeting persons to whom we are attached, particularly if we have not seen them for a long time, and finding ourselves in their proximity is a powerful drive satisfying (consummatory) stimulus. Being homesick is also a most powerful drive, being satisfied by very complex and sophisticated stimulus-patterns. Similarly, in our relations to loved persons, mere caressing and kissing may provide strong drive satisfaction, and these acts do not necessarily lead to "induction" of a specific sexual drive ending in the sexual intercourse. After all, sexual drive is only one of many kindred drives representing love or affection, and each of them is satisfied by different stimuli. The problem whether all these drives "derive" from the sexual drive is outside the scope of our present discussion.

Another penetrating criticism of the drive-reduction theory of the formation (and preservation) of instrumental CRs was pointed out by D. E. Berlyne (personal communication). Assuming that an animal is in a state of strong hunger drive and a given movement is followed by a firmly established negative CS producing a clearcut hunger antidrive, Berlyne asks why in that situation the instrumental response will probably not be formed, although the movement *is* "reinforced" by drive reduction.

We are unable to answer this question without having appropriate experimental results. As it was pointed out in Chapter VII, a no-food CS is not necessarily an antidrive CS; on the contrary it may increase and not decrease the hunger drive. Therefore, when making experiments explaining this problem we must be certain that the stimulus used as a "reinforcer" actually produces the true appeasement of the animal, inhibition of hunger contractions of the stomach, and so on. If the result of such an experiment is negative, it would mean that "drive satisfaction" is not necessarily tantamount to "drive reduction," and that various antidrive states may have quite different functional properties.

animal has no tendency to apply the instrumental movement established in response to the fear CS to get rid of the fear US.

The probable explanation of this seemingly paradoxical fact is that in our experimental situation the noxious stimulus elicits a powerful motor unconditioned response: an air-puff into the ear produces strong head shaking, and the introduction of acid into the mouth gives rise to vigorous mouthing movements. It may be assumed that these motor acts which are in some sense natural instrumental responses, because they help to get rid of the noxious stimulus, suppress the tendency to perform the instrumental conditioned response established to the fear CS. Needless to say, if by special training we teach the animal to perform that response to get rid of the noxious stimulus, this can be easily achieved—the procedure denoted as escape training.

Incidentally, it should be noted that the thesis of the necessity of drive action for the performance of a type II conditioned response has often been questioned, particularly in respect to avoidance conditioning. It was claimed that if an avoidance CR is firmly established, the instrumental movement may appear in the absence of drive, simply in response to the external stimuli to which it was trained. We postpone the discussion of this point until Chapter X in which the significance of these external stimuli will be described.

The last of our theses, that the drive reduction produced by the food consummatory response or the cessation of fear *stops* the performance of the trained movement, is again largely documented by many experimental results presented in the previous chapter. Therefore we shall discuss here only a phenomenon which seems to contradict this thesis. It is provided by the experimental procedure originated by Skipin.[14] The task with which his experimental animals (dogs) were confronted was that the instrumental response (lifting the foreleg) served, not only for presentation of a portion of food, but also for its *availability* during the whole act of eating. This was achieved by attaching the foreleg to a lever connected with a bowl. In this way the bowl with food remained in the aperture of the feeder only when the animal kept his leg lifted. Since, according to our concept, during the act of eating the hunger drive is inhibited, the movement of the leg should *ipso facto* be discontinued.

It seems that the explanation of this fact is that in Skipin's method the animal is trained, not to *perform* a movement during the act of eating, but to keep the leg in a certain *position*. As a matter of fact, there are many situations in which the animal, in order to reach food, has to take a definite, sometimes even quite uncomfortable posture. For instance, when the food is in a deep hole the animal must keep his head immersed in this hole during the whole act of eating; on the contrary, if food is situated on a small elevated platform, the animal has to climb this platform with his forelegs and eat the food standing on his hindlegs. All these postures are kept during the act of eating, since their maintenance does not need the actual drive. Of course, if this posture has to be changed from time to time, the act of eating is interrupted and then the drive reflex is released.

To sum up, it seems that although there are certain facts which seem to cast some doubt upon the above specified theses and which require some additional assumptions to be explained adequately, the overwhelming body of evidence fully supports them. In consequence we shall accept these theses as a basis for our further discussion.

3. The control of alimentary instrumental responses by hunger drive

As shown in Section 2, we can reasonably assume that instrumental responses are drive-bound, being elicited by that drive which has caused their formation. Since, as noted in Chapter I, drive reflexes, in contradistinction to consummatory reflexes, do not possess any easily observable unconditioned effects, instrumental conditioning may be utilized as an important tool of the study of unconditioned and conditioned drive reflexes, the instrumental responses serving as indicators of particular drives. Thus, on the one hand, a number of facts concerning classical drive CRs which were discussed in Chapters VI and VII may be now better substantiated by the technique of instrumental conditioning; on the other hand, a number of peculiar properties of instrumental CRs presented in Chapter VIII can be now adequately explained. We shall start our discussion with an analysis of alimentary type II CRs.

To begin, let us remember that if in a given situation food is repeatedly presented to the animal in small portions, with or without being preceded by a sporadic CS, the unconditioned hunger reflex is elicited after each consummatory act, and the conditioned hunger reflex is established to the whole situation. Accordingly, if in a given situation a type II CR is trained, the instrumental response will usually appear immediately after the cessation of the act of eating. If each such response is followed by food, the instrumental CR will be formed extremely rapidly and will be exceedingly stable and regular, because it will exploit the unconditioned hunger drive after each consummatory response.

If the instrumental CR is formed to a sporadic CS, in the first stage of training the intertrial responses will always occur, being particularly crowded after each food intake and being more frequent in more voracious animals.

Since during the intertrial intervals the dog never receives food, the hunger CR in these intervals will become gradually inhibited, and therefore the intertrial movements will disappear, to be performed only in response to the sporadic stimulus at which they are followed by food. However, if the dog will once or twice receive food "gratis" in the absence of the CS, the hunger drive CR to the experimental situation will be restored, and the intertrial movements will immediately reappear.

The strength of the hunger drive CR can also be manipulated by providing the animal with more or less attractive (or "tasty") food. If in the first trial the dog finds that the food is more attractive than usual (for example, if the meat-biscuit powder contains more meat), the instrumental responses in all subsequent trials will be more vigorous and the intertrial movements will reappear. On the contrary, if the food offered in a given session is less tasty than usual, the animal may even refuse to work for food at all, although he will take this food if offered "gratis."

The explanation of these facts is based on our considerations on the nature of tastiness of food presented in Chapter I and its effects on hunger drive CRs discussed in Chapter VI. It was shown there that the more attractive the food offered to the animal—that is, the better the satisfaction of the given kind of hunger drive—the stronger the unconditioned drive released after the food is consumed, and the stronger the conditioned drive to the situation and/or stimuli in whose presence this food was presented. Accordingly, the alimentary instrumental activity becomes proportionately more intense.

These rules are faithfully followed when hunger drive is elicited artificially by electric stimulation of the lateral hypothalamus.[15] If a goat is trained to perform an instrumental movement in response to an experimental situation, this movement will be repeatedly elicited in a satiated animal by stimulation of the hypothalamic hunger center (Figure IX-2a). If, however, the goat is trained to perform the movement only in response to a sporadic stimulus, hypothalamic stimulation in the satiated animal will elicit it only in the presence of the CS and not in intervals, provided that stimulation is not too strong (Figure IX-2b).

In the preceding chapter it was shown (Experiments VII and VIII) that the formation of type II CR to a sporadic stimulus S_E does not occur if that stimulus is simply followed by movement M and reinforced by food. In order to establish this reflex, S_E has to be occasionally presented alone without M and without offering food. According to our discussion in Chapter VI (Section 4), the occasional non-reinforcement of S_E prevents the formation of the consummatory food CR to this stimulus and preserves its hunger-drive–producing character, in-

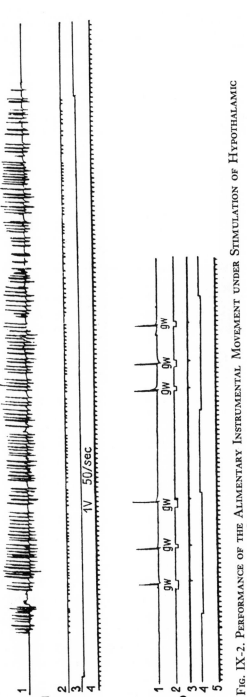

1V 50/sec

Fig. IX-2. Performance of the Alimentary Instrumental Movement under Stimulation of Hypothalamic Hunger Center in Satiated Goat

a) Instrumental response conditioned to the experimental situation. 1, lifting the foreleg; 2, presentations of food; 3, hypothalamic stimulation; 4, time in 5 seconds.

b) Instrumental response conditioned to a sporadic auditory stimulus. 1, lifting the foreleg; 2, CS (whistle); 3, presentations of food; 4, stimulation of hypothalamus; 5, time in 5 seconds.

(Wyrwicka, Dobrzecka, and Tarnecki, in *Acta Biol. Exper.*, 20 [1960]: 121.)

dispensable for the formation of the instrumental CR. Thus, the thesis of the partial inhibitory character of the type II CS (in respect to the consummatory food CR) is in some sense true, since inhibition of the consummatory food CR allows the hunger CR to be manifested. On the contrary, inhibitory effect of a "pure" consummatory food CS upon instrumental responding manifested in Experiment XIV (cf. Figure VIII-7) of the preceding chapter is further proof of the unidirectional antagonism of the food CR and the hunger CR discussed in Chapter VI.

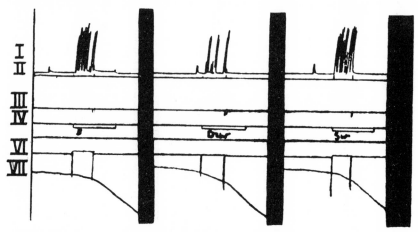

FIG. IX-3. THE TYPE II CR TO THE ORIGINAL TYPE II CS AND TO THAT TRANSFORMED FROM TYPE I CS

I, instrumental response (lifting the right foreleg); II, CS-US interval; III, presentation of food; IV, CS; VI, CS-US interval; VII, salivation (downward).

First and third graphs denote CR to the original type II CS; second graph denotes CR to the type II CS transformed from the type I CS.

(J. Konorski and W. Wyrwicka, in *Acta Biol. Exper.*, 15 [1950]: 193.)

In good agreement with this interpretation of the relations between the type I food CR and the type II hunger CR is the strong resistance to the transformation of the classical food CR into an instrumental CR.[16] It has been shown that such a transformation is much more difficult than the formation of the instrumental CR to a new stimulus, and that the type II CS converted from the type I CS for a long time retains a weaker "motogenic power" than the original type II CS does (Figure IX-3). Moreover, when the instrumental CR to the original type II CS and to the converted type II CS are subjected to extinction, the motor response to the first stimulus is much more resistant to extinction than that to the second stimulus.

The explanation of this fact is that, once a strong consummatory food CR has been established to a given stimulus, this stimulus produces the hunger antidrive which handicaps the formation of the hunger drive CR controlling the instrumental response. If the type I CR is partly inhibited by non-reinforcement (when the trained movement is not performed), the hunger drive CR is released; but thereafter the reinforcement of the CS when the movement *is* performed restores the former reflex and handicaps the performance of the movement. On the other hand, an original type II CR is not always a pure hunger drive reflex. In fact, once an instrumental response has been firmly established, each presentation of the CS is regularly followed by food; this increases the tendency of that stimulus to become the consummatory CS.

Thus, it is clear that in usual instrumental training the hunger drive CR and the consummatory CR are mixed in various proportions, one of these reflexes prevailing, depending on the original training and some other circumstances (see Section 4, below). These relations are schematically represented in Figure IX-4.

Our present discussion throws light on another essential difference between classical and instrumental conditioning connected with the schedule of reinforcement.

It is well known that classical food CRs measured by the amount of salivation are most sensitive to non-reinforcement and require the presentation of food in practically every trial. On the other hand, instrumental CRs do not require such a rigorous procedure, as is documented by the fact that the so-called partial reinforcement under various schedules became a routine experimental practice in all those experiments which required keeping the animals working for food during prolonged periods of time.

Similarly, it is well known that in consummatory food CRs the success of conditioning depends largely on the portions of food presented as reinforcement in each trial. If these portions are too small, the CR is poor or even completely absent. Furthermore, there is much experimental evidence collected in Pavlov's laboratories to show that the CS-US trials should not be too crowded and that the optimal intertrial interval is not less than four or five minutes. On the contrary, even the smallest portions of food, consumed in about one second, are sufficient reinforcement of instrumental CRs, and my strong impression is (unfortunately not supported by any systematic experimental findings) that these reflexes are more stable and reliable if the portions of food are small and the trials frequent.

The explanation of all these facts from the point of view of our concept is again quite evident. Large portions of food used as reinforcement strongly favor the dominance of consummatory CRs over

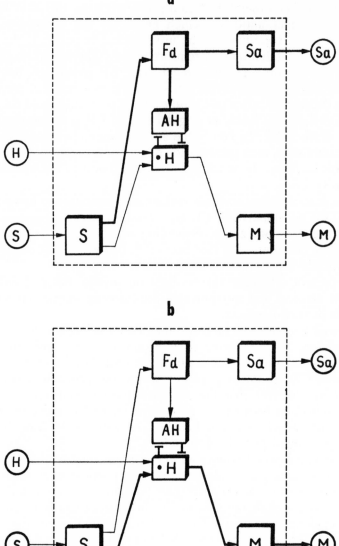

Fig. IX-4. Mixed Type I and Type II CR Arc

Thick arrows, strong connections; thin arrows, weak connections.

a) Preponderance of the type I CR connections over the type II CR connections.

b) Preponderance of the type II CR connections over the type I CR connections.

Denotations as in Figure IX-1.

hunger CRs. On the other hand, small and frequent portions produce a repeated anticipatory drive CR at the moment the food is offered and post-consummatory drive UR at the moment it is swallowed, this strongly increasing the general "tonus" of the hunger drive. Similarly, the irregular reinforcement may even improve the instrumental responding, because it tends to diminish the consummatory food CR and does not harm the drive CR, which is more tonic and resistant to extinction.

To end this discussion, we should mention still another interesting fact, discovered by Wyrwicka,[17] which at first glance seems even to contradict the principles presented above. Wyrwicka's experiment runs in the following way.

In the first stage of training an instrumental CR is firmly established to a given sporadic stimulus in a naïve dog. Thereafter, a new stimulus is introduced, which after a few seconds is reinforced by food according to the classical CR procedure. It may be seen that after a few trials this new stimulus starts to evoke by itself the trained instrumental response; if this response is immediately reinforced by food, the type II CR is soon consolidated by a mere transfer from the old CR. This result seems to be even more paradoxical when we recall that if the type II CR is established *after* the formation of a type I CR, the transfer of the instrumental response to the type I CS almost never occurs, since the latter stimulus *inhibits* the instrumental response established to the type II CS.

The explanation of the Wyrwicka phenomenon, as we have called it, is as follows. As pointed out in Chapter VI, when in an alimentary situation a new stimulus is introduced and accompanied by food, at first the hunger CR is formed to it because this stimulus is immediately followed by increased hunger due to visual presentation of food. In the routine type I conditioning procedure the hunger CR is soon replaced by the food CR and becomes partly suppressed. However, if earlier in the given situation a type II CR has been established, the hunger CR elicited by the new CS immediately releases the instrumental response, which, if reinforced by food, soon becomes fixed.

4. The interrelations between salivary and motor responses in type II conditioning

As indicated in the preceding chapter, our method of type II conditioning has offered an excellent opportunity, not only to study the instrumental responses in a convenient experimental condition, but also to examine the interrelations between salivary and motor responses in various experimental schedules. From the material presented in that chapter it may be seen that two somewhat different problems arise in this respect. One problem is that of the relations between the salivary and instrumental responses in various stages of type II conditioning. The other problem is that of the relations between these two responses when the classical and instrumental reflexes are separately established to different stimuli.

Let us start with an analysis of the second problem. It seems that the best model of the relations between the two types of CRs is provided by Experiment XIV, in which type I positive or negative CS was presented against the background of continuous type II responding (cf. Figure VIII-7). It appeared that whereas the positive type I CS produced copious salivation and inhibition of type II responses, the negative CS, on the contrary, produced no inhibition (and perhaps even augmentation) of these responses although the salivary effect was clearly diminished. If it is assumed that inhibition of the instrumental responses during the operation of the positive type I CS is due to the suppression of the hunger CR by the consummatory CR, the intense performance of the instrumental movements in response to a not firmly established negative CS shows that the operation of that stimulus evokes the hunger CR. The fact that the salivary response was during that time strongly decreased was perhaps the first proof that the hunger reflex is not necessarily accompanied by salivation.

An analogous result was obtained in Experiment XV when to various sporadic stimuli a positive type I CR, negative type I CR, and positive type II CR were established respectively. The positive type I CS elicited copious salivation and no instrumental response, whereas the negative type I CS elicited instrumental responses accompanied by very slight salivation. Similarly, acute extinction of the positive type I CR produced intense instrumental responding to each presentation of the CS, continuing in spite of the strong decrease of salivation (Experiment XVI).

We shall now proceed to the other problem—that of interrelations between salivary and motor responses in instrumental conditioning. As pointed out in the previous chapter, these interrelations are far from being clear. In some experiments the salivary response strongly prevailed over the motor response; in others, the reverse relations were manifest. Similarly, experiments with extinction or differentiation of type II CRs also gave unpredictable results as to which of these responses was more, or less, resistant to extinction.

It seems now that, in view of our present concept, the disentangling of this problem has become possible.

As noted in the preceding section, in the usual type II conditioning procedure the character of the CS is ambiguous. On the one hand, it is obviously a drive-producing stimulus, because otherwise it would fail to elicit the instrumental response. On the other hand, when the type II CR is already firmly established and in consequence the CS is always reinforced by food within a short CS-US interval, it of course tends to become also a type I food CS, its manifestation being the salivary response. It is clear that the relations between the two partly antagonistic CRs may fluctuate, because the preponderance of the food CR over the drive CR causes the delay of the instrumental movement and consequently the delay of the food reinforcement, whereas the reverse relationship leads to the earlier performance of the movement and thus to the shortening of the CS-US interval.

The problem arose as to whether it would be possible to design an experimental set-up in which the type II CR would not be contaminated with the type I CR. It was found that this set-up is indeed possible. Following are the results of these experiments.[18]

The training of the dogs ran as follows. First, a strong type I CR was established to a stimulus situated close to the feeder. Then the animals were trained to press, with the right foreleg, a lever situated on the right side of the feeder to secure the presentation of the type I CS and then food. When the animals learned to perform this movement, a new stimulus was introduced (type II CS), and only the movements performed in its presence were followed by the type I CS. This being achieved, the type II CS was protracted until nine lever pressings were executed and the type I CS-US interval was protracted to eight seconds. Thus, when the type II CS was presented, the animal had to perform nine trained movements; then this stimulus was turned off and the type I CS was presented, followed after eight seconds by food.

The results of these experiments were most significant. The type II CS produced a general motor excitement of the animal, accompanied by vigorous lever-pressings. Salivation was either totally absent or very poor. When the type II CS was turned off and the type I CS turned on, the animal's behavior changed immediately: he calmed down, stared intently at the feeder, and salivated copiously. No trained movements ever appeared in response to this stimulus (Figure IX-5).

In this way we succeeded in achieving total separation of the instrumental CR driven by the hunger drive and classical food CR without visible contamination by the drive CR. It is worth mentioning that when, in the next series of experiments, the type II CS was reinforced by food after the required number of lever-pressings without the intermediary of the type I CS, the type II CR was soon contaminated by the type I CR. The animal began to salivate in the presence of the stimulus, and the motor responses were somewhat extended in time. Very often the animal, after performing a few movements, turned to the feeder, salivated, and then again returned to pressing the lever, thus

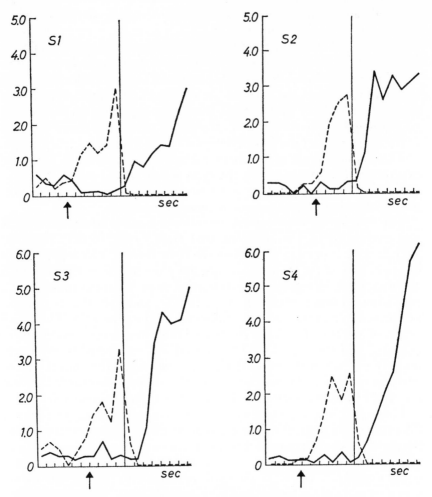

FIG. IX-5. SEPARATION OF INSTRUMENTAL AND SALIVARY
CONDITIONED RESPONSES

Mean rate of lever-pressing (presses per second) is denoted by dashed lines; mean rate of salivation (drops per second) is denoted by continuous line. Each graph represents average of a typical session (about 15 trials) late in the training of each dog. The vertical line represents the onset of the classical CS. The curves end at the time of reinforcement. The arrows indicate the median time (in seconds) of onset of the instrumental CS.

(From G. D. Ellison and J. Konorski, in *Science*, 146 [1964]: 1071–72.)

completing the required number of movements. In many cases (but not always), clear antagonistic relations were observed between the salivary and instrumental response.

The present experiments settle, among other things, the so far uncertain question as to whether salivation can be considered one of the effects of the hunger drive. The answer is negative. If salivation does appear during hunger drive, this means that the food CR was mixed with it. Since, as indicated in Chapter V, in normal life associations are formed between the hunger center and the food CS units, the subject, under a strong hunger drive, may easily imagine various feeding situations and in this way provide himself with the food CS.

Another important experiment concerning the interrelation between salivary and motor responses in type II conditioning was performed by Wolf.[19] The animals were first trained to perform a single movement of flexion of the foreleg in response to a type II CS, this movement being immediately followed by food. Then two such movements were required for obtaining food; thereafter the number of movements required for one reinforcement was gradually increased until the animal refused to work altogether.

When the required number of movements was not significant (not more than ten), the animals performed them with maximal speed, salivating copiously. When, however, the number was still further increased, the delay of the first movement became more and more protracted, until it reached one or two minutes. Thereafter the animal began to work, first slowly but then with a gradually increasing rate of movements. Salivation followed closely and precisely the motor performance. During the delay period, no salivation was observed; but the first performed movement was accompanied by a definite "quantum" of salivation (Figure IX-6).

The explanation of these results seemingly contradictory to the previous ones is the following. In the preliminary training, the proprioceptive stimulus S_{Pr} generated by the learned movement closely preceding the presentation of food became a strong type I CS. When the number of movements required was gradually increased, the animal did not learn to react to their fixed ratio but continued to react with a short type I response to S_{Pr} of *each* movement. The increasing delay of the performance of movements was a true inhibition of delay of instrumental responses due to the prolongation of the CS-US interval. Since this delay still more protracted this interval (the required number of movements being definite), a vicious circle was easily produced with the result that the animals refused to work altogether.

Comparing these two series of experiments, we see that, depending on the procedure, the trained instrumental movements may either

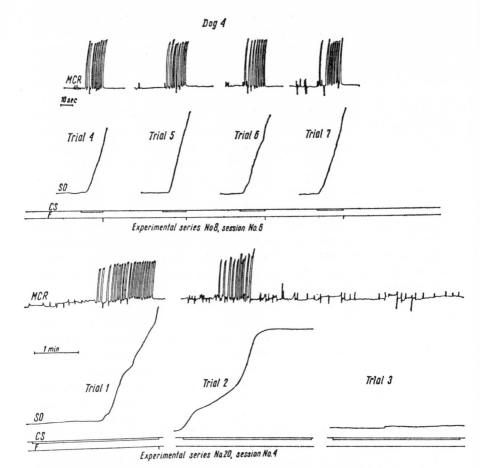

Fig. IX-6. Voluminograms of Salivary Outflow Correlated with Multiple Instrumental Responding

MCR, tracing of the multiple CR (lifting the right foreleg); SO, tracing of salivary outflow; CS, conditioned stimulus; F, food presentation.

Above: 8 movements are required for food reinforcement; note the prompt onset of both salivary and motor responses in all the trials.

Below: 20 movements are required for food reinforcement; in trial 1 both salivation and motor response begin after considerable latency; in trial 2, after performing 11 movements, the dog stops working and salivary response abruptly drops to zero; in trial 3 the dog refuses completely to perform the instrumental response and does not salivate.

(From K. Wolf, in *Acta Biol. Exper.*, 23 [1963]: 133–50.)

appear without being accompanied by salivation if proprioceptive stimuli generated by them are not made type I CSs or may be closely and precisely connected with salivation if the animal learns that the performance of the movement is the immediate signal for the presentation of food. The major issue emerging from this discrepancy is that whether or not a proprioceptive stimulus generated by the instrumental response becomes a consummatory food CS, this does not influence in any way the very process of instrumental conditioning. This is in clear opposition to all theories (including our own original theory) which claim that the proprioceptive feedback of the performed movement is essential for instrumental conditioning as a sort of secondary reinforcement.[20]

It should be added that when in another series of experiments[21] the dogs were trained under the fixed ratio schedule (thirty-three instrumental responses) for a prolonged time, the results were intermediate between the two series just described: salivation was only partly dissociated from instrumental responding, since it started after about half the required number of responses.

5. The mechanism of the defensive type II conditioned reflexes

In the preceding chapter we have described two varieties of defensive instrumental CRs. In one, the animal resisted performing a given movement when this movement was followed by a fear-producing stimulus (Experiments IX and X); in the second, the animal learned to perform a movement when it was followed by the state of relief (Experiments XXI and XXII). These two types of procedures are usually referred to as passive and active avoidance respectively.* Our aim now is to explain these two varieties in accordance with our present concepts.

Begin with the analysis of the second variety (active avoidance or escape method), because its mechanism seems to be more clear.

In our routine procedure described in Experiments XXI and XXII, the training consists of two stages. In the first stage, a sporadic stimulus is reinforced by a noxious agent, and consequently a fear CR is established to that stimulus. If this preliminary training is long-lasting and

---

* It should be noted that the term "passive avoidance" in its general usage is ambiguous. It has at least three meanings: (1) the active restraining from the performance of a movement with clear concomitance of the antagonistic movement (as in our Experiments IX and X); (2) the freezing type of fear response inhibiting *all* movements; and (3) the restraining from the performance of hunger-driven movements because of the fear-hunger drive antagonism, as manifested in the CER method. In the present discussion we shall deal only with the first kind of "passive avoidance," since the mechanism of the others do not present any special difficulty for explanation and have been discussed in other contexts.

the US not very strong, the fear CR in the intertrial intervals is gradually inhibited, as the animal learns that he is secure in the absence of the CS. Thereafter, in the second stage of training, we elicit a certain movement in the presence of the CS, and then the aversive US is omitted. Since this movement, being followed by relief, has from the very beginning a clear drive-reducing significance, the animal soon learns to perform it instrumentally. Because the fear drive in the intertrial intervals has been inhibited in the first stage of training, the intertrial movements are scarce. Of course, when we administer the noxious US unexpectedly at the beginning of a session, the fear drive will be increased, the avoidance responses will become more vigorous, and the intertrial movements may appear. Similarly, if we introduce a new stimulus and reinforce it by the same noxious US, then after a few trials it starts to elicit the same instrumental response (Experiment XXII). The explanation of this fact is that the new stimulus becomes a fear CS.

Unfortunately, the explanation of the first variety of the defensive instrumental CRs ("passive avoidance") is not so clear. The question may be asked as to according to what mechanism the animal learns to perform a movement, antagonistic to that followed by an aversive US. When the aversive US acts directly upon the part of the body involved in the provoked movement (for instance, the water-puff directed upon the mouth when the animal seizes food in Experiment X), the antagonistic reflex is either innate, or learned in the animal's early experience; therefore, its instrumentalization, when it is followed by relief, is obvious. If, however, the aversive US is not contiguous with the performed movement (as it is in Experiment IX) the situation is more complex and its elucidation requires more rigorous experiments than those we have performed. In any event, whatever the *origin* of the instrumental response involved in "passive avoidance," its properties are exactly the same as those of the active avoidance response.

Now we shall turn to the explanation of the extraordinary stability of the avoidance CR, which, with a proper experimental procedure, does not extinguish despite its total lack of reinforcement.

It should be noted that an important factor securing the stability of the avoidance CR is the cessation of the CS immediately after the performance of the instrumental response. As a result this response closely precedes the abrupt reduction of the fear drive; in effect the proprioception of that response becomes a strong relief CS.

It seems that precisely this fact is crucial for the stability of the avoidance response. According to our theory of association, the actual connections between two sets of gnostic units can be formed if, and only if, the activation of these sets overlaps; in the case of conditioning, the US must follow the CS in the overlapping sequence, or at least after a short delay, but it cannot be separated from the CS by any other not neutral stimulus. Yet, in avoidance procedure the CS, originally trained as a fear CS, is separated from the state of relief by the proprioceptive stimulus heralding this relief, and in consequence its extinction (that is its transformation into the fear antidrive CS) is not possible. In effect the CS continues to be a fear producing stimulus and, as such, elicits the avoidance response which in turn precludes its own extinction. In other words, the avoidance response constitutes a "barrier" preventing the association between the fear CS and the state of relief to be established.

Mutatis mutandis, the situation is here not very different from that encountered in alimentary instrumental conditioning. If an alimentary instrumental motor response to a sporadic CS closely precedes the food intake (that is, the hunger antidrive), the hunger-producing role of this CS is well preserved, because the proprioception of the movement being a strong consummatory food CS forms a safe "barrier" preventing the conversion of the hunger CS into the food CS.

Both in the alimentary and in the defensive instrumental CRs the impermeability of this barrier depends largely on the closeness of the relation between the trained movement and the antidrive state. If in alimentary type II conditioning the presentation of food involving the hunger antidrive state does not closely follow the trained movement, the CS tends to be converted into the consummatory (that is, hunger antidrive) CS and consequently the movement tends to decrease. Similarly, it may be expected that if the tie between the avoidance movement and fear reduction becomes loosened, this would lead to the CS being closer followed by the state of relief. In consequence, the avoidance CR will be "extinguished" because of the transformation of the fear drive CR into the fear antidrive CR.

The available data strikingly confirm this conclusion. Fonberg and Bregadze[22] have independently found that when the avoidance CS is prolonged to a definite period of time and is discontinued regardless of whether the animal performs the trained movement, the instrumental response is gradually extinguished. As shown by Sołtysik,[23] this extinction is due either to the attenuation of the fear drive elicited by the CS, as judged by the lack of acceleration of the heart rate formerly produced by that CS (Figure IX-7), or to a substitution of the old instrumental response by another one of a more tonic character (cf. Chapter X).

To end these considerations, we would discuss the problem of interrelation between the instrumental response as an indicator of the fear CR on the one hand, and the increase of the heart rate as a reliable

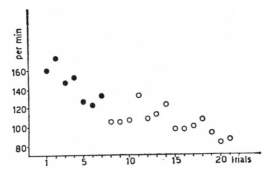

FIG. IX-7. "EXTINCTION" OF AN AVOIDANCE CR BY PROLONGATION OF THE ACTION OF CS TO 10 SECONDS

Each circle represents the maximal heart-rate (measured in 3-second intervals) observed during the 10-second action of the CS. Black circles denote heart-rate in trials in which the CS elicited the instrumental responses (placing the fore-leg on the platform); white circles denote those trials in which no responses were elicited.

For extinction a new stimulus similar to the original CS was used. This is why extinction occurred relatively rapidly. Note that the disappearance of movements occurred when the pulse-rate decreased.

(S. Sołtysik, in *Acta Biol. Exper.*, 20 [1960]: 171–82.)

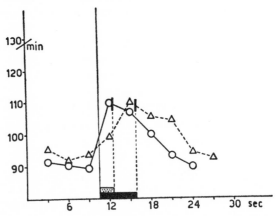

FIG. IX-8. RELATION OF THE LATENCY OF AVOIDANCE RESPONSE (VERTICAL BARS) TO THE RISE OF THE HEART-RATE

Abscissae, time; ordinates, heart-rate.

Latencies of the instrumental response in one group of trials were about 2 seconds (circles), in another group 5 seconds (triangles). In both groups the response occurs when cardioacceleration reaches a definite level.

Note that the CS (dotted block or black block respectively) ends immediately after the performance of movement and that the heart-rate falls dramatically after the trial is terminated.

(S. Sołtysik and M. Kowalska, in *Acta Biol. Exper.*, 20 [1960]: 157–70.)

effect of classical fear CR on the other. This problem was studied by Sołtysik et al.,[24] who found that there is in fact a striking positive correlation between the two responses: in most instances the instrumental motor act appears exactly at the moment when increased heart rate achieves a certain level, and stops being elicited when this level is not achieved. An example of this correlation is presented in Figure IX-8.

In contrast to this close correlation between the instrumental and autonomic fear CR, there is no correlation whatsoever between the instrumental fear CR and the defensive consummatory CR. Thus, as shown in Experiment XXII, when an instrumental response protecting the animal from the introduction of acid into the mouth is established, it is elicited *ad infinitum* by the corresponding CS, although the salivary acid conditioned response has been long abolished. Similarly, when the dog is trained to lift his left foreleg in response to a sporadic stimulus to avoid an electric shock to the right hindleg, then, when the instrumental CR is established, the CS produces only the movement of the foreleg but no longer the movement of the previously shocked right hindleg.[25] Thus, it may be inferred that, after the avoidance CR is set up, there is a complete separation between the fear CR which is fully preserved and the consummatory defensive CR (acid CR, shock CR, and so on) which is extinguished because the CS is no longer followed by the US.

6. Summary and conclusions

In this chapter, we have been concerned with the problem of the relations between drive activities on the one hand and instrumental conditioning on the other. According to numerous data indicating the close relationship between the two phenomena, a thesis was advanced that particular drive centers constitute *intermediary links* between the central representation of the type II CS and the central representation of the given motor act. In other words, it has been assumed that between the highest levels of the drive centers situated in the limbic system and the particular centers of the motor behavioral system connections are formed because of which the operation of the given drive produces a definite instrumental response.

The mechanism of the formation of these connections was visualized in the following way. Excitation of a drive center produces a state of arousal in the central motor behavioral system. If against this background a particular movement is provoked and it coincides with the cessation of drive, the conditioned connections between the two corresponding centers are formed, whereas other movements performed during the drive operation are retroactively inhibited. In alimentary type II CRs the cessation of the hunger drive is accomplished through inhibition of the drive center provided by the food UR (act of eating) or its substitute, the type I CR. In defensive type II CRs the inactivation of the fear drive is achieved by termination of the fear CS immediately after the performance of the instrumental response.

Thus, our concept implies that the type II CR can be formed and elicited only on the basis of a certain drive, and that its formation and preservation requires the reduction or inhibition of drive (being tantamount to the occurrence of the antidrive) after the instrumental response has been performed.

Since the instrumental response may be considered a reliable indicator of a drive reflex (either unconditioned or conditioned), the relations between drive CRs and consummatory CRs described in earlier chapters may be substantiated by experiments utilizing the combined method involving type I and type II CRs.

Since in alimentary activity there is a unidirectional antagonism between the consummatory food reflexes and the hunger drive reflexes, this antagonism is reflected in the relations between classical and instrumental CRs. Whenever the consummatory CR prevails over the hunger CR, the instrumental responding is poor whereas the salivary response is abundant. On the contrary, the dominance of the hunger drive CR over the consummatory CR makes the instrumental responding stable and intense whereas the salivary response is poor. Generally speaking, small portions of food presented at short intervals favor the occurrence of the instrumental responses even if they are not regularly reinforced, whereas large portions of food at long intervals regularly coinciding with the presentation of a CS favor the occurrence of classical CRs. The full separation of a hunger CR manifested by instrumental responding and consummatory CR manifested by salivation is possible if the two appropriate CSs operate in non-overlapping sequence.

Since in defensive activity the consummatory and drive reflexes are not antagonistic, the type I CS may produce the instrumental response under the appropriate training. However, when this response is established and the animal avoids the presentation of a noxious stimulus by instrumental responding, the close parallelism between the two CRs disappears because the classical consummatory CR becomes readily extinguished whereas the instrumental CR, under the proper experimental procedure, lasts indefinitely. The lack of extinction of the fear CR elicited by the type II CS in a proper avoidance procedure is explained by the fact that the instrumental response, being a strong relief

CS, forms a barrier separating the original fear CS from the state of relief.

In the next chapter it will be shown that the control exerted upon the type II CRs by the emotive system does not exhaust the mechanism of these reflexes, because the direct associations established between the external CSs and the motor behavioral system play an equally important role in their formation and occurrence.

References to Chapter IX

1. I. P. Pavlov. 1928. *Lectures on Conditioned Reflexes.* Translated by W. H. Gantt. Chap. 13. New York: International.
2. W. R. Hess. 1957. *The Functional Organization of the Diencephalon.* New York and London: Grune & Stratton.
   J. W. Papez. 1937. A proposed mechanism of emotion. *Arch. Neurol. Psychiat.* (Chicago), 38: 725–43.
   B. K. Anand and J. R. Brobeck. 1951. Hypothalamic control of food intake in rats and cats. *Yale J. Biol. Med.*, 24: 123-40.
3. H. W. Magoun. 1958. *The Waking Brain.* Springfield, Ill.: Charles C Thomas.
4. G. Moruzzi and H. W. Magoun. 1949. Brain stem reticular formation and activation of the EEG. *Electroenceph. Clin. Neurophysiol.*, 1: 455–73.
5. W. Wyrwicka, C. Dobrzecka, and R. Tarnecki. 1960. Elaboration of alimentary conditioned reflex type II with the use of electrical stimulation of the hypothalamus. *Bull. Acad. Pol. Sci.*, Ser. Sci. Biol., 8: 109–11.
6. J. Olds and P. Milner. 1954. Positive reinforcement produced by electrical stimulation of septal area and other regions of rat brain. *J. Comp. Physiol. Psychol.*, 47: 419–27.
7. J. A. Deutsch. 1960. *The Structural Basis of Behavior.* Chicago: University of Chicago Press.
8. C. I. Howarth and J. A. Deutsch. 1962. Drive decay: The cause of fast "Extinction" of habits learned for brain stimulation. *Science*, 137 (No. 3523): 35–36.
9. J. M. R. Delgado, W. W. Roberts, and N. E. Miller. 1954. Learning motivated by electrical stimulation of the brain. *Am. J. Physiol.*, 179: 587–93.
10. N. E. Miller and M. L. Kessen. 1952. Reward effects of food via stomach fistula compared with those of food via mouth. *J. Comp. Physiol. Psychol.*, 45: 555–64.
    A. N. Epstein and P. Teitelbaum. 1955. Regulation of food intake in the absence of taste, smell and other oropharyngeal sensation. *J. Comp. Physiol. Psychol.*, 55: 753–59.
    P. Teitelbaum. 1964. "Appetite." *Proc. Am. Physiol. Soc.*, 108: 464–72.
11. F. D. Sheffield, J. J. Wulff, and R. Backer. 1951. Reward value of copulation without sex drive reduction. *J. Comp. Physiol. Psychol.*, 44: 3–8.

12. W. Wyrwicka, C. Dobrzecka, and R. Tarnecki. 1960. The effects of electrical stimulation of the hypothalamic feeding centre in satiated goats on alimentary conditioned reflexes type II. *Acta Biol. Exp. Vars.*, 20: 121–36.

13. E. Fonberg. 1962. Transfer of the conditioned avoidance reaction to the unconditioned noxious stimuli. *Acta Biol. Exp. Vars.*, 22 (No. 4): 251–58.

14. Г. В. Скипин. 1947. О механизме образования условных пищевых рефлексов. (On the mechanism of the formation of alimentary conditioned reflexes.) Moscow: Izdat. "Sovetskaia Nauka."

15. W. Wyrwicka, C. Dobrzecka, and R. Tarnecki. 1960 (see note 12 above).

16. J. Konorski and W. Wyrwicka. 1950. Research into conditioned reflexes of the second type. I. Transformation of conditioned reflexes of the first type into conditioned reflexes of the second type. *Acta Biol. Exp. Vars.*, 15: 193–204.

    G. D. Ellison and J. Konorski. 1966. Salivation and instrumental responding to an instrumental CS pretrained using the classical conditioning paradigm. *Acta Biol. Exp. Vars.*, 26: 159–65.

17. W. Wyrwicka. 1952*a*. Studies on motor conditioned reflexes. V. On the mechanism of the motor conditioned reaction. *Acta Biol. Exp. Vars.*, 16: 131–37.

    ———. 1952*b*. Zagadnienie mechanizmu warunkowej reakcji ruchowej. (The problem of the mechanism of the conditioned motor reaction.) *Acta Physiol. Pol.*, 3: 39–62. English and Russian summaries.

18. G. D. Ellison and J. Konorski. 1964. Separation of the salivary and motor responses in instrumental conditioning. *Science*, 146 (No. 3647): 1071–72.

    ———. 1965. An investigation of the relations between salivary and motor responses during instrumental performance. *Acta Biol. Exp. Vars.*, 25: 297–315.

19. K. Wolf. 1963. Properties of multiple conditioned reflex type II activity. *Acta Biol. Exp. Vars.*, 23: 133–50.

20. O. H. Mowrer. 1960. *Learning Theory and Behavior.* New York: Wiley.

21. G. D. Ellison and D. R. Williams. 1962. Conditioned salivation during FI and FR lever-pressing for food. Paper presented at Eastern Psychological Association meetings, Philadelphia.

22. А. Н. Брегадзе. 1953. К вопросу выработки оборонительного условного рефлекса у собак. (A problem of the formation of a defensive reflex in dogs.) *Trudy Inst. Fiziol. Akad. Nauk Gruz. SSR.*, 9: 43–59.

    E. Fonberg. 1953. Unpublished data.

23. S. Sołtysik. 1960. Studies on the avoidance conditioning. I. Differentiation and extinction of avoidance reflexes. *Acta Biol. Exp. Vars.*, 20: 171–82.

24. S. Sołtysik and M. Kowalska. 1960. Studies on the avoidance conditioning. I. Relations between cardiac (type I) and motor (type II) effects in the avoidance reflex. *Acta Biol. Exp. Vars.*, 20: 157–70.

25. Г. В. Скипин. 1957. О физиологических механизмах, лежащих в основе образования оборонительных условных рефлексов. (On physiological mechanisms underlying the formation of defensive conditioned reflexes.) *Zhurn. vyssh. nervn. dejat.*, 7 : 877–88. English summary.

————. 1959. О взаимодействии различных форм двигательных оборонительных условных рефлексов у животных. (On the interaction between different forms of motor conditioned reflexes in animals.) *Ibid.*, 9 : 429–35. English summary.

CHAPTER X

STRUCTURE OF THE TYPE II
CONDITIONED REFLEX ARC

1. Introductory remarks

In the preceding chapter it was shown that the *spiritus movens* for instrumental responses is provided by emotive factors or drives which not only enable the formation of particular type II CRs but are also indispensable for their elicitation. Further, it was shown that the given drive not only is the factor eliciting a given instrumental act but it also determines which of various instrumental acts is performed; in fact, in our previous discussion (Chapter VIII, Section 7) we brought evidence to show that in principle the instrumental response is evoked by the operation of that specific drive whose reduction was brought about by that response.

However, the question may be asked as to whether the type II CRs depend exclusively on the emotive factors which brought them into existence or whether there are also other agents which determine what instrumental act is elicited at a given moment.

The following general consideration leads us to the assumption that these other agents determining both the formation and elicitation of particular instrumental responses do actually exist and that they play an important role in the motor behavior of animals and men.

Examining our own motor behavior and that of our pet animals, we may observe that each individual has at his disposal a number of instrumental acts subserving the satisfaction of each drive and that different acts are thrown into operation in different external conditions, or even in the same condition when the preceding acts were ineffective. To give a most typical example, a cat will perform quite different movements to secure food when he is directly confronted with it, when he sees a piece of meat outside the cage in which he is enclosed, when he sees it on an elevated platform, or when he smells a mouse. In the first instance, he grasps it in his mouth; in the second, he uses his forepaw; in the third, he jumps upon the platform; and in the fourth, he creeps and then jumps upon the prey. *Mutatis mutandis*, our own way of bringing various kinds of food into the mouth is no less varied: we perform quite different instrumental acts when we have in front of us a sandwich, a plate of soup, a hot dish, or a bunch of grapes.

Therefore, there is no doubt that although a given drive can throw into operation all the instrumental acts which are at its disposal, the particular act produced at a given moment is determined largely by the external situation with which the subject is confronted.

Taking these considerations into account, we see that our paradigm presented in Figure IX-1 is not sufficient for the determination of which instrumental response will be elicited by a given type II CS. We should accept that the CS center is connected with the center of the instrumental movement, not only through the intermediary of the drive center, but also, so to speak, directly, bypassing this center. New paradigms representing this situation are shown in Figures X-1 and X-2.

Accepting the existence of a "direct" connection between the CS center and the M center, we may immediately observe that this connection is exactly the same as that discussed in much detail with regard to human beings in Chapter V, Section 5. There we were not much concerned with the connections running from the emotive brain to the kinesthetic gnosis, postponing a consideration of these connections to the discussion on instrumental conditioning; but we were much concerned with the connections linking various exteroceptive gnostic fields with the kinesthetic gnostic fields involved particularly in oral and manual behavioral acts. We have proposed a hypothesis that these intergnostic associations are based chiefly on axosomatic synaptic contacts whereas the less "specific" drive-gnostic associations are based on the axodendritic facilitatory connections. Whether this is true or not, it does seem reasonable to assume that, with regard to the instrumental motor acts, the direct CS-M connections play a determining role, specifying which movement can be elicited in a given external situation, whereas the drive-M connections play an "energizing" role, facilitating the performance of the movement designated by the determining factor. We should be reminded once again that when these determining connections, developed mainly by conditioning, are still

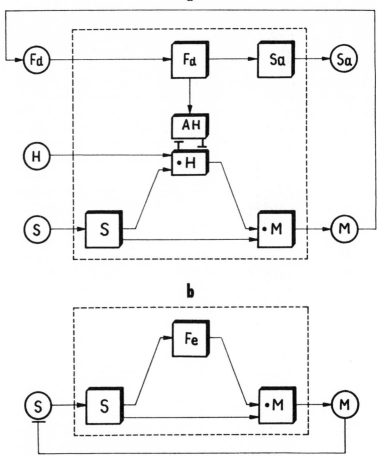

Fig. X-1. A Completed Block Model of Type II CR Arc

All denotations as in Figure IX-1 (p. 398).
a) Alimentary type II CR.
b) Defensive type II CR.

Note that the difference between this model and the previous one is that the center of the CS (S) is connected with the center of the instrumental response (M) not only through the drive center (H and Fe, respectively) but also directly. The point in the instrumental response center denotes that it is activated by the joint operation of drive→M connections and S→M connections.

A similar model of instrumental alimentary CRs involving both "direct" connections and "indirect" connections was proposed by Wyrwicka (*Acta Biol. Exper.*, 16 [1952]: 131–37), except that in her theoretical concepts the intermediary link between CS and M is represented not by the hunger drive center but by a general "alimentary center."

not established (either in general in a newborn organism or in a particular situation), the drive action produces a chaotic behavior due to the general arousal of the whole central motor behavioral system.

The discussion in the present chapter will be concerned mainly with the functional significance of each of the two branches of the type II CR arc $(CS \rightarrow D \rightarrow M$ and $CS \rightarrow M)$ and their interrelations. In particular we shall concentrate our considerations: (1) on the cooperation of the two channels of messages converging upon the motor

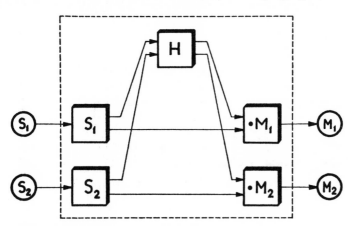

Fig. X-2. Block Model of Two Type II CRs Established under the Same Drive (H)

S_1, S_2, receptors and centers of two type II CSs; M_1, M_2, centers and effectors of instrumental responses.

center (or, to be more precise, kinesthetic units) controlling the given instrumental act; (2) on the mechanism of the selectivity of $CS \rightarrow M$ connections in designating a proper instrumental act; and (3) on inhibitory processes developing in the process of extinction or differentiation of instrumental CRs.

2. The cooperation of the CS-D-M and CS-M connections in instrumental conditioned reflexes

We have many reasons to believe that, in order for a given established instrumental response to be elicited, the joint operation of CS-M and CS-D-M connections is indispensable: in the absence of CS-M connections the animal does not "know" what to do in order to satisfy the acting drive, whereas in the absence of CS-D-M connections he has no "motivation" to perform the movement designated by the CS-M connections.

In usual experimental conditions, when we establish a given instrumental response in a given situation (with or without a sporadic CS), both these types of connections are trained *pari passu*. When the given situation (denoted by ΣCS) is an actual CS (as is the case in Experiment III of Chapter VIII or in the Skinner box procedure), the animal learns to perform the trained movement constantly in that situation, stopping only during the consummatory acts. However, being under the action of the same drive, he will never perform that movement in a situation different from the original one. He will also stop performing the trained movement in that situation in the absence of drive, thus showing that the ΣCS-M connections alone are not sufficient for its elicitation.

More complex is the state of affairs when the animal is trained to perform an instrumental movement in response to a sporadic CS. As shown in the preceding chapters, the animal learns first to perform that movement in response to the whole situation, because of the formation of both ΣCS-D and ΣCS-M connections. However, later, when the movement M is followed by drive reduction only in the presence of a sporadic CS, the role of the situation is changed. This is because in the intertrial intervals the drive (whether hunger or fear) becomes weakened by the formation of classical ΣCS-antidrive CR (cf. Chapter VII). This weakening of drive prevents the performance of the instrumental response, but the originally established ΣCS-M connections remain intact. This is why presenting the US in the intertrial interval often "disinhibits" the given drive and causes the reappearance of the trained movements.

According to the "principle of strength of the CS effect," the stronger the sporadic CS, the more intense the drive CR produced by it and the more vigorous the instrumental response. However, since the CS has a double association with the instrumental movement, it is possible to arrange the experiment in such a way as to strengthen selectively the CS-M connection, leaving the CS-D-M connection unchanged.

The experiment has been programed in such a way that the dogs were trained to place the right foreleg on the platform under food reinforcement in response to auditory stimuli (buzzer, metronome, and so on), a rhythmic tactile stimulus applied to the body, and a rhythmic tactile stimulus applied to the distal part of the right forepaw (hereinafter called specific tactile stimulus, STS).[1]

It was found that whereas in regular experiments there was hardly any difference between the instrumental responses elicited by these stimuli, this was not true when special tests were given.

First, it was found that when the dogs were moderately satiated before the experimental session the instrumental response to the STS was still preserved, whereas the response to an auditory stimulus or to a tactile stimulus applied to the body had already disappeared. Similarly, if an auditory stimulus and the STS were subjected to parallel extinction (either acute or chronic), the resistance to extinction of the STS was much stronger than that to the auditory stimulus or to a tactile stimulus applied to the trunk (Figure X-3).

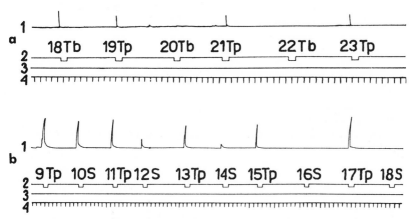

FIG. X-3. RESISTANCE TO EXTINCTION OF TYPE II CRs TO VARIOUS CSs

1, lifting of the leg; 2, CSs: Tp, specific tactile stimulus; Tb, tactile stimulus to the body; S, auditory stimulus; 3, food reinforcement; 4, time in 5 seconds.

Records present final stages of extinction, the numbers denoting the successive extinction trials.

a) Extinction of the CRs to STS and to tactile stimulus to the body.

b) Extinction of the CRs to STS and to auditory stimulus.

(Dobrzecka and Wyrwicka, in *Bull. Acad. Pol. Sci.*, 8 [1960]: 363.)

It was assumed that the unusually strong resistance to extinction and to satiation of the STS in comparison to other CSs is due to the existence of particularly strong connections linking the STS units with M units. The anatomical substrate of these connections was supposed to be the U fibers connecting the sensory and the motor area of the cortex. Consequently, a cut was made dividing these two areas in the region of the foreleg cortical representation (Figure X-4).[2]

The effect of this operation was most dramatic. The instrumental responses either to the specific tactile stimulus or to the control auditory stimulus were not impaired, and it might seem that the surgery had no effect at all on the type II CR. However, both the satiation test and the chronic extinction test have shown that the specific tactile

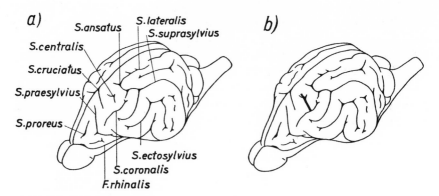

FIG. X-4. LINE OF INCISION BETWEEN THE SENSORY AND
MOTOR CORTEX IN DOG

a) Map of dog's cortex.
b) Place of incision.
(Cz. Dobrzecka, B. Sychowa, and J. Konorski, in *Acta Biol. Exper.*, 25
[1965]: 91–106.)

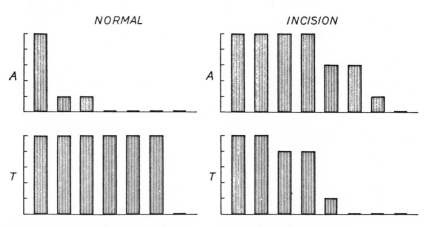

FIG. X-5. RESISTANCE TO EXTINCTION OF TYPE II CR TO STS (T) AND
AUDITORY STIMULUS (A) BEFORE AND AFTER SEPARATION OF
THE SENSORY AND MOTOR CORTEX

Each column denotes the number of positive responses in five trial blocks.
Note the weak resistance to extinction of CR to the auditory CS and strong
resistance to extinction to the STS before operation and partially reverse situation after operation.
(Cz. Dobrzecka, B. Sychowa, and J. Konorski, in *Acta Biol. Exper.*, 25 [1965]:
91–106.)

stimulus completely lost its extraordinary reflexogenic power and did not now differ from the control stimulus (Figure X-5). Therefore, we may claim that we have found a small part of the type II CR arc which was responsible for precisely the particular strength of that reflex when elicited by the specific tactile stimulus (Figure X-6).

The general inference which may be drawn from these experiments is rather important. It appears that in spite of the quite different physiological significance of CS-M and CS-D-M connections, the former being "gnostic" and the latter "emotive," their joint effect depends on the relative strength of each of them. If the CS-M connections are relatively weak, the CS-D-M connections must be strong in

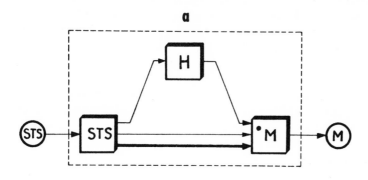

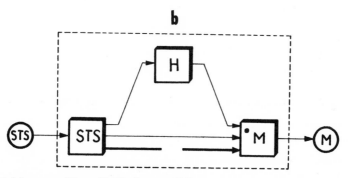

Fig. X-6. Model of Type II CR Arc to STS

STS, receptor and center of specific tactile stimulus; H, hunger center; M, motor center and effector.

The direct connection between STS and M has an additional pathway (a) which is cut by separation of the sensory and motor areas (b).

(Cz. Dobrzecka, B. Synchowa, and J. Konorski, in *Acta Biol. Exper.*, 25 [1965]: 91–106.)

order to evoke the instrumental response and vice versa; if the CS-M connections are very strong, the instrumental response may still persist in spite of the fact that the drive facilitating this response is very weak. This important principle may be expressed also in psychological terms by stating that the easier the performance of the given instrumental movement (because of associations established between the exteroceptive stimuli and that movement), the weaker has to be the motivation inspiring that movement.

Thus, we come to the conclusion that the strength of drive is not the only factor determining the vigor of the instrumental response. As a matter of fact, this vigor is determined by the *product* (not only in the logical but also in the algebraic sense) of the density of impulses arriving at the M center through the CS-M and the D-M channels. If this density in one of these channels is zero, then the instrumental response does not occur. However, if it is very small, it can be compensated for by the density of impulses running through the other channel.

To end our considerations, we should like to draw attention to one curious fact, manifested in Figure X-5, which was regularly observed in our experiments. If in a dog the instrumental CR is established to an auditory stimulus and the specific tactile stimulus, the reflex to the latter stimulus tends to suppress in some way the reflex to the former stimulus.[3] For instance, we often observed that it is difficult or even impossible to establish the type II CR to an acoustic stimulus when the reflex to the STS is already established. In Figure X-5 this suppressing effect is manifested by the exceedingly weak resistance to extinction of the auditory stimulus before the surgery. Curiously, after the incision made between the sensory and motor cortex, together with the "normalization" of the reflex to the specific tactile stimulus, this suppressing effect upon the other reflex has been totally abolished.

3. The relation of type II conditioned reflexes to the experimental situation

In the preceding section it was mentioned that if in a given situation a type II CR is established, the trained instrumental response does not occur under the same drive if the animal is brought to a quite different situation. This fact is documented by the following experiment performed by Wyrwicka.[4]

An instrumental alimentary CR of placing the right foreleg on the feeder to the sound of a flute was trained in dogs in a standard CR chamber. When it was firmly established, the animal was brought to another room in which only a table and a chair for the experimenter were placed (test situation). The dogs were allowed to run freely in that room for ten minutes daily for a few days without any stimuli being presented. Thereafter the sound of the flute and the sound of a rattle (never presented before) were tested.

As shown in Table X-1, whereas the rattle produced only an orientation response, the flute elicited a quite clear natural hunger drive response, but without any tendency to perform the trained movement.

Analogous experiments were performed on other dogs with defensive type II CRs. Each animal was trained to lift his hindleg in response to a whistle to avoid an electric shock applied to that leg.

TABLE X-1

EFFECT OF NEW AND TYPE II CONDITIONED STIMULI
IN "INDIFFERENT" SITUATION

Time	Stimulus	Reaction
	Protocol No. 1: The Dog Runs Freely around the Room	
1 min., 30 sec........	Rattle for 15 sec. (never used before)	A slight orientation reflex to the place of the rattle, then the dog continues running
3 min..............	Flute for 15 sec. (alimentary type II CS)	The dog comes to the flute, sniffs it, wags his tail, then jumps putting his forelegs on the knees of the experimenter
Time	Stimulus	Reaction
	Protocol No. 2: The Dog Moves Freely	
5 min..............	Rattle for 15 sec. (never used before)	A slight orientation reflex in first seconds, then the dog continues walking around the room
7 min..............	Whistle for 15 sec. (defensive type II CS)	The dog almost immediately runs to the wall, retracts his tail, then sits at the wall

SOURCE: Wyrwicka, in *Acta Biol. Exper.*, 18 (1958): 175–93.

Again, when the dog was brought to the test situation, the CS produced a fear response consisting in running away without any tendency to lift the leg.

Only when some essential elements of the experimental situation were introduced into the test situation (for example, the platform and the bowl of food placed on it) did the animal perform the trained movement.

Another series of experiments performed by Wyrwicka was concerned with the relations between type II CRs trained in different situations.[5] Situation I was a standard CR chamber with a dog being placed on the stand and fed from the feeder; situation II was an ordinary room with the dog standing on the floor and having pieces of bread thrown at him by the experimenter. In situation I the dog was trained to perform movement M_1 to stimulus S_1; in situation II, he was trained to perform movement M_2 to stimulus S_2. When both these type II CRs were firmly established, stimulus S_1 was tested in situation II, and stimulus S_2 was tested in situation I.

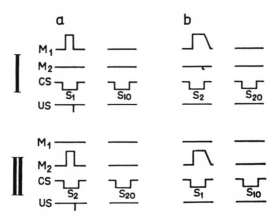

FIG. X-7. RELATIONS BETWEEN ALIMENTARY TYPE II CRs ESTABLISHED IN TWO DIFFERENT EXPERIMENTAL SITUATIONS (SCHEMATIC KYMOGRAPHIC RECORDS)

I, situation I; II, situation II; M_1, instrumental response trained in situation I; M_2, instrumental response trained in situation II; S_1, S_2, corresponding positive CSs; S_{10}, S_{20}, negative CSs.

a) Normal course of experimental session in situation I and II, respectively.

b) CSs from situation II were presented in situation I, and vice versa.

Note that S_2 presented in situation I elicits movement M_1; S_1 presented in situation II elicits movement M_2. Both negative CSs presented in different situation preserve their inhibitory significance.

The results of this transposition were unequivocal. A CS presented in the foreign situation evoked a short orientation reaction followed by the movement proper to the situation in which it was elicited. On the other hand, if in situation I differentiation was established by reinforcing stimulus S_1 and non-reinforcing a similar stimulus S_{10}, this differentiation was preserved in situation II; this means that whereas S_1 produced in that situation movement M_2, stimulus S_{10} after slight disinhibition remained negative. These relations are diagrammatically shown in Figure X-7.

All these experiments are most instructive. They show that type II CSs, both positive and negative, both attractive and aversive, do not lose their corresponding *drive* significance if presented in quite different situations. The positive alimentary type II CS still produces hunger drive; the negative one produces hunger antidrive; and the aversive type II CS produces fear drive. However, the motor manifestations of these drives are different and are determined by specificity of a given situation or, rather, by the sort of previous experience to which the animal was subjected in that or in a similar situation.

How are these facts to be explained?

According to the general principles of associations, when the animal is trained, under a given drive, to perform a certain movement in a given situation, the association between the situation and the movement is established. Thus, in situation I the animal is prepared to perform the movement M_1, in situation II, movement M_2. Yet, the actual execution of each of these movements occurs only when a drive producing CS is in operation. In consequence, *any* type II CS connected with a given drive, when operating in situation I, will elicit movement M_1 and, when operating in situation II, will elicit movement M_2. On the other hand, a CS connected with another drive or with the antidrive will not elicit either of these movements.

The same role which is played by environmental stimuli in determining which instrumental response is performed in a given situation can be played also by some drugs, for instance curare[6] or pentobarbital.[7] It is amazing that exactly the same rules are obeyed in experiments with these drugs as those which were found in Wyrwicka's experiment on type II CRs in two situations. One can assume that these drugs strongly influence a number of receptive structures of the central nervous system, and in consequence the receptive background against which the CR is established under the given drug is totally different from that without the drug. Therefore, the drug or no-drug condition plays the role of a powerful determining factor selecting the instrumental movement to be performed under each of these conditions.

4. M₁-M₂ differentiation under the same US reinforcement

We turn now to the elucidation of the next problem—that of interrelations between two (or more) instrumental responses trained in the same situation under the same drive to different type II CSs. This procedure is usually denoted as "discrimination learning." We should, however, remember that, as explained in Chapter II (Section 8), by "discrimination" we mean the purely perceptive process concerned with the discerning of two similar stimuli, whereas by "differentiation" we mean the process of utilization of the perceived differences between CSs for associative aims. In Chapter VII (Addendum) we dealt with Pavlovian differentiation of classical CRs in which the positive CS is reinforced by the US whereas the negative CS is not. The same type of differentiation with regard to instrumental CRs will be discussed in Section 6, below; here we shall deal only with differentiation of two instrumental responses reinforced by the same US. As we shall presently see, this problem is far from being simple and is only now becoming understandable.

To avoid terminological confusion, the term "differentiation" will be always preceded by specifying a sort of task with which the animal is confronted. Thus, the classical Pavlovian procedure in which one of the two stimuli is reinforced by food and the other one is not will be referred to as food–no-food differentiation (or, more generally, US–no-US differentiation), whereas the analogous procedure in instrumental CRs will be called go–no-go differentiation (or, more generally, M–no-M differentiation). On the other hand, the situation in which the animal has to choose between two different responses, each of them if properly chosen being reinforced by the same attractive US (or not reinforced by the same aversive US), will be referred to as go-left–go-right differentiation (or, more generally, M_1-M_2 differentiation). We shall see that this terminology will be both unequivocal and convenient.

Our present task is to specify all the experimental procedures in which the M_1-M_2 differentiation takes place and then try to understand the mechanism involved in it.

(1) *Go-left–go-right simultaneous differentiation.* This is perhaps the most common form of experimentation in animal psychology, applied to many species of animals. It was originally developed for the study of the capacity of the given animal to discriminate between various visual (or sometimes olfactory) cues. It may be noted that the conclusions reached on the basis of this test are only one-sided. If the animal is able to solve the test, this means that he certainly distinguishes the two cues presented; if, however, he does not solve it, this does not mean that this failure is due to the lack of discrimination, because it may be due to a number of other factors. In any event, even if the animal discerns clearly between the two cues from the very beginning of the experiments, he must nevertheless learn in a number of trials which of these cues should be approached and which one avoided.

In most cases, especially in those where the cues simply cover the food-wells (full contiguity case), what the animal learns is to approach one cue and to avoid the other one. In consequence, the task presented is not a true M_1-M_2 differentiation but as a matter of fact the go–no-go differentiation in which the go-trials and the no-go–trials are compressed, so to speak, into a single trial. Instead of the animal's being presented the positive and negative cues in succession, he is given them at the same time. After the animal has mastered the task, he may either look at once at the positive cue and go there, or may look first at the negative cue, resist going there, and only then look at the other one and approach it. The realization of this point is important, because if for some reason (for example, prefrontal lesion) the animal is not able to inhibit its go-responses to the negative cue, he will make errors in spite of the fact that his discriminative power is unimpaired.

In other cases, however, especially in those in which no contiguity exists between the food-well and the cue and in which the cues are close to one another, the animal may perceive the two cues as a whole, one Gestalt being produced by one arrangement of the cues and another one by the reverse arrangement. What the animal does learn now is to react by going left when seeing one Gestalt and by going right when seeing the other one. In this way the whole task is reduced to exactly that type of successive go-left–go-right differentiation that we have under discussion in the present section.

Thus, it may be concluded that, from our point of view, the simultaneous go-left–go-right differentiation is not a clear and unambiguous experimental set-up, because, depending on the procedure, it is either a particular case of the go–no-go differentiation (which will be dealt with in the next section) or of successive go-left–go-right differentiation. This being so, all the types of experiments we shall presently be concerned with will involve successive differentiation, in which two stimuli requiring two different instrumental responses will be presented in separate trials. Therefore, the adjective "successive" will no more be needed.

(2) *Go-left–go-right differentiation with food-contiguous cues* (*choice method I*). We shall present here for illustration our own experimental procedure, since experiments of this kind were routinely performed in our laboratory on dogs and cats as a preliminary step for delayed responses. The experimental set-up is presented in Figure XII-1 (p. 498). Three feeders are situated on three walls of the room, with the starting platform on the fourth wall. The CSs are buzzers or lights operating from those feeders which should be approached in the given trial. The animal is taught to remain on the starting platform until the CS is presented and then to run to that feeder from which it is operating. When the animal approaches the proper feeder, the bowl with food is put into position.

It has been found that the choice of the correct feeder does not provide any difficulty for the animals, even with the triple choice, so that the task should hardly be called differentiation (Figure X-8a). It is worth mentioning that in experiments with visual cues the dogs had some difficulties in localizing the source of light and went occasionally to the wrong feeder, until they learned to find the proper direction by scanning.[8] These errors had, however, a purely perceptual character and are beyond the scope of our present considerations.

(3) *Go-left–go-right differentiation with directional cues* (*choice method II*). These experiments were performed on dogs by Ławicka,[9] who taught the animals to go to the left or to the right feeder in response to the same tone sounding from two different places; both loudspeakers producing the tone were situated at the starting platform; one

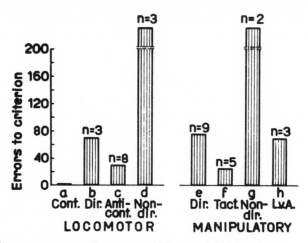

FIG. X-8. PERFORMANCES OF ANIMALS IN VARIOUS M_1-M_2 DIFFERENTIATION PROCEDURES

  a) Go left–go right differentiation with food-contiguous cues.
  b) Go left–go right differentiation with directional cues.
  c) Go left–go right differentiation with food-anticontiguous cues.
  d) Go left–go right differentiation with non-directional cues.
  e) Left leg–right leg differentiation with directional cues.
  f) Left leg–right leg differentiation with specific tactile cues.
  g) Left leg–right leg differentiation with non-directional cues.
  h) Left leg–right leg differentiation with visual and auditory cues.

on the floor, the other suspended at the height of six feet. As shown in Figure X-8b the dogs used for these experiments mastered the task relatively easily, and after about ten experimental sessions (180 trials) they reached the criterion of 90 per cent correct runs in ninety trials. Thus, the problem, although not so obvious as the preceding one, was nevertheless easily solved.

(4) *Go-left–go-right differentiation with food anticontiguous cues* (*choice method III*).[10] In this procedure the auditory stimulus operating from the left feeder signaled the presentation of food in the right feeder and vice versa. This problem also appeared to be solvable for

the dogs and was within the same range of difficulty as the preceding one (Figure X-8*c*).

(5) *Go-left–go-right differentiation with nondirectional cues* (*choice method IV*). This is the method which is usually called "successive" discrimination. Behavioristic experiments were performed usually on rats (in the Lashley jumping apparatus) and on monkeys (in the Wisconsin General Test Apparatus) with visual stimuli. The stimuli were presented between two feeding places. One stimulus signified that the food was on the left; the other that the food was on the right. Depending on the degree of dissimilarity between the cues, the problem was solvable with differing degrees of ease.

Quite different were the results of experiments performed by Ławicka with auditory stimuli.[11] In her experiments a loudspeaker was situated in front of the starting platform; two tones greatly differing in frequency (300 cps versus 900 cps) denoted food in the left or right food tray respectively. The problem appeared to be practically insolvable for the animals (Figure X-8*d*) and was eventually mastered only when the difference of tones was still further increased. But then it appeared that the high tone elicited a much stronger orienting reaction than the low tone and that this was the basis on which the differentiation was established; for, when the reaction to the high tone was weaker than usual, or that to the low tone stronger, the dog was likely to make mistakes. These results are in strong contrast to the food–no-food (or go–no-go) differentiation in dogs, who, as is well known, are great masters at this task and are able to react correctly to tones of much smaller difference in frequency. Thus, it seems that go-left–go-right tone differentiation (or, more generally, sound quality differentiation) is not achievable for dogs unless they base their responses on a difference in orienting reaction, as in the case of directional cues. The same has appeared to be true in respect to monkeys.[12]

(6) *Lifting-the-left-leg–lifting-the-right-leg differentiation.* In order to see whether the same rule holds in the case when the animal performs, not locomotor, but isolated instrumental responses and when the food is offered from one place, the following study was undertaken.[13]

Experiments were performed in the Pavlovian CR chamber. Each dog was trained to lift the right foreleg in response to a metronome situated in front of him, and to lift the left foreleg in response to the sound of bubbling from behind him. Eight trials were given each day, half with the metronome, half with the bubbling, in random order. The intertrial intervals were about one minute.

After about twenty sessions the task was mastered and the animals' performance became correct in 100 per cent of the trials (Figure X-8*e*). It was observed that all the dogs displayed a clear orienting reaction toward the source of the stimulus before performing the instrumental movement. Thus, looking forward toward the metronome was followed by the movement of the right foreleg; turning back toward the bubbling was followed by the movement of the left foreleg.

When the differentiation was firmly established and no erroneous responses were performed, the places of the stimuli were interchanged, so that now the metronome was situated behind the stand and the bubbling apparatus in front of it. The result was that now the animals reacted with lifting the right foreleg to bubbling and with lifting the left foreleg to the metronome.

The results of these experiments seem to be very instructive. It was clear from the behavior of the animals that they "knew" that the sound of the metronome should come from in front and the sound of bubbling from behind—that is, that the associations between the quality of the stimuli and their positions had been established. This was manifested, among other things, by the clear orientation reaction ("surprise") displayed by some of the animals when the stimulus operated for the first time from the unusual place. Nevertheless, they could not utilize the stimulus-quality information for determining the type of response they performed, whereas they could easily use the stimulus-position information for this aim.

In another type of experiment, rhythmic tactile stimuli were applied to the wrists of both forelegs, each serving as a type II CS eliciting the movement of the corresponding leg. As shown in Section 2, above, such stimuli are strongly reflexogenic in respect to the type II conditioned response displayed by the same leg; therefore, we have called them "specific tactile stimuli." It has now been found that when we train the animal to perform the movement of the left foreleg in response to the left tactile stimulus and the movement of the right foreleg in response to the right stimulus, it is very easy to establish the appropriate instrumental CRs and the number of "wrong" responses is negligible (Figure X-8*f*).

Finally, an attempt was made to teach the dogs to lift the right foreleg in response to the metronome and the left one in response to the bubbling when both these stimuli were operating from the same place in front of the stand. It appeared that, similar to the analogous task presented in the go-left–go-right procedure, this task too was extremely difficult (Figure X-8*g*). The situation was different, however, when one of the two discriminative stimuli operating from the same place was auditory (bubbling) and the other visual (rhythmic light). In that case the task was easily mastered, and the left-leg–right-leg differentiation became quite stable (Figure X-8*h*).[14]

We see from all these experiments that, depending on the character of the cues, the results of M_1-M_2 differentiation may be divided into the following three categories:

(1) In some cases the establishment of two different type II CRs, $S_1 \rightarrow M_1$ and $S_2 \rightarrow M_2$, under the same reinforcement does not present any difficulty, since the instrumental responses have no tendency to interchange and since both CRs become specific without (or with a very short) differential training. This occurs when: (a) two instrumental locomotor CRs (go-left–go-right) are trained to food-contiguous stimuli; (b) two instrumental CRs consisting of lifting different legs are trained to tactile stimuli applied to these legs; and (c) two instrumental CRs are trained in quite different situations.

(2) In other cases the establishment of two different type II CRs under the same reinforcement, however possible, is not accomplished at once but requires a more or less prolonged differentiation training. This happens when (a) visual cues are used as type II CSs (experiments performed on rats and monkeys in the choice method); (b) the two CSs are of different modality (experiments performed on dogs with auditory and visual stimuli); and (c) auditory directional cues are used as type II CSs (experiments performed on dogs and monkeys both by the locomotor choice method and by the method of isolated movements).

(3) In still other cases the establishment of two different type II CRs under the same reinforcement is very difficult or hardly possible at all. This occurs when two auditory cues differing only in quality but not in orienting reactions serve as type II CSs in dogs.

How are these various results to be explained?

It seems that the most reasonable explanation may lie in assuming the different strengths of potential connections directly linking the CS units with the units representing the instrumental responses. If these connections are strong (category (1)), the actual connections between both centers are formed very readily by the appropriate training and easily determine the instrumental movement to be performed in response to the given CS (cf. Figure X-2). In two cases the existence of particularly strong CS → M connections may be easily understood. When we have to do with food-contiguous CSs (choice method I), the natural orienting reaction to the source of the stimulus is *allied* with the locomotor conditioned response to the feeding place, both of them having the same direction. Similarly, when we deal with specific tactile stimuli serving as CSs, again they are subliminal in respect to flexion of the corresponding leg* and therefore allied with the instrumental response. Less clear is the third case, in which the character of the trained movement appears to be closely bound with the situation in which it is performed. The reason for this affinity and its nature remains to be elucidated in special experiments.

In category (2) the situation is somewhat different. The "natural" connections between the CS center and the center representing the trained movement are not so close as in the preceding category. Since the drive center common to both CRs is connected with both movements and since the direct connections linking each CS with the corresponding movement are not yet established, the animal is likely to make errors and perform the "wrong" movements. The reasons for these errors are easily detectable. They are determined by the temporary preponderance of one of the trained movements over the other, owing to some accidental factors—such as the first trial in a given session, a few successful responses, and so on. In fact, it may be observed that in the early periods of training the animal performs the same response in a number of successive trials regardless of the presented stimulus (perseverative errors). Only after some time does the animal learn *not* to perform the wrong response to the given CS, and in this way is he able to master the task (Figure X-9a).

Finally, in category (3) the animal is unable to establish M_1-M_2 differentiation. This may be explained by assuming that there are no potential connections discriminatively linking the units representing the given CSs with the units representing the trained movements

---

* In fact, the tactile stimulus applied to the anterior aspect of the wrist elicits in a hanging animal the placing response. Although this response is inhibited by the animal's standing on the floor, the subliminal impulses certainly activate the motor area of the cortex.

FIG. X-9. VARIOUS MECHANISMS OF DIFFERENTIATION

H, hunger center; AH, antihunger center; S_1, S_2, receptors and centers of CSs; M_1, M_2, centers and effectors of instrumental responses; $\sim M_1$, $\sim M_2$, the movements antagonistic to instrumental responses; Or, Or_1, Or_2, targeting responses to CSs; PS, PS_1, PS_2, receptors and centers of proprioceptive stimuli generated by these responses; S+, S−, receptors and centers of positive and negative CSs, respectively; points in squares denote logical product; arrows, excitatory connections; stopped lines, inhibitory connections. Broken contour denotes the events within the central nervous system. For the sake of simplicity some connections are omitted.

a) Simple M_1-M_2 differentiation.

b) Failure of M_1-M_2 differentiation because of lack of direct connections between the centers of CSs and the centers of instrumental movements.

c) M_1-M_2 differentiation based on different targeting reflexes elicited by each CS.

d) Drive–no drive differentiation shown for comparison.

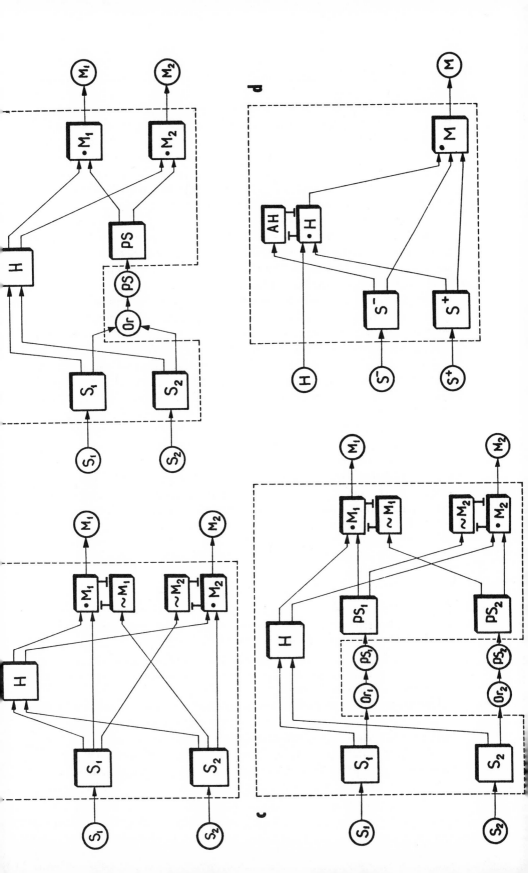

(Figure X-9b). In consequence, the animal is helpless in such a situation, since, although clearly discerning the two CSs, he cannot utilize the difference for the given task—that is, learn which of them means which movement. (In this respect he resembles a patient with auditory-visual aphasia who discriminates the words symbolizing the given objects and the objects themselves but fails to learn which word corresponds to which object, cf. Chapter V, Section 2.)

As shown by our experiments, the dogs, in spite of being endowed with an excellent and most precise analysis of sounds, cannot apply this analysis for the task of M_1-M_2 differentiation, because of a presumable lack of potential connections linking the auditory analyzer with the kinesthetic analyzer. On the other hand, he is quite capable of forming associations between various stimuli of the kinesthetic analyzer itself, in particular between the kinesthesis of a given orienting response and a given instrumental response. In consequence, when the animal is confronted with the M_1-M_2 differentiation of the different auditory stimuli, he must forego the direct solution of the problem, since it is unavailable for him, and base his solution on the different orienting reactions elicited by the two stimuli (Figure X-9c). This is obviously easy when the position of the two stimuli in space is different, but it is much more difficult, and surely not always possible, when both auditory stimuli are operating from the same place.

On the other hand, the situation is quite different if we deal with go–no-go differentiation. Here both differentiated stimuli act on the hunger drive center: the positive stimulus activating this center, and the negative one inhibiting it by activation of the antidrive center. Since the auditory analyzer *is* well connected with the limbic system, even very subtle differentiation may be reached without any help from the side of the kinesthetic analyzer (Figure X-9d).

5. M_1-M_2 differentiation under different US reinforcements

We were so far concerned with the problem of transfer and differentiation of instrumental conditioned responses when they were reinforced by the same attractive US (or served for avoidance of the same aversive US). Now we shall discuss the problem of the relations between particular instrumental responses established on the basis of different reinforcing agents.

Unfortunately, the problem we have now to discuss was not subjected to any systematic and exhaustive investigations. Although we have at our disposal a number of separate experimental results concerning particular cases of differentiation of heterogeneous type II CRs, these are not sufficient to draw any safe conclusions as to their mechanisms. Therefore, we are not able at the present time to propose any documented solution of this important problem, and the only thing we have to do is to propose some general hypotheses which may be the point of departure for future experimentation.

The general problem we are now confronted with is the following. From our whole discussion on instrumental conditioning presented so far it is clear that the instrumental response can be produced if, and only if, there are determining factors which specify the movement to be performed, and energizing factors which give the order of its performance. But the clear separation of these two types of factors has as yet not been done. In particular, we have no clear answer to the essential question as to whether a particular drive is the energizing factor only for those instrumental acts which have been established under its auspices, or whether an instrumental act, once established, *can* be released also by heterogeneous drives.

As was shown in Chapter VIII, Section 7, if in a given situation two different type II CRs are established to two different CSs under the hunger drive and the fear drive respectively, the mutual interchange of both instrumental responses is rather exceptional.[15] This is in clear contrast to the very strong interchange of instrumental responses established under the same drive. But since in our experimental procedure each of the two CSs signaled a different drive, it could be conjectured that each of these drives played a role of a strong *determining* factor designating a particular motor act, this role being independent from its energizing role which may be entirely unspecific.

More conclusive are the experiments of Żernicki and Ekel,[16] who trained the dogs to perform different instrumental movements—one for obtaining food, and the other for obtaining water. When the animal was hungry but water-satiated, the food instrumental CR was trained. When he was thirsty but food-satiated, the water instrumental CR was trained. Both food and water were offered in the same bowl, being placed there automatically from a container. No other cues determining the quality of the movement except hunger and thirst were provided.

It has been shown that the differentiation between the two instrumental responses under these conditions was very difficult and required a lengthy training. In some dogs a 100 per cent correct performance was never achieved. In particular, when after a series of thirst sessions a hunger session followed, the water movements tended to appear instead of the food movements, and vice versa. Similarly, if the reinforcement was not presented after a given movement, the other movement invariably followed it.

Since hunger and thirst must be considered distinct drives, this interchange of food movements and water movements proves that, at least in the domain of appetitive drives, the energizing factor is not bound to a specific drive.

The lack of specificity of energizing factors in instrumental conditioning is also supported by our everyday experience. In fact, many well-trained instrumental responses—such as opening a closed door, getting up from a chair, or particular locomotor acts—may of course subserve any drive, depending on the situation in which they are executed. Incidentally, the same is true of the behavior of a house dog who scratches at the closed door under a great variety of drives both appetitive and aversive.

All these separate bits of information induce us to think that the energizing factor providing a "fiat" for any instrumental movement to be performed is the *unspecific arousal of the motor behavioral system,* accomplished through axodendritic synaptic contacts. This arousal may be produced by every drive, and not necessarily by that which was involved in the formation of a given instrumental response. Which of the multitude of instrumental movements the organism has at its disposal is performed at a given moment depends entirely on the presence of the determining factors—that is, on those stimuli which are associated, directly or indirectly, with the given movement. This association is established between those agents which operate in the presence of instrumental learning and that movement which terminates the drive under which it was executed. It is assumed that the respective connections are based on axosomatic synaptic contacts.

We can distinguish three categories of determining factors (Figure X-10).

(1) Type II CSs. As shown in the preceding sections of this chapter, the sets of gnostic units representing these stimuli form actual connections with the set of units representing the kinesthesis of the instrumental motor act.

(2) Drives under whose control the given instrumental CRs have been established. In Chapter V (Section 5) we have indicated that particular sets of emotive units can form connections with particular kinesthetic gnostic units as well as with gnostic units of other modalities. Therefore, we assume that a drive which is involved in the formation of the instrumental CR plays a dual role in it: first, it provides the general arousal of the whole behavioral system through axodendritic synaptic contacts; second, its units become connected, through axosomatic contacts, with kinesthetic units representing a particular motor act.

(3) The gnostic representation of the US involved in a given instrumental conditioning. Again, as was explained in Chapter V, the particular emotions become strongly associated with those stimuli

which gave rise to them. So, the conditioned hunger drive produced in a dog in the experimental situation certainly activates the sets of gnostic units representing the sight, smell, and taste of food in the feeder; similarly, the conditioned fear drive activates the sets of units representing the gnostic aspects of aversive agents—for instance, the taste of acid or the pinprick on the skin.

Thus, if in a given experimental condition two different instrumental responses are established to two different CSs, each one under

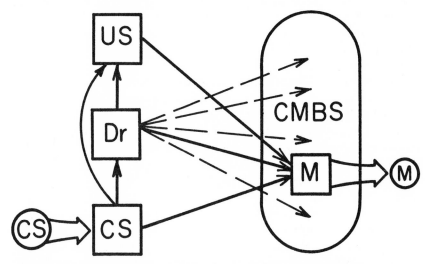

FIG. X-10. FINAL VERSION OF THE BLOCK MODEL OF TYPE II CR ARC

CS in circle denotes the type II CS; CS in square, its central representation. Dr in square denotes the central representation of a given drive; US in square, central representation of the US. CMBS in oval, central motor behavioral system. M in square, central representation of instrumental response (including its kinesthesis); M in circle, instrumental response. Continuous-line arrows denote specific connections between centers; broken-line arrows, unspecific (facilitatory) connections; double-line arrows, connections between receptive surface and center, or center and effector.

Note that the center of drive sends specific (determining) connections to the center of particular instrumental response and unspecific (energizing) connections to the whole CMBS.

a separate drive, the determining role of each of these CSs is not limited only to its perceptual qualities, but includes also the corresponding drive CR elicited by it and the image of the US elicited by this drive. The second and third determining factors may have an even greater importance than the quality of the CS itself. In fact, we know that it is quite easy to elaborate two different instrumental CRs to two different tones under different drives, whereas this task is almost impossible if both CRs are trained under the same drive.

This is because in the latter case *only* the quality of each CS is a cue for differentiation, whereas in the former the character of the drive and of the US contribute to the separation of both instrumental responses.

It is interesting to report in this context the experiment performed by Fonberg in which she succeeded in establishing without any difficulty two different avoidance responses to two different CSs, each of these stimuli being a signal of a different aversive US.[17] This differentiation is hardly possible if the same US is used as reinforcement. In Fonberg's experiment the cue for differentiation was a different image of each US (that is, different sets of gnostic units activated by association), whereas the fear drive was common to both of them.

6. The problem of inhibition of type II conditioned reflexes

After having constructed the model of type II CR arc which accounts for the main properties of this type of behavior, we shall now turn to the consideration of the model of *inhibitory* type II CRs which are produced by the appropriate changes in the CR procedure. Entering into this problem we should remember that, according to our consideration brought out in Chapter VII, we have come to the conclusion that, as far as type I conditioning is concerned, there is no evidence of *inhibitory conditioned connections* being formed between the appropriate centers. The so-called inhibitory CR was assumed to be either the no-US CR or the antidrive CR—that is, another excitatory CR reinforced by an agent eliciting inhibition in the corresponding US center or drive center respectively. We shall now see how these rules operate in respect to type II conditioning.

Taking into account our model of type II CRs (Figure X-1) we can easily observe that the inhibitory processes may be interposed in it at the following points of its circuit.

First, according to the concept held in the present book, the connections between the drive center and the central representation of the given motor act are established if this motor act marks the termination of that drive, owing either to its inhibition by the consummatory reaction or to its cessation by the removal of a fear-producing stimulus. In consequence, in the case in which the termination of a given drive is not secured by the performance of the given instrumental response, and therefore other motor acts follow it, that response becomes retroactively inhibited. We shall, accordingly, call this kind of inhibitory training of the type II CR *retroactive inhibition* training.

Second, we have stressed now and again that, if the alimentary type II CS is repeatedly not followed by food, this stimulus will eventually become a hunger antidrive CS and thus the hunger drive CR will be reciprocally inhibited. In consequence, the CS will fail to evoke the given instrumental response. We shall call this kind of inhibitory training *drive inhibition* training.

Third, it is also possible that the inhibitory training of the type II CR may occur through inhibition of the motor act itself along the "direct" CS → M pathway. We shall see below that this kind of inhibitory training does in fact exist; we shall call it *motor act inhibition* training.

Now we shall discuss all these three kinds of inhibitory training by presenting experimental situations in which each of them is most clearly manifested.

(1) *Retroactive inhibition training*. The important phenomenon based on this type of inhibition is M_1-M_2 differentiation or reversal learning with intra-trial corrections. The general procedure of this kind of learning is that the incorrect instrumental response performed in the presence of the type II CS is not followed by satisfaction of drive and in consequence the animal performs some other movements. If one of these movements signals the termination of drive, then after a number of such trials the animal will learn to perform that movement at once in the presence of the given CS.

Most experiments with reversal training were performed on rats and monkeys with the double-choice technique. In a given situation the animals were confronted with the possibility of performing two motor acts—for example, to go left or to go right. One of these acts was made an instrumental response leading either to food or to avoidance of an electric shock. Then the procedure was changed in such a way that the learned response failed to secure the drive reduction but the other response did so. After a number of trials the first response was abandoned by the animal and the second one was adopted instead.

The same principle is in operation when the animal is trained by the aid of the intra-trial correction method to react differently to two different stimuli. In many types of such experiments the animal learns to react properly to each stimulus by "trial and error"—that is, by performing the wrong and then the correct movement. The first movement is then retroactively inhibited by the second movement, and in consequence this second movement is performed at once in the presence of the given CS.

A particular case illustrating this kind of inhibitory training is provided by the experiments of Fonberg and Bregadze[18] concerning defensive type II CRs. These authors have shown that the avoidance CRs can be easily extinguished or differentiated when the CS, instead of being discontinued at the moment of the performance of the trained movement, lasts for a definite time and ceases to operate irrespective of what the animal does. According to our present considerations, the explanation of this fact is that, since the trained movement does not lead to the termination of the fear drive, it is retroactively inhibited by other activities following it. According to the observation of Sołtysik and Zieliński, in a number of cases the movement replacing the original instrumental response is some tonic type of activity which lasts until the end of the CS.[19]

(2) *Drive inhibition training.* Let us analyze now what happens when an alimentary type II CR is extinguished by non-reinforcement or differentiated by the food–no-food procedure (cf. Figure X-9d). It may be conjectured that in the early period of the extinction training the instrumental response tends to be retroactively inhibited since it does not terminate the hunger drive elicited by the CS. However, this stage, if present at all, is certainly only transient, because what really does occur is the extinction of the hunger CR elicited by the CS. In fact, the non-reinforcement of this stimulus by food leads to the gradual development of the antidrive CR to it, and in consequence the instrumental CR disappears. The best proof of the correctness of this reasoning is brought forth by the experiments of Wyrwicka,[20] repeated routinely in our laboratory. Wyrwicka has found that when an alimentary type II CR to a certain CS is either chronically or acutely extinguished, it may be restored by mere re-reinforcement of that CS. In other words, it is not necessary to teach the animal anew to perform the instrumental response to that stimulus by resorting to the original training, because this response reappears spontaneously when the CS is again followed by food. This fact certainly shows that there is no inhibition of the instrumental response itself accomplished through the direct pathway $CS \rightarrow M$, because in that case the type II CR should be reestablished only by special training.

The fact that extinction of a type II CR is accomplished through inhibition of drive and not of the movement itself may be understood in view of the following considerations. As indicated in the preceding sections, the $S \rightarrow M$ association is represented by connections established between the CS units and kinesthetic units representing the given movement. It follows that as long as the movement is performed in response to the CS, this association is sustained quite independently of whether food reinforcement is or is not presented. The movement stops being performed because no messages from the drive center are supplied to the kinesthetic center, but until this happens the $CS \rightarrow M$ connections are not affected. In consequence, when in that early period of extinction the CS is re-reinforced and the drive CR restored, the movement reappears instantaneously.

It may, however, be expected that the situation is quite different in the case when extinction is overtrained—that is, when many trials are given in which the movement is not performed. In that case the CS is not followed by M in many trials, and therefore the association between the CS and no-M is established. It should be anticipated that now the type II CR would not be restored by mere re-reinforcing of the CS.

The experimental evidence, although meager, seems to confirm this expectation. Whereas in Wyrwicka's experiments the restoration of the extinguished CR occurred immediately after the instrumental response disappeared, in some experiments of Szwejkowska[21] the extinction was much overtrained. In that case spontaneous recovery of the instrumental CR did not occur, and returning to the original training appeared to be necessary.

In summary, it seems that in the regular extinction procedure of the type II CR all three inhibitory mechanisms are in operation. In the early stage of extinction the retroactive inhibition caused by the protraction of hunger after the performance of the movement may take place; then the hunger CR established to the CS gradually disappears, being replaced by the hunger antidrive CR, and eventually, if extinction trials are repeatedly given after the movement has disappeared, motor act inhibition occurs. Whereas the first inhibitory mechanism is only conjectural, the other two may be tested by the appropriate experiments.

It should be noted that the same mechanism of drive inhibition may also be in operation in avoidance CRs when the duration of the CS is prolonged and does not coincide with a given movement. As shown in the preceding chapter, after such a procedure the fear drive may become inhibited, as judged from the lack of acceleration of the heart rate (cf. Figure IX-7). This will happen mostly in those cases when, not the primary, but the secondary CS is subjected to extinction, because then the conditioned fear drive is not very strong (cf. Chapter IX, Section 5). In other cases the retroactive type of inhibition is dominant, as indicated above.

In Chapter VII it was pointed out that antidrive CRs are controlled by higher order emotive fields belonging to particular antidrive subsystems, with which the appropriate external stimuli form conditional connections (cf. Figure I-3 and I-4). This assumption implies that lesions sustained in these fields should impair or abolish the corresponding antidrive CRs, leaving the drive CRs unaffected. It may be further inferred that this impairment will be unnoticed in those cases in which a given stimulus was an originally established antidrive CS (cf. Chapter VII, Section 5), whereas it will be most manifest when this stimulus has been converted from a drive CS.

Experimental findings fully confirm this thesis.[22] The dogs were trained in positive and negative instrumental CRs under food reinforcement. Negative CRs were established to stimuli similar to the positive CSs and to the compounds composed of an extra-stimulus (conditioned inhibitor, CI) and a CS. The interval between CI and CS was prolonged to several seconds. After both positive and negative CRs were firmly established, the prefrontal ablations (limited by the presylvian sulcus) were made.

After the surgery the general behavior of the animals did not differ very much from that before the operation, but their CR activity was very disordered. Whereas the positive CRs were quite normal, the negative ones were dramatically disinhibited (Figure X-11). The animals also performed many intertrial instrumental responses, which never occurred in the period preceding the operation. On the other hand, the conditioned inhibitor, being a primary negative CS, never elicited the instrumental response.

With the course of retraining, the CR activity gradually improved: first, the intertrial responses disappeared, then the responses to the negative CSs. The finer the differentiation, the more difficult was the restoration of the negative CR (Figure X-12). This restoration may be due to the fact that either the field concerned with hunger drive inhibition was only partially destroyed (in fact, the larger the lesion, the stronger was the disinhibitory effect), or that some other field could compensate for the defect.

Further studies have shown that in dogs the crucial field responsible for hunger drive inhibition is situated in the medial part of the prefrontal area.[23] Analogous disorders of the negative instrumental CRs were found in monkeys after lesions sustained on the orbital surface of the frontal lobes.[24]

The presented results hardly need comment. In a go–no-go differentiation training the units representing a no-go CS make connections with both hunger drive units and hunger antidrive units with the preponderance of the latter connections; in consequence the destruction of the antidrive units leads to disinhibition of the drive CR. The stronger the connections between the CS units and the drive units, the stronger the disinhibitory effect. If no connections are formed between the CS units and the drive units (as is the case with the primary negative CS), disinhibition is not present.

(3) *Motor act inhibition training.* We can discern the following situations in which this type of inhibition occurs.

(a) The case discussed above when the CS is no longer followed by the instrumental response, because of the lack of drive previously elicited by the CS. On such an occasion the excitation of the CS units does not coincide with the excitation of kinesthetic units representing the movement M, but does coincide with the excitation of units representing the antagonistic movement or posture. As a result, the connections between the CS units and those representing the latter movement are established, and in consequence the old movement is reciprocally inhibited.

(b) Motor act inhibition plays an important role in the M_1-M_2 differentiation without intra-trial corrections (cf. Figure X-9a, c). As has been pointed out in the previous section, this differentiation is achieved when the animal learns not to go to the incorrect feeder or not to perform the incorrect movement in response to the corresponding CS. Again, this occurs by the response "don't go there" prevailing over the response "go there." If in the given period of training, the correct response is not well established or is inhibited by generalization, the animal will perform no response at all. According to our experience, such no responses happen quite often in the course of a difficult M_1-M_2 differentiation.

(c) Finally, the motor act inhibition plays a substantial role in the formation of those varieties of type II conditioning in which the movement provoked by the experimenter has to be inhibited in order to avoid an aversive US, or to secure an attractive US.

Now we come to a crucial question of the mechanism of the motor act inhibition: whether inhibitory connections are formed between the CS center and the M center, or whether, as in all other cases of internal inhibition, this process occurs, here too, through primary excitation of the antagonistic center.

Not being able to answer this question definitely, we are rather inclined to maintain the unitary theory of internal inhibition, proposed in Chapter VII, and to believe that inhibition of the center controlling a given motor act occurs through excitation of the antagonistic center. It is worth remembering that in all our experiments dealing with motor act inhibition the antagonistic movement was always conspicuous. When the dog had been trained not to take food from the bowl during the action of the buzzer, because this movement was followed by an aversive US, the buzzer always elicited the movement of turning away (Experiment X); similarly, when the dog had been trained not to flex his foreleg in the presence of the metronome, because its flexion prevented receiving food, the metronome began to elicit a strong extension movement of that leg (Experiment XVII, Figure VIII-9); on the contrary, after this extension response had been extinguished and extinction was overtrained, the flexion of the foreleg appeared instead (Experiment XIX and Figure VIII-11); it is also a

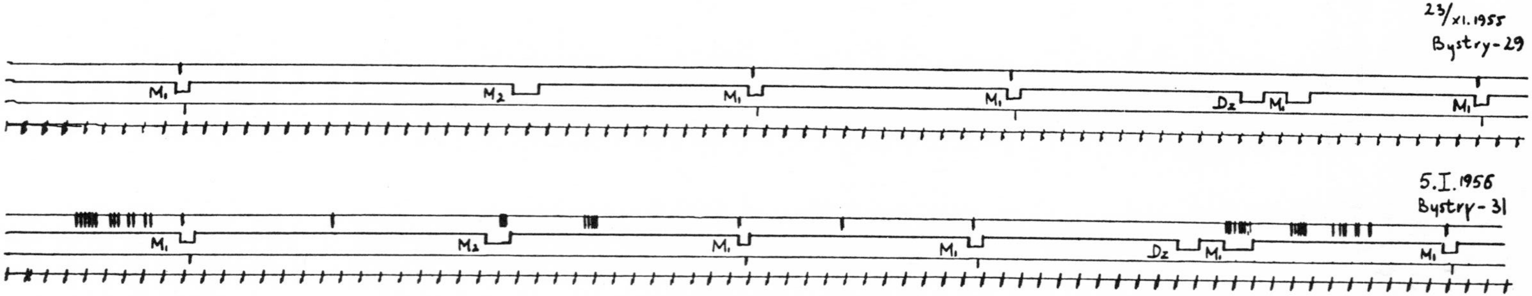

FIG. X-11. IMPAIRMENT OF INSTRUMENTAL CR AFTER PREFRONTAL LESION IN DOG

Fom top to bottom: instrumental responses (barks); CSs: M₁, positive metronome; M₂, negative metronome; Dz, bell (conditioned inhibitor); food reinforcement; time in 5 seconds.

Upper graph: the record of an experimental session before operation. Note that the animal performs instrumental responses (barks) only to the positive metronome, while he is silent in response to the differentiated metronome and to the inhibitory compound.

Lower graph: first period after prefrontal lesion. Note that the dog barks occasionally in the intertrial intervals, as well as in response to the negative metronome and to the positive metronome preceded by the conditioned inhibitor. The latter response is more disinhibited than the former one. Also note that the conditioned inhibitor itself (primary negative CS) does not elicit barking. The positive CRs are not changed.

(W. Ławicka, in *Acta Biol. Exper.*, 17 [1957]: 317–25.)

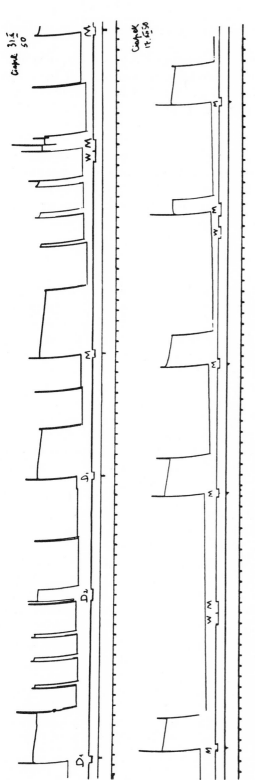

FIG. X-12. GRADUAL RESTORATION OF INHIBITORY CRs AFTER RETRAINING IN PREFRONTAL DOG

From top to bottom: instrumental response (placing the right foreleg on the food tray); CSs: D₁, positive CS (bell); D₂, differentiated CS (another bell); M, positive CS (metronome); W, conditioned inhibitor (rotor); food reinforcement; time in 5 seconds.

Upper graph: soon after prefrontal lesion the animal is very disinhibited. The instrumental movements appear in intertrial intervals, to the differentiated CS (D₂) and to the positive CS (metronome) immediately following the conditioned inhibitor (rotor).

Lower graph: 1½ month later. No intertrial movements. Inhibitory compound is not disinhibited when CS immediately follows the conditioned inhibitor, but is still disinhibited when the interval between them is 5 seconds.

Note that even in the first period after operation the conditioned inhibitor itself did not elicit the instrumental response. The CRs to positive CSs are normal. The protracted motor response to the positive CSs (in comparison to the negative CSs) is due to the fact that the animal was in the habit of keeping his leg on the food tray throughout the period of eating; so putting down the leg marks the termination of food intake.

(W. Ławicka's experiment.)

455

common observation that the overtrained extinction of the instrumental flexion movement leads to the extension movement. All these facts seem to support the view that the motor act inhibition occurs through the formation of excitatory connections between the CS units and the kinesthetic units of the antagonistic movement; the excitation of these units exerts the reciprocal inhibitory influence upon the kinesthetic units of the original movement. Thus, the motor act inhibition follows exactly the same general principles as those governing all S-S associations, in which the reciprocity between mutually incompatible units was observed. In this way we arrive at some unitary system of concepts applicable to a large range of inhibitory phenomena within the whole nervous system.

7. Summary and conclusions

This chapter was devoted to an attempt to construct a model of a type II CR arc based on contemporary evidence concerning the neurophysiological mechanisms of drives on the one hand and on new data obtained in the field of type II conditioning on the other.

On the basis of general observation of the behavior of animals and man, it was shown that the pathway connecting the CS units with the kinesthetic units of the instrumental response through the intermediary of the drive center ($CS \rightarrow D \rightarrow M$) is not sufficient to account for all the properties of type II CRs, and that the direct pathway between the CS center and the M center, bypassing the D center, should be also postulated. It was indicated that only the joint operation of both kinds of connections may lead to the performance of the instrumental response.

Although the drive-mediated activation of the M center and its direct activation by the CS center play different roles in the accomplishment of the instrumental response, they may mutually compensate each other in the sense that the stronger the direct activation of the M center the weaker the drive necessary for the elicitation of the motor act. This rule is clearly manifested in experiments in which a tactile stimulus administered to the leg involved in the instrumental response is used as a CS. This stimulus is strongly motogenic because of direct connections linking the sensory and the motor cortical areas. After separating the two areas, this peculiar property of the specific tactile stimulus is lost.

Owing to the existence of direct connections between the CS center and the M center, the selection of different instrumental responses to different type II CSs under the same drive operation is possible. Depending on the properties of the CSs, two (or more) instrumental responses may be selectively established to two (or more) stimuli either without any differentiation procedure or by means of a special differentiation training. No special differentiation training is needed when the two type II CRs are established in quite different experimental situations or when there is an inborn "affinity" between a CS and a given motor response (for example, touching the leg → lifting this leg). Differentiation training is necessary when such an affinity does not exist and the animal must learn which movement should be performed to which stimulus. In some cases, however, the M_1-M_2 differentiation based on the same drive is practically impossible, in spite of the fact that the animal perfectly distinguishes the two stimuli concerned, as may be judged from the very easy M–no-M differentiation. These different results of the M_1-M_2 differentiation procedure depend on whether there are potential connections linking the gnostic fields representing the CSs with the gnostic kinesthetic fields representing the instrumental responses. For instance, it has been shown that in the dog the auditory analyzer seems to have no direct connections with the kinesthetic analyzer, and therefore the animal is unable to establish an M_1-M_2 differentiation to two purely auditory cues, even if he can easily distinguish them. On the other hand, the dog is quite able to base the M_1-M_2 differentiation on different orienting reactions evoked by both stimuli. In consequence, when two— even identical—auditory stimuli are operating from different places, or when they differ so much from one another that they elicit different orienting reactions (for example, a stronger and a weaker one), then the M_1-M_2 differentiation is possible.

The analysis of experimental facts concerning the M_1-M_2 differentiation based on different reinforcing stimuli has allowed us to make a clearer distinction between determining and energizing factors involved in type II conditioning than was hitherto possible. The hypothesis was advanced that the arousal of the whole motor behavioral system produced by *any* drive is the energizing factor releasing the instrumental response. On the other hand, the determining factors specifying which instrumental response is elicited at a given moment are: (1) the CS to which this response was established; (2) the drive under which the instrumental training was carried out; (3) the gnostic aspect of the US involved in the instrumental training. Whereas the energizing factor operates on the basis of innate axodendritic connections linking particular drive centers with the motor behavioral system, the determining factors operate on the basis of acquired axosomatic connections linking the sets of units representing these factors with the kinesthetic units of the given instrumental act.

On the basis of our type II CR model, the formation of not only positive but also negative instrumental responses may be accounted for. There are three different mechanisms on which the inhibitory training in type II CRs may be based. First is the retroactive inhibition of the instrumental response occurring when the operation of the drive is protracted beyond the execution of the response. A typical example of the operation of this mechanism is reversal training or M_1-M_2 differentiation, with intra-trial corrections. The second mechanism is inhibition of the drive CR and its substitution by the antidrive CR. This mechanism is in operation in all those cases in which the instrumental response elicited by a given CS is not reinforced by the attractive US; the drive CR to that CS is then extinguished, leading to the disappearance of the instrumental response. The drive inhibitory mechanism is impaired or destroyed after lesions sustained in the higher order antidrive center; such lesions produce dramatic disinhibition of negative type II CRs. The third mechanism is the motor act inhibition occurring by establishing connections linking the CS with the antagonistic movement. This inhibition takes place when the performance of a given movement in response to a given stimulus does not lead to the satisfaction of drive, whereas its nonperformance does. It also occurs in overtrained extinction, when the CS is repeatedly presented after the disappearance of the instrumental response.

It is assumed that the inhibitory training in respect to type II CRs is based on the same general principles as those postulated in Chapter VII in respect to type I CRs. This is that in type II conditioning, just as in type I conditioning, no inhibitory conditioned connections are formed between the two centers involved, but excitatory conditioned connections are formed between the transmittent (CS) units and the recipient units reciprocally related to the original recipient units. In type II conditioning, these are the units representing a movement antagonistic to that originally performed in response to the CS.

The models presented in this chapter concerned only the *connections* between various nervous centers involved in type II conditioning but not the internal organization of these centers. The organization of the drive center was discussed in Chapter I and that of the perceptive centers in Chapter II; the organization of the centers belonging to the central motor behavioral system has so far been almost unmentioned. This difficult and hitherto poorly explored problem will be undertaken in the next chapter.

References to Chapter X

1. C. Dobrzecka and W. Wyrwicka. 1960. On the direct intercentral connections in the alimentary conditioned reflex type II. *Bull. Acad. Pol. Sci.*, Cl. II, Ser. Sci. Biol., 8: 373–75.

C. Dobrzecka and J. Konorski. 1962. On the peculiar properties of the instrumental conditioned reflexes to "specific tactile stimuli." *Acta Biol. Exp. Vars.*, 22 (No. 3): 215–26.

2. C. Dobrzecka, B. Sychowa, and J. Konorski. 1965. The effects of lesions within the sensory-motor cortex upon instrumental response to the "specific tactile stimulus." *Acta Biol. Exp. Vars.*, 25: 91–106.

3. C. Dobrzecka and J. Konorski. 1962 (see note 1 above).

4. W. Wyrwicka. 1958. Studies on the effects of the conditioned stimulus applied against various experimental backgrounds. *Acta Biol. Exp. Vars.*, 18: 175–93.

5. ———. 1956. Studies on motor conditioned reflexes. VI. On the effect of experimental situation upon the course of motor conditioned reflexes. *Ibid.*, 17: 189–203.

6. E. Girden and E. A. Culler. 1937. Conditioned responses in curarized striate muscle in dogs. *J. Comp. Psychol.*, 23: 267–74.

7. D. A. Overton. 1964. State-dependent or "dissociated" learning produced with pentobarbital. *J. Comp. Physiol. Psychol.*, 57: 3–12.

8. W. Ławicka. 1959. Physiological mechanism of delayed reactions. II. Delayed reactions in dogs and cats to directional stimuli. *Acta Biol. Exp. Vars.*, 19: 199–219.

9. ———. 1964. The role of stimuli modality in successive discrimination and differentiation learning. *Bull. Acad. Pol. Sci.*, Cl. II, Ser. Sci. Biol., 12: 35–38.

J. Konorski. 1964. Some problems concerning the mechanism of instrumental conditioning. *Acta Biol. Exp. Vars.*, 24: 59–72.

10. I. Stępień. Unpublished experiments.

11. W. Ławicka. 1964 (see note 9 above).

12. ———. Unpublished experiments.

13. C. Dobrzecka, G. Szwejkowska, and J. Konorski. 1966. Qualitative versus directional cues in two forms of differentiation. *Science*, 153 (No. 3731): 87–89.

C. Dobrzecka and J. Konorski. 1967. Qualitative versus directional cues in differential conditioning. 1. Left leg–right leg differentiation to cues of a mixed character. *Acta Biol. Exp. Vars.*, 27 (No. 2), in press.

14. C. Dobrzecka and J. Konorski. 1967. Qualitative versus directional cues in differential conditioning. 3. Right leg–left leg differentiation to non-directional cues. *Acta Biol. Exp. Vars.*, in preparation.

15. Ю. Конорски и С. Миллер. 1936. Условные рефлексы двигательного анализатора. (Conditioned reflexes of the motor analyzer.) *Trudy Fiziol. Lab. I. P. Pavlova*, 6 (No. 1): 119–278. English summary, pp. 285–88.

J. Konorski. 1939. O zmienności ruchowych reakcji warunkowych. (Zasady przełączania korowego.) (Sur la variabilité des réactions conditionnelles motrices. [Les principes d'aiguillage cortical].) *Przegl. Fizjol. Ruchu.*, 9: 1–51. French summary.

16. B. Żernicki and J. Ekel. 1959. Elaboration and mutual relations between alimentary and water instrumental conditioned reflexes in dogs. *Acta Biol. Exp. Vars.*, 19: 313–25.

17. E. Fonberg. 1961. On the transfer of two different defensive conditioned reflexes type II. *Bull. Acad. Pol. Sci.*, Cl. II, Ser. Sci. Biol., 9: 47–49.

18. A. H. Брегадзе. 1953. К вопросу выработки оборонительного условного рефлекса у собак. (Problem of the formation of a defensive reflex in dogs.) *Trudy Inst. Fiziol. Akad. Nauk Gruz. SSR.*, 9: 43–59.
    E. Fonberg. 1952. Unpublished experiments.

19. S. Sołtysik and K. Zieliński. 1962. Conditioned inhibition of the avoidance reflex. *Acta Biol. Exp. Vars.*, 22 (No. 3): 157–67.

20. W. Wyrwicka. 1952. Studies on motor conditioned reflexes. V. On the mechanism of the motor conditioned reaction. *Acta Biol. Exp. Vars.*, 16: 131–37.

21. G. Szwejkowska. 1960. Transformation of differentiated inhibitory reflexes of type II into excitatory reflexes. *Acta Biol. Exp. Vars.*, 20: 147–55.

22. S. Brutkowski, J. Konorski, W. Ławicka, I. Stępień, and L. Stępień. 1955. Wpływ usuwania okolic czołowych na ruchowe odruchy warunkowe u psów. (The effect of the removal of prefrontal areas of the cerebral hemispheres on the conditioned motor reflexes in dogs.) *Pr. łódz. Tow. Nauk Wydz.* III (1955), No. 37. Russian and English summaries.
    ———. 1956. The effect of the removal of frontal poles of the cerebral cortex on motor conditioned reflexes. *Acta Biol. Exp. Vars.*, 17: 167–88.
    W. Ławicka. 1957. The effect of the prefrontal lobectomy on the vocal conditioned reflexes in dogs. *Acta Biol. Exp. Vars.*, 17: 317–25.

23. G. Szwejkowska, J. Kreiner, and B. Sychowa. 1963. The effect of partial lesions of the prefrontal area on alimentary conditioned reflexes in dogs. *Acta Biol. Exp. Vars.*, 23: 181–92.
    S. Brutkowski and J. Dąbrowska. 1966. Prefrontal cortex control of differentiation behavior in dogs. *Acta Biol. Exp. Vars.*, 26 (No. 4), 425–39.

24. S. Brutkowski, M. Mishkin, and H. E. Rosvold. 1963. Positive and inhibitory motor conditioned reflexes in monkeys after ablation of orbital dorso-lateral surface of the frontal cortex. In E. Gutmann and P. Hnik, eds., *Central and Peripheral Mechanisms of Motor Functions: Proceedings of the Conference held at Liblice near Prague, May 15–21, 1961*, pp. 279–84. Prague: Publ. House of the Czechoslovak Acad. of Sci.
    W. Ławicka, M. Mishkin, and H. E. Rosvold. In preparation. The effects of prefrontal lesions on differentiation in monkeys.

CHAPTER XI

THE ORIGIN AND PHYSIOLOGICAL BASIS
OF INSTRUMENTAL MOVEMENT

1. Introductory remarks

In the preceding chapters, when dealing with the interneural organization of type II conditioning, we were largely concerned with connections linking various brain centers with the center of the motor response. We found that for the formation and elicitation of a given instrumental movement two types of connections leading to its central representation should be established: those providing impulses which release this movement, and those which select which movement has to be released. It was assumed that the connections of the first type run from the units of the emotive brain to the whole motor behavioral system, whereas those of the second type run from the gnostic units of particular analyzers (including the emotive analyzer) to the gnostic units of the kinesthetic analyzer, which pass their orders to the executive centers. We were, however, not concerned with the intimate nature of the centers responsible for the movements taking part in type II conditioning or with the ways of their operating. This very problem will be dealt with in this chapter.

The questions to be answered in our present discussion are: (1) which types of motor activities can be transformed into type II conditioned responses (or, to put it briefly, may be "instrumentalized")? (2) what is the role of kinesthesis in the formation and execution of type II conditioned responses? and (3) what are the localization and organization of the nervous structures controlling these responses?

If we make a general survey of movements which can be performed by the animals, we can divide them either according to their origin or according to their character.

According to the origin of the performed movements, they may be roughly divided into the following categories:

(1) Movements produced as effects of unconditioned reflexes: flexion of the leg in response to a noxious stimulus administered to it; scratch movements in response to a specific irritation of the skin of the body; sneezing in response to an irritation of the nasal mucous membrane; barking in dogs as a display of aggression or other drives; masticating food present in the mouth; placing and hopping reflex; and so on.

(2) Movements produced as a result of already established instrumental CRs. Examples of such movements established in the natural life of animals are: manipulatory movements of the forelimbs providing food; running toward a visible place of feeding; running away from "danger"; running around an obstacle; jumping up on elevated objects, or jumping down from them.

(3) Movements produced as the result of an external force administered to the limbs or body: passive flexion of the leg; passive lying down, produced by pressing the body from above, and the like.

(4) Movements induced by electrical stimulation of the central nervous system, and particularly of the brain, such as movements produced by stimulation of the motor cortex, caudate nucleus, and many other central fields.

This classification of movements is neither exhaustive nor perfect. It is clear that no precise boundaries can be drawn between the unconditioned and conditioned reflex movements; passive movements may be either purely passive or contaminated by myotatic reflexes, and some of the electrically induced movements may have a reflex character. However, this division will provide a good basis for our further discussion concerning the problem of instrumentalization of particular movements.

According to their character, motor acts may be divided into: (1) locomotor acts, changing the position of the animal in space; (2) isolated movements of limbs, changing the position of a limb in relation to the rest of the body; and (3) postural movements, changing the position of the whole body.

As far as the character of movements is concerned, there is no doubt that all their categories can be instrumentalized. We are able to establish type II conditioned responses from the locomotor acts as well as from isolated movements of the limbs and postural changes. However, as far as the origin of movements is concerned, the problem of their instrumentalization is far from being simple, and its full solution is still impossible. Therefore, on the basis of the categorization of the origins of movements specified above, we shall try to determine which of them can and which cannot be transformed into type II CRs.

2. Instrumentalization of the reflex movements

Perhaps the first author to show that motor URs can be transformed into instrumental CRs was Thorndike.[1] He placed a cat into a box from which the animal tried to escape; whenever the animal displayed the scratch reflex he was released or offered food. After some time Thorndike noticed that the cat began to perform the scratch-like movements when put into the box and in this way he achieved his goal.

Since in our laboratory the transformation of various UR movements into type II conditioned responses is a routine experimental procedure, we shall briefly describe this process and the changes they undergo when the training is accomplished.

In our first experiments it was shown that when flexion of the leg elicited by an electric shock is reinforced by food, the animal easily learns to perform the same movement instrumentally (cf. Chapter VIII, Experiment 1). This procedure was often used with the same result, and the training was successful when flexion of either the foreleg or the hindleg was utilized. The method may be slightly modified by tightly binding the distal part of the leg with a band. The animal begins to perform vigorous jerking movements with this leg to get rid of the band. If these movements are followed by food, the animal very soon learns to perform them instrumentally; at the beginning he does so only when the band is attached; then the pressure of the band may be loosened, and finally it can be taken off altogether. It is characteristic that the kind of movement remains roughly the same as it was when provoked by the US: the hindleg is thrusted backward by the jerky movement in the same way as it was when the band was attached. This method is particularly useful when we want to establish the type II conditioned response of the hindleg in both dogs and cats.

Another UR often utilized for instrumental conditioning in cats is the scratch reflex.[2] After the animal has been habituated to the experimental situation, a piece of cotton is put into his ear, soon evoking scratching movements directed to that ear. These movements are immediately followed by presentation of morsels of meat. At the beginning of such training, the antagonistic relations are sometimes observed between the hunger drive and the scratch reflex, causing a nearly total disappearance of scratching. However, since the food is not presented then, the balance between the two is restored and the scratch movements reappear. After some time it is clearly seen that they become type I food CSs, since after each scratching the animal immediately turns to the feeding place. When now the piece of cotton is removed from the ear the animal continues to perform scratch movements which are always reinforced by food. In the early period of training, even when the instrumental scratch response is already established, it sometimes needs facilitation by placing cotton again into the ear. This usually happens at the beginning of a session, when the animal cannot start to perform the trained movement without this help. However, after a few days this is no longer needed and the animal begins to "work" with utmost regularity and speed immediately after he is placed in the experimental situation. The recurrence to the original US to evoke the movement is never needed again.

The conditioned pseudo-scratch movements are not quite identical with those evoked by the US itself. First, the animal rarely touches his neck or ear with the hindleg, but most often performs the movement "in the air." The rhythmic character of the movement is also usually lost. Thus, the learned motor response consists of: assuming the posture appropriate for ear scratching, with the body slightly bent and turned to the direction of the hindleg, raising that leg, and extending it forward in the direction of the ear (Figure XI-1a). Since we usually do not require that the animal perform a "better" movement for food reinforcement, this movement is regularly performed in the experimental situation. It is easy, however, to force the cat to perform a better movement by not offering him the food immediately: then the animal will "correct himself" by making a movement of larger amplitude with some rhythmic component, with or without touching the neck near the ear.

It should be added that in the first stage of instrumental training, when the pseudo-scratching response is not firmly established, the cats occasionally perform other movements which are in some respect equivalent to the scratch movement, such as rubbing the ear with the foreleg, head shaking, pinna movements, although cotton is no longer placed into the ear. This important phenomenon will be commented upon in a later section.

Another instrumental CR similar to that described above has its origin in cleaning the anus in response to wetting it either with water or with a soap solution. The original UR consists of lying down on one side, turning the head toward the anus and licking it, while the free hindleg extends maximally upward. Again, when such a motor act is repeatedly reinforced by food, then after a few sessions the cleaning UR is transformed into the instrumental pseudo-cleaning CR in which the animal lies down on his side and maximally raises the extended hindleg upward without licking the anus (Figure XI-1b). This CR becomes after a short time stable and regular.[3]

It is worth stressing once more that although both these type II CRs may be trained and overtrained for a long time and in both of them the chief component is the movement of the hindleg, they usually preserve their different character indefinitely, so that seeing the animal's performance one has no doubt whether the origin of the CR was the scratching or the cleaning UR.

Still another type II CR often used in cats consists in rubbing the face with the foreleg. It originates in the UR produced by the animal's cheek being smeared with gum arabic (Figure XI-1c).

In dogs we have frequently used vocal instrumental CRs established by food reinforcement of emotional barking either in the experimental situation or in the presence of a sporadic stimulus (cf. Chapter VIII, Experiment III).

In the same way we can utilize for instrumental conditioning various natural instrumental responses which were acquired by the animal in his pre-experimental life. We can teach a dog or a cat to press a pedal, to push a button, to draw in from outside the cage some object with his foreleg, and so on. The best method of this training is that the manipulanda are first baited, and when the animal performs a proper movement to get the bait he receives food from another place. After a few trials the animal learns to perform the required movement without bait. Similarly, the animals are taught to perform various locomotor responses, to jump on platforms, and so on.

Although all these type II CRs differ largely among themselves, both in the character of the responses (locomotor, postural, or manipulatory) and their origin, they possess a number of common properties which should be emphasized.

First, the transformation of all these movements into the alimentary instrumental responses is very rapid (provided that the animal acts under a strong hunger drive), and once established they are displayed with the same speed and regularity as the natural food-securing reactions. The fact that such motor acts as scratching, licking the anus, or flexing the hindleg were never before used by the organisms for securing food and that they originally had a defensive character shows the unexpected range of flexibility of motor behavior and its remarkable adaptability. Of course, the manipulative responses of the forelegs are most readily established as type II CRs; but this is due to the fact that these responses already possessed the food instrumental character, and their training consists merely in their transfer into the experimental situation.

The second important point to be stressed is the preservation of the original character of the response, which may be reduced and simplified in comparison with its primordial model but is usually not distorted. This seems to suggest that perhaps the center controlling that response is also in some way involved in the type II CR. The simplification of the learned movement in comparison with its prototype may be explained as due to the fact that various components of the original UR are in evident incompatibility with the alimentary response. Thus, whereas simple raising of the hindleg and/or even the slight turning the head is not incongruent with taking food, such a movement as licking the anus certainly is; therefore, the animal tends to omit it if the experimenter permits him to do so. If, however, the food is not presented after this simplified version of the movement, the animal resorts to its more perfect execution, thus showing that its other components are reciprocally inhibited by the alimentary response rather than erased by the instrumental training.

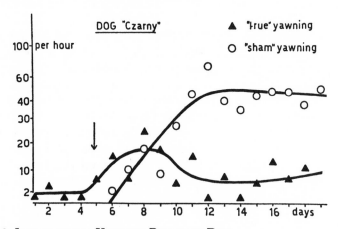

Fig. XI-2. Instrumental Yawning Reflex in Dog

Abscissae, experimental sessions; ordinates, rate of yawning per hour. Arrow denotes the beginning of reinforcing each yawn by food. Note that the number of yawning movements increases, but in addition sham yawning movements appear which soon outnumber the true yawning responses.

(Sołtysik's experiment.)

The important question arises as to whether *all* the motor effects of URs can be made instrumental by the appropriate procedure. The answer to this question remains so far unknown simply because of the lack of corresponding experimental evidence. The following considerations, however, force us to assume that there are probably such unconditioned motor responses whose instrumentalization is not possible.

To begin with, there are some URs whose instrumentalization is very difficult. For instance, when in dogs the yawning reflex is reinforced by food, the tendency to display this reflex in the experimental situation is increased but true instrumental yawning is performed with

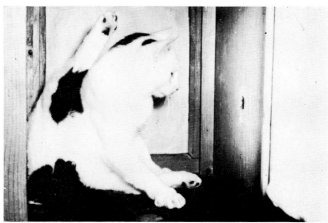

Fig. XI-1. Instrumental CRs Derived from Particular
Unconditioned Reflexes in Cats

    a) Instrumental pseudo-scratch reflex.
    b) Instrumental pseudo-licking the anus reflex.
    c) Instrumental pseudo-rubbing the face reflex.
    (T. Górska, E. Jankowska, and M. Mossakowski, in *Bull. Acad. Polon. Sci.,*
12 [1964]: 413–17.)

obvious difficulty. Instead, the animals perform a pseudo-yawning movement consisting of simple opening of the mouth. If this movement is reinforced, it is repeatedly executed and the full yawning responses decrease (Figure XI-2).[4] An analogous situation arises when attempts to instrumentalize sneezing movements are made.[5] Turning to a human experience, we can hardly perform a swallowing movement when the mouth is completely dry and there is nothing to be swallowed; nor can we accommodate our vision to a short distance if there is no object in our visual field to be focused upon. One has the impression that the more a given reflex action is yoked to a stimulus eliciting it, the more difficult is its emancipation from that stimulus.

3. Instrumental responses originating in passive movements

The problem of instrumental conditionability of passive movements is of the utmost importance for the whole theory of type II conditioning. Therefore, we must carefully analyze all the available evidence, both in favor and against such a possibility, and try to draw the most plausible conclusions at the present stage of our knowledge in this field.

It should be remembered that, according to Miller's and my original concept, the formation of instrumental CRs by passive movements was considered as a theoretically most adequate method for this aim. In fact, according to this concept, if the displacement of the limb becomes the alimentary type I CS, this automatically leads to the animal's executing the movement resulting in this displacement. The fact that this method occasionally proved unsuccessful, particularly with regard to the movements of the hindleg, was attributed to its improper usage. In fact, since passive flexion of the leg involves not only the proprioceptive feedback but also the pressure upon the skin, the latter stimulus could easily mask the former one and prevent its classical conditioning (cf. Chapter VIII, Section 3). However, this explanation of the occasional failure to instrumentalize the passive movement of the leg was by no means conclusive, and it could be suspected that this failure might be due to some other, more essential factors.[6]

The doubt as to whether the passive movement procedure is indeed proper for instrumental conditioning was increased by the extreme difficulty or even total failure of instrumentalization of the passive flexion of the hindlegs in cats.[7] This fact may seem even more puzzling if we take into account that, as shown in the previous section, the instrumentalization of the movements of the hindleg induced by way of reflex (scratch reflex or cleaning the anus reflex) is very easy in these animals. On the other hand, in goats the formation of instrumental CRs by passive movements of both the foreleg and the hindleg does not encounter any difficulty.[8]

All these facts suggest the following explanation of the formation of type II CRs by passive movements. If we are dealing with animals with long limbs (goats or large dogs), the passive raising of the leg endangers the preservation of the balance of the body, and therefore the animal actively opposes it. When, however, the tugging of the leg upward is strong enough, the resistance of the animal is broken and flexion of the leg is executed. This flexion has, however, not a passive but a purely reflex character: the extensors being stretched by the external force finally give way, and the typical "clasp-knife" phenomenon takes place. This is Sherrington's shortening reflex observed in decerebrated animals with increased extensor tonus but certainly present also in normal standing animals. When such a myotatic flexion reflex is repeatedly reinforced by food, we observe that the animal begins slightly to raise this leg itself, and then a light tugging of the leg is enough to provoke a high movement. Therefore, we have good reasons to believe that the animal learns in this condition actively to raise his leg, not because the source of the movement was passive flexion, but rather because it was a myotatic flexion reflex. This explanation accounts for the discrepancies of the results of training in various dogs, depending on whether the passive bending of the leg did or did not elicit the myotatic reflex. It also made clear the failure of establishing the type II CR by passive displacement of the hindleg in cats, since their hindlegs are totally flaccid and no resistance to their passive bending is ever felt.

This conclusion is well supported by a quite different line of evidence provided by Held et al.[9] in experiments carried out on humans with prismatic glasses put on their eyes. In the preliminary training one group of subjects was allowed to observe only passive movements of their arms placed in a special apparatus, but could not perform any active movements; the subjects of the second group were allowed to perform analogous movements of their arms actively. Thereafter, pointing the targets placed in the visual field of the subjects was tested. It was found that only those subjects who were allowed to perform active movements of the arm learned new visuo-motor relations caused by the prismatic glasses.

Analogous experiments were performed by Held and Hein[10] on newborn kittens: some of the animals were allowed to move actively within an experimental compartment, whereas the others were subjected to the same displacements in space on vehicles. Subsequent tests of visually guided movements showed that the second group failed to cope with those visuo-motor problems which were easily solved by the first group.

All these experiments seem to indicate that a passive displacement of the body or limbs followed by drive reduction does not lead to the formation of an instrumental response imitating that displacement. One is compelled to conclude that the individual has to perform the given movement *by himself* in order to reproduce it in instrumental conditioning.

On the other hand, there are some facts which apparently contradict the generality of this conclusion. There is a large body of evidence that when the animal, which is well acquainted with a given environment, is transported from one place to another and receives food there, he is quite able to go to that place even if in the conditioning trial his eyes were covered. Beritoff[11] has convincingly shown that labyrinths are indispensable in solving the problem. This would show that the animal is able to utilize in his locomotor response the labyrinthine and/or visual cues which he acquired during the passive displacement. It was also shown that when a rat is transported through a watery maze on a small "boat," he learns to run along the corresponding path, although the experience was quite passive.

Two possible explanations of these findings may be offered. One is that if an alert animal is transported from one place to another, the visual and labyrinthine perceptions produce corresponding reflex turns of the head and eyes, which are unobserved by the experimenter but which can guide the animal when he is allowed to move freely. In other words, it is suggested that, in acquiring the habit of moving from one place to another, only movements of the head and eyes matter, whereas the means of locomotion is quite irrelevant; in consequence, the animal can change his method of locomotion from swimming to walking and vice versa without affecting his proper performance. Similarly, the animal is probably able to utilize in walking the directional movements acquired while he was being transported.

The other supposition is that in this type of phenomena we have to do with quite another mechanism of learning going beyond the ordinary type II conditioning. This type of learning (which, as a matter of fact, could be called "type III conditioning") was referred to by various investigators as "insight," "reasoning," or "problem solving." Its analysis, presented in detail in our earlier paper,[12] led us to a conclusion that these phenomena are based on associations between particular motor acts and their immediate consequences. In other words, if the animal, on the basis of his earlier experience, "knows" that a given neutral stimulus (visual or proprioceptive) appears when he performs a certain movement, he is able to utilize this "knowledge" if this stimulus becomes a signal of an attractive US. For instance, it may be assumed that a dog or a cat has learned in his early experience that when he is confronted with an elevated platform and lifts his foreleg in a definite manner this leg will be placed on the platform. Then he finds out that whenever the leg is on the platform he obtains food. In consequence, by the mechanism just described, he is able to perform "spontaneously" the movement leading to that position of the leg which secures the attractive US. Similarly, if the animal is familiar with a certain environment and "knows" what locomotor response is needed to reach a definite place, he will find his way to that place after he has been fed there.

It should be realized that even if an animal *is* capable of using such a mechanism in certain cases. of instrumental conditioning, he can apply it only when he has a good experience of manipulation with the given set of stimuli. This would explain why dogs and cats are able to utilize passive displacement of the limbs for instrumental learning when movements of the forelegs but not of the hindlegs are involved and why rats can utilize passive displacement of the body in space when they are placed in an environment with which they are familiar.

To sum up, we may reach the conclusion that in a *regular* type II conditioning the truly passive movements cannot be utilized as a source of the formation of an instrumental response. When this apparently does occur, it may mean either that the myotatic reflex is here in operation, or that the animal performs some responses which are invisible to us, or that some mechanism different from that of type II conditioning is involved in a given learning procedure.

4. Instrumentalization of movements obtained by brain stimulation

Electrical stimulation of the brains of animals to produce movements was first used in experiments performed by Fritsch and Hitzig on dogs in acute experiments almost a hundred years ago. These authors have shown that stimulation of the cortical area situated laterally or behind the cruciate sulcus produces movements of the contralateral hindleg or foreleg or of the face, depending on the place in which the electrodes are situated. This study opened up a vast field of further investigation in which numerous authors electrically stimulated various parts of the cerebral cortex of various animals, in this way mapping the so-called motor area of the cortex.

Experiments concerned with electrical stimulation of the motor area by implanted electrodes in *waking* animals were first performed in the beginning of this century by Ewald,[13] who succeeded in placing chronic electrodes on the sensorimotor area in dogs and was able to elicit cortically induced movements. Yet, there were only a few experimental studies in which such a stimulation was utilized for the formation of instrumental CRs.[14] According to these studies, a movement produced by electrical stimulation of the motor cortex or its vicinity, after being repeatedly reinforced by food, *can* become a type II conditioned response. Since this was in agreement with our early supposition that movements produced in any way could be made instrumental, these experiments were simply considered a confirmation of the apparently well-established general principle.

The experiments were resumed a few years ago by Tarnecki[15] on cats with the aim of verifying the role played by the stimulated motor "center" in type II conditioning. For this purpose electrodes were implanted in the pericruciate area, the movements of the contralateral foreleg or hindleg were elicited by stimulation of the appropriate points, and the instrumental training was carried out by reinforcing each movement by presentation of food. Alternating current, with rectangular pulses of 50 cycles per second and one millisecond pulse duration, was used. Electrodes were unipolar or bipolar, and in most cases they were placed epidurally.

The experiments were fully successful in that stimulation always produced isolated movements of either the foreleg or the hindleg with no side-effects in the form of autonomic symptoms or pain. In fact, the animals were amazingly indifferent to the stimulation and were able to consume immediately the food offered to them when the movement was performed. The results of the instrumental training were, however, quite unexpected.

In view of their unambiguous results, we shall be concerned here only with those experiments in which the cortical area of the hindleg was stimulated.

First, it was noted that the movements of the hindleg produced by stimulation had a different character depending on the place in which the stimulating electrode was implanted (Figure XI-3). If it was placed in the rostral part of the area, just behind the cruciate sulcus, the latency of the motor response was short, the threshold, low and the movement was prompt and high, terminating immediately with the end of stimulation. When the cat was inexperienced, it often happened that the "unexpected" high lifting of the leg produced by stimulation caused the animal to lose balance and fall over. On the other hand, if the electrode was placed more caudally, near the ansate sulcus, the threshold of the movement was higher, its rise and decline was less abrupt, and its amplitude was smaller. It certainly had less "artificial" character than that produced by stimulation of the rostral part of the excitable area.

The CR training has shown that only the movements of the second category could be converted into instrumental responses. This occurred relatively rapidly, the training lasting usually as long as the instrumental training of scratch movements or cleaning the anus movements. The instrumental movement originating from the cortically induced motor response was so similar to that response that from mere observation it was often not possible to tell whether the movement was "spontaneous" or produced by stimulation. Its formation took exactly the same course as the formation of other type II CRs did. When it first appeared, it was performed with long intervals and was easily fatigable. Thereafter it became prompt and regular.

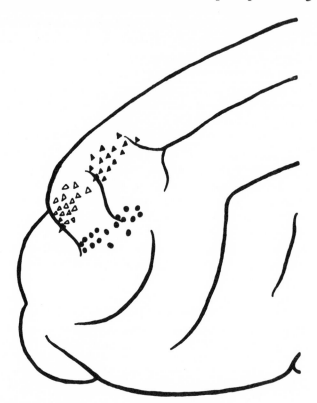

Fig. XI-3. Places of Stimulating Electrodes on a Cat's Cortex Provoking Movements of the Contralateral Foreleg (Circles)
or Hindleg (Triangles)

Black circles, points whose stimulation led to the instrumentalization of the foreleg movement. Black triangles, points whose stimulation led to the instrumentalization of the hindleg movements. White triangles, points whose stimulation did not lead to the instrumentalization of the hindleg movements.

Note that stimulation of points situated in front of the central dimple which provokes the movements of the hindleg does not lead to the instrumentalization of that movement.

(R. Tarnecki and J. Konorski, in Central and Peripheral Mechanisms of Motor Functions [Prague, 1963].)

The picture was totally different when the stimulating electrodes were implanted in the rostral part of the area. In spite of the fact that the cortically induced movements were high and prompt and the animals manifested a clear alimentary behavior after their elicitation, the cats were completely incapable of learning to perform the analogous movements without stimulation. They did not display any tendency to do so, and in the interstimulation intervals they were quite quiet, not performing even abortive movements of the legs. The difference between the two groups was so sharp that there was no doubt that quite different neural mechanisms were involved in both cases.

TABLE XI-1

RATE OF "INSTRUMENTALIZATION" OF CORTICALLY INDUCED MOTOR REACTIONS

NUMBERS OF TRIALS NEEDED TO ESTABLISH ICR	NUMBERS OF ANIMALS			
	Foreleg		Hindleg	
	Motor Area	Sensory Area	Motor Area	Sensory Area
5–10	7	6	0	4
10–20	5	3	0	10
20–30	0	1	0	3
30–40	0	0	0	6
40–50	0	0	0	1
Not established	0	0	17	0

SOURCE: R. Tarnecki, in *Acta Biol. Exp. Vars.*, 22 (1962) (No. 2): 35–45.

It should be noted in parenthesis that the instrumental training with stimulation of the foreleg area gave the positive results regardless of whether the electrodes were implanted in the rostral or the caudal part of the excitable zone. However, since feeding of the animals was accomplished by putting the bowl into position, and the animals displayed a tendency for manipulatory movements with the forelegs, it would be more cautious to withhold from the final evaluation of these results (Table XI-1).

Analogous experiments were performed on dogs in a standard CR chamber.[16] Only stimulation of the sensori-motor area for the hindleg was applied. In two dogs, the movements of the leg were very prompt and high and did not disturb the animal at all. However, in spite of hundreds of trials, the dogs failed to display any tendency to perform these movements actively. In one of these dogs, after the training proved hopeless, the type II CR training was begun by tightly attaching a band to that leg. After a few sessions a very good instrumental response was established consisting of raising the leg and extending it backward. Since the two movements—the cortically induced one and the instrumental one—were easily discernible, it was possible to study their mutual relations. It was found that they could be easily produced in a quick succession or even superimposed, but neither facilitation nor inhibition of one movement upon the other one was observed.

In the second dog, in which the instrumental training by cortical stimulation was also unsuccessful, salivary fistula was made and the type I food CR to cortically induced movements was observed. For this aim each trial consisted of three movements with intervals of two or three seconds. It was quite clear that the animal manifested a strong alimentary response, looking intently at the feeder and salivating when the movements were elicited.

In a third dog, the result of the experiment was quite different. After a few trials in which the cortically induced movement of the hindleg was reinforced by food, the dog started to perform a quite similar movement spontaneously; after a few sessions this movement became stable and regular. Post-mortem examination of the brain of this dog showed that the electrode was placed in the sensory cortex.

All these results seem now to be quite comprehensible and in good agreement with the results presented in the two preceding sections. Stimulation of the motor area of the cortex elicited movements through the direct activation of pyramidal cells. In consequence, the movement evoked had no reflex character, since it was produced by the efferent part of the appropriate reflex arc. The stability of its threshold, latency, and amplitude substantiates its purely efferent character. On the other hand, stimulation of the sensory area of the cortex or the thalamic nuclei has a quite different character. Although it does not act upon receptors or afferent peripheral nerves, it presumably acts upon the structures belonging to the afferent side of the corresponding reflex arcs. Accordingly, the movement elicited by such stimulation falls under the category of reflex movements described in Section 2, above.

Thus, summing up all our results, we may reach the general conclusion that only those movements can become instrumentalized which are accomplished by the intermediary of the central nervous system—in other words, which have a reflex character in the broad sense of the word. Neither the pure passive movements not contaminated by a myotatic reflex nor the movements elicited by stimulation of the efferent parts of the nervous system can be instrumentally conditioned. Of course, this conclusion has a far-reaching significance for the explanation of the physiological mechanism of type II conditioning, a subject which will be undertaken in a later section of this chapter.

5. The role of proprioceptive feedback in type II conditioning

Remembering that in our original concept the proprioceptive feed-back of the provoked movement played an essential role in type II conditioning, we must now say that, according to our new data, this role should be very much restricted. First, we have stated in Section 3, above, that the somesthetic proprioception provided by passive displacement of the limb which generates messages from joints plays no role in type II conditioning, since its pairing with feeding does not lead to the instrumentalization of a movement involving the same positional effect. Second, the failure to instrumentalize the cortically induced movement when the motor area is stimulated suggests that even the muscular proprioceptive feedback which is generated by such a movement does not suffice for this aim.

Thus, we have ascertained that the feedback generated by a movement reinforced with food is not *sufficient* for the formation of the type II CR. This, however, does not exclude a possibility that it is *indispensable* for achieving this aim. In other words, it might be assumed that reinforcement of the given reflexly produced movement leads to the formation of the type II CR only if the messages about its performance reach the brain.

The best way to solve this problem is to make a full deafferentation of the limb taking part in the given motor response and to see: (1) whether the instrumental CR established before the operation will be preserved; and (2) if so, whether it is possible to establish a type II CR involving the movement of the deafferentated limb.

These experiments were performed in a number of studies on cats, dogs, and rats by Jankowska et al.[17] and gave unequivocal results. Here are the chief types of experimentation performed by these authors.

(1) In cats and rats, after the instrumental pseudo-scratch CR was established by means of putting a piece of cotton into the ear, full deafferentation of the corresponding hindleg was performed. After this operation the unconditioned scratch reflex was preserved, although its character was drastically changed. The animal failed to reach the ear with his hindleg, performing the scratch movements "in the air" with a stiffly extended leg. Exactly in the same manner the instrumental pseudo-scratch CR was changed. The movement was clumsy and was performed with the extended leg, but there was no doubt about its full preservation. The same was true when deafferentation affected both hindlegs.

(2) The same result was obtained with regard to the type II CR originating from the cleaning-the-anus UR. Here too the instrumental response was fully preserved after deafferentation of, not only

the hindleg taking part in this response, but also of both hindlegs. This last result is highly important because the bilateral deafferentation of the hindlegs extended also to the region of the anus. In consequence, the unconditioned cleaning-the-anus reflex was completely lost and the animals did not make any attempts to lick the anus region, which remained dirty if it was not washed by a technician. Thus, in spite of the fact that the *unconditioned* response could not be produced because of denervation of its receptive field, the *conditioned* instrumental response was preserved: the animal lay down on his side, turned his head toward the anus, and lifted his extended hindleg as if preparing to lick the anus, a movement which never occurred.

(3) Making profit of the fact that unconditioned scratch reflex was preserved after deafferentation of the hindlimb, although in a distorted form, the experimenters made an attempt to establish a pseudo-scratch CR in deafferentated naïve animals. This attempt proved to be fully successful. The instrumental CR was established in cats with the deafferentated hindleg within the same time as in normal animals.

(4) The instrumental CR performed by the deafferentated limb could be extinguished and restored in the same way as in normal animals.

(5) Experiments concerning the formation and preservation of the type II CR after deafferentation of the limb were conducted in dogs according to the standard type II conditioning procedure. The animals were trained to lift either the foreleg or the hindleg by various methods either in the food situation or the avoidance situation. Deafferentation of the foreleg affected the dorsal roots from C_5 to Th_3; deafferentation of the hindleg affected the dorsal roots from L_2 to S_4. The type II CRs in dogs were established to sporadic auditory stimuli so that the experimenters would not be misled by some unidentified fidgeting movements not connected with instrumental responding. Another precaution consisted in the presentation of a control negative CS never reinforced by food, in response to which the animal did not perform the trained movement. Precautions were also made to prevent the animal from seeing his leg.

In all experiments in which the preservation of the instrumental CR after deafferentation was tested, the trained movement was present in the very first experimental session carried out after deafferentation. Although the animal had no sensory feedback from the leg involved in conditioning, the motor response was quite stable and did not deteriorate even after many post-operative sessions. If in some trials the performed movement was small, the CS was prolonged without reinforcement and the animal improved his performance. Repeated non-reinforcement led to the extinction of the trained movement, which was restored when the CS was again followed by food.

In other words, the properties of the instrumental CR involving the deafferentated limb did not differ in any way from those involving the unimpaired leg, except in the clumsiness of the movement owing to the rigidity of the distal portions of the leg.

In some dogs, after deafferentation of the foreleg a regular type II CR training was conducted by placing the deafferentated limb on the food-tray and reinforcing this passive movement by food.[18] This training turned out to be completely unsuccessful, although the animal was able to see his leg being placed on the food-tray and occasionally he displayed a type I food CR to this sight. On the other hand, if an *active* movement of the foreleg, caused by general motor excitement of the animal or electrical stimulation of his ear, was reinforced by food, the type II CR was readily established.

Similar results to those described for dogs and cats were obtained in another experimental series performed on monkeys by Knapp et al.[19]

All these data leave no doubt that, for both the formation of the type II CR and its preservation, the sensory feedback from the limb involved in the trained movement is not necessary. The generally held misconception concerning this point, widespread among neurologists and neurophysiologists, probably has its source in the observation that the deafferentated limb is of no use in any skillful, manipulatory movements, such as reaching a goal with the forelimb, pulling or pushing objects, or seizing them. Since such activities are composed of successive motor acts in which a feedback from the fulfillment of one segment provides a stimulus for eliciting the next one, they obviously cannot be performed by the deafferentated limb. As a matter of fact, the deafferentated limb does not take part even in locomotion which involves at least proprioceptive information about its position and tactile information concerning its touching the ground. In consequence, the non-employment of the deafferentated limb because of its inutility is easily mistaken for the inability of this limb to perform *any* instrumental movements. Thus, precise evidence showing the preservation of the instrumental performance in the deafferentated limb can be provided only by the "artificial" experimental condition in which the animal is required to perform a movement which obviously plays no practical role in his life, since it does not involve any precision connected with the sensory feedback. In other words, a movement which in normal life is completely useless in artificially simplified conditions remains fully instrumental for achieving a goal consisting in obtaining the food or avoiding an aversive US. Therefore, its utility is totally preserved, and in consequence its performance is not inhibited.

A good example showing how misleading may be the superficial observation of an animal without applying special tests for discovering his true motor abilities is as follows.[20] A cat sustained a bilateral radical deafferentation of both forelimbs. This lesion totally disabled his walking, because alternating movements of the limbs require their proprioception. Therefore, the animal permanently lay on his side without any possibility or any attempt to get up. Both forelimbs were totally immobile and gave the impression of being paralyzed.

The experimenter blew air into the animal's face with a rubber bulb. The cat immediately made a vehement movement with his free fore-paw toward the bulb, and when such trials were repeated, he very promptly developed a strong defensive CR consisting in vigorous hit-ting of the bulb whenever it was in his visual field. The contrast between the total helplessness of the cat in such simple activity as standing on his forelegs (requiring the tactile feedback from the feet) and very good performance of the hitting movement by the foreleg in response to a visual stimulus was indeed most striking.

Yet, although we have certainly dismissed the necessity of the peripheral sensory feedback for the performance of an instrumental movement, we cannot exclude the significance of the *intercentral* feedback signaling, not the execution of the movement, but the order sent for this execution.

Assuming the existence of such an intercentral feedback, we thought that it might be accomplished in at least two ways. For one thing, as known from anatomical and physiological studies, the py-ramidal fibers give off collaterals which reach the *nucleus gracilis* and *cuneatus*.[21] For another, bidirectional relations between the motor cortex and the cerebellum might be thought to be a source of such a feedback. In consequence, it was decided to destroy the correspond-ing thalamic nuclei in order to see the effects of these lesions upon type II CRs.[22]

Cats were used for these experiments, and the pseudo-scratching and cleaning-the-anus instrumental responses were established. Then either the VPL or VL thalamic nuclei or both were bilaterally de-stroyed by electrocoagulation.

The following results were obtained. The VL lesions did not seri-ously affect either of the trained motor responses. The VPL lesion, on the other hand, apparently had a strong detrimental effect on the pseudo-scratch CR leaving the other one practically undisturbed.

Closer observation of the animals could easily show the source of this discrepancy. The pseudo-scratching instrumental movement is usually executed from a sitting position of the animal. It was found that after a bilateral VPL lesion the animals could not afford to dis-engage the hindleg from its supporting role. In consequence, the trained movements, although in most cases present, were very small and difficult to be identified. On the other hand, the pseudo-cleaning movement is always accomplished from the lying position; hence the hindleg taking part in it is free. Proof was provided by the fact that in some cases the animals of the first group trying to perform the required movement lost their balance and turned over on the opposite side, thus unblocking the hindleg which had to execute this movement. In this way the movement became successful, and soon the cats learned to use this trick of "deliberately" turning over on their sides before performing the instrumental response. The same results were obtained when both VL and VPL nuclei were jointly impaired.

Thus, our attempt to find an intercentral feedback which would be responsible for the performance of the instrumental movement was unsuccessful. Consequently, the question may be raised as to whether such a feedback does actually exist; in the next section we shall show that the assumption of its existence is in fact superfluous.

6. The mechanism of instrumental movement

In Chapter I we have introduced a notion—"central motor behavioral system"—denoting by it the system controlling the whole set of behavioral acts, innate and acquired, which the organism has at its disposal in a given period of life. We have assumed that this system is brought into the state of arousal under the influence of drives, and we have shown that particular behavioral acts belonging to that system may become instrumental responses under the appropriate type II CR training.

It seems that the data described in the present chapter are in full agreement with our preceding considerations and help us clarify in more detail the mechanism of instrumental motor acts.

First, it has been clearly stated in our present discussion that only those movements can be instrumentalized which are mediated by the central behavioral system—in other words, which are performed by the organism itself and are not forced upon it, as is the case with passive movements or movements elicited by stimulation of efferent pathways.

Second, it was established that if a given motor act has a unitary character, no peripheral feedback is necessary for its instrumentalization, since this process occurs owing to the formation of connections between the CS units and drive units on the one hand and the "center" of this motor act on the other.

Our aim now is to elucidate what nervous structures represent recipient units in instrumental conditioning.

Taking into account the full range of motor behavioral acts speci-fied at the beginning of this chapter, from which the instrumental re-sponses can be formed, we may divide them into the following cate-gories.

(1) Simple behavioral acts such as: locomotion toward a given stimulus (visual, auditory, olfactory), turning right or left in the course of locomotion, jumping upon or from an elevated platform under the guidance of vision, climbing, such manipulatory movements as placing the foreleg on the platform, pressing a pedal, grasping some-thing in the mouth. Many of these movements are preserved after lesions involving the sensorimotor cortex, but they may be annihilated after lesions localized in the basal ganglia. For instance, in experiments performed by Sołtysik and Zieliński on cats the simple avoidance re-sponse of pedal pressing was abolished after striatal lesions, although the fear drive was unaffected;[23] on the other hand, this instrumental act was preserved in both dogs and cats even after extensive cortical lesions or after pyramidectomies.[24] The contrast between the animals with sensorimotor or pyramidal lesions and those with striatal lesions was indeed striking. Although the animals of the first group (particu-larly dogs) were often strongly handicapped in their motor per-formances (especially when the lesion was extensive), the general pro-gram of the trained movement was fully preserved. On the other hand, the striatal animals, although quite skillful in all their movements, be-haved as if the instrumental response was never trained in them.

Comparing the behavior of cats deprived of neocortex with those in which the basal ganglia are additionally removed, we may easily come to the conclusion that the former have preserved the basic behavioral acts and therefore do not differ radically from normal cats; the latter are drastically different, displaying only simple reflexes in an automa-ton-like fashion.[25] Therefore we propose the hypothesis that the most primitive behavioral patterns, similar to the most primitive perceptual patterns (cf. Chapter VI, Section 9), are represented in the basal gan-glia—in other words, that these structures comprise kinesthetic units programing the simplest forms of animal behavior.

(2) More complex behavioral acts formed by integration of ele-mentary movements are represented in the so-called premotor cortex (cf. Chapter III, Section 8). This area comprising gnostic units of kinesthetic analyzer is of course highly developed in man and other primates, whereas it is much less so in lower animals. Nevertheless, we may present a good example of the role of the premotor area in instru-mental CRs.

In a series of studies carried out by Stępień et al.[26] the role of par-ticular regions of the sensorimotor (including premotor) cortex in instrumental CRs was investigated. A simple motor act consisting of placing the foreleg on an elevated platform was used as the instrumental response. It was found that lesions in the sensory and motor cortex impair the *performance* of the trained movement (making it atactic or paretic respectively), but this impairment has a purely "technical" character, not at all affecting the very program of the instrumental response.

Quite different, however, were the effects of lesions sustained in the premotor area. In contradistinction to lesions in the sensorimotor region, the skillful character of the motor acts was preserved. The animals were neither paretic nor atactic, and they easily performed movements which were difficult for the former dogs, as, for instance, jumping on or jumping off a stand. However, their instrumental CR activity was strongly impaired in a peculiar way: the presentation of the CS, instead of eliciting the prompt placing of the right foreleg on the platform, produced either strong targeting response toward the source of a CS or a direct response to the bowl. The instrumental response to the CS was absent, although the animal occasionally performed this response in intertrial intervals. When the instrumental CR to the CS was gradually restored, it clearly consisted of three separate phases, namely: (1) the targeting response toward the source of the CS; (2) turning to the bowl and occasionally licking or gnawing it; and (3) placing the foreleg on the feeder. At first this separation of the three motor acts caused a strong prolongation of the latency of the trained movement and its utmost irregularity. Gradually the responses became more regular and prompt, but the separation of the three phases was clearly seen during the whole postoperative period.

The symptom just described may be considered a simple model of apractic disorder. In well-trained normal animals the short targeting reflex, the turn to the bowl, and lifting the leg become integrated into a unitary behavioral act and are hardly discernible as separate elements. After ablation of the premotor cortex they are disintegrated, and as such they may even become antagonistic to each other.

(3) Finally, it is necessary to discuss a third category of instrumental motor acts, which take their origin from particular URs, such as scratching, licking the anus, or yawning. As a basis of our consideration, take the type II CR transformed from the scratch reflex.[27]

It is clear that when the scratch movement elicited by a stimulus irritating the ear is followed by food, there is not only the coincidence between the hunger drive and that movement but also the coincidence between that drive and the irritating stimulus. Therefore, according to the general principles of associations, we should expect that strong connections are formed between the drive units and the somesthetic units representing the US (in our case itching stimulus). In consequence, the hunger drive produced in a given situation leads not only to the excitation of *kinesthetic* units representing the drive reducing movement (pseudo-scratching) but also to the excitation of *somesthetic* units representing the itching stimulus, giving rise to its image or hallucination. Thus, it may be assumed that the animal starts to perform the motor response because he "feels" the stimulus provoking that response although this stimulus is no longer administered.

Convincing evidence that the above mechanism is actually in operation, at least in the first stage of instrumental conditioning, was mentioned above. It can be observed that in that stage, when the instrumental pseudo-scratch response is not yet routinized, the animal performs a number of vicarious movements aiming at the removal of a non-existing irritating agent, such as rubbing the ear against the wall, rubbing it with the foreleg, or shaking the head, although these movements were never reinforced by food. Only in a later stage of training do these other responses disappear, and the cat performs exclusively the pseudo-scratch movement in a machine-like fashion.

Since the detailed analysis of this peculiar type of conditioning has not yet been undertaken, we cannot answer a number of questions which arise in respect to it. The first question is whether the discussed mechanism is in operation in all instrumental responses originating from clear-cut URs or only in some of them. Then, it is not clear whether this mechanism is maintained permanently, in spite of the fact that the original US is no longer applied, or whether it gives way to the typical mechanism of instrumentalization of a given motor act. It may be that both mechanisms are jointly in operation, corroborating each other. In this respect the instrumental pseudo-yawning reflex is most instructive (cf. Figure XI-2).

It may be noticed that the phenomenon now under discussion has an immediate bearing on the long-debated problem of instrumentalization of autonomic responses. Since we have no evidence that these responses have a special analyzer analogous to the kinesthetic analyzer for somatic movements, we do not believe that they can be instrumentalized in the same way as are the motor acts. We may assume, however, that if some stimuli provoking a definite autonomic response (for instance, salivation or a change in the heart rate) coincide with a certain drive, they are prone to form association with it; in consequence, this drive plus the situation in which this coincidence repeatedly took place will evoke by association the activation of units representing that stimulus (giving rise to its image or hallucination), and this in turn will produce the given autonomic response. The recent data obtained in Miller's laboratory[28] seem to confirm the existence of such a mechanism.

The above described mechanism of instrumentalization of "involuntary" motor acts (such as reflex scratching or yawning) as well as, probably, autonomic responses may be considered a *sui generis* physiological artifact brought forth by a peculiar coincidence of two heterogeneous unconditioned factors (for instance, hunger drive and itching stimulus) which hardly occurs in natural life. This, however, is not quite true. Although certainly the arrangement of the external world hardly provides the organism with the situations in which yawning or scratching the body would be instrumental for securing food or a sexual partner, in some exceptional conditions such coincidences may occasionally occur and may lead to peculiar neurotic symptoms. For example, a soldier who suffered a strong fear shock in a battle is able to produce afterward, during a prolonged period, a number of pathological motor and autonomic responses (such as paleness, trembling, tics) which are instrumental for obtaining an invalid pension; similarly, a child who suffered from pertussis is able, after the disease is gone, to develop a quasi-deliberate cough in order to blackmail his parents and extort from them his demands. A similar analysis of these abnormal reactions was presented by Kretschmer.[29]

As seen from our discussion, if we put aside the latter, rather exceptional, mechanisms of instrumentalization of normal or pathological URs, in natural conditions, we have to do with two sources of instrumental movements depending on two major divisions of the central motor behavioral system.

The first, phylogenetically older, division, localized probably in particular regions of the basal ganglia, is concerned with relatively simple and innate behavioral acts such as turns of the body, jumping up and down, climbing onto an elevated platform with the forelegs, and the like. All these acts may become instrumentalized and serve for satisfaction of particular drives in particular situations. The extrapyramidal character of these acts (at least in cats and dogs) is well documented by the fact that they are totally preserved after bilateral pyramidectomies.[30] The topography of kinesthetic units programing these motor acts is so far completely unknown; hence most diversified and contradictory are the findings following striatal lesions in particular experimental studies.

The second division of the system, phylogenetically more recent, is localized in the kinesthetic gnostic fields of the cerebral cortex. Here the more complex behavioral patterns are represented: those patterns which are as a rule composed of more elementary movements represented in the projective "motor" area. These elements have a purely transit character and therefore cannot be called behavioral acts; they correspond to "sensations" of the exteroceptive analyzers. It may be reasonably assumed, however, that this is not the only input to the units of kinesthetic gnostic fields, because probably the simple behavioral acts of the extrapyramidal system can be also combined and integrated in these fields.

It is quite natural to assume that, *pari passu* with the phylogenetical development of animals' motor behavior the role of the second kinesthetic system becomes more and more dominant over the first system. This is due to the fact that whereas in subprimate species the behavioral acts are relatively simple, the behavior in primates—above all in man —becomes most complex and is composed of serial elementary motor acts characteristic for manual praxis involved in skillful movements and oral praxis involved in speech. This is why the striatal lesions seem to produce much more severe behavioral symptoms in dogs and cats than in monkeys and man.

To end our considerations on the mechanism of instrumental movements, the problem of the *information* about the performance of these movements should be commented upon—information indispensable for the occurrence of type II CRs. For, as follows from our previous discussion, the animal *must* know that the instrumental movement has been performed, or at least ordered, because otherwise that movement would be doomed to suppression: in fact, in the alimentary type II CR, the type II CS would be transformed into the type I food CS; in the avoidance type II CR, this stimulus would be transformed into the type I relief CS (cf. Chapter IX, Section 5). But, as stated above, both alimentary and avoidance type II CRs are fully preserved after deafferentation of the limb involved and do not display any symptoms of deterioration in further training. Moreover, we have no evidence that any intercentral feedback is in operation that is responsible for the preservation of the instrumental response.

It seems that in view of our present concept this apparent contradiction may be easily removed. In the normal occurrence of the instrumental reflex the drive units and CS units send impulses to the recipient kinesthetic units which program the pattern of the movement and give orders for its performance. As already explained in Chapter IV (Section 8) in respect to voluntary movements in man, the activation of these units provides the information about its intention and initiation, which is tantamount to the information on its performance, provided that no contrary information is obtained from the periphery. Speaking psychologically, we may say that in spite of deafferentation the animal "feels" that the movement is executed, not because of the peripheral feedback, but because of the very fact that the appropriate kinesthetic units have been centrally activated.

Incidentally, one should notice that in dogs and cats both in alimentary and defensive type II CRs the instrumental response appears in the very first session after deafferentation, and does not need to be retrained. This shows that in a normal animal too the information of the trained movement indispensable for the formation of the type II CR derives, not so much from periphery, but rather from this "decision making" and programing central mechanism. Otherwise, the animal would have to change the cue informing him on the performance of the trained movement, and some period of relearning would be necessary. According to the experiments of Berman et al. this may be true in respect to monkeys.[31]

7. Summary and conclusions

This chapter was concerned with the problem of the functional organization of the centers controlling the instrumental motor acts. It was earlier postulated that all these acts are represented in the "central motor behavioral system," and it was suggested that they are patterned and programed on the afferent side of the circuit (kinesthetic analyzer), the efferent part having only the executive role.

First, the specification of various categories of movements was carried out, taking into account their character and origin, and it was shown that only those movements can be transformed into instrumental responses which are mediated by the central nervous system—that is, which have a reflex character in the broadest sense of the word. Accordingly, it was shown that the purely passive movements, not being contaminated by the myotatic reflex, and cortically induced movements elicited by stimulation of the motor area of the cortex cannot be instrumentalized. The usual successfully applied method of instrumentalization of passive movements was explained as being due to the myotatic clasp-knife reflex (lengthening reflex) in the standing animal.

A large body of experimental evidence on cats, rats, and dogs was presented to show that the sensory feedback of the limb taking part in the trained movement is not necessary for preservation of the already established type II CR; deafferentation of the limb does not destroy the instrumental response, although it somewhat changes its character. Only those motor acts are destroyed by deafferentation which have a more complex serial character and in which proprioception is an indispensable link connecting their successive phases. This is why most of the purposive or skillful movements cannot be executed properly after deafferentation.

If the receptive field for elicitation of a given reflex is outside the zone of afferentation of the limb, as it is with scratch reflex directed to the ear, then the instrumental CR can be established after deafferentation of that limb, the training requiring as much time as in normal conditions.

The type II CR, either alimentary or defensive (avoidance), is as stable after deafferentation as in normal condition and can be submitted to extinction and restoration by the usual procedures.

In order to find out whether a shortened, intercentral feedback may be substituted for the peripheral one, the VL and VPL thalamic nuclei as well as *lemniscus medialis* were destroyed in cats. This did not seriously affect the instrumental responses, although the response originating from the scratch reflex was handicapped by the VPL lesion owing to the postural difficulties. These experiments proved that there is no intercentral feedback running through these nuclei and responsible for the maintenance of the type II CR.

We have discerned two divisions of the kinesthetic analyzer in which the instrumental responses are programed and initiated. One division, phylogenetically older, is thought to be localized in some regions of the basal ganglia. It is concerned with the programing of the more primitive behavioral acts, probably mostly of an innate character. The kinesthetic units representing these acts may become connected with the CS units and drive units, and in this way the relatively primitive instrumental responses are formed. The other division, phylogenetically more recent and particularly well developed in higher primates, is localized in the cortical kinesthetic gnostic area (premotor area). It is concerned with more complex behavioral acts integrated of simple elements represented in the motor area or in the basal ganglia.

Further, the instrumental responses transformed from particular unconditioned reflexes, such as scratch reflex, may have still another mechanism—that in which the CS and drive become associated with the *stimuli* eliciting those reflexes. In consequence, the joint operation of the CS and drive produces activation of the somesthetic units representing the irritating focus and in this way elicits the corresponding UR or its equivalents. Some pathological neurotic symptoms are based on this mechanism.

It may be noticed that the experimental evidence presented in this chapter and the conclusions reached on its basis are in striking harmony with those conclusions which were reached by us earlier (Chapter IV, Sections 8 and 9) on the basis of psychological and neurological evidence. This circumstance strongly increases the probability that the concepts concerning the mechanisms of instrumental (alias voluntary) motor acts proposed in this book may be correct.

References to Chapter XI

1. E. L. Thorndike. 1911. *Animal Intelligence.* New York: Macmillan.
2. E. Jankowska. 1963. Znaczenie informacji zwrotnej z efektora w odruchach instrumentalnych. (The role of the kinesthetic feedback from effectors in the instrumental conditioned reflexes.) Sc.D. Thesis, Warsaw, Inst. Biologii Dośw. im. M. Nenckiego PAN (Nencki Inst. of Experimental Biology).
3. T. Górska, E. Jankowska, and W. Kozak. 1961. The effect of deafferentation on instrumental (type II) cleaning reflex in cats. *Acta Biol. Exp. Vars.,* 21: 207–17.
4. S. Sołtysik. Unpublished experiments.
5. В. К. Федоров. 1952. Основные принципы взаимных влияний между различными двигательными реакциями. (Basic principles of mutual influences between various motor reactions.) *Fiziol. Zh. SSSR.,* 38: 559–65.
6. C. B. Woodbury. 1942. A note on "passive" conditioning. *J. Gen. Psychol.,* 27: 359–61.
7. W. Kozak and E. Jankowska. Unpublished experiments.
8. W. Wyrwicka, C. Dobrzecka, and R. Tarnecki. 1960. Elaboration of alimentary conditioned reflex type II with the use of electrical stimulation of the hypothalamus. *Bull. Acad. Pol. Sci.,* Cl. II, Ser. Sci. Biol., 8: 109–11.
9. R. Held and N. Gottlieb. 1958. Technique for studying adaptation to disarranged hand-eye coordination. *Percept. Mot. Skills,* 8: 83–86.
   R. Held and A. V. Hein. 1958. Adaptation of disarranged hand-eye coordination contingent upon re-afferent stimulation. *Percept. Mot. Skills,* 8: 87–90.
   R. Held and M. Schlank. 1959. Adaptation to disarranged eye-hand coordination in the distance-dimension. *Amer. J. Psychol.,* 72: 603–5.
10. R. Held and A. V. Hein. 1963. Movement-produced stimulation in the development of visually guided behavior. *J. Comp. Physiol. Psychol.,* 56: 872–76.
11. I. S. Beritoff (Beritashvili). 1965. *Neural Mechanisms of Higher Vertebrate Behavior.* Translated and edited by W. T. Liberson. Boston: Little, Brown & Co.
12. J. Konorski. 1950. Mechanisms of learning. In: *Physiological Mechanisms in Animal Behaviour,* pp. 409–31. Symp. Soc. Exp. Biol., No. 4.
13. J. R. Ewald. 1898. Über künstliche Reizung der Grosshirnrinde. *Dt. med. Wschr.,* Bd. 24, Vereinbeil. No. 25.
14. R. B. Loucks. 1936. The experimental delimitation of neural structures essential for learning: The attempt to condition striped muscle responses with faradisation of the sigmoid gyri. *J. Psychol.,* 1: 5–44.
    J. Konorski and L. Lubińska. 1939. Sur un procédé nouveau d'élaboration et réflexes conditionnels du II type et sur les changements d'excitabilité du contre cortical moteur au cours de l'apprentissage. *Acta Biol. Exp. Vars.,* 13: 143–52.

15. R. Tarnecki. 1962. The formation of instrumental conditioned reflexes by direct stimulation of sensori-motor cortex in cats. *Acta Biol. Exp. Vars.*, 22 (No. 2) : 35–45.

    R. Tarnecki and J. Konorski. 1963. Instrumental conditioned reflexes elaborated by means of direct stimulation of the motor cortex. In E. Gutmann and P. Hnik, eds., *Central and Peripheral Mechanisms of Motor Functions: Proceedings of the Conference held at Liblice near Prague, May 15–21, 1961*, pp. 177–82. Prague: Publ. House of the Czechoslovak Acad. Sci.

16. R. Tarnecki, G. D. Ellison, and J. Konorski. Unpublished experiments.

17. E. Jankowska. 1959. Instrumental scratch reflex of the deafferentated limb in cats and rats. *Acta Biol. Exp. Vars.*, 19: 233–47.

    T. Górska, E. Jankowska, and W. Kozak. 1961 (see note 3 above).

    T. Górska and E. Jankowska. 1961. The effect of deafferentation on instrumental (Type II) conditioned reflexes in dogs. *Acta Biol. Exp. Vars.*, 21: 219–34.

18. ———. 1960. The effect of deafferentation on the instrumental conditioned reflexes established in dogs by reinforcing passive movements. *Bull. Acad. Pol. Sci.*, Cl. II, Ser. Sci. Biol., 8: 527–30.

19. H. D. Knapp, E. Taub, and A. J. Berman. 1958. Effect of deafferentation on a conditioned avoidance response. *Science*, 128 (No. 3328) : 842–43.

20. T. Górska and E. Jankowska. Unpublished experiments.

21. F. Magni, R. Melzack, G. Moruzzi, and C. J. Smith. 1959. Direct pyramidal influences on the dorsal-column nuclei. *Arch. Ital. Biol.*, 97: 357–77.

    H. G. J. M. Kuypers. 1960. Central cortical projections to motor and somato-sensory cell groups. *Brain*, 83: 161–84.

22. R. Tarnecki. 1963. Wpływ uszkodzeń jąder brzuszno-bocznego i brzuszno-tylno-bocznego wzgórza na instrumentalne odruchy warunkowe. (The effect of lesions of ventro-lateral and ventro-postero-lateral thalamus upon instrumental conditioned reflexes.) Sc.D. thesis, Warsaw, Inst. Biologii Dośw. im. M. Nenckiego PAN (Nencki Inst. of Experimental Biology).

23. S. Sołtysik and K. Zieliński. Unpublished experiments.

24. I. Stępień, L. Stępień, and J. Konorski. 1961. The effects of unilateral and bilateral ablations of sensori-motor cortex on instrumental (type II) alimentary conditioned reflexes. *Acta Biol. Exp. Vars.*, 21: 121–40.

    T. Górska, E. Jankowska, and M. Mossakowski. 1966. Effects of pyramidotomy on instrumental conditioned reflexes in cats. I. Manipulatory reflexes. *Acta Biol. Exp. Vars.*, 26 (No. 4) : 441–50.

    T. Górska. 1967. Instrumental conditioned reflexes after pyramidotomy in dogs. *Acta Biol. Exp. Vars.*, 27 (No. 1) (in press).

25. G. H. Wang and K. Akert. 1962. Behavior and reflexes of chronic striatal cats. *Arch. Ital. Biol.*, 100: 48–85.

26. I. Stępień and L. Stępień. 1959. The effect of sensory cortex ablations on

instrumental (type II) conditioned reflexes in dogs. *Acta Biol. Exp. Vars.*, 19: 257–72.

I. Stępień, L. Stępień, and J. Konorski. 1960*a*. The effects of bilateral lesions in the motor cortex on type II conditioned reflexes in dogs. *Acta Biol. Exp. Vars.*, 20: 211–23.

———. 1960*b*. The effects of bilateral lesions in the premotor cortex on type II conditioned reflexes in dogs. *Ibid.*, 20: 225–42.

———. 1961. The effects of unilateral and bilateral ablations of sensorimotor cortex on the instrumental (type II) alimentary conditioned reflexes in dogs. *Ibid.*, 21: 121–40.

I. Stępień, L. Stępień, and J. Kreiner. 1963. The effects of total and partial ablations of the premotor cortex on the instrumental conditioned reflexes in dogs. *Acta Biol. Exp. Vars.*, 23: 45–60.

27. З. Янковска и С. Солтысик. 1960. Двигательные условные рефлвксы, выработанные из безусловных двигательных рефлексов, подкрепляемых пищей. [(Motor conditioned reflexes established from unconditioned motor reflexes reinforced by food.) In *Central'nye i periferičeskie mechanizmy dvigatel'noj dejatel'nosti životnych* (Spisok dokladov meždunarodnogo Simpoziuma Pol'sa, 1958), pp. 61–69. Moscow: Izdat. Akad. Nauk SSSR.]

28. N. E. Miller and A. Carmona. 1967. Modification of a visceral response, salivation in thirsty dogs, by instrumental training with water reward. *J. Comp. Physiol. Psychol.*, 63: 1–6.

J. A. Trowill. 1967. Instrumental conditioning of the heart rate in the curarized rat. *Ibid.*, pp. 7–11.

N. E. Miller and L. DiCara. 1967. Instrumental learning of heart rate changes in curarized rats: shaping, and specificity to discriminative stimulus. *Ibid.*, pp. 12–19.

29. E. Kretschmer. 1960. *Hysteria, Reflex and Instinct.* New York: Philosophical Library.

30. T. Górska. 1965. Znaczenie czynnościowe dróg piramidowych w ruchowych odruchach warunkowych. (The role of the pyramidal tract in motor conditioned reflexes in dogs.) Sc.D. Thesis, Warsaw, Inst. Biologii Dośw. PAN (Nencki Inst. of Experimental Biology).

31. H. D. Knapp, E. Taub, and A. J. Berman. 1958 (see note 19 above).

CHAPTER XII

TRANSIENT (OR DYNAMIC) MEMORY

1. Introductory remarks

Writing a work like the present one devoted to a comprehensive survey of a given field of science compels the author to take into consideration not only those phenomena which are more or less ready for a synthesis but also those whose incorporation into a coherent system is, in the present stage of our knowledge, not readily feasible. The phenomena of recent memory belong to the latter category of events. In fact, if we make a cursory survey of the problems which have been dealt with so far by the behavioral sciences, and the methods which have been developed for their study, we may readily observe that most of these problems concern the formation and properties of stable memory traces involved in conditioning and learning, whereas the methods devoted to the problems of recent memory have been relatively scarce. This fact is in clear disproportion to the important role which is played by the phenomena of recent memory both in our own mental processes and in those of other animals.

An impulse for investigation of recent memory in animals in the past two decades was supplied by the discovery of dramatic effects exerted upon the memorization processes by an electroconvulsive shock (ECS) or anoxia.[1] It was shown that if these agents closely follow a training session, the memory traces of what the animal has learned are completely or nearly completely erased. On the contrary, if these agents are administered after several hours, the memory traces are preserved.

On the basis of anatomical evidence showing that there exist in the brain closed chains of neurons enabling the nerve impulses to circulate along them for long periods of time,[2] the reverberation theory of recent memory accounting for the above results was proposed. According to this theory: (1) the circulation of impulses along the closed circuits of neurons is assumed to be the physiological basis of recent memory; and (2) this circulation leads to the transformation of dynamic memory traces into stable ones, a process referred to as *consolidation*. ECS or anoxia was thought to stop this circulation of impulses and thus prevent the process of consolidation.[3]

A serious doubt as to the correctness of this theory was cast recently by Albert,[4] who has convincingly shown that the process of consolidation of memory traces is independent of recent memory. He also confirmed the hypothesis earlier advanced by Hydén[5] of the biochemical nature of stable memory.

Without entering here into a discussion of this debatable hypothesis, we should like to emphasize only that the idea of clear separation and complete independence of the processes of recent memory on the one hand and the formation of stable memory traces on the other seems to us quite sound and, as we shall presently see, it is fully supported by psychological and behavioral data. Thus, in our further discussion we shall hold the view that recent memory (or, as we shall call it, *transient* memory) has a dynamic character depending on the activation of closed, self-reexciting chains of neurons, whereas the consolidation of memory is a quite separate and independent process whose intimate nature is still poorly understood. After all, it should be remembered that transient memory traces following a single event are not always— in fact, rather seldom—followed by consolidation of the stimulus pattern, especially in older age. Otherwise the brain would be overburdened with the tremendous amount of information which would handicap its normal activity. For, as it will be seen in the following sections, most of our transient memory traces do not *need* to be consolidated, and they may vanish (and they do vanish) when their role is fulfilled.

In our present discussion we shall first make a survey of the phenomena of transient memory in humans, basing our considerations on introspective experiences and pathological data, and then we shall turn to the results obtained in experimentation on animals. We shall be concerned exclusively with the "pure" phenomena of transient memory, putting the problem of consolidation processes aside because, according to our view, it does not pertain to the topic of our present consideration.

2. Transient memory of perceptions

If while in a state of alertness we pay attention to a number of new stimulus-objects—for instance, when visiting a foreign city we notice the faces of unknown persons, hear the unknown language, or look at new surroundings—we vividly remember some of these for a certain period of time, being able to evoke their images at will. Sometimes, if the perception was tinted by a strong emotion, we cannot get rid of the corresponding image which obsessively occurs to us even against our will. These experiences indicate that if a given stimulus-object belongs to a category of patterns well represented in one of our gnostic fields, its single exposition may lead to the establishment of appropriate gnostic units. These units, however, in contradistinction to the gnostic units discussed in earlier chapters, are only *transient*, because, as we know, in many cases they do not become "consolidated" and transferred to the files of our stable memory. In fact, we may observe that after some hours or days we do not remember any longer the exposed stimulus-object—that is, we can neither evoke it in our imagination nor recognize it if it is presented to us once more.

The question arises as to what is the mechanism of the formation and existence of these transient gnostic units and what is their relation to the stable gnostic units.

To begin, it should be noted that the experience we have when we evoke the image of a stimulus-object soon after its presentation does not differ phenomenologically from images returning to us after a long time by way of association. In fact, when I imagine a face or a picture I have recently seen, I do not know whether it belongs to my stable memory file or whether it will vanish completely after some time. This shows that gnostic units are formed in our gnostic fields both as a result of temporary and reversible processes and as a result of permanent and irreversible states of neurons concerned.

According to the reverberation theory of the transient memory, the simplest conjecture would be that the postulated closed circuits are represented by *cortico-thalamic loops*. In fact, we know that each gnostic area is bidirectionally connected with a corresponding "associative" thalamic nucleus, and there is some evidence, unfortunately scarce, to show that lesions in these nuclei are as harmful for a given kind of gnosis as cortical lesions. Thus we assume that when a given stimulus-object is presented, the impulses traveling from the lower levels of the afferent system concerned reach the appropriate gnostic field, impinge upon the free units that are the points of their convergence and throw into operation the corresponding cortico-thalamic loops. As long as these loops are active, the transient memory of the given stimulus-object persists. This activity may be thought to die out spontaneously after a lapse of time or to be suppressed by conflicting perceptions. The latter mechanism is usually referred to as "retroactive inhibition."

Now we should ask the question as to why the image of a recently perceived stimulus-object is not experienced permanently throughout the period of reverberation but appears only from time to time and may even not appear at all if we do not evoke it. The answer to this question is readily at hand. Precisely as the perception of a stimulus-object with which we are confronted occurs only under the influence of attention—that is, an arousal produced in a given gnostic field by appropriate drive—so it is with images. In fact, the image of a recently perceived event whose trace is kept in the transient store of the recent memory behaves in much the same way as the object confronting our receptive surface—we "perceive" it only when we pay attention to it.

The reverberation theory of transient memory implies that during the operation of the cortico-thalamic circuits the gnostic units temporally occupied by a given stimulus-pattern are in a state of sensitization, because they are continuously bombarded by the circulating impulses. Consequently, if a given stimulus-pattern which gave rise to this sensitization is presented again, the impulses originated by it will impinge upon the same units and the pattern will be recognized. This is because, as assumed in Chapter II, potential synaptic contacts between the transmittent and recipient units are not completely impassable for incoming impulses, and, in consequence, these impulses may produce the actual excitation of the recipient units if the latter are in a state of sensitization. In this way the sensitized gnostic units may be activated by the appropriate stimulus-pattern, although stable actual contacts linking them with the units of the lower level have not been established and the pattern will be totally forgotten after some time.

The sensitization of gnostic units by the reverberating circuits allows us to understand another important phenomenon—that of the ease of evocation of appropriate images and even their obsessive appearance. We assume that during the operation of recent memory traces the images appear, not on the basis of *associations*, but on the basis of *sensitization* of the appropriate units and their arousal by unspecific facilitating impulses. In fact, when after our day's work we are lying in bed and we call to mind all the events we experienced during that day, we "behold" the corresponding images in exactly the same way as we behold the actual stimulus-objects selecting them according to our current interest.

Let us examine in more detail imagery of this kind.

First, we may behold in our imagination some *new* stimulus-objects with which we were confronted for the first time, provided that they are represented in a well-elaborated gnostic field and can be perceived at a single exposure. Thus, we recall new persons we have met or new places we have visited, or a new bunch of flowers presented to us on our birthday. Yet, in our routine everyday life these new stimulus-objects are relatively rare. Most often we meet persons we know very well, we stay in rooms familiar to us, and nobody offers us any bunches of new flowers. Nevertheless many of these stimulus-objects, although perfectly known to us, are revived owing to their recent perception.

Thus, we come to an important point which has been completely overlooked by all recent-memory theorists. This is that a well-known stimulus-object which has its well-established representation in the appropriate gnostic field can be, and usually is, reappealed by the transient memory mechanism when it was recently perceived, in exactly the same way as are new objects. This shows that transient memory is not the privilege of only new stimulus-objects (being said to serve for their consolidation), but it is a normal process following *each perception*.

The occurrence of transient memory processes is not limited to such phenomena as those of loose and often futile reminiscences of recent events. The constructive and most important role of these processes is that all short-term planning is effectuated by their assistance. A most typical model of this sort of behavior follows. In the morning nearly everyone establishes a program of those activities which are unique—that is, which do not belong to our routine acts accomplished by means of simple instrumental CRs. I decide (or I am instructed) to do some shopping, to meet someone in order to discuss something with him, to write some letters which are the replies to letters kept in the store of either my transient or stable memory. I prepare in my thought a lecture I shall have to deliver or what I shall answer to my discussants. All these and a host of other images of future tasks are held in my transient memory store, and I direct my behavior in such a way as to fulfill them. After this is done, their memory is no longer preserved and they "make room" for other images. Precisely this type of behavior in experiments on animals is called the *delayed response procedure*. It is clear that it is entirely based on recent memory; if the neural mechanism securing it were lacking or impaired, a large part of our normal conduct would be impossible. We would be then doomed to the performance of well-trained routinized motor acts, in which, by the way, we might be quite skillful. We shall call this role of transient memory its *prospective* role.

There is still another domain of phenomena where transient memory plays a decisive role. It may be observed that in our everyday life we frequently perform some single motor acts which should not be repeated although we have no external cues indicating that they have been actually performed. When we leave our apartment and close the door, we must remember that it has been closed; otherwise we would have a tendency to return in order to check it. We should remember that we have already taken our medicine, and with which of our colleagues we have shaken hands after coming to a meeting. All these seemingly natural phenomena of not repeating the already terminated activities are undoubtedly controlled by the transient memory of their performance. Thus our transient memory plays no lesser role in remembering the already completed actions than in remembering those actions which have to be fulfilled in future. Whereas the impairment of transient memory involved in the latter actions leads to the failure in planning the future behavior, the impairment of the memory of fulfilled actions leads to their perseveration. We propose to call this role of transient memory its *retrospective* role.

The question arises as to what is the localization of transient memory traces. In accordance to our present discussion, we can assume that recent memory of stimulus-objects of particular modalities simply depends on the gnostic fields involved in their perceptions and images.[6] This would mean that, for instance, damage of the visual facial gnostic field (V-F) would *ipso facto* destroy the transient memory of particular physiognomies simply because their visualization is impossible, and damage of the audioverbal gnostic field (A-W) would destroy the transient memory of words.

According to this view, lesions sustained in the prefrontal area have a special significance since they affect the images of *particular types of behavioral acts* (cf. Chapter III, Section 8) and therefore they severely impair the planned (i.e. delayed) motor behavior. In fact, if a patient is unable clearly to imagine by his kinesthetic gnosis the tasks he is ordered to perform, he is much handicapped in their fulfillment, although he is perfectly able to remember or to repeat the instruction. This is the cause of the puzzling behavior of those patients who seemingly understand the instruction and know what they should do (because this "knowledge" is kept in gnostic fields of their auditory or visual analyzers) but in spite of this fail to fulfill it because of their lack of kinesthetic imagery. In effect their routine reactions to the actual stimuli very easily suppress their planned actions, producing the so-called perseverative behavioral responses.[7]

From this point of view the dramatic impairment of recent memory encountered after bilateral hippocampal lesions in man[8] should be considered in the following way.

Anatomically the hippocampus belongs to the emotive brain, being closely connected with nearly all structures of the limbic system directly involved in drive and antidrive functions. Therefore it may be assumed that the hippocampus is concerned with some higher processes involved in emotive functions—for instance, it supplies reverberating circuits responsible for transient memory traces of emotions produced by drive and antidrive stimuli. In consequence, hippocampal lesions, impairing these traces would *ipso facto* affect transient memory of gnostic events for which the emotional factor is indispensable. Of course this concept should be considered as quite tentative and is proposed for the sake of speculative filling the gap in our knowledge rather than as a true explanation.

3. Transient memory of associations

It seems that the principles of functioning of transient memory described above in respect to perceptions are exactly the same for associations. In fact, in our discussion in the preceding section we often recurred to the examples which involved, not only perceptual processes, but also associative processes, simply because they can hardly be separated.

If in a new environment (for instance, in a new city) we discover the relations between its parts, we preserve these relations in the transient memory store and utilize them for our behavior in exactly the same way as we do in respect to our stable memory storage. Similarly, if being for a short time in a foreign country we memorize some most important words (perceptual recent memory) and associate them with particular meanings (associative recent memory), again we are able to utilize this knowledge, although it may appear to be totally transient. Whether the associations we have acquired will become stable is a quite different matter which does not in the least affect our actual behavior. Again, although the transient associative store and the stable associative store are phenomenologically indiscernible, the difference between them is quite clear because those people who are poor in consolidation processes will soon completely forget their acquired knowledge, whereas those whose mental plasticity is good will preserve it to the end of their life.

Transient memory of associations plays no less important role in our life than transient memory of perceptions. A good example of such associations is provided by our temporary memorization of multidigital numbers. As is well known we have a good ability to do so either on the basis of the acoustic memory (associations within the A-W field) or on the basis of the visual memory (associations within the V-Sn field). In some cases these associations are stable; in others our memory of digital sequences is only temporary and they are remembered only so long as they are needed.

The physiological mechanism of associative transient memory should be conceived in the same way as perceptual recent memory. Suppose that two sets of gnostic units A and B (both belonging to the stable memory storage) are activated in overlapping sequence. Then each of these sets will become sensitized through reverberating circuits, and in consequence, if there exist potential connections between them, they will become temporarily actualized. In effect a perception activating the transmittent set of units A will temporarily activate the recipient set B, producing the image of the corresponding stimulus-object. If no stable connections are formed between these two sets, the memory of this association will be erased when the sensitization of the recipient set will vanish.

4. Transient memory in experimentation in animals

If we omit the whole category of phenomena connected with consolidation of memory traces as not directly concerned with transient memory, we may see that experimental methods involving that kind of memory are scarce. The procedure which may be considered as a specific test for transient memory is that introduced into psychological research by Hunter[9] and denoted by him as "delayed response." The essence of the procedure is that an animal is confronted with the task of choosing one of several possible responses leading to food reinforcement, the correct response being determined by a cue which ends *well in advance* of its performance. Therefore, at the moment when the animal is allowed to perform the response, he must remember the cue given earlier.

In most delayed response procedures the animal who is immobilized on a starting platform is confronted with two or more food-wells. Then a stimulus is given, determining in which well the food will be available, and after a more or less prolonged period of delay the animal is released and is able to make a choice. Visual, auditory, or kinesthetic stimuli are used as cues determining the delayed response. Visual and auditory stimuli may be either contiguous with the appropriate food-well (for instance, placing food in the sight of the animal or a buzzer sounding from the feeder) or separate from it. A kinesthetic cue is utilized in the delayed alternation procedure in which the preceding response is a cue for the next response.

From this short description of the delayed response procedure it is clear that it consists of a set of instrumental CRs in which the CSs are compound stimuli composed of two elements:[10] (1) a trace of the "preparatory stimulus" determining which of several instrumental responses the animal has to perform, and (2) the "releasing stimulus" common for all the instrumental responses.

Accordingly the paradigm of the delayed response procedure with triple choice may be presented as follows.

$$[S_{Pr1}] S_{Re} \rightarrow R_1 - F$$

$$[S_{Pr2}] S_{Re} \rightarrow R_2 - F$$

$$[S_{Pr3}] S_{Re} \rightarrow R_3 - F$$

$[S_{Pr}]$ here denotes the recent memory trace of a given preparatory stimulus; S_{Re}, the releasing stimulus; R, the delayed response; F, presentation of food.

It is clear that in the absence of $[S_{Pr}]$—that is, when the animal at the moment of release does not remember the cue determining the proper response—he is unable to solve the problem.

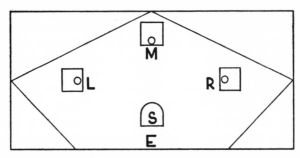

Fig. XII-1. Schema of the Experimental Room Used for Experiments with Delayed Responses

E, the seat of the experimenter; S, starting platform; L, M, R, left, middle, and right feeders, respectively.

As a basis of our further consideration we shall utilize the experiments on dogs and cats performed by Ławicka[11] in which the triple choice procedure was used (Figure XII-1). Before each trial the animal was immobilized on the starting platform (a dog on a leash and a cat in a cage). Then the buzzer placed on a particular feeder operated for three seconds. After a definite period of time the animal was released and, if he approached the signaled feeder, the bowl with food was put into position by remote control. If the animal approached a wrong feeder, food was not presented even if he corrected himself and ran to the proper feeder.

The most important facts obtained in these experiments are the following.

(1) In normal animals (both dogs and cats) the correct delayed response occurs regardless of the bodily orientation assumed by the animal during the delay period. In other words, in order to make a

correct response the animal does not need to be oriented to the feeder signaled in a given trial.

(2) The correct delayed responses in normal animals generally occur after a delay period of as long as three minutes for cats and of ten minutes or more for dogs.

(3) Distractions introduced during the delay period, such as the experimenter's caressing the dog, giving him food on the starting platform, or even taking him away for a while from the experimental room, do not generally impair his delayed response performance.

(4) The delayed response also remains correct (in dogs) when the starting platform is surrounded by a screen so that the animal does not see the feeders.

(5) When in the same trial two feeders are signaled in immediate succession, then, after the delay period, the animal usually goes first to the most recently signaled feeder, and then, after consuming the portion of food there, he approaches the other feeder (the double signal test).

It was noticed that in experiments performed on dogs some subjects behave in the delay period in such a way that they preserve their bodily orientation toward the feeder signaled by the preparatory stimulus and then, after being released, they run in the proper direction. We have called such behavior a "pseudo-delayed response," because it is not necessarily based on the memory traces of the cue but on the actually operating postural stimulus. In order to see whether the animal *has* the memory traces of the cue determining the delayed response, it is necessary to compel him to change the body position by diverting his attention to a different direction. Normal dogs are generally not disturbed by such measures, showing that their delayed responses are really controlled by memory traces of the cue.

The essential question to be asked here is: what is the cue which guides the animal in his delayed response performance? Although we have no conclusive evidence on which to base an answer to this question, we propose the hypothesis that in dogs and cats the corresponding cue is provided by *the spatio-kinesthetic image of the itinerary to a given feeder*. In other words, we assume that, according to the animal's experience in the testing room, he has developed in his spatial-kinesthetic gnostic field (K-Sp), three sets of units representing the approach to each of the three feeders. Now, when one of the feeders is signaled by the corresponding preparatory stimulus, this stimulus evokes by way of association the activation of the corresponding set of spatial-kinesthetic units, and this activation is maintained owing to the transient memory reverberating circuits throughout the delay period. Thus, the appropriate response is programed in the brain and is fulfilled when the animal is released.

The following data seem to favor this assumption.

(1) When the feeders were situated not at right angles, as they were in our regular experiments, but at acute angles, the delayed response performance of the animals was strongly impaired, although they could perfectly discern which feeder was signaled by each preparatory stimulus and reacted correctly if released immediately after that stimulus. The explanation of this impairment is that the discrimination of similar spatial-kinesthetic cues was more difficult and therefore their transient memory traces became less distinct.[12]

(2) The delayed response performance in dogs is best when the preparatory stimuli are contiguous to the feeders. On the contrary, when other directional cues are used (for instance, a buzzer operating from above signaling the left feeder and a buzzer from below signaling the right one), the delayed responses are much poorer.[13] This is due to the fact that association between a stimulus contiguous to the feeder and the corresponding locomotor response is much stronger than association between a stimulus in a neutral place and that response (cf. Chapter X, Section 4). In consequence, the activation of the corresponding set of gnostic units by the preparatory stimulus is much stronger in the first case than in the second, and it can more easily resist the long delay period and/or distractions. Psychologically, the animal has a much clearer or stronger image of his itinerary when this image is produced by a buzzer situated at the goal than if it is produced by a buzzer situated in a different place.

(3) Last but not least, it seems that the dramatic impairment of the delayed response performance after prefrontal lesions also speaks in favor of our hypothesis. In fact, in Chapter III, Section 8, we presented evidence that spatial-kinesthetic gnosis in both animals and man is localized in the prefrontal area; it seems that the impairment of the delayed response test after removal of this area is in good agreement with this concept.

The impairment of delayed responses after prefrontal lesions was first observed in monkeys by Jacobsen in his classical work.[14] The experiments were then repeated by many authors with the aim to elucidate the mechanism of this impairment and to find the particular zone within the prefrontal area whose removal is responsible for this defect.

In Ławicka and Konorski's experiments on dogs and cats a thorough analysis of the impairment of delayed responses in a triple choice procedure was made.[15] It was found that dogs immediately after lesion are totally unable to make a proper choice, unless they are released during or immediately after the operation of a preparatory stimulus. After some time they learn to solve the problem by keeping their head and body directed toward the signaled food-tray throughout the delay period. But when their attention is diverted by a distracting stimulus (e.g. offering food on the platform), they are again completely lost. Similarly, they fail to solve the double signal test, approaching only the second signaled feeder; and they are lost when the starting platform is surrounded by screens.

In experiments on cats a strong perseverative tendency of prefrontal animals was observed which was manifested in either approaching only one feeder and totally neglecting the other ones (in severe cases) or approaching that feeder in which they received food in the preceding trial (one-trial-learning errors).

All these facts seem to show that simple locomotor responses either to an actual exteroceptive CS or to the animal's bodily orientation are mediated by lower parts of the kinesthetic analyzer (basal ganglia?) and do not require their programing in the prefrontal gnostic field. This programing is necessary when the actual CS is not in operation and the animal has to preserve in his transient memory store the kinesthetic image of a response to be executed after release.

One point which remains unclear is that prefrontal cats, in contradistinction to dogs, are well compensated after some retraining and may even achieve a pre-operative level of performance. This may be either due to less radical lesions or to the involvement of another mechanism (for example, spatio-visual) which can substitute for the lack of spatio-kinesthetic gnosis (cf. Chapter III, Section 8).

If our assumption concerning the mechanism of the delayed response is correct, then this test concerns not the transient memory in general but only spatial-kinesthetic transient memory. So the problem arises as to what tests would be suitable to examine in animals transient memory of stimuli of other analyzers.

It seems that these tests should be based on the animal being compelled to compare two stimuli of the same analyzer following one another at some interval when 'no significance is attached to their absolute values. For instance, when two identical tones following one another (whatever their frequency) represent a positive compound CS while two different ones represent a negative compound CS, or vice versa, then the animal must base the solution of this task on remembering the first tone and comparing it with the other one.[16] Experiments along this line are still scarce, but they show that lesions in the areas considered as gnostic areas for particular qualities of stimuli are indeed indispensable for the solution of these tasks.[17]

To end our considerations on transient memory phenomena involved in animal experimentation, it should be emphasized that according to casual observations these phenomena are much more numerous than it is generally acknowledged, judging from the relevant
papers. Indeed, every experimenter working on conditioning according to Pavlov's procedure knows how changeable animals' responses
are depending on recent memory traces.

A few examples follow.

We have a dog trained in classical CRs (alimentary or defensive)
with long CS-US intervals; in consequence his conditioned responses
have a rather long latency. In one trial we reinforce the CS much
earlier than usual. It is nearly certain that in the next trial, following
after a few minutes, the latency will be much shortened, showing that
the animal perfectly remembers the change which occurred in the
preceding trial and adjusts his response accordingly. Similarly, if in
one positive trial the reinforcement is omitted, it is very probable that
the CR to that stimulus in the next trial will be diminished. If a rat
trained in frequent reversals of a CR has developed two opposite
conditioned responses (for instance, in go left–go right procedure),
then a single "instructing" trial may be enough for switching his response to the opposite one. Generally speaking, we think that the
overbalance of one of the two conditioned responses to a CS possessing a double CR meaning is largely under the control of transient and
not stable memory. To conclude, there is no doubt that all our CR
experiments are strongly permeated by transient memory phenomena
which are not manifested when a session takes a routine course but
are immediately noticeable when an intentional or unintentional
change is introduced.

5. Summary and conclusions

When a set of gnostic units representing a certain stimulus-pattern is
activated by the corresponding perception, this activation considerably outlasts the operation of the stimulus, giving rise to its transient
memory trace. It is assumed that this phenomenon is due to throwing
into action closed, self-reexciting circuits of neurons (probably cortico-thalamic loops) which are in operation for a shorter or longer time
(of the order of hours or days) and are stopped either spontaneously
or under the influence of activation of competitive circuits according
to the principle of lateral inhibition. This post-stimulatory activation
of gnostic units may give rise to images of the corresponding stimulus-
objects when these units are additionally stimulated by the arousal
system. Thus, at every moment of life a great number of gnostic units
of various analyzers are temporarily activated, constituting a transient

memory store which, in contradistinction to the stable memory store, has a dynamic character and constantly changes its contents.

Transient memory usually concerns those stimulus-patterns which are already represented in the appropriate gnostic field, causing the temporal activation of the corresponding units. Yet, if a new stimulus-pattern is presented which belongs to a well-developed gnostic field (and therefore is likely to be grasped by a unitary perceptual act), this pattern will temporarily "occupy" the appropriate potential gnostic units and activate corresponding neuronal loops. Consequently, in a given gnostic field, beside the stable gnostic units whose existence is due to the static connections converging on them from the lower level of the given analyzer, there are also temporary gnostic units depending on activation of self-reexciting neuronal loops.

There is no evidence that transient memory traces are *transformed* into stable memory traces by the process of consolidation. On the contrary, it seems that the two processes (that of transient memory and that of consolidation) are independent of one another, being based on quite different mechanisms.

Transient memory of associations follows exactly the same rules as those governing transient memory of perceptions.

In human life transient memory is best manifested in planned behavior, when a subject has to perform some behavioral acts programed in advance (prospective role of recent memory), and in resistance to the perseveration of behavioral acts already performed (retrospective role of recent memory).

In animal experimentation the only well-known test for transient memory is that of delayed response, being a simple model of planned behavior in humans. It is assumed that the delayed response is based on the transient memory of spatial-kinesthetic cues represented in the appropriate gnostic field of the kinesthetic analyzer. The tests for studying transient memory of stimulus-objects of other analyzers are still poorly developed.

Since, according to our concept, the cortico-thalamic loops responsible for transient memory are attached to the gnostic units representing particular stimulus-objects, the transient memory of these objects is affected by lesions sustained in the corresponding gnostic fields. It is assumed that a dramatic impairment of delayed responses following prefrontal lesions in animals is precisely due to the destruction of units representing their spatio-kinesthetic gnostic functions.

References to Chapter XII

1. C. P. Duncan. 1949. The retroactive effect of electroshock on learning. *J. Comp. Physiol. Psychol.*, 42: 32–44.

R. Thompson and W. Dean. 1955. A further study on the retroactive effect of ECS. *J. Comp. Physiol. Psychol.*, 48: 488–91.

R. Thompson and R. S. Pryer. 1956. The effect of anoxia on the retention of a discrimination habit. *J. Comp. Physiol. Psychol.*, 49: 297–300.

2. R. Lorente de No. 1938. Analysis of the activity of the chains of internuncial neurons. *J. Neurophysiol.*, 1: 187–94.

3. S. E. Glickman. 1961. Perseverative neural processes and consolidation of the memory trace. *Psychol. Bull.*, 58: 218–33.

4. D. J. Albert. 1966a. The effect of spreading depression on the consolidation of learning. *Neuropsychologia*, 4: 49–64.

——. 1966b. Memory in mammals: Evidence for a system involving nuclear ribonucleic acid. *Ibid.*, 4: 79–92.

5. H. Hydén. 1959. Biochemical changes in glial cells and nerve cells at varying activity. In: *Proceedings of the Fourth International Congress of Biochemistry, Vienna 1958.* Vol. III: *Biochemistry of the Central Nervous System*, pp. 64–89. London and New York: Pergamon Press.

6. J. Konorski. 1961. The physiological approach to the problem of recent memory. In J. F. Delafresnaye, ed., *Brain Mechanisms and Learning*, pp. 115–32. Oxford: Blackwell Sci. Publ.

7. H. L. Teuber. 1964. In J. M. Warren and K. Akert, eds., *The Frontal Granular Cortex and Behavior*, pp. 287–88. New York: McGraw-Hill. Discussion following chap. 13.

A. R. Luria and E. D. Homskaya. 1964. Disturbances in the regulative role of speech with frontal lobe lesions. *Ibid.*, pp. 353–71.

8. B. Milner and W. Penfield. 1955. The effect of hippocampal lesions on recent memory. *Trans. Amer. Neurol. Ass.*, 80: 42–48.

W. B. Scoville and B. Milner. 1957. Loss of recent memory after bilateral hippocampal lesions. *J. Neurol. Neurosurg. Psychiat.*, 20: 11–21.

9. W. S. Hunter. 1913. The delayed reaction in animals and children. *Behav. Monogr.*, 2 (No. 1): 1–86.

10. J. Konorski and W. Ławicka. 1959. Physiological mechanism of delayed reactions. *Acta Biol. Exp. Vars.*, 19: 175–97.

11. W. Ławicka. 1959. Physiological mechanism of delayed reactions. II. Delayed reactions in dogs and cats to directional stimuli. *Acta Biol. Exp. Vars.*, 19: 199–219.

12. ——. Unpublished experiments.

13. ——. Unpublished experiments.

14. C. F. Jacobsen. 1936. Studies of cerebral function in primates. *Comp. Psychol. Monogr.*, 13 (No. 3; Ser. No. 63): 1–60.

15. W. Ławicka and J. Konorski. 1959. Physiological mechanism of delayed reactions. III. The effects of prefrontal ablations on delayed reactions in dogs. *Acta Biol. Exp. Vars.*, 19: 221–31.

——. 1961. The effects of prefrontal lobectomies on the delayed responses in cats. *Ibid.*, 21: 141–56.

——. 1962. The properties of delayed responses to double preparatory signals in normal and prefrontal dogs. *Ibid.*, 22 (No. 2): 47–55.

J. Konorski and W. Ławicka. 1964. Analysis of errors by prefrontal animals on the delayed-response test. In J. M. Warren and K. Akert, eds., *The Frontal Granular Cortex and Behavior*, pp. 271–94. New York: McGraw-Hill.

16. J. Konorski. 1959. A new method of physiological investigation of recent memory in animals. *Bull. Acad. Pol. Sci.*, Cl. II, Ser. Sci. Biol., 7: 115–17.

———. 1961 (see note 6 above).

17. L. Stępień, J. P. Cordeau, and T. Rasmussen. 1960. The effect of temporal lobe and hippocampal lesions on auditory and visual recent memory in monkeys. *Brain*, 83: 470–89.

H. Chorążyna and L. Stępień. 1961. Impairment of auditory recent memory produced by cortical lesions in dogs. *Acta Biol. Exp. Vars.*, 21: 177–87.

CHAPTER **XIII**

THE GENERAL ARCHITECTURE
OF THE INTEGRATIVE
BRAIN FUNCTION

1. Introductory remarks

As explained in the Introduction, research work on brain functions
follows two separate lines, which, although complementary to each
other, pursue different aims and utilize quite different experimental
methods. One line of research, which may be called analytical, is concerned with minute details of structure and function of various parts
of the brain and their interconnections, studied by histological and
electro-physiological methods. The other line of investigation, which
may be called synthetic, is concerned with the brain as the organ of
control and integration of the whole animal's activity and is mainly
conducted by behavioral methods.

Each of these two approaches is encumbered by different handicaps
and exposed to different dangers. Analytical study is in danger of
being completely drowned in the bulk of particular facts, showing
the tremendous complexity of the functional organization of the brain
but failing to contribute to its elucidation. On the contrary, the synthetic approach is in danger of the tendency to remain blind to this
complexity and grossly to oversimplify the intricate and most diversified relations existing in the actual brain function. In fact, to engage
in the synthetic study of the brain function with taking into full
account its physiological and anatomical complexity seems at the

present stage of our knowledge simply impossible. Therefore, our only aspiration now is that our ideas concerning the integrative action of the brain should not be controverted by new discoveries in the analytical studies, but on the contrary that they would find in these discoveries a further support.

This being so, it seems reasonable now to recapitulate clearly the principal ideas proposed here, omitting those which seem more controversial. If these ideas appear correct, they will perhaps contribute to the further development of brain physiology and provide a systematizing principle for further research.

2. Afferent systems and perceptual learning

The gross correlative anatomy of the brain teaches us that this organ is composed of three kinds of functional systems: (1) the *afferent systems* (analyzers) built according to the hierarchical convergence-divergence principle; (2) *associative systems* linking particular afferent systems and their parts; and (3) *efferent systems* controlling the executive organs. In each of these systems two types of intercentral connections may be discerned: in one type the synaptic contacts between nerve cells are fully transmissible because of the ontogenic development of the nervous system; in the other type the ontogenetically determined transmissibility of the synaptic contacts is only potential, and their actualization depends on animal's individual experiences accomplished by learning processes.

The function of the afferent systems is to provide the brain with information concerning the external environment in which the organism is situated and the feedback generated by its own activity. The well-being of the organism requires that this information should be highly selective, picking up particular combinations of elements of the external world and neglecting the other ones. According to our concept—which is an extrapolation and generalization of recent results of the studies of the visual system—this selectivity is provided by convergence of messages arising in particular elements of the receptive surface upon particular neurons (units) of higher levels of a given system, and by inhibition of those messages which are incongruent with the stimulus-pattern represented by these units.

Since the stimulus-patterns impinging upon each afferent system belong to various categories or various aspects of the events of the external world, each category having a different significance for the organism, these systems must be endowed with powerful *sorting* mechanisms distributing the messages delivered by the receptors to particular aggregates of units (centers or fields) for their proper utilization accomplished by associative systems. This is why each afferent

system not only has a hierarchical structure but also is amply rami-
fied, forming different hierarchies for different categories of stimuli.

Some of these aggregates deal with relatively simple and phylogenetically determined stimulus-patterns possessing stable functional
significance. Therefore the transmissibility of connections linking the
receptors with corresponding afferent units, as well as these afferent
units with the efferent neurons, are developed in ontogenesis in the
form of more or less complex unconditioned reflex arcs. However,
the overwhelming majority of stimulus-patterns with which the organism must deal does not possess such a pre-established nature, and
their very existence and functional significance depends largely on
the particular conditions of individual life. Consequently, the transmissibility of connections linking the receptive organs with the appropriate units and linking these units with units of other systems is
completed by learning processes. These processes occur predominantly in the cerebral cortex for highly elaborated stimulus-patterns and
in subcortical structures for more primitive patterns. Thus the cerebral
cortex is the main organ for perceptions of complex and not phylogenetically stereotyped stimulus-patterns and for their associations with
other patterns according to the requirements of individual life.

Since the stimulus-patterns dealt with by the cerebral cortex are
ipso facto most complex, their integration must be accomplished in
several stages, each stage providing more and more elaborated elements of which the final perceptual products are composed. Thus,
in every afferent system we discern transit levels in which these partial
products are built and exit levels in which the functionally meaningful
patterns, ready for utilization in associative functions, are integrated.
We call the units representing functionally meaningful patterns of
events perceptive or gnostic units, and the transmission of messages
from the receptive surface to these units unitary perceptions. The
cortical areas in which gnostic units (potential or actual) are situated
are called gnostic (associative) areas. They are distributed in the
vicinity of the projective cortical areas of corresponding analyzers,
which are predominantly transit areas providing the gnostic areas with
elements for the formation of gnostic units.

We assume that gnostic units are formed by transformation of
potential synaptic contacts, linking the units of lower levels of the
given afferent system with the units of the appropriate gnostic area,
into actual synaptic contacts. New gnostic units representing new
stimulus-patterns are formed from potential gnostic units—that is
those units which are so far unengaged by other patterns. Since all
the possible stimulus-patterns impinging upon a given afferent system
belong to particular categories determined chiefly by the character

of elements of which they are composed, the cortical gnostic area of that system is subdivided into gnostic fields representing each of these categories. It is further assumed that each meaningful stimulus-pattern (represented either in a gnostic field of the cerebral cortex, or in other parts of the afferent system) is always represented by a number of equivalent units (called a set of units), securing the given afferent system against its partial impairment.

Each afferent system is furnished with special types of reflexes, which may be called perceptive recurrent reflexes because they are concerned with modulating the sensory input provided by a stimulus impinging upon the receptive surface. Two kinds of these reflexes may be specified: one is the targeting reflex consisting in adaptation of sensory organs to the optimal reception of the given stimulus; the other one is the inhibitory reflex producing habituation—a tendency to neglect the stimulus if it has no significance for the organism.

3. Inborn associative systems (unconditioned reflexes)

Unconditioned reflexes represent those forms of activity of the organism which follow relatively rigid patterns established in ontogeny to cope with those agents and situations which require a more or less stereotyped response. They may be divided into two not sharply separable categories which have been called preservative and protective reflexes. On the other hand, both preservative and protective reflexes may be divided into consummatory reflexes serving for the immediate adaptation of the organism to actual biologically significant agents, and preparatory reflexes procuring those agents or situations which elicit preservative reflexes or forestalling those agents or situations which elicit protective reflexes. The central mechanisms controlling the preparatory reflexes are denoted as drives or emotions. Accordingly, the preparatory reflexes are called drive reflexes.

The chief difference between the consummatory and drive reflexes is that whereas each consummatory reflex follows its own more or less rigid and phylogenetically established course with small variability, the inborn effects of drive reflexes are much less specific. In fact, in higher animals they have mainly facilitatory character in respect to both afferent and efferent systems: on the one hand, they increase the susceptibility of the organism to the operation of external stimuli of particular analyzers and facilitate the targeting reflexes; on the other hand, they produce the general activation of the motor behavioral system manifested by hypermotility and increased efficiency of the motor acts.

If the consummatory reflex is accomplished—that is, the agent producing the preservative reflex is used up, or the agent producing the protective reflex is removed—then the corresponding drive is assumed to be replaced by the antagonistic process which we have denoted as antidrive.

In protective activities the stimuli eliciting consummatory defensive reflexes are also the elicitors of drive reflexes; hence these two reflexes occur *pari passu*. In consequence, the antidrive reflex, which may be called here a relief reflex, occurs when the aversive reflexogenic stimulus is terminated.

On the other hand, in preservative activities two different antidrive mechanisms can be discerned. First, the antidrive reflex, called satiation reflex, comes into being when the consummatory reflex has been terminated in a natural way—that is, when the drive producing factors (mainly humoral) are no longer present. Second, the satisfaction of drive (that is, the state of antidrive) occurs when the consummatory stimulus is in operation; it is momentarily replaced by induction of drive when this stimulus is withdrawn before satiation.

To explain this dual mechanism of preservative antidrives, it is assumed that in preservative reflexes the drive controlling center is composed of on-drive units and off-drive units which are in reciprocal relations. Whereas in the absence of the consummatory stimulus the on-drive units are activated by drive-producing factors, during its operation off-drive units are activated while on-drive units are reciprocally inhibited. Both on-drive units and off-drive units are under the common control of the satiation antidrive center, which regulates in the same direction their excitability.

The satisfaction of drive—that is a steep replacement of a strong drive by its antidrive antipode—is what is subjectively experienced as pleasure or comfort, whether it is an excellent dish or a sudden relief from anxiety. In other words, whereas the pure quality of a stimulus— its "epicritic" aspect—is perceived by the gnostic system, its emotional or "protopathic" aspect (either comforting or discomforting) is perceived by the emotive system. Thus many stimuli impinging upon receptors possess this dual character, having their gnostic specificity tinted by emotional evaluation. The latter depends of course on the emotional significance of a given stimulus, and may greatly change under the influence of both unconditioned and conditioned factors.

The drive and antidrive reflexes are controlled by the part of the brain which may be denoted as emotive brain. Its lower level is situated in the hypothalamus and is probably concerned with unconditioned drive and antidrive reflexes, whereas its higher level, situated in the limbic region, is involved chiefly in corresponding conditioned reflexes and perhaps in highly elaborated unconditioned reflexes.

4. Acquired associative systems (associative learning)

As indicated earlier, learning processes—that is the transformation of potential connections into actual connections—can occur either in afferent systems themselves (perceptual learning) or in associative systems (associative learning). Associative learning occurs when two units (one of them being a transmittent unit, the other one a recipient unit) linked by potential connection are synchronously activated and consists in increasing the transmissibility of their synaptic contacts.

In the present work we do not enter into the problem of the intimate nature of this process. Intuitively we believe that it is based either on the growth of synaptic knobs or in biochemical attuning of the units involved or on these two processes occurring *pari passu*. Whatever the nature of the learning process, it does *not* occur immediately in the moment of coincidence of both stimuli but develops later as the aftermath of this coincidence. In consequence, if the consolidation process of the memory traces is obstructed by some disturbing factors, the transformation of potential connections into actual connections will be prevented.

It is assumed that the indispensable condition for the formation of actual connections between two synchronously activated units is that the recipient unit is brought into a state of arousal by the impact of impulses delivered by the emotive (unspecific) system. To account for the clear difference of the role played by specific connections between the units involved in association and facilitatory connections making this association possible, it is assumed that the former ones are axosomatic and the latter axodendritic. The same type of cooperation between specific and unspecific connections is thought to operate in perceptual learning and perceptual processes.

Associations in the cerebral cortex may be formed between particular sets of units of the same gnostic field, between units of different gnostic fields of the same analyzer, or of different analyzers. Naturally, associations can be formed only when the units concerned have already been established—in other words, the perceptual learning precedes the associative learning. It is assumed that long pathways in the white matter of the cortex linking particular gnostic fields provide the anatomical substrate for associations between different analyzers. Most associations in the cerebral cortex are bidirectional—that is, each set of gnostic units involved may play the role of either a transmittent set or a recipient set.

If association is formed between particular units of two gnostic fields A and B (A being transmittent and B recipient), it will be "utilized" only if both these fields are in a state of arousal produced by the emotive system. This is because arousal of field A is necessary for activation of the transmittent units by a corresponding stimulus-object (paying attention to this object), whereas arousal of field B is necessary for activation of the recipient units through associative ways established between two sets of units. If a given set of transmittent units has formed associations with a *number* of sets of recipient units, then the perception represented by the former units will activate by association only that recipient set which is at the given moment under arousal.

Whereas the psychological aspect of the activation of a given set of gnostic units by presentation of the corresponding stimulus-object is denoted as perception, the psychological aspect of the activation of this set by association is denoted as image. The problem may be raised of what is the physiological difference between the two processes. A proposed solution of this problem is that perception is brought about by the combination of activation of gnostic units with the targeting reflex directed toward the actual stimulus-object and mediated by lower levels of the given afferent system, whereas image is brought about by activation of gnostic units in the absence of the targeting reflex. If for some reason the targeting reflex is in operation in spite of the absence of the actual stimulus-object, the phenomenon called hallucination is produced.

Associations can be formed, not only between cortical gnostic fields, but also between exit fields of other ramifications of the afferent systems representing cruder aspects of the stimulus-objects impinging upon receptors. It is thought that basal ganglia are the site of these ramifications forming another anatomical substrate for associative functions.

5. Classical conditioned reflexes as particular instances of acquired associations

By classical (or type I) conditioned reflex we denote association (or rather its utilization) between two sets of units of which the recipient set gives rise to an unconditioned reflex. In this way the formation and functioning of a given association may be directly observed by recording the effect of the recipient stimulus appearing in response to the transmittent stimulus.

Since the unconditioned reflexes may be classified into consummatory reflexes and drive reflexes, the same classification is relevant to conditioned reflexes.

The drive conditioned reflex is established if any stimulus represented in the cortex or subcortical structures coincides with a drive-producing stimulus. Since the latter stimulus *ipso facto* produces arousal of the structures involved, the actual connections between the transmittent units representing the conditioned stimulus and the recipient units representing a given drive are readily formed.

The consummatory conditioned reflex is established if a given stimulus coincides with a stimulus producing a consummatory unconditioned reflex. The connections are then formed between the corresponding sets of units, provided that both of them are aroused by unspecific impulses. These impulses are usually provided by the drive reflex related to the given consummatory reflex. In consequence, usually the formation of the drive conditioned reflex precedes the formation of the consummatory reflex.

The relations between drive CRs and consummatory CRs reflect the relations between corresponding unconditioned reflexes. Since drive URs usually have a more "tonic" character than consummatory URs, so it is with corresponding conditioned reflexes. Further, whereas protective drive CRs are allied with consummatory CRs, preservative drive CRs are to some extent antagonistic to the corresponding consummatory CRs. In consequence, as far as protective CRs are concerned, the drive CSs are represented both by sporadic stimuli immediately preceding a noxious US and by continuous stimuli constituting a background against which that stimulus is presented. On the other hand, in preservative CRs the sporadic CS closely preceding the US "substitutes" its effect and consequently tends to inhibit the drive CR which is in operation as a "tonic" reflex before this CS is presented.

6. Instrumental (type II) conditioned reflexes

Another type of associations is in operation in instrumental conditioned reflexes—those reflexes in which the animal, being under the action of a particular drive, learns to perform a certain motor act when this act leads to the corresponding antidrive. The mechanism of the formation of instrumental CRs is conceived in the following way.

According to our earlier discussion, one of the major effects of drive reflexes is hypermotility produced by arousal of the motor behavioral system. If in this condition a given movement is followed by immediate satisfaction of drive, connections are established between the units representing that drive and kinesthetic units representing that movement. On the contrary, if satisfaction of drive does not follow the movement, hypermotility continues and the association fails to be formed because of retroactive inhibition preventing the process of its consolidation.

The proposed concept, being a version of the drive reduction theory, fulfills at the same time the requirements of the hedonistic view claiming that the instrumental movement is learned and performed because the subject anticipates the pleasure of the "reward" or of the cessation of anxiety. In fact, since, according to our concept, a stimulus is pleasant only if it leads to satisfaction of drive, the two formulations are more or less equivalent.

The above described mechanism of instrumental conditioning represents its most simplified version, which hardly ever occurs in normal life. For in reality the instrumental responses are formed and performed always in certain external situations in which a given drive is produced and satisfied. Accordingly, a given situation becomes associated on the one hand with a drive which is elicited against its background and on the other hand with a movement which leads to its satisfaction. Thus, the instrumental response is normally determined by two factors: by a situation (or a sporadic stimulus) in whose presence it is elicited, and by the drive which is terminated by it.

It is assumed that drive plays a dual role in instrumental conditioning. On the one hand, it becomes a determining factor specifying which instrumental movement should be performed in a given situation. On the other hand, it is the energizing factor which by arousal of the central motor behavioral system elicits that movement which is selected by the actual determining factors. Whereas the first role of drives is played owing to associations formed between emotive units and kinesthetic units, the second role is played owing to the innate connections linking the drive systems with the central behavioral system.

7. Transformations of associations

In the normal life of animals and man the coincidence between particular stimulus-patterns is most manifold, giving rise to innumerable associations established between particular sets of gnostic units as well as between gnostic units and emotive units. In many cases these associations do not interfere with each other, and therefore a transmittent set of units may simultaneously activate a number of recipient sets, the selection being dependent on which of these sets are aroused in a given moment. However, in other instances the particular sets of recipient units are in antagonistic relations, and then the activation of one association is incompatible with the activation of the other one.

A most usual case of the formation of such incompatible associations, encountered in experimental practice and in life, is due to the transformation of conditioned reflexes. The general pattern of such procedure is that first a given CR (classical or instrumental) is established to a given stimulus, and thereafter either the unconditioned stimulus or the movement required for satisfaction of drive is changed.

Following are typical instances of such transformations.

(1) A given CS is first regularly followed by presentation of the US, and then this presentation is withdrawn (extinction).

(2) A CS is first regularly followed by presentation of one US (for instance, of food) and then by presentation of another US (for instance, of an electric shock to the paw).

(3) A subject is first trained to perform a definite instrumental response to a given CS to secure satisfaction of certain drive, and then another response antagonistic to it is required for this aim (reversal learning).

According to our concept in all these cases the old intercentral connections established in the original training are fully preserved while new connections linking the same transmittent units with new recipient units are formed. Thus, in the case of extinction of the food CR, the connections between the CS units and the no-food-taste units are formed which antagonize the old connections between the CS units and the food-taste units. In the case of transformation of heterogeneous CRs, the connections between the CS units and the new drive units are formed which antagonize the connections between the CS units and the former drive units. Finally, in reversal training, the connections between the CS units and kinesthetic units representing a new movement are formed which antagonize the connections between the CS units and the units representing the previous instrumental act.

In all these cases, transformation of the CR usually occurs more slowly than the formation of an original CR, because the new set of recipient units is originally inhibited by associative activation of the old set of recipient units. Hence the resistance to transformation is observed which is characteristic for all transformations of CRs into antagonistic CRs but not to the allied CRs. However, when after the new CR is established we restore the old CR, the restoration is prompt because it consists simply in giving the advantage to the previously established connections which are now made predominant.

The above concept implies that: (1) every transformation of conditioned reflexes is based on the formation of new intercentral connections with no annihilation or reduction of old connections; and (2) no inhibitory connections are formed between the transmittent and recipient units, but instead the inborn inhibitory connections between the antagonistic sets of units are utilized. In consequence we maintain that both the term "inhibitory CR" or "internal inhibition" and the term "transformation of CRs" are somewhat misleading and may be applied in the phenomenological sense but do not reflect the mechanism of the processes involved.

8. The mechanism of efferent systems

Since the efferent systems subserving the unconditioned reflexes as well as classical conditioned reflexes do not present any major problems for our current consideration, we have concentrated our attention only on the mechanism of motor behavioral acts performed by animals and man, the acts whose experimental prototype is provided by the instrumental conditioned response.

We hold the view that the chief source of information on the performance of movements is provided by kinesthetic proprioception represented by muscular and tendon receptors and not by somesthetic proprioception represented by articular receptors. The spindles and tendon receptors deliver information to the cerebellum on the tensions in muscles and tendons whose combination is directly related to the type of movement the muscle performs. The translation from the language of tensions into the language of movements is performed in the cerebellum, which in this respect may be regarded as a true kinesthetic receptive surface informing the brain about the movements performed by the subject and their character. From the cerebellum the messages travel through the brain stem and thalamic nuclei to the precentral cortex, which may be regarded as the projective area of the kinesthetic analyzer, exactly as the postcentral cortex is the projective area of the somesthetic analyzer. In front of the projective precentral area, which is the transit area of the kinesthetic analyzer, the kinesthetic gnostic fields are situated (for mouth, hand, and body) symmetrical to the somesthetic gnostic fields situated behind the projective somesthetic area.

Although the kinesthetic feedback from the cerebellum is assumed to play the essential role in the performance of skilled movements, the joint-somesthetic feedback providing information on the postural changes of a limb concerned may play an additional role in this respect. It may be thought that the latter role would grow in importance when the kinesthetic feedback is absent.*

The operation of the kinesthetic analyzer is somewhat different from that of other analyzers, because it provides information, not about the external events, but about the motor activity generated by the central nervous system itself. It is assumed that the more or less chaotic movements produced by lower levels of the motor behavioral

---

* This thesis has been recently confirmed in our laboratory by Jaworska, Słowik, and Konorski on cats. It has been found that joint lesions in the cerebellar cortex and in the somesthetic area of the cerebral cortex (S I) produce a dramatic and long-lasting impairment of skilled movements, while each of these lesions separately may produce only a slight and easily compensated effect.

system after birth become integrated in the gnostic fields of the kinesthetic analyzer into definite patterns, a process analogous to the formation of unitary perceptions in the exteroceptive analyzers. When these sets of units representing particular kinesthetic patterns are formed, they receive connections from gnostic units of other analyzers and so may be activated by them.

The kinesthetic analyzer also differs from exteroceptive ones in that it is directly connected with the motor efferent system represented in the cortex by pyramidal and extrapyramidal neurons. In consequence, when the kinesthetic gnostic units representing a given motor pattern are activated through associative fibers coming from other gnostic fields, that pattern is dispatched to the motor projective area, where it is disintegrated into its elements and delivered to spinal motoneurons for execution. And so the kinesthetic gnostic units may be regarded as a programing device for skillful movements which the subject has learned to perform.

The important inference which emerges from this discussion is that the performance of a unitary skillful movement, once its pattern has been established owing to the peripheral kinesthetic reception, no longer needs this reception and may be programed and executed in its absence. The full analogy with the functioning of the exteroceptive afferent systems may be immediately seen, since here too, once a gnostic pattern has been established by perception, it can be evoked by association in the form of image or hallucination even if the receptive surface is totally destroyed. Therefore, once the patterns of skillful movements have been established in the kinesthetic gnostic area, the role of peripheral feedback is reduced to a correcting mechanism adjusting the movements to a given situation and regulating the successive performance of the segments of serial movements.

It was said that the activation of recipient units through association is accomplished only if the recipient field is aroused by the drive system. Accordingly, the programing of the skilled movement and its execution are possible only when the given drive urges a subject to perform it—that is when the subject is appropriately motivated.

It may be seen that the experimental evidence derived from instrumental conditioning fully confirms these considerations and makes them even more lucid. In instrumental conditioning connections are formed between the gnostic units representing the given situation (or a sporadic stimulus) and the kinesthetic units representing the motor act. These connections, however, are not sufficient for the performance of this act, unless the animal is appropriately motivated—that is, unless he is under the action of drive whose satisfaction is provided by that movement.

It should be added that the kinesthetic gnostic area is not the only place in which behavioral motor acts are programed. It is known that removal of that area in animals does not deprive them of the execution of more primitive behavioral acts. These acts may be made instrumental under appropriate training, showing that the corresponding associations can be formed beyond the cerebral cortex. It is assumed that basal ganglia are endowed with this capacity and that they represent the exit fields both for the primitive aspects of exteroceptive stimuli and for primitive patterns of behavioral acts.

Finally, one more problem should be commented upon—the problem of activation of kinesthetic gnostic units representing a given movement without its actual performance. This activation occurs regularly in human beings in their "internal speech," but it is also present in those cases when we program a motor act postponing its execution. It seems reasonable to assume that this phenomenon takes place when the efferent output from the kinesthetic units is blocked. This occurs, for instance, when the given movement is unfeasible because of an inappropriate posture. Internal speech *can* be explained in this way by assuming that it occurs when the actual posture of the mouth and glottis prevents vocalization.

9. Transient (or recent) memory

Our considerations on recent memory (which should be more properly called transient memory) led us to some revision of the current concepts on its functional role and its relation to stable memory. Here we recapitulate very briefly our main theses.

(1) Transient memory traces arise as an after-effect of *every* perceptive process, either exteroceptive or proprioceptive, enabling the subject to revive (imagine) the corresponding stimulus-pattern some time after its withdrawal. In agreement with the general belief, we assume that these traces are due to reverberating circuits attached to the appropriate gnostic units, which are thrown into operation by activation of those units and keep them activated after the perception is over: Thus, transient memory is not a privilege peculiar to new perceptions but concerns old perceptions as well.

(2) Transient memory has no relation to consolidation of the learning process, either perceptive or associative, which is based on a quite different mechanism.

(3) The functional role of transient memory is to hold temporarily the traces of perceptions or images for their immediate utilization. This occurs particularly in all planned behavior, in which a subject estab-

lishes a program of his activity which is later performed (according to the delayed response principle), for comparison of perceptions which follow one another at some interval, or for remembering that a definite motor act has been already fulfilled and should not be repeated.

INDEX

Abrahams, V. C., 62
Acoustic analyzer, *see* Auditory analyzer
Actual connections, definition, 86
Afferent systems
  adaptation in, 69–70
  adequate stimulus, 71–73
  divergence-convergence principle in, 64–65
  in general, 507–9
  lateral inhibition in, 71–72, 84
  on-units and off-units, 68
  perceptive function, definition, 65, 105
  receptive function, definition, 65, 105
  rules of functioning, 64–73
  transit and exit levels, 64–66, 105
  unspecific (emotive) control of, 67–68
Aggressive reflex, *see* Offensive unconditioned reflex
Agnosia
  alexic, 85, 120–22
  audioverbal, 130–31
  of faces (prosopagnosia), 85, 119
  hand-kinesthetic (apraxia), 148, 195
  limb-somesthetic (asomatognosia), 134
  of melodies (amusia), 131
  oral-somesthetic (Luria aphasia), 138
  of shapes (astereognosia), 85, 135–36
  spatiovisual, 114–15
  of textures (ahylognosia), 134
  of visual objects, 116
  word-kinesthetic (Broca aphasia), 149–50
Agraphia, 148
Ahylognosia, *see* Agnosia, of textures
Ajuriaguerra, J. de, 116, 135, 163, 164
Akert, K., 163, 165, 488, 504, 505
Alajouanine, T., 120, 163
Albert, D. J., 109, 491, 504
Alexejeff, A., 309
Alimentary unconditioned reflex
  consummatory, 11–14
  preparatory, 18–29

Amusia, *see* Agnosia, of melodies
Amygdala control
  of fear, 33–34
  of hunger, 26, 28
  of satiation, 26, 28
Analyzers, *see* Afferent systems
Anand, B. K., 60, 394, 421
Anarthria, 150–51
Anatomical controversies, 5
Angelergues, R., 163
Anger, definition, 34
Anger reflex
  central mechanism of, 35
  and sympathetic tonus, 35
Anokhin, P. K., 343
Anosognosia, 195
Anrep, G. V. (ed.), 6, 59, 307, 351, 392
Antidrive
  definition, 41
  mechanism of alimentary, 49–53
  mechanism of defensive, 53–54
Aphasia
  amnestic, 248–51, 252
  auditory-somesthetic, 238
  auditory-verbal (central), 244–46
  auditory-visual, 227–29
Appetite, definition, 22
Appetitive reflex, definition, 10
Apraxia, *see* Agnosia, hand-kinesthetic
Arousal
  of afferent systems, 23–24, 32
  of motor behavioral system, 23, 32, 35
  role in type I CR, 289
  role in type II CR, 395–99
Asomatognosia, *see* Agnosia, limb-somesthetic
Asratian, E. A., 343
Associations
  audioverbal-gustatory, 237
  audioverbal–limb-somesthetic, 237–38
  audioverbal-somatotextural, 237

521

INDEX OF RUSSIAN PROPER NAMES